Historical Foundations
of Educational Psychology

PERSPECTIVES ON INDIVIDUAL DIFFERENCES

CECIL R. REYNOLDS, *Texas A&M University, College Station*
ROBERT T. BROWN, *University of North Carolina, Wilmington*

DETERMINANTS OF SUBSTANCE ABUSE
Biological, Psychological, and Environmental Factors
Edited by Mark Galizio and Stephen A. Maisto

HISTORICAL FOUNDATIONS OF EDUCATIONAL PSYCHOLOGY
Edited by John A. Glover and Royce R. Ronning

THE INDIVIDUAL SUBJECT AND SCIENTIFIC PSYCHOLOGY
Edited by Jaan Valsiner

METHODOLOGICAL AND STATISTICAL ADVANCES IN THE STUDY OF INDIVIDUAL DIFFERENCES
Edited by Cecil R. Reynolds and Victor L. Willson

THE NEUROPSYCHOLOGY OF INDIVIDUAL DIFFERENCES
A Developmental Perspective
Edited by Lawrence C. Hartlage and Cathy F. Telzrow

PERSONALITY AND INDIVIDUAL DIFFERENCES
A Natural Science Approach
Hans J. Eysenck and Michael W. Eysenck

PERSONALITY DIMENSIONS AND AROUSAL
Edited by Jan Strelau and Hans J. Eysenck

PERSPECTIVES ON BIAS IN MENTAL TESTING
Edited by Cecil R. Reynolds and Robert T. Brown

THEORETICAL FOUNDATIONS OF BEHAVIOR THERAPY
Edited by Hans J. Eysenck and Irene Martin

A Continuation Order Plan is available for this series. A continuation order will bring delivery of each new volume immediately upon publication. Volumes are billed only upon actual shipment. For further information please contact the publisher.

Historical Foundations
of Educational Psychology

Edited by

John A. Glover
and
Royce R. Ronning
University of Nebraska
Lincoln, Nebraska

Plenum Press • New York and London

Library of Congress Cataloging in Publication Data

Historical foundations of educational psychology.

(Perspectives on individual differences)
Includes bibliographies and index.
1. Educational psychology—History. I. Glover, John A., 1949–   . II. Ronning,
Royce R. III. Series.
LB1051.H537   1987   370.15   87-7875
ISBN 0-306-42354-5

© 1987 Plenum Press, New York
A Division of Plenum Publishing Corporation
233 Spring Street, New York, N.Y. 10013

Printed in the United States of America

Contributors

Thomas Andre
Department of Psychology
Iowa State University
Ames, Iowa

Ludy T. Benjamin, Jr.
Department of Psychology
Texas A & M University
College Station, Texas

Sidney W. Bijou
Department of Psychology and Special Education
University of Arizona
Tucson, Arizona

Robert D. Brown
Department of Educational Psychology
University of Nebraska
Lincoln, Nebraska

John B. Carroll
Department of Psychology
University of North Carolina
Chapel Hill, North Carolina

Don C. Charles
Department of Psychology
Iowa State University
Ames, Iowa

Emily S. Davidson
Department of Psychology
Texas A & M University
College Station, Texas

Walter Dick
Department of Educational Research
Florida State University
Tallahassee, Florida

Francis J. Di Vesta
Division of Counseling and Educational
    Psychology
Pennsylvania State University
University Park, Pennsylvania

David N. Dixon
Department of Educational Psychology
University of Nebraska
Lincoln, Nebraska

Carolyn M. Evertson
Department of Teaching and Learning
Peabody College
Vanderbilt University
Nashville, Tennessee

Robert M. Gagné
Department of Educational Research
Florida State University
Tallahassee, Florida

John A. Glover
Department of Educational Psychology
University of Nebraska
Lincoln, Nebraska

Don E. Hamachek
Department of Counseling, Educational
  Psychology, and Special Education
College of Education
Michigan State University
East Lansing, Michigan

Ernest R. Hilgard
Department of Psychology
Stanford University
Stanford, California

John E. Horrocks
Department of Psychology
Ohio State University
Columbus, Ohio

Lloyd G. Humphreys
Department of Psychology
University of Illinois
Champaign, Illinois

Arthur R. Jensen
School of Education
University of California
Berkeley, California

Jack J. Kramer
Department of Educational Psychology
University of Nebraska
Lincoln, Nebraska

Thomas R. Kratochwill
Department of Educational Psychology
University of Wisconsin
Madison, Wisconsin

Richard E. Mayer
Department of Psychology
University of California, Santa Barbara
Santa Barbara, California

Gerald J. Melican
Educational Testing Service
Princeton, New Jersey

Barbara S. Plake
Department of Educational Psychology
University of Nebraska
Lincoln, Nebraska

Royce R. Ronning
Department of Educational Psychology
University of Nebraska
Lincoln, Nebraska

Mark A. Smylie
Department of Curriculum Instruction and
  Evaluation
University of Illinois
Chicago, Illinois

Robert L. Williams
Department of Educational and Counseling
  Psychology
University of Tennessee
Knoxville, Tennessee

Preface

This volume represents a beginning effort to compile a history of educational psychology. The project began, innocuously enough, several years ago when we decided to add more material about the history of educational psychology to the undergraduate course we were teaching. What seemed like a simple task became very complex as we searched in vain for a volume dealing with the topic. We ended up drawing on various histories of psychology that devoted anywhere from a few paragraphs to several pages to the topic and on a very few articles addressing the issue. We were startled, frankly, by the apparent lack of interest in the history of our field and decided to attempt to compile a history ourselves.

As is the case with any edited volume, the contributing authors deserve credit for its positive features. They uniformly made every effort asked of them and taught us much about educational psychology. Any errors or omissions are our responsibility alone.

In retrospect, it seems that we misread the field when we began working on this volume. That is, we presumed that educational psychology was a much more coherent and readily defined field than it is. In fact, there is little agreement about what educational psychology is and who or what educational psychologists are. The ambiguous nature of the field is not something new, arguments about its identity have been a part of the literature since the turn of the century. Even so, our attempt to piece together a history of educational psychology has been fascinating and given us far more insight into educational psychology than we could have gained in any other way. It is our hope that the readers of this volume will also gain a knowledge of the field different from what is available in the journal literature and traditional textbooks.

Given the lack of agreement about what educational psychology is, we devoted the first chapter to defining the field and examining issues that influence its definition. The second chapter explored the development of early departments of educational psychology. Then, because of the diverse nature of the field, we were faced with a difficult decision. We could attempt to follow Chapter 2 with chapters on topics such as educational psychology in the 1930s, educational psychology during World War II, or we could solicit chapters that focused on the history of specialties closely related to educational psychology. We decided on the latter course.

After reviewing available materials on the history of educational psychology, it seemed that our field was largely derivative, depending on work in individual differences, measurement, cognitive psychology, instructional design, and other areas for much of its growth. Because of this, we chose chapters on the history of specialty areas closely related to educational psychology, with particular emphasis on how these areas influenced educational psychology. These chapters comprise the second section of the volume. Their topics, the child study movement, individual differences, measurement, the guidance movement, school psychology, behavioral psychology, humanistic psychology, instructional design, and the cognitive movement describe, in large part, what educational psychology has been and what it is becoming.

The problem of defining educational psychology also led us to expand the volume beyond what we had originally envisioned. Rather than attempting to define the field as it is in the late 1980s, we decided to include a series of state-of-the-art chapters on topics representative of educational psychologists' interests. These chapters, dealing with reading, teacher effectiveness, classroom management, measurement, evaluation, and problem solving, are not all inclusive but they do provide a sampling of the wide range of research interests incorporated in educational psychology.

The last section of the volume provides a much more personalized attempt to deal with the history of the field and its status. Here, we asked notable contributors to educational psychology to give us their own perspectives. Each of these chapters is unique, offering insights into educational psychology not available from standard sources. The illness of some potential contributors, unfortunately, cut this section shorter than we had planned.

A large number of people were involved in the development of this volume—too many to list in this brief space. Grateful thanks, however, must be extended to some scholars who were especially helpful. We thank Cecil R. Reynolds for helping get the project off the ground and a whole series of discussions about the shape of the volume. We thank J. B. Stroud for his many insights into the evolution of the field. A very large debt of gratitude is owed to David C. Berliner for his grace, good will, and analytic skills in evaluating a wide-ranging discussion of the history of educational psychology. We are also grateful to E. Paul Torrance and Terry B. Gutkin for thoughtful analyses of the project. We also must express our appreciation and heartfelt gratitude to a very special group of scholars who graciously gave their time and expertise to reviewing chapters in this volume: Larry A. Braskamp, Roger H. Bruning, Joel Dill, Robert L. Egbert, Gene V. Glass, Elizabeth M. Goetz, Robert L. Linn, Wesley C. Mierhenry, William J. Moore, Wayne C. Piersel, Ernst Z. Rothkopf, and John W. Zimmer, Finally, we also must thank our editor at Plenum, Eliot Werner, whose unflagging enthusiasm helped us enormously.

We view this volume as a first step. As with any project, hindsight shows gaps and omissions that should have been foreseen but that were not. In particular, we hope to be able to devote a future volume to a decade-by-decade chronology of educational psychology with specific emphasis on educational psychology's relationship to professional organizations. We also hope to be able to expand the individual perspectives on the field, which we believe give otherwise unobtainable information. We do hope that our readers will find the history we present to be as fascinating and illuminating as we did.

JOHN A. GLOVER
ROYCE R. RONNING

Contents

PART I   BEGINNINGS

Chapter 1   **Introduction** **3**

    John A. Glover and Royce R. Ronning

Definitions of Educational Psychology   5
Influences on the Definition of Educational Psychology   6
Who Are Educational Psychologists?   10
Summary   14
References   14

Chapter 2   **The Emergence of Educational Psychology** **17**

    Don C. Charles

Nineteenth-Century Psychology and Its Role in Education   19
The Turn of the Century   21
The New Discipline   27
Development of Educational Psychology in Principal Institutions   28
Concluding Observations   35
References   36

PART II   THE DEVELOPMENT OF EDUCATIONAL PSYCHOLOGY

Chapter 3   **A History of the Child Study Movement in America** **41**

    Emily S. Davidson and Ludy T. Benjamin, Jr.

Eighteenth- and Nineteenth-Century Views of Education   41
The Industrial Revolution and the Growth of Cities   44
The Founding of Child Study   46

Child Study and the New Psychology 48
Influence of the Child Study Movement: 1890–1910 54
The Demise of the Child Study Movement 55
The Legacy of the Child Study Movement 57
Summary 58
References 59

Chapter 4   **Individual Differences in Mental Ability** **61**

      Arthur R. Jensen

The Prescientific Era 63
The Factor Analysts 72
References 86

Chapter 5   **Measurement and Educational Psychology: Beginnings and
              Repercussions** **89**

      John B. Carroll

Introduction 89
Methods of Testing 90
Theory of Measurement 91
Test Theory 94
Factor Analysis 97
Test Validity 98
Research Design 99
Computational and Test Scoring Technology 100
Institutional and Organizational Arrangements 101
Summary Comments 102
References 103

Chapter 6   **From Parsons to Profession: The History of Guidance and
              Counseling Psychology** **107**

      David N. Dixon

The Counseling Professions 108
A River Story 111
Historical Contributions 112
References 118

Chapter 7   **School Psychology: A Developmental Report with Special
              Attention to Educational Psychology** **121**

      Jack J. Kramer

Introduction 121
School Psychology: A Developmental Analysis 121
The Nature and Extent of the School Psychology–Educational Psychology
Connection 125

Summary and Conclusions: Maintaining the Diversity and Maximizing the
Interaction 128
References 129

Chapter 8   **The Impact of Behaviorism on Educational Psychology** 131

            Thomas R. Kratochwill and Sidney W. Bijou

Introduction 131
Philosophical, Biological, and Physiological Origins 132
Operant Conditioning and Development of the Experimental Analysis of
Behavior: B. F. Skinner 138
Development of Applied Behavior Analysis 141
Professional Developments in Behaviorism 147
Concluding Perspectives 149
Summary 153
References 154

Chapter 9   **Humanistic Psychology: Theory, Postulates, and Implications for
            Educational Processes** 159

            Don E. Hamachek

Prologue 159
What is Humanistic Psychology? 160
Early Humanism: Parent of the Humanistic Spirit 160
Emergence of the Humanistic Orientation as Psychology's "Third Force" 161
Basic Humanistic Views about Human Behavior 165
Role of the Self in Humanistic Thinking 166
Major Contributors to the Growth of Humanistic Psychology 167
Some Common Criticisms of Humanistic Psychology 168
Strengths and Virtues of the Humanistic Position 169
Beginnings of the Humanistic Movement in Education 170
Implications of the Humanistic Movement for Educational Processes 171
Toward Facilitating Teaching and Learning within a Humanistic Framework 172
Implications for Educational Psychology 176
Epilogue 179
References 180

Chapter 10   **A History of Instructional Design and Its Impact on Educational
            Psychology** 183

            Walter Dick

The Beginnings of Instructional Design—World War II to 1958 183
The Late Fifties—Sputnik and Programmed Instruction 184
The Conceptual Revolution of the Sixties 186
From Instructional Design to Instructional Systems in the Seventies 189
Current Status of Instructional Design 192
The Instructional Designer: 1960 and 1987 194
The Current Impact of Instructional Design on Educational Psychology 196
A Comparison of the Current Orientations of Educational Psychology and
Instructional Design 199

Summary 200
References 200

Chapter 11   **The Cognitive Movement and Education** 203
      Francis J. Di Vesta

The Nature of Understanding 204
Education: Two Philosophies 204
The Transition from Philosophy to Educational Psychology 206
The Current Cognitive Movement 208
Information Processing 210
Facilitating Understanding by External Aids 213
Cognitive Skills and Control Processes 218
Illustrative Cognitive Strategies 220
Cognitive Skills Training 222
The Psychology of School Subjects 223
Expertise: Procedural Knowledge and Declarative Knowledge 225
Motivation 226
Summary 228
References 230

PART III   CURRENT ISSUES AND FUTURE DIRECTIONS

Chapter 12   **Program Evaluation: Agendas for Discussion of Issues and for Future Research** 237
      Robert D. Brown

Historical Perspective 237
An Issue Agenda 239
A Research Agenda 249
Conclusion 255
References 256

Chapter 13   **Processes in Reading Comprehension and the Teaching of Comprehension** 259
      Thomas Andre

Educational Psychology and the Study of Reading: A Brief Historical Overview 261
Models of Reading Comprehension 263
Issues in Reading Comprehension Research 272
Teaching Reading Comprehension Skills 282
Summary and Conclusions 288
References 290

Chapter 14   **Current Issues in Classroom Behavior Management** 297
      Robert L. Williams

Types of Participants 297
Target Behaviors 298

Treatment Strategies 299
Evaluation of Classroom Management Research 317
References 321

Chapter 15   **The Elusive Search for Teachable Aspects of Problem Solving** .. **327**

      Richard E. Mayer

Introduction 327
Definitions 328
Cognitive Analysis of Problem Solving 329
Historical Example 332
Teaching for Transfer: Rote versus Meaningful Learning 334
Teaching Problem Solving in Reading 338
Teaching Problem Solving in Writing 339
Teaching Problem Solving in Math 340
Teaching Problem Solving for Intelligence Gains 342
The Future of Problem-Solving Research 343
References 345

Chapter 16   **Research on Teaching and Classroom Processes: Views from
Two Perspectives** **349**

      Carolyn M. Evertson and Mark A. Smylie

Two Lenses—Different Perspectives 350
Planning and Decision Making 354
Classroom Management 357
Academic Instruction 362
Conclusion 367
References 367

Chapter 17   **Future of Educational Measurement** **373**

      Barbara S. Plake and Gerald J. Melican

Introduction 373
Aptitude and Achievement Testing 375
Future of Computers in Educational Measurement 377
Testing for Decision Making 383
Implications of the Revised Joint Technical Standards on the Future of
Educational Measurement 385
Conclusions 388
References 389

PART IV   PERSPECTIVES ON EDUCATIONAL PSYCHOLOGY

Chapter 18   **Peaks and Valleys of Educational Psychology: A Retrospective
View** **395**

      Robert M. Gagné

Early Postwar Research 397
Research on Training of Military Personnel 397

School Subjects as Learning Tasks 398
The Period of Development of Laboratories and Centers 399
Development of Ideas about Instructional Psychology 400
Some Reflections on Educational Psychology 401
References 402

Chapter 19   **Quantitative Methodology: Then, Now, and the Future** **403**

        Lloyd G. Humphreys

Methodology Then 403
What We Have Added 407
Problems in Psychological Research 410
References 414

Chapter 20   **Perspectives on Educational Psychology** **415**

        Ernest R. Hilgard

The Nineteenth-Century Background in America 415
The Influence of Global Perspectives 416
Instructional Psychology in the Late Twentieth Century 420
The Future of Educational Psychology 422
References 422

Chapter 21   **Retrospect and Prospect in Educational Psychology** **425**

        John E. Horrocks

Chapter 22   **Conclusion** **431**

        Royce R. Ronning and John A. Glover

Overview 431
The ''Splinter'' Groups 431
Problems of Definition 432
Early Educational Psychology Content 433
Educational Psychology 1960–1987 435
The Future of Educational Psychology 436
References 438

Index **439**

PART I

Beginnings

Only two chapters are included in this section. The first examines the definition of educational psychology and how it has evolved. The second surveys the emergence of departments of educational psychology.

CHAPTER 1

Introduction

John A. Glover and Royce R. Ronning

It would be as absurd for one to undertake to educate the young with no knowledge of . . . psychology, as for one to attempt to produce a sonata while ignorant of the phenomena of sound.
—Louisa Parsons Hopkins, *Educational Psychology,* 1886, p. 3.

In the past 100 years, there have been many changes and innumerable arguments about what educational psychology should be. Still, a common thread for all of us who call ourselves educational psychologists is the belief clearly expressed by Hopkins in the first text to be entitled "Educational Psychology." That is, we believe that the best teaching can occur only when teachers cogently apply principles of psychology.

Educational psychology is much more than the simple application of already discovered psychological principles to educational systems. We believe it is its own discipline with its own goals, research agenda, and infrastructure. It has a unique history in academia and has been blessed with contributors of uncommon ability and foresight. This volume was designed (a) to provide a history of the many components that have made up educational psychology and (b) to present a series of reflections on the state of the discipline in the late 1980s. The project has five major goals.

The first goal is to describe a long and honorable history that has not been well documented. Educational Psychology, that middleman between education and psychology (Bagley, Bell, Seashore, & Whipple, 1910; Grinder, 1978), has existed for more than 100 years. Courses in our discipline have been given since 1839 (see Brett, 1912; Cole, 1950; Dexter & Garlick, 1898; Hall, 1883; Hopkins, 1886; Joncich, 1968; Sully, 1896/1977). Journals devoted solely to the topic have been published since 1910 (Bagley *et al.,* 1910). Professorships in the area have existed since 1895 (Goldenstein, 1958), and departments of educational psychology have functioned as independent units since 1902 (Goldenstein, 1958). In fact, it can be argued that American educational psychology as a separate discipline is as old as experimental psychology (Henderickson & Blair, 1950).

The second major goal is to obtain the perspectives of influential psychologists who have made significant contributions to educational psychology. The first generation of educational psychologists has long since departed from the scene, but we are still able to obtain perspectives on the development of the field from senior second-generation educational psychologists, many of whom had direct contact with the early luminaries in educa-

John A. Glover and Royce R. Ronning • Department of Educational Psychology, University of Nebraska, Lincoln, NE 68588-0440.

tional psychology and who have helped shape what our field has become. These insights are invaluable and irreplaceable.

A third goal is to provide an orientation for people newly entering our field. Most contemporary educational psychologists have had a history and systems course or a learning theories course. The former provides a broad history of psychology, whereas the latter details the evolution of theories of learning. Neither adequately provides educational psychologists in training with the history of the field they are entering, to say nothing of its goals and methods. From our perspective, graduate students in educational psychology and, indeed, psychology more generally, have much to gain from a study of the history of this field. Not only can a history help our students avoid dead ends and blind alleys, it can also provide a much clearer perspective for examining contemporary issues.

A fourth goal is to review the nature of the field itself. Seemingly, educational psychology has suffered from an identity crisis since its formation. A comprehensive treatment of its history may prove fruitful in conceptualizing future directions for the discipline. Since at least 1898 (see Dexter & Garlick, 1898, pp. 1–15) scholars have been debating the nature of the field, its definition, and its unique features. In 1913, for example, Henmon wrote an overview of the area that raised "the question as to whether educational psychology has a distinctive field and a specific problem not covered by other branches of psychology" (p. 70). In 1915, Hall-Quest carried out a national survey of how the undergraduate course in educational psychology was taught and concluded that although there was a trend toward more scientifically oriented courses, there was still an incredible diversity in the contents of these offerings. Only a few years later, Remmers and Knight (1922) concluded that "there is no general agreement on terminology or on the structure of courses in educational psychology" (p. 405).

The debate over this issue, both in terms of what the undergraduate course should be (e.g., Douglas, 1925; Feldhusen, 1970; Hertzberg, 1928; Watson, 1926; Weeks, Pickens, & Roudebush, 1930; Worcester, 1927) and what the overall field is (e.g., Ausubel, 1968a; Feldhusen, 1976; Grinder, 1978; Page, 1974) has continued to this day. Almost 20 years ago, for example, Travers (1969, p. 414) concluded that "one cannot clearly identify a body of knowledge as representing a discipline

which can be appropriately named educational psychology." More recently, Grinder (1978, p. 285) stated that "Educational psychologists have never agreed upon who they are or what they are about." Certainly, a review of undergraduate educational psychology texts of the 1980s reveals (if that is possible) even greater diversity than has been the case in the past. Basic questions about what our field is have become especially acute in light of increasing specialization by psychologists.

The fifth goal for this volume is to examine current and historical relationships among educational psychology and closely related disciplines. The evolution of the field can only be understood by reviewing these relationships. As we will see in later chapters, educational psychology has always been closely related to those areas that have since become developmental psychology, guidance and counseling, tests and measurements, and school psychology (Roweton, 1976).

Although the scope of the current volume is broader than prior efforts to provide a history of educational psychology, there are some very real limits. First, only minimal attention will be devoted to the evolution of the undergraduate course. An analysis of all the psychology applied to education and educational psychology texts from Hopkins' *Educational Psychology* and James Sully's *Outlines of Psychology with Special Reference to the Theory of Education* (1884) to contemporary texts would require a massive volume all its own. Second, little effort will be devoted to identifying the kinds of vocations that educational psychologists have entered. Even though occasional papers have been published on this topic (e.g., Feldhusen, DiVesta, Thornburg, Levin, & Ringness, 1976), it is too far away from the central emphasis of the current project to warrant inclusion. Third, except as they relate to other issues, no attempt will be made to deal with the short-lived American Association for Applied Psychology or the abortive Society for Educational Psychology (see Page, 1974; Tobias & Farley, 1977). We also will not focus on the relationship of the American Psychological Association's (APA) Division 15 (that division devoted to educational psychology) to APA and other professional organizations. Grinder (1967) has addressed these issues in some detail and, according to our own research and that by others, only about 40% of the people who actually teach educational psychology are members of APA (see also Ball, 1971; Jones, Symonds, Klausner, Horrocks, & Noll, 1952). Finally, the state-of-the-art chapters in the third section of this book were chosen to represent the diversity of research being conducted by educational psychologists. No attempt was made to represent all the research interests of the field.

Definitions of Educational Psychology

Despite the publication of numerous texts and papers on the general topic, the consensus of scholarly opinion is that educational psychology was first clearly defined by E. L. Thorndike in his 1903 *Educational Psychology* (see, for example, Travers, 1969; Watson, 1961). Thorndike's goal, "offering the knowledge of human nature to students of educational theory" (p. 11) did not, at first glance, seem to be a radical departure from very similar sounding goals such as Judd's (1903, p. 1) "to acquaint teachers with the scientific study of mental development," or Harris's (1898, p. x) "to provide the psychological foundations of . . . educational factors in civilization and its schools." What was different was how Thorndike proceeded to apply psychology to education (Grinder, 1978).

Thorndike was influenced by the writings of William James and emphasized the biological nature of human capabilities (Grinder, 1978; Joncich, 1968; Watson, 1961). Thorndike also put distance between educational psychology and the child study movement (see Professor Davidson and Professor Benjamin's Chap. 5), by insisting on a highly empirical, theory-based approach to research. Finally, Thorndike's best known contribution was his adaptation of Herbartian psychology in developing a wide-ranging theory of learning that guided research through an approach that emphasized the interaction of the person and the environment.

These elements of Thorndike's views were directly incorporated into his definition of educational psychology in his classic 1913 text, reappearing without change in his short course versions of 1914 and 1921:

The arts and sciences serve human welfare by helping man to change the world, including man himself, for the better. The word education refers especially to those elements of science and art which are concerned with changes in man himself. Wisdom and economy in improving man's wants and in making him better able to satisfy them depend on knowledge—first of what his nature is, apart from education, and second, of the

laws which govern changes in it. It is the province of educational psychology to give such knowledge of the original nature of man and of the laws of modifiability or learning, in the case of intellect, character and skill. (Thorndike, 1913, p. 1)

This two-pronged definition together with the implicit emphasis on a scientific method of gathering data has had a powerful influence on the field that can clearly be seen in how texts appearing from 1911 to 1919 changed.

Educational psychology . . . treats the application of psychology to education. (William Henry Pyle, 1911, p. 7)

Educational psychology . . . gives guidance in the methods of helping students learn. (James Welton, 1911, pp. 6–7)

Educational psychology is the application of methods and facts known to psychology to the questions which arise in pedagogy. (Kate Gordon, 1917, p. 1)

The field of educational psychology is divided into large divisions which we may designate as: I. The native equipment of human beings; II. The psychology of learning. (Daniel Starch, 1919, p. 3, see also 1927)

The texts by Pyle (1911) and Welton (1911) were only minimally affected by Thorndike and closely resemble pre-Thorndike texts. Gordon's (1917) volume provided a rigorous research base and devoted chapters to the "laws of learning." The clearest break with pre-Thorndikian tradition is seen in Starch's (1919, 1927) texts. Starch, who apparently was Thorndike's greatest competitor in terms of book sales in the 1920s (Feldhusen, 1978), very clearly adhered to the definition of educational psychology first espoused by Thorndike.

By 1920, texts in educational psychology were almost uniformly based on theoretically driven research bases. In addition, the topics of basic human abilities and how to modify them had become central components. From about 1920 on, the basic model of educational psychology remained constant, although tremendous advances have been made in our understanding of "basic equipment" and how learning proceeds.

In addition to Thorndike's overwhelming influence on educational psychology, the foundation of the *Journal of Educational Psychology* in 1910 had a stabilizing effect on the field. For the first time, a journal specifically devoted to the publication of educational psychology research existed. The *Journal* emphasized theoretically based, empirical contributions and stated that the term "Educational Psychology" will, for our purposes, be interpreted in a broad sense as covering all those phases of the study of mental life which concern education. Educational psychology will then be regarded as including not only the well-known field covered by the average text-book—the psychology of sensation, instinct, attention, habit, memory, the technique and economy of learning, the conceptual processes, etc.—but also problems of mental development—heredity, adolescence and the inexhaustible field of child-study—the study of individual differences, of retarded and precocious development, the psychology of the "special class," the nature of mental endowments, the measurement of mental capacity, the psychology of mental tests, the correlation of mental abilities, the psychology of special methods in the several school branches, the important problems of mental hygiene; all these, whether treated from the experimental, the statistical or the literary points of view, are topics and problems which we deem pertinent for consideration in a Journal of Educational Psychology. (Bagley *et al.*, 1910, pp. 2–3)

Influences on the Definition of Educational Psychology

Theory and Application

The basic assumption underlying Thorndike's original definition of the field was the need for an empirical, theory-driven approach to educational problems. Over the years, educational psychology has generally met this assumption, drawing on the research of other psychologists and developing its own programs of investigation. As any educational psychologist can attest, however, it is one thing to have a research base and another thing altogether to convince nonresearchers of its utility.

By defining itself as the "middleperson" who applied the principles of psychology to education, educational psychology has put itself in the position of justifying its existence to the rest of psychology and justifying psychology to education. On the one hand, education has criticized educational psychology for being too theoretical and too concerned with research. On the other hand, psychology has accused the field of being too concerned with applications and not possessing clearly articulated programs of research (see, for example, Grinder, 1967; Roweton, 1976; Watson, 1961). These conflicting demands have led educational psychologists to attempt the nearly impossible task of achieving parity with other areas of psychology in theory and research, while at the same time being seen as highly relevant and directly applicable to education. Not surprisingly, the relative emphases on theory/research and applications have waxed and waned over the years. A review of state-of-the-discipline papers (e.g., Scandura *et*

al., 1978) and an analysis of current journal contents would suggest that our field has swung, at least for a brief time, toward the theoretical.

These swings from a research/theory focus to an educational perspective do not alter the basic definition of the field. And yet, the "feel" of the discipline changes as our perceptions of how educators and other psychologists view us change. It seems unlikely that educational psychology will alter its cyclic nature. The essence of the discipline appears to be such that it will continue to be closely scrutinized by psychologists and educators. These two groups appear to have very different world views and attempts to satisfy both will continue to create stress in the discipline.

Native Equipment

In addition to a theoretically sound research base, Thorndike's original definition of the field included coverage of human nature or, as Starch (1919) later put it, "native equipment." The ways in which this native equipment have been studied have influenced the field's definition. Two research areas in particular have shaped our self-image—development and individual differences.

Even though developmental psychology has evolved and separated from educational psychology, an accounting of human development is a significant component in thinking about the application of psychology to educational settings. The vast majority of educational psychology texts contain from one to four or five chapters outlining aspects of intellectual, social, emotional, moral, and physical development. Most departments of educational psychology include developmental faculty and the education of educational psychologists almost inevitably includes at least one developmental course. Further, the discipline's journals regularly publish developmental studies even though several high quality journals are available that devote themselves solely to developmental research.

The study of individual differences also has long been an integral part of educational psychology (see Professor Jensen's Chap. 3). Individual differences in intellectual ability, achievement, temperament, and so on have always been a part of the description of native equipment. Inextricably intertwined with the study of individual differences, of course, is measurement. A major component of most undergraduate texts, training programs, and an important area of application and research, measurement has historically been linked to educational psychology.

The close linkages among educational psychology, development, the study of individual differences, and measurement have on occasion led to acrimonious debates over what educational psychology is and is not and have even threatened the field with dissolution (see Grinder, 1967 for a discussion of these debates within APA). Despite the close relationships to these areas, educational psychology is not merely the study of age-related changes, or the study of how quantifiable characteristics differ among people, or the quantification of those characteristics. Rather, these areas are collateral fields drawn on by a discipline that seeks to employ elements of each in educational applications and in coherent patterns of research studies focusing on the interface of psychology and education. Hence, development, individual differences, and measurement are all vital parts of educational psychology, but the definition of our field is more than an amalgam of the definitions of these related areas.

Laws Governing Human Nature

The third element of Thorndike's definition of educational psychology was "laws governing human nature." Traditionally, these laws have been couched in terms of learning theory and theories of motivation. Learning theory has always been closely associated with educational psychology (see Shulman, 1982; Watson, 1961), forming a major component of our research and classroom applications. In fact, Thorndike himself is best known to most psychologists not as the founder of educational psychology, but as the proponent of one of the most important early learning theories (see Hilgard & Bower, 1975, p. 28). The study of motivation has also had a long relationship with educational psychology in terms of applications and research (e.g., Shulman, 1982).

A full accounting of learning theories and theories of motivation is far beyond the scope of this volume. Nonetheless, these theories have had considerable impact on the definition of the field. Here, we will restrict ourselves to examining two perspectives on learning—behavioral and cognitive—and examine their influence on educational psychology. Our discussion of how theories of motivation have effected views of educational psychology will also be restricted, focusing specifically on humanistic perspectives.

Behaviorism. Behaviorism itself is usually dated back to the early part of the century in the work of Ivan Pavlov and John B. Watson. As we will see in the chapter by Professors Kratochwill and Bijou, the dominant versions of behavioral psychology have shifted over the years from a Pavlovian/Watsonian view based largely on respondent conditioning, to a Hullian logico-deductive perspective, to an operant/behavior analytic emphasis, to the more recently emerging cognitive-behavioral position. Here, we will not attempt to cover Professors Kratochwill and Bijou's ground by discussing the evolution of behaviorism. Instead, we will briefly review the impact of behaviorism on the definition of educational psychology.

Behaviorally based views of educational psychology began to appear in the 1920s (Thorndike, of course, being an associationist). Edward Kellogg Strong's *Introductory Psychology for Teachers* (1920), as an early example, presented a view of learning that was Watsonian in nature. David Kennedy-Issacs' *The Psychology of Education* (1924) was similar in that it described learning in behavioral terms. Later, Peter Sandiford, in his *Educational Psychology: An Objective Study* (1928), wrote that the field "utilizes the laws and principles discovered by 'pure' psychology. Its subject matter is the behavior of human beings undergoing the process of education" (p. 9). An even more behavioral focus soon appeared in Rudolf Pintner's *Educational Psychology: An Introductory Text* (1929), in which he stated that the field consisted of the "study of the behavior of the individual in response to educational situations" (p. 4). In the mid 1930s, J. S. Gray (1935) published his *Psychological Foundations of Education,* which was designed as a strictly behavioral handbook of educational psychology. Nowhere is the influence of behaviorism easier to discern, however, than in A. M. Jordan's first three editions of *Educational Psychology* (1928, 1934, 1942). In 1928 (p. 3) Jordan defined educational psychology as "a concentrating of all knowledge of mental life upon the activities of the growing child, particularly as he goes and comes within the environment of the school." By 1942, however, behaviorism had become Jordan's central focus on learning. He saw psychology as the study of the behavior of the individual resulting from his adjustment to the environment. Educational psychology, in his view, was the study of behavior in educational settings (see 1942, p. 3).

The emphasis on behaviorism, however, did not change the essence of educational psychology as a discipline devoted to the application of psychology to education. Instead, the impact of behaviorism was on how learning, one component of the field, was viewed. Texts written in the 1920s, 1930s, 1940s, and 1950s continued to stress the basic coverage established by Thorndike. That is, they were research based, they outlined the basic equipment of human beings (which typically included discussions of development and individual differences), and described how the characteristics of learners might be altered through the principles of learning.

It is fair to suggest, then, that behavioral psychology, as dominant as it may have been in other areas of American psychology, never really reached a position of ascendency in educational psychology. Additional evidence for this view comes from an analysis of the contents of journals covering the 1920s and 1930s conducted by R. I. Watson (1961). He concluded that "one is left with the impression that behaviorism during these years did not have much specific effect on educational psychology" (p. 232). Our own analysis of the contents of journals covering 1920 to 1960 supports Watson's statement. With the exception of a very lively area of educational psychology—that concerned with industrial and military training—that has been dominated by behavioral approaches, articles on programmed instruction, and work on behavioral objectives, Watson's (1961, p. 232) assertion, that "no article of this sort (i.e., behavioral) seems to have reached the stature of being considered as a major contribution to educational psychology," rings very true—at least up until the development of a highly effective behavioral intervention technology in the early 1960s.

As we will see in the chapter by Kratochwill and Bijou and in Williams's chapter, behavioral psychology has made some important contributions to educational psychology since 1960. In addition, a few texts in the last 20 years have taken an extremely behavioral perspective, such as Francis Kelly and John Cody's *Educational Psychology: A Behavioral Approach* (1969), and Julie Vargas's *Behavioral Psychology for Teachers* (1977). It seems clear, however, that educational psychology has consistantly retained a much more eclectic perspective than that afforded by behaviorism, despite occasional critics who decry the amount of behavioral coverage in textbooks (e.g., Gaite, 1975).

Cognitive Influences. A different flavor of educational psychology comes from the various versions of cognitive psychology. Even though the influence of cognitive psychology was relatively minor on American psychology in general during the 50-year reign of behavioral psychology, the vast majority of educational psychology textbooks continued to cover cognitively oriented topics such as Gestalt psychology, memory, reasoning, and problem solving. In particular, texts such as Crow and Crow's *Educational Psychology* (through four editions, 1963), Cummins and Fagin's *Principles of Educational Psychology* (1937, 1954), Gates, Jersild, McConnell, and Challman's *Educational Psychology* (1949, a book related to previous volumes by Gates), and Kelly's *Educational Psychology* (through four editions, 1956) all gave extensive coverage to topics such as memory, problem solving, and reasoning. Similarly, the trend in the 1960s, 1970s and 1980s was to maintain a broad coverage of behavioral and cognitive topics (see Biehler & Snowman, 1982; Gage & Berliner, 1984; Hamachek, 1985; Worrell & Stillwell, 1984; also see earlier editions of these volumes).

With the exception of Robert Morris Ogden's *Psychology and Education* (1926), however, no primarily cognitive texts were published in the United States until Ausubel's *Educational Psychology: A Cognitive View* (1968b, Ausubel, Novak, & Hanesian, 1978) and Ausubel and Robinson's (1969) *School Learning*. From Ausubel's (1968b, p. 8) perspective, educational psychology was to be concerned "with those properties of learning that can be related to efficacious ways of deliberately effecting stable cognitive changes which have social value." As was the case with behavioral influences, however, the real definition of educational psychology was not changed—instead, presumptions about the nature of learning had shifted.

In the years since Ausubel's first edition, the cognitive movement has had considerable influence on all of psychology. Certainly, an analysis of the contents of the *Journal of Educational Psychology, Contemporary Educational Psychology,* and the *Educational Psychologist* over the past 10 years does suggest that far more cognitively oriented studies are being published in our journals than are behavioral studies. In addition, the coverage of texts in the mid-1980s has included more and more cognitive content (see Biehler & Snowman, 1982; Glover, Bruning, & Filbeck, 1983). Even so, it is too soon to determine what the ultimate impact of the cognitive movement will be on how we define educational psychology.

Motivation. Educational psychologists have long been interested in motivation, especially because of its direct relevance to classroom situations. A recounting of all the various theories of motivation and the relative influence they have had on educational psychology, however, is beyond the scope of this volume.

Of all of the central issues in psychology, perhaps none has proven as recalcitrant to human understanding as those dealing with motivation. . . . In spite of the best thoughts of some of the best minds in psychology, the emergence of satisfactory explanations of [such] . . . motivational phenomena has been slow relative to those in other areas of psychology, such as learning, sensation, and perception. This fact may account for the observation that the history of motivation psychology has never been written. The absence of a consensus in the field has inhibited efforts at summing up. (Russell, 1970, p. 1)

In our view, Russell's comments are as accurate now as when they were written. Because of the massive scope of the area, we will restrict ourselves here to commenting only on one general view of motivation—that of humanistic psychology.

As we will see in Professor Hamachek's chapter, humanistic views have had a profound effect on many educational practices. Books such as Carl Rogers' *Freedom to Learn: A View of What Education Might Become* (1969) have reached educational audiences that more traditional treatises missed. Further, a significant number of humanistic texts have appeared over the years (e.g., Hamachek, 1985, through three editions; Morris, 1978) and most undergraduate educational psychology texts include humanistic views of motivation. And, although we will not presume to discuss material better left to Professor Hamachek's chapter, it is important to note that humanistic psychology has had a significant influence on how we view ourselves and how we structure classroom interventions.

Other Influences of the Field's Development

A part of how we view ourselves, of course, includes our relationships with various other subspecialties in psychology. As we will see in the chapter by Professor Kramer, school psychology has had a long and often confusing relationship with educational psychology. And, although there is still no broad agreement as to what our relationship should be, our interactions with school psychology have and will continue to alter educational psychology's view of itself.

Another closely related discipline is guidance and counseling, from which counseling psychology arose (Super, 1955). As will be described by Professor Dixon later in this volume, the guidance and counseling area has roots outside of educational psychology and its development into the mature field of counseling psychology has taken it and its agenda apart from educational psychology—an event that has influenced educational psychology's self-view.

New relationships have also had an impact. In particular, instructional design (with strong linkages to behavioral psychology) and evaluation are two specialties that have become associated with educational psychology and that have had and will continue to have an impact on the field. Professor Dick will examine the development of instructional design more closely whereas Professor Brown will review the growth of evaluation.

A Contemporary Definition of Educational Psychology

There are essentially two views that can be taken in defining contemporary educational psychology. The pessimistic perspective dates back to Henmon's (1913) questions about whether or not educational psychology is a distinctive field with its own research agenda. The rise of developmental psychology, school psychology, counseling psychology, and measurement (to a lesser extent, perhaps) as independent areas with their own organizations, conventions, journals, research agendas, and applications would seem to suggest that very little "pure" educational psychology is left over—primarily the study of learning and cognition. If this is truly the case, it can further be argued that other areas (applied behavior analysis for those so inclined and cognitive science, see the lead editorial in the first issue of *Cognition and Instruction*) cover learning and cognition, leaving nothing at all.

We do not accept this pessimistic view. Educational psychology is the field that applies the principles of psychology to education. More than being a simple conduit of information, however, educational psychology conducts psychological research relevant to education, thereby contributing original knowledge to the bases of both psychology and education. As long as there is a discipline of education and a science of psychology, educational psychology will endure. Some "middleperson" must translate psychological findings into educational relevance and focus psychological research on educational problems.

Educational psychology is an empirical discipline. In terms of theory, educational psychologists work within the framework of psychological theories (much as, say, astronomers work within the theories of physics) but may also be theory constructors (e.g., E. L. Thorndike, R. M. Gagné, E. Z. Rothkopf). Further, educational psychology reflects the strengths and weaknesses of the larger field of psychology as well as its fads and trends. Just as there is no one theory of psychology there is no one theory of educational psychology. As is the case in the larger field, there are educational psychologists of every theoretical persuasion. In terms of empirical background, educational psychology draws on data gathered by psychologists and educators but the field includes a large number of researchers who contribute works of their own.

The broad definition we employ here includes a large number of psychologists who find the application of psychological principles to education to be the major locus of their professional efforts—people specializing in learning, cognition, measurement, social behavior, development, and personal adjustment. There are, however, many people who fit our criterion but who do not think of themselves as educational psychologists. It seems to us that a psychologist must not only have educational applications as a professional emphasis but also that one must think of her/himself as an educational psychologist.

Who Are Educational Psychologists?

Given the broad definition we have employed for educational psychology, a reasonable question is Who are educational psychologists? In this section we will briefly consider professional organizations, professional standards, and educational programs in educational psychology as a means of shedding light on the question of who we are. Then, we will attempt to synthesize some demographic data and describe the prototypical educational psychologist.

Professional Organizations

One way to obtain information about a profession is to study the makeup of its professional organizations. Although there are many organizations that educational psychologists belong to (e.g., the American Educational Research Association, the International Reading Association, the Psychonomic Society, the Association of Applied Behavior Analysis), there is only one specifically devoted to educational psychology: Division 15 of the American Psychological Association, which has 2,040 members and fellows (APA Directory, 1984). The membership of Division 15 seems impressive until we consider it in context. Although it is probably not possible to identify precisely how many educational psychologists there are, more than 11,000 people have attained the doctorate in the area since 1960 (Harmon, 1978; National Research Council, 1985). We assume that some of these 11,000 people have died, retired, or left the profession. However, it is also reasonable to assume that many of the individuals who took their doctorates in educational psychology prior to 1960 (approximately 3800 between 1920 and 1960; Harmon, 1978; National Research Council, 1985) are still in a professional capacity. Thus, it is apparent that Division 15 is not an organization that reflects the totality of the field. Further, the membership figure for Division 15 is somewhat inflated because a number of individuals whose primary areas are outside educational psychology belong to the division as a second or third choice. It would seem, then, that a study of the membership of Division 15 would provide an inadequate picture of educational psychologists because we have no way of knowing whether the membership represents the field.

Professional Standards

Another way of describing the members of any profession is to examine their professional standards. The American Psychological Association, for example, has set fairly rigorous standards for doctoral programs in clinical, counseling, industrial, and school psychology. In these areas, the degree programs must retain faculty with certain skills, provide specific course work, furnish practicum experiences that fit specific guidelines, and require internships that fit within some standard parameters. Thus, we can be fairly certain that all new school psychologists, for example, will have much in common. As of this writing, however, there are no professional standards that we are aware of for attaining the status of educational psychologist, despite occasional calls for the development of such standards (e.g., Scandura *et al.*, 1978). Consequently, we cannot be assured of common experiences among educational psychologists even though most good programs do resemble each other.

Educational Programs

Very closely related to professional standards are questions about educational programs. Bachelor's programs in educational psychology are rare. Of the 23 we were able to locate (see Cass & Birnbaum, 1983), most are educational psychology degrees in name only. That is, special education, counseling (of one sort or another), or media specialists happen to be housed in departments of educational psychology and so degrees are given in educational psychology even though they might better be labeled in other ways. In addition, some departments of psychology housed in colleges of education offer their general psychology degree for undergraduates under the label of educational psychology. Unlike the broader field of psychology, then, educational psychology is almost totally a graduate course of study.

A cross tabulation of available documents (e.g., Conley, 1983; Graduate Records Examination Board, 1981; Professional and Reference Books, 1983) allows us to estimate that about 180 colleges and universities offer the master's degree in educational psychology. About one third of these programs are housed in departments of psychology (Arts and Sciences colleges) with the remainder in colleges of education. A survey of these programs (via a review of college and university catalogs) indicates an amazing diversity, ranging from experimental psychology training to therapeutic training, to special education—all referred to as educational psychology. Not included in our survey, of course, are programs not identified as educational psychology in which it is possible to gain a degree (e.g., psychology, education, curriculum) with a specialization in educational psychology.

At the doctoral level there are approximately 60 programs in educational psychology (another 30 or so programs in educational measurement and school psychology are closely related). The majority of these 60 programs are located in departments of educational psychology, although some are found in departments of psychology, foundations, curriculum, educational administration, counseling psychology, or educational measurement. In addition, doctoral level education in educational psychology can be obtained in various multidepartmental organizations and as a specialization in some departments even though no formal program exists. As was the case in master's programs, there is tremendous variation among the doctoral programs in educational psychology, ranging from the highly experimental to the highly applied, with all sorts of content area differences.

Typically, we think of learning, development, individual differences, measurement, and statistics as a common core for educational psychologists. Our review of program requirements, however, indicates that even such basic courses may not necessarily form a base of common experiences for doctoral students. For instance, requirements of different programs range from zero to 15 hours of statistics, from zero to 15 hours of development, and from zero to 15 hours of learning. Further, the theoretical frameworks of different programs vary considerably. Both the newly graduated applied behavior analyst and the freshly matriculated cognitive scientist may refer to themselves as educational psychologists.

Demographic Characteristics

The major source of demographic data on students receiving the doctorate in the United States is the National Research Council's Doctorate Records Project. For our purposes, we obtained data on people earning the doctorate during the years from 1973 to 1983 in the areas of educational, experimental, and clinical psychology. We chose experimental and clinical psychology as contrasting subdisciplines because both have long histories and because they represent two of the larger areas in the broader field of psychology. An examination of the data yield some interesting observations.

Age. Persons earning the doctorate in educational psychology traditionally have tended to be older than their counterparts in experimental or clinical psychology (Harmon, 1978). In 1983, the median age of new educational psychologists was 35.12 years, as compared to 30.63 for experimental psychologists and 31.18 for clinicians. In the years 1973 to 1983, the median age of both experimental and clinical psychologists increased by nearly 2 years, reducing the gap between them and educational psychologists. The median age for new educational psychologists has generally fluctuated between about 33 and 36 years of age since 1950.

Number of Doctorates. There has been a steady decrease in the number of new doctorates in educational (from 592 in 1973 to 427 in 1983) and experimental psychology (from 333 in 1973 to 209 in 1983) since 1973. Concomitantly, there has been an increase in the number of new doctorates in clinical psychology over this same time period (from 746 in 1973 to 1209 in 1983). The decrease in educational psychology degrees, however, has been experienced primarily in colleges of education rather than in departments of psychology. In 1973, 477 of the 592 doctorates (81%) were granted in colleges of education. By 1983, only 274 of 427 (64%) degrees were awarded in colleges of education. In fact, within departments of psychology, the number of degrees granted in educational psychology increased from 115 in 1973 to 153 in 1983. The significance of this trend in educational psychology is hard to determine but we would expect that because a larger and larger proportion of new educational psychologists are matriculating in departments of psychology there may be an increased emphasis on the theoretical end of the field. A similar speculation arises when we examine the type of doctoral degree being earned.

Type of Doctoral Degree. Historically, a large proportion of educational psychologists have earned the Doctor of Education (Ed.D.) degree. Over the past 30 years, however, there has been a decided trend away from the Ed.D. to the Doctor of Philosophy (Ph.D.) degree. By 1973, approximately 40% of new graduates in our field earned the Ed.D. with about 58% earning the Ph.D (Each year a small percentage of doctorates are categorized as "other"). In 1983, 80% of the doctorates in educational psychology were Ph.D.s and only about 19% were Ed.D.s. The meaning of the shift away from the Ed.D. to the Ph.D. is also difficult to determine. Traditionally, the Ph.D. has been considered as the research degree, whereas the Ed.D. has been thought of as suiting the needs of practicioners. If doctoral degree granting programs are indeed requiring more research of Ph.D. than Ed.D. students, it would seem to suggest that there should be an overall increase in research emphasis in the field.

Other than school psychology and counseling psychology, of course, educational psychology is the only area in psychology in which the Ed.D. is given. More than 99% of the doctorates awarded in experimental and clinical psychology during 1973 to 1983 were Ph.D.s. Even though there has been a swing away from the Ed.D. in educational psychology, a significant proportion of all educational psychologists continue to earn this degree. The differences in degree requirements between the Ed.D. and the Ph.D. help point up some of the important differences between educational and experimental and clinical psychology.

Undergraduate Degree Areas. Another difference among educational, experimental, and clinical psychology can be seen in the areas in which students took their undergraduate degrees. In 1983, more than 70% of those attaining the doctorate in clinical psychology had undergraduate degrees in psychology. Similarly, more than 75% of new experimental psychologists in 1983 took their undergraduate work in psychology. In contrast, only about 40% of new educational psychologists in 1983 had undergraduate degrees in psychology. The remaining new doctorates in educational psychology had obtained undergraduate degrees in almost all possible areas of study with education (18%), history (5%), and English (5%) being the most common. In the years between 1973 and 1983, very little change in undergraduate degrees was seen among experimental or clinical psychologists. In educational psychology, however, there was a noticeable drop in those who took their undergraduate work in education (from 28% in 1973 to 18% in 1983). This reduction in the percentage of new doctorates who had undergraduate degrees in education was accompanied by an increase in diversity across all degree areas with no one area showing growth at the expense of others.

Master's Degrees. When master's degrees are considered, some interesting differences show up among educational, experimental, and clinical psychology. About one quarter of clinical (23.2%) and experimental (27.3%) psychology students attaining the doctorate in 1983 did not receive master's degrees. In contrast, only about 7% of new educational psychologists in 1983 had not received a master's degree. The most common master's degree among clinical (63.5%) and experimental (66%) psychologists was in psychology. Less than 10% of those receiving the doctorate in clinical or experimental psychology in 1983 had received master's degrees outside of psychology. A very different pattern was seen among new educational psychologists in 1983. Thirty-nine percent received their master's in psychology, 44% in education, and 10% took their master's degrees in other areas. The general patterns of master's degree work were stable between 1973 and 1983.

Employment. One last area of contrast among the different subspecialties in psychology comes from patterns of employment of new doctorates. From 1973 to 1983 there was a steady decrease in firm employment plans among new graduates in all three areas (from 66% to 58% in educational psychology; from 61% to 46% in experimental psychology; and from 66% to 50% in clinical psychology). This general trend may indicate a general reduction in the job market or a saturation of the existing market. If so, educational psychology seems to have been the least affected of the three areas.

When considering only those 1983 graduates who had firm employment plans, we find that 57% of educational psychologists entered academe, 12% took positions working for government agencies, 13% went to work in business or industry, 16% obtained employment with nonprofit organizations, and the remainder were scattered across a wide variety of settings. Among new experimental psychologists, a similar pattern is seen. Forty-eight percent entered academe, 17% went to work for government agencies, 26% entered business or industry, and 7% were employed by nonprofit agencies. New clinical psychologists, as one might expect, showed a different employment pattern. Twenty-two percent entered academe, 26% were employed by government agencies, 20% entered business or industry, and about 30% took positions with nonprofit organizations.

Summary of Demographic Data. The typical new educational psychologist is older than his/her peers in experimental or clinical psychology. Most educational psychologists now earn the Ph.D., but a significant proportion receive the Ed.D. The primary areas of undergraduate work for new doctorates in our field are psychology and education, although more than 40% took their work in other areas. The vast majority complete the master's, typically in education or psychology. Further, more than half have firm employment plans upon graduation, with a high proportion taking positions in academe. In general, the 1970s and early 1980s saw a decrease in the overall number of doctorates granted but an increase in the proportion of educational psychology students matriculating in psychology departments and an increase in the proportion earning the Ph.D. And, although there has been a decrease in the proportion of new educational psychologists who had firm employment plans upon graduation, our graduates have not been affected by the difficulty of finding employment as much as new graduates in experimental or clinical psychology.

Who Are We?

When we return to the question of who educational psychologists are, Grinder's (1978, p. 285) observation that, "Educational psychologists have never agreed upon who they are or what they are about," is especially pertinent. No one organization represents the whole of educational psychology. Rather, our colleagues apparently belong to many different organizations or no organization at all. No official set of professional standards for educational psychologists exists, and there seems to be little commonality in the educational programs that produce new colleagues. Educational psychologists come from all undergraduate fields, although psychology and education are the most heavily represented. Most obtain the master's, typically in education or psychology. Our new colleagues most frequently earn the Ph.D., but a large proportion gain the Ed.D. A surprisingly large number enter academe, but notable proportions also are employed in business and industry, take positions with government agencies, or work for nonprofit organizations.

Educational psychology is characterized by diversity. Apparently, there is no prototypical educational psychologist and the question of who we are can only be answered by returning to the definition of the field. Regardless of other factors, educational psychologists are those individuals who find the application of the principles of psychology to education to be the central focus of their professional lives.

In many ways, the diversity that seems to be our major characteristic is a very powerful strength. Education and psychology are extremely broad fields that we must interface in many ways. The principles of psychology that we apply span the breadth of psychology in our attempts to deal with issues in every facet of education. Only a highly diverse field could be capable of serving as the middleperson between such massive and complex disciplines. As we turn now to the history of our field, the diversity in how the principles of psychology are applied to education will become readily apparent.

Summary

Even after nearly 100 years, common agreement on a definition of educational psychology does not exist. To the extent that there is some consensus, it appears in definitions that direct psychology to the study of problems of learning, motivation, etc., that occur in school settings. Topics frequently seen as the purview of educational psychology include human development, individual differences, measurement, learning, motivation, and humanistic approaches to education. Contemporary educational psychology is both data and theory driven.

In spite of the decreasing demand for doctoral level persons in academic settings, a large proportion of recent doctoral graduates took positions in colleges and universities, though significant numbers entered government and industry. Educational psychology doctorates differ particularly from doctorates in experimental or clinical psychology in the diversity of their undergraduate majors. Whereas about 40% hold undergraduate psychology degrees, the next highest rate of mention, education, accounted for only 18% with the remaining new educational psychologists holding undergraduate degrees in a wide variety of areas.

In spite of (or perhaps because of) the lack of clear definition of the field, educational psychology appears to continue to flourish as a discipline. The remainder of this volume will provide historical views of a number of areas of educational psychology, an assessment of the present status of the field, and will conclude with a series of personal discussions of the field presented by a number of eminent persons who have been intimately involved with the field.

References

American Psychological Association. (1984). *Membership Directory*. Washington, DC: Author.

Ausubel, D. P. (1968a). Is there a discipline of educational psychology? *Educational Psychologist, 5,* 1–9.

Ausubel, D. P. (1968b). *Educational psychology: A cognitive view.* New York: Holt, Rinehart, & Winston.

Ausubel, D. P., & Robinson, F. G. (1969). *School learning: An introduction to educational psychology.* New York: Holt, Rinehart, & Winston.

Ausubel, D. P., Novak, J. D., & Hanesian, H. (1978). *Educational psychology: A cognitive view* (2nd. ed.). New York: Holt, Rinehart, & Winston.

Bagley, W. C., Bell, J. C., Seashore, C. E., & Whipple G. M. (1910). Editorial. *Journal of Educational Psychology, 1,* 1–3.

Ball, S. (1971). Educational psychology. In L. C. Deighton (Ed.), *The encyclopedia of education* (Vol. 3, pp. 199–202). New York: Macmillan.

Biehler, R. F., & Snowman, J. (1982). *Psychology applied to teaching* (4th. ed.). Boston: Houghton-Mifflin.

Brett, G. (1912). *A history of psychology.* London: Allen & Unwin.

Cass, J., & Birnbaum, M. (1983). *Comparative guide to American colleges* (11th. ed.). New York: Harper & Row.

Cole, L. (1950). *A history of education.* New York: Holt, Rinehart, & Winston.

Cole, L. E., & Bruce, W. F. (1950). *Educational psychology.* Yonkers-on-Hudson, NY: World Book.

Conley, D. (1983). *Peterson's annual guides/graduate study: Book 2* (18th ed.). Princeton, NJ: Peterson's Guides.

Crow, L. D., & Crow, A. (1963). *Educational psychology* (4th ed.). New York: American Book Company.

Cummins, W. & Fagin, B. (1937). *Principles of educational psychology.* New York: The Ronald Press.

Cummins, W., & Fagin, B. (1954). *Principles of educational psychology* (2nd ed.). New York: The Ronald Press.

Dexter, T. F. G., & Garlick, A. H. (1898). *Psychology in the schoolroom.* New York: Longmans, Green.

Douglas, O. B. (1925). The present status of the introductory course in educational psychology in American institutions of learning. *Journal of Educational Psychology, 16,* 396–408.

Feldhusen, J. F. (1970). Student views of the ideal educational psychology course. *Educational Psychologist, 8,* 7–9.

Feldhusen, J. F. (1976). Educational psychology and all is well. *Educational Psychologist, 12,* 1–13.

Feldhusen, J. F. (1978). Two views of the development of educational psychology. *Educational Psychologist, 12,* 297–304.

Feldhusen, J. F., DiVesta, F. J., Thornburg, H. D., Levin, J. R., & Ringness, T. A. (1976). Careers in educational psychology. *Educational Psychologist, 12,* 83–90.

Gage, N. L., & Berliner, D. C. (1984). *Educational psychology* (3rd ed.). New York: Rand-McNally.

Gaite, A. J. H. (1975). Review: Approaches to educational psychology—Some recent textbooks. *Educational Psychologist, 11,* 197–204.

Gates, A. I., Jersild, A. T., McConnell, T. R., & Challman, R. L. (1949). *Educational psychology.* New York: Macmillan.

Glover, J. A., Bruning, R. H., & Filbeck, R. W. (1983). *Educational psychology: Principles and applications.* Boston: Little, Brown.

Goldenstein, E. H. (1958). *The University of Nebraska: The first 50 years.* Lincoln, NE: University of Nebraska.

Gordon, K. (1917). *Educational psychology.* New York: Holt.

Graduate Records Examination Board. (1981). *Graduate programs and admissions manual.* Princeton, NJ: Educational Testing Service.

Gray, J. S. (1935). *Psychological foundations of education.* New York: American Book.

Grinder, R. E. (1967). The growth of educational psychology as reflected in the history of division 15. *Educational Psychologist, 4,* 12–35.

Grinder, R. E. (1978). What 200 years tell us about professional priorities in educational psychology. *Educational Psychologist, 12,* 284–289.

15

Hall, G. S. (1883). Aspects of child life and education. *Princeton Review, 2,* 249–272.

Hall-Quest, A. L. (1915). Present tendencies in educational psychology. *Journal of Educational Psychology, 6,* 601–614.

Hamachek, D. E. (1985). *Psychology in teaching, learning, and growth* (3rd ed.). New York: Allyn & Bacon.

Harmon, L. R. (1978). *A century of doctorates.* Washington, DC: National Academy of Sciences.

Harris, W. T. (1898). *Psychological foundations of education.* New York: D. Appleton.

Henderickson, G. M., & Blair, G. M. (1950). Educational psychology. In W. S. Monroe (Ed.), *Encyclopedia of educational research* (2nd ed., pp. 346–352). New York: Macmillan.

Henmon, V. A. C. (1913). Educational psychology. In E. Blond (Ed.), *Encyclopedia of education* (pp. 70–72). Belfast: W & G Baird.

Hertzberg, O., E. (1928). The opinion of teacher training institutions concerning the relative value of subject matter in educational psychology to the elementary school teacher. *Journal of Educational Psychology, 19,* 329–342.

Hilgard, E. R. & Bower, G. H. (1975). *Theories of learning* (4th ed.). Englewood Cliffs, NJ: Prentice-Hall.

Hopkins, L. P. (1886). *Educational psychology.* Boston, MA: Lee & Shepard.

Joncich, G. (1968). *The sane positivist: A biography of Edward L. Thorndike.* Middleton, CT: Wesleyan University Press.

Jones, R. S. (1964). *Instructional handbook for educational psychologists.* Urbana, IL: University of Illinois, College of Education.

Jordan, A. M. (1928). *Educational psychology.* New York: Holt.

Jordan, A. M. (1934). *Educational psychology* (2nd ed.). New York: Holt.

Jordan, A. M. (1942). *Educational psychology* (3rd ed.) New York: Holt.

Judd, C. H. (1903). *Genetic psychology for teachers.* New York: D. Appleton and Company.

Kelly, F. J., & Cody, J. J. (1969). *Educational psychology: A behavioral approach.* Columbus, OH: Merrill.

Kelly, W. A. (1956). *Educational psychology* (4th ed.). Milwaukee, WI: Bruce.

Kennedy-Issacs, D. (1924). *The psychology of education.* New York: Boni & Liverwright.

Morris, J. (1978). *Psychology and teaching: A humanistic view.* New York: Random House.

National Research Council (1985). *Summary of earned doctorates.* Washington, DC: National Research Council.

Ogden, R. M. (1926). *Psychology and education.* New York: Harcourt, Brace.

Page, E. B. (1974). Should we re-design our discipline? A major question for educational psychologists. *Educational Psychologist, 11,* 52–56.

Pintner, R. (1929). *Educational psychology: An introductory text.* New York: Holt.

Professional and Reference Books. (1983). *The college blue book.* New York: Macmillan.

Pyle, W. H. (1911). *The outlines of educational psychology.* Baltimore, MD: Warwick & York.

Remmers, H. H., & Knight, F. B. (1922). The teaching of educational psychology in the United States. *Journal of Educational Psychology, 13,* 399–407.

Rogers, C. R. (1969). *Freedom to learn: A view of what education might become.* Columbus, OH: Merrill.

Roweton, W. E. (1976). *Revitalizing educational psychology.* Chicago, IL: Nelson-Hall.

Russell, W. A. (1970). *Milestones in motivation: Contributions to the psychology of drive and purpose.* New York: Appleton-Century-Crofts.

Sandiford, P. (1928). *Educational psychology: An objective study.* New York: Longmans, Green.

Scandura, J. M., Frase, L. M., Gagne, R. M., Stolurow, K., Stolurow, L., & Groen, G. (1978). Current status and future directions of educational psychology as a discipline. *Educational Psychologist, 13,* 43–56.

Shulman, C. S. (1982). Educational psychology returns to the school. In A. G. Kraut (Ed.), *The G. Stanley Hall Lecture Series* (Vol. 2, pp. 73–118). Washington, DC: American Psychological Association.

Starch, D. (1919). *Educational psychology.* New York: Macmillan.

Starch, D. (1927). *Educational psychology* (2nd ed.). New York: Macmillan.

Strong, E. K. (1920). *Introductory psychology for teachers.* Baltimore: Warwick & York.

Sully, J. (1884). *Outlines of psychology with special reference to the theory of education.* New York: D. Appleton.

Sully, J. (1896/1977). *Studies of childhood.* Washington, DC: University Publishers of America (reprint).

Super, D. E. (1955). Transition: From vocational guidance to counseling psychology. *Journal of Counseling Psychology, 2,* 3–9.

Symonds, P. M., Klausner, S. Z., Horrocks, J. E., & Noll, V. A. (1952). Psychologists in teacher training institutions. *American Psychologist, 7,* 24–30.

Thorndike, E. L. (1903). *Educational psychology.* New York: Lemcke & Buechner.

Thorndike, E. L. (1913). *Educational psychology: Vol. I. The original nature of man.* New York: Teachers College, Columbia University Press.

Thorndike, E. L. (1914). *Educational psychology: Briefer course.* New York: Teachers College Press.

Throndike, E. L. (1921). *Educational psychology.* New York: Teachers College Press.

Tobias, S., & Farley, F. H. (1977). On a proposed reorganization of the division of educational psychology. *Educational Psychologist, 12,* 248–261.

Travers, R. M. W. (1969). Educational psychology. In R. L. Ebel (Ed.), *Encyclopedia of educational research* (4th ed., pp. 413–420). New York: Macmillan.

Vargas, J. S. (1977). *Behavioral psychology for teachers.* New York: Harper & Row.

Watson, G. B. (1926). What shall be taught in educational psychology? *Journal of Educational Psychology, 17,* 577–599.

Watson, R. I. (1961). A brief history of educational psychology. *Psychological Record, 11,* 209–242.

Weeks, H. G., Pickens, H. D., & Roudebush, R. I. (1930). A comparative study of recent texts in psychology, educational psychology, and principles of teaching. *Journal of Educational Psychology, 21,* 327–340.

Welton, J. (1911). *The psychology of education.* London: Macmillan.

Worcester, D. A. (1927). The wide diversity of practice in first courses in educational psychology. *Journal of Educational psychology, 18,* 11–17.

Worrell, J., & Stillwell, W. E. (1984). *Psychology for teachers and students* (2nd ed.). New York: McGraw-Hill.

CHAPTER 2

The Emergence of Educational Psychology

Don C. Charles

To the scholar or practitioner in any mature discipline, it seems normal and inevitable that the discipline should exist in its current form. But disciplines, like persons, have their own individual histories, and current status reflects accumulated experience for both categories. Psychology and education have origins lost in the mists of history; education in some form is as old as civilization, and Brett's massive three-volume *History of Psychology* (1912–1921) barely mentions the 20th century. It is the purpose of this chapter to describe some of the social and academic circumstances of psychology and education that led to the emergence of a new discipline, educational psychology.

Psychology grew out of philosophy and physiology, attempting to answer questions that neither discipline could answer alone. As psychology emerged, some of the practitioners felt that their knowledge and skill would be useful to education, and began to carry out research and to offer practical advice to the often-beleaguered schools. For our history, then, we need to examine the activities of early psychologists who involved themselves in the problems of education. Until the 1920s, at least, we simply had psychologists, some of whom, some of the time, paid particular attention to problems of an educational nature.

The scholarly world in which educational psychology grew did not emerge in the late 19th century fully developed but evolved from antecedents appearing in much earlier centuries. These beginnings are relevant to what the discipline became, and they will be examined briefly before considering the current century.

Historical Precursors

In the broadest sense, psychology is ancient in origin. We find psychological concepts and concerns in the work of Aristotle, Bacon, Descartes, and other ancients.

But it was Juan Vives (1492–1540) whose work was clearly and directly related to the questions that psychology began to deal with 350 years later. Vives employed "a self-conscious emphasis on induction as a method of inquiry and discovery in philosophical and particularly psychological questions," according to his translator and biographer, F. Watson (1915, p. 334). Vives was born in Spain, but like most scholars of the period, lectured in the various intellectual centers of Europe: Paris, Bruges, England, and spent his later years in Switzerland.

The first work of relevance is his *De Anima et Vita,* published in 1538 but written earlier. In this book he considered manifestations of reality, not what *is* but what could be observed. This is a psy-

Don C. Charles • Department of Psychology, Iowa State University, Ames, IA 50011.

chology that is introspective and empirical, dependent on the association of ideas in an attempt to discover laws. He presents a twofold nature of memory, an apprehending function and a maintaining function, plus fourfold laws of forgetfulness. Two more books followed to complete his psychology, one on intellectual faculties and another on emotions.

Educational psychology, in the form he gave it, is set forth in *De Tradendis Disciplinus* (Vives, 1531), apparently written earlier than the books described above, despite the later publication date. The way he applied psychology to education can be summarized as follows:

1. He recommended an orderly arrangement of facts to impress contents on the memory. Here he anticipated Herbart.

2. He emphasized practice, for example, saying material to be learned aloud, writing it down—in other words, exercising it.

3. He reported that interest was absolutely vital to acquisition of new material.

4. He emphasized practical knowledge, which he described as preparation for "moral excellence."

5. He recommended adjusting teaching to individual differences, paying considerable attention to problems of teaching children who were "feeble-minded," "deaf-and-dumb," blind, and the like.

6. He suggested that basic learning depends on self-activity.

7. He recommended that a student be evaluated in terms of his own past accomplishments, and not in comparison to another student.

A teacher or educational psychologist would find little to quarrel with in these conclusions. Vives addressed not only teachers, but also physicians, politicians, historians, and economists on the grounds that all of these professionals dealt with other persons, and thus had need for psychology (Watson, 1915).

Closer in time were two turn-of-the-century thinkers, Pestalozzi and Herbart. Although quite unlike each other in experience and character, both wanted to ground education in psychology as that philosphically-based discipline was understood at the time.

Johan Pestalozzi (1746–1827) planned to enter the ministry, but a failed sermon changed his aim (like the later identical experience of G. S. Hall in America). After reading Rousseau's *Emile* (1762/1883), he was attracted to pedagogy.

Eventually he became a teacher, and he created the first modern elementary school (Meyer, 1965, p. 350). He soon distilled his experience into a book, *How Gertrude Teaches Her Children* (1802/1898) and developed a new school that prospered for 20 years. His attempt to psychologize education was based on an inadequate understanding of the faculty psychology of the day, but somehow it succeeded and his school and ideas were stimulating to educators for the rest of the century. His influence on the development of educational psychology lay primarily in his emphasis on the centrality of the child, rather than the content of the school, and on the role of observation in learning rather than the rote memory then extant in the classroom (Cole, 1966, pp. 454–506).

One of the visitors to the school was Johann Herbart (1776–1841), who was to organize and systematize education in a scholarly fashion beyond the capacities of his forerunner. He worked at Konigsberg where he occupied the chair once held by Immanuel Kant. He was a prodigious worker: in addition to teaching his subject, seminars, advising doctoral students, and supervising a practice school, he produced a series of notable books. Those of interest here include a *Manual of Psychology* (1816), *Psychology as a Science* (1824), and *General Metaphysics* (1828). His psychology rested on the idea that learning was powered by interest, both self-generated and manufactured by the teacher. The catchword for Herbart's notion was apperception. Interest and apperception were combined and worked to form his teaching method, called the Formal Steps, of which there were eventually five. By the last quarter of the 19th century this notion had reached its summit, according to Mayer (1965, p. 362). Translations and commentaries spread his ideas to American educators well into the 20th century (e.g., his *Outlines of Educational Doctrines,* presented as helpful to actual teaching, translated by A. F. Lange and annotated by C. DeGarmo, was published in 1901 and reprinted in 1904, 1909, and 1913—obviously there was still an audience and a market).

The growth of what became behavior science in the 20th century, of course did not occur in a social vacuum. In the 19th century in the United States especially, suggests Silver (1983, p. 136), the luster of science was such that academic respectability was secured in part by labeling a discipline accordingly; thus there was political science, economic science, historical science, and the like. So the new pedagogical science, based on psychology, emerged from the moral philosophy that preceded it.

Nineteenth-Century Psychology and Its Role in Education

Wilhelm Wundt did not invent psychology, any more than Henry Ford invented the automobile, but like Ford he turned his vision into something new. Wundt stated in the preface to his *Principles of Physiological Psychology* (1904, 1874 preface) that he was presenting work that would "mark out a new domain of science." Watson (1978, p. 275) comments that "Wilhelm Wundt was the first man one can call a psychologist without qualifying the statement by reference to another, perhaps stronger, interest."

Wundt's immediate predecessors of psychological note were the psychophysiologist Gustav Fechner (1801–1887), and the neural physiologist Hermann von Helmholtz (1821–1891). Wundt described Fechner as having made the first conquest of experimental psychology (Watson, 1978, pp. 239–250). Helmholtz, interested in physics, was too poor to study it at a university, so instead he took up tuition-free medical training, and eventually became an army surgeon. But he studied physics on his own and began to experiment; in time he was able to hold rank as professor of anatomy and physiology in a number of German universities. He, like Fechner, was an experimenter and an empiricist, and used measurement techniques to specify results. It was, if not inevitable, entirely logical and reasonable that the problems and methods generated by these scientists would evolve into experimental psychology.

was the first as is frequently reported is somewhat questionable because William James had established one for teaching purposes at Harvard in 1875. James had little interest in laboratory work, however, and his venture languished whereas Wundt's flourished and attracted worldwide academic attention.

A scholar almost anywhere in the world had few choices of places to go to learn about psychology. There was an absence of almost anything resembling graduate education in American colleges and universities. Thus it was that anyone who had a serious interest in scholarship, especially in the developing discipline of psychology, pretty much had to go to Europe to pursue the interest, and Wundt's laboratory was a magnet for many Americans who made up the early cadre of psychologists in this country. Among the founders and shapers of early American psychology who worked and studied with Wundt were G. Stanley Hall (Clark), J. McKeen Cattell (Columbia), Edward Scripture (Yale), Lightner Witmer (Pennsylvania), and Charles Judd (Chicago). Although Wundt expanded his work to include social or cultural psychology, he was most influential in work with sensation and perception, reaction time, attention, and feeling and association. But it was the stimulation students received experiencing his laboratory that had the greatest impact on American psychology (Watson, 1978, pp. 275–295).

Evans (1984, p. 55) observes that Wundt's philosophical orientation, "mind-as-contents" did not survive the ocean voyage his students made in returning to America. At the universities to which they dispersed, they were soon talking about "mind-in-use," but trying to study it with methods they learned in Germany.

Wundt (1832–1920)

Wundt advanced and modified both the methods and the orientation of his predecessors. His method was introspection, an ancient process he tried to change from meditation to a precise, experimental approach emphasizing discrimination responses, reaction time, emotional responses, and the like.

He had arrived at his eminence by way of medical and physiological training. At Heidelberg he published the previously mentioned *Principles;* the first half in 1873, the second half the next year. His last revision was published in 1911. His growing fame brought him to Leipzig, where he established his famous laboratory in 1879. Whether it

Galton (1822–1911)

Another strong influence on what became American psychology was not a psychologist at all, but a wealthy and somewhat eccentric Briton named Francis Galton.

Stimulated by his cousin Charles Darwin's new evolutionary ideas, he pursued interests that led to the field of eugenics. Specifically, he published a book called *Hereditary Genius* (1869), in which he considered the whole range of human ability, and offered as evidence of the hereditary nature of intelligence the disproportionate number of eminent relatives possessed by men of importance. He also made some twin comparisons. However shaky the assumptions on which his hereditarian concepts were based, his work was sufficient to set off what continues to be one of the enduring controversies (and thus, sources of stimulation for research) in psychology, the primacy of "nature or nurture." His anthropological concerns led to the collection of large amounts of quantitative data; the distribution of human measures in what came to be known as the "normal curve" fascinated him, as did the relationship of one set of measures with another. In order to look at relationships of these data in human subjects, he developed a primitive kind of correlation technique, later refined by his associate Karl Pearson, into the product-moment coefficient of correlation, a tool much used by psychologists. He dabbled also in memory and association, mental tests, and other psychologically related topics, but his major contribution to the development of psychology was the work and stimulation on the inheritance of psychological traits in human beings, and the development of statistical ways of making sense of quantities of data from human subjects (Watson, 1978, pp. 323–333).

Galton did not, like Wundt, attract students. Although he was visited by a number of Americans, only J. McKeen Cattell acknowledged Galton's profound influence (Watson, 1978, p. 333). For educational psychology, it is appropriate to recall that Thorndike was Cattell's student, and that Thorndike became a major early producer of research on abilities, and of statistical evaluation of data.

Psychology in Teacher Training

The idea of a science of the mind appealed to educators, and through various routes and by various names, psychology began to enter the teacher-training curriculum.

Apparently the first educational psychology in America was in a course at Lexington, Massachusetts; in 1839 a course was offered in Mental Philosophy, a name for the new psychology. The Oswego, New York normal school offered a course in child study as early as 1863 (Crabb, 1926, p.10). The Normal Department of Iowa University offered a mental philosophy course in 1866, and the University of Missouri in 1869 (Luckey, 1903, pp. 68–69). In 1870, the Bridgewater, Massachusetts Normal School required psychology of all its students (Robinson, 1930, p. 8). Educational psychology was offered

as Applied Psychology in 1886 by the Department of Pedagogics at Indiana, and in the same year the University of North Carolina offered a Methods of Culture course for teacher trainees. The University of Minnesota had a course in 1893 called The Development of Child Mind (Luckey, 1903, pp. 83–90).

A course described as Educational Psychology was taught at Illinois in 1890 by Charles DeGarmo, and was later taught by an early psychological clinician, a Professor Krohn. The text used by Krohn was Sully's 1887 *Handbook of Psychology* (Catalog and Circular of the University of Illinois, 1890–1891, pp. 65–66).

Psychology was wide-spread enough in normal schools to stimulate people to try to define the discipline and its role in education. In 1887 two speakers commented on educational psychology in addresses to the National Education Association convention. One was S. S. Parr on "The Normal School Problems": "Educational psychology is commonly interpreted to mean the study of general psychology, with stray observations about children's minds." Joseph Baldwin noted that "Educational psychology is made the basis of distinctive normal-school work. Through self the normal student studies the race, and thus becomes familiar with the laws of mental activity and mental growth." (National Education Association, 1888, pp. 670–677).

The presence, nature, and content of textbooks of this period tell something about the nature of the discipline. Apparently, the first to be called "Educational Psychology" was a booklet published by Louisa Hopkins in 1886 (Roback, 1952, p. 378). Bain published *Education as Science* in 1884, and Claparede, a book on experimental pedagogy in 1905 in French, later translated and revised (Claparede, 1911). Shortly before and after 1900, a number of American texts appeared: one was Baldwin's *Elementary Psychology and Education* (1891). Baldwin espoused the faculty psychology widely accepted at the time, commenting that "it is evident that psychology can make no progress whatever without introspection" (Baldwin, 1891, p. xx). The divisions of Baldwin's book include six sections. Another representative text was written by Dexter and Garlick and published in 1908. Their point of view was expressed in the phrase, "Psychology is the science of consciousness . . . there is a connection between mind and body." (Dexter & Garlick, 1908, pp. 7, 17).

The Turn of the Century

American psychology was beginning to form itself into a discipline in the years on either side of 1900. Whereas most of the early departments or programs were being developed by psychologists who had experience in Wundt's laboratory, the tone, orientation, philosophy, and continuity stemmed largely from the influence of William James.

William James (1842–1910)

William James was a member of a distinguished New England family. After dabbling in many areas of interest, James eventually took a degree in medicine at Harvard, but interested himself primarily in philosophy.

He was invited to teach physiology at Harvard in 1872, and by 1875 had offered his first course in psychology (he was aware of the work of Fechner and others in Europe). As he later put it, the first lecture on psychology he ever heard, he gave himself! In the same year, he founded the laboratory mentioned earlier, a laboratory little used except for student demonstrations (Allen, 1967).

James described Herbert Spencer as an "ignoramus," and Wundt was dismissed with the comment that he was "The finished example of how much *mere* education can do for a man" (Perry, 1935, p. 69). European psychologists with whom he was friendly and whose ideas he responded to included James Sully, James Ward, Theodore Flournoy, and Carl Stumpf. He was no follower, but worked out his own concepts. These concepts were presented in papers published from time to time and eventually were presented in a more organized fashion in his *Principles of Psychology* (1890), which had been under contract to Henry Holt for 12 years at the time of publication. His ideas were appealing to the American mind, and the book was widely read and used; it helped determine the direction of American psychology.

In his view, mind is not a passive adapter to circumstances, but is active, spontaneous, and selective. *Habit* is central to his views, and is his way of explaining the workings of the nervous system; his chapter begins, "Habit is thus the enormous fly-wheel of society, its most precious conservative agent" (James, 1890, p. 79). Although he was not an associationist, because of his rejection of its atomism and elementarism, he did recognize the role of association or contiguity on memory; in this context he rejected the then popular faculty psychology, later demolished by Thorndike and others. In total, his psychology was functional and pragmatic, and so American psychology became (Barzun, 1983; Watson, 1978, pp. 370–393). Gardner Murphy (1971) observed that James' "central importance" was due to his "rich, beautiful and very modern concept of how the will actually operates" (p. 254).

But his influence was greater and more focused than such generalizations suggest. Woodward (1984) has identified Jamesian concepts in the work of the succeeding generation of psychologists. These include work in learning concepts, habits, and ideo-motor action by Edward Thorndike, which led to the "law of exercise"; the motivational theory of volition developed by R. S. Woodworth; Mary Calkins developed James' will, faith, and belief concepts into a personality theory following his volitional ideas; Gordon Allport, also a personality theorist, took from James traits, functional autonomy, and a unifying philosophy of life; John Dewey, Josiah Royce, William Macdougal, Floyd Allport, and George H. Mead were other borrowers in the social sciences.

The influence of James on educational psychology can be identified at this period in terms of his influence on the whole fabric of American psychology, in which educational psychology was embedded. But James also had a more direct hand in psychology applied to education; he both lectured and wrote for teachers and teacher trainees specifically, and adapted his theoretical system to applications in the classroom. It would be tempting to say that education, in the public school sense, was one of his central interests, but there is no evidence that is so. James had a large family and needed money, and he earned it where he could. In 1892 he was invited, for a fee, to discuss education with the teachers of Cambridge. The lectures were well received, and next he took them on the Chatauqua circuit.

James did not find association with teachers stimulating or rewarding. His lack of enthusiasm for the activity was expressed in a letter commenting on the female teachers in his audience: "I have never seen more women and less beauty, heard more voices and less sweetness, perceived more earnestness and less triumph than I ever supposed possible." In another letter to his wife, he further commented on his teacher audiences: "Meeting minds so earnest and helpless that it takes them half an hour to get from one idea to its immediately adjacent next neighbor, and then they lie down on it . . . like a cow on a doormat, so that you can get neither in nor out with them.'' (James, 1967, 1896). Despite his distaste for the process, the lectures prospered, and 1889 they were published as *Talks to Teachers on Psychology and to Students on Some of Life's Ideals* (James, 1899).

James' psychology for teachers was functional: the child was seen as an active organism and it was education's obligation to be consistent with the child's instincts and yet fit him for life in society. Although the instinct notion was abandoned, his position made inroads into the existing faculty psychology, and the success of what he attempted in lectures and in his book—practical, concrete application of psychology for teachers—helped bring the attention of later psychologists to the child in the classroom.

James had many students in his classes, but not many advisees and he supervised few doctoral dissertations. Among his students who did go on to make names for themselves in psychology were Mary Calkins, William Healy, Edward Thorndike (a student, but no follower), and Robert S. Woodworth (Watson, 1967, p. 376).

G. Stanley Hall (1846–1924)

Hall was a contemporary of James, but very different temperamentally and intellectually. After an abortive start at the ministry, Hall went to Europe to study, first at Bonn and then at Berlin. In 3 years he returned to the United States without a degree, and then worked at Harvard long enough to earn a Ph.D. in psychology by way of philosophy. He worked as a tutor, read Wundt and returned to Germany to work with Wundt briefly and also with Helmholtz. Back in America, he somehow got the opportunity to give Saturday lectures on education at Harvard. These lectures went well, and led to an invitation to repeat them at Johns Hopkins. Again they were successful, and he joined the faculty there. Later he became first president and developer of Clark University.

Hall's influence was more that of enthusiast and promoter than that of scientist or researcher. He founded the *American Journal of Psychology* and later the *Pedagogical Seminary* (now known as the *Journal of Genetic Psychology*), founded and was first president of the American Psychological Association, encouraged the study of psychoanalysis

and later taught psychoanalysis himself. But his influence on psychology in general and educational psychology in particular stemmed from two sources: his orientation toward the study of children, and the stimulation he provided a series of students who became eminent psychologists and educators of succeeding generations.

Hall was fascinated by children and their development, and consequently, their education. It was his ambition for educators to study children, learn what children were trying to accomplish, and then help children reach their own goals. He described his approach as ''scholiocentric'' rather than the existing ''pedocentric'' orientation to education by advising educators:

The guardians of the young should strive first of all to keep out of nature's way and to prevent harm . . . they should feel profoundly that childhood . . . is not corrupt . . . there is nothing else so worthy of love, reverence, and service as the body and soul of the growing child. (Hall, 1901–1902, pp. 24–25)

Somewhat later he expressed his interest in adolescence in his two-volume work on the subject, *Adolescence* (1904). After these developmental books, he pulled together his child and education ideas in a volume called *Educational Problems* (1911). All during this period, of course, the journal he founded, now called *Journal of Genetic Psychology,* was publishing research and analytical pieces on children and on education; this was important because up until Hall, all the psychological journals were German and would not have published this kind of material.

As observed earlier, Hall had many students who distinguished themselves, unlike James, who towers over him intellectually. Hall was described recently by Mortimer Appley as a sometimes ''Mean, vain and self-serving man, [but] Hall could also be generous and supportive of others'' (Fisher, 1983, p. 29).

His students form a roster that is almost a ''Who's Who'' of early century psychology: James McKeen Cattell, John Dewey, Joseph Jastrow, William H. Burnham, Edmund C. Sanford, and others who attended his seminar at Clark, including Lewis Terman. Cattell and Dewey, however, did little work with him (Fisher, 1983, p. 29).

When Hall moved to Clark, he brought Burnham with him to teach pedagogics, which in this setting was educational psychology and mental hygiene. Many of his students found him stimulating and supportive: Lewis Terman, who later developed the Stanford-Binet scales, studied gifted children, and in general led the investigation of intelligence in America, commented in his autobiography that "For me, Clark University meant briefly three things: freedom to work as I pleased, unlimited library facilities, and Hall's Monday evening seminar" (Terman, 1932, p. 315). The secret of Hall's extraordinary influence on American psychology is revealed in Terman's further discussion of that famous seminar; he observes that "it was unique in character and about the most important single educational influence that ever entered their lives" (p. 315). The roster of students includes a host of names still familiar today, among them Arnold Gesell and E. B. Huey of later educational fame (Terman, 1932).

James McKeen Cattell (1860–1944)

Cattell was ambitious and enterprising, beginning his graduate study by appointing himself the assistant Wundt did not know he needed (Watson, 1978, pp. 285–286)! Although he worked productively with Wundt, he found greater stimulation with Francis Galton, "The greatest man whom I have known," as he described his mentor (Cattell, 1930, p. 116). He became, in 1888, not only the first psychology professor in America, but in the world (the others were in philosophy). He advanced rapidly: at 28, professor at Pennsylvania, at 31 chairman of the department at Columbia, at 35 president of the American Psychological Association, and at 40 elected to the National Academy of Sciences (Watson, 1978 p. 409).

Cattell, like Hall, was something of a promotor, although he did considerable scientific work. He began studying reading with Wundt, attempting to measure various components of the process. He went on to study words, time needed for impression on the retina, and the legibility of type (Woodworth, 1914, pp. 341–343). He had no love for G. S. Hall or his journals, and in 1894 founded the first of what became several competing journals, the *Psychological Review,* (Watson, 1978, pp. 407–413).

At Columbia Cattell was associated for many years with Robert S. Woodworth, and of course Edward Thorndike. Although Thorndike came as a student, it can hardly be said that he was influenced a great deal by Cattell: Thorndike was always a loner, and made his own way intellectually (Travers, 1983, p. 261). But perhaps it is more than accidental that he emphasized and developed

individual differences and measurement, two of Cattell's special concerns.

A New Movement: Functionalism. Men like James, Hall, and Cattell had their own theoretical orientations and numerous followers, but none founded a school or movement (possibly excepting Hall's curious genetic psychology) like functionalism, which emerged at the turn of the century. Any brief description of a philosophical or psychological view will be oversimplified and somewhat misleading, but we need to be aware of it because the attitude or orientation (perhaps a better term than "theory") of functionalism was essential for the development of American psychology, and especially for the emergence of educational psychology. Functionalism concerned itself with the mind as it acted or functioned. From this orientation it becomes possible to consider— and then realize—application of psychology to a host of real-life problems and situations. John Dewey and J. R. Angell, both familiar names in education, were among the leading figures of the new movement; indeed, Dewey might be called the first psychologist to be identified with functionalism as a separate school or theory of psychology.

The Functionalist Period

John Dewey (1859–1952) was a major figure in the development of functionalism, and its role in the emergence of educational psychology. As was reported earlier, Dewey took his Ph.D. at Johns Hopkins when Hall was there, but except for a stint in Hall's laboratory was little influenced by him. He taught psychology and philosophy at Michigan after his graduation, and published a general psychology text during his tenure there (Dewey, 1886), but his influence began to rise after his move to Chicago in 1894. During the years he spent at Chicago his psychological work peaked and here he was instrumental in the development of the orientation that made educational psychology possible in its American form (Boring, 1953).

Dewey, and Angell after him, were influenced by James' conviction that consciousness was a causal factor in life and biological survival; thus consciousness is related to the environment on both sensory and motor sides. He therefore taught at Chicago a James-like philosophy of wholeness of activity and adjustment (Murphy, 1951, p. 212).

Adaptation to the environment was Dewey's

psychological interest and orientation. He had a high level of concern for the adjustment of human beings—physical, mental, and moral—these concerns, coupled with functional psychology, appealed to educators and were factors in the development of educational psychology. Dewey's pioneering work in progressive education grew out of his adaptation-to-the-environment orientation, and out of his belief that education should be based on an understanding of the child's needs as they develop. In 1904, Dewey left Chicago for Columbia where he appeared to abandon psychological work and gained greater fame as a philosopher.

James R. Angell (1869–1949) replaced Dewey at Chicago (at the latter's request) within a year of Dewey's departure. Angell had studied under James at Harvard and after the customary contact with European psychologists—in his case, Ebbinghaus and Helmholtz—he became Dewey's assistant at Michigan. The James–Dewey exposure impelled him towards functionalism, which he further developed.

In 1906, Angell's American Psychological Association presidential address provided a definition of functionalism: it is concerned with the how and why of consciousness, mind—consciousness—mediates between the needs of the organism and the environment and this helps to solve problems (herein we find the roots of applied—including educational—psychology), and finally it is psychophysiological and thus requires that mind–body relations be considered (Angell, 1907). A somewhat earlier text also presented his views in a fashion set forth by the subtitle: *An introductory study of the structure and function of human consciousness* (Angell, 1904).

Under his guidance, the University of Chicago became the leader of the functionalist movement and a center of psychological, philosophical, and intellectual stimulation. Angell stayed at Chicago until 1919 and supervised 50 doctoral dissertations during those years, including those of John B. Watson, the founder of the behaviorist movement, Walter Hunter, a leading experimentalist of succeeding decades, and Walter Van Dyke Bingham, who became a leader in applied psychology and aptitude testing. After leaving Chicago, he was for 16 years president of Yale University.

Harvey Carr (1873–1954) replaced Angell, his former teacher, and remained head of the department until 1938. About 150 students received Ph.D.s during this time, and of course brought their Chicago orientation with them to various parts of the United States. Although Carr continued Angell's functionalist orientation, it gradually lost importance as a movement. This occurred in part because of the rise of behaviorism, but also in part because all movements in American—and other—psychology have had a period of development and enthusiastic reception, followed by a period when much of the new orientation is absorbed into the mass of what everybody knows in the field, and the lesser peculiarities of the position fade into history.

But the residual effect of functionalism on American psychology was a desire to make psychology useful. A concern with learning, and the development of learning theory, had long-term effects on psychology and education.

Robert S. Woodworth (1869–1962) of Columbia was not a functionalist like the foregoing—he was independent and eschewed all "schools"—but he was making his contributions during the period discussed. Although not accepting the label or agreeing in all the dimensions (as was true of his response to behaviorism) he was in the broadest sense of the term a major American functionalist.

He collaborated in his early work at Columbia with Thorndike on research on transfer of training, a concept contrary to the then current faculty psychology. Thorndike, of course, continued at various times in his career to work in the transfer area, and it became an important part of the developing educational psychology. Along the way Woodworth assisted the anthropologist Franz Boas in a study of individual differences in primitive peoples. At various times he developed psychological tests, produced a stream of books on experimental and physiological psychology, edited the *Archives of Psychology* from 1906 to 1948, developed an orientation (not a theory, but an emphasis, in his view) that he called dynamic psychology, and through his teaching—his real love—helped to integrate and organize psychological knowledge, and helped shape the destiny of scientific psychology (Poffenberger. 1962; Shaffer, 1956).

Edward L. Thorndike (1847–1949)

Although it is difficult, as we shall see, to pin down just when specific institutions defined educational psychology as a separate discipline, it is not difficult to determine who defined educational psychology through his own research and writing: it was, of course, Edward L. Thorndike of whom Travers said, "No psychologist has ever had a greater impact on education than Edward L. Thorndike'' (p. 249). Travers goes on to point out that this was in part a product of the general rise to fame of Teachers College, Columbia early in the century.

What became Teachers College was created in 1887 with a faculty of three; it expanded rapidly and eventually offered degrees of Bachelor of Pedagogy, Master of Pedagogy, and Doctor of Pedagogy. In 1894, a reorganized college appeared in a new building across the street from and tied to Columbia College; eventually the aggregate became Columbia University (Cremin, Shannon, & Townsend, 1954). For more than four decades, Thorndike and Teachers College together led American education into a science-based age of teacher education and pupil instruction.

Thorndike was one of several scholarly children of a Methodist minister. After education at Wesleyan, he attended Harvard for a year. It was James' lectures that turned Thorndike to psychology. Although he never became a Jamesian, he was intellectually excited by James' presentation of ideas, and James in turn let Thorndike raise his experimental laboratory chickens in the basement of the family home; the James children were reportedly fascinated by these feathered subjects.

Thorndike did not go to Europe to study but, on the advice and recommendation of James, went to Columbia to work with J. McKeen Cattell. Cattell gave him an assistantship and space in the psychology department's building attic for his chicken research, but not much direction or help. This was satisfying to Thorndike, who liked to work alone. He already had some thesis ideas when he arrived, and soon settled on a learning study with his birds. The thesis, *Animal Intelligence,* quickly became ''a classic in psychology'' as his biographer describes it (Joncich, 1968, p. 126). Its subtitle, ''Association in Animals'' tells what his orientation was. The study was published as a monograph in 1898, as one of the early Columbia Contributions to Education, and later revised and expanded as a book (Thorndike, 1911).

The thesis focused on learning (i.e., adaptive change in behavior) that occurs as the animal forms and strengthens associations. Later he would call these connections; his theory of connectionism was descended from the work of the British empiricists Locke, Bain, and Berkeley. The work excited the psychological community. John B. Watson cited this work frequently as part of the background for his own new behaviorism, and the

work also played a role in developing the ideas of Yerkes at Harvard, and later B. F. Skinner. His emphasis on motivation and the learning process helped orient American psychology of succeeding decades up to the present.

Thorndike taught briefly at Western Reserve College for Women as a Special Lecturer in Education. At this time, however, Thorndike had little use for pedagogy and psychology's role in it, finding it neither ''profuse nor profound,'' as his biographer put it (Joncich, 1968, p. 157). Psychology had no division in the National Education Association at that time, and although there was talk of using psychological data in education, little was actually done by way of gathering data through experimentation. Charles Judd recalls asking William James, whose *Talks to Teachers* had just been published (1899), what he thought of educational psychology. James' reply: ''Educational psychology? I think there are about six weeks of it'' (Judd, 1932, p. 226). Thus, despite James' writing and Hall's more educationally oriented work, educational psychology did not have much status as a scientific discipline, or as an interesting field to enter.

In 1899, Thorndike succeeded in getting what he wanted: an appointment in psychology at Teachers College, Columbia, where he could do research. The research, of course, was to be done only after he had completed his principal duties, teaching 15 hours per term.

Thorndike became a compulsive and tremendously productive worker. As mentioned earlier, he began studying transfer of training with Woodworth and continued this line of research for years. All his course outlines turned into books. In child psychology, he rejected the questionnaire method of the Child Study Movement, and advised them to observe, using objective methods only. In teacher training, he emphasized attention, memory, habit, mental training, and experimental approaches in general. In applied psychology, he put his students to work analyzing teaching materials to determine how they conformed to psychological principles (Travers, 1983, pp. 263–266). His mind and work habits enabled him to produce, by 1940, more than 500 publications, a majority of them research based (Cremin *et al.,* 1954, p. 44).

The early and continuing transfer of training studies are especially important, because the question of how learning topic A affects learning topic B is central to almost every major question in education, including curriculum. The data accumulated, and Thorndike summarized his early work in *Educational Psychology* (1903); the book was successful, Thorndike was promoted, and he continued his efforts. This book succeeded in killing formal discipline, which had dominated education for decades. With accumulated research, Thorndike in 1913–1924 published his three-volume *Educational Psychology*. Travers comments that the 1913 book was "a landmark publication and reflects Thorndike at his best, and Thorndike at his best was brilliant" (Travers, 1983, p. 272). With the accumulation of Thorndike's work, educational psychology became a respectable, science-based discipline that had much to do with the character of education from early to mid-20th century.

In addition to the transfer work that was at the base of his educational psychology, Thorndike carried out the first scientific study of animal intelligence and learning, helped demolish faculty theory and the theory of formal discipline, developed laws of learning that marked the end of the mental-process approach in psychology, formulated the laws of readiness and law of effect, introduced statistical methods in education and psychology and invented a performance scale, stimulated the achievement test, developed group methods of intelligence testing, explored heredity and environment as causes of behavior, explored individual differences, did pioneer research in adult learning, developed methods and materials for many school subjects, studied children's vocabulary—the list goes on and on to include the development of modern learning curves, the importance of feedback and reinforcement, the effect of massed versus distributed learning, and the nature of forgetting (Cremin *et al.*, 1954, p. 44). His work was "one of the great milestones of education" (Travers, 1983, p. 277).

Others of the Period

Charles Judd (1873–1946) was a contemporary of Thorndike and Terman, and was another Wundt Ph.D. of the period. He commented that he tried to mold himself after the master (Judd, 1932, pp. 218–219). He taught at Wesleyan, New York University, Cincinnati, and Yale before his final move to Chicago. Although he had an enormous range of interests, he began to publish in education, beginning at Yale, and is remembered for his contributions to that field. In 1903 he published *Genetic Psychology for Teachers*. This was a Darwinian

attempt to explain how the teacher perceives the classroom, and included advice on discipline, an emphasis on imitation, discussion of the origins of reading (a continuing interest) and other topics, all with a very different orientation than Thorndike's, whose work did not impress him. He also had little admiration for James or Hall.

In 1907 he moved to Chicago, where he became head of the School of Education. Chicago was in decline, according to Travers (1983, p. 328) and Judd tried to raise standards to the level of the Arts and Science faculty. He developed several journals, published *Psychology of School-Subjects* (1915), *Introduction to Scientific Study of Education* (1918), *Psychology of Secondary Education* (1927), and *Educational Psychology* in 1939, after his retirement. He was opposed to the concept of transfer that Thorndike espoused and usually ignored it, but did confront the idea in his education text: his explanation for the phenomenon was not identical elements (Thorndike's view), but rather the degree to which generalizations were taught. Among his students were William S. Gray, Guy Buswell, and Karl Holzinger (Judd, 1932; Travers, 1983, pp. 320–330).

Another contemporary of this group was Edmund B. Huey (1870–1913), whose early work on reading was definitive and has remained influential up to the present. Huey began investigating reading when a fellow student at Clark, Guy Whipple, asked him about the possibility of reading without inner speech. Huey began his research on the problem about 1898, and in 1908 he published *The Psychology and Pedagogy of Reading*. In this book he reviewed existing published research, and presented his views buttressed by his own and other laboratory work. It was his thesis that children should, from the beginning, get the meaning of content, rather than emphasize the pronunciation of words, which had been the major concern of the then current elocution approach. Besides emphasis on inner speech, he discussed limits on the span of attention, the difference between perception and recognition cues used in word recognition, and other topics still familiar in the reading field (Good & Teller, 1973, pp. 402–403). Lewis Terman recalled in his autobiography many men who had been his fellow students at Clark. Among those to whom he felt most indebted intellectually were Fredrick Kuhlman and E. B. Huey. Of the latter, Terman commented that he was "one of the most promising for science" (Terman, 1932, p. 317).

Undoubtedly, Huey's influence would have been even greater on education and psychology if he had not died so early, in 1913, at age 43.

The New Discipline

From the foregoing description of the views and work of a number of psychologists, it is apparent that from the turn of the century to the post World War I period, educational psychology had become identified as a scientific discipline, complete with theoretical orientations, methods and procedures, several areas of focus, and an accumulated body of knowledge. The areas of study generally were learning, tests and measurements, human development, child clinical, including the study of exceptional children, and in general, a focus on the scientific study of the child in school.

Psychology Departments Training Early Educational Psychologists

In the first decade of the century, the American Psychological Association appointed a committee to study the teaching of psychology in colleges. The committee, chaired by Carl Seashore, included Guy Whipple whose assignment was normal schools. Whipple was a Clark product, a student of G. S. Hall. He sent a 33-item questionnaire to 259 normal schools listed by the Commissioner of Education in 1907. The questionnaire concerned content, techniques, and the like, and also included questions about the training of the instructor. Replies were received from 100 institutions. The source of instructors' degrees was also reported. Thus, a list of institutions training educational psychology instructors was generated and reported (Whipple, 1910). These instructors were educational psychologists only in that they were teaching psychology in teacher-training institutions, of course. The schools training more than one instructor are presented in Table 1.

In 1927, Clara Robertson, in pursuit of a doctorate at Columbia Teachers College, replicated the Whipple study for her dissertation. She sent out her questionnaire to 195 institutions: 110 normal schools and 85 teachers colleges, with a response from 91 schools (129 instructors replying). Her returns on sources of degrees are presented in Table 2 (Robinson, 1930). Not all schools contacted replied to Robinson, but her list seems to

Table 1. Institutions in Which Psychology Was Studied by Instructors Teaching Educational Psychology in 1907 in 100 Professional Schools for Teachers[a]

Institution	n	Institution	n
Chicago	19	Iowa	3
Columbia	14	Wisconsin	3
Clark	13	Yale	3
Harvard	11	Berlin	2
Michigan	8	Cornell	2
Indiana	5	Gottingen	2
Pennsylvania	4	Illinois	2
California	3	Minnesota	2
Jena	3	Stanford	2
Leipzig	3	Zurich	2
New York University	3	Other institutions (1 each)	30

[a]Data from the teaching of psychology in normal schools, by G. M. Whipple, 1910, *Psychological Monographs*, *12*, Whole #51, p. 8.

Table 2. Institutions in Which Psychology Was Studied by Instructors Teaching Educational Psychology in 1927 in 91 Professional Schools for Teachers[a]

Institution	n	Institution	n
Columbia	41	Stanford	4
Chicago	29	Missouri	4
Harvard	9	California	4
Clark	8	Boston University	4
Iowa	8	Nebraska	3
Peabody	6	Minnesota	3
Indiana	5	Yale	3
New York University	5	Michigan	3
Pennsylvania	5	Tufts	2
Cornell	4	Ohio State	2
Wisconsin	4	Other institutions (1 each)	29

[a]Data from Psychology and the preparation of the teacher for the elementary school, by C. L. Robinson, 1930, *Teachers College Columbia University Contributions to Education*, *418*, pp. 32–34. New York: Columbia University.

offer a reasonable description of faculty teaching psychology for teacher trainees in institutions of the 1920s, at which time the discipline was developing rapidly.

The Robinson list provided the starting point for finding out more about the way in which educational psychology was handled by institutions early in the century. The writer contacted schools that had produced more than one instructor of psychology for teacher trainees—21 in all—and queried them about the organization of educational psychology in their early days. Specifically, they were asked if a separate department of educational psychology was organized in the institution, and if so, when, and if the teaching was not done in a separate department, how it was handled. They were asked further for any general information about the role of educational psychology in their school. Heads of appropriate departments were addressed first, and when they were unable to provide information, other channels were used. Of the 21 institutions, one (Boston University) made no reply to repeated queries, and another (University of Iowa) could not provide any historical information. The remaining 19 provided a variety of kinds of information: printed material from department files, recollections of emeritus professors, references to published documents, and in more than one case, a book or monograph.

Because the information received takes many forms, it does not lend itself well to any kind of neat tabular ordering, so each institution's early way of handling educational psychology will be presented in brief narrative form.

Development of Educational Psychology in Principal Institutions

University of California: Berkeley

The School of Education goes back to 1892. Its title was changed in 1901 to Department of Education and in 1916 to School of Education. The first Ph.D. in Education was awarded to Millicent Shinn in 1898; her dissertation, a baby biography, was widely studied and remains readable and interesting today. In the late 1890s the departments of Pedagogy and Philosophy cooperated in offering Philosophy 2 (General Psychology), described as a "valuable" prerequisite to education; in 1898 it became a degree requirement, and by 1903 students were expected to take it prior to admission, for it was a prerequisite to all undergraduate courses in the Department of Education. Additional courses appeared by the 1920s: tests and measurements (Cyrus D. Mead), educational psychology (Joseph Breitwisser), educational statistics (Raymond Franzen). Later, Giles Ruch, Noel Keys, and Luther Gilbert worked in educational psychology, Edna Bailey and Anita Laton taught growth and development of the child, and Richard French taught a course on atypical children. During the first 20 years, the faculty of the School of Education functioned as a common faculty rather than as a group of departments in a school. In time, a divisional identity emerged, with Psychology of Education as a field for the doctorate, probably the first such specialization in the school. By 1930, more than a dozen dissertations had been produced on topics of an educational psychology nature (Nadine Lambert, personal communication, December 15, 1983).

University of Chicago

The development of educational psychology in this institution has been discussed earlier in considering the work of Dewey, Angell, and Carr. The special field of educational psychology was founded in 1892 as part of the Department of Philosophy. In 1896, Education became a formal part of the Department of Philosophy; the new name reflected the change, for it was subsequently called the Department of Philosophy and Education. In 1900, Education was separated and thereafter remained alone. During all this time, educational psychology was a specialization with the departments (Tom Trabasso, personal communication, October 3, 1983).

Columbia University

Some aspects of Columbia's role in the field can be inferred from the earlier discussion of Edward L. Thorndike, who was employed by Teachers College, Columbia, in 1899 as Instructor in Genetic Psychology. In 1902, his title was changed to Adjunct Professor of Educational Psychology (Thorndike, personal communication, 1983). This title reflected a change in the college structure, when Dean James Russell broke the Division of Education into five administrative departments, of which Educational Psychology was one (Cremin *et al.*, 1954, p. 63). In 1921, the college embarked on an extensive program of research. Administratively, there were three divisions: Educational Psychology (headed by E. L. Thorndike), School Experimentation, and Field Studies. In the next few years the educational psychology enterprise developed College Board examinations, carried out a study of intelligence measurement, and did a study of exceptional children (Cremin *et al.*, 1954, pp. 81–82).

Clark University

The intertwining of education and psychology at Clark can be inferred from G. S. Hall's work there. Although they never had a separate department of educational psychology, there was never a time when education did not include psychology. By Hall's second year there as president, 1890–1891, and with the appointment of his former Johns Hopkins student William Burnham, development began and by 1893 education was made a subdepartment within the psychology department—by 1904–1905, education gained full departmental status. The first course in educational psychology *per se* appears to have been offered in 1894–1895, although the content was always present to some extent in Hall's work (Koelsch, personal communication, 1983). In an 1899 report, Burnham commented that "pedagogy is based upon psychology and owes to it the inspiration and stimulus to scientific work, and psychology owes to pedagogy the suggestion of some of its most fruitful fields of education" (Burnham, 1899, p. 161). He comments favorably on lectures in educational psychology in the institution, and discusses desirable qualities of a training program for producing professors of pedagogy, one of these being "an acquaintance with elementary psychology" (p. 162). In a footnote to the paper he also comments, "Many of the papers mentioned in this list are quite as much products of the department of psychology as of that of pedagogy; and, on the other hand, the pedagogical department has contributed to many of the psychological studies mentioned above" (p. 163).

Cornell University

Cornell responded to the late 19th-century work of psychologists in laying the foundation for a scientific basis of education by emphasizing education in the Arts and Science College, and by development of a Department of Education in the

Agriculture College. A geologist early offered courses in teaching, and was succeeded by Charles DeGarmo. DeGarmo was joined by Guy Whipple, a Clark product who was a pioneer in the testing movement.

In 1907 a School of Education was formed, whereas Arts and Science and Agriculture continued to offer courses in education. The School offered work in principles of education, educational psychology, methods of teaching and mental tests. In 1914 the first Professor of Educational Psychology, P. Kruse, was appointed, and in time four faculty positions were created. Educational psychology was presented under the aegis of the Department of Education, and was also allied with other psychology units on campus (Stutz, 1981).

Harvard University

Harvard University has never had a program officially named educational psychology, but educational psychology has been taught as a course there since early in the century, and as White (personal communication, Sept. 19, 1983) notes, "a good number of psychologists on the faculty have addressed themselves to education in one way or another."

By 1906 a separate Division of Education existed (with two faculty) and by 1909 enough expansion had occurred so that the Board felt justified in endowing a graduate school of education. James and Royce were on the faculty, but neither they nor any other members encouraged interest in research in education; this attitude encouraged forward-looking graduate students to go to Columbia or Clark rather than Harvard. In 1910, Robert Yerkes was dragooned into teaching a course in educational psychology, an assignment he resisted and tried to turn over to someone else when he could. Although the subject was taught, it was not included among the four basic fields required for a Ph.D. in Education. In the course of time, psychological science, and especially measurement, became a matter of concern to President Lowell, and he offered a post to Edward Thorndike, who rejected it (not enough money), and then to Walter Dearborn of Chicago, who also turned it down, but later was induced to accept. Dearborn's eventual acceptance filled the position, but his interests evolved away from classroom learning, and educational psychology never became an area of emphasis (Powell, 1980, pp. 84–107).

Psychology *per se* was a part of philosophy at

Harvard as at most schools in the early 1900s, with James, of course, the great name in American psychology. James was followed by Munsterberg, whose work had no discernible effect on education. Psychology did not separate from philosophy until 1934 (Allport & Boring, 1946; Kuklick, 1977, pp. 180–195). Educational psychology has had no role in these arrangements.

Although there has been no institutional commitment to educational psychology, individual psychologists in the Education School have taught the coursework of the discipline. Besides Yerkes, these include Walter Dearborn, Truman Kelley, Philip J. Rulon, O. Hobart Mowrer, Robert R. Sears, and John B. Carroll (White, personal communication, 1983). In addition, besides James, Jerome Bruner and B. F. Skinner have contributed to educational theory and practice.

Indiana University

Indiana was very early in the field, having some educational psychology instruction before 1900, mainly in child study. A three-term course was offered in 1911 by the School of Education. Indiana's president from 1902 to 1937, William Lowe Bryan, was a Hall student from Clark and had become a well-known researcher (best known for his Morse code learning curve research, done with Harter). He established a psychological laboratory in the philosophy department in the 1890s, described by Lynch (personal communication, Oct. 7, 1983) as "the oldest continuous center of experimental psychology in the United States." Sidney Pressey, who had worked with Munsterberg and Yerkes at Harvard, was a research associate in this laboratory from 1917 to 1922, when he went to Ohio State. Lewis Terman received his BA and AM at Indiana (1903) and went to Clark in part at Bryan's urging.

By 1913, educational psychology offered three courses and was listed as a unit in the Graduate School. All courses were taught by W. F. Book, the major figure in educational psychology there from 1912 to 1934. He too was from Clark, and taught learning, mental development, intelligence measurement, and general educational psychology courses; he also directed the laboratory during most of his tenure, and carried out his own experiments, especially in acquisition of typing skill. He also published a number of volumes relevant to the field during this period. Other early faculty in the area, besides Book and Pressey, included Herman

Young (from Pennsylvania), Grover Somers (Columbia, where he was reputedly Thorndike's favorite student), and Douglas Scates (Chicago).

Through the 1920s and 1930s, the program consisted of one elementary course and more advanced courses for upper-level undergraduates and graduate students; these courses included work in individual differences, mental measurements, individual mental testing, psychology of elementary school subjects, psychology of exceptional children, diagnostic teaching, and other advanced educational and research-oriented courses.

Many of the courses were cross-listed between Education and Psychology and some faculty had appointments in either or both of the areas. By 1913 educational psychology was a regular part of the training of teachers at Indiana, and the possibility of a Ph.D. specifically in educational psychology has existed there since 1913 (Lynch, personal communication, 1983).

University of Michigan

In 1879, a chair in the Science and Art of Teaching was established at Michigan, "the first permanent chair in any American College or university devoted exclusively to the preparation of teachers" (Whitney, 1931, pp. 27–28).

In 1899, Allen Whitney introduced a course in child study and social education, but the first course labeled educational psychology was offered by Irving King in 1906, and more advanced work began with Charles Johnston's "seminary," (a common nineteenth century term for the modern "seminar") "Psychological Investigations of Educational Processes" in 1909. By 1910 a general advanced course in educational psychology was offered by Fredrick Breed, and was repeated occasionally thereafter. Arthur Irion, a visiting instructor in the summer of 1925, gave the first course in the psychology of learning, and from 1926 on, William Clark Trow continued this course for many years (School of Education Bulletin, undated, pp. 108–109).

Clark Trow (as he was usually called) was a major figure in the field at Michigan and in the nation. His career spanned the years from the World War I period to the 1970s. He was an innovator in concerning educational psychology with the real problems teachers faced in the classroom, the teaching of specific subject matters, and with social behavior and values. He had a lifelong concern with methodology and with technologies. He was instrumental in establishing school psychology as a discipline in Michigan, and, in general, strove to integrate technology from psychology with applied education (Morse, 1983).

As educational psychology expanded, the Michigan work also diversified. Social education, later called social learning, was offered nearly from the beginning. Exceptional child work began in 1911, and continued with considerable involvement with other schools and institutions. Psychology of elementary subjects was introduced in 1912, and a reading clinic was established along the way. Mental measurements, emphasizing statistics, appeared in 1912 and evolved into more statistics and measurement courses, and other aspects of educational measurement began to be an important part of the curriculum.

Research and experimentation was always important. As early as 1910 Experimental Education was offered; by 1914 it became Experimental Educational Psychology, and was expanded by Guy Whipple in 1921, and by Howard McClusky in 1924 (Whitney, 1931).

University of Minnesota

In 1905, a formal college of education was established in the university. Educational psychology courses were offered as early as 1915, and such courses became the backbone of teacher training. Beck (1980) observed that "Underlying all . . . programs was of course educational psychology" (p. 188). The early courses included a general educational psychology course, mental testing with laboratory, mental diagnosis, and an educational psychology seminar (all taught by the same man every semester, Melvin Haggerty). From 1924 to 1928, the department had a 4-year undergraduate program for the training of school psychologists; the term is not defined in available material, so it is not clear what they were trained to do, or actually did in the schools (pp. 187–188).

From 1925 on, the Institute of Child Welfare carried out research and clinical work with children. A number of psychologists were attached to the Institute, and although it did not join the College of Education administratively for some years, there was a good bit of interaction between the academic educational psychologists and the Institute staff. By 1919, 10 credits were required in psychology for all teacher trainees, at least five of which had to come from educational psychology (Beck, 1980, p. 12).

University of Missouri

A Normal College was established shortly after the Civil War, but this institution was short-lived. In 1883, education reappeared in the university, under the Department of English. By 1903, it had become a separate department (in another year named "Teachers College") and in 1904 one of the dozen or so areas offered was educational psychology, taught by the department head, A. Ross Hill (Viles, 1939, p. 363). Under the aegis of the Graduate College, both AM and Ph.D. degrees were offered in education, including educational psychology; the first Ph.D. was granted in 1916. The institutional name changed again, to School of Education during this period. Viles reports that the functional psychology of John Dewey was the dominant orientation of the school at this time (p. 367). The education college, and especially educational psychology, flourished through the 1920s.

A Department of Experimental Psychology was established in the Arts and Science College in 1909, headed by Max F. Meyer, and education students also took courses in this area (Stephens, 1962, p. 360).

University of Nebraska

In 1901–1902, the Regents of the University of Nebraska established a College of Education. In the listing of departments of the new college was a department named Educational Psychology. About a year or two later, the phrase "and Measurements" was added to the title; early in the century, in the eyes of many educators, psychology *was* primarily measurement. In another year or two, the Regents removed the addition. During the early years, the Arts and Science College had been the parent of Education, and was the degree-granting authority, but in March 1921, Teachers College was freed from this tie, and was granted authority to grant its own degrees. By 1924 eight departments existed in the College, including Educational Psychology and Measurements (the addition having been restored in 1921), headed by Charles Fordyce (Baller, personal communication, March 27, 1972; Sawyer, 1973).

New York University

The School of Pedagogy (later called the School of Education) was founded in 1890 at New York University. Educational Psychology of the time was a part of the program from the beginning: when the school opened, a course was offered called "The Practical Applications of the Psychology of Expressional Activities." By 1910, 25% of the school's program was made up of psychology courses. By 1915 the catalog listed Child and Adolescent Psychology, Physiological and Experimental Psychology, and Elementary and Advanced Psychoanalysis. As early as 1920, references to "special education" appeared in course offerings. The faculty in these early years consisted of James E. Lough and Robert MacDougall. In 1921, the school was renamed as noted above, and the traditional academic degrees—BS, MA, and Ph.D.—were authorized.

In a typical year from the early period, 1924–1925, the following courses were offered: Psychology of Elementary School Subjects; Psychology of High School Subjects; Experimental Study of the Learning Process: Habit, Skill, and Memory; Genetic Psychology: Mental Development of the Individual; Principles of Educational Psychology; Psychology for Childhood; Psychology for Teachers of Backward and Deficient Children; Systematic Psychology; Social Psychology; Elementary Psychoanalysis; Educational Psychology (Advanced), and Research in Psychology.

In 1919, the Department of Educational Psychology was established, with Charles E. Benson as Chairman. Charles E. Skinner and Paul V. West were early faculty members in the department. In 1926, Benson, Lough, Skinner, and West published *Psychology for Teachers*.

Some special programs introduced before 1940 included training for school psychologists (1929), research experts in educational psychology (1932), teachers of mentally retarded children (1933), and introduction to clinical psychology (1937) (Goldner, 1984; Hug, 1970).

Ohio State University

Educational psychology has not been a separate department at Ohio State, but many courses that could be considered educational psychology have been taught in the College of Social and Behavioral Sciences, which has had a specialty area in educational psychology as one of its subareas (Osipow, personal communication, Dec. 20, 1983).

Educational psychology content first appeared at Ohio State in a course taught by John Short; this was in the department of philosophy. The course was later taught sequentially by two university

presidents, and a laboratory (with four pieces of equipment) existed as early as 1900. A course in educational psychology was offered by John Gordy in 1896 in the department of pedagogy, and other educational psychology courses were later taught in philosophy.

A psychology department, for many years administered by the College of Education, was established in 1907, primarily as a universitywide undergraduate service department. Between 1913 and 1920, graduate work began with the first MA in 1915 and the first Ph.D. in 1917. By the middle 1920s, the department was considerably larger and began to distinguish itself. Several familiar names appeared during this period: Pressey, Williams, Toops, Warfield, and Renshaw, and for a brief time Luella Cole and Edgar A. Doll. By 1927, the date of the survey reported earlier, 67 MAs had graduated, and 30 Ph.D.s. In educational psychology alone, 39 MAs and 21 Ph.D.s had been granted under Sidney Pressey's direction by 1937. Pressey was a sometimes eccentric but creative and productive educational psychologist, who kept the discipline stirred up in a variety of ways for decades (Wherry, 1968).

George Peabody College for Teachers

Peabody began its psychological work in education early in the century. In 1915, the college dedicated Jesup Psychological Laboratory: according to E. K. Strong, the first Professor of Psychology at Peabody, "Never before, in any institution in this country or in Europe has there been a building called a psychological building, and devoted and dedicated to psychology" (Peabody Alumni News, 1916). Both psychology and educational psychology were housed in the building. A few years later it was reported of faculty members Joseph Peterson in Psychology and S. C. Garrison in Educational Psychology that "Both hold to the experimental type of psychology rather than the old philosophical theories" (Peabody Reflector, 1922).

S. C. Garrison, the faculty member mentioned earlier, had received the first Ph.D. from the Department in 1919. He later became president of the college. Other faculty members, and visiting professors over the years, included Edgar James Swift, E. L. Thorndike, Truman Lee Kelley, Robert Morris Ogden, Henry Woodburn Chase, William McCall, Arthur I. Gates, Charles E. Spearman, Karl Garrison, A. S. Edwards, Paul

Boynton, Joseph Moore, Norman Munn, Lyle H. Lanier, and others. Besides S. C. Garrison, several of these names are of Peabody graduates: Karl Garrison, Paul Boynton, Joseph Moore, and Lyle Lanier (Hobbs, 1954). By 1930, 19 Ph.D.s had been granted (Stanley, 1954).

University of Pennsylvania

No formal program in the content areas of educational psychology appeared at Pennsylvania until the 1960s (Dole, personal communication, Sept. 22, 1983), but the psychology department is one of the very old ones in the United States. In 1888, James McKeen Cattell was appointed to a Chair in Psychology, the first such in the world. In the previous year, he had established at Penn the first psychological laboratory, one of the very early ones in America.

During these early years, teachers took some courses in the psychology department. In 1895–1896, Lightner Witmer, Cattell's successor, gave a course on child psychology to a class composed primarily of teachers. One of these teachers brought to class a bright boy who had been unable to learn to read. Witmer and the class were interested and worked with the boy. Other such experiences occurred. In the summer of 1896, in an extension class, a horde of problem youngsters were brought in for help, and parents also began to bring in their own children who had various difficulties—usually school problems. Out of this demand came the establishment of the Psychological Clinic, the first in America, if not in the world. By 1909, the department had been reorganized and university appropriations were granted to the clinic. A professional staff was built up, and thus a link was forged between academic psychology and the needs of children (Cheney, 1940, pp. 353–355; Dowlin, 1940, pp. 22–24).

Stanford University

Stanford opened in 1891, and presumably worked in teacher training from the beginning, but not until 1897–1898 was there any statement in the catalog on education. The earliest information concerns Earl Barnes, who studied child psychology in this department. He later became Professor of Education, and was Secretary of the Faculty from 1891 to 1897 (Thoresen, personal communication, Nov. 8, 1983). The field began to develop with the appointment of Ellwood P. Cubberley in 1898

(Sears & Henderson, 1957, pp. 60–64). His goal was to develop a truly professional school of education, and by 1907 began to enlarge the faculty; a number of his appointees became eminent in education and associated fields.

Before training psychologists were appointed, Cubberly included some psychology in his introductory course: one of his lectures was entitled "Apperception-principles of Psychology Applied," and he spoke on James' "Talks to Teachers." Lewis Terman later observed that although Cubberly had no training in psychology, he obviously had a good general grasp of the discipline (Sears & Henderson, 1957, p. 60). One of Cubberly's appointees was Lewis Terman, in 1910. Terman, a Clark product, had been teaching at Los Angeles Normal School with his friend Arnold Gesell, of later developmental psychology fame at Yale. E. B. Huey was an old friend of Terman from graduate school, and it was Huey who stimulated Terman to begin thinking about mental testing and clinical work with children. A position in education at Stanford was first offered to Huey, who did not want to leave his work at Johns Hopkins. He in turn recommended Terman, who accepted (Seagoe, 1975, pp. 36–37). Other psychologists were added later, including Truman L. Kelley in 1919. In addition to Terman and Kelley, Reginald Bell, a graduate student there at one time, became Assistant Professor of Education and Assistant Director of Citizenship; he taught child psychology (Thoresen, 1983). Only nine master's degrees were granted in the first 17 years by the Education school, and the first doctorate was granted in 1916 (Sears & Henderson, 1957, pp. 84–85). As the staff and student body expanded, courses were added in educational psychology, mental testing, educational measurement, statistics, guidance, and in other aspects of educational psychology (p. 90).

Terman began developing new courses at once. Among his first courses were those in child and adolescent psychology, for example, "Social and Moral Education," and "The Literature of Child Psychology." He moved next to school health and hygiene, and then to clinical aspects of child psychology and a special course in mental tests. Next he added educational psychology through courses in experimental pedagogy, educational psychology, and educational problems. Finally he worked in teacher training and supervision of teachers. But eventually, of course, his interest in individual differences and intelligence dominated his work (Seagoe, 1975, pp. 34–39). By 1916 he had published his version of the Binet test, was a full Professor and was becoming widely known. A few years later, he began his Genetic Studies of Genius, the landmark (and still continuing) longitudinal study of the gifted. In 1922, he was appointed to succeed Frank Angell as head of the Psychology Department (he retained his Education professorship), which he quickly expanded and upgraded. In 1923 he was elected president of the American Psychological Association.

The School of Education has never had departments as such, but functions with an area committee system. Psychological Studies in Education is one area with three different subareas: Educational Psychology, Child Development and Early Education, and Counseling Psychology (Thoresen, personal communication, 1983).

Tufts University

Psychology instruction began very early at Tufts, but until 1932, when a separate department was established, courses appeared under a variety of titles, and in often confusing combination with other subjects, usually theology and philosophy.

A course was offered to juniors in 1854 in Moral Science, with text by Alexander, and taught by President Ballou, followed in the second semester by Intellectual Philosophy, with text by Wayland. The first course listed as psychology was offered in 1869–1870, with a text by Porter; the course was called Human Intellect; by 1875 a text by Bain was being used.

For the next three decades, psychology continued to appear in philosophy and theology under a variety of titles. In 1892, psychology was listed as a Department of Instruction, offering but one course. In the late 1890s physiological psychology appeared, and James' text began to be used in some courses. In 1899, Robert Cushman became philosophy chairman, and psychology was no longer primarily a preparatory area for philosophy.

In 1910–1911, psychology was temporarily removed from philosophy; a new Department of Education and Psychology was created with Dr. Colin A. Scott as Chairman. In succeeding years, however, courses still appeared in philosophy, including a course in experimental psychology with a 9-hour laboratory requirement. This was taught by Professor Schmidt of philosophy. Educational psychology was taught in the Department of Edu-

cation, by the same Professor Schmidt, who was also listed as a mathematics instructor.

Things continued in this fashion for several years. More courses were added in the 1920s; Leonard Carmichael was by this time a member of the faculty. In 1925–1926, the department was renamed the Department of Philosophy and Psychology, and eight courses were listed, though not all were taught, and a major was possible. Fred Keller was an instructor during this period. As noted earlier, in 1932 psychology was made a separate department, and a straight major was possible, without philosophy or education involvement (Memorandum on the History of the Department of Psychology, Tufts College, undated).

University of Wisconsin

In addition to training teachers in the middle of the 19th century, Wisconsin forced improvement of education in the state through the structure of their entrance requirements. In earliest times, teachers were trained in a Normal Department, but were later cast into a ghetto called the Female College. But with changes in administration, teacher trainees (presumably all female) came to be awarded the same degrees as other students of the university in 1869, and by 1873 the Female College had disappeared (Pyre, 1920, pp. 181–189).

Psychology was a regular part of teacher training. A Professor was appointed in 1849 and assigned to deal with mental philosophy (psychology), logic, rhetoric, and English literature; this was the Normal Professor (Curti & Carstensen, 1949, 1. p. 73). One of the early enthusiasts for psychology was the president, John Bascom, who published several psychology texts between 1869 and 1881. During these years, he regularly taught a course in psychology, one that "baffled and intrigued" students (Curti & Carstensen, 1949, 1. pp. 281–282).

In 1884, a Chair of Pedagogy was established, and in 1888 a Chair of Psychology. The appointee to this Chair was Joseph Jastrow from Johns Hopkins; he was hired to establish a psychology laboratory and organize an active experimental psychology program. Jastrow and the University were not always happy together. His interests in experimental psychology declined, whereas his interest in education increased (Curti & Carstensen, 1, 1949, pp. 334–335). However, the department progressed. Clark Hull, who took his Ph.D. in

1918, began to attract attention before he left for Yale in 1929. Daniel Starch, a 1906 graduate from Iowa under Carl Seashore, published *Experiments in Educational Psychology* in 1911; this book was described as being objective in a fashion similar to Thorndike's. Starch later moved to advertising as a major interest. V.A.C. Henmon was a Columbia product of Cattell and Thorndike, and came in 1910 to represent educational psychology on the faculty. During World War I he worked at aviation psychology, taught briefly at Yale, and then returned to Wisconsin (Curti & Carstensen, ll, p. 334).

Yale University

Prior to 1891, occasional courses in psychology were offered (in philosophy) by George T. Ladd and others, but in this year the Graduate School came into being. Professors Hershey Sneath and E. F. Buchner taught Pedagogics and included Bain and Herbart in their readings, but in 1894 Edward Scripture, with a Ph.D. from Leipzig, began to teach what he called "Research work in Pedagogy"; he had earlier been appointed director of the Yale Psychological Laboratory. At about the turn of the century, Carl Seashore was on the staff, as well as other trained psychologists. The administration unit under which this work was offered was called at various times The Department of Philosophy, The Department of Philosophy and Psychology, and The Department of Philosophy, Psychology, and Education.

New faculty appeared and offerings were expanded. Charles H. Judd joined the faculty in 1902, taught psychology, and inaugurated a summer session aimed primarily at teachers in 1905. From 1908 to 1910, however, only a single course in educational psychology was taught, by Edward H. Cameron. Judd was discouraged at the lack of support he found at Yale, and moved to Chicago to carry out a distinguished career there. E. C. Moore came in 1910, followed by Arnold Gesell in 1912, and Charles Kent a year later.

When the doctoral program in education matured in the late 1920s and early 1930s, the general background required of all Ph.D. candidates included the history and philosophy of education, educational psychology, and basic educational issues. Educational psychology was one of the nine specialization areas most frequently chosen by candidates (Brownell, personal communication, Sept. 16, 1983). It was not until 1920 that psychology was freed from its bondage to philosophy and became a department in its own right. New appointments, expansion, and a growing reputation followed quickly (Pierson, 1955, p. 521).

Concluding Observations

It would be unrealistic to assume that the schools described in the latter part of this chapter constituted all the important producers of psychologists working in teacher education early in the century. Other institutions of consequence in the field may have failed to respond to the 1927 queries of Robinson (1930) and so escaped notice as preparers of psychologists working in education during the period. However, the listed schools certainly were among the primary producers of such professionals and would seem representative of the rest.

Who should be included as an early educational psychologist is very much a matter of judgment. A high proportion of all psychologists from the turn of the century onward saw their discipline as a potentially useful one, and were eager to apply it. In part, of course, this was an aspect of the zeitgeist, the optimistic assumption pervading Western culture in the late 1800s and early 1900s that science and technology of all kinds had the capacity to alleviate or solve many of the problems of society, and to improve nearly every aspect of life. The school seemed a particularly appropriate locus for application of the developing science of behavior. Need was high because the schools were burgeoning, expanding rapidly in number and size, and increasingly responsible for new kinds of students (e.g., immigrant children and the culturally deprived) and were seeking help wherever promise seemed to exist. Thus many psychologists who had little intrinsic interest in education or the schools became involved in the process through professional obligation or perceived opportunity.

Searching for early manifestations of psychology or educational psychology requires some ingenuity because the nomenclature is not clear. Early in the century, psychology was likely to appear in departments of philosophy, where it lingered in some institutions until well into the 1930s or beyond. Courses carried a variety of innovative labels: (Mental Philosophy was a favorite, and Mental Science another, with Moral Science and Intellectual Philosophy also appearing in some programs). Educational applications of psychology often emerged in schools or departments of education, with traditional psychology remaining in the philosophy department. In at least one institution, work in education was administered by the College of Agriculture.

It should be clear that psychologists were not just trying to hawk their product to the education enterprise: many educators were actively seeking and supporting psychology because of their perceptions of its value. A good example of this attitude was that of Elwood P. Cubberley, a figure of considerable importance in early 20th-century education. He acquired a good basic understanding of psychology on his own, attracted Lewis Terman to his school, Stanford, and encouraged and supported Terman's work in intelligence, and that of other psychologists.

Who were the major figures in the emergence of educational psychology as a discipline? William James must be included because his views established a direction and orientation for generations of American psychologists, an orientation that made use and application of the discipline not only possible, but probable. James' own work in education is interesting to observe, but had little long-term effect other than to reduce the influence of faculty psychology. G. S. Hall was of major importance for two reasons. One was his emphasis on the centrality of the child in the educational process, relegating content to second place. This emphasis had long-term effects because of the second reason for his importance: his roster of distinguished studnets, including Jastrow, Burnham, Sanford, Terman and to a lesser degree Cattell and Dewey. These men realized in their life work what Hall suggested in his teaching. Edward L. Thorndike is the dominant figure in the emergence of educational psychology as a discipline. In his Columbia laboratory, for the first time, all the scientific rigor and sophisticated measurement emerging in the field was applied to the child, and specifically to the child as learner in school. If one wishes to review the literature of the major aspects of educational psychology today, one usually starts with Thorndike, or encounters his work as a major early exploration of the matter under consideration. James Angell at Chicago (followed by Harvey Carr) resembles G. S. Hall in that the Chicago students were influential for years in American education. They carried with them a clear orientation to a useful (functional) psychology and a devotion

to learning and learning theory; the work of their teacher was important in its own right, but the students spread out to institutions all over America, bringing with them the Chicago orientation. Dewey of course had preceded Angell at Chicago and set the tone for the movement that followed, but his own psychological work had less impact than his theoretical orientation. James, Hall, Thorndike, and the Chicago group then seem to be leaders without whose influence the discipline would not have emerged, or would have taken a very different form than it did.

To delineate the emergence of educational psychology as a discipline, this chapter has necessarily focused on ways in which individuals and institutions taught, applied, or promoted educational psychology as a source of help for education. But no discipline can flourish—or even survive—if it is "applying what it doesn't know" or is borrowing its content from some other discipline. So most early educational psychologists were producers as well as consumers of research. Thorndike of course is the model, with his lifetime accumulation of more than 500 publications, most of them research based. But he was unusual only in volume, not in having a basic concern for scholarly work. Space does not permit any exploration of the specifics of early educational psychology research, but relevant work appeared in most of the general psychological journals of the period as well as in more specialized periodicals, such as Hall's *Pedagogical Seminary*, first published in 1891 and later named *Journal of Genetic Psychology*, the Murchison *Journal of Educational Psychology*, with Volume 1 appearing in 1910, and the *Journal of Educational Research*, first appearing in 1910. Educational psychology indeed was a research-based discipline.

The discipline had not reached its maturity by the end of the period discussed in this chapter. It was the next generation of educational psychologists—students from this early period—who brought the movement to fruition by their research, teaching, and writing. But theirs is another story.

References

Allen, G. W. (1967). *William James: A biography.* New York: Viking.

Allport, G. W., & Boring, E. G. (1947). Psychology and social relations at Harvard University. *American Psychologist, 2,* 239–243.

Angell, J. R. (1904). *Psychology: An introductory study of the structure and function of human consciousness*. New York: Holt.

Angell, J. R. (1907). The province of functional psychology. *Psychological Review, 14*, 61–91.

Bain, A. (1884). *Education as a science*. New York: Appleton.

Baldwin, J. (1891). *Elementary psychology and education*. New York: Appleton.

Barzun, J. (1983). The masterpiece. In J. Barzun, *A Stroll with William James* (pp. 34–82). New York: Harper & Row.

Beck, R. H. (1980). *Beyond pedagogy: A history of the University of Minnesota College of Education*. St. Paul, MN: North Central.

Boring, E. G. (1953). John Dewey, 1859–1952. *American Journal of Psychology, 47*, 145–147.

Brett, G. S. (1912–1921). *History of psychology* (Vols. 1–3). London: George Unwin.

Burnham, W. H. (1899). Pedagogy. In W. E. Strong, L. N. Wilson (Eds.), *Clark University 1889–1899*, Decennial Volume (pp. 161–163). Worcester, MA: Clark University.

Catalog and circular of the University of Illinois. (1890–1891). Urbana, IL.

Cattell, J. M. (1930). Psychology in America. *Scientific Monthly, 30*.

Cheney, E. P. (1940). *History of the university of Pennsylvania*. Philadelphia, PA: University of Pennsylvania.

Claparede, E. (1911). *Experimental pedagogy and the psychology of the child* (4th ed.). London: Edward Arnold.

Cole, L. (1966). *A history of education*. New York: Holt, Rinehart & Winston.

Crabb, L. C. (1926). A study in the nomenclature and mechanics employed in catalog presentation in courses in education. *Peabody Contributions to Education*, No. 21.

Cremin, L. A., Shannon, D., & Townsend, M. (1954). *A history of Teachers College Columbia University*. New York: Columbia University.

Curti, M., & Carstensen, V. (1949). *The University of Wisconsin: 1848–1925 a history*. Madison: University of Wisconsin (Vol. l-ll).

Dewey, J. (1886). *Psychology*. New York: Harper and Brothers.

Dewey, J. (1896). The reflex arc concept in psychology. *Psychological Review, 3*, 357–370.

Dexter, T. F. G., & Garlick, A. H. (1908). *Psychology in the schoolroom*. New York: Longmans-Greene.

Dowlin, C. M. (1940). The University of Pennsylvania today. Philadelphia: University of Pennsylvania.

Evans, R. B. (1984). The origins of American academic psychology. In J. Brozek (Ed.) *Explorations in the history of psychology in the U.S.* pp. 17–60. Lewisburg: Bucknell Univ. Press.

Fisher, K. (1983). Hall: man remembered, science celebrated. *APA Monitor, 14*(12) 29.

Freeman, F. N. (1919). Courses in educational psychology in college, universities and normal schools. *Yearbook of the National Society of College Teachers of Education, 8*, 43–62.

Galton, *Sir* Francis. (1869). *Hereditary genius: An inquiry into its laws and consequences*. London: Macmillan.

Gates, A. I. (1932). The place of educational psychology in the curriculum for the education of teachers. *Studies in Education Yearbook, 20*, 21–43.

Good, H. G., & Teller, J. D. (1973). *A History of American Education*. New York: Macmillan.

Hall, G. S. (1901–1902). The ideal school as based on child study, *The Forum, 32*.

Hall, G. S. (1904). *Adolescence*. New York: Appleton.

Hall, G. S. (1911). *Educational problems*. New York: Appleton.

Herbart, J. (1913). *Outlines of educational doctrine*. A. F. Lange, Trans. Annotated by C. DeGarmo. New York: Macmillan. (Original version published 1901).

Hobbs, N. (1954). Peabody's program in human development and guidance. *The Peabody Reflector, 28*, 4.

Huey, E. B. (1908). *The psychology and pedagogy of reading: With a review of reading and writing and of methods, texts and hygiene in reading*. New York: Macmillan.

Hug, E. (1970). *The department of educational psychology, a partial review 1929–1970*. Unpublished report. New York: New York University.

James, W. Letter to his wife, July 24, 1896. Cited in G. W. Allen (1967) *William James* (p. 384). New York: Viking.

James, W. Letter to Rosina Emmet, August 2, 1896. Cited in G. W. Allen (1967) *William James* (p. 384). New York: Viking.

James, W. (1890). *Principles of psychology*. New York: Henry Holt.

James, W. (1899). *Talks to teachers on psychology and to students on some of life's ideals*. New York: Holt.

Jarrett, R. P. (1928). Status of courses in psychology in state teachers college in the United States. *Peabody Contributions to Education*, No. 47, p. 136. Nashville, TN: George Peabody College for Teachers.

Joncich, G. (1968). *The sane positivist: A biography of Edward L. Thorndike*. Middletown, CT: Wesleyan University.

Judd, C. H. (1915). *The psychology of high school subjects*. New York: Ginn.

Judd, C. H. (1918). *Introduction to scientific study of education*. New York: Ginn.

Judd, C. H. (1932). Autobiography. In C. Murchison (Ed.), *A history of psychology in autobiography* (Vol. 2, pp. 207–235). Worcester, MA: Clark University.

Judd, C. H. (1939). *Educational Psychology*. New York: Houghton-Mifflin.

Kuklick, B. (1977). *The rise of American philosophy*. New Haven: Yale University.

Luckey, G. W. A. (1903). *The professional training of secondary teachers in the United States*. New York: Macmillan.

MacDondald, M. E. (1927). A catalog study of courses in psychology in state normal schools and teachers college. *Educational Administration and Supervision, 13*, 272–282.

Memorandum on the History of the Department of Psychology, Tufts College. (Undated) Unpublished manuscript. Boston: Tufts University.

Meyers, A. E. (1965). *An educational history of the western world*. New York: McGraw Hill.

Morse, W. C. (1983). William Clark Trow (1894–1982). *American Psychologist, 38*, 849–850.

Murphy, G. (1951). *Historical introduction to modern psychology*. New York: Harcourt, Brace.

Murphy, G. (1971). William James on the will. *Journal of the History of the Behavioral Sciences, 7*, 249–260.

National Education Association. (1888). *Journal of Proceedings and addresses* (Vol. 27). Topeka: Kansas Publishing House.

Peabody Alumni News (1916, October). Jesup psychological laboratory dedicated, 2(1), 7.

The Peabody Reflector (1922). Cover, *3*, January 25, No. 2.

Perry, R. B. (1935). *The thought and character of William James* (Vol. 2). Boston, MA: Little, Brown.

Pestalozzi, J. H. (1898). *How Gertrude teaches her children*.

(L. E. Holland & F. C. Turner, Trans.) Syracuse, NY: C. Bordeen. (Original work published 1802)

Pierson, G. W. (1955). *Yale College, 1921–1937*. New Haven, CT: Yale University.

Poffenberger, A. T. (1962). Robert Sessions Woodworth, 1869–1962, *American Journal of Psychology, 75*, 677–692.

Powell, A. G. (1980). *The uncertain profession*. Cambridge: Harvard University.

Pyre, J. F. A. (1920) *Wisconsin*. New York: Oxford University.

Robinson, C. L. (1930). Psychology and the preparation of the teacher for the elementary school: A survey and an analysis of practices in the teaching of psychology in certain professional schools for the preparation of teachers. *Teachers College Contributions of Education*, No. 418. New York: Teachers College, Columbia University.

Rousseau, J. J. (1883). *Emile* (E. Worthington, Trans.). Boston, MA: D. C. Heath. (Original work published 1762)

Sawyer, R. M. (1973). *Centennial history of the University of Nebraska*. Lincoln, NE: Centennial Press.

School of Education Bulletin. (undated). Ann Arbor: University of Michigan, pp. 108–112.

Seagoe, M. V. (1975). *Terman and the gifted*. Los Altos, CA: William Kaufmann.

Sears, J. B., & Henderson, A. D. (1957). *Cubberley of Stanford*. Stanford, CA: Stanford University.

Shaffer, L. F. (1956). Presentation of the first gold medal award. *American Psychologist, 11*, 587–589.

Silver, H. (1983). *Education as history*. New York: Methuen.

Stanley, J. (1954). Peabody Ph.D.s in Psychology, 1919–1953. *The Peabody Reflector, 28*, January, p. 25.

Stephens, F. F. (1962). *A history of the University of Missouri*. Columbia, MO: University of Missouri.

Stutz, F. M. (1981). *The study of education at Cornell: role of the department of education, CALS*. Unpublished manuscript. Ithaca, New York: Department of Education, Cornell University.

Sully, J. (1817). *Teachers handbook of psychology, or the basis of the "Outlines of Psychology" by James Sully*. New York: Appleton.

Terman, L. M. (1932). Trails to psychology. In C. Murchison (Ed.), *A History of psychology in autobiography*. (Vol. 2, pp. 297–332). Worcester, MA: Clark University Press.

Tilton, J. W. (1960). *The Department of Education at Yale University, 1891–1958*. New Haven, CT: Yale University.

Travers, R. M. (1983). *How research has changed American schools*. Kalamazoo, MI: Mythos.

Viles, J. (1939). *The University of Missouri, a centennial history*. Columbia, MO: University of Missouri.

Vives, J. L. (1531). De tradendis disciplinis. In F. Watson Trans. *Vives on education*. Cambridge: Cambridge University Press, 1913.

Watson, F. (1915). The father of modern psychology. *Psychological Review, 22*, 333–353.

Watson, G. (1926). What shall be taught in educational psychology? *Journal of Educational Psychology, 17*, 577–599.

Watson, R. I. (1978). *The great psychologists* (4th Ed.) New York: Lippin.

Wherry, R. J. (1968). *A statistical history of the department of psychology at The Ohio State University 1907–1968*. Columbus, OH: Ohio State University.

Whipple, G. M. (1910, April). The teaching of psychology in normal schools. *Psychological Monographs, 12* (Whole #51).

Whitney, A. S. (1931). *History of the professional training of teachers*. Ann Arbor, MI: George Wahr.

Woodward, W. R. (1984). William James' psychology of will: Its revolutionary impact on American psychology. In J. Brozek (Ed.), *Explorations in the history of psychology in the United States* (pp. 148–195). Lewisburg, PA: Bucknell University Press.

Woodworth, R. S. (1914). The psychological research of James McKeen Cattell. *Archives of Psychology*, No. 30.

Woodworth, R. S., & Sheehan, M. R. (1964). *Contemporary schools of psychology*. New York: Ronald.

Wundt, W. (1904). *Principles of physiological psychology* (5th German ed.), (Vol. 1, E. G. Titchener, Trans). New York: Macmillan. (Original work published 1874)

PART II

The Development of Educational Psychology

The nine chapters in this section focus on the histories of areas that have had profound influences on educational psychology. The study of individual differences, measurement, and the various approaches to learning have formed the core of our discipline. The relatively short-lived child study movement affected early development of the field and our ongoing relationships with school psychology and guidance continue to have important implications for our identity.

CHAPTER 3

A History of the Child Study Movement in America

Emily S. Davidson and Ludy T. Benjamin, Jr.

The child study movement constitutes an important chapter in the history of educational psychology. Although goals of the movement were diverse, its principal purpose was to establish a scientific pedagogy, to bring the methods of experimental psychology to bear in discovering all that could be known about the child: sensory capabilities, physical characteristics, humor, play, religious ideas, memory, attention span, and so forth. With this new knowledge, education would no longer be guesswork but a science. Pedagogical practices would be restructured in such a way as to be maximally effective for all kinds of students. In this context, child study was seen as a natural bridge between the universities and the schools, a link that would aid in the acceptance of an educational psychology.

In this chapter we will describe the development of the child study movement from the work of G. Stanley Hall, beginning in 1883, through the establishment of the Child Welfare Research Station at the State University of Iowa in 1917. Foundings are rarely unequivocal and child study is no exception; the continuity of ideas that is the intellectual history of child study began long before the writings of Hall and continues today. A myriad of forces related to industrialization, immigration, and urbanization, as well as changing philosophies of education and of human nature, were antecedent to this movement. This chapter will discuss those antecedents to child study as well as the legacy of child study for contemporary psychology and education. But the focus of this history will be on the years 1883–1917, with emphases on the goals of the movement, the methods used in pursuit of those goals, the accomplishments and failures of the movement, and the effect of the movement on the psychology and education of its time.

Eighteenth- and Nineteenth-Century Views of Education

A new round in the centuries-old debate on human nature (and particularly the nature of children) was being conducted in the later decades of the 18th century. One of the most enthusiastic and influential participants for our purposes was Jean-Jacques Rousseau (1712–1778). The publication of *Julie ou la nouvelle Héloïse* in 1761 and *Emile* in 1762 provided Rousseau's major statements on the nature and education of children, or at least male children. The child was basically good; the purpose of education was to use reason to develop nature. Further, education should take place in the

Emily S. Davidson and Ludy T. Benjamin, Jr. • Department of Psychology, Texas A & M University, College Station, TX 77843.

country (an emphasis on the benefits of rural life for children is a theme that runs throughout the history of education) largely through direct interaction with the objects in the world. The teacher, in a one-on-one relationship, by staying alert to the child's individual talents and needs could present the child with new objects and new information. The child would never be forced to learn anything, even reading or writing; rather education was to be self-directed. The nature of the female was quite different; it was markedly inferior to that of the male. She was to be given only as much education as necessary to fit her to her life as helper to the male (Sahakian & Sahakian, 1974).

Although Rousseau was roundly condemned by the Paris parliament after the publication of *Emile,* his works were immensely popular throughout Europe. His ideas stimulated model schools, such as the one founded by German educator Johan Bernhard Basedow in 1774. Among the most important individuals influenced by Rousseau was Johann Heinrich Pestalozzi.

Pestalozzi (1746–1827) received the traditional, grim schooling of the time, with its emphasis on catechism and rote learning. He, like many other young people of the time, greeted the publication of *Emile* with great enthusiasm (he even named his son for Rousseau). Pestalozzi's first response to Rousseau's call for a return to the natural life was to become a farmer. This effort was not a success and after disposing of his own money and most of his wife's inheritance, he turned his efforts in new directions, founding a school for poor children at Neuhof in 1774. Although this school failed in 1780, Pestalozzi later worked for and founded other schools. A school at Stans for orphans, begun in 1799, was short-lived and Pestalozzi became a teacher at another school in Burgdorf that same year. He became director of that school the following year, a position he retained until 1804, when he founded an experimental school at Yverdon. That school provided the demonstration of Pestalozzi's ideas about education until 1825, shortly before his death in 1827 (Downs, 1975).

Pestalozzi's philosophy of education was heavily influenced by Rousseau, but differed from it in important ways. Pestalozzi was strongly committed to education for the poor; his first school at Neuhof was for the poor and 50 years later, near the end of his life, he left Yverdon to return to Neuhof, founding another school for poor children. Poor children had to learn a trade and the rudiments of reading and writing. But the method was to be similar; learning should be self-generated through direct observation. Rote learning of the catechism was not accepted. In addition, Pestalozzi recognized the importance of emotional development and viewed the relationship between teacher and learner (especially the first teacher, the mother) as the critical base for the education of the child (Downs, 1975).

Of course, the demonstration schools were not the only way Pestalozzi communicated his philosophy of education. He published a number of books expressing his ideas, including an early baby biography in 1774 about his young son, Jean-Jacques, a novel, *Leonard and Gertrude,* which went through several editions as Pestalozzi's ideas changed, and *How Gertrude Teaches Her Children* in 1801. These works were among the best sellers of their day and in addition to their influence, also brought many visitors to Pestalozzi's schools, among them Froebel and Herbart (Downs, 1975).

Friedrich Froebel (1782–1852) also had an unhappy childhood and unsuccessful early experiences with school, which may have fueled his interest in education. He visited Pestalozzi's school at Yverdon for 2 weeks in 1805 and spent 2 years there from 1808 to 1810. He was impressed by the emphasis on direct observation, but was also impressed by the lack of organization and the disconnectedness of different subjects. In 1817, he founded a school in Keilhau, Germany in which he could put his own ideas into effect. Because his financial abilities were on a level with Pestalozzi's, the early years were difficult. Although the school was not a financial success, it was an educational one and in 1831, Froebel received an invitation to set up a school in Switzerland (Downs, 1978).

During the years in Switzerland, from 1831 to 1836, Froebel became increasingly convinced of the importance of early experiences and envisioned a situation in which an educated mother worked with her child until the child entered school. He left Switzerland in 1836, in part because of religious opposition to his ideas, and returned to Germany, prepared to set up his first institution for very young children. Like Pestalozzi and Rousseau before him, Froebel believed that children were essentially good and needed to be nurtured and cared for at an early age. Like young plants, their own nature would allow them to develop properly, hence the name *kindergarten* for these institutions. The titles infant school and nursery school were deliberately avoided because they implied the imposition of formal education and lessons.

Froebel's kindergartens combined work and

play. The work, at least in the kindergartens with which Froebel was directly involved, was gardening. Froebel felt that this taught the child about nature through direct observation; and also taught the child responsibility and cooperation, because each child's plot was part of a larger garden. The main emphasis however was play, but carefully directed play.

While still in Switzerland, Froebel had begun to develop the "gifts" and "occupations" for which he became famous. The "gifts" were a series of objects; balls, building blocks, sticks, rings, paper, etc. of increasing complexity. The first gift was a set of six wool balls, in six different colors, to be given to a child as early as 2 months of age. A later gift was a wooden cube, made up of eight smaller cubes; by playing with these objects, the child would learn form, color, whole–part relations, number, and the bases for the later study of mathematics. The "occupations" were the formal activities that used the gifts. Froebel and his assistants devised dozens of games that used the gifts, often deriving the games from their observations of children in free play (children in Froebel's kindergartens did not spend all their time in gardening and organized play; they had many opportunities for free play as well).

Another component of Froebel's system of early education was music. Songs were to accompany various exercises and songs could teach about the world (e.g., songs about the moon, or birds, or plants). The culmination of Froebel's efforts was *Mother's Songs, Games, and Stories,* published in 1843. In this book, Froebel described the many activities in which a mother should engage her child. Although Froebel is known as the founder of the kindergarten, he emphasized the importance of the family, particularly the mother, in the early education of children.

Johann Friedrich Herbart (1776–1841), another visitor to Pestalozzi's school at Yverdon, although writing during the same time as Pestalozzi and Froebel, had quite different ideas about education. Pestalozzi and Froebel believed in the inherent good nature of the child; the purpose of education was to allow this goodness to develop freely. Herbart, by contrast, viewed the child as essentially neutral; the purpose of education was to instill moral values. Herbart, unlike Pestalozzi and Froebel, had relatively little experience teaching children (2 years as a tutor); instead, most of his career was spent as a university professor (Dunkel, 1970).

Herbart was deeply interested in psychology and believed strongly that theories of education should be based on psychology, in particular, on an empirical psychology. As an associationist, Herbart's ideas about the apperceptive mass (the mass of thoughts and ideas already in the mind) and about the five steps toward acquiring new knowledge (preparation, presentation, association, generalization, and application) were very influential in educational circles of the 19th century. It was his emphasis on psychology as science, however, that helped to lead to the child study movement 50 years later. The publication of *Psychology as a Science* in 1824–1825 marked his major statement on the subject. Herbart's view of psychology as science was that it was empirical, based on direct observation, and mathematical; it was not, however, experimental. His views on empiricism later influenced the child study movement via Fechner and Wundt, but his rejection of experiment led to a rift between the child study movement and the American Herbartians (Dunkel, 1970).

This resurgence of interest in the nature of children in the late 1700s and early 1800s combined with the accelerating development of psychology as a science led a few educators and/or scientists to attempt systematic observations of children, in these cases, their own. These were the baby biographies of the 19th century. A very early one was by Pestalozzi, *Diary on the Education of his Three-year Old Son* (1774), in which he detailed his intensive teaching of his young son. This work contained the beginnings of Pestalozzi's ideas about education, but on the whole had relatively little impact compared to Pestalozzi's other writings and the schools that he ran.

At the beginning of the 19th century, education was still largely the province of the middle class or the wealthy; universal education was not the norm. The major goal of the elementary school was to teach reading, and to a lesser extent writing. There was only sporadic interest in teaching mathematics, science, or the arts. The secondary schools, even more elite than the elementary schools, were intended largely as preparation for the university and were heavily focused on classical humanism. In the United States, religion and education were closely tied, and the orthodoxy of the teacher's religious beliefs was as important a qualification for teaching as the teacher's own level of education, which varied widely (Pounds, 1968).

Systems of education in Europe and the United States began to diverge as the century progressed. The class system of Europe led to the establishment of a dual system of education, with separate schools for upper and lower classes. In the United States, a system developed in which, at least in theory, every level of education would be available to those with the ability to take advantage of it. The poor would be educated for free, establishing, after many battles at local levels, the principle of free education. A concurrent fight led to the gradual separation of religion from education. Following the idea of making education freely available to all (dependent on ability) came the idea of requiring that all take advantage of it. Massive immigration, especially from Europe, gave the schools a new role, that of teaching the American culture to the new arrivals. Many of the new arrivals had little inclination for this indoctrination and had to be forced to attend. Massachusetts passed the first compulsory school attendance law in 1852 and by the close of the century, most states had such laws (Pounds, 1968).

Although one of the purposes of the compulsory attendance laws was to change the immigrants, the immigrants were also changing the schools. The ideas of Pestalozzi, Froebel, and Herbart had their influence partly through Americans who went to Europe to study these new ideas. But an equally important force for change were the immigrants, in particular German immigrants who established Froebel's kindergarten system in the United States.

The massive number of students required a massive number of teachers as well, and as the century progressed there was increasing concern over the qualifications of those teachers. States began to establish normal schools, separate from the colleges and universities, whose purpose was to teach the methods of teaching. These schools were dominant through much of the 19th century, but gradually came to be viewed as inadequate, particularly for the preparation of secondary school teachers. Slowly, the functions of the normal schools began to be transferred to already established colleges and universities or to newly established teachers colleges.

The Industrial Revolution and the Growth of Cities

The American Revolution established a new political and economic entity, but one with strong roots in English political and economic philosophy. The political system was one that protected individual freedoms and encouraged individual initiatives; the Industrial Revolution was one of the results. The technological advances necessary were made in the 1700s and early 1800s and industrialization continued its growth in the middle of the century. But truly explosive growth occurred between the Civil War and World War I. In that time period, the number of manufacturing jobs more than tripled, from 1.8 million to 6.3 million. Manufacturing required concentrations of workers and, as a consequence, the United States became increasingly urban. At the beginning, about one quarter of the population lived in towns and cities; by the end almost half did. The increase in city populations came partly from workers moving from the country to the city, the dominant pattern in Europe, but in the United States many of the new city dwellers were immigrants (Hughes, 1970).

The new city dwellers faced very different living conditions than those of their agricultural parents. Agricultural work was usually a family's work, tied to the home. In contrast, the factory worker was separated from family members, who were probably working in other factories. Whether at work or at home, the working class existed in abysmal conditions. The work day was long, 12 to 15 hours, even for children, and the work itself was brutal and dangerous. Conditions at home were little better; cities had not been planned to house so many people, buildings were crowded, and sanitation totally inadequate (Stearns, 1967).

The middle class also grew during this time, both in numbers and in relative wealth. The great industrialists usually came from that group, and within the middle class as a whole, mobility was fairly high. The contrast in living conditions was marked in most cities; the middle class responded in several ways. For many, the initial response was a denial that conditions for workers were really that bad; this strategy was difficult to maintain for any long period of time. Other responses were to explain the discrepancy as being the result of the natural order of things or to try to change the conditions.

The publication of Darwin's *The Origin of Species* provided the basis for justifying differences of outcome for different people. Herbert Spencer, writing during the same period, provided a comprehensive philosophy of science, incorporating Darwin's biology as well as new discoveries in physics, which would explain the workings of humans and their societies. Just as plant and animal life had evolved through natural selection and survival of the fittest, so too did human societies evolve. That evolution, if left unchecked, should lead, eventually, to greater and greater progress by society. Many writers of the period equated fitness with socioeconomic status: the poor were poor because they were unfit. The harsh conditions of their lives were a natural consequence of their incompetence, and it was not merely unnecessary to alleviate those conditions but actually unnatural and inhumane. It was natural for the poor to die early and efforts to change this would retard the progress of society (Hofstadter, 1945).

Social Darwinism, like biological Darwinism before it, had its critics. Some tried to establish the roots of altruism in its evolutionary value, others challenged the notion that economic status could be equated with fitness. Still others focused their attention directly on changing the conditions of the working poor.

The child welfare movement was part of this larger effort for reform. Paralleling the rise of industrialization and urbanization was the rise of the progressives, who attempted to change working and living conditions. The progressives were ambivalent about the poor; they blamed poverty and poor living conditions on moral attitudes that led to continuing poverty. As a consequence, not only did the physical conditions have to be changed (more and better housing, improved sanitation), the poor themselves had to change in order to benefit from these improvements. No group seemed more appropriate for help than children (Lubove, 1962).

Children who were particularly vulnerable had to be protected. The latter half of the 19th century saw the rise of a variety of institutions and laws designed to protect them (Siegel & White, 1982). Orphanages or foster homes provided care for otherwise normal children not receiving adequate care from their families. Special institutions were established for retarded children, for the deaf, blind, or otherwise physically handicapped. The growth of such institutions slowly accelerated as the century came to a close, accompanied by considerable debate about the most appropriate treatment for such children.

Children less physically disadvantaged still had to be protected from the psychological consequences of poverty. They needed to be prevented from vice and instilled with the moral values of middle-class society (which provided most of the reformers). The institution most responsible for these changes was the school. The passage of child labor laws got children out of factories, considered good in and of itself (it also reduced competition for jobs); passage of compulsory attendance laws got them into schools.

Although schools were the major means of training children in moral values, they were not the only means. Adult society was faced with the problem of what to do with city children after school. One reaction was the development of boys clubs (clubs were founded for girls as well, but boys were the major focus because they tended to get into more serious trouble). Clubs for working class boys were largely aimed at providing alternatives to being out on the street (Macleod, 1983). Most of these clubs, unlike those for middle-class children, did not try to build character; if the activities provided kept boys off the streets and in a state of relative calm, that was sufficient. The YMCAs, originally founded to serve the needs of young adult men, gradually expanded with junior departments to serve boys. They excluded poor boys as much as possible, partly through the imposition of fees that the poor simply could not afford. The YMCAs did try to build character— through religious training, educational programs, and physical exercise. Boys' Brigades, with a quasi-military structure and an emphasis on temperance pledges, also served the middle class and foreshadowed the Boy Scout movement.

The schools and the youth organizations were intended to produce model citizens/workers. When that effort failed, another set of institutions took over. Although social Darwinist thought dominated theories of criminality and suggested a strong genetic component in crime, those who actually worked with young criminals held onto the belief that juvenile delinquents could be rehabilitated. Beginning in the 1840s and 1850s, state-supported reform schools, located in the country, away from the vice of the cities, were established (Kett, 1977). Intended to provide a stable home-like environment for the lower-class criminal, who, presumably, had never experienced it, most reform schools quickly developed a prison-like atmosphere.

Concurrent with the development of the manufacturing economy and the intellectual ferment that accompanied it was the development of empiricism. In Europe, Darwinian theory, (as well as a number of other intellectual trends) had suggested that individual humans might differ as much as examples of other species. The social Darwinists developed these ideas philosophically; the empiricists demonstrated them.

One of the most important of these early empiricists was Francis Galton, whose particular interest was the relationships between individual difference and heredity (Anastasi, 1965). In his early work, he used family history questionnaires, both with the talented (*Hereditary Genius, 1869;* and *English Men of Science,* 1874) and with the general population (*Natural Inheritance,* 1889). He was also concerned with the actual measurement of different abilities, especially sensory abilities. He devised a number of ways of measuring such things as pitch discrimination, reaction time, and strength of movement.

During the same period, Wundt established his laboratory in 1879. Although much of the work of the first psychologists was aimed at demonstrating similarities in human capacities and behavior, some students did look at individual differences. James McKeen Cattell did his dissertation on individual differences in reaction time, and before returning to the United States, made contact with Galton in England.

In the latter part of the 19th century, these forces combined to push for the scientific study of children. Immigration and industrialization heightened the need for schooling, the increasing enrollment of students sparked a demand from parents and teachers for information about how to teach children; the social Darwinists and individual difference psychologists wanted to know about how adult differences started, and the child welfare workers wanted help in planning programs to help children. The child study movement attempted to meet these diverse needs.

The Founding of Child Study

Credit for the founding of the Child Study Movement in America has historically been accorded to Granville Stanley Hall (1844–1924). Hall's commitment to child study covered the years 1883 through 1918, although after 1911 his involvement lessened. It began in Germany where he studied for two years after receiving his doctorate from Harvard in 1878. Hall planned to use the trip to enhance his knowledge of physiology, and indeed he was able to work with Hermann von Helmholtz at Berlin and Carl Ludwig at Leipzig. But characteristic of his broad intellectual interests, Hall found himself drawn to other subjects, including the German educational system and its underlying view of the nature of the child (Hall,

1923). He became familiar with the German studies of the knowledge of beginning school children (Bartholomai, 1870) and these questionnaire studies became the basis for his similar work with Boston public school children.

Hall admired Preyer's work and was responsible for the English translation of his *Die Seele des Kindes* (Bradbury, 1937). His familiarity with the problems of education uncovered in the Bartholomai study and his respect for Preyer's scientific approach to the study of children led him to propose child study as the nucleus of a new approach to pedagogy. He made his initial call to arms in an address before a gathering of school superintendents at a meeting of the National Education Association in the spring of 1882 (Ross, 1972). Later that year he would begin his study of Boston school children that would culminate in "The Contents of Children's Minds," published in an 1883 issue of the *Princeton Review*. That paper is acknowledged as the formal beginning of the child study movement (Dennis, 1949).

For the Boston study, Hall developed a questionnaire of 134 items, nearly double what Bartholomai had used in his survey. But although the questions increased, the nature of the survey was very similar, with Hall's questions largely drawn from the same seven areas used in the German study (e.g., astronomy, animals, plants, mathematics). However, he added some other questions that tested children's beliefs, including their understanding of right and wrong. Considerable care was taken in both the construction of the questionnaire and in its administration. The items were pretested to determine their comprehensibility for children. Further, the school teachers used to collect the responses were given a standardized administration procedure and the principal examiners coordinating those teachers were given additional training. Once the responses were collected, the questionnaire results were divided and reliability checks done on the various subsets. For its time, Hall's study was reasonably sound methodologically, but has been criticized for its content (Ross, 1972) and its interpretation of the results (Siegel & White, 1982).

Like the German study, Hall's questionnaire sought to establish what city school children knew upon entering school. His questions asked these Boston children about beehives, sunsets, brooks, crows, rainbows, and growing wheat. Not surprisingly he found much ignorance among the children tested. For example, 80% did not know what a beehive was, 93% did not know that leather products came from animals, and 92% could not define dew. Indeed, many of the questions favored children from a rural existence due to Hall's belief that "knowledge of country life constituted 'general' knowledge and that it formed a superior mental training to knowledge of city life." (Ross, 1972, p. 127). So convinced was he of the values of knowledge gained from country life that he urged city parents to take their children for visits in the country to improve their intelligence (Hall, 1883).

Although some may have taken issue with Hall's study, there were many, both educators and parents, who viewed the results as strong evidence of the need for educational reform in America, and in the 1880s, the voices for that kind of reform were growing in strength (Hendricks, 1968). How could education be effective if teachers were unaware of the nature of the child? How might knowledge of the mind of a child aid parents in providing the proper rearing to assist children in reaching their full potential? How might this knowledge motivate teachers and ensure greater sensitivity and enthusiasm in them? Those were some of the questions raised in support of the need for child study and its relationship to educational reform.

Hall's study of the contents of children's minds was much in demand, so much so that he authored a similar version under the title "The Study of Children," which was privately published in the same year (Hall, 1883). Eight years later the survey was republished in Hall's journal, *Pedagogical Seminary,* a version that also contained some corroborating data from a survey conducted in the public schools of Kansas City (Hall, 1891). Two years later the 1883 study was reprinted again as a separate booklet and sold for 25 cents. It was referred to as a classic study that "should be in the hands of every teacher" (Wolfe, 1896a, p. 11).

Such studies were not conducted without resistance, in some cases from teachers, but mostly from parents. Some critics argued that studies of the kind encouraged by Hall and others advocating child study would make children self-conscious and would take away the "natural naivete" of children. Child study was seen as a kind of "mental vivisection" that should be opposed. Opponents called for children to be loved, not studied (Hall, 1900).

Child study involved not only the mind, but the body as well. Henry P. Bowditch, one of Hall's professors at Harvard and an eminent physiologist,

had conducted a large-scale study of the physical measurements of children in the Boston schools in 1879. His study established some of the earliest norms for school children, by age and sex, in physical dimensions, such as body size and length of arms, in motor skills, such as strength of grip and running, and in perceptual capabilities including tests of vision, audition, and smell. Bowditch's study, and those that followed, were part of an emphasis on physical hygiene as it related to the development of mental abilities or as an indicator of the state of a child's mental development. Although these anthropometric studies were of lesser importance in the child study movement, they reinforced the belief in physical health as a condition for maximizing learning and stimulated studies to discover how school environments could be altered (e.g., ventilation, lighting, temperature) to enhance education (Wolfe, 1896a).

The child study advocates, primarily influenced by Hall's work, were able to establish a Committee on Pedagogy as a Science, which issued its report at an 1884 meeting of the National Education Association. There was some opposition to the report from educators who resented the implication that pedagogy to date was unscientific. But support for child study was strong and eventually there was something of a consensus in the NEA that called for educators joining with those specialists who were seeking to construct a scientific pedagogy (Ross, 1972).

Interestingly, Hall would be little involved for the remainder of the decade. He had been offered a faculty position at Johns Hopkins University in 1882 and would spend the next few years building experimental psychology there. Organizational efforts with the *American Journal of Psychology* and then the move to Clark University as its president would occupy him in the decade to come. These duties deprived child study of its most influential and vocal advocate and for most of the 1880s the movement was hardly a movement at all. Rather, there were pockets of interest, mostly centered around educational reform, particularly the reformers who had returned from their study abroad with Herbartian disciples. In 1885, at Hall's suggestion, the Worcester State Normal School began a program of child study using students in the normal school to study children in the local schools (Wolfe, 1896a); a Bureau of Child Study was established in the Chicago schools in 1889 (Mullen, 1981); and in 1890, Harry Kirke Wolfe began a formal program in child study at the

University of Nebraska, training education majors in the methods of child study (Benjamin & Bertelson, 1975). These events, as well as others, signalled the growing interest in child study, but there was no leader who seemed able to coalesce the diverse groups (teachers, principals, psychologists, physicians, physical education instructors, parents) into one, that is, until Hall returned to child study in 1891.

The event was the annual meeting of the NEA, which Hall had not attended since 1885. At the 1891 meeting in Toronto, he placed a notice on a bulletin board announcing a gathering of those interested in discussing child study. Approximately 150 of the NEA attendees were present at that discussion. The movement had its leader and it was a role Hall was ready to assume, partly because of his interest in attracting public support for Clark University (Ross, 1972), but also because he believed that experimental psychology had reached a state of development that allowed the establishment of a true science of child study (Hall, 1894). In support of that belief he established a new journal, *Pedagogical Seminary,* in 1891 to publish the results of scientific pedagogy. Hall, himself, dated the child study movement to this date (1891) and not to the "contents" study of 1883. The exact founding is of little importance; what is clear is that the movement had considerable momentum in the 1890s and enjoyed its greatest successes during that decade. It was bold in its hopes and in its promises, a boldness that attracted supporters and participants, as well as detractors.

Child Study and the New Psychology

In the early 1890s, the science of psychology, largely imported from the new German laboratories in Leipzig and Berlin, was barely a decade old in America. Not surprisingly, there were many critics of the laboratory work in this philosophical discourse turned experimental science. The proponents of this "new psychology" encountered much resistance in establishing their laboratories and were called upon to demonstrate the applicability of their science. In reacting to the critics, some psychologists, such as William James, acknowledged the fledgling nature of experimental psychology, whereas others believed psychology was now fully established as a science. For example, in an appeal for funding for laboratory equip-

ment and space, H. K. Wolfe wrote to the University of Nebraska Board of Regents in 1890: "the study of the mind is the most universally *applied* of all sciences. Because we learn so much about it from everyday experience is the reason perhaps that it only recently has become an 'exact' science" (Benjamin, 1975, p. 376).

G. S. Hall may not have agreed with Wolfe's assessment of psychology as an exact science but his 10 years of laboratory work at Johns Hopkins and Clark universities had convinced him of psychology's potential for application in education. He made that pronouncement at a meeting on education in Chicago in 1893, held in conjunction with the World's Columbian Exposition. In her historical treatment of child study, Dorothy Ross (1972) calls that meeting one of the most significant events in spreading the gospel of child study throughout the country. Hall (1894) followed that with an article in *Forum* entitled "The New Psychology as a Basis of Education." In his summary of the value of the new psychology he wrote, "The one chief and immediate field of application for all this work is its application to education, considered as the science of human nature and the art of developing it to its fullest maturity" (p. 718).

The Goals of Child Study

To this point we have treated child study as a program in the service of education. That emphasis is deserved but not wholly accurate. Definitions of child study differed, although most were similar to that of G. W. A. Luckey (1896), who wrote that the goal of child study is "to make common property the best and truest in educational practices from the earliest times to the present, and to bring our teaching into harmony with the natural stages of the growing child as determined by its spontaneous interests" (p. 2).

One of the beliefs of the rational approach to education was that teaching was an art and that knowledge of child nature and skill in teaching were acquired in only one way—by teaching. Those in child study opposed that belief, arguing that such a practice was bad for children and teachers alike. They felt the skills of teaching could be acquired in a much shorter time period when teachers were taught the laws of development of child nature before they were permitted to teach. For many parents and teachers, the attraction of the child study movement was its promise for an effective and painless education. The improvement of educational practices was clearly of highest priority.

Whereas the rank and file of the movement were working for a better education for their children and students, some of the leaders of the movement had other ambitions. We have already mentioned that child study offered an obvious link between the universities and the schools, a link that was probably looked upon with more favor by the university side. Schools of education in universities were expanding and the beliefs about teacher training and teaching as a profession supported their growth. Child study offered a means to strengthen the ties between teachers at the two levels.

Another goal of child study was to provide the knowledge necessary to change parenting techniques. A. E. Winship (1892) described the goal of child study as knowing "the present relative maturity and immaturity of the child, physically, intellectually, socially, and religiously, with a view to knowing how best to secure the most complete maturity at the proper time" (p. 141). Knowledge of the child would help parents to see that children attained their highest mental, moral, and physical development. As noted earlier, the end of the 19th century marked significant changes in the nature of the American family, especially with removal of many children from the work force and increasing their time spent in school. Parents looked to professionals for help and child study offered the promise of that help (Schlossman, 1976).

Child study coexisted with the beginnings of mental testing in America and the two were closely related (Mullen, 1981). One anticipated outcome of child study was a classification system of children based on the huge normative studies encouraged by Hall (1903) and others (e.g., Bruce, 1903). Interest was growing in the psychopathology of the child and it was felt that child study might uncover the secrets of such pathology. Although Freud's influence in America was still some years away, there were child study advocates (e.g., James Mark Baldwin) who espoused a belief in the importance of early experiences for adult behavior. As such, the child study movement made some contributions to the development of American clinical psychology (Siegel & White, 1982), but we would not label this contribution a goal of the movement.

In assessing its goals, we should recognize that the child study movement was a conglomerate of people with diverse interests. It attracted experimental psychologists, teachers, parents, physicians, and social workers. Hall (1900) described the movement as composed of psychology, anthropology, ethics, philosophy, biology, medico-hygiene, pedagogy, with a touch of folklore, religious evolution, and gossip. Not surprisingly the coalition was an uneasy one. Some groups were better served and would remain with the movement for many years, whereas others would desert the cause in dismay or dissatisfaction. We will treat those issues in a later section of this chapter.

Scientific Pedagogy at Clark University

With renewed interest in a national campaign of child study research, partly stimulated by the interest shown from those at the 1891 NEA meeting, Hall began attempts at a formal organization of the movement. At the 1891 NEA meeting, Hall had called for a national society for scientific pedagogy and the proposal was enthusiastically received. Attempts to establish such a group failed, apparently due to the narrowness of views represented in those individuals Hall chose to serve as directors. Although no national child study organization was ever founded, the NEA did establish a Child Study Department in 1894 as part of the association and Hall was elected its first president (Ross, 1972).

An important step in fostering child study was to make significant contacts with teachers. One approach to that end was the establishment of child study programs, typically held on college and university campuses during the summer months. The most prominent of these summer programs was initiated by Hall at Clark University in 1892.

Sixty-eight attended this first session, including a half-dozen principals of normal schools, a like number of city school superintendents, generally from small towns in the East, a few university professors of pedagogy, and the rest generally normal school teachers. The entire Clark faculty led these eager students from 8 a.m. to 10 p.m. through cram courses in the new psychology and progressive educational ideas, and left them, according to report, enthusiastic supporters. (Ross, 1972, p. 281)

These summer programs, typically 2-weeks in length, were an annual feature at Clark through 1903. Similar programs for teachers were established a few years later in Illinois, California, and Nebraska.

The focus of scientific pedagogy was the questionnaire. Although Hall did not originate the technique, his extensive use of questionnaires has caused the method to be associated historically with his name. The first of the Clark University child study questionnaires was on anger and it was printed in October of 1894. This questionnaire, like the many that followed, was designed by Hall, his colleagues, and students. By 1903, 96 questionnaire studies had been completed and by 1915 that number had swelled to 194 (Hall, 1903, 1923). Attendees at the summer conferences at Clark often participated in collecting the data for these surveys and in some cases contributed to the content of the questionnaires themselves.

These 194 questionnaire studies carried out over a period of 20 years would be used by Hall in four books that he published between 1904 and 1911: the two-volume work on adolescence (1904), a condensed version of that work entitled *Youth, Its Education, Regimen and Hygiene* (1906), a book on children and education (1907), and another two-volume work on educational problems (1911).

Child Study in Other Areas of the United States

Hall encouraged states to form their own child study societies and eventually about half of them formed such groups. The first of these was the Illinois Society for Child Study, which was founded at Champaign, Illinois, in May of 1894. That society was spawned by Hall's speech at the Columbian Exposition the year prior. The Illinois society held an annual summer conference, lasting from four days to a week, which attracted large audiences. F. W. Parker, head of the Cook County Normal School, W. O. Krohn of the University of Illinois (a Hall student from Clark), and C. C. Van Liew of the Illinois State Normal University were the chief organizers for these early conferences. By 1896, membership in the society numbered 1,300.

Although few state societies would become as large as that of Illinois, most would model their organization after it. The organization was dominated by teachers and by teacher trainers from the normal schools. Psychologists played a minor role. The first work of the Illinois society was to establish contacts with the regional educational societies in the state and to ask that those groups place the subject of child study on their respective programs. In two years, child study was a standard feature at all of the regional educational meetings. The state organization also sponsored and encouraged the formation of local child study groups with a person designated from each group to maintain contact with the state society. To aid the local groups, the state society arranged roundtables in local communities that included parents, physicians, teachers, and others interested in child study issues on a community level.

The Illinois society also published several volumes on child study that included papers presented at the summer conferences, sample questionnaires to be used in child study, papers from "leading child study specialists" around the country, and some original child study work generated within the state (Wolfe, 1896b). But publications from the state societies were the exception, rather than the rule. These societies existed principally to organize interested parties within the state and to promote the concept of the value of child study. Scientific pedagogy was not one of their purposes, although they contributed to such efforts in their cooperation with educators and psychologists at colleges and universities. They existed in part to disseminate the latest scientific discoveries in child study to their public, namely principals, teachers, and parents.

Following the lead in Illinois, state child study societies were formed in Iowa in 1894, in Nebraska in 1895, and in Kansas and Minnesota in 1896. By 1910, approximately another 20 states had followed suit. Several publications emerged to report the activities of these groups. One that was prominent in the child study field was the *Northwestern Journal of Education,* which began focusing on child study in 1896, publishing child study research and state society activities from the midwestern part of the United States.

University-based research units also emerged in the 1890s. The best known of these, outside of Clark, was headed by Earl Barnes, a professor of education at Stanford University. Barnes conducted summer courses for teachers at Stanford and in other locations in California. He began working with teachers in 1891, using them to collect data from their classes. By 1896 he had gathered responses to various questionnaires from more than 75,000 students on topics such as play, color choice, ambitions, and theological ideas. His evaluation of this work was that it was "most unsatisfactory, but it has made a beginning" (Wolfe, 1896a, p. 7). Barnes was principally critical of the untrained teachers who had gathered much of the data. Still, this research was incorporated into 10 separate issues of the journal, *Studies in Education,* which Barnes edited in 1896 and 1897.

Like Hall, Barnes relied primarily on the questionnaire method, although he recognized the value of other child study techniques. He generated a great number of surveys that would offer direct comparisons between children in the West and those in the East, tested in Hall's studies. Rigor of method was extremely important to Barnes and much of his writing was spent in emphasizing high standards for questionnaire research. However, in using untrained or semitrained "researchers" this standard was more an ideal than a reality.

In Nebraska, child study was in the hands of Harry K. Wolfe, who had earned his doctorate in the new psychology from Wundt in 1886. Wolfe came from a family of educators and in his initial year as professor of philosophy at the University of Nebraska (1889) he instituted a course in pedagogy. Wolfe was an early convert to child study and the following year he added a course for teachers and would-be teachers on the literature and methods of child study. Wolfe had begun his own research on child study in 1886 with a study of color sense in children (Wolfe, 1890). He adopted the label "scientific pedagogy" to describe his work. All of his students in the child study course were required to conduct original research projects and many of those studies were published in the *Northwestern Journal of Education,* a journal that Wolfe edited for a time. Wolfe made use of the questionnaire method, but unlike Hall and Barnes, it was used to supplement the data collected using other techniques. Wolfe's investigations of child nature were essentially of three varieties: (a) naturalistic observation of children involving well-delineated categories of data collection, (b) aptitude and ability testing, and (c) psychophysical studies, principally involving visual judgments. The influence of Wundt is clear and sets Wolfe apart, on methodological grounds, from some of the other psychologists doing child study research. But he was a great admirer of Hall and Barnes and he shared their vision of child study and the importance of scientific pedagogy in that endeavor. In addition to his own research, he traveled throughout Nebraska and neighboring states, preaching the value of child study and organizing local groups for action (Benjamin, 1976).

The Literature of Child Study

As child study swept the country in the 1890s, publication outlets were needed for the rapidly growing body of studies. Some extant journals, such as *Educational Review, American Journal of Psychology,* and *Journal of Education* would include child study research among their pages. We have already mentioned the *Northwestern Journal of Education,* which in 1896 changed its content to focus on child study work. But new journals were needed to handle the vast amount of research on this topic. In addition to Hall's *Pedagogical Semi-*

nary, W. O. Krohn began publication of the *Child Study Monthly* in 1895, and in 1908, another journal entitled *Child Study* began publication.

Indicative of the volume of literature being generated were the annual bibliographies compiled by L. N. Wilson at Clark University from 1898 through 1912 (see Wilson, 1975). These bibliographies were intended to include all articles and books on child study published in the particular year. The first several bibliographies contained about 350 references but by 1910 that number had increased to around 1,900 separate titles. Hall had tried to collect all these publications for the child study library at Clark but "their number soon transcended the resources we desired to devote to this subject" (Hall, 1923, p. 392).

By the turn of the century the child study literature contained a number of handbooks on child study, some intended for parents, but most written for teachers (see Kirkpatrick, 1903). These books were of two varieties, one intended to teach the science of child study to would-be investigators and the other to summarize the findings of child study for interested parties. These manuals became the standard textbooks in departments of pedagogy that had formed in most universities at the end of the 19th century. Child study was at its peak at this time. It boasted its own journals, training manuals, a collection of influential expert scientists, well-organized groups of parents and teachers on a national scale, and the claim that it was uncovering the secrets of child nature. But it was not without its detractors, some of whom campaigned vigorously against the dangers, if not evils, of child study. Much of the criticism concerned the methods of child study, which are considered in the next section.

The Methods of Child Study

The methods of child study were diverse and sometimes difficult to categorize. Luckey (1896) suggested 5 types of work:

1. Work without method. In this category, Luckey put unplanned observation.
2. The normal method. This involved observation of children by teachers and Luckey implies that its major worth is to the teacher because it "increases her sympathy for children and leads her to respect their individuality" (p. 34).

The remaining three categories were the ones that would be helpful to science.

3. Statistical method. By this Luckey meant questionnaire studies; he referred specifically to the work of Hall and Barnes.
4. The individual method. These were systematic observations of individual children over a long period of time.
5. Psychological method. This included laboratory studies of children, much along the lines of the experiments being done with adults.

Barnes (1896, cited in Siegel & White, 1982) had a more elaborate system of nine categories, but discounted the first six, which included reminiscences, journals of children, literary treatments, etc. He agreed with Luckey that the three methods useful to scientists were "direct studies on children" (i.e., experiments), biographies of young children, and "statistical studies, on the lines of a syllabus." These three methods will be described in more detail.

The baby biography, in particular Preyer's *The Mind of a Child*, had helped to inspire the child study movement and retained an honored place within it. It is difficult to determine exactly how it differed from other efforts at observation. Presumably, a useful baby biography was one in which observations were recorded as they occurred, and observations were made repeatedly on the same aspects of the child. Barnes refers to Preyer's; Luckey refers to one produced by Millicent Shinn, who considered herself part of the child study movement (Shinn, 1900).

Shinn pointed out the advantage of the baby biography—it was the major form of longitudinal study of its day. She accepted the evolutionary doctrine of the child study movement and defended the baby biography as an important way of studying it:

The biographical method of child study has the inestimable advantage of showing the process of evolution going on, the actual unfolding of one stage out of another, and the steps by which the changes come about. No amount of comparative statistics could give this. (p. 11)

Shinn wrote of "our baby's" (the child was her niece) changes in vision, in motor development, particularly grasping and walking, and in speech. She was familiar with the work of many psychologists and related that work to the development of the baby she observed.

The experimental method was also being applied to children. These studies simply took the experimental methods being used with adults and used children as subjects. Thus, many of the studies focused on sensation, perception, and learning. These studies were done in psychological laboratories, including Hall's at Clark University, but they were not considered the major method of child study; the method most associated with child study was the questionnaire.

The questionnaire or syllabus was the heart of the child study method, and its fortunes parallel those of the child study movement as a whole. It was devised as an alternative to the two chief methods of academic psychology of the period, the experiment and introspection. According to Hall (1897) "We can neither excite the stronger emotions in the laboratory nor coolly study ourselves while they are under natural conditions" (p. 147). Unfortunately, most were not constructed with the same care as Hall's first study on the contents of children's minds. The questionnaires usually asked for accounts of the phenomenon under study, including the age, intensity, eliciting stimulus, and consequences. In addition, a large number of possible eliciting stimuli were usually listed. Hall's study of fear listed nearly 100 specific fear objects; in the study of pity, Saunders and Hall (1900) asked about responses to a large number of specific situations (e.g., "animals that were tortured, found dead, killed, cold, hungry or friendless" (p. 535).

The questionnaires were distributed in a variety of ways. Sometimes they were published in educational journals, duplicated by teachers for use with classes, or sent to individuals who requested them. The instructions that accompanied them suggested a variety of ways of administration, including adults recalling their own childhoods, adults answering the questions regarding their children, teachers assigning the questions to students as writing exercises, and principals turning it over to teachers. Respondents were requested to mail them in, usually to Hall; if they wished the respondents could study the results themselves and use them "for a lesson in psychology, for a discussion in a meeting of teachers or mothers, or an address, or an article for the press" (Hall, 1897, p. 149).

As might be expected, the results were a hodgepodge of questionnaires. The results considered in the "fear" paper were mostly written by high school students, but of 266 papers sent by one source "134 were original observations, 88 reminiscence, 39 hearsay, and the rest from literature" (p. 149). In the paper on pity, most of the returns were from adults, but "others have questioned young children in order to gather directly and indirectly their experiences with this sentiment" (p. 534). These returns were from a variety of sources "the identity of which has unfortunately been lost."

Hall described the process of data analysis for fears: "The data . . . consists of the records of the chief fears of 1,701 people, mostly under 23 years of age, gathered in different places and by methods without great uniformity" (p. 151).

Hall went through the returns, "copying every salient or typical phrase and word" (p. 151); these were cut into thousands of slips of paper that were "brought into natural groups, and thus allowed to classify themselves." In the fear paper, the data were presented in tables, giving frequencies of different types of fears, sex differences, and age differences. The bulk of the article consisted of examples of different fears. In the paper on pity, even the tables were omitted.

As noted earlier, almost 200 questionnaire studies were completed by Hall and his students. A selective listing of these studies illustrates the breadth of child study as conceived by Hall: crying and laughing, 1894; toys and playthings, 1894; early sense of self, 1895; appetites and foods, 1895; feelings about old age, disease, and death, 1895; the only child, 1896; home and school punishments, 1897; obedience and obstinancy, 1898; perception of rhythm, 1899; straightness and uprightness of body, 1900; reactions, thoughts, and feelings, toward animals, 1902; interest in flowers, 1902; ideas about the soul, 1903; stuttering and other speech defects, 1904; imagination, 1905; aesthetic interest, 1906; shame, 1908; ambition, 1909; belief in immortality, 1910; and dreams, 1912.

Criticisms of the Child Study Movement

Critics of the child study movement included some prominent educators and psychologists. Among the latter group were William James and James Mark Baldwin. Baldwin had initially been a supporter and contributor to the movement (see Baldwin, 1895) but would later condemn it as "a fad" and would argue that teachers conducting child study research were being deceived in "thinking that they are making contributions to science" (Baldwin, 1898, p. 219). The harshest of the critics from psychology was Hugo Münsterberg, director of the psychology laboratory at Harvard University. Writing in an 1898 issue of *Atlantic Monthly,* he warned teachers:

> This rush toward experimental psychology is an absurdity. Our laboratory work cannot teach you anything which is of direct use to you in your work as teachers; and if you are not good teachers it may even do you harm, as it may inhibit your normal teacher's instincts. . . . You may collect thousands of experimental results with the chronoscope and kymograph, but you will not find anything in our laboratories which you could translate directly into a pedagogical prescription. (p. 166)

Münsterberg may seem surprising as a critic because he spent much of his career in applied psychology, especially industrial and forensic psychology, and in promoting the value of psychology for the general public (Moskowitz, 1977). But he opposed the study of children because he believed that it depersonalized the child and would alter the way teachers reacted to children. An analysis of the individual abilities of children would lead to their personalities being dissolved into elements and "love and tact have nothing to do with a bundle of elements" (Münsterberg, 1898a, p. 165).

But Münsterberg's principal objection to child study was the use of teachers and parents as data collectors. In reference to child study he wrote, "the work must be done by trained specialists or not at all" (Münsterberg, 1898b, p. 114). Further, he was critical of the lack of theory guiding child study research, noting that "child study . . . has for its aim only the collection of curiosities about the child, as an end in itself" (1898b, pp. 114–115). In his view child study's value to psychology was akin to the value of hunting stories for scientific biology.

Not surprisingly, Münsterberg's denouncement of the new psychology produced a flurry of responses disputing his claims (see, for example, Bliss, 1898; Davies, 1899). Much of Münsterberg's criticism was directed at Hall and his students, and after a brief delay, Hall responded with his own defense in an article in *Forum* (1900). He argued that child study is in itself an act of love of children as parents and teachers are motivated to gain the new knowledge which will better help them raise and teach these children. Hall criticized those parents "who do not love their children intelligently enough to study them" (Hall, 1900, p. 692).

Hall also reacted to the criticism that data collected by untrained observers would have little value in pointing to the use of lay observers in anthropology and biology. He noted that even

Charles Darwin relied on the observations of non-scientists. Further, he argued that the familiarity parents and teachers had with their children could lead them to make observations that might be missed or misinterpreted by a scientific observer not acquainted with the child.

Clearly Hall recognized the variance of quality in the scientific work in child study, work that he described as ranging from "utter worthlessness to the very highest value" (1900, p. 693). But he was dismayed that child study critics chose to focus their attacks on the poorest of the work, "vanquishing the weaklings" as he referred to it.

Finally, Hall made reference to methodological approaches in child study and the misunderstanding and misrepresentation of those methods. In spite of these failings, child study was having a significant impact on those concerned with children.

Influence of the Child Study Movement: 1890–1910

The child study movement was, in some respects, the "pop psychology" of its day, and scientific psychologists and nonscientific public alike responded in much the same way they do today. Scientific psychology almost totally rejected it; the public embraced it with great enthusiasm. The child study movement had as two of its central goals the collection of data about children and the enlightenment of the data collector, usually the teacher. Critics felt that it could not achieve either one.

The public felt a need for information and advice and the child study movement provided it, when more scientific psychologists were unwilling to address the need. The public, in the form of middle-class mothers, were early advocates (Ross, 1972). A Society for the Study of Child Nature was formed in 1889 and women's groups discussed child study, very occasionally collecting data as well. Hall accepted and encouraged their support; he was the main speaker at the first meeting of the National Congress of Mothers in 1897.

In between the scientific community and the public were those who worked directly with children: teachers, teacher trainers, and child welfare workers. Although they lacked the scientific training of the psychologists, they had a professional interest in child study, unlike the more purely personal interest of parents' groups. And it was on the

child care professionals that the child study movement had its biggest impact.

The child study movement presented a stage theory of development, which emphasized using children's own interests to educate them (data collected with the syllabi often addressed these topics). Teacher training journals often had articles that discussed how to teach particular subjects in different grades. Francis Parker, an early advocate of child study, began in 1900 to publish *The Course of Study* (which evolved into the *Elementary School Journal*); every issue of that first year of publication contained a series of articles on what and how subjects should be taught in each of the elementary grades.

Hall's interest in children's physical development helped lead to a greater emphasis on what was called "manual training" and "physical culture" (Parker, 1900), as did his interest in children's music and art. These subjects began to be viewed as appropriate areas for the schools. The child study movement influenced not only content, but also method. Children were not to be drilled, rather they should learn through free expression of their own ideas (Ross, 1972). The schoolroom was changing; the emphasis was no longer on rote recitation but on exploration of the new and interesting. Münsterberg, so vociferous in his criticism of the child study movement for its methodology, and its effects on teachers, was as harsh in his attack on school reform (Münsterberg, 1900), which, he argued, extended kindergarden throughout the school years. Children do not learn what they need to know, but only what they want to know. More importantly:

A child who has himself the right of choice, or who sees that parents and teachers select the courses according to his tastes and inclinations, may learn a thousand pretty things, but never the one which is the greatest of all: to do his duty. He who is allowed always to follow the paths of least resistance never develops the power to overcome resistance: he remains totally unprepared for life. (p. 665)

According to Münsterberg, the new school reform was only making a bad situation worse. The *real* problem was that the teachers were of low quality, undereducated, and poorly trained for teaching (indeed he argued against any training because it would interfere with the "natural instincts" of teaching).

Educators counterattacked vigorously. Wilbur Jackman of the Chicago Institute (Jackman, 1900) pointed out that the European system Münsterberg defended was incompatible with American ideals and the United States was filled with people for whom that system had failed. Joseph Lee (Lee, 1900) defended the elective system as one in which "the greatest breadth of culture is obtained, not by ignoring the individual bent, but by studying to give to each mind, not culture in general, but the broadest special culture of which that particular mind is capable" (p. 130).

Hall also made suggestions about school reform, but they were more compatible with the ideas of teachers themselves. In 1896, using data from a questionnaire sent to teachers throughout the country, Hall, like Münsterberg, called for improved basic education for teachers, and pointed to the low qualifications of many teachers. However, he also pointed out that, if qualifications were to be raised, salaries must be raised as well and teachers freed from the burdens of overcrowded classrooms and political interference (Hall, 1896). Hall and the child study movement were trying to make teaching a profession.

Teacher training was changing; teachers were learning the new methods coming out of the child study movement. New teachers were getting these ideas in normal schools and departments of pedagogy; they were also being disseminated through journals, such as *Educational Review* and the *Elementary School Teacher*. These education journals, unlike the child study journals, tended to publish technique articles based on personal experience rather than the "data-based" articles of child study journals.

But the psychologists and educators agreed on the importance of child study in the training of teachers. Parker (1900), describing the purposes of the Chicago Institute, suggests that even if the teacher cannot "avail himself of a thorough laboratory course in psychology" (p. 21), the teacher should use the results of others and engage in child study at the individual level. Albert Boyden, principal of a normal school in Massachusetts, listed as one of the four goals of normal schools that "the normal student should be led to make a practical study of children" (Boyden, 1900, p. 4). Luckey (1896) suggested that by that time "the subject [child study] is considered . . . in nearly all of the leading universities."

Although child study had its greatest impact in education, child welfare workers were also influenced. A particular concern, as noted earlier, was what to do with children, especially adolescents, when they were not in school. The child study

movement's emphases on physical development and the importance of play fit in well with the needs and interests of those trying to organize non-school activities. Physical activity was closely tied to moral development and children and adolescents needed the discipline of organized play (Cavallo, 1981). The relationship between child study and the play movement was fairly direct: Henry Curtis and George Johnson, two of the movement's founders, were students of Hall's at Clark University and Luther Gulick, the first president of the Playground Association of America, was a good friend of Hall's (Cavallo, 1981).

The play movement had its peak between 1906 and 1917; hundreds of cities supported thousands of playgrounds and even more thousands of play directors (Cavallo, 1981). Through the leaders of the movement they were heavily influenced by Hall's theories of biological development. Play organizers used recapitulation theory as a way of organizing their own thinking about play. Joseph Lee regarded play as part of the instinctive life of the primitive boy (Kett, 1977); the purpose of organized play was to channel these instincts in directions which would be safe and lead to moral development (Cavallo, 1981). The tribal character of the adolescent boy made him a particularly good candidate for team games.

The playground movement was one approach to dealing with children's leisure time. Many of the same people were associated with other organizations. Luther Gulick was also involved in the further development of YMCAs. Hall himself served on the first National Council of Boy Scouts in 1910 (Murray, 1937) and both organizations justified their emphases on physical exercise and the outdoor life with Hall's theories. Hall and the child study movement had so much influence in large part because most child welfare workers were relatively unfamiliar with the work of other psychologists (Macleod, 1983). As the child study movement waned, so did that influence.

The Demise of the Child Study Movement

Earlier we have shown that a multitude of factors gave rise to the child study movement; similarly many factors would contribute to its demise. Siegel and White (1982) have described child study as an amalgam of six different groups, each with their own motives for child study: (a) scientists who looked for the laws of human behavior in child study; (b) university administrators seeking better means of teacher training; (c) educators desiring better quantitative measures of school performance; (d) social workers looking to child study data as a base for political advocacy for their work and as a means for planning their services; (e) clinical psychologists wanting normative data on emotional and cognitive development, criticial periods, and reactions to stress; and (f) parents who needed information on child rearing. Despite the diversity of their backgrounds and the differences in their motives, these groups came together to encourage and foster child study. But the cement that held these groups together, that made child study a movement, was G. Stanley Hall. From the beginning it was his movement and when his interests turned to other topics the coalition dissolved and the member groups went their separate ways. The studies that were the literature of child study would form the beginnings of a host of new areas focusing on the child, such as experimental child psychology, educational psychology, school psychology, physical education, social work, mental retardation, mental hygiene, mental testing, and early education (Ross, 1972; Siegel & White, 1982). These are the legacies of the child study movement, some of which will be discussed in the final segment of this chapter.

The reasons for Hall's leaving child study are not entirely clear. Paradoxically, his two-volume work on adolescence (1904), which drew on the wealth of extant child study research, would cause substantial rumblings among the movement's followers. In describing that book, Ross (1972) wrote it "was his crowning effort in child study, but it followed his far-ranging mind quite beyond the pedagogical purposes and mental limits of the movement" (p. 325). The book was quite explicit in its discussions of adolescent sexuality, too explicit for many readers, especially many teachers involved in the movement, and it was banned from some libraries. Hall urged teachers to understand sexual urges of children and to help them redirect those sexual energies into socially acceptable ends. It was not a task teachers were willing to undertake. The condensed version of the adolescence volumes, published in 1906, eliminated the sexual content and other passages and was thus appropriate for use as a textbook in normal schools. But the adolescence book presented other problems for the child study followers, as Hall used its pages to defend his views on a number of controversial topics, such as corporal punishment, tolerance for male misbehavior as natural and acceptable, separate educational curricula for women, opposition to coeducational high schools, the unfortunate predominance of women as school teachers, the belief that education was to be reserved for those who could intellectually profit from it, and a call for education to include moral and religious training (Ross, 1972).

America was changing rapidly in the early days of the 20th century. Progressive education would find more value in the ideas of John Dewey. Environmentalism was gaining in favor as a major tenet of behaviorism and the genetic psychology of Hall was fast becoming outmoded. The status of women was changing, which would also contribute to the unpopularity of Hall's ideas.

Hall persisted in his attempts to hold the child study movement together through 1911, despite the fact that Clark University had been unable to support financially Hall's efforts in this regard. The criticisms of child study had weighed heavily on Hall and, to some extent, had demoralized him. He harbored a vision that the nature of Clark University might be changed so that it could "devote all its funds ultimately to the cult of the child. . . . As, however, all hopes of realizing ideals in this direction failed, I can now see that I passed through something of a crisis, though without realizing it at the time, and that my interests slowly took a new tack" (Hall, 1923, p. 405). Following publication of his 1911 book, *Educational Problems,* Hall ceased to lecture on education. He turned to interests in psychoanalysis, psychology of aging, psychology of religion, and ultimately to the self-reflection provided in his two autobiographies. He would continue to publish occasionally on the topic of child study but by 1911 he had effectively abandoned the movement, a ship that he clearly recognized as sinking.

Changes marking the final days of the movement included the rise in prominence of other universities in training education faculty, notably Teachers College of Columbia University; the change of NEA's Child Study Department to the Department of Child Hygiene; the emergence of the mental testing movement, largely fostered in America by three of Hall's students, Henry Herbert Goddard, Lewis Terman, and Frederick Kuhlmann; the experimental methods for child study offered by Edward L. Thorndike (1903) and John B. Watson (1916); and, perhaps most important, the establishment of child research centers to use those new observational and experimental methods (see Anderson, 1956).

With the establishment of these new centers, such as the Iowa Child Welfare Research Station founded in 1917, the child study movement gave way to the child development movement. Thus child study ''bridged the gap between pseudo-scientific, philosophical speculations and a true science of the child, between 'rational' education and educational psychology, between sentimental and scientific principles of child rearing'' (Belden, 1965, p. 2).

The Legacy of the Child Study Movement

The child study movement's long-term effects were, to a large extent, indirect. Its methodology and data were rejected by many circles even at the height of the movement. But it did establish the need to study children scientifically. Others, briefly or not so briefly associated with the child study movement, proved more able to meet that need. Through them, child study particularly influenced education, educational psychology, and child development. Those developments are detailed elsewhere in this volume; the purpose of this section is to discuss their relationship to the child study movement.

John Dewey and J. M. Baldwin were to have a significant impact on American education and both were touched by the child study movement. Dewey studied briefly with Hall at Johns Hopkins; the relationship was not a happy one (Ross, 1972). Dewey had other contacts with people in child study; he worked with Baldwin at the University of Chicago and was influenced by Francis Parker, a prominent educator and advocate of child study (Boyd & King, 1975). He shared with Hall an interest in the role of evolution in child development and an interest in the scientific study of children (Boyd & King, 1975). He shared with Baldwin an interest in the social psychology of children. His early work was an effort to join these ideas in the development of the ideal school. Unlike Hall, Dewey attempted to create his ideal school in the University Laboratory School, founded in 1896.

J. M. Baldwin, an early member of the movement, was also one of the first to reject it on methodological grounds. He also had a somewhat difficult, if not acrimonious, relationship with Hall. In contrast with the other critics, however, Baldwin continued to study children, even though he was not involved in the child study movement. He shared Hall's concern to develop a genetic psychology and was particularly interested in social aspects of child development; a major emphasis was imitation, which he viewed as a central process.

The biological slant of child study and its effort to provide normative data about children (Sears, 1975) had its most noticeable impact on the work of Arnold Gesell. His work, more than that of most of Hall's students, appeared to do what the child study movement had originally promised to do. After receiving his doctoral degree, he felt limited to positions in pedagogy; in order to increase his job opportunities, he began work toward a medical degree. In 1911 he went to Yale to teach education and to finish his medical degree. He remained there, collecting huge amounts of data on normal children, through the rest of his career (Ross, 1972). Gesell actually collected the data the original child study movement was supposed to provide; he remained consistent with the broad emphasis of child study on the importance of biological maturation in child development (Dixon & Lerner, 1984).

Although child development under Gesell was to collect the basic scientific data on children, a new discipline emerged from child study that more successfully joined the science of academic psychology to the practical needs of education: educational psychology. Educational psychology, under the leadership of E. L. Thorndike, had more limited and more realistic goals. Educational psychology, when it began, focused on efforts to quantify abilities and achievements and to establish a scientific basis for learning (Ross, 1972). Both developments were spurred by people who began by identifying themselves as part of child study. Thorndike's first book was entitled *Notes on Child Study*. Having studied under James, and more importantly Cattell, he brought a methodological sophistication that so many in the field lacked. He attempted, in his early work, to organize the findings of child study, pointing out when results were inconclusive. He strongly criticized recapitulation theory in particular and the biological thrust of the movement in general at the expense of learning. His own research, especially his animal experiments, were leading him to emphasize the importance of learning in development. In 1903, he published the first edition of *Educational Psychology*. The following year, he published *Introduction to the Theory of Mental and Social Measurements,* which "first made the Galton-Pearson biometrical statistical methods readily available for the run-of-the-mill mental tester" (Boring, 1950). In this book, Thorndike also presented general procedures for test construction. Over the next decade, Thorndike and his students applied those principles to the development of a number of tests of school achievement (Linden & Linden, 1968).

Others with connections to child study were also involved in the development of educational psychology, particularly the testing component. Two of Hall's students, Terman and Goddard, were especially influential. Hall himself was not very enthusiastic about the testing movement (Ross, 1972) but as his students and others developed it and it became successful, he attempted to claim it as a part of child study. Terman wanted to do his dissertation on tests but Hall's lack of encouragement and methodological deficiencies led him to work with Sanford. Goddard, who received his degree from Hall in 1899, and other Hall students took positions at schools for the retarded, Goddard at the Vineland Training School for the Feebleminded. When Binet's work became known in the United States Goddard translated the test and used it successfully. Terman also continued his work on testing at Stanford. Both Terman and Goddard maintained their ties to the child study movement, in spirit if not methodology, and presented their work to the NEA meetings of the child study departments in 1910 and 1911 (Ross, 1972).

Ten years after Thorndike published the first *Educational Psychology* the discipline, now completely independent of, and to a large extent, replacing child study, was flourishing. Thorndike incorporated the findings of the previous decade into a new three volume edition of *Educational Psychology: The original nature of man, The psychology of learning,* and *Individual differences and their causes.* Boring (1950), writing on the history of educational psychology, said that "Hall's compelling dynamism was what got it started." Thorndike, more usually considered the founder of educational psychology, continued to admire Hall, unlike many others who broke from Hall and the child study movement. In the 1913 edition of *Educational Psychology* he wrote of "Stanley Hall, whose doctrines I often attack, but whose genius I always admire." Child study tried to do too much, with too little adequate meth-

odology, but it was exciting and set goals that required several new fields to meet.

Summary

The child study movement was a product of a variety of intellectual trends and social needs. Educational theorists, such as Rousseau and later, Pestalozzi and Froebel, offered a view of children as curious, enthusiastic learners, who should be pulled into learning by addressing their interests, rather than pushed into learning by rote. The evolutionary theory of Darwin was invoked by the social Darwinists to explain the development of society and eventually the development of the individual. The empiricists, such as Galton, began to develop the methodology to evaluate individual differences in adults, and were joined by psychologists in considering how these differences arose.

Whereas the intellectuals were considering the nature of children in the abstract or in the laboratory, those who worked with children were forced to consider the nature of children in very concrete, practical terms, in the classroom and on the streets. The combining forces of industrialization, immigration, and compulsary school laws faced teachers with thousands of sometimes reluctant learners. Child welfare workers struggled with what to do with those children after they left the control of the teachers. Intellectual needs for data to confirm or refute theories and social needs for data to suggest practical solutions to real problems came together in the child study movement.

Inspired by questionnaire studies and baby biographies published in Germany, G. Stanley Hall published his first questionnaire study on the contents of children's minds in 1883. If this date marks the beginning of the child study movement, then its development was sporadic until 1891, when Hall announced a meeting for those interested in child study. Interest was high and remained so for the remainder of the century. Questionnaire studies and experiments with children were conducted in great numbers, new journals were established to publish the growing body of research, child study was introduced into curricula of many normal schools and teachers' colleges, states formed their own child study societies, and Hall and Barnes conducted child study workshops.

As child study grew, so did the number of critics. They attacked both its goals, saying that child study would destroy the special relationship between children and their parents or teachers and, particularly, its methodology, arguing the questionnaire was so unstandardized as hardly to be a method at all. Early psychologist advocates, such as Baldwin, began to distance themselves from child study (although not necessarily from the study of children). Although Hall attempted to respond to these criticisms, he was largely unsuccessful; the goals of child study were taken over by others, particularly educational psychology and child development.

The child study movement itself was never successful in fulfilling its grandiose ambitions. Too many people from too many diverse perspectives with too many different needs made those ambitions impossible to realize. But child study was the first effort to study children scientifically and to apply psychology to the practical problems of those who deal with children.

References

Anastasi, A. (1965). *Individual differences*. New York: John Wiley.

Anderson, J. E. (1956). Child development: An historical perspective. *Child Development, 27,* 181–196.

Baldwin, J. M. (1895). *Mental development in the child and race: Methods and processes*. New York: Macmillan.

Baldwin, J. M. (1898). Child study. *Psychological Review, 5,* 218–220.

Bartholomai, F. (1870). The contents of children's minds on entering school at the age of 6 years. *Städtisches Jahrbuch, Berlin und Seine Entwicklung* (Vol. 4).

Belden, E. (1965). *A history of the child study movement in the United States, 1870–1920, with special reference to its scientific and educational background*. Unpublished doctoral dissertation, University of California, Berkeley.

Benjamin, L. T. (1975). Psychology at the University of Nebraska, 1889–1930. *Nebraska History, 56,* 375–387.

Benjamin, L. T. (1976). *Scientific pedagogy: The psychology of Harry Kirke Wolfe*. Paper presented at the annual meeting of the Nebraska Psychological Association, Lincoln, NE.

Benjamin, L. T., & Bertelson, A. D. (1975). The early Nebraska Psychology Laboratory, 1889–1930: Nursery for presidents of the American Psychological Association. *Journal of the History of the Behavioral Sciences, 11,* 142–148.

Bliss, C. B. (1898). Professor Münsterberg's attack on experimental psychology. *Forum, 25,* 214–223.

Boring, E. G. (1950). *A history of experimental psychology* (2nd ed.). New York: Appleton Century Crofts.

Boyd, W. & King, E. J. (1975). *The history of western education* (11th ed.). Totowa, NJ: Barnes & Noble.

Boyden, A. G. (1900). The problems which confront the normal school at the opening of the twentieth century. *Education, 21,* 1–4.

Bradbury, D. E. (1937). The contribution of the child study movement to child psychology. *Psychological Bulletin, 34,* 21–38.

Bruce, H. A. (1903). The educative function of empirical psychology. *Bookman, 18,* 189–192.

Cavallo, D. (1981). *Muscles and morals*. Philadelphia, PA: University of Pennsylvania Press.

Davies, H. (1899). The teacher's attitude towards psychology. *Education, 19,* 476–485.

Dennis, W. (1949). Historical beginnings of child psychology. *Psychological Bulletin, 46,* 224–235.

Dixon, R. A., & Lerner, R. M. (1984). A history of systems in developmental psychology. In M. H. Bornstein & M. E. Lamb (Eds.), *Developmental psychology: An advanced textbook* (pp. 1–35). Hillsdale, NJ: Erlbaum.

Downs, R. B. (1978). *Friedrich Froebel*. Boston, MA: Twayne.

Downs, R. B. (1975). *Heinrich Pestalozzi*. Boston, MA: Twayne.

Dunkel, H. B. (1970). *Herbart and Herbartianism*. Chicago, IL: University of Chicago Press.

Hall, G. S. (1883). The contents of children's minds. *Princeton Review, 2,* 249–272.

Hall, G. S. (1891). The contents of children's minds on entering school. *Pedagogical Seminary, 1,* 139–173.

Hall, G. S. (1894). The new psychology as a basis of education. *Forum, 17,* 710–720.

Hall, G. S. (1896). The case of the public schools. *Atlantic Monthly, 77,* 403–413.

Hall, G. S. (1897). A study of fears. *American Journal of Psychology, 8,* 147–249.

Hall, G. S. (1900). Child study and its relation to education. *Forum, 29,* 688–702.

Hall, G. S. (1903). Child study at Clark University. *American Journal of Psychology, 14,* 96–106.

Hall, G. S. (1904). *Adolescence: Its psychology and its relations to physiology, anthropology, sociology, sex, crime, religion, and education* (Vols. 1–2). New York: Appleton.

Hall, G. S. (1906). *Youth, its education, regimen and hygiene*. New York: Appleton.

Hall, G. S. (1907). *Aspects of child life and education*. Boston, MA: Ginn.

Hall, G. S. (1911). *Educational problems* (Vols. 1–2). New York: Appleton.

Hall, G. S. (1922). *Senescence: The last half of life*. New York: Appleton.

Hall, G. S. (1923). *Life and confessions of a psychologist*. New York: Appleton.

Hendricks, J. D. (1968). *The child study movement in American education, 1880–1910: A quest for educational reform through a systematic study of the child*. Unpublished doctoral dissertation, Indiana University.

Hofstadter, R. (1945). *Social Darwinism in American thought*. Philadelphia, PA: University of Pennsylvania Press.

Hughes, J. (1970). *Industrialization and economic history*. New York: McGraw-Hill.

Jackman, W. S. (1900). Professor Münsterberg on school reform. *Educational Review, 20,* 85–89.

Kett, J. F. (1977). *Rites of passage: Adolescence in America 1790 to the present*. New York: Basic Books.

Kirkpatrick, E. A. (1903). *Fundamentals of child study*. New York: Macmillan.

Lee, J. (1900). Münsterberg on the new education. *Educational Review, 20,* 123–140.

Linden, K. W., & Linden, J. D. (1968). *Modern mental measurement: A historical perspective*. Boston, MA: Houghton-Mifflin.

Lubove, R. (1962). *The progressives and the slums*. Pittsburgh, PA: University of Pittsburgh Press.

Luckey, G. W. A. (1896). A brief survey of child study. *North-Western Journal of Education, 7*, 2–8.

Macleod, D. I. (1983). *Building character in the American boy*. Madison, WI: University of Wisconsin Press.

Moskowitz, M. J. (1977). Hugo Münsterberg: A study in the history of applied psychology. *American Psychologist, 32*, 824–842.

Mullen, F. A. (1981). School psychology in the USA: Reminiscences of its origin. *Journal of School Psychology, 19*, 103–119.

Münsterberg, H. (1898a). The danger from experimental psychology. *Atlantic Monthly, 81*, 159–167.

Münsterberg, H. (1898b). Psychology and education. *Education Review, 16*, 105–132.

Münsterberg, H. (1900). School reform. *Atlantic Monthly, 85*, 656–669.

Murray, N. D. (1937). *The history of the Boy Scouts of America*. New York: The Boy Scouts of America.

Parker, F. W. (1900). Syllabus of a course of lectures upon the philosophy of education. *The Course of Study, 1*, 16–28.

Pounds, R. L. (1968). *The development of education in Western culture*. New York: Appleton-Century-Crofts.

Ross, D. (1972). *G. Stanley Hall: The psychologist as prophet*. Chicago, IL: University of Chicago Press.

Sahakian, M. L., & Sahakian, W. S. (1974). *Rousseau as educator*. New York: Twayne.

Saunders, F. H., & Hall, G. S. (1900). Pity. *American Journal of Psychology, 11*, 534–589.

Schlossman, S. L. (1976). Before home start: Notes toward a history of parent education. *Harvard Educational Review, 46*, 436–467.

Sears, R. R. (1975). Your ancients revisited: A history of child development. In E. M. Hetherington (Ed.), *Review of child development research: Vol. 5* (pp. 1–70). Chicago, IL: University of Chicago Press.

Shinn, M. W. (1900). *The biography of a baby*. New York: Houghton Mifflin. (Reprinted edition 1975 by Arno Press)

Siegel, A. W., & White, S. H. (1982). The child study movement: Early growth and development of the symbolized child. In H. W. Reese & L. Lipsitt (Eds.), *Advances in child development and behavior* (Vol. 17, pp. 233–285). New York: Academic press.

Stearns, P. N. (1967). *European society in upheaval*. New York: Macmillan.

Thorndike, E. L. (1903). *Educational psychology*. New York: Columbia University Teachers College Press.

Watson, J. B. (1916). The place of the conditioned reflex in psychology. *Psychological Review, 23*, 89–116.

Wilson, L. N. (1975). *Bibliography of child study: 1898–1912*. New York: Arno Press (reprinted edition).

Winship, A. E. (1892). Why child study? *Journal of Education, 36*, 141.

Wolfe, H. K. (1890). On the color-vocabulary of children. *University Studies* (University of Nebraska), *1*, 205–234.

Wolfe, H. K. (1896a). Historical sketch of child study. *North-Western Journal of Education, 7*, 9–12.

Wolfe, H. K. (1896b). The state societies for child study. *North-Western Journal of Education, 7*, 42–48

CHAPTER 4

Individual Differences in Mental Ability

Arthur R. Jensen

One of the most obvious "facts of life" to all teachers, at every level of education, is the phenomenon of individual differences—in mental abilities, special talents, and traits of personality. Especially salient are those characteristics of pupils that are the most clearly related to the success of teachers' efforts to impart knowledge and intellectual skills. The most prominent of such characteristics is general mental ability, or intelligence. Consequently, the study of individual differences, especially differences in intelligence, has been one of four major themes of educational psychology (along with development, learning, and measurement) ever since this field was formally recognized as a branch of psychology. The ideal of universal education, which first gained impetus and implementation in America, literally forced educators' practical and humane concern with the problem of making formal schooling a successful and rewarding experience for the whole school-age population, which ranges widely in mental abilities and other characteristics that are importantly related to scholastic performance.

This chapter centers its focus on the history of attempts to understand only one of these differential variables—intelligence. The concept of intel-

ligence has a longer, more complex, and much more controversial history than is found for any other theme within the whole purview of educational psychology. The history of the concept of intelligence therefore merits a whole chapter in its own right. Indeed, a large book could well be devoted to the topic. Other dimensions of individual differences are relatively latecomers to educational research, and their importance, in terms of their relative contribution to variance in scholastic performance, is minor in comparison with the role of individual differences in intelligence. Moreover, the basic concepts and methodology of measurement and research developed in connection with the study of intelligence have considerable generality, because they have been applied as well to the investigation of other educationally relevant traits, particularly in the domains of personality and motivation.

Few psychological phenomena, however, are as highly relevant to education as individual differences in mental ability. Probably because of the practical consequences of individual differences for scholastic performance and all of its occupational, economic, and social correlates, this subject has had perhaps the most tumultuously controversial history of any topic in psychology and education.

There is really no argument about the prominence or importance of the topic itself. The argu-

Arthur R. Jensen • School of Education, University of California, Berkeley, CA 94720.

61

ments today involve quite different issues. In the past half-century, millions of school children in America and the Western world have been given tests called "IQ" tests, "intelligence" tests, "scholastic aptitude" tests, and the like. (Quotation marks seem advisable early in this discussion, first, to indicate loosely defined popular terms, as contrasted with precisely defined technical terms, and second, to warn against the risk of improper reification of terms that represent abstract concepts.)

Whatever these tests "measure," which we will let remain an open question for the time being, two things are now definitely known beyond dispute: (a) The majority of such tests (labeled "IQ," "intelligence," or "general aptitude") all measure pretty much the same source of variance as indicated by high correlations among scores on such tests; correlations typically fall in the range of .70 to .90, averaging close to .80. (b) No other single item of information that we can obtain about children is as highly correlated with assessments of scholastic performance as the children's scores on these tests. No other kind of information concerning children's background is as highly predictive—not the socioeconomic status of the children's parents, or the parents' education, or occupation, or race, or the national origin of children's ancestry, or their gender. Children's scores on "IQ" tests account for more of the total variance (i.e., individual differences) in overall scholastic achievement than all of these background variables combined, independent of IQ. This appears to be true in every country, for every type of educational system, and for every method of instruction yet devised. No attempts, by means of varied instructional techniques, to completely overcome the correlation between individual differences in scholastic performance and scores on "IQ" tests, when a fully representative sample of the school-age population is considered, have come anywhere near success. The fact that this is so is scarcely disputed today. But *why* this is so and what it means have long been, and still are, questions of intensive inquiry and heated debate in educational psychology.

Through it all, the use of numerous tests of "mental abilities" has become widely entrenched in education, in connection with "streaming" or "tracking" pupils, for placement in special classes, for individual diagnosis of learning problems, for vocational counseling, and for selection for higher education. The lives of countless persons have undoubtedly been affected to some degree by "mental tests." Just what do such tests actually "measure" that would seem to justify such widespread use?

Similar tests, often called "aptitude" tests, are also now commonly used with adults outside the school setting, in screening job applicants for industry, and for selection and allocation to various training programs in the armed services. The tests commonly used for these purposes have also been shown, through correlation analysis, to measure much the same individual differences as are measured by the IQ tests administered in schools. There is no longer any question that such tests possess some practical validity for predicting job performance and success in training programs. The persisting question is why such tests have predictive validity for so many practical, real-life criteria.

The fundamental question implied here, we know, has existed long before mental tests were ever invented. Stated bluntly in laymen's terms, it is the simple question: Why are some people smarter than others? Many other questions that need to be answered naturally spring from this single question, which many persons have viewed as the Pandora's box of psychology. Yet for more than a century, it has remained, and continues to remain, a central question in that branch of psychology now known as differential psychology, or the scientific study of individual and group differences in psychological traits. The current status of research, theories, and controversies on this topic is highly complex and perhaps even perplexing to newcomers to this field. It seems likely that the present scene can be more clearly understood when viewed in historical perspective. The history of thought about the nature of individual differences in human abilities should essentially enlighten the question, how did we arrive at our present state of knowledge and theory on this topic? A historical overview might also suggest the most promising avenues for future research. It is the writer's belief that the modern era of research in this field has been evincing lively progress toward addressing, with advanced statistical and laboratory methods, a number of the key questions that have come down from the past. It seems unlikely that a historical survey of the thinkers and their theories and researches that have led up to the present state of the field could justify the wiseacre's definition of history as "a chronology of events that never should have happened."

The Prescientific Era

The concept of mental ability, as we conceive of it today, is of surprisingly recent origin in the history of human thought. There is little evidence of association between the concept of *mind* and the concept of *ability* in the literature of theology and philosophy prior to the latter half of the 19th century. It is the ability aspect of mental ability that was so delayed in making its appearance. The notion of individual differences in mental ability is even more scarce in philosophical thought prior to the nineteenth century. The leading theologians, philosophers, and political and social thinkers before that time apparently did not concern themselves with the subject of individual differences in mental abilities.

Yet it seems almost impossible to imagine that since the dawn of history people have not noticed differences among their fellows in characteristics that today we would think of as constituting mental ability. Indeed, the concept of individual differences, although not of concern to early philosophers, is evident in literature throughout history. Characters have been described in literature by a variety of adjectives, such as clever, keen-witted, and discerning, or dull-witted, addled, and stupid; also, geniuses and feebleminded persons have figured in literature for centuries. There seems little doubt that individual differences in mental traits have always been recognized. Why then, we must wonder, did it take so long for such an evidently well recognized human phenomenon as individual differences in mental traits to become a subject for systematic thought by the leading thinkers in history before about 1850?

Even after psychology became a formal discipline, with its own textbooks and dictionaries of specialized terminology, the ideas of mental ability and individual differences were slow to enter. The first prominent American psychologist, William James (1842–1910), at Harvard University, published his famous textbook *The Principles of Psychology* in 1890, yet it makes only three brief and scattered mentions of "intelligence," but only in the philosophic sense of "intellect" or "reason," and James never makes any reference to individual differences. One will search in vain for any mention of intelligence or individual differences of any kind in William James's later *Talks to Teachers* (1899). James wrote extensively on such topics as perception, association, emotion, will, habit, and the "stream-of-thought," but there is no evidence that he ever entertained any notion of individual differences in abilities. At that time, the subject of individual differences was evidently not considered within the purview of formal psychology. Another comprehensive text of that period, *Handbook of Psychology* (1890) by James Mark Baldwin (1861–1934) contains two pages on "intellect" and nothing at all about individual differences. Baldwin's encyclopedic *Dictionary of Philosophy and Psychology* (1901) does not accord the word *intelligence* a separate entry, but refers to it merely as a synonym of *intellect*. To understand this surprisingly late entry of the concepts of mental ability and individual differences into psychology, we must look back to the earliest recorded beginnings of psychological thought.[1]

Origins of Psychology

The great philosopher Plato (427–347 B.C.) is credited as the first thinker to distinguish (in *The Republic*) three parts or aspects of the human soul, corresponding, in modern terms, to intellect, emotion, and will, or the cognitive, affective, and conative aspects of the human psyche. Dualism, or the distinct separation of mind and body, as a formal philosophic doctrine in Western thought, probably originated with Plato. Intellect, or reason, was regarded as an attribute of the perfect or divine soul, not of the physical person or the person's observable behavior. Therefore, the soul was thought to remain untouched by the existence of individual differences that were manifested in man's overt behavior. Mind, reason, thought, and intellect— all more or less synonymous concepts in Plato's thinking—were seen as part of the immaterial soul, or *nous,* as Plato called it. The soul, according to Plato, transcends mundane activity and distinguishes man from the lower animals. Thus it was viewed as a universal quality incompatible with the notion of individual differences. In Plato's day, philosophers were mainly concerend with the essences that distinguish humans from animals, rather than distinctions between individual humans. Physical distinctions were recognized, of course, as were differences in moral character. In *The Republic,* Plato clearly recognized psychological differences in classifying people into three

[1]Besides the sources specifically cited, material on the early history of the concepts of mind and intellect were obtained mainly from the following: Boring (1950), Burt (1955), Guilford (1967), Matarazzo (1974), Peterson (1925), Stoddard (1943), Watson (1963).

types. Plato likened these types, in terms of their rarity, to gold, silver, and brass, and held that the ideal society would assign people to occupations on the basis of this classification. The three main divisions were first the philosophers, who would govern; then the warriors; and lastly, the artisans. But the basis for such a classification of people was not made clear, nor were the means of achieving it. But Plato's idea is probably the first major expression of opinion regarding the recognition of individual differences as being related to a society's general welfare.

Plato is also credited as the first thinker to suggest a hierarchical structure of mental functions—an idea that comes down to the present day. He regarded reason, or intellect, as the highest aspect of the soul, which ideally dominated the lower functions of emotion and drive. In *Phaedrus,* he depicts intellect as the charioteer who holds the reins, the emotion and drive are likened to the team of horses that draw the vehicle. The charioteer is the *cybernetic* element, the horses the *dynamic* element. Here already we can see some of the basic ingredients of modern psychology.

Plato's illustrious student, Aristotle (384–323 B.C.), was really the first formal psychologist, in that he wrote the first books on the subject, *De Anima, De Sensu et Sensili, De Memoria et Reminiscentia,* and *On Psyche.* Aristotle clearly distinguished various psychological functions, such as sensation, reaction, desire, memory (recognition and recall), knowing, and thinking. Unlike Plato, Aristotle recognized thinking as directly dependent upon what he regarded as the lower processes of sensation and memory. Thought was viewed as deliberation preceding action. Aristotle might also be regarded as the first cognitive theorist. He constrasted actual activity with the hypothetical capacity or mental activity on which it depends; this is the first introduction of the concept of ability as a latent trait, distinct from its behavioral expression.

Aristotle reduced Plato's threefold classification of the soul to only two broad divisions, which he termed *dianoetic* (cognitive functions) and *oerectic* (emotional and moral functions). It was the Roman author, orator, and statesman, Cicero (106–43 B.C.), who, in translating Aristotle's Greek terminology, coined the almost exact equivalent of ''dianoetic'' in Latin as *intelligentia*—hence the origin of the word *intelligence.* But neither Aristotle nor other ancient Greek philosophers said anything about individual differences in the various psycho-

logical qualities that they propounded. Besides the fact that these qualities were thought of largely as qualities of the soul and hence were exempt from human frailty, the social systems of the ancient and medieval world, consisting of aristocracies and serfdoms, probably afforded little scope for the salience of individual differences in abilities. A person's occupation and station in society were determined by the circumstances of his birth. Formal education was the privilege of only an elect few, and the great inequality of opportunities for education and vocational choice could largely obscure the perception of human differences as representing characteristics that are intrinsic to individuals.

Indeed, the first clear statement concerning individual differences in mental abilities came some years following the heyday of Greek philosophy, from the Roman philosopher, Quintillian (A.D. 35–95), who might well be called the first real educational psychologist. He wrote the following advice to teachers, which would not look out of place in a modern textbook of educational psychology.

It is generally, and not without reason, regarded as an excellent quality in a master to observe accurately differences of ability in those whom he has undertaken to instruct, and to ascertain in what direction the nature of each particularly inclines him; for there is in talent an incredible variety, and the forms of mind are not less varied than those of bodies. (As quoted in Stoddard, 1943, p. 79)

It would be a long time, however, before anyone else systematically considered the subject of individual differences in mental abilities. (*Mental* means simply that individual differences are not mainly due to differences in sensory or motor capabilities *per se.*) The mind–body dualism propounded by the early Greek philosophers, and the idea of mind as a spiritual essence or soul independent of physical or organic cause, was elevated and perpetuated by the Christian scholastics. Most prominent among them was the Catholic theologian Thomas Aquinas (1225–1274), who followed Aristotle in subdividing the functions of mind. The first division was between the intellectual and the appetitive functions. The intellectual function was further subdivided into sensation, perception, memory and reproductive imagination, and reasoning and creative imagination. This structure of the mind, with minor variations, persisted in philosophical writings down to the 19th century. But throughout this period, these categories of mind remained philosophic abstractions without being viewed in relation to human differences in their individual manifestations. That conceptual leap would have to await a major revolution in human thought, namely, a fully biological conception of the human species, and of human behavior, as fundamentally continuous with the rest of the animal kingdom, as a product of organic evolution rather than of special creation.

Among early philosophers, John Locke (1632–1704) has had a lasting influence on this field through his most famous work, the *Essay Concerning Human Understanding* (1690). Essentially, Locke brought mind closer to naturalistic explanation. He opposed the notion of innate ideas and viewed the human mind at birth as a blank tablet, or *tabula rasa,* which is gradually filled with impressions through the avenues of the special senses. All knowledge, Locke claimed, comes from only two sources, *sensation* and *reflection,* or "the association of ideas." He wrote,

Let us suppose the mind to be, as we say, white paper, void of all characters, without any ideas; How comes it to be furnished? Whence comes it by that vast store, which the busy and boundless fancy of man has painted on it with an almost endless variety? Whence has it all the materials of reason and knowledge? To this I answer, in one word, from *experience*. In that all our knowledge is founded, and from that it ultimately derives itself. (Quoted by Boring, 1950, p. 172)

Thus the line was clearly drawn between *nativism,* or the idea that the mind comes equipped with certain built-in qualities, and *empiricism,* according to which the properties of the mind are wholly attributable to individual experience. Although there is nothing explicit in this empiricist philosophy concerning intelligence and individual differences, the implications of Locke's *tabula rasa* conception were that both intelligence and human differences therein must arise entirely from differences in people's experiences—an idea that has come down to the present day in the research and controversy concerning the relative effects of "nature" and "nurture" (or heredity and environment) on mental abilities and other psychological characteristics.

The British philosopher Herbert Spencer (1820–1903) was the immediate precursor of the scientific era in the study of intelligence and individual differences. He was a Lamarkian evolutionist, who propounded his own pre-Darwinian ideas about evolution. After the publication of Darwin's *Origin of Species* (1858), Spencer was converted from Lamarkism to the theory of natural selection, and he became the leading philosopher of the Darwinian revolution. Because Spencer was never himself an empirical scientist, we must assign him to the prescientific era as regards his contributions to psychology. However, his textbook, *The Principles of Psychology* (1855), was the first psychology book to resurrect the term *intelligence* and to pay specific attention to individual differences. Spencer viewed human intelligence as a unitary trait that emerged through the differentiation of adaptive functions in the course of biological evolution. Later, with the publication of Darwin's theory of natural selection as the explanation of evolution and the "survival of the fittest" as its principal mechanism of evolution, Spencer perceived the biological significance of individual differences as the essential raw material on which evolution depends. Spencer's extension of this line of thought to the human social conditions of his time has been termed "Social Darwinism," often in a pejorative context. However, Spencer's idea of intelligence as a biologically adaptive function for achieving the "adjustment of internal to external relations" is a progenitor of the detailed modern efforts to understand both animal and human intelligence in an evolutionary perspective, as seen, for example, in Harry Jerison's chapter, "The Evolution of Biological Intelligence" in the recent *Handbook of Human Intelligence* (Sternberg, 1982). The concept of the *phylogeny* of intelligence, the idea that intelligence increases progressively throughout the phylogenic scale of the animal kingdom, is also attributable to Spencer. His view of the *ontogeny,* or individual development, of intelligence in humans, from birth to maturity, is that it has three main aspects, (a) an increase in the accuracy of inner adjustments to outer demands, (b) an increase in the number of items of simple knowledge, and (c) an increase in the complexity of consciousness of the external environment. The idea of accuracy of perceptions was likely a precursor of Francis Galton's (1822–1911) emphasis on sensory discrimination as a measure of intelligence, and the ideas of number and complexity were much later relabeled and empirically researched by Edward L. Thorndike (1874–1949) as breadth and altitude of intellect (Thorndike, Bregman, Cobb, & Woodyard, 1927). But it was actually Spencer, rather than Galton, who is so often credited (or blamed) for the concept of intelligence as a unitary or general ability. As Guilford (1954) has put it, "The conception of intelligence as a unitary entity was a gift to psychology from biology through the instrumentality of Herbert Spencer'' (p. 471). This unitary conception of intelligence was destined for a turbulent history. It is still a pivotal theoretical issue in contemporary psychology.

The Scientific Era

The scientific era in the study of individual differences is marked by the advent of objective measurement and the quantitative treatment of data. Systematic, objective observation and some form of measurement are partly what distinguish empirical psychology from speculative philosophy. Although measurement does not guarantee the advancement of a science, without measurement a science seldom advances beyond a rudimentary or purely descriptive and taxonomic stage. The idea of the measurement of mental attributes was particularly crucial for the development of the psychology of individual differences.

The first actual measurement of any kind of psychological individual differences was performed not by a philosopher or a psychologist, but by a German astronomer, F. W. Bessel (1784–1846), in 1822. He was fascinated by the discovery, made in 1795 at the Greenwich Observatory, that individual astronomers differed systematically in the exact time at which they recorded the transit of a star across a hairline in the field of a telescope. Telescopic observers could not voluntarily correct their errors of observation in order to bring their time measurements into perfect agreement. Bessel systematically investigated this phenomenon, estimating differences in visual reaction times between individuals in milliseconds. He discovered reliable individual differences in reaction time, to which he gave the name *personal equation,* which could be used to correct the astronomical observations of different individuals, thereby improving the accuracy of measurement. Bessel discovered not only that individuals differed reliably in reaction time, but that there was considerable variability among a number of reactions by the same individual, hence the distinction between *inter*individual and *intra*individual variability. The temporal constancy or accuracy of the personal equation (i.e., interindividual differences in reaction time) was seriously limited by the fact that an individual's reaction time varies from one occasion to another. To read through this intraindividual variability and discern consistent differences between individuals required averaging a large number of

reaction time measurements obtained from each individual. Students of psychometrics will immediately recognize that the basic concepts of classical test theory, such as true score and error components, are latent, if not actually explicit, in this early research on reaction time.

The chronographs and chronoscopes invented by astronomers for the precise measurement of reaction time were soon adopted by physiologists, and shortly thereafter, in the 1880s, they became standard apparatus in the first psychological laboratory, established in 1879 in Leipzig by Wilhelm Wundt (1832–1920). In adopting the reaction time technique that astronomers specifically developed for studying individual differences, however, experimental psychologists failed to adopt also the astronomers' primary interest in individual differences. The primary aim of experimental psychology was to discover general laws of mental functioning; individual differences were regarded merely as error, noise, or nuisance variance in this endeavor, to be minimized as much as possible through experimental control, careful selection of subjects, and the refinement of procedures. Reaction time became an important technique for the objective measurement and analysis of reflexes, attention, sensory discrimination, choice decision making, association, and recall memory. This line of research has come down through a spotty history to modern times, where, known as mental chronometry, it has taken on new life as the chief methodology of experimental cognitive psychology (e.g., Posner, 1978).

Reaction time has also figured in the study of individual differences in mental abilities, but through a quite different tradition of scientific psychology, instigated mainly by Sir Francis Galton in the 1860s. The work of Galton marks the real beginning of scientific research on individual differences, that is, the fields of differential psychology and psychometrics.[2]

In what is probably the most frequently cited presidential address by any president of the American Psychological Association, Lee Cronbach (1957) in ''The Two Disciplines of Scientific Psychology,'' deplored the theoretical and methodological gulf that, throughout the history of psychology, has separated experimental psychology, on the one hand, and differential psychology and psychometrics, on the other. The founding fathers of these two branches were Wundt, in Germany,

---

[2]Burt (1962) provides the most useful source on Galton's contributions to psychology.

and Galton, in England. Until recent years, these two lines have shown only occasional and casual interaction. The one subject on which the "two disciplines of scientific psychology" have finally become focused in a fruitful merger, only within the last decade, is the study of human intelligence. But the threads of this development really go back to Galton in the latter half of the 19th century.

Sir Francis Galton

Galton was born the same year as Gregor Mendel (1822–1884), the father of modern genetics, and he died the same year as Alfred Binet (1857–1911), the inventor of the first practical test of intelligence. Interestingly, Galton was the first investigator of the genetics of intelligence and the first to attempt the objective measurement of abilities.

Galton was born into a wealthy English family. A half-cousin of Charles Darwin (1809–1882), they both were grandsons of the philosopher, physiologist, and poet, Erasmus Darwin (1731–1802). Galton was a prodigy who could read and write by the age of three. After attending medical school and earning a degree in mathematics at Cambridge University at 21, he fell heir to a family fortune that allowed him freely to pursue his extremely wide and varied scientific interests for the rest of his long life, without need to earn a living. He used his fortune to travel, to finance his research, to found journals (*Biometrika* and *Annals of Human Genetics,* which are still in existence today), to endow a chair in genetics (occupied by such luminaries as Karl Pearson and Sir Ronald Fisher) and the famous Galton Laboratory at the University of London. He also founded the Eugenics Society, which still exists.

Galton was one of the greatest scientific dilettantes of all time. Because he was also a genius, he made original contributions to a variety of fields: exploration and geography (of Africa), meteorology, photography, fingerprint classification, genetics, statistics, anthropometry, and psychometry. His prolific achievements and publications brought him worldwide recognition and many honors, including knighthood, Fellow of the Royal Society, and several gold medals awarded by various scientific societies in England and Europe.[3]

[3]The chief sources on the life of Galton are Galton's *Memoirs* (1908), Pearson's (1914–1930) three-volume biography, and a modern biography, containing also a complete bibliography of Galton's publications, by Forrest (1974).

What is Galton's legacy to the psychology of individual differences? Above all, he vigorously promoted the idea of objective measurement and quantitative analysis of data, whether by mere counting, or by ranking, or by true measurement. His favorite motto was, "When you can, count." He acted accordingly, some would say, to an almost eccentric extreme. He applied this predilection for quantification mainly to the study of human variation in just about every physical and mental characteristic that was within his power to count, rank, or measure. Unlike Wundt, the father of experimental psychology, who saw individual differences as a nuisance to be overcome in the search for general laws, Galton regarded human variation as of paramount importance and as perhaps the most interesting of all phenomena for scientific study in its own right. Hence the "two disciplines of scientific psychology," stemming respectively from Wundt and Galton.

As a result of Galton's pursuit, he was led to invent a number of the statistical and psychometric concepts and methods familiar to all present-day researchers, including the bivariate scatter diagram, regression and correlation, multiple correlation, percentile ranks, standardized or scale-free scores, rating scales, the use of the normal, or Gaussian, distribution as a basis for the interval scaling of traits, and the use of the median and geometric mean as measures of central tendency. But the details of these contributions more properly belong in the history of measurement and statistics *per se.*

Galton's main substantive contributions, which depended heavily on his quantitative inventions, are found essentially in two works: *Hereditary Genius: An Inquiry into Its Laws and Consequences* (1869), his most famous and most influential work, and *Inquiries into Human Faculty and Its Development* (1883). The second work is of interest from our standpoint for its descriptions of the odd assortment of "tests" Galton invented for measuring human capacities. Successful or not, they were the very first objective "mental" tests. Like every scientific innovator, Galton was also a product of his time. This is reflected in his choice of "tests." The prevailing doctrine at the time was *faculty psychology,* which traces back to the ancient Greek philosophers, who conceived of the mind as consisting of a number of distinct and separate powers or faculties, such as sensation, discrimination, perception, memory, and reason. And the chief techniques of experimental psychology at the time were the so-called brass instrument apparatuses of Wundt's laboratory, gadgets for measuring various types of sensory discrimination and speed of reactions. In keeping with the psychology of his time, Galton believed that because all the contents of intellect must come through the sense organs, the capacity for fineness of sensory discrimination was one of the two main aspects of mental ability; the other, because of its supposed adaptive evolutionary significance, was sheer speed of reaction to an external stimulus. In *Human Faculty* (1883), he argued,

The only information that reaches us concerning outward events appears to pass through the avenue of our senses; and the more perceptive the senses are of difference, the larger is the field upon which our judgment and intelligence can act. (p. 19)

Hence, Galton's battery of tests consisted mostly of devices for measuring auditory, visual, and kinesthetic discrimination, short-term memory span, as well as simple reaction time to visual and auditory stimuli. These various tests, along with a number of physical measurements, were obtained during the brief period between about 1884 and 1890, on more than 9000 individuals, who paid threepence apiece to be run through all the tests in Galton's "Anthropometric Laboratory" in the South Kensington Science Museum. Galton expressed his notion of the aim of such tests as follows:

One of the most important objects of measurement . . . is to obtain a general knowledge of the capacities of a man by sinking shafts, as it were, at a few critical points. In order to ascertain the best points for the purpose, the sets of measures should be compared with an independent estimate of the man's powers. We thus may learn which of the measures are the most instructive. (Quoted in Anastasi, 1965, p. 25)

Galton's idea was quite sound, and presages the modern psychometric concept of external validity.

Unfortunately, however, Galton's particular collection of tests of sensory discrimination and reaction time did not prove to be very fruitful in his own day. Such simple tests could often distinguish the mentally deficient, but differences among persons of normal and superior intelligence, as judged by educational and occupational attainments, were generally so slight and seemingly unreliable as to afford scarcely any evidence for the claim that they measured intelligence. At least so it seemed at the time. Mere visual inspection of the data yields an unpromising picture. Reliability theory had not yet been conceived, and modern analyses of Galton's data reveal exceedingly low reliability of many of his tests. The reaction time tests, for example, were based on only a few trials and therefore

yielded measurements with an average reliability of only 0.18 in the total sample. Tests with such low reliability could hardly show impressive correlations with any criterion, and mean differences between different age groups and occupational categories look unimpressive to casual inspection. Unfortunately, multiple regression analysis and statistical tests of significance had not yet been invented. When, in recent years, modern statistical analyses have been applied to Galton's old data, there were found to be highly significant mean differences by age group and by five occupational categories (ranging from professional to unskilled) on many of Galton's measurements.[4] Still, Galton's simple tests, at least in their original primitive form, proved to be practically useless for individual assessment. The first practically useful test for mental ability was still waiting to be invented by Alfred Binet, some 15 years later.

It was not until almost a century after Galton's failed attempt that psychologists have looked with renewed interest at Galton's ideas in search of more refined techniques for fathoming the nature of individual differences in mental abilities. One of the leading modern cognitive theorists, Earl Hunt, has stated, "We believe that Galton, not Binet, had the right approach. Measurement in science should be dictated by theory. What is needed is a better theory" (Hunt, Frost, & Lunneborg, 1973, p. 195). The statement is somewhat reminiscent of John Dalton's comment to the effect that the most important thing for a scientist is not necessarily to be right, but to have the right idea. And Galton had the right idea. But he lacked the necessary technical and statistical apparatus to make it work.

Galton's ideas about the nature of intelligence were not very formalized as a theory in the usual sense. Deeply impressed by Darwin's theory of evolution and the central role of individual variation in natural selection and "fitness for survival," Galton thought of intelligence as having developed in the course of evolution as a general, heritable fitness trait in the Darwinian sense, attaining its highest development in *Homo sapiens,* while still evincing variation between individuals and between various subspecies, or races. (One chapter

---

[4]Nearly all of Galton's original data had been secured by Professor Gerald McClearn, while at the University of Colorado's Institute of Behavior Genetics. Various specialists in genetics and psychometrics are in the process of analyzing the data with modern statistical techniques. The information reported here was provided by one of those who are reexamining Galton's data, Professor Ronald Johnson of the University of Hawaii.

of Galton's *Hereditary Genius* is given a title that today would surely be viewed as quite unacceptable, "The Comparative Worth of Different Races.") Galton's view of intelligence stemmed much more from his evolutionary philosophy than from the disappointing empirical findings based on his battery of sensory and motor tests. But Galton's view of intelligence was also influenced by his study of "hereditary genius," in which he found that the blood relatives of men who were eminent for their intellectual achievements showed a markedly higher probability of also attaining eminence than would be expected by chance or social advantage, and that the probability decreased in a regular stepwise fashion the remoter the degree of kinship—a pattern that Galton observed as well in the case of various physical characteristics, for example, stature and athletic prowess. From this he concluded that mental ability was inherited in much the same manner and to the same degree as physical traits. The fact that eminent relatives in the same family line were often eminent in quite different fields of endeavor (for example, mathematics, literature, and music) was seen by Galton as supporting his idea that mental ability, or at least its hereditary component, is a *general* ability that can be channelled, by circumstance or interest, into any kind of intellectual endeavor.

Thus, Galton's conception of intelligence can be summarized as innate, general, cognitive ability. The specification *cognitive* is intended to distinguish it from the other two aspects of the Platonic triarchic division of mind—the affective and conative. Because Galton thought the inheritance of general ability followed the same laws as physical inheritance, and because Galton found that individual variation in physical traits, such as stature, was distributed approximately in accord with the Gaussian, or normal, bell-shaped distribution, he assumed that the same type of distribution held also for general ability. He thereby scaled genius and lesser levels of ability on a graded continuum by dividing the baseline of the normal curve into 18 equal intervals. Galton's conception of ability as a perfectly continuous trait, aside from the assumption of a normal distribution, represented a break with the typological thinking of his contemporaries, who viewed genius and mental deficiency as distinct types, separate from the general run, rather than as the upper and lower extremes of the continuous distribution of a single trait. The ideas of the continuity of traits and of the normal curve have had a profound and enduring influence in differential psychology and psychometrics.

Galton also recognized the existence of special abilities, such as linguistic, mathematical, memorial, and artistic, although he regarded them as of secondary importance, believing that general ability was the primary factor in all intellectual achievements, though it is more important in some types of achievement than in others. In *Hereditary Genius* (1869), he stated,

Numerous instances recorded in this book show in how small a degree eminence can be considered as due to purely special powers. People lay too much stress on apparent specialities, thinking that because a man is devoted to some particular pursuit he would not have succeeded in anything else. They might as well say that, because a youth has fallen in love with a brunette, he could not possibly have fallen in love with a blonde. As likely as not the affair was mainly or wholly due to a general amorousness. (p. 64)

Thus Galton replaced the doctrine of mental faculties by the formulation of mental ability as consisting of a *general ability* and a number of *special abilities*. It is apparent today that virtually none of Galton's theoretical ideas concerning mental ability—the hypothesis of general and special abilities, the normal distribution and inheritance of general ability—were rigorously tested or established scientifically by Galton's own researches, which fall far short of the methodological requirements for attaining that goal. Nevertheless, most of the key research questions that presently occupy contemporary researchers in this field stem directly from Galton. It is doubtful that anyone else has had a greater influence on our theories of intelligence, although Binet unquestionably had the greater influence on the measurement of intelligence for practical purposes.

Galton's methods were introduced to America by James McKeen Cattell (1860–1944). Cattell (who was no relation to the contemporary psychologist Raymond B. Cattell) was the first American to earn a Ph.D. in psychology under Wundt, in 1886. In 1888, he spent a postdoctoral year in England and worked with Galton, whom Cattell greatly admired, later referring to Galton as "the greatest man whom I have ever known" (Cattell, 1930). Cattell coined the term *mental tests* (in 1890 in the British journal *Mind*) in reference to Galton's battery of techniques for measuring various sensory acuities and reaction times. In 1891, he founded the psychological laboratory at Columbia University and headed the psychology department there for 26 years. He early on emphasized research on individual differences along Galtonian lines. But his own research with "mental tests" of the Galtonian "brass instrument" variety and, in particular, a study published in 1901 by one of his Ph.D. students, Clark Wissler (1870–1947), led to the early demise of Galtonian methods of mental testing in America.

Wissler, working in Cattell's lab, administered to between 90 and 252 Columbia College undergraduates a battery of Galtonian tests measuring various simple sensory and motor capacities, discrimination, short-term memory, color-naming speed, and simple visual and auditory reaction time, as well as several physical measurements. These simple measures were correlated with class standing and grades in classics, foreign language, and mathematics courses, which were assumed to reflect individual differences in general mental ability, or intelligence. Pearsonian correlations were calculated between each of the "mental tests" and the academic criteria. It was the very first use in psychology of the product-moment coefficient of correlation, invented in 1896 by Karl Pearson (1857–1936), protégé of Galton. Few of Wissler's correlations significantly exceeded zero. Unfortunately, Wissler's results, interpretation, and conclusions largely reflected psychometric and statistical naiveté. With the clarity of hindsight, modern students can easily see that the deck had been strongly stacked against finding significant or substantial correlations. Each test score was based on an average of only three to five measurements, which we now know would result in exceedingly low reliability; the "range of talent" was very restricted in this highly selected group of Ivy League students, a fact that greatly attenuates correlations; and the reliability and validity of course grades as a measure of intelligence leave much to be desired. (The best present-day IQ tests generally show correlations of less than .50 with grades in selective colleges.) Wissler's and Cattell's disappointing results, coming from the most prestigious psychological laboratory in America, cast a pall over the whole Galtonian approach to studying individual differences in abilities. Galton's methods might have survived this blow and been developed further, however, had it not been for a momentous development in France, just 4 years later.

Alfred Binet

Binet (1857–1911) was France's greatest psychologist, an investigator of remarkably broad interests, insight, and ingenuity.[5] Trained in experi-

mental and physiological psychology, as well as in medicine, Binet was the first major figure in our field of interest who could be called a clinical psychologist, who thought and acted like a clinician in the best sense of that term. All his predecessors perceived themselves either as philosophers or as natural scientists. Binet was not a strong theorist, and he developed no formal theory of intelligence; but his numerous writings afford a fairly clear impression of his conception of intelligence, and his methods of developing the first practically useful intelligence test have provided many followers, as well as critics, grist for theoretical inference about the nature of intelligence as conceived by Binet.

Binet was already eminent when he was drawn to the study of intelligence. The story is well known, how he and his co-worker, Théodore Simon (1873–1961), a psychiatrist, were commissioned in 1904 by the Minister of Education, to devise a practical, objective means for assessing mental subnormality in primary school children. Contrary to some of the later lore that has grown up about Binet, largely through the interpretations of American followers who wished to sharpen the contrast between Binet and the Galtonian school in Britain, Binet, in fact, greatly admired and was profoundly influenced by the British evolutionists Darwin, Spencer, and above all, Galton. The idea that Galton and Binet were at opposite poles is false, although their disciples have often been at odds. Binet accepted Galton's idea of intelligence as a general ability that enters into "nearly all the phenomena with which the experimental psychologist has previously concerned himself—sensation, perception, memory, as well as reasoning," and Binet also distinguished special abilities, which he termed "partial aptitudes" (Binet & Simon, 1905a). Binet was also a hereditarian regarding the basis of individual differences and claimed that his intelligence scale was expressly devised to reflect innate differences, in contrast to "pedagogical scales" that measure specifically educational attainments (Binet & Simon, 1905b).

It was when Binet actually set about devising a test of intelligence that he became truly innovative, taking a quite different approach from the one suggested by Galton. Binet was well informed of the unimpressive results obtained using the Wundtian and Galtonian "brass instrument" techniques of measuring simple processes as a means for assessing intelligence.

In looking around for more promising measures, Binet was impressed by a new sentence completion test devised by the German psychologist Hermann

[5]The best account of Binet's life and work is the biography of Binet by Theta H. Wolf (1973).

Ebbinghaus (1850–1909), who is best remembered for his experimental studies of verbal learning and memory. The completion test consisted of sentences with missing words that the subject had to fill in with words selected so as to make good sense of the incomplete sentence. This was probably the first successful test of higher mental abilities; it quite clearly discriminated between primary school pupils when they were classified by their teachers as being good, average, or poor in scholastic standing. (A sentence completion test is still in use today, for example, as part of the well known Lorge-Thorndike Intelligence Test; and it generally shows a higher correlation with the total IQ than any other type of subtest.) Ebbinghaus emphasized the importance of complexity of a task's cognitive demands as being essential for the assessment of the higher mental functions thought of as intelligence. Complexity thus became a key idea in Binet's effort. He abandoned Galton's and Cattell's simple sensorimotor tests (except Galton's test for discriminating weights) and devised instead a large number of single-item "tests" based, not on laboratory apparatus, but on brief tasks children could perform with such commonplace things as pencil, paper, coins, blocks, pictures of familiar objects, and the like. Each task posed a problem involving attention, adaptability, memory, judgment, reasoning, or some common item of information.

Binet's most original contribution was the concept of mental age as a device for selecting and scaling items so as to permit a meaningful interpretation of the child's performance. As it was obvious to Binet that children's mental capability increases with age, he used age as a criterion for selecting and grading his test items. By calibrating items in terms of the percentage of each normative group of children sampled at one-year age intervals from age 3 to 15 years who passed the item, it was possible to express a child's raw score (i.e., number right) on the whole battery of items in terms of mental age. A 6-year-old who got as many items right as the average 8-year-old, for example, would be said to have a mental age of 8 years. It was the German psychologist, William Stern (1871–1938), who suggested dividing the child's mental age (MA) by his chronological age (CA) in order to express his *relative* standing, in comparison with other children, in rate of mental development. The ratio of MA/CA (× 100, to remove the decimal), was termed the "mental quotient" by Stern, and was later translated by Lewis M. Terman (1877–1956) as "intelligence quo-

tient," or IQ. The Binet-Simon intelligence scale, consisting of a graded series of heterogeneous items, was the prototype of virtually all subsequent tests of intelligence down to the present time.

Binet never attempted to develop a consistent or unified theory, or even a formal definition, of intelligence, but from his voluminous writings one can discern Binet's implicit conception of intelligence. This effort, however, may be a bit like describing a Rorschach inkblot, with different writers emphasizing different aspects of Binet's rather unsystematic views. Those aspects of Binet's ideas about intelligence that show the least similarity to the Galtonian and British lines of thought have been the most emphasized by Binet's followers in America. Although at times Binet writes of intelligence as a general ability, at other times he emphasizes its heterogeneity, which seemingly (but mistakenly) justifies the heterogeneous item content of his test. General intelligence, in Binet's thinking, is not a single function, but the resultant of the combined effects of many more limited functions, such as attention, discrimination, and retention. In his later writings, he put greater emphasis on the more complex mental functions—logical processes, comprehension, judgment, and reasoning—as the *sine qua non* of intelligence. He argued that intelligence could be measured efficiently only by using a great variety of items that "sample" these higher processes. As Tuddenham (1962) has aptly put it: "Regarding intelligence as a product of many abilities, Binet sought in his tests to measure not an entity or single dimension—'general intelligence'—but rather an average level—'intelligence in general' " (p. 489).

Tuddenham's characterization of Binet's view probably represents the prevailing conception of intelligence among the majority of American psychologists and especially among clinical psychologists. But there are also serious theoretical and psychometric problems with this Binetian view, as first pointed out by the first really important theoretical successor to Galton, Charles Edward Spearman (1863–1945). The question of whether intelligence is a unitary process or is a resultant of the complex interaction of a great many different, more specialized processes is one of the chief issues of contention by contemporary theorists. But before bringing in Spearman, who begins a whole new line of investigation, this would seem the right place to mention Binet's main intellectual heirs in America. There is not much that needs to be said about them in the present context, however, because, like Binet, they were mainly applied psychologists and test developers, rather than major theorists of intelligence.

The Binet-Simon Intelligence Scale was translated into English and introduced to American psychology by Henry H. Goddard (1866–1957), a leading researcher on mental retardation. Ironically, although Goddard was impressed by the usefulness of Binet's test in his research with retarded children, he was actually a follower of Galton and was an ardent evolutionist and hereditarian, imbued with enthusiasm for Galton's idea of eugenics, or the improvement of the human species through genetic means. He was also the most energetic early promoter of the use of mental tests in clinics and schools in America. His contributions to theory and measurement, however, were nil.

Lewis Madison Terman (1877–1956) was the most important representative of the Binet tradition in America. As a professor at Stanford University, he translated and reworked the Binet-Simon scales, adapting, extending, and norming them for the American population, to produce the Stanford-Binet Intelligence Scale. It was first published in 1916, with revised editions appearing in 1937, 1960, and 1972.

Terman was not a very explicit or original theorist in this field; he largely echoed Binet's notions about the nature of intelligence, although he attached greater importance than did Binet to the capacity for abstract thinking as a necessary attribute of intelligence. Terman was mainly preoccupied with investigating the validity of the IQ, not only for predicting scholastic performance, but for predicting occupational and personal success in adult life as well. His truly monumental study of gifted children, published in five volumes under the general title *Genetic Studies of Genius,* had this purpose. This famous longitudinal study of more than 1,500 children selected on the basis of Stanford-Binet IQs of 140 and above (i.e., the top 1% of the school-age population) is still in progress, now under the supervision of Robert Sears and Lee Cronbach at Stanford University, both of whom, interestingly, were themselves subjects in Terman's study. Terman's intellectually gifted subjects are now in their late 60s and early 70s. The group as a whole shows much higher levels of occupational and intellectual achievements than a random sample of the general population, or even when randomly selected subjects are matched with the parental socioeconomic and educational background of the gifted group.

David Wechsler (1896–1981) followed in essentially the same tradition as Binet and Terman, mainly as an applied psychometrician and constructor of tests, rather than as a theorist or researcher on the nature of intelligence (Matarazzo, 1974; Wechsler, 1958, 1975). Wechsler is best known for the intelligence scales that bear his name: The Wechsler Preschool and Primary Scale of Intelligence (WPPSI), the Wechsler Intelligence Scale for Children (WISC), and the Wechsler Adult Intelligence Scale (WAIS). They are now the most widely used individual tests of intelligence. Wechsler was the first to abandon Binet's mental age scale, which not only seemed indefensible for the measurement of adult intelligence, but has other psychometric defects as well. (The Wechsler IQ scales are all based on standardized scores within narrow age groups of the normative population.) Wechsler conceived of intelligence perhaps more broadly than any of the formal theorists, as an aggregate or global capacity for purposeful action, rational thought, and effective interaction with the environment, a view that broadens the concept of intelligence beyond the strictly cognitive sphere into the realm of affect, motivation, and personality. Wechsler's conception was probably too all-inclusive to attract serious theoretical or scientific interest and, although it has been the favored view of clinical psychologists for half a century, it has been virtually a cipher in the theoretical development of differential psychology.

The Factor Analysts

Charles Edward Spearman

Spearman (1863–1945) was the first really major theorist of human ability. His interest was in founding an empirically based scientific theory of mental ability. Although test development and other aspects of applied psychometrics were, for Spearman, necessary for the realization of his aim, they were quite incidental adjuncts, never holding the center stage in his thinking and research. Yet he was the first important theoretical psychometrician. He presented the first clear conception of what today is referred to as "classical test theory"; he developed the modern concept of reliability, invented the correction of the correlation coefficient for attenuation, formulated precisely the relationship between the length of a test and its reliability (i.e., the Spearman-Brown prophesy formula), and derived the formula for the nonparametric rank-order correlation coefficient. But his greatest methodological contribution was the invention of factor analysis, a methodology that has developed and dominated the study of human abilities ever since it was first introduced by Spearman in 1904.

Spearman came to psychology relatively late in life. After a career as a British Army officer, from which he retired, at age 34, with the rank of major, he began a new career by earning a Ph.D. degree in psychology at the University of Leipzig, under Wundt. He then joined the psychology faculty at the University of London, and soon thereafter he was appointed successor to William McDougall as professor and head of the psychology department, a chair he held for 25 years. In terms of the importance of the topics he researched, his great originality, and his enduring influence, Spearman was unquestionably Britain's greatest psychologist. Besides his intellectual brilliance and mathematical talent, the traits that characterized his career were his clear, no-nonsense, scientific style of thinking about psychological problems and his unalloyed impatience with armchair philosophizing and speculation. This hard-nosed attitude led Spearman into conflict with much of the psychological thought of his day. In his autobiography, Spearman (1930a, p. 330) described his career as "one long fight." For the present purpose, unfortunately, it is impossible to do more than summarize Spearman's contributions rather too briefly and hence inevitably with considerable simplification. Spearman's major works, however, are still worth reading, as many of the issues he raised are still very much alive in contemporary research on intelligence (Spearman, 1904, 1923, 1927, 1930b; Spearman & Jones, 1950). Spearman's most famous book, in which he most completely explicates his main contributions, is *The Abilities of Man* (1927). It still ranks near the top of the list of "must" reading for students of individual differences. Virtually all the basic questions that continue to occupy contemporary researchers and theorists of human ability were first clearly posed by Spearman.

When Spearman began his career in psychology, the doctrine of formal faculties was the generally accepted view of individual differences in abilities. Persons differ in the powers of the many distinct "faculties" that constitute the mind, such as perception, discrimination, memory, recollection, attention, reason, common sense, language, imagination, invention, comprehension, motor control, kinesthetic sense, visualization, and so on. One theorist even listed as many as 48 distinct mental faculties, including "sense of the ridiculous."

Spearman questioned whether the numerous listed faculties were truly distinct components of the mind. Are "memory" and "recollection" really different abilities, or "imagination" and "invention," or "reason" and "comprehension"? If so, mental ability could be objectively measured only by devising special tests for each of the many faculties. But there were endless armchair debates among psychologists concerning the number and names of the faculties. Spearman saw an objective solution to this problem by the use of correlation. If two (or more) nominal faculties were claimed to be distinct, it should be possible to devise tests of each one, to administer the tests to a group of persons who show individual differences in the power of the faculties in question, and show that the measurements of the different faculties are uncorrelated.

Spearman performed this type of study with school children, using tests, examination marks, and teacher ratings on a variety of variables, including classics, French, history, geography, mathematics, "common sense," musical talent, and measures of auditory, visual, and kinesthetic (weight) discrimination. The matrix of correlations among all of these tests revealed all positive intercorrelations, suggesting to Spearman that all of the measures reflect a common factor, that is, a common or unitary source of the covariance among the variables. Individuals who scored exceptionally high on any one variable tended to score above average on all the others as well. Moreover, the correlation matrix displayed a quite regular variation among the sizes of the correlation coefficients, such that by arranging the variables in the matrix in the order of their average correlation with every other variable, the correlations displayed what Spearman referred to as a hierarchy, that is, the correlations in the matrix decreased regularly in both the horizontal and vertical directions from the diagonal, going from the upper left to the lower right corner of the matrix. It especially impressed Spearman that in this hierarchical pattern of correlations there was no clear discontinuity between the scholastic measures (classics, etc.) and the measures of musical ability and of sensory discrimination. This observation seemed to confirm Galton's notion that discrimination ability is a basic aspect of general intelligence. Spearman showed mathematically that such a hierarchical correlation matrix could be "explained" in terms of a single *factor* (i.e., source of variance) that every test in the matrix has in common. He later assigned the label *g* to this *general factor,* which he identified with general intelligence. Spearman hypothesized that every type of cognitive test measured *g* in addition to one other source of variance (besides error), labeled *s* (for *specific*). The *s* is entirely specific to a particular test (or a very narrow class of highly similar tests). This hypothesis became known as Spearman's "two-factor theory" of ability, according to which the total true-score variance (σ_t^2) on any test is expressed as the sum of two components, *g* variance (σ_g^2) and *s* variance (σ_s^2), hence $\sigma_t^2 = \sigma_g^2 + \sigma_s^2$.

Spearman invented a method, now known as *factor analysis,* but actually a rather simple forerunner of the modern techniques under this name, that made it possible to determine precisely the proportion of *g* variance in each of the variables that are entered into a correlation matrix. The square root of this proportion can be interpreted as the test's correlation with the hypothetical ability represented by *g;* this correlation between a test and a factor is commonly termed the *loading* of the test on a given factor (in this case *g*).

Much of Spearman's subsequent research consisted of determining the *g* factor loadings of numerous diverse tests. As many as 94 various tests were factor analyzed in one study (Spearman & Jones, 1950, Chap. 8). Various tests differed widely in their *g* loadings, even when the loadings were corrected for attenuation, ranging from slightly greater than zero up to .80 and above. Spearman regarded the differences in tests' *g* loadings as a basis for discovering the essential nature of *g*. He attempted to do this by comparing high and low *g*-loaded tests for their similarities and differences. The types of tests with the highest *g* loadings, he found, were those that require inductive or deductive reasoning and have a quality of abstractness. In general, the *g* loadings of tests were found to increase, going from tests of simple sensorimotor abilities, to tests of rote and associative memory, to tests involving the grasping of conceptual or abstract relationships, as typically found in verbal and figural analogies tests. Hence, Spearman characterized *g*, or general intelligence, as the "eduction of relations and correlates," that is to say, inductive and deductive reasoning. But this is merely a description of the types of tests that best measure *g;* these are tests requiring fairly complex mental manipulations in order to arrive at the correct answer. But this empirical observation

can hardly be called a theory of *g*. It does not tell us what *g* is, independently of the very mathematical operations of factor analysis, by means of which we have determined the "existence" of *g* and the extent of its loading in various tests. Nor does the description of *g* in terms that characterize the most highly *g*-loaded tests tell us why even tests that involve no reasoning or conceptual content, such as pitch discrimination and choice reaction time, also have some moderate *g* loading. Spearman fully admitted that factor analysis does not, and logically cannot, permit a declaration of the nature of *g*, but can only point to those tests that measure it best. This "defining of *g* by site rather than by nature," he wrote, is a "way of indicating what *g* means . . . just as definite as when one indicates a card by staking on the back of it without looking at its face" (1927, p. 76).

Spearman (1927, Chap. 7) considered many different speculative hypotheses of the nature of *g*. He settled on the hypothesis of a unitary mental energy. This "energy" was deployed to whatever specific "engines" or brain processes were involved in different mental tasks, some tasks requiring more energy, and some less, and hence their different *g* loadings. In Spearman's view, this unitary source of energy enters into every kind of mental task, and the observed positive correlation between all tests is a result of individual differences in the amount of mental energy that people brought to bear on the tests. The specificity peculiar to different tests was attributed to localized or specific energies. "Successful action would always depend partly on the potential energy developed in the whole cortex and partly on the efficiency of the specific group of neurons involved" (1923, p. 6).

The main problem with Spearman's theory of *g* as "mental energy" is not that it is necessarily wrong, but that no means have been found to test it empirically. Theories are scientifically useful only when opposing theories can be pitted against one another in an empirical test. Thus, without an empirical means of being tested, Spearman's theory of *g* remains only speculative and problematic to this day. The *g* factor itself, however, remains secure as an established empirical phenomenon, summarizing the observation that virtually all mental tests that are scorable according to an objective standard of performance are positively intercorrelated in an unrestricted sample of the general population.

The application of Spearman's method of factor

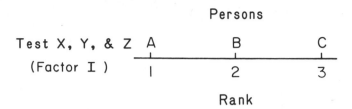

Figure 1. Representation of the rank order (i.e., 1,2,3) of three persons (A,B,and C) on three tests (X, Y, and Z) in a hypothetical one-dimensional (i.e., one factor) test correlation matrix.

analysis to a variety of test batteries by other pioneers of factor analysis, such as Sir Cyril Burt (1883–1971), as well as by Spearman and his students, soon made it apparent that the two-factor theory of ability was too simple to account for the data.[6] Spearman had proven that if only one factor, say g, accounted for all of the intercorrelations among a collection of tests, the correlation, r_{xy}, between any two tests, x and y, would be equal to the product of their g factor loadings, g_x and g_y (i.e., $r_{xy} = g_x \times g_y$). Hence, if g were partialled out of the correlations between tests, the resulting residual correlations should be reduced to zero. But often, this outcome would not be found; after g was partialled out, the residual matrix, although markedly reduced in total variance, would reveal a number of significant correlations, usually among tests of similar content, such as verbal tests, or numerical and mathematical tests, or spatial visualization tests, or tests of memory. This meant that there were actually other factors in addition to g, a fact that Spearman reluctantly conceded. He termed these additional factors *group factors,* because, unlike the general factor, g, which is loaded on every test, the other factors showed substantial loadings on only certain groups of tests. The so-called group factors could be easily named in terms of the similar features of the tests with the largest loadings on a given factor. Among the main group factors identified by Spearman were verbal, mechanical (or spatial), mathematical, and memory factors. When these group factors were viewed as residual sources of test variance, that is, the remaining reliable variance after g is partialled out, they usually accounted for a relatively small proportion of the total variance in test scores, as compared with the amount of variance accounted for

by g. Thus we have a *hierarchical* factor model, in the sense that g, at the pinnacle, is correlated with every test, whereas each group factor is correlated with only a limited domain of tests that are quite similar to one another. In this system, g and each of the group factors are said to be *orthogonal* (i.e., uncorrelated) dimensions.

To those who are not familiar with the mathematical operations of factor analysis, the idea of factors can be made less mysterious if they are thought of as *dimensions*. The question, then, is how many dimensions are needed to represent the covariation (or correlation) among a number of tests. The conceptually simplest example can be illustrated by assuming three tests, labeled X, Y, Z, given to three persons, named A, B, C. Rather than using scores, for simplicity we can simply rank these persons' performance on the tests, giving ranks 1, 2, 3. Consider the following data matrix; the correlation matrix is below.

		Person		
		A	B	C
	X	1	2	3
Test	Y	1	2	3
	Z	1	2	3

Test	X	Y	Z
X		1.0	1.0
Y	1.0		1.0
Z	1.0	1.0	

Only one dimension (or factor) is needed to describe these results; the persons show the same rank order on every test. One dimension can be represented by a straight line (see Figure 1).

---

[6]A detailed critique of Spearman's two-factor theory and of later developments and results of factor analysis can be found in two articles by Burt (1949a, b).

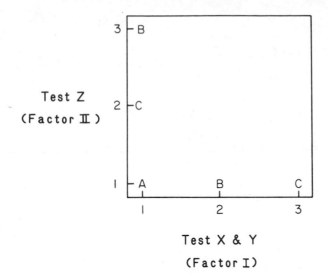

Figure 2. Representation of the rank order of three persons on three tests in a hypothetical two-dimensional (i.e., two factors) test correlation matrix.

A two-factor (2-dimensional) case:

		Person	
	A	B	C
Test X	1	2	3
Test Y	1	2	3
Test Z	1	3	2

Test	X	Y	Z
X		1.0	0.5
Y	1.0		0.5
Z	0.5	0.5	

A 2-dimension space is needed to represent these data (see Figure 2).

A three-factor (3-dimensional) case:

		Person	
	A	B	C
Test X	1	2	3
Test Y	1	3	2
Test Z	2	3	1

Test	X	Y	Z
X		0.5	−0.5
Y	0.5		0.5
Z	−0.5	0.5	

And a 3-dimension space is needed to represent these data (see Figure 3).

One can go on adding dimensions, although it becomes impossible to depict more than three dimensions graphically, and the geometry of n-dimensional space can be treated only in purely mathematical terms. The scientifically desirable economy of factor analysis as a means of describing the "structure" of a correlation matrix results from the fact that most of the covariance among a large number of tests can be accounted for in terms of a relatively much smaller number of factors, because many different tests share some of the same factors in varying degrees.

It is important to recognize just what factor analysis does and does not tell us. It tells us which tests "go together," that is, it parsimoniously describes the correlations among a number of diverse tests in terms of a limited number of uncorrelated common sources of individual differences variance, called factors, that are shared by all mental tests (in the case of *g*) or by particular groups of tests (in the case of group factors). Thus factor analysis is es-

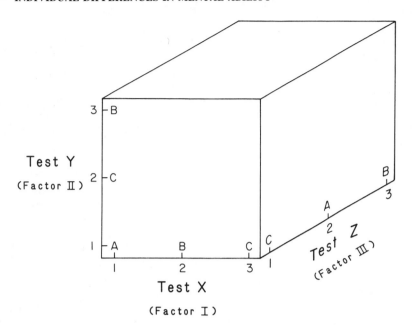

Figure 3. Representation of the rank-order of three persons in a hypothetical three-dimensional (i.e., three factors) test correlation matrix.

sentially descriptive. It is said to describe the structure of abilities. It is not an explanatory theory. It does not explain why various tests are correlated as they are, or why various tests show quite different average correlations with all the other diverse tests in a battery. Factors merely afford a systematic description of phenomena with unknown causes. Factors themselves are not the causes of anything; they are simply descriptive abstractions. The basic empirical phenomena from which factors are derived are individual differences in test scores and their intercorrelations among diverse tests. It is these phenomena, and consequently the factors to which they give rise, that are in need of scientific explanation in causal terms.

If we accept *g,* the largest common factor, as a working definition of intelligence, then a major aim of a theory of intelligence is the explanation of *g.* This boils down to an explanation of why different tests are correlated with one another and why some tests are correlated more highly than others. As already noted, Spearman put forth a unitary or monistic explanation of *g* in terms of a hypothetical "mental energy." He hoped that future neurophysiological research would discover individual differences in some form of general neural energy in the cerebral cortex. Spearman's monistic

theory of *g* as mental energy was soon challenged by rival theories.

Edward Lee Thorndike. The leading American educational psychologist, Thorndike (1874–1949) was best known for his studies of learning. But he also played a major role in the development of intelligence tests and was the first American to espouse a theory of intelligence, the elements of which were borrowed directly from his theory of learning as the formation of new stimulus–response (S–R) bonds under the influence of reward, or positive reinforcement. For Thorndike, learning was a process of "selecting and connecting"; hence his term *connectionist theory.* An individual's behavioral and intellectual repertoire was made up, basically, of innumerable S–R connections in the nervous system, the specific connections being acquired through experience in the environment. Thorndike's theory of intelligence was set forth in his major contribution to this field, *The Measurement of Intelligence* (Thorndike *et al.,* 1927), which is also one of the major classics of this field that is still rewarding to read. According to Thorndike, individual differences in intelligence reflect the number of S–R bonds that persons acquire by a given age. He hypothesized that persons differ innately in the number of potential neural connections that they possess, so that even given the same environment and experience, two individuals may differ markedly in the number of S–R bonds they can acquire, and hence they will differ accordingly in intellect.

In Thorndike's theory, the ubiquitous positive correlations between tests, and the g factor that can be extracted from all their intercorrelations, result from two hypothetical conditions: (a) various tests draw on different numbers and combinations of neural bonds, and (b) there is overlapping of the bonds "sampled" by different tests. Thus, according to Thorndike, there is no unitary factor, such as Spearman's "mental energy," that underlies g. The g factor, and all other factors as well, are artifacts resulting from different tests sampling common bonds. The elemental bonds themselves could be entirely uncorrelated, differing only in their quantity from one individual to another. A person's score on an intelligence test represents an average of all the particular connections tapped by the test items.

Spearman (1927, Chap. 5) termed this kind of theory "anarchic." He argued that it was a scientifically inadmissable basis for the measurement of intelligence. Taking an average of what he termed a "hotchpot" of test items, which was the method of the Binet tests, for example, did not meet essential criteria of scientific measurement. How could one claim that any given item or class of items measured intelligence? What rational basis is there for giving all types of items equal weight in the composite average? Should memory items and reasoning items be weighted equally? Questions such as these could be debated endlessly or decided arbitrarily. Factor analysis provided an objective means for dealing with them. The fact that "hotchpot" tests such as the Binet and Wechsler scales actually turn out to be quite good measures of intelligence, or g, and show substantial correlations with real-life, commonsense criteria of intelligence is explained by Spearman's principle of "the indifference of the indicator" of g. Because every kind of mental task involves g to some extent (in addition to any other more specific factors), the larger and more diverse that the collection of tasks is, the greater is the cumulative proportion of g variance relative to the variance attributable to the many task-specific factors, which, being uncorrelated across diverse tasks, cancel each other out, so to speak. Hence the summed scores over a wide variety of tasks may represent a rough approximation to the measurement of g.

In the early days of factor analysis, a great deal of argument was wasted on the question of whether g did or did not "exist." The answer now is clear: certainly g exists as a product of the factor analysis of any sizable collection of diverse mental tests.[7] The fact that a very substantial g, in the sense of proportion of total variance accounted for, is found in virtually any sizable collection of diverse tests, and that the g is highly similar for different collections of tests, provided each collection is reasonably diverse in form and content, is a fundamental and important empirical discovery.

The crucial issue that remains worth considering is the question, What causes g? That is to say, what are the mechanisms or processes, entirely independent of factor analysis, that could explain the positive intercorrelations among individual differences in performance on virtually all mental tasks and hence make possible the extraction of a predominant g factor from any large collection of mental tasks? To argue, as do some psychologists, that because g is a mathematical abstraction, it cannot be thought of as having a cause, is fallacious, in that it fails to take account of the fact that a g factor need not be found at all. If all mental tasks involved only specific abilities, no g factor could emerge by any method of factor analysis, and persons' scores on tests would vary solely as a function of the particular collection of tasks (or items) included in the test, plus errors of measurement. All the correlational evidence, however, completely contradicts this possibility. But this fact alone cannot prove that the g factor has a single or unitary cause. The g factor could be explained, as did Thorndike, by hypothesizing a multitude of independent components (S–R bonds, neural elements, or whatever) of ability, a number of which are necessarily sampled by any task, and a larger number being sampled by the more complex tasks. Indeed, it is observed that complex tasks are more highly correlated with one another than simple tasks are correlated with one another. This is just what one would predict from the hypothesis that complex tasks sample more elements than do simple tasks, and therefore increase the proportion of overlapping elements between the tasks. It could also be argued equally well that more complex tasks are more g loaded because

---

[7]By far the most profound and sophisticated discussion of the logical and metaphysical status of the mental factors yielded by factor analysis that I have found is in *The Factors of the Mind* by Burt (1940).

they require more mental energy. From the viewpoint of sampling theory, however, the factors revealed by factor analysis really describe the characteristics of tests rather than factors of the mind. Although "sampling theory," as it later came to be known, originated with E. L. Thorndike, it was formalized mathematically by the British psychometrician and educational psychologist, Sir Godfrey H. Thomson (1881–1955), who had spent a year (1923–24) at Columbia University working with Thorndike. Thomson's (1951) "sampling theory" of g was seen as a challenge to Spearman's "mental energy" theory. It has gained considerable popularity among psychometricians, especially in the United States. Although the "sampling theory" has been around since at least 1914, when first introduced by Thorndike, it has never given rise to any empirical research that could put it to a significant test. Its appeal is entirely intuitive. The typical criticism of Thorndike's and Thomson's sampling theory has been cogently expressed by Jane Loevinger (1951):

The sampling theory hardly qualifies as a true theory, for it does not make any assertion to which evidence is relevant. Perhaps the large number of adherents to this view is due to the fact that no one has offered evidence against it. But until the view is defined more sharply, one cannot even conceive of the possibility of contrary evidence, nor, for that matter, confirmatory evidence. A statement about the human mind which can be neither supported nor refuted by any facts, known or conceivable, is certainly useless. Bridgman and other philosophers of science would probably declare the sampling theory to be meaningless. (p. 595)

Louis L. Thurstone. The leading American psychometrician and factor analyst, Thurstone (1887–1955) developed a method of "multiple factor analysis" (Thurstone, 1947) that facilitated the extraction of a number of factors from a correlation matrix of numerous diverse tests, and along with it he proposed an objective criterion for the "rotation" of the factor axes that he called *simple structure,* intended to yield psychologically interpretable factors. Rotation of the factor axes to the simple structure criterion maximized the loadings of certain tests on particular factors and minimized the tests' loadings on other factors, making it relatively easy to describe the various uncorrelated factors in terms of the particular tests on which they had the largest loadings. Ideally, each factor would load only on certain tests and each test would be loaded on only one factor, in which case it could be called a "factor pure" test.

Applying his method of multiple factor analysis to large batteries of tests, Thurstone (1938) extracted a number of factors that he termed *primary mental abilities:* verbal fluency, verbal comprehension, numerical, spatial, reasoning, perceptual speed, and associative memory. There was no g factor in this structural model of abilities, for the simple reason that the criterion of simple structure mathematically precludes the extraction of a general factor. This limitation of Thurstone's method became a point of considerable contention between British and American psychometricians. The appropriateness of the simple structure criterion in the domain of human abilities was soon challenged. It was noted that a good simple structure could not be achieved with orthogonal (uncorrelated) factor rotation; allowing oblique rotation of the factor axes, so that the axes were at less than right angles and were thus oblique, or correlated, factors, permitted a much closer approximation to the ideal simple structure. Thurstone himself resolved the conflict with Spearman. By factor analyzing the intercorrelated primary factors, Thurstone showed that the g factor emerged as a second-order factor, or superfactor. Thurstone's method of multiple factor analysis with orthogonal rotation to simple structure had merely scattered the large g factor among the so-called primary factors. When Eysenck (1939) reanalyzed Thurstone's correlation matrix of more than 50 diverse tests, using a method of factor analysis that allows the appearance of a general factor and various group factors, he found that the g factor accounted for more of the total variance in all the tests than the variance accounted for by all of the remaining group factors combined. In fact, it has proved impossible to construct factor-pure tests of Thurstone's primary mental abilities that do not also measure Spearman's g, and usually each test is more highly loaded on g than on the primary factor it was specially devised to measure. At best, so-called factor-pure tests measure g plus the one primary factor they were devised to measure.

Contemporary Theorists

The two leading contemporary factor analysts of the abilities domain are Joy Paul Guilford (b. 1897) and Raymond Bernard Cattell (b. 1905).

Guilford (1959, 1966, 1967, 1977) has proposed a complex scheme, or "facet" model, for the classification of abilities that he has called the Structure of Intellect (SOI) model. The hypothetical abilities of the SOI model represent the intersections of 5 different mental *operations* (cognition, memory, divergent production, convergent production, and evaluation) × 5 different types of *contents* (visual, auditory, symbolic, semantic, and behavioral) × 6 different types of *products* (units, classes, relations, systems, transformations, and implications), making for $5 \times 5 \times 6 = 150$ abilities in all. Guilford regards each of the SOI abilities as unique, or factorially distinct from all the others. The SOI model thus suggests a possible 150 types of tests, and from year-to-year new tests are reported as having been devised to measure still a few more of the abilities suggested by this model. The number of such tests must now exceed 100. If all these tests were subjected to a type of factor analysis that does not mathematically prohibit the extraction of a general factor, it seems virtually certain that a large g would emerge. Yet the SOI does not admit a g factor. A model with 150 hypothesized unique abilities, however, is actually beyond the reach of factor analysis for all practical purposes, and so the 150 abilities have not come anywhere near being substantiated by factor analysis. The testability of the SOI model poses such staggering problems that it seems unlikely that it will ever be able to face the challenge of empirical verification (Undheim & Horn, 1977). Scientifically, the SOI model has not really advanced beyond a purely formal system (one of many possible rational systems) for the generation and classification of mental tests. Although Guilford's SOI is apparently a quite comprehensive and fine-grained system of categories into which an extremely great variety of tests may be classified, it is highly arguable whether it actually tells us anything about the nature of intelligence. It completely evades the central question: Why are all tests correlated with one another, thereby giving rise to g?

Cattell (1963, 1971) has distinguished two aspects of g, which he has termed fluid (g_f) and crystallized (g_c). Tests based on specific knowledge and cognitive strategies acquired prior to taking the test, such as general information, vocabulary, arithmetic, scholastic knowledge and skills, and the like, are most heavily loaded on the g_c factor. Tests with little or no knowledge content but that depend on short-term memory for novel material presented in the test situation (e.g., digit span memory) and novel problem solving involving reasoning about figural materials (e.g., figure analogies, matrices, series completion) are the most heavily loaded on the g_f factor. People reach their peak power on g_f in their late teens or early twenties, whereas g_c gradually increases until old age, provided persons are not entirely cut off from experiences that afford opportunities for new learning. The g_c factor can be interpreted as reflecting the knowledge and skills acquired through the individual's investment of g_f in specific forms of learning and experience. Consequently, individual differences in g_f and g_c will be more or less highly correlated depending on the degree of similarity in people's educational experience and in the cultural values that influence the types of experience in which g_f will be invested. The correlation between g_f and g_c again yields the superfactor g. Recent studies (Gustafsson, 1984; Undheim, 1981) based on a hierarchical type of factor analysis of collections of tests well representative of fluid and crystallized abilities suggest that g_f is "absorbed" into the g (a "neo-Spearmanian" g) at the top of the factor hierarchy; that is, when g is partialled out of g_f, the residualized g_f is reduced to zero, and hence it is concluded that g_f is the same factor as Spearman's g (or vice versa). The g_c factor remains as one of two or three second-order factors in the hierarchy.

In contrast to the factor analytic school, a quite different approach, clinical and qualitative, to the study of intelligence was taken by the noted Swiss child psychologist Jean Piaget (1896–1980). In his major work on this subject, Piaget (1950) viewed intelligence as a biological process of adjustment between the conscious organism and its physical and social environment. The term *intelligence* indicates the forms of organization or equilibrium by which the organism cognitively structures its sensory and motor experiences. The complexity of the cognitive structures increases and changes qualitatively through different stages of the child's mental growth. Piaget's descriptions of the stages of mental growth developed from his observations of children when confronted by various problems cleverly devised by Piaget to reveal the "logic" of children's thinking at different stages of their mental development. Briefly, Piaget viewed the mental development of the child as going through four main stages, which are invariant in sequence for all children: (a) the *sensorimotor* stage (onset from birth to about 1 year) is the first phase of intellectual development, in which knowledge and thought are intimately tied to the content of specific sensory input or motoric activity of the child; it includes conditioning, stimulus–response learning, reward learning, perceptual recognition, and associative or rote learning and memory. (b) The *preoperational* stage (onset ages 1 to 2 years) is a transitional period between the sensorimotor stage and the next stage and is mainly characterized by symbolic play and cognitive egocentrism, that is, the child in this stage can view objects and relationships only in terms of his own relation to them. (c) *Concrete operations* (onset 6 to 7 years) is the first stage of what Piaget called operational thinking, which characterizes his view of intelligence. It involves the capacity for performing mental operations on concrete objects, such as numeration, seriation, and classification or other forms of grouping, and the ability to conceive the invariant structure of classes, relations, and numbers. (d) *Formal operations* (onset 11 to 13 years) is the final level of operational thinking, manifested in logical reasoning (not dependent on the manipulation of concrete objects), propositional thinking, combinatorial and inferential thinking that involve using hypothetical possibilites, abstractions, and imaginary conditions, as well as the mental manipulations of symbols for real or experiential knowledge. The main stages are claimed to be invariant in sequence for all children, but there are individual differences in the rate of progress from one developmental stage to the next, attributable to both innate factors and environmental influences. In the light of numerous empirical studies by other experimental child psychologists, Piaget's theory of qualitatively distinct stages of mental growth has come under increasingly severe criticism and doubts in recent years (e.g., Brainerd, 1978).

Piaget's *méthode clinique,* consisting of various tasks administered individually with careful inquiry to elicit the child's thought processes, has been psychometrized, in the fashion of the Binet scale, by Tuddenham (1970), Vernon (1965), and others. When the Piagetian tasks have been factor analyzed along with a large number of conventional psychometric tests, they show quite large loadings exclusively on the *g* factor; there is no group factor that is unique to the Piagetian tasks. Thus even Piaget's quite different approach to the study of intelligence, in the final analysis, reveals essentially the same *g* factor as originally discovered by Spearman. (For a review of the relevant research, see Jensen, 1980, pp. 669–677). The behavioral manifestations of *g* are almost infinitely multifarious, and much has been written, and will no doubt continue to be written, by way of describing the many behavioral aspects of *g* throughout the course of development from infancy to old age. An understanding of the essential nature of *g,* however-

er, would depend on approaching the problem from a different level of analysis than that afforded either by Piaget's *méthode clinique* or by the application of factor analysis to conventional psychometric tests.

Information Processing Theories

By the mid-1940s, the factor analysis of abilities had about run its course in its potential conceptual contribution to the study of human intelligence. From the viewpoint of theoretical development, the whole field went into the doldrums for nearly a quarter of a century. Strictly methodological and statistical developments and refinements in factor analysis and test theory came to occupy the center stage, whereas the substantive issues of differential psychology remained virtually at an impasse. It became increasingly clear that the factor analysis of psychometric tests alone could serve only a descriptive function and could not compel any particular structural model. Such basic questions as whether intelligence is singular or plural could not be settled by any methodology available in traditional psychometrics. The explanation of the descriptive factors yielded by the factor analysts would have to be explained by means that are entirely independent of factor analysis itself. It is important to recognize that the results of factor analysis describe individual differences in abilities rather than the abilities themselves. Abilities can show up as factors only to the extent that there is individual variation in the abilities. If there are abilities, even very crucial abilities, which everyone possesses to much the same degree, they will not be revealed as important abilities by factor analysis. Hence, not all of the operating features of the mind—call them *cognitive processes*—are necessarily revealed by factor analysis. Theoretically, all mental processes could not be revealed by factor analysis as it is traditionally used, unless it were assumed that there are substantial individual differences in all of the processes.

In the 1960s, psychologists whose chief interests were not individual differences or psychometrics, but the experimental psychology of learning, memory, and problem solving, turned to the newly developed information processing theory as a model for the intervening variables, or hypothetical constructs, needed to explain the complex types of behavior that strictly behavioristic S–R theories seemed inadequate to cope with. Information processing theory, or cognitive theory, is a "black box" approach, in which the processing of information, from sensory reception to motor response, is explained in terms of the operations of a number of hypothetical constructs termed "elementary information processes," which act in sequence (or, on occasion, in parallel) to mediate problem solving (Newell & Simon, 1972).

Because tests involving problem solving are among the most highly g loaded, it is not surprising that the information processing approach to problem solving was soon perceived as a promising new paradigm for the study of intelligence. Information processing research on human abilities sprang up like mushrooms in the 1970s and has since become one of the liveliest fields in contemporary psychology. Among the leading pioneers in this relatively new field that brings the information processing paradigm to bear on the problems of differential psychology on which traditional psychometric approaches had run out of steam are J. B. Carroll (1976, 1980), E. B. Hunt (Hunt, 1976; Hunt et al., 1973), and R. J. Sternberg (1977, 1979). An introduction to the major developments in this approach can be found in several multi-authored books edited by Resnick (1976), R. J. Sternberg (1982a, 1982b, 1984), and Eysenck (1982a).[8]

Processing theory attempts to analyze various cognitive tasks in terms of a limited number of "information processes" (or "components" in Sternberg's theory) having the status of intervening variables or theoretical constructs that are hypothesized to execute different cognitive functions termed elementary information processes. Among the more prominently invoked processes are visual search, stimulus encoding, discrimination-comparison, scanning short-term memory, storing information in intermediate and long-term memory, and memory search and retrieval of information. Metaprocesses are those executive functions that deploy and integrate the elementary processes, direct and monitor performance, and invoke acquired learned strategies for more efficient information processing, such as chunking or grouping stimuli, use of S–R mediators and verbal mnemonics, rehearsal of associations, and the like. These hypothesized elementary information processes are operationally definable, and individual

differences in them can be measured, at least indirectly, by various chronometric techniques that measure reaction times in the performance of simple tasks that are contrived to elicit certain information processes. Because the experimental tasks are usually so very simple that error rates are extremely small, individual differences must be measured in terms of reaction time (RT) or response latency, usually in milliseconds. For example, the speed of scanning for an item in short-term memory has been measured by displaying a set of anywhere from 1 to 5 digits, which the subject studies for 2 seconds. The series then disappears from the screen, and immediately a single probe digit appears. The subject responds as quickly as possible by pressing one of two keys labeled "yes" or "no," as to whether the probe digit was or was not a member of the previously presented set (S. Sternberg, 1966).

According to the information processing view, there are individual differences in the speed or efficiency of the various elementary processes and in the presence or absence of certain metaprocesses, and these differences account for the differences in performance on psychometric tests and the kinds of educational and occupational performance criteria predicted by conventional test scores. The as yet unrealized task of information processing research is to show that individual differences in the same limited number of elementary cognitive processes are indeed involved in a wide variety of superficially different kinds of test items and can thereby afford an adequate explanation of the sources of variation in, and correlations between, standard psychometric tests. The g yielded by factor analysis of psychometric tests, according to information processing theory, results from there being certain elementary information processes and perhaps also certain metaprocesses that are required for successful performance on virtually all test items (Sternberg & Gardner, 1982). But it turns out that measures of the elementary cognitive processes are themselves intercorrelated, and when factor analyzed they yield a g factor that is correlated with the g of psychometric tests. If the elementary processes are themselves g loaded, the explanation of g is merely passed on to another level of analysis. At the end of this reductionistic regress of g to more and more elemental levels of analysis, presumably, is some physiological substrate, the precise nature of which is still highly speculative. Research on the electrical potentials of the brain evoked by simple auditory stimuli

---

[8]A comprehensive discussion of the educational implications of information processing conceptions of intelligence, as contrasted with the psychometric and Piagetian views, is presented by Wagner and Sternberg (1984).

("clicks") while the conscious subject does nothing overtly has shown remarkably high correlations between psychometric *g* and certain indexes derived from the average evoked potential. Both Eysenck (1982b) and Schafer (1985), in independent studies, have found that the degree to which indexes of the average evoked potential are correlated with each of the 11 diverse subtests of the Wechsler Adult Intelligence Scale is directly related (with correlations of +0.90 and +0.95) to the size of the *g* loadings of each of the subscales. In other words, the Wechsler subtests with the highest *g* loadings also show the largest correlations with the average evoked potential. The specific neural mechanisms that mediate this impressive relationship between evoked potentials and psychometric *g* are not yet known and the field is wide open for theoretical speculation and empirical investigation. It is entirely possible, some would even say likely, that the basis of *g* at the level of brain physiology could be much simpler than the multifarious manifestations of *g* that we can observe at the psychological or behavioral level of analysis.

The Inheritance of Mental Ability

The correlation of *g* with measures of the brain's electrophysiological response to sensory input is surely consistent with Galton's view of intelligence as a biological phenomenon and is therefore influenced by hereditary factors. Although the belief that mental traits are inherited much as are physical characteristics can be traced at least as far back as the philosophers of ancient Greece, it was Galton who first tried to put this idea on an empirical, scientific footing. He can therefore be claimed as the founder of behavioral genetics, which is now recognized as the application of the principles and methodology of quantitative genetics to the study of individual differences in behavioral traits. The essential features of quantitative genetic analysis are seen in their present form in Galton's own work in *Hereditary Genius* (1869). Inferences concerning the relative effects of genetic and environmental factors on individual variation are based on quantitative estimates of the varying degrees of resemblance, or correlation, between relatives of different degrees of genetic kinship. Galton was also the first scientist to recognize the value of monozygotic (MZ) and dizygotic (DZ) twins for genetical analysis.

With the advent of psychometric tests and the development of quantitative genetics by Sir Ronald A. Fisher (1890–1962) and others, it became possible, using various kinship and twin correlations, to analyze the variance in any given metric trait into its genetic and environmental components. The second quarter of this century brought forth a number of now classic studies in this vein, most of them showing that a substantial proportion of the population variance in IQ, at least half and perhaps as much as three quarters, is attributable to polygenic inheritance. Consider such findings with respect to IQ as the following: the pattern of various kinship correlations rather closely approximates the pattern of correlations predicted by a simple ploygenic model; MZ twins reared apart are much more similar in IQ than DZ twins or full siblings reared together; the IQs of genetically unrelated children reared together show a much lower correlation than the correlation of full siblings reared together; the IQs of adopted children are more highly correlated with the IQs of their biological parents than with the IQs of their adoptive parents; inbred children born to genetically related parents (e.g., incestuous matings and cousin matings) show lower IQs, on average, than children born to genetically unrelated parents—a genetically predictable phenomenon known as "inbreeding depression" (Jensen, 1978, 1983). Such findings virtually defy explanation in strictly environmental terms; yet rather simple polygenic models fit these data remarkably well. The methodology and typical findings of quantitative genetic research on human abilities have been explicated in a nontechnical fashion by Jensen (1981), Plomin, De-Fries, and McClearn (1980), and Vernon (1979). A more technical and comprehensive review of the evidence is provided by Scarr and Carter-Saltzman (1982).

At the same time that the early classic studies of the inheritance of intelligence were taking place, a new development, radical behaviorism, under the leadership of John Broadus Watson (1878–1958), was on the ascendance in American psychology. Watson hoped to explain all behavior, including individual differences, in terms of Pavlovian conditioning and learning. Watson's bold challenge, in *Behaviorism* (1925), to the Galtonian idea of inherited mental capacity has been often quoted:

Give me a dozen healthy infants, well-formed, and my own specified world to bring them up in and I'll guarantee to take any one at random and train him to become any type of specialist I might select—doctor, lawyer, artist, merchant-chief, and yes, even beggar-man and thief, regardless of his talents, penchants, tendencies, abilities, vocations, and race of his ancestors. (p. 82)

Watson's view, although usually expressed in less brash tones, became the dominant sentiment in American psychology, sociology, and cultural anthropology. The heated polemics of opposition and conflict between the hereditarian and environmental positions in all their aspects regarding the explanation of individual differences, as well as of social class and racial differences, in mental test scores and scholastic achievement have long been known as the nature–nurture controversy. The controversy, with roots going back at least to Locke's *tabula rasa* theory of the mind and the egalitarian philosophy of 19th century liberalism, has actually been fueled more by philosophical, political, and ideological values than by the intrinsic scientific problems of behavior-genetic analysis. An excellent account of the history of the nature–nurture controversy is provided by Loehlin (1984). Researchers in behavioral genetics are confronted with a quite different order of theoretical and methodological issues than those that are paraded under the popular banner of the nature–nurture controversy. The real scientific questions now are not whether genetic factors are importantly involved in human variability in mental abilities, but concern the details of the genetic architecture and its evolutionary basis, the specific nature of the pathways from genes to behavior, and the forms of interaction and covariance of genetic and environmental factors. The controversies engendered in this endeavor are of a highly technical nature intrinsic to the scientific issues, and bear little resemblance to popular hereditarian or environmentalist ideologies.

Along with the decline of interest in the theory of intelligence following World War I, there was a corresponding waning of genetic studies of intelligence. Interest in this field almost completely disappeared from the psychological scene. However, in the late 1950s and early 1960s, the increasing national concern over the quality of public education and the increasingly conspicuous inequalities in scholastic performance among different segments of the population stimulated a renewed interest in the improvability of intelligence, educability, and scholastic achievement by means of environmental interventions, especially during the crucial developmental period in early childhood. Research and action programs in this vein, made possible under the War on Poverty and the Great Society programs of Presidents Kennedy and Johnson, received a level of federal support previously unknown in the behavioral and social sciences.

Probably the single most influential publication of the 1960s, with respect to the thinking of the psychologists and educators who were concerned with bringing about greater equality of educational performance, was *Intelligence and Experience* (1961) by J. McVicker Hunt (b. 1906). A scholarly and persuasively argued work, it greatly minimized the role of genetics and strongly emphasized the effects of early environmental stimulation on intellectual development. Hunt's thesis was perceived by many as the needed theoretical rationale for innovative programs in early childhood education and compensatory education.

By the late 1960s, after such educational programs had already been in effect for several years, the evidence from various large-scale compensatory education programs and Head Start had not shown the theoretically predicted effects of markedly raising the IQs or scholastic achievements of the children these programs were specifically intended to benefit. Intellectual development and its manifestation in scholastic performance, it appeared, were not as easily alterable as the then prevailing theory led many psychologists and educators to believe. In 1969, the present writer, at the request of the editors of the *Harvard Educational Review,* prepared a lengthy critique (Jensen, 1969) of the overly extreme environmentalist theory that had engendered unrealistic expectations regarding the susceptibility of human differences in ability to psychological and educational manipulation.[9] This article, entitled "How Much Can We Boost IQ and Scholastic Achievement?" included a fairly comprehensive review of the then available research on the heritability of intelligence. Largely because the article not only revived what, since the 1930s, had become an unpopular view—that IQ differences have a genetic basis—but also because it conjectured that genetic as well as environmental factors were probably involved in the observed statistical differences between social class and racial groups, the article became widely cited and stirred up a storm of protests and criticisms and debates. Some of these events have been detailed in the Preface of *Genetics and Education* (Jensen, 1972), a volume that also contains the original article that set off all the commotion. These events also coin-

---

[9]A recent review of the evidence on attempts to raise IQ is provided by Spitz (1986).

cide with the beginning of what appears as a new era of scientific interest, research, and publication concerned with the theory of intelligence and the behavior-genetic analysis of individual differences. Besides many dozens of books and hundreds of articles published on these topics since 1970, and numerous research programs addressed to fundamental issues, there also now are two quarterly journals that publish research exclusively in these areas: *Intelligence* and *Behavior Genetics*. By the mid-1980s, the era of vehement controversy on these topics seemed a thing of the past. The arguments that we can expect in the future of this thriving branch of science will most likely be more the kind of intrinsic controversy that is seen as a normal and necessary aspect of every lively and developing science.

Intelligence and Education

Theories of education, of its proper aims and the means for achieving them, have been strongly influenced, implicitly or explicitly, by theories of the nature of intelligence. Throughout the history of education, theories of intelligence and of the nature of individual differences therein have ranged between polar opposites: the notion of individual differences as completely innate and immutable, and the notion of almost unlimited plasticity. The idea that individual differences in intelligence are predominantly a product of differences in the opportunities for learning and in cultural privileges afforded by the environment and, by the same token, can be markedly shaped by educational means has been a dominant theme in American educational philosophy. Yet scholastic achievement, and, by inference, scholastic aptitude, or intelligence, persistently vary over a wide range. Quite large differences are often seen even between full siblings reared together in the same family, the *average* IQ difference between siblings being 11 to 12 IQ points (after correction for errors of measurement). And these IQ differences are highly correlated with scholastic performance. IQ differences are manifested in different rates of learning scholastic subject matter, in the level of cognitive or conceptual complexity of the material that can be mastered at a given age, and probably, for all practical purposes, in the level of complexity of the material that can ever be mastered with any amount of training. Obviously, not everyone can become a Shakespeare, a Beethoven, or an Einstein, however excellent their training and plentiful their opportunities.

The ubiquity of large individual differences in pupils' performance in every type of instructional program that has ever been tried inevitably raises the question whether education should attempt to overcome or minimize individual differences so as to shape all children to similar educational goals and attainments or should itself be shaped to meet the needs of children varying widely in abilities. The preponderance of the research evidence to date inescapably supports the view that schooling, by every method of instruction yet tried, is capable of inculcating knowledge and skills, interests and attitudes, but has relatively negligible effects on the wide spread of differences in the rates of acquisition of knowledge and skill and in the levels of subject-matter complexity that can be comprehended at any given age. The problem of individual differences may well be one of those many aspects of reality that have no universally satisfactory solution from the standpoint of individual aspirations.

To the best of our present knowledge, it appears that some substantial part of the variance in IQ and scholastic achievement—probably somewhere between 50% and 70%, according to the best evidence on the heritability of IQ—is probably not subject to manipulation by strictly psychological or educational treatment. The reason for this, presumably, is that the main locus of control of that apparently unyielding variance is more biological than psychological or behavioral. At an even more fundamental level, we might ask why variance in intelligence should be so surprisingly resistant to experimental manipulation. This apparent resistance to manipulation seems less surprising if we view human intelligence as an outcome of biological evolution. Genetic variation is the one absolutely essential ingredient to enable evolution to occur. If intelligence has evolved as a fitness characteristic in the Darwinian sense—that is, as an instrumentality for the survival of humankind— it is conceivable that the biological basis of intelligence has a built-in stabilizing mechanism, rather like a gyroscope, that safeguards the individual's behavioral capacity for coping with the exigencies of survival. If that were the case, mental development would not be wholly at the mercy of often erratic environmental happenstance. A too malleable fitness trait would afford an organism too little protection against the vagaries of its environment. Thus, as humanity evolved, processes may also have evolved to buffer human intelligence from being pushed too far in one direction or another, whether by adventitiously harmful or by intentionally benevolent environmental forces.

What many contemporary educational psychologists would consider a realistic position regarding the broad implications for education of our present knowledge of intelligence can be summarized as follows. Individual differences in measured intelligence are reflected in the child's performance in school in a variety of ways: in the age at which he reaches optimal readiness for beginning classroom instruction in certain school subjects (especially reading and arithmetic), in the ease and speed with which he learns scholastic subjects under ordinary conditions of instruction, in his generalization and transfer of learning from one lesson to the next and from one subject to another, and in his ability to apply principles learned in one context to somewhat novel situations. Given other necessary conditions of learning, such as good motivation and good study habits, differences in intelligence are also reflected not only in the rate of attainment but also in the levels of mastery and complexity that are generally reached. The learning of addition and subtraction, for example, will not reflect IQ differences to as great an extent as the more complex operations of multiplication and long division, which in turn are not as discriminating as the still more complex and abstract concepts of algebra, geometry, and calculus. Similarly, penmanship and spelling ability are much less differentiated along the lines of IQ than is ability in written composition.

Despite real differences in ability, however, a diversity of appropriate instructional programs and flexibility in the age grading of school subjects can make it possible for the vast majority of children to attain at least the basic scholastic skills during their years in school.

Because mental abilities are distributed over a wide range and are reflected in differences in educability, and because most of this variability is related to both genetic and environmental factors that are not directly under the school's control, it seems a reasonable conclusion that schools and society must provide a range and diversity of educational methods, programs, and goals, and of occupational opportunities, just as wide as the range of human abilities. Equality of educational opportunity accordingly is not to be interpreted as uniformity of instructional facilities and techniques for all children. Diversity rather than uniformity of

approaches holds greater promise for making education rewarding for children over the full range of abilities. The reality of individual differences should not mean educational rewards for some children and frustration and defeat for others. If the ideal of universal education is to be successfully pursued, the extent to which all children can be beneficiaries of the educational system will depend in large part on the proper recognition of individual differences.

References

Anastasia, A. (Ed.). (1965). *Individual differences*. New York: Wiley.

Binet, A., & Simon, Th. (1905a). Méthodes nouvelles pour le diagnostic du niveau intellectuel des anormaux. *L'Année Psychologique, 11*, 199–244.

Binet, A., & Simon, Th. (1905b). Application des méthodes nouvelles au diagnostic du niveau intellectuel chez des enfants normaux d'hospice et d'école primaire. *L'Année Psychologique, 11*, 245–336.

Boring, E. G. (1950). *A history of experimental psychology* (2nd ed.). New York: Appleton-Century-Crofts.

Brainerd, C. (1978). *Piaget's theory of intelligence*. New York: Prentice-Hall.

Burt, C. (1940). *The factors of the mind*. London: University of London Press.

Burt, C. (1949a). The two-factor theory. *British Journal of Psychology* (Statistical Section), *2*, 151–178.

Burt, C. (1949b). The structure of the mind: A review of the results of factor analysis. *British Journal of Educational Psychology, 19*, 100–199.

Burt, C. (1955). The evidence for the concept of intelligence. *British Journal of Educational Psychology, 25*, 158–177.

Burt, C. (1962). Francis Galton and his contributions to psychology. *British Journal of Statistical Psychology, 15*, 1–49.

Carroll, J. B. (1980). *Individual difference relations in psychometric and experimental cognitive tasks*. Chapel Hill, NC: L. L. Thurstone Psychometric Laboratory, University of North Carolina.

Cattell, J. McK. (1930). Psychology in America. *Scientific Monthly, 30*, 114–126.

Cattell, R. B. (1963). Theory of fluid and crystalized intelligence: A critical experiment. *Journal of Educational Psychology, 54*, 1–22.

Cattell, R. B. (1971). *Abilities: Their structure, growth and action*. Boston, MA: Houghton-Mifflin.

Cronbach, L. J. (1957). The two disciplines of scientific psychology. *American Psychologist, 12*, 671–684.

Eysenck, H. J. (1939). Review of *Primary mental abilities* by L. L. Thurstone. *British Journal of Educational Psychology, 9*, 270–275.

Eysenck, H. J. (Ed.). (1982a). *A model for intelligence*. Heidelberg: Springer-Verlag.

Eysenck, H. J. (1982b). The psychophysiology of intelligence. In C. D. Spielberger & J. N. Butcher (Eds.), *Advances in personality assessment* (Vol. 1, pp. 1–33). Hillsdale, NJ: Erlbaum.

Forrest, D. W. (1974). *Francis Galton: The life and work of a Victorian genius*. New York: Taplinger.

Galton, F. (1869). *Hereditary genius: An inquiry into its laws and consequences*. London: Collins.

Galton, F. (1883). *Inquiries into human faculty and its development*. London: Macmillan.

Galton, F. (1908). *Memories of my life*. London: Methuen.

Guilford, J. P. (1954). *Psychometric methods*. New York: McGraw-Hill.

Guilford, J. P. (1959). Three faces of intellect. *American Psychologist, 14,* 469–479.

Guilford, J. P. (1966). Intelligence: 1965 model. *American Psychologist, 21,* 20–26.

Guilford, J. P. (1967). *The nature of human intelligence*. New York: McGraw-Hill.

Guilford, J. P. (1977). *Way beyond the IQ: Guide to improving intelligence and creativity*. Buffalo, NY: Creative education Foundation.

Gustafsson, J.-E. (1984). A unifying model for the structure of intellectual abilities. *Intelligence, 8,* 179–203.

Hunt, E. (1976). Varieties of cognitive power. In L. B. Resnick (Ed.), *The nature of intelligence* (pp. 237–259). Hillsdale, NJ: Erlbaum.

Hunt, E., Frost, N., & Lunneborg, C. (1973). Individual differences in cognition: A new approach to intelligence. In C. Bower (Ed.), *Advances in learning and motivation* (Vol. 7, pp. 81–110). New York: Academic Press.

Hunt, J. McV. (1961). *Intelligence and experience*. New York: Ronald Press.

Jensen, A. R. (1969). How much can we boost IQ and scholastic achievement? *Harvard Educational Review, 39,* 1–123.

Jensen, A. R. (1972). *Genetics and education*. London: Methuen.

Jensen, A. R. (1978). Genetic and behavioral effects of nonrandom mating. In R. T. Osborne, C. E. Noble, & N. Weyl (Eds.), *Human variation: Psychology of age, race, and sex*. New York: Academic Press.

Jensen, A. R. (1980). *Bias in mental testing*. New York: The Free Press.

Jensen, A. R. (1981). *Straight talk about mental tests*. New York: The Free Press.

Jensen, A. R. (1983). Effects of inbreeding on mental-ability factors. *Personality and Individual Differences, 4,* 71–87.

Loehlin, J. C. (1984). Nature/nurture controversy. In R. J. Corsini (Ed.), *Encyclopedia of Psychology* (Vol. 2, pp. 418–420). New York: Wiley.

Loevinger, J. (1951). Intelligence. In H. Helson (Ed.), *Theoretical foundations of psychology* (pp. 557–601). New York: Van Nostrand.

Matarazzo, J. D. (1974). *Wechsler's measurement and appraisal of adult intelligence* (5th ed.). Baltimore, MD: Williams & Wilkins.

Newell, A., & Simon, H. (1972). *Human problem solving*. Englewood Cliffs, NJ: Prentice-Hall.

Pearson, K. (1914–1930). *The life, letters and labours of Francis Galton* (3 vols.). Cambridge: Cambridge University Press.

Peterson, J. (1925). *Early conceptions and tests of intelligence*. Yonkers, NY: World Book.

Piaget, J. (1950). *The psychology of intelligence*. London: Routledge & Kegan Paul.

Plomin, R., DeFries, J. C., & McClearn, G. E. (1980). *Behavioral genetics: A primer*. San Francisco: W. H. Freeman.

Posner, M. I. (1978). *Chronometric explorations of mind*. Hillsdale, NJ: Erlbaum.

Resnick, L. B. (1976). *The nature of intelligence*. Hillsdale, NJ: Erlbaum.

Scarr, S., & Carter-Saltzman, L. (1982). Genetics and intelligence. In R. J. Sternberg (Ed.), *Handbook of human intelligence* (pp. 792–896). Cambridge: Cambridge University Press.

Schafer, E. W. P. (1985). Neural adaptability: A biological determinant of *g* factor intelligence. *The Behavioral and Brain Sciences, 8,* 240–241.

Spearman, C. E. (1904). ''General intelligence'' objectively determined and measured. *American Journal of Psychology, 15,* 201–293.

Spearman, C. E. (1923). *The nature of ''intelligence'' and the principles of cognition*. London: Macmillan.

Spearman, C. E. (1927). *The abilities of man*. New York: Macmillan.

Spearman, C. E. (1930a). Autobiography. In C. Murchison (Ed.), *A history of psychology in autobiography* (Vol. 1, pp. 299–333). Worcester, MA: Clark University Press.

Spearman, C. E. (1930b). *Creative mind*. New York: Cambridge.

Spearman, C. E., & Jones, LL. W. (1950). *Human ability*. London: Macmillan.

Spitz, H. H. (1986). *The raising of intelligence: A selected history of attempts to raise retarded intelligence*. Hillsdale, NJ: Erlbaum.

Sternberg, R. J. (1977). *Intelligence, information processing, and analogical reasoning: The componential analysis of human abilities*. Hillsdale, NJ: Erlbaum.

Sternberg, R. J. (1979). Intelligence research at the interface between differential and cognitive psychology: Prospects and proposals. In R. J. Sternberg & D. K. Detterman (Eds.), *Human intelligence: Perspectives on its theory and measurement* (30–60). Norwood, NJ: Ablex.

Sternberg, R. J. (Ed.). (1982a). *Handbook of human intelligence*. Cambridge: Cambridge University Press.

Sternberg, R. J. (Ed.). (1982b). *Advances in the psychology of human intelligence* (Vol. 1). Hillsdale, NJ: Erlbaum.

Sternberg, R. J. (Ed.). (1984). *Advances in the psychology of human intelligence* (Vol 2). Hillsdale, NJ: Erlbaum.

Sternberg, R. J., & Gardner, M. K. (1982). A componential interpretation of the general factor in human intelligence. In H. J. Eysenck (Ed.), *A model for intelligence* (231–256). Heidelberg: Springer-Verlag.

Sternberg, S. (1966). High speed scanning in human memory. *Science, 153,* 652–654.

Stoddard, G. D. (1943). *The meaning of intelligence*. New York: Macmillan.

Thomson, G. D. (1951). *The factorial analysis of human ability* (5th ed.). Boston, MA: Houghton-Mifflin.

Thorndike, E. L., Bregman, E. O., Cobb, M. V., & Woodyard, E. (1927). *The measurement of intelligence*. New York: Bureau of Publications, Teachers College, Columbia University.

Thurstone, L. L. (1938). Primary mental abilities. *Psychometric Monographs* (No. 1). Chicago, IL: University of Chicago Press.

Thurstone, L. L. (1947). *Multiple factor analysis*. Chicago, IL: University of Chicago Press.

Tuddenham, R. D. (1962). The nature and measurement of intelligence. In L. Postman (Ed.), *Psychology in the making: Histories of selected research problems* (pp. 469–525). New York: Knopf.

Tuddenham, R. D. (1970). A ''Piagetian'' test of cognitive development. In W. B. Dockrell (Ed.), *On intelligence* (pp. 49–70). London: Methuen.

Undheim, J. O. (1981). On intelligence II: A neo-Spearman

model to replace Cattel's theory of fluid and crystallized intelligence. *Scandinavian Journal of Psychology, 22,* 181–187.

Undheim, J. O., & Horn, J. L. (1977). Critical evaluation of Guilford's Structure-of-Intellect theory. *Intelligence, 1,* 65–81.

Vernon, P. E. (1965). Environmental handicaps and intellectual development: Part II and Part III. *British Journal of Educational Psychology, 35,* 1–22.

Vernon, P. E. (1979). *Intelligence, heredity, and environment.* San Francisco: W. H. Freeman.

Wagner, R. K., & Sternberg, R. J. (1984). Alternative conceptions of intelligence and their implications for education. *Review of Educational Research, 54,* 179–223.

Watson, J. B. (1925). *Behaviorism.* New York: Norton.

Watson, R. I. (1963). *The great psychologists from Aristotle to Freud.* Philadelphia, PA: Lippincott.

Wechsler, D. (1958). *The measurement and appraisal of adult intelligence* (4th ed.). Baltimore, MD: Williams & Wilkins.

Wechsler, D. (1975). Intelligence defined and undefined: A relativistic appraisal. *American Psychologist, 30,* 135–139.

Wolf, T. H. (1973). *Alfred Binet.* Chicago, IL: University of Chicago Press.

CHAPTER 5

Measurement and Educational Psychology

BEGINNINGS AND REPERCUSSIONS

John B. Carroll

Introduction

Insofar as educational psychology was to make a contribution to the use of scientific principles and methods in education, it was early realized that it was necessary to develop the theory and practice of educational measurement. The most notable statement of this idea was written by Edward L. Thorndike, the founder of scientific educational psychology in America:

Whatever exists at all exists in some amount. To know it thoroughly involves knowing its quantity as well as its quality. Education is concerned with changes in human beings; a change is a difference between two conditions; each of these conditions is known to us only by the products produced by it—things made, words spoken, acts performed and the like. To measure any of these products means to define its amount in some way so that competent persons will know how large it is, better than they would without measurement. . . . This is the general *Credo* of those who, in the last decade, have been busy trying to extend and improve measurements of educational products.

This is obviously the same general creed as that of the physicist or chemist or physiologist engaged in quantitative thinking—the same, indeed, as that of modern science in general. And, in

general, the nature of educational measurements is the same as that of all scientific measurements. (Thorndike, 1918)

Thorndike went on to remark, however, that

in detail . . . there are notable differences. An educational product . . . is commonly a complex of many sorts of things. . . . What we do, of course, is . . . to measure the amount of some feature, *e.g.*, the general merit of the composition or the richness of its vocabulary. . . . Every measurement represents a highly partial and abstract treatment of the product.

He expressed concern that educational measurements usually lack zero points and have ill-defined units of measurement. Nevertheless he felt that carefully made measurements could be of great practical use to educators.

Thorndike realized that measurements of many sorts would be indispensable in scientific research on educational problems. He was among the first to develop scientifically based procedures of measurement for such research. With his *Introduction to The Theory of Mental and Social Measurements* (Thorndike, 1904, 1913) he was the first to offer a treatment, comprehensive for its time, of statistical methods in educational research.

Space does not permit presenting a complete history of the beginnings and development of mea-

John B. Carroll • Department of Psychology, University of North Carolina, Chapel Hill, NC 27514.

surement in educational psychology. There are numerous sources for facts and interpretations of this history (Cook, 1952; DuBois, 1970; Ebel & Damrin, 1960; Engelhart, 1952; Linden & Linden, 1968; Ross & Stanley, 1954, Chap. 2; Travers, 1983). Jončich's (1968, Chap. 13) biography of Thorndike gives an illuminating account of his role in the development of educational measurement. Monroe (1945) contrasted the status of educational measurement in 1945 with that in 1920. In the early years of its existence, the National Society for the Study of Education published several yearbooks devoted to educational measurement issues; for example, Whipple (1918) edited one on the measurement of "educational products" in which Thorndike contributed the previously quoted homily on educational measurement and its uses. The periodic reviews of educational and psychological testing research in the *Review of Educational Research*, starting with that in Volume 3 (1933) and ending with that in Volume 39 (1969) (after which the journal changed its format), can be consulted for details and bibliographies.

The focus here is on the development of educational measurement as a technology. I note and comment on what I regard as major breakthroughs and influential contributions. Because another chapter in this volume discusses the history of research on individual differences in intelligence and aptitudes, I confine my attention chiefly to technology in the measurement of educational achievement, but the problems and methods discussed apply in other areas, including the study of individual differences in intelligence, aptitudes, personality, and interests. I mention the history of statistical method only to the extent that it relates to developments in educational measurement as such. Treatments of the history of statistics by Walker (1929) and Dudycha and Dudycha (1972) may be consulted for further details.

The purpose is to make readers aware of the antecedents of present-day practices and trends and thus to encourage them to realize that most of the basic problems in educational measurement have been recognized, and have been persistent, throughout the whole history of this art and science.

Methods of Testing

In hindsight, the development of contemporary methods of testing has had a long and tortuous history. From time immemorial—even in ancient China (DuBois, 1970), Greece, and Rome—the traditional way of assessing students' progress in learning has been some form of oral or written examination, and this mode of testing is still widely used, though perhaps with more observance of standards and safeguards than in earlier times (Coffman, 1971). Examinations have been of many kinds, ranging from simple spelling and arithmetic tests to the writing of long essays in response to questions or problems posed. But even the written examination was not widely used until means of writing (paper, pens, pencils) became readily available in schools in the 19th century (Travers, 1983, pp. 96ff.) It was not until the 20th century that the use of "new-type" or "objective" examinations became at all prevalent.

The objective or new-type test, consisting of series of completion, true-false, or multiple-choice items, grew mainly out of early efforts to measure mental abilities (Whipple, 1910). Ebbinghaus (1896–1897) was the originator of the completion or fill-in test—the forerunner of the cloze technique later developed by Taylor (1953) to measure the readability of prose. Using the completion technique, Trabue (1916) developed scales for measuring the level of language knowledge and understanding. Other types of objective test items were derived, in part from the work of Binet, by Yerkes, Bridges, and Hardwick (1915). Just before the entry of the United States into World War I, Otis had developed a group intelligence test for elementary school children that was completely objective in the sense that it could be scored by checking responses against an answer key. His tests, and related materials, were models for the Alpha and Beta examinations rather hastily constructed for testing mental abilities of Army recruits (Yerkes, 1921). Otis (1918) published an account of his group intelligence test, interesting for the statistical methods of scaling and item analysis that he used.

The success of objective-type items in the measurement of abilities encouraged educators to import this type of test into the measurement of school learning and achievement. McCall (1920) described "a new kind of school examination" that was actually nothing more or less than the true-false test (the multiple-choice item was not even mentioned, even though this type had been used, at least in an elementary form, in the Army tests). The multiple-choice type of achievement-test item started to become prevalent in the mid-1920s. It was also in this period that test standardization procedures were developed and became widely used, although even as early as 1917 a textbook on educational measurements by Monroe, DeVoss, and Kelly (1917) listed ''standardized'' tests in a variety of school subjects—tests that did not, however, generally use objective-type items.

Methods and guidelines for the actual writing of objective tests were slow to appear. Little or no information on this matter is to be found, for example, in the text by Monroe *et al.* (1917) just cited, but McCall (1922) treated the topic fairly extensively. Starting in 1927, Ruch and Rice (1930) conducted a nationwide contest in the construction of objective examinations; they published an extensive sample of examinations that were awarded prizes. In evaluating the entries, no explicit consideration was given to whether the examinations covered specified educational objectives; apparently appropriateness to educational objectives was taken for granted. Much more consideration of educational objectives, and methods of writing items to test them, was given in a collection of articles edited by Hawkes, Lindquist, and Mann (1936) under the auspices of a committee of the American Council on Education. In these articles, authors suggested ways of testing understanding and other ''higher mental processes,'' but in general, the many achievement tests constructed during the 1930s were limited to the testing of elementary skills and factual knowledge. The tests used in the well-known Pennsylvania Study of high school and college students' subject-matter attainments (Learned & Wood, 1938) were of this type. A departure from this tradition came with the tests constructed for the so-called Eight-Year Study (Smith & Tyler, 1942), to measure higher mental processes, social sensitivity, appreciation, and personal and social adjustment.

During the early years of educational measurement, there was considerable ambiguity and confusion as to what kind of measurement could be called objective. At first, objectivity was defined simply in terms of ''freedom from personal opinion in scoring.'' McCall (1922, p. 312) stated that ''a test is perfectly objective when identical results are secured from two applications of the same test to the same pupils by *different* examiners.'' Later, objectivity came to be defined in terms of whether tests could be scored by clerks, or even by machine.

Restricting attention to the process of test writing, I see at least two important trends in the period since about 1935 (that is, the last 50 years):

1. Gradual acceptance and implementation of the idea that tests must be closely geared to the measurement of specified educational objectives. Bloom's (1956) *Taxonomy of Educational Objectives* played an important role here, as did later work (e.g., Bloom, Hastings, & Madaus, 1971) on the specification of behavioral objectives, inspired by programmed instruction and similar developments. Tests were planned in terms of grids or outlines specifying contents and item types in relation to objectives. Standardized achievement tests paid more attention to common elements in curricula nationwide, and this led to criticisms of these tests as forcing undue uniformity of curricula and as not adequately reflecting local curriculum variations.

2. There was more knowledge about, and greater appreciation of, characteristics of good as opposed to poor test items in terms of wording, format, dependence on the objective to be tested, and the influence of specific determiners (attributes of items that might bias the examinee's response apart from content). In the 1930s and 1940s, there was much research on characteristics of various types of objective items, and on their validity as compared to that of free-response and essay tests. Manuals of item-writing techniques also became available (e.g., Wood, 1961), a trend culminating in such more recent works as those of Bormuth (1970) and Roid and Haladyna (1982) offering a ''technology for test-item writing.''

Although test item writing may have become more of an established discipline for professional test constructors, it is anybody's guess how well this discipline has penetrated into the actual practices of teachers in the schools. To be sure, departments and colleges of education have long offered courses in educational measurement and statistics for teachers, and occasionally schools conduct workshops on the subject for their staffs, but there has been continued failure on the part of many teachers to address themselves to the preparation of well-designed classroom tests and the use of simple statistical procedures, such as item analysis, to make effective diagnostic and evaluative instruments.

Theory of Measurement

In his *Introduction to the Theory of Mental and Social Measurements* (Thorndike, 1904, 1913)—which may be characterized as an early textbook on statistics rather than one on educational measurement—Thorndike pointed out the ''special difficulties'' of mental measurements, ''due chiefly to (1) the *absence or imperfection of units* in which to measure, (2) the *lack of constancy in the facts* measured, and (3) the *extreme complexity* of the measurements to be made'' (1913, p. 4). His chapter ''Units and Scales'' pointed out ''common defects in scales for measuring mental and social facts,'' such as the arbitrariness of a scale from 0 to 100 or from 0 to 10. He distinguished objective from subjective scales, absolute from relative scales, discrete from continuous series, and absolute from arbitrary zero points. He hinted at notions of reliability and validity of measurements, although he did not use those terms. (In a later chapter, ''The Reliability of Measures,'' *reliability* referred to what would now be called the standard errors of statistics. In 1904, the theory of test reliability was only beginning to be explored.)

In Thorndike's early work, the ideal scale for an educational measurement was perceived as one that presented specimen educational products of different degrees of quality from very poor to excellent, with numbers assigned to these different products in such a way that they formed approximately what would now be called an interval scale with equal units of measurement. Thorndike (1910) presented a handwriting scale following this scheme. In use, samples of handwriting were to be matched as accurately as possible to specimens on the scale. The equality of units was established by analyzing judges' ratings according to Fullerton and Cattell's (1892) theorem that differences that are equally often noticed are equal. Inspired by this work, scales for other kinds of educational products, such as drawings and English compositions, were constructed by Thorndike or his students (Hillegas, 1912), and apparently put into fairly wide use. It seems, however, that in the subsequent history of educational measurement relatively little use has been made of this technique, at least not in the careful way that Thorndike and his students employed it. For example, the technique can be used in the measurement of public speaking performances, foreign language speaking and writing proficiency, and the excellence of mathematical proofs.

The problem of measurement scales arose in a more critical way when points were assigned to answers to a series of discrete items, resulting in test scores. Here there was no satisfactory way, as Thorndike realized, to assume equality of units. Based on statistical work done in the 19th century on distributions of personal attributes like height and weight, it was widely assumed that underlying distributions of ability and school achievement would approximate normality; witness a statement by Monroe, DeVoss, and Kelly (1917, p. 276): ''It is a well-known fact that when a group of pupils is measured with respect to a mental or physical characteristic they are found to be distributed as shown in [a figure representing a normal distribution].'' There was concern, therefore, with how test scores could be evaluated with reference to a normal distribution. Thorndike (1904, 1913) presented methods for translating scores into percentiles (the percentile was a concept originated by Galton) and then to normal curve equivalents. Monroe *et al.* presented (p. 260) a method of translating test scores into school mark scales.

There was also the question of assessing and scaling difficulty of particular questions, exercises, or items. Monroe *et al.* (1917) refer to methods used by Buckingham (1913), Trabue (1916), and Woody (1916) in translating percent of correct responses into P. E. (probable error) equivalents. (The P. E. is .6745 times the Standard Deviation). Apparently these authors were the first to convert proportions correctly into normal curve equivalents, at least to create something like a reasonable interval scale. Strangely, however, they were also concerned with establishing an absolute zero point on this basis. Monroe *et al.* state that

to express the absolute value of an exercise a zero point must be established. This is done by constructing an exercise which calls for zero ability. The other exercises are then compared with this one. (p. 277)

According to current theory, of course, such a procedure makes little sense, or would be considered invalid.

These early procedures formed the basis for expressing scores in terms of *norms,* whether in percentiles, P. E. scores, T scores (McCall, 1922), or scaled scores (Flanagan, 1939a). By the 1960s, many tests were being criticized as ''norm-referenced'' because their results could be interpreted only with reference to norms. Yet, it should be pointed out that early educational measurers had a strong desire to express tested educational outcomes in terms of what would now be called criterion referencing (Berk, 1980), that is, in terms of what actual kinds of performance a score would refer to. In the early years of the century, there were many attempts to make test scores criterion-referenced in the contemporary sense of the term.

The logical problems of establishing measuring scales began to be formalized with the work of Stevens (1946, 1951, 1968) in distinguishing four basic scale types: nominal, ordinal, interval, and ratio. (Actually, even in 1904 Thorndike had already perceived differences among some of these scale types.) This work has had more importance in the use of measurement scales in statistical research than in the actual construction of classroom tests. The importance has been in connection with the assumptions underlying various statistical procedures, such as correlation (Carroll, 1961) or analysis of variance. It has been argued that data that are no more than ordinal are inappropriately analyzed with parametric statistics, or at least, that much caution must be used in using such statistics with them. The question of the necessity of observing rules about scale types has been debated for many years. The latest exchange has been between Gaito (1980) and Townsend and Ashby (1984), the former arguing, with Lord (1953), that "the numbers do not know where they come from" and therefore that they can be treated as pure numbers without regard to type of measurement scale, and the latter pointing out that ignoring scale type can, at least in some circumstances, lead to serious errors in interpreting statistical results. On the other hand, even though many test scores are technically no more than ordinally scaled, most educational researchers believe that it usually does little violence to use parametric statistics with them, providing their distributions are approximately normal.

Even more formal considerations of measurement problems have been made by philosophers and logicians who have attempted to construct an axiomatic system for defining scales (Krantz, Luce, Suppes, & Tversky, 1971a; Suppes & Zinnes, 1963). I am not aware, however, that any of this work has as yet influenced educational measurement or educational research.

One basis for establishing a scale of ability, proficiency, or achievement is to select a series of tasks, all of which are considered or demonstrated to measure the same trait, but which vary in apparent difficulty or complexity, and then to determine the proportion of individuals in some representative sample who are able to perform, solve, or master each task. The ability scale is then formed by arranging the tasks in order of proportion correct. On the assumption that the underlying ability is normally distributed in the sample of individuals tested, the tasks are assigned difficulty values in terms of normal deviate units corresponding to the proportions. (We have already seen that this technique was used by early test constructors, except that "probable error" units were employed.) Kelley (1916) presented a curve relating "proportion missed" to the difficulty of spelling words. In their work on the construction of a scale of intelligence, Thorndike, Bregman, Cobb, and Woodyard (1927, Chapter 11) were impressed with the fact that for a group of persons at any given ability level, there was a regular curve of relation between task difficulty and percent correct for that particular group. In fact, by shifting origins for different groups, curves for different groups coincided and appeared to have the same (reverse normal ogive) form. It was on this basis that Thorndike *et al.* established a scale for specifying the "altitude" of an individual's intellect.

A problem with this approach (apparently not recognized even by Thorndike) was that the procedures did not guarantee that the scale was unidimensional. Almost any series of tasks, as long as they have some correlation among themselves, could generate an "altitude" scale like Thorndike's. The tasks assigned to different levels, however, might measure somewhat different traits. The first breakthrough in solving this problem was made by Walker (1931, 1936, 1940) in a series of papers appearing in the *British Journal of Psychology*. Walker noticed that at least for certain tests, the students' answers followed a systematic pattern when they were studied in relation to item difficulty. Students who were able to perform the most difficult tasks could also perform all or nearly all tasks of less difficulty. Likewise, students who failed easy tasks also failed all or nearly all tasks of greater difficulty. Tests that had this characteristic, according to Walker, were called "unig"; tests that did not were said to have an element of "hig" (from "higgledy-piggledyness", as suggested by Godfrey Thomson). Thus, Walker anticipated the work of Guttman (1941), who regarded a series of tasks or items showing the previously described answer pattern as being unidimensional. In fact, the scalogram technique developed by Guttman is simply a way of seeing the extent to which Walker's "unig" pattern is displayed by a set of data. Perhaps the so-called Guttman scale should be renamed the Walker scale.

Eventually there were further developments along these lines; for the most part, the various contributors were unaware of each other's work. A Walker scale was assumed by Ferguson (1941) and

Carroll (1945) in their work on the variance and correlational properties of such scales. Ferguson was concerned with the effects of using tasks on such scales in item factor-analysis; Carroll considered the additional complications introduced when items, or sets of them, could be passed by chance guessing. Mosier (1940, 1941) related such mental test scales to psychophysical scales, by pointing out that they constituted a relation between the nature of the stimulus (its difficulty, complexity, or whatever) and the individual's characteristic level of ability. Loevinger's (1947) index of homogeneity was a measure of the extent to which a test conforms to the properties of a perfect Walker-Guttman scale; Carroll (1951) pointed out, however, that Loevinger's index could be seriously depressed by unreliability and chance guessing effects. The full ramifications of this line of research on unidimensional tests have never been worked out, even today. (Item response theory, to be discussed later, concerns relations between proportion correct and *ability* rather than task difficulty, without necessarily assuming unidimensionality of the items or of the ability measured.)

Test Theory

Some of the topics mentioned in the preceding section might more properly be considered under what has come to be known as "test theory," or sometimes, "the theory of mental tests." Test theory concerns the particular problems of statistical analysis associated with the construction of tests and other kinds of variables dealt with in psychological and educational research, such as ratings, questionnaire responses, and the like. The problems dealt with in the preceding section, on units of measurement, have close relations with problems of test theory; it is difficult to draw the line, in fact. Nevertheless, in test theory it is possible to distinguish between problems having to do with *variables* as such, and problems having to do with *composites of variables,* which is, in reality, what many tests are. That is, much of test theory concerns how tests should be constructed as composites of *items,* each item usually consisting of a stimulus and a response that is scored dichotomously, that is, as either 1 or 0 (for example) depending on whether the response is considered correct or incorrect. The total test score is a sum of the item scores, or sometimes a sum of the weighted item scores. First we consider that part of test

theory that concerns scores, ratings, or other measures as variables rather than as composites. Later, theories of test scores as composites of items will be considered; this part of test theory was developed somewhat more recently than the former. Actually, all of this theory is considered as part of classical test theory, as opposed to what has come to be called item response theory (to be considered still later).

Most of classical test theory can be derived from certain elementary theorems about the correlation of sums, the sums being regarded as containing both true scores and error scores. It thus harks back to a period when applications of correlation theory were being developed. It is perhaps difficult for the present-day student to realize that the theory of correlation is less than 100 years old. As discussed by Walker (1929), the idea of correlation arose in the mind of Francis Galton (as it had also in the minds of various mathematicians in the early 19th century), but the actual mathematical formulation of the theory was done by Karl Pearson, an associate of Galton, around 1895. The ordinary, familiar correlation statistic is called the Pearsonian product-moment correlation because it was formulated by Pearson as the mean of the products of standard deviation scores of two variables. Pearson and his students also developed (in the period 1900–1910, approximately) variants of the correlation coefficient such as the biserial and the tetrachoric coefficients, and worked out the theory of multiple and partial correlation. Thus, the groundwork was already laid for developing a theory of test reliability when, shortly after 1900, Charles Spearman began his studies of tests of mental abilities.

The basic theory of reliability was set forth in a paper by Spearman (1904a). The term *reliability* was not used in that paper, however; it did not appear in print until 1910, when Spearman defined it as "the coefficient between one-half and the other half of several measurements of the same thing." (Strictly speaking, this would now be called the reliability of a half-length test.) The modern student of test theory, working through the derivations presented by Spearman and others, will see this development as rather tortured; the derivations given by Spearman seem much more complicated than they need to be. Nevertheless, the basic idea of a test score as a composite of a true score and an error score is certainly implicit in Spearman's discussion in 1904; in fact the other paper that Spearman (1904b) published that year, on the concept of intelligence, provided an example of the use of what would now be called the correction for attenuation. The correction for attenuation and the so-called Spearman-Brown prophecy formula, however, were not formalized until 1910 in papers independently published by Spearman (1910) and Brown (1910), coincidentally in the same issue of the *British Journal of Psychology.*

Use of the term *reliability* as referring to the correlation between equivalent measures, and thus as an indication of the accuracy of a measurement, was slow to penetrate educational measurement procedures in the United States. Even in the revised edition of his textbook on mental measurements, Thorndike (1913) used the term only to refer to standard errors of statistics. Similar use of the term was made by Rugg (1917) in his text on statistics. Monroe, DeVoss, and Kelly's text (1917) used the term in its general sense, but not with reference to actual coefficients of reliability. Otis (1916) concluded that the most "reliable" measures of an ability (spelling) are obtained by using items for which there is an average of 50% correct answers. He also remarked that he believed it was

better to express the unreliability of scores in terms of a median deviation or "probable error" of the scores than in terms of a coefficient of correlation, since the latter is affected by the degree of heterogeneity of the group. (p. 796)

Working without knowledge of Spearman and Brown's efforts, Truman Kelley (1916) developed a formula for the "index of reliability" (the correlation between an observed score and the true score), and in a footnote offered a formula similar to the Spearman-Brown prophecy formula. It was not until about 1921, however, that usage of the term reliability as the name of a particular kind of correlation coefficient began to be standardized and widely recognized among test constructors (see Kelley, 1921, 1923, who defined reliability as "the extent to which the test measures what it in reality does measure—not necessarily that which it is claimed to measure"). Only by the time of Kelley's (1927) *Interpretation of Educational Measurements* can one find a more or less complete discussion of reliability coefficients and their use, including formulas for the standard error of measurement and the effect of the range of talent on the reliability coefficient. Kelley even went so far as to specify certain values for "minimal satisfactory reliabilities as measured by a reliability coefficient determined from the pupils in a single school grade" for tests serving different purposes.

One of the clearest, simplest presentations of classical test theory, with derivations, was given by Thurstone (1931b); later and more advanced presentations are those of R. L. Thorndike (1949) and Gulliksen (1950). Further, a discussion of classical reliability forms the early part of Lord and Novick's (1968) authoritative text.

It is interesting that in the first several decades of the test movement there was much controversy and empirical research concerning the accuracy and utility of the Spearman-Brown prophecy formula in predicting the reliability of lengthened tests. Some of this research was briefly treated by Osburn (1933, p. 36) and subsequent reviewers in the *Review of Educational Research.* Evidently the problem was not really resolved until Gulliksen (1950) pointed out that the accuracy of the formula depends on the degree to which its assumptions are valid for a particular use of the formula.

Prior to the work of Kuder and Richardson (1937), estimates of test reliability were generally made by split-half, test-retest, or alternate form techniques. Using theorems associated with variances and correlations of sums, Kuder and Richardson showed how test reliability could also be determined from internal item statistics. Their formulas 20 and 21 (the numbers are those of the actual formulas in their mathematical development) are now regularly used in this connection, although the assumptions underlying their use are not always recognized. For about the next 10 years, the journal *Psychometrika* contained numerous articles concerned with issues of test reliability. Articles by Wherry and Gaylord (1943, 1944) are of note, concerned with the effect of factorial composition on reliability. An article by Tucker (1946) led to concern with the "attenuation paradox" (Loevinger, 1954) to the effect that under certain conditions test validity can seem to *decrease* as reliability increases, contrary to classical test theory predictions. This problem was not resolved until the advent of Lord and Novick's (1968) item response theory; it was seen that the paradox arose because of the incorrect assumption of linearity in test validity coefficients.

Early educational researchers occasionally encountered the problem of assessing the reliability of multiple measures, such as a series of ratings. Commonly this was done by finding the average correlation among such measures and using the Spearman-Brown prophecy formula to estimate the reliability of the composite of the ratings; Edgerton and Toops (1928) presented a short-cut for these computations. It was not until 1951 that Ebel (1951) perceived the applicability of ANOVA techniques to this problem. Already in 1941 Jackson and Ferguson (1941) had applied such techniques to test scores. Later presentations by Stanley (1971) and Winer (1972) have shown how variances due to trait, item difficulty, rater bias, and error can be computed and used in the assessment of the reliability with which a variable is measured.

In the meantime—in fact as early as 1908 with Stone's (1908) arithmetic tests—test constructors were concerned with the properties of particular test items as contributing to measurements of variables. One problem was the distribution of item difficulties. We have already mentioned Otis's (1916) observation that the most reliable test would be composed of items of 50% difficulty. This seemed, to some, to be contrary to common sense and logic, and the usual practice among early test constructors was to compose tests from items graded in difficulty from fairly easy to fairly difficult. Others, however, felt that all items should be fairly easy, in order to detect pupils who were not able to pass items "crucial" for a given grade. For most of the history of test construction, the tendency has been to use item difficulty distributions peaked at about the mean difficulty level expected for the sample or population to be tested, although it can be shown that this policy is unwise under certain conditions.

In assessing the validity of an item—that is, the effectiveness of an item in measuring a trait or an educational achievement, techniques in an almost startling variety were devised. J. A. Long and Sandiford's (1935) survey and analysis of these methods will be found instructive. One easy method was to split the total score distribution at the median and compare percents correct in the two halves. A somewhat more sophisticated technique was developed by Flanagan (1939b) on the basis of a proof by Kelley (1939) that in general, and under certain assumptions, maximum accuracy would result from comparing percents correct from the upper and lower 27% portions of the distribution. Brigham (1932) used the Pearson- and Kelley-developed biserial correlation in his work on developing the Scholastic Aptitude Test.

My consideration of the latter-day history of test theory can be brief. Credit goes to Lord (1952) for making test theory into a discipline soundly based on statistical theory and a general mathematical model of the functioning of items in measuring "latent traits" of ability or achievement. The central idea of item response theory (IRT), as introduced in Lord and Novick's (1968) classic text, is that subjects' likelihoods of correct response to an item can be described by a functional equation that may have one or more parameters—usually three. The most important parameter is one representing the item's overall level of difficulty on the scale of the latent trait measured by the item. (The latent trait may be either unidimensional or multidimensional.) Two other parameters are one describing the slope of the function as ability varies and one representing the probability of correct response for a subject whose ability is infinitely low, but who may nevertheless perform the item correctly through guessing or other chance phenomena. As Lord (1980) has shown, IRT has many applications, as in developing more reliable, better scaled tests, in equating tests, in using "tailored" tests, in studying item bias, and so forth. IRT involves highly technical computations, and generally requires large samples to fit and test models. Its main virtue is that it resolves, or claims to resolve, many of the difficulties presented in classical test theory.

Test theorists have divided into several schools of thought and interest. One school, led by Wright and Stone (1979), puts emphasis on a one-parameter item response model derived from the work of Rasch (1960, 1980). Another school of thought, led by Popham (1978), Berk (1980), and others, has devoted its attention to the development of criterion-referenced tests based on domains of items. A *criterion-referenced* test is one whose outcomes help to indicate and describe students' performances with reference to educational objectives more directly and substantively than do the scores of norm-referenced tests, which only indicate students' performances relative to norms. It is claimed that special procedures for determining reliability and validity are required for such criterion-referenced tests. Cronbach, Gleser, Nanda, and Rajaratnam (1972) elevated reliability theory into what they call *generalizability theory,* concerned with the replicability of measurements over samples of items and examinee populations.

In the midst of the excitement, many readers were startled to see Lumsden's (1976) evaluation of test theory as having "few major ideas," "dominated by an inappropriate and unfruitful model." What Lumsden seems to have been calling for would be a test theory more concerned with construct validity and trait measurement than with matters of reliability, scaling, and other nice mathematical properties. In some ways, Lumsden's critique brings test theory full circle back to the concerns voiced by Edward L. Thorndike in the early years of the century. But even Thorndike was perhaps unduly distracted by his attempts to develop ''scientific'' measurements with defined, equal units.

Factor Analysis

Factor analysis has been intimately involved in the history of educational measurement. The term *factor analysis* refers to a collection of techniques for determining the latent dimensionality of a set of measures (variables) applied to a sample of persons or objects and for assessing the extent to which each variable measures each of the latent dimensions. In simple terms, factor analysis can help one decide how many different kinds of ability traits or dimensions of learning there are, and how different tests measure those traits or dimensions.

Although the variables studied in factor-analytic investigations have most often been measures of mental abilities and attributes of personality, they have also included measures of students' educational achievement, attributes of schools or school systems, and characteristics of educational materials and products.

Factor analysis originated in a famous paper by Spearman (1904b), which presented an analysis of a small matrix of correlations among certain tests of sensory discrimination, reaction time, and school marks. (This long and detailed paper is well worth reading even today, since it includes a critique of earlier attempts to measure intelligence.) Spearman claimed that his matrix could be accounted for by a single latent dimension of general intelligence, especially if the correlations were corrected for errors of measurement. Over the years 1904 to 1927 Spearman developed his two-factor theory of intelligence, which proposed that any test of intelligence measured a factor of general intelligence, designated *g,* and a factor specific to that test, designated *s*. This theory was presented in detail in his book *The Abilities of Man* (1927), but the term *factor analysis* does not appear in that book. Nevertheless, various British statisticians addressed the mathematical problems of testing the two-factor theory and determining factor loading coefficients, sometimes criticizing Spearman's theory (e.g., Emmett, 1936). Gradu-

ally, factor analysis became a recognized field of statistical psychology. It seems that Thurstone (1931a) was the first to use the term *factor analysis.*

During the period of Spearman's domination of the field, the principal debate concerned whether intelligence could be satisfactorily accounted for by the two-factor theory. Even Spearman (1931) was finally led to admit that some group factors of intelligence existed alongside *g.* In the United States, Holzinger (1931; Holzinger & Harman, 1937) developed a bi-factor method of finding factors and factor loadings. (Holzinger had been a student of Spearman and was associated with him in a study of unitary traits; Holzinger, 1936). Kelley (1928, 1935) was another American educational psychologist who developed methods of factor analysis that could yield multiple factors. Holzinger and Kelley's methods, however, did not gain wide acceptance, partly because they seemed to present computational difficulties and partly because they did not have the clarity and force of the multiple factor analysis model presented by Thurstone (1931a, 1935, 1947).

Over the period 1935 to about 1970 the dominant model and method of factor analysis was Thurstone's; as characterized by Tucker (1955) it would now be called a model and method for *exploratory* factor analysis, as opposed to *confirmatory* factor analysis (to be mentioned later). Exploratory factor analysis proposes to take any given correlation matrix and determine the number of meaningful common factors in it, as well as the coefficients of equations specifying the factorial composition of the variables. Thurstone recommended use of his *centroid* method for determining an orthogonal factor matrix that would approximately reproduce the given correlation matrix; the coordinates on which this factor matrix was based were then to be rotated to what Thurstone called *simple structure.* Thurstone and his students conducted a number of classic factor-analytic investigations using this method (e.g., Thurstone, 1938). He saw that it was often desirable to allow factors to be correlated. In this way, one could arrive at second- and higher-order factors to account more satisfactorily for the correlations of a set of variables. Schmid and Leiman (1957) developed this idea further to arrive at hierarchical factor solutions in which the independent contributions of higher-order factors could be expressed in the factorial equations for variables.

After Thurstone's death in 1955, research workers continued to perform many exploratory factor analysis studies using his model and methods. Thurstone had been aware of the contribution of Hotelling (1933) in developing the principal component method, that relied on finding the eigenvalues and eigenvectors of the correlation matrix (with unities on the diagonal). For large matrices, this method could not readily be used with hand computation methods, however. When high-speed computers became available, the principal component method, or several variants of it (chiefly, the principal factor method, analyzing common factor variance rather than total variance) were applied to numerous data sets. The question of whether principal component or principal factoring procedures are preferable is still unresolved (Velicer, Peacock, & Jackson, 1982).

Thurstone's concept of simple structure has given rise to much controversy and investigation. Although the principle of simple structure has generally gone unquestioned, some workers (e.g., Guilford, 1967) have questioned whether factors should be allowed to be correlated. A number of investigators, being dissatisfied with the largely subjective, graphical methods developed by Thurstone, have attempted to develop more objective, "analytic" methods of factor rotation (e.g., Carroll, 1953). Kaiser's (1958) *Varimax* solution became the most generally accepted procedure for orthogonal rotation of axes, but it has not been possible for research workers to decide which of numerous available procedures is preferable for oblique rotation to correlated factors (Hakstian & Abell, 1974). Exploratory factor analysis has been plagued with the number-of-factors problem, that is, the decision as to the number of significant common factors to be analyzed in a correlation matrix. With his scree test, Cattell (1966, 1978) has offered one solution to this problem, as have Montanelli and Humphreys (1976), but experience with applying these criteria to real data sets does not indicate that any final and general solution is yet in sight.

It has been claimed (e.g., J. S. Long, 1983) that most of the problems of exploratory factor analysis vanish when confirmatory techniques are employed. *Confirmatory* techniques derive initially from the work of Lawley and Maxwell (1963), and others, in providing maximum likelihood methods of factor extraction, accompanied by statistical tests of hypotheses as to number of factors and factor structure. Even statistical tests, however, merely indicate probabilities, which are a matter of degree. Confirmatory techniques have received their greatest development at the hands of Jöreskog and his associates (Jöreskog & Sörbom, 1979). With his techniques, and with use of the so-called LISREL program, it is possible to set up and test hypotheses concerning the factorial structure of a set of variables, and to gain information as to how those hypotheses might be modified to obtain more satisfactory fit of model to data. Because of the recency of these developments, they have not as yet been applied to sufficiently varied samples of data to permit definitive evaluations of their utility, but it can be said that they are highly promising.

Despite the methodological problems inherent in factor analysis, of either the exploratory or the confirmatory kind, factorial results cannot be dismissed as having little or no significance. If methods are used carefully and intelligently, the findings have the same general patterns with different methods, and can make a distinct contribution to the understanding of educational measurement data (Carroll, 1985).

Test Validity

The idea that a test, or other educational measurement procedure, should yield information on what is claimed to be measured is a very old one, certainly implicit in discussions going back to the days of E. L. Thorndike or earlier. Nevertheless, it was not until the 1920s that the term *validity* acquired anything like the technical meaning it possesses now, nor can one find extended discussion of the concept of validity before that time. Validity was viewed as being supported by either or both of two kinds of evidence: (a) chiefly in the case of achievement tests, *judged* faithfulness of the test content to the curricular objectives covered, and (b) chiefly in the case of mental ability and aptitude tests, correlations of measurements with external criteria, such as other measurements intended to measure the same thing, school achievement, or judgments of job performance. The former came to be called content validity, and the latter, predictive validity. As an example of predictive validity, we may cite the concern of the developers of the Army Alpha test to demonstrate its high correlations with individual scales of intelligence such as the Binet (Yerkes, 1921). One of the first extended discussions of the concept of validity was given by Kelley (1927, pp. 29–32). He felt that tests—even particular items in tests—

should be shown to be valid in terms of both content and correlations with external criteria. Among other matters, he discussed the relative emphasis that ability and achievement tests should give to "speed" and "power," pointing out that speed elements might often interfere with valid measurement of the abilities and achievements one might wish to tap. Further discussions of test validity can be found in works by Hawkes *et al.* (1936) and Smith (1938). The validity of particular tests, and the evidence or lack of evidence for it, was a favorite topic for test reviewers in the *Mental Measurement Yearbook* series initiated by O. K. Buros in 1935.

More modern concepts of validity developed out of much experience in attempting to evaluate the validity of various types of tests—mental ability, scholastic aptitude, school achievement, and personality tests, among others—in a wide variety of situations. It was recognized, for example by R. L. Thorndike (1949) and Cureton (1951), that the concept of validity presented many logical and even philosophical problems, in addition to statistical ones such as that of cross-validation (validation of tests, item scoring keys, or batteries on samples other than those used in initial validation). The first edition of *Technical Recommendations for Psychological Tests and Diagnostic Techniques* (American Psychological Association, 1954) distinguished four types of validity—content, predictive, concurrent, and construct, and noted that "the vagueness of [a] construct is an inevitable consequence of the incompleteness of current psychological theory, and cannot be rectified faster than theory grows and is confirmed" (p. 15). The next version (1966), compilation of which had been conducted with the collaboration of educational measurement groups, collapsed predictive validity and concurrent validity into a single category, criterion-related validity. The evolution of the concept of validity was influenced by considerations from the logic and philosophy of science as reviewed by Cronbach and Meehl (1955); an advanced treatment of the topic is to be found in a chapter by Cronbach (1971).

Research Design

Most research designs in educational psychology prior to about 1950 would be regarded as relatively primitive by contemporary standards. Often they involved small groups matched on some variable thought to be in need of experimental control. If it was necessary to evaluate a difference in means, most often a "critical ratio" of the difference to its probable error was determined and evaluated. Monroe (1934, fn. p. 40) stated that "a difference is commonly called statistically significant when it is equal to or greater than four times its probable error." Because a critical ratio of 4 is approximately equivalent to a t value of 2.7, $p < .005$ for 40 degrees of freedom, early statistical tests of significance may be characterized as suitably conservative in avoiding Type I errors.

Occasionally more involved designs were used; for example Campbell and Stanley (1963) cited a study by Thorndike, McCall, and Chapman (1916) that used a "rotation experiment" design that was essentially equivalent to what would now be called a Latin square. Campbell and Stanley praised McCall's (1923) book *How to Experiment in Education* as "an undervalued classic," pointing out that it recommended random selection as the best procedure for obtaining equated groups.

In the meantime, more sophisticated procedures of experimental design were being developed in Great Britain by R. A. Fisher (1925), chiefly in agricultural research. The introduction of Fisherian designs, small-sample statistics, and analysis of variance and covariance (ANOVA) procedures into educational and psychological research was slow. Rucci and Tweney (1980), in a comprehensive historical analysis of the period from 1925 to 1950, suggest three stages:

(a) an initial, expository phase lasting until the onset of World War II, (b) a wartime interregnum during which use of ANOVA declined, and (c) a postwar resurgence, characterized by the institutionalization of ANOVA training.

Leaders in introducing these techniques included Jackson (1940), working in an educational research setting in Toronto, and Lindquist (1940, 1953), with influential textbooks on statistics and experimental design. Deemer and Rulon (1942) conducted one of the earliest large-scale educational experiments using the Johnson and Neyman (1936) technique to find regions of an aptitude space where differences in performance were significant as a function of type of training in shorthand, but use of the Johnson-Neyman technique is still fairly infrequent, even in aptitude–treatment interaction (ATI) studies (Cronbach & Snow, 1977).

It was recognized that small-sample statistics and ANOVA techniques had the possible drawback of requiring strong assumptions about the scaling and distributional characteristics of variables. As one way of circumventing this drawback, educational researchers were introduced to nonparametric statistics by Siegel (1956).

It is probably not worthwhile to recount the more recent history of experimental design and statistical methods in educational and psychological research. A classic statement on experimental and quasi-experimental designs in research on teaching (and other topics) was published by Campbell and Stanley (1963); it has continued to have a strong influence on research practices. Increasingly complex designs have come into use, and many researchers have become thoroughly familiar with various forms of multivariate analysis as detailed in texts like those of Cooley and Lohnes (1971) and Tatsuoka (1971).

Computational and Test Scoring Technology

It is almost banal to remark that most of the present-day advances in educational measurement technology could not have come about had it not been for advances in devices for performing computations and various data collection and clerical functions, mechanically or electronically. Nevertheless, present-day students need to realize that around the beginning of the century, desk-top hand (mechanical) calculators had only recently become available. These machines were used by Pearson and his students in performing statistical calculations and preparing statistical tables. Presumably, they were also available to Thorndike and other early researchers; yet, Thorndike (1913) deemed it advisable to supply his readers with multiplication and square root tables to aid in hand calculations. Until well into the 1950s, most psychological and educational research computations were performed either by hand, by slide rule, or with the aid of desk-top mechanical calculators. Motor-driven calculators (favorite brands were Friden, Marchant, and Monroe) facilitated such work from about 1930 on. Correlations were often computed with the use of various worksheets whereby one would make a scatterplot of the data and follow certain rather involved algorithms to find the value (e.g., Toops, 1921). All such computations were highly error prone and it is indubitable that substantial numbers of published results were inaccurate.

Early in the century, the U. S. Census Bureau began using machines for tabulating data recorded on punched cards. Warren and Mendenhall (1929) developed a method for using tabulating machines for computing the sums and sums of squares and cross-products required for correlation tables, but the final computations still had to be done with hand calculators. These and related procedures were extensively employed in the personnel research programs of World War II.

It was not until the advent of high-speed electronic calculating machines, in the middle 1950s, that educational and psychological researchers were readily able to process large quantities of data and make elaborate statistical computations. For example, Lord (1956) reported using the Whirlwind I computer, sponsored by the Office of Naval Research, to perform a factor analysis of 39 variables by Lawley's maximum likelihood method. Since that time, various computer packages for performing all sorts of statistical computations for educational and psychological research have become available, and the speed of mainframe computers has increased by several orders of magnitude. The latest advance, of course, has been the introduction of microcomputers and associated software. (For example, I find that with a desktop microcomputer I can perform a factor analysis with nearly the same speed and capacity that I had available in 1956 with a mainframe computer that occupied a very large area.) Unfortunately, the available hardware and software is not always used as competently and intelligently as it might be, and some software programs continue to have errors and bugs of various sorts that unsuspecting users may not recognize.

Similar technological advances have been made in the scoring of tests and the handling of test data. The test scoring template, for use with objective tests, was introduced in 1918 for the Army Alpha examination (Yerkes, 1921), and shortly after World War I most published standardized tests began to include scoring stencils in sets of materials for users. In 1935, the IBM Corporation marketed a test scoring machine based on measuring the conductivity of graphite marks made by examinees on special answer sheets. These IBM scoring machines were in wide use until about 1970, when optical scanning machines for test scoring had become perfected. Since 1970 or even earlier, there have been attempts to use computers for scoring and otherwise evaluating outcomes of tests and examinations other than those of the purely objective type, for example, essays and English compositions. Thus far, there has not been unqualified success in this effort. However, mention should be made of uses of computers (either large-frame or micro) in the administration and scoring of "tailored" tests in which items are presented and sequenced dependent on examinee's responses (Lord, 1970, 1980). As of this writing, both the underlying measurement theory and the hardware technology are available, but tailored testing with computers is only beginning to be put into wide use.

Institutional and Organizational Arrangements

As a specialty, measurement (or psychometrics) has taken somewhat different directions in departments of psychology and in departments or schools of education, although actually the connections have generally been close.

In psychology, the study of measurement and statistics has usually been part of the regular training of all psychologists, though only a small proportion of psychologists have specialized in it. Departments of psychology where there was a strong emphasis on psychological measurement in the first decades of the century included those at Clark, Columbia, Johns Hopkins, and Stanford Universities. Later, psychometrics flourished notably at Stanford University (under L. M. Terman, T. L. Kelley, and Q. McNemar), the University of Chicago (under L. L. Thurstone), and the University of Southern California (under J. P. Guilford).

In education, the main line of development derives from E. L. Thorndike's work and teaching at Teachers College, Columbia University; many Ph.D. dissertations appeared under his auspices in the *Teachers College Contributions to Education.* Many of the early standardized tests in education were developed by Thorndike's students. Since the early decades of the century, there has been a gradual evolution of educational measurement as a specialty. Lindquist (1951, p. vii) remarked that in 1945 very few institutions offered advanced graduate level courses in educational measurement. At present, however, many university departments and schools of education maintain programs of graduate study in measurement.

Professional Organizations and Journals

The earliest organization devoted to educational research as such, and thus incidentally to problems of measurement, was the Society of Educational Research, founded in New York City in 1903 (Travers, 1983, p. 122), but it was short-lived. A more successful organization was the National Association of Directors of Educational Research, founded in 1915 and devoted largely to problems of conducting school surveys—a prevalent concern in those days. This association became a department of the National Education Association (NEA) in 1930, and at that time changed its name to the American Educational Research Association (AERA). Shortly thereafter, in 1931, the AERA founded the journal *Review of Educational Research,* which, as has been mentioned, published periodic reviews of educational research and measurement topics for many years. As the AERA became more interested in scholarly, psychological, and technical issues, in 1968 it severed its ties with the NEA and formed divisions of membership, one of which (Division D) was devoted to measurement and research methodology. In its publication program, the AERA exhibited its strong interest in educational research and measurement, continuing the *Review of Educational Research* (but in a different format from previously), and founding such journals as the *American Educational Research Journal* (from 1964) and the *Journal of Educational Statistics* (from 1976). Still another organization devoted to measurement was the National Council on Measurements Used in Education (founded in 1938 and in 1961 renamed the National Council on Measurement in Education), responsible for publishing the *Journal of Educational Measurement* (from 1964).

In the meantime, the American Psychological Association, which had been founded in 1892, had in 1945 formed itself into divisions, Division 5 being that devoted to psychological and educational measurement. Psychological and educational measurement concerns were centered in the APA's publication of the *Journal of Educational Psychology* (which it took over from a private publisher in 1957) and a statistical section of the *Psychological Bulletin.* Independent of the APA, scholars concerned with psychological measurement, especially factor analysis and test theory, founded the Psychometric Society in 1935, which has published the increasingly technical journal *Psychometrika* since 1936. There is also a Society for Multivariate Experimental Psychology, founded by R. B. Cattell in 1960, which has concerned itself extensively with psychological and educational measurement problems, publishing the journal *Multivariate Behavioral Research* from 1966.

Thus, persons interested in psychological and

educational measurement have increasingly had a wide choice of organizations, conventions, and journals, to the point that it is now quite difficult to keep abreast of the great diversity of activities and journal articles. The privately published journal *Educational and Psychological Measurement* (from 1941) also deserves mention as influential in the development of the field.

Test Publishing

The first successful commercial test publication in the United States was that of the Courtis Standard Research Tests in Arithmetic, by the World Book Company (now a division of Harcourt Brace Jovanovich), in 1918. Starting as early as the 1920s, a number of publishers have had extensive test development departments devoted to the construction, analysis, and standardization of tests. The Psychological Corporation, founded in 1921 by J. McK. Cattell, E. L. Thorndike, and R. S. Woodworth, has provided an outlet for many psychological tests; it has now been acquired by Harcourt Brace Jovanovich. Science Research Associates (from 1938) was another large commercial test publishing organization, now a division of the IBM Corporation. Important nonprofit testing organizations have included the Cooperative Test Service, the Graduate Record Examination, and Educational Records Bureau; in 1947 these three organizations were absorbed into the newly founded Educational Testing Service, which has continued important practical and theoretical work in measurement.

The role of profit and nonprofit testing organizations in education was examined by Holmen and Docter (1972). They concluded that despite some shortcomings and problems, the influence of these organizations on education has been generally salutary and wholesome. They remarked, however, that "the good practices at the test-research and development level are not sufficient at this time to offset testing system inadequacies at the test user level" (p. 171).

Test Review and Evaluation Procedures

There has been a persistent problem in monitoring the testing industry, and all makers of tests, even individual scholars, for the quality and excellence of the products. Probably the most important and effective method of meeting this problem is represented in the series of *Mental Measurement Yearbooks* edited by O. K. Buros over the period 1934 to 1978 (Buros, 1978). (With Buros's death in 1978, the series is being continued by the Buros Institute of Mental Measurement at the University of Nebraska.) Expert reviews have served to point out to the profession, and to test users, the strengths and weaknesses of published tests and other measurement procedures. In the long run this has improved the quality of these materials. Parallel to this, professional organizations (APA, AERA, and NCME) have published, starting in 1954, guidelines and standards for psychological and educational tests (APA, 1954, 1966); it can hardly be questioned that these standards have had an important influence on test makers and publishers.

Even with such arrangements to maintain the integrity and scientific excellence of the testing profession, many tests in print fail to meet high standards, and there is a certain tendency for tradition and inertia to cause undesirable or outdated materials and techniques to persist after their time.

Summary Comments

Viewing the whole history of the testing movement in education, one can see many substantial advances and breakthroughs in the field since the time of Edward L. Thorndike. Were he alive today, I believe Thorndike would be more pleased than displeased with the current state of the art and science that he set in motion. Certainly he would be pleased with the great advances in the technology of test preparation, the theory of measurement, test theory, factor analysis, the theory of test validity, and computational methods that have been reviewed here. He would note with approval the great expansion of institutional and organizational arrangements surrounding the testing movement, for Thorndike himself was a great organizer. But he would probably voice some complaints about developments in the field.

He might have reason to complain that educational measurement has not yet approached the fulfillment of many of its promises. He might be disturbed that most psychological and educational measurements still are not based on scientifically grounded units of measurement. He would deplore the fact that psychological measurements often do not have well-established construct validity, and that there are insufficient links between educational measurements and the educational objectives that need to be assessed. He would lament that measurement procedures—for example, available standardized tests—are all too frequently not kept up to date with technological advances. He would be dismayed that teachers and school personnel are insufficiently trained in measurement techniques, and that they frequently misuse or misinterpret measurement information.

Probably Thorndike's greatest disappointment would come with his realization that educational and psychological measurement does not now have the degree of public approval and support that he firmly believed it would come to deserve. He might be genuinely perplexed by the fact that whereas, on the one hand, the public seems to attach great significance to comparative test score statistics and highly publicized scholastic aptitude score declines, on the other hand it does not fully approve, and along with the media and certain activist groups often attacks, the use of tests for selection, placement, guidance, and diagnosis of learning difficulties.

Thorndike's response to all this, I think, would be to offer the opinion that the profession of educational measurement has done great things, but that it still has a long way to go in reaching the goals he set out for it. He would emphatically urge, in addition, that the profession do a better job of selling itself to its clientele and to the public.

References

American Psychological Association. (1954). *Technical recommendations for psychological tests and diagnostic techniques.* Washington, DC: Author. (*Psychological Bulletin, 41*(2, Part 2, Supplement).

American Psychological Association. (1966). *Standards for educational and psychological tests and manuals.* Washington, DC: Author.

Berk, R. A. (Ed.). (1980). *Criterion-referenced measurement: The state of the art.* Baltimore, MD: Johns Hopkins University Press.

Bloom, B. S. (Ed.). (1956). *Taxonomy of educational objectives; The classification of educational goals. Handbook I: Cognitive domain.* New York: Longmans, Green.

Bloom, B. S., Hastings, J. T., & Madaus, G. F. (Eds.). (1971). *Handbook of formative and summative evaluation of student learning.* New York: McGraw-Hill.

Bormuth, J. R. (1970). *On the theory of achievement test items.* Chicago, IL: University of Chicago Press.

Brigham, C. C. (1932). *A study of error: A summary and evaluation of methods used in six years of study of the Scholastic Aptitude Test of the College Entrance Examination Board.* New York: College Entrance Examination Board.

Brown, W. (1910). Some experimental results in the correlation of mental abilities. *British Journal of Psychology, 3,* 296–322.

Buckingham, B. R. (1913). *Spelling ability: Its measurement and distribution.* New York: Teachers College Columbia University Contributions to Education, No. 59.

Buros, O. K. (Ed.). (1978). *The eighth mental measurements yearbook.* Highland Park, NJ: Gryphon Press.

Campbell, D. T., & Stanley, J. C. (1963). Experimental and quasi-experimental designs for research on teaching. In N. L. Gage (Ed.), *Handbook of research on teaching* (pp. 171–246). Chicago, IL: Rand McNally.

Carroll, J. B. (1945). The effect of difficulty and chance success on correlations between items or between tests. *Psychometrika, 10,* 1–19.

Carroll, J. B. (1951). Criteria for the evaluation of achievement tests: From the standpoint of their internal statistics. In *Proceedings of the 1950 Invitational Conference on Testing Problems* (pp. 95–99). Princeton, NJ: Educational Testing Service.

Carroll, J. B. (1953). An analytical solution for approximating simple structure in factor analysis. *Psychometrika, 18,* 23–38.

Carroll, J. B. (1961). The nature of the data, or how to choose a correlation coefficient. *Psychometrika, 26,* 347–372.

Carroll, J. B. (1985). Exploratory factor analysis: A tutorial. In D. K. Detterman (Ed.), *Current topics in human intelligence. Vol. 1: Research methodology* (pp. 25–58). Norwood, NJ: Ablex.

Cattell, R. B. (1966). The scree test for the number of factors. *Multivariate Behavioral Research, 1,* 245–276.

Cattell, R. B. (1978). *The scientific use of factor analysis in behavioral and life sciences.* New York: Plenum Press.

Coffman, W. E. (1971). Essay examinations. In R. L. Thorndike (Ed.), *Educational measurement* (2nd ed., pp. 271–302). Washington, DC: American Council on Education.

Cook, W. W. (1952). Tests, achievement. In W. S. Monroe (Ed.), *Encyclopedia of educational research* (rev. ed., pp. 1461–1478). New York: Macmillan.

Cooley, W. W., & Lohnes, P. R. (1971). *Multivariate data analysis.* New York: Wiley.

Cronbach, L. J. (1971). Test validation. In R. L. Thorndike (Ed.), *Educational measurement* (2nd ed., pp. 443–507). Washington, DC: American Council on Education.

Cronbach, L. J., Gleser, G. C., Nanda, H., & Rajaratnam, N. (1972). *The dependability of behavioral measurements: Theory of generalizability for scores and profiles.* New York: Wiley.

Cronbach, L. J., & Meehl, P. E. (1955). Construct validity in psychological tests. *Psychological Bulletin, 52,* 281–302.

Cronbach, L. J., & Snow, R. E. (1977). *Aptitudes and instructional methods: A handbook for research on interactions.* New York: Irvington.

Cureton, E. E. (1951). Validity. In E. F. Lindquist (Ed.), *Educational measurement* (pp. 621–694). Washington, DC: American Council on Education.

Deemer, W. L., & Rulon, P. J. (1942). *An experimental comparison of two shorthand systems.* Cambridge: Harvard University Press. (*Harvard Studies in Education,* vol. 28.)

DuBois, P. H. (1970). *A history of psychological testing.* Boston, MA: Allyn & Bacon.

Dudycha, A. L., & Dudycha, L. W. (1972). Behavioral statistics: An historical perspective. In R. E. Kirk (Ed.), *Statistical issues: A reader for the behavioral sciences* (pp. 2–25). Monterey, CA: Brooks/Cole.

Ebbinghaus, H. (1896–1897). Über eine neue Methode zur Prüfung geistiger Fähigkeiten und ihre Anwendung bei

Schulkindern. *Zeitschrift für Psychologie und Physiologie der Sinnesorgane, 13,* 401–459.

Ebel, R. L. (1951). Estimation of the reliability of ratings. *Psychometrika, 16,* 407–424.

Ebel, R. L., & Damrin, D. E. (1960). Tests and examinations. In C. W. Harris (Ed.), *Encyclopedia of educational research* (3rd ed., pp. 1502–1517). New York: Macmillan.

Edgerton, H. A., & Toops, H. A. (1928). A formula for finding the average intercorrelation coefficient of unranked raw scores without solving any of the individual intercorrelations. *Journal of Educational Psychology, 19,* 131–138.

Emmett, W. G. (1936). Sampling error and the two-factor theory. *British Journal of Educational Psychology, 26,* 362–387.

Engelhart, M. D. (1952). Examinations. In W. S. Monroe (Ed.), *Encyclopedia of educational research* (rev. ed., pp. 407–414). New York: Macmillan.

Ferguson, G. A. (1941). The factorial interpretation of test difficulty. *Psychometrika, 6,* 323–329.

Fisher, R. A. (1925). *Statistical methods for research workers.* Edinburgh & London: Oliver & Boyd.

Flanagan, J. C. (1939a). *A bulletin reporting the basic principles and procedures used in the development of their* [Cooperative Test Service's] *system of scaled scores.* New York: Cooperative Test Service of the American Council on Education.

Flanagan, J. C. (1939b). General considerations in the selection of test items and a short method of estimating the product-moment coefficient from the data at the tails of the distributions. *Journal of Educational Psychology, 30,* 674–680.

Fullerton, G. S., & Cattell, J. McK. (1892). *On the perception of small differences with special reference to the extent, force, and time of movement.* Philadelphia, PA: Philosophical Series of the Publications of the University of Pennsylvania, No. 2.

Gaito, J. (1980). Measurement scales and statistics: Resurgence of an old misconception. *Psychological Bulletin, 87,* 564–567.

Guilford, J. P. (1967). *The nature of human intelligence.* New York: McGraw-Hill.

Gulliksen, H. (1950). *Theory of mental tests.* New York: Wiley.

Guttman, L. (1941). The quantification of a class of attributes: A theory and method for scale construction. In P. Horst (Ed.), *The prediction of personal adjustment* (pp. 319–348). New York: Social Science Research Council.

Hakstian, A. R., & Abell, R. A. (1974). A further comparison of oblique factor transformation methods. *Psychometrika, 39,* 429–444.

Hawkes, H. E., Lindquist, E. F., & Mann, C. R. (1936). *The construction and use of achievement examinations: A manual for secondary school teachers.* Boston, MA: Houghton Mifflin.

Hillegas, M. B. (1912). A scale for the measurement of quality of English composition by young people. *Teachers College Record, 13,* 331–384.

Holmen, M. G., & Docter, R. F. (1972). *Educational and psychological testing: A study of the industry and its practices.* New York: Russell Sage Foundation.

Holzinger, K. J. (1931). On factor theory. In National Research Council, *Conference on individual differences in special and general abilities.* Washington, DC: National Research Council.

Holzinger, K. J. (1936). Recent research on unitary mental traits. *Character & Personality, 4,* 335–343.

Holzinger, K. J., & Harman, H. H. (1937). Relationships between factors obtained from certain analyses. *Journal of Educational Psychology, 28,* 321–345.

Hotelling, H. (1933). Analysis of a complex of statistical variables into principal components. *Journal of Educational Psychology, 24,* 417–441, 498–520.

Jackson, R. W. B. (1940). *Application of the analysis of variance and covariance method to educational problems.* Toronto: Department of Educational Research, University of Toronto, Bulletin 11.

Jackson, R. W. B., & Ferguson, G. A. (1941). *Studies on the reliability of tests.* Toronto: Department of Educational Research, University of Toronto, Bulletin 12.

Johnson, P. O., & Neyman, J. (1936). Tests of certain linear hypotheses and their application to some educational problems. In J. Neyman & E. S. Pearson (Eds.), *Statistical Research Memoirs, 1,* 57–93.

Jonçich, G. (1968). *The sane positivist: A biography of Edward L. Thorndike.* Middletown, CT: Wesleyan University Press.

Jöreskog, K. G., & Sörbom, D. (1979). *Advances in factor analysis and structural equation models.* Cambridge, MA: Abt.

Kaiser, H. F. (1958). The varimax criterion for analytic rotation in factor analysis. *Psychometrika, 23,* 187–200.

Kelley, T. L. (1916). A simplified method of using scaled data for purposes of testing. *School & Society, 4,* 34–37, 71–75.

Kelley, T. L. (1921). The reliability of test scores. *Journal of Educational Research, 3,* 370–379.

Kelley, T. L. (1923). *Statistical method.* New York: Macmillan.

Kelley, T. L. (1927). *The interpretation of educational measurements.* Yonkers-on-Hudson, NY: World Book.

Kelley, T. L. (1928). *Crossroads in the mind of man: A study of differentiable mental abilities.* Stanford, CA: Stanford University Press.

Kelley, T. L. (1935). *Essential traits of mental life.* Cambridge, MA: Harvard University Press. (*Harvard Studies in Education,* No. 26.)

Kelley, T. L. (1939). The selection of upper and lower groups for the validation of test items. *Journal of Educational Psychology, 30,* 17–24.

Krantz, D. H., Luce, R. D., Suppes, P., & Tversky, A. (1971). *Foundations of measurement* (Vol. 1). New York: Academic.

Kuder, G. F., & Richardson, M. W. (1937). The theory of the estimation of test reliability. *Psychometrika, 2,* 151–160.

Lawley, D. N., & Maxwell, A. E. (1963). *Factor analysis as a statistical method.* London: Butterworth. (2nd edition, 1970)

Learned, W. S., & Wood, B. D. (1938). *The student and his knowledge.* New York: Carnegie Foundation for the Advance of Teaching, Bulletin No. 29.

Linden, K. W., & Linden, J. D. (1968). *Modern mental measurement: A historical perspective.* Boston, MA: Houghton Mifflin.

Lindquist, E. F. (1940). *Statistical analysis in educational research.* Boston, MA: Houghton Mifflin.

Lindquist, E. F. (1951). *Educational measurement.* Washington, DC: American Council on Education.

Lindquist, E. F. (1953). *Design and analysis of experiments in psychology and education.* Boston, MA: Houghton Mifflin.

Loevinger, J. (1947). A systematic approach to the construction and evaluation of tests of ability. *Psychological Monographs, 61*(4).

Loevinger, J. (1954). The attenuation paradox in test theory. *Psychological Bulletin, 51,* 493–504.

Long, J. A., & Sandiford, P. (1935). *The validation of test items*. Toronto: Department of Educational Research, University of Toronto, Bulletin No. 3.

Long, J. S. (1983). *Confirmatory factor analysis: A preface to LISREL*. Beverly Hills, CA: Sage.

Lord, F. M. (1952). A theory of test scores. *Psychometric Monographs, No. 7*.

Lord, F. M. (1953). On the statistical treatment of football numbers. *American Psychologist, 8*, 750–751.

Lord, F. M. (1956). A study of speed factors in tests and academic grades. *Psychometrika, 21*, 31–50.

Lord, F. M. (1970). Some test theory for tailored testing. In W. H. Holtzman (Ed.), *Computer assisted instruction, testing and guidance* (pp. 139–183). New York: Harper & Row.

Lord, F. M. (1980). *Applications of item response theory to practical testing problems*. Hillsdale, NJ: Erlbaum.

Lord, F. M., & Novick, M. R. (1968). *Statistical theories of mental test scores*. Reading, MA: Addison-Wesley.

Lumsden, J. (1976). Test theory. *Annual Review of Psychology, 27*, 251–280.

McCall, W. A. (1920). A new kind of school examination. *Journal of Educational Research, 1*, 33–46.

McCall, W. A. (1922). *How to measure in education*. New York: Macmillan.

McCall, W. A. (1923). *How to experiment in education*. New York: Macmillan.

Monroe, W. S. (1934). Controlled experimentation as a means of evaluating methods of teaching. *Review of Educational Research, 4*, 36–42.

Monroe, W. S. (1945). Educational measurement in 1920 and 1945. *Journal of Educational Research, 38*, 334–340.

Monroe, W. S., DeVoss, J. C., & Kelly, F. J. (1917). *Educational tests and measurements*. Boston, MA: Houghton Mifflin.

Montanelli, R. G., Jr., & Humphreys, L. G. (1976). Latent roots of random data correlation matrices with squared multiple correlations on the diagonal: A Monte Carlo study. *Psychometrika, 41*, 341–348.

Mosier, C. I. (1940). Psychophysics and mental test theory: Fundamental postulates and elementary theorems. *Psychological Review, 47*, 355–366.

Mosier, C. I. (1941). Psychophysics and mental test theory, II: The constant process. *Psychological Review, 48*, 235–249.

Osburn, W. J. (1933). The selection of test items. *Review of Educational Research, 3*, 21–32.

Otis, A. S. (1916). The reliability of spelling scales, involving a 'deviation formula' for correlation. *School & Society, 4*, 676–683, 716–722, 750–756, 793–796.

Otis, A. S. (1918). An absolute point scale for the group measure of intelligence. *Journal of Educational Psychology, 9*, 238–261, 333–348.

Popham, W. J. (1978). *Criterion-referenced measurement*. Englewood Cliffs, NJ: Prentice-Hall.

Rasch, G. (1960). *Probabilistic models for some intelligence and attainment tests*. Copenhagen: Danmarks Paedagogiske Institut.

Rasch, G. (1980). *Probabilistic models for some intelligence and attainment tests* (expanded edition). Chicago, IL: University of Chicago Press.

Roid, G. H., & Haladyna, T. M. (1982). *A technology for test-item writing*. New York: Academic.

Ross, C. C., & Stanley, J. C. (1954). *Measurement in today's schools* (3rd ed.). New York: Prentice-Hall.

Rucci, A. J., & Tweney, R. D. (1980). Analysis of variance and the "second discipline" of scientific psychology: A historical account. *Psychological Bulletin, 87*, 166–184.

Ruch, G. M., & Rice, G. A. (1930). *Specimen objective examinations: A collection of examinations awarded prizes in a national contest in the construction of objective or new-type examinations, 1927–1928*. Chicago, IL: Scott Foresman.

Rugg, H. O. (1917). *Statistical methods applied to education: A textbook for students of education in the quantitative study of school problems*. Boston, MA: Houghton Mifflin.

Schmid, J., & Leiman, J. M. (1957). The development of hierarchical factor solutions. *Psychometrika, 22*, 53–61.

Siegel, S. (1956). *Nonparametric statistics for the behavioral sciences*. New York: McGraw-Hill.

Smith, B. O. (1938). *Logical aspects of educational measurement*. New York: Columbia University Press.

Smith, E. R., & Tyler, R. W. (1942). *Appraising and recording student progress*. New York: Harper.

Spearman, C. (1904a). The proof and measurement of association between two things. *American Journal of Psychology, 15*, 72–101.

Spearman, C. (1904b). "General intelligence", objectively determined and measured. *American Journal of Psychology, 15*, 201–293.

Spearman, C. (1910). Correlation calculated from faulty data. *British Journal of Psychology, 3*, 271–295.

Spearman, C. (1927). *The abilities of man: Their nature and measurement*. New York: Macmillan.

Spearman, C. (1931). What the theory of factors is *not*. *Journal of Educational Psychology, 22*, 112–117.

Stanley, J. C. (1971). Reliability. In R. L. Thorndike (Ed.), *Educational measurement* (2nd ed., pp. 356–442). Washington, DC: American Council on Education.

Stevens, S. S. (1946). On the theory of scales of measurement. *Science, 103*, 667–680.

Stevens, S. S. (1951). Mathematics, measurement, and psychophysics. In S. S. Stevens (Ed.), *Handbook of experimental psychology* (pp. 1–49). New York: Wiley.

Stevens, S. S. (1968). Measurement, statistics, and the schemapiric view. *Science, 161*, 849–856.

Stone, C. W. (1908). *Arithmetical abilities and some factors determining them*. New York: Teachers College, Columbia University Contributions to Education, No. 19.

Suppes, P., & Zinnes, J. L. (1963). Basic measurement theory. In R. D. Luce, R. R. Bush, & E. Galanter (Eds.), *Handbook of mathematical psychology* (Vol. 1, pp. 1–76). New York: Wiley.

Tatsuoka, M. M. (1971). *Multivariate analysis techniques for educational and psychological research*. New York: Wiley.

Taylor, W. L. (1953). "Cloze procedure": A new tool for measuring readability. *Journalism Quarterly, 30*, 415–433.

Thorndike, E. L. (1904). *Introduction to the theory of mental and social measurements*. New York: Teachers College, Columbia University.

Thorndike, E. L. (1910). *Handwriting*. New York: Columbia University Press.

Thorndike, E. L. (1913). *Introduction to the theory of mental and social measurements* (2nd ed.). New York: Teachers College, Columbia University.

Thorndike, E. L. (1918). The nature, purposes and general methods of measurements of educational products. In G. M. Whipple (Ed.), *The measurement of educational products*. National Society for the Study of Education Yearbook, *17* (Part 2), 16–24.

Thorndike, E. L., Bregman, E. O., Cobb, M. V., Woodyard, E., & Staff of the Division of Psychology of the Institute of Educational Research of Teachers College, Columbia University. [1927]. *The measurement of intelligence*. New York:

Bureau of Publications, Teachers College, Columbia University. (undated)

Thorndike, E. L., McCall, W. A., & Chapman, J. C. (1916). *Ventilation in relation to mental work.* New York: Teachers College, Columbia University Contributions to Education, No. 78.

Thorndike, R. L. (1949). *Personnel selection: Test and measurement techniques.* New York: Wiley.

Thorndike, R. L. (Ed.). (1971). *Educational measurement* (2nd ed.). Washington, DC: American Council on Education.

Thurstone, L. L. (1931a). Multiple factor analysis. *Psychological Review, 38,* 406–427.

Thurstone, L. L. (1931b). *The reliability and validity of tests.* Ann Arbor, MI: Edwards Brothers.

Thurstone, L. L. (1935). *The vectors of the mind.* Chicago, IL: University of Chicago Press.

Thurstone, L. L. (1938). Primary mental abilities. *Psychometric Monographs,* No. 1.

Thurstone, L. L. (1947). *Multiple factor analysis: A development and expansion of* The Vectors of Mind. Chicago, IL: University of Chicago Press.

Toops, H. A. (1921). Eliminating the pitfalls in solving correlation—A printed correlation form. *Journal of Educational Psychology, 4,* 434–446.

Townsend, J. T., & Ashby, F. G. (1984). Measurement scales and statistics: The misconception misconceived. *Psychological Bulletin, 96,* 394–401.

Trabue, M. R. (1916). *Completion-test language scales.* New York: Teachers College, Columbia University Contributions to Education, No. 77.

Travers, R. M. W. (1983). *How research has changed American schools: A history from 1840 to the present.* Kalamazoo, MI: Mythos.

Tucker, L. R. (1946). Maximum validity of a test with equivalent forms. *Psychometrika, 11,* 1–13.

Tucker, L. R. (1955). The objective definition of simple structure in linear factor analysis. *Psychometrika, 20,* 209–225.

Velicer, W. F., Peacock, A. C., & Jackson, D. N. (1982). A comparison of component and factor patterns: A Monte Carlo approach. *Multivariate Behavioral Research, 17,* 371–388.

Walker, D. A. (1931). Answer pattern and score scatter in tests and examinations. *British Journal of Psychology, 22,* 73–86.

Walker, D. A. (1936). Answer pattern and score scatter in tests and examinations. *British Journal of Psychology, 26,* 301–308.

Walker, D. A. (1940). Answer pattern and score scatter in tests and examinations. *British Journal of Psychology, 30,* 248–260.

Walker, H. M. (1929). *Studies in the history of statistical method.* Baltimore, MD: Williams & Wilkins.

Warren, R., & Mendenhall, R. M. (1929). *The Mendenhall-Warren-Hollerith correlation method.* New York: Statistical Bureau, Columbia University, Document No. 1.

Wherry, R. J., & Gaylord, R. H. (1943). The concept of test and item reliability in relation to factor pattern. *Psychometrika, 8,* 247–264.

Wherry, R. J., & Gaylord, R. H. (1944). Factor pattern of test items and tests as a function of the correlation coefficient: Content, difficulty, and constant error factors. *Psychometrika, 9,* 237–244.

Whipple, G. M. (1910). *Manual of mental and physical tests.* Baltimore, MD: Warwick & York.

Whipple, G. M. (Ed.). (1918). *The measurement of educational products.* National Society for the Study of Education Yearbook, *17* (Part II).

Winer, B. J. (1971). *Statistical principles in experimental design* (2nd ed.). New York: McGraw-Hill.

Wood, D. A. (1961). *Test construction: Development and interpretation of achievement tests.* Columbus, OH: Merrill.

Woody, C. (1916). *Measurements of some achievements in arithmetic.* New York: Teachers College, Columbia University Contributions to Education, No. 80.

Wright, B. D., & Stone, M. H. (1979). *Best test design: Rasch measurement.* Chicago, IL: Mesa.

Yerkes, R. M. (Ed.). (1921). Psychological examining in the United States Army. *Memoirs of the National Academy of Sciences,* No. 15.

Yerkes, R. M., Bridges, J. W., & Hardwick, R. S. (1915). *A point scale for measuring mental ability.* Baltimore, MD: Warwick & York.

CHAPTER 6

From Parsons to Profession

THE HISTORY OF GUIDANCE AND COUNSELING PSYCHOLOGY

David N. Dixon

Counseling psychology, counselor education, and guidance and counseling as representative of different professional areas in counseling share much common history with other areas of applied psychology and education. These counseling fields share much of the same history, both in terms of societal factors, significant events, and important people. Counseling shares much with educational movements such as vocational education and individual education. Psychology has provided counseling a theoretical base for understanding and changing human behavior. These factors do little to separate counseling from educational psychology as elaborated earlier in this book. However, a strong case could be made for the striking lack of commonality between counseling and educational psychology. Educational psychology has become less interested in application whereas counseling is by definition oriented toward change and the application of principles of change. Educational psychology has always been closely tied to undergraduate teacher education, its very existence arising from the early application of psychology to teacher training. The scope of its knowledge base is reflected in, if not identical with, the content that undergraduate teacher trainees are expected to

master (as defined by the required educational psychology courses). No such direct tie between teacher training and counseling exists (except in the case of school counseling). Counseling is almost exclusively a graduate program with, in some cases, no tie to colleges of education. As this chapter develops the history of the guidance movement and counseling psychology, further points of commonality and distinctiveness can be seen.

In looking at the history of guidance and counseling psychology, a plausible case could be made for including a number of contributive events in a story of complex developments. It is difficult to look back and select those people, circumstances, and events that provide a history for guidance and counseling. In like manner, it is difficult to look forward from a place in history (e.g., the publication of Parson's *Choosing a Vocation*) and trace the impact of particular people, events, and cultural circumstances. A particular key event may have direct and indirect consequences for not only guidance and counseling, but may also be part of the history of other areas as well. To write a history of a professional area the author must choose not only from antecedents but also a set of consequences or outcomes. In order to limit the historical scope, one must first determine the phenomena one is attempting to explain.

This chapter will first examine the current status

David N. Dixon • Department of Educational Psychology, University of Nebraska, Lincoln, NE 68588-0345.

of guidance and counseling, recognizing that there are other professional areas that incorporate many similar techniques and goals. It is clear that the training of counseling professionals has become increasingly divergent. Counseling professionals are trained at undergraduate, masters, and doctoral levels, with the majority of direct service providers being trained at the masters level. Each of the levels is based on different assumptions and resultant models of what is needed for effective intervention. This description will restrict itself to those professional areas variously described as: (a) counseling psychology, (b) counselor education, and (c) guidance and counseling. This chapter will then trace those significant factors that contributed to and focused the development of the current situation.

The Counseling Professions

The counseling psychology area includes only those doctoral programs meeting APA-accreditation standards. The counselor education area includes all other doctoral programs in counseling. Guidance and counseling will be used as an inclusive category for all subdoctoral programs, including such programs as school counseling, agency counseling, college counseling, marital and family counseling, and rehabilitation counseling. We will look first at the status of counseling psychology as a professional field.

Counseling Psychology

One of the major indexes of status is the growth of the number of APA-accredited programs in counseling psychology. The *American Psychologist* (Committee on Accreditation, 1984) lists 41 doctoral programs as being either fully accredited (34) or provisionally accredited (7). Of these programs nine were accredited in the 1950s, three in the 1960s, 11 in the 1970s, and 18 have received accredited status in the 1980s. Obviously, the impetus to become an accredited doctoral program has greatly increased and generally reflects an increased identity with psychology in those programs.

The identity with psychology has been greatly influenced by the credentialing process. Licensure laws for psychology exist in 48 states, with graduation from an accredited program allowing for access to the examination process in most states. Access to third-party payments for the provision of mental health services is also greatly enhanced by graduation from an accredited program. Further, the majority of 275 accredited predoctoral internship training programs in psychology (with no distinction made between clinical and counseling internships) either require or highly prefer applicants who have graduated from accredited programs. It appears that the professional stature and access provided by the doctoral degree in counseling psychology clearly make it the preferred degree for counseling professionals. Both career and training opportunities are enhanced by credentials made more available through APA accredited programs. Further, it appears that those programs with adequate strength and resources have moved in this direction. In fact, some of the more recently accredited programs were not too long ago identified as leading counselor education programs.

The identity with psychology has also required curriculum that ensures adequate psychology content. Hollis and Wantz (1983) summarize the APA criteria:

Professional psychology programs generally are located in universities or schools of professional psychology that offer doctoral training and are approved by one of the six regional accreditation bodies recognized by the Council on Post-Secondary Accreditation (COPA).

Program must be clearly identified and labeled as a psychology program and must be a recognizable, coherent organization entity.

Faculty must be well qualified and must have clear authority and primary responsibility for all aspects of the program.

The plan of study must be integrated and organized with assurance of breadth of exposure to the field of psychology including a curriculum with equivalency of at least three academic years of full-time resident graduate study. The coursework must include scientific and professional ethics and standards, research design and methodology, statistics and psychological measurement, biological bases of behavior, cognitive-affective bases of behavior, social bases of behavior, individual bases of behavior, and courses in specialty areas.

Supervised practicum, internship, and field or laboratory training must be included. The minimum practicum experience is 300 hours, of which at least 150 hours are in direct service experience and 75 hours of formally scheduled supervision. Internship must be full-time for one year or the equivalent with an experience of at least 1500 hours. (pp. 65–66)

Counseling psychology as a recognized specialty in psychology (Committee on Professional Standards, 1981) is also represented by a research literature through the *Journal of Counseling Psychology* (an official publication of APA) and *The Counseling Psychologist* (a publication of the Division of Counseling Psychology). The *Journal of Counseling Psychology* is primarily concerned with "reporting the results of empirical studies about counseling processes and interventions, theoretical articles about counseling, and studies dealing with the evaluation of applications of counseling and counseling programs" (Gelso, 1982). *The Counseling Psychologist* is a theme-oriented journal that requests and approves proposed issues dealing with timely topics related to counseling.

Division 17 of APA represents the Counseling Psychology field within APA and also to the public. Membership in Division 17 of APA lists 224 Fellows, 2,182 Members, and 148 Associates (APA Membership Register, 1984). The American Board of Professional Psychology offers diplomate status in Counseling Psychology with 262 individuals so recognized (APA Membership Register, 1984).

Another parallel professional group is the Council of Counseling Psychology Training Programs. This group is concerned with training issues and with representing counseling psychology student and program interests with the Association of Psychology Internship Centers (APIC), state licensing boards, the Veterans Administration (VA) and with other specialty areas in psychology.

Counselor Education

Hollis and Wantz (1983) surveyed 506 institutions and 584 administrative units offering counselor preparation programs. Units surveyed offered a wide range of counseling specialties, (e.g., counseling psychology, counseling and guidance, community counseling, marriage and family counseling, rehabilitation counseling, and school counseling). From the reported data, Hollis and Wantz extrapolated that 222 doctoral degree programs are offered. From the large number of programs it is not difficult to conclude that nearly every university, college, or professional school that offers a doctoral degree offers one in a counseling related area. From this frequency it could also be assumed that counseling doctoral programs are cost efficient from the institution's perspective, (i.e., they take few resources to establish other than faculty, they have high enrollments, and they generally make money). From the graduates surveyed, 19% of them were identified with counseling psychology. The other 81% were identified as counseling, counselor education, counseling and guidance, or some other related designation.

Counselor education doctoral programs are more diverse than those in counseling psychology,

so it is more difficult to assess the status of these doctoral programs. Counselor education programs are best represented by the Association of Counselor Education and Supervision (ACES), a Division of the American Association of Counseling and Development (AACD; previously the American Personnel and Guidance Association). AACD is the major professional organization representing counselors at the masters level and counselor education at the doctoral level. Although AACD membership is predominantly made up of master's level professionals, membership in ACES is primarily doctoral.

ACES first approved training standards for Advanced Preparation (Doctoral) in Counselor Education in 1977. Hollis and Wantz (1983) summarize the standards as follows:

> The doctoral program consists of a minimum of four academic years of graduate preparation, including the entry program and a year of internship. A minimum of one academic year of full-time graduate study beyond the entry program (masters and specialists) is required.
> Supervised experiences include the completion of at least one academic year (36 weeks) of full-time internship.
> Competencies in statistics, research design, and other research methodology are to be obtained by all students.
> In addition to the core areas of preparation, students are to gain a depth of knowledge and skills in one or more areas such as learning theory, career guidance, research, testing, or evaluation.
> Beyond coursework and seminars students are to be provided opportunities to participate in conferences, workshops, special training programs, and other professional activities that will assist in bridging the gap between the campus and the professional world. (pp. 67–68)

Sixteen programs have received accreditation for doctoral studies from the Council for Accreditation of Counseling and Related Educational Programs (CACREP; 1984). Thus, only a minority of doctoral level counselor educators have graduated from a program that has met national training standards and been the subject of external peer evaluation (a few other programs may have been accredited by the American Association for Marriage and Family Therapy, AAMFT, the Council of Rehabilitation Education, CORE, or other accreditation groups).

The utility of CACREP (and also AAMFT and CORE) accreditation is still uncertain. Certainly such standards assist a doctoral training program in self-evaluation studies, but whether it serves a credentialing function for graduates is unclear. Many graduates of non-APA approved doctoral programs seek licensure as psychologists, often unsuccessfully and frequently with a great deal of questioning from state licensing boards. Several states have passed counselor licensing bills, but these have not clearly facilitated the collection of third-party payments or allowed the licensed counselor any special privileges. They have served to restrict the title and thus protect the public by ensuring that those with such credentials have met minimal standards.

Counselor Education as a professional field is represented by the *Journal of Counseling and Development* and other AACD publications. The *Journal of Counseling and Development* (formerly the *Personnel and Guidance Journal*) has been primarily a practitioner-oriented journal with little theoretical, empirical research reported. However, with the recent change of editorship a more scholarly emphasis is evident. The editor, associate editor, and column editors are also professionals with heavy involvement in counseling psychology.

Current leadership in AACD and its divisions is decidedly void of individuals who also are leaders in counseling psychology. This has not always been the case as early leaders in APA Division 17 and AACD were often drawn from the same leadership pool.

Counseling and Guidance

Based on the 418 units analyzed by Hollis and Wantz (1983), 407 programs offered one or more masters and specialists degrees. They estimated that more than 24,000 master's students with some type of counseling major are graduated each year. Of these, approximately half seem to be prepared for jobs in school settings, although not all these graduates are finding employment in schools. The remainder are preparing for positions outside the school setting in such areas as rehabilitation counseling, student personnel development, and community and agency counseling.

Again, it would not be presumptuous to conclude that nearly every postsecondary institution offering graduate degrees offers a master's degree in guidance and counseling or a similarly named field. Many of the programs began in response to a tremendous demand for counselors in the schools and once developed, have continued to graduate large numbers of counselors despite an imbalance between demand for graduates and the number of graduates.

One response has been a great expansion of the number of specialties offered by the programs. Many employers have also gradually raised requirements from the paraprofessional level to the master's degree as the preferred entry level preparation. Vocational rehabilitation counseling increased its standards during the 1970s and the same change is currently evident in the substance abuse area. Alcohol treatment centers are increasingly seeking people with greater credentials and training, with a similar trend becoming evident in correctional settings.

The master's degree in counseling and guidance is also viewed as a robust degree. Teachers, needing additional coursework for advancement, see a counseling degree as a way to increase salary and expand options. With the degree, the person is eligible for a position as a school counselor and also has a credential that may allow for work outside the elementary/secondary school environment. Additionally, many people find master's degree programs interesting and applicable to their own lives and their environments. They are perceived as providing a set of skills that can be used in a range of noncounseling settings from real estate sales to business management. Unfortunately, because of the demand/graduate imbalance, students with more focused vocational goals may find that the degree fails to result in the career credential sought.

The Association for Counselor Education and Supervision accepted standards for the entry preparation (master's and specialists) of counselors and other personnel services specialists in 1973. Hollis and Wantz (1983) summarize the training standards as follows:

The Program must have objectives that were developed by the faculty in the institution of higher education where offered. The institution must provide a graduate program in counselor education with opportunity for full-time study throughout the academic year.

The program of study includes a core of courses with content applicable to the following areas: human growth and development, social and cultural foundations, helping relationship, groups, lifestyle and career development, appraisal of the individual, research and evaluation, and professional orientation.

The program must provide specialized studies necessary for practice in different work settings so that each student may gain skills needed to work effectively in the professional setting where the student plans to practice.

Supervised experiences include laboratory, practicum, and internship. The minimum practicum requirement is sixty clock hours extended over a minimum nine-month period. Internship is a postpracticum experience where the intern spends in the field placement a minimum of 300 clock hours on the job under supervision by a qualified supervisor.

Research facilities must be available within the counselor preparation institution to faculty and students. (p. 67)

A small percentage of master's level programs are accredited by ACES (27 as of Jan. 1, 1984, CACREP, 1984). However, several others have met AAMFT, CORE, or other standards and a large number of them meet minimal standards set by their state departments of education in order to recommend graduates for credentials as guidance counselors.

These programs differ widely in the extent of psychological content in their curriculum. Some by virtue of administrative location include significant coursework in psychology or educational psychology whereas others, often housed independently from a psychology or educational psychology department, may be openly antagonistic toward psychology and are regarded with disdain by psychologists on campus. The controversy over the relevance and adequacy of psychology as the primary discipline base for counselor training has been a controversial one and the "gulf between counseling psychology and counselor education appears to be growing" (Dowd, 1984, p. 303) over this issue.

Master's degree training of counselors often exists within the context of teacher training. The genesis of many of the programs was the training of school counselors; thus, these programs developed almost exclusively in colleges of education. Several recent national studies of education have suggested that teacher training would be improved if many of the less equipped institutions would get out of the business (e.g., National Commission for Excellence in Teacher Education, 1985). This same recommendation would certainly apply to graduate training in counseling. There are far too many programs with less than minimal faculty and other resources, with ill-defined curricula, and without adequately supervised practicum experiences producing poorly prepared graduates.

The training of master's degree counselors is, however, an important function. The profession would be ill-served to devote all resources to doctoral training. In nearly all situations, (e.g., employment services, community mental health centers, schools, correctional facilities, and mental health institutions) a great percentage (in most cases a majority) of direct services are provided by subdoctoral personnel. A master's degree program can provide entry level preparation for these roles. As identified earlier, many areas are undergoing increased professionalization (e.g., substance abuse, corrections), and the master's level professional represents a level of formal training well beyond the current, typical service provider. Just as the position of school counselor evolved from the teacher who showed a knack for counseling, to the 90-day wonder with limited training, to the master's degree as the minimal entry requirement, the master's degree represents a significant increase in professionalization in many settings. There is, however, no longer a need for programs that cannot provide rigorous, well-developed academic and practical experiences.

What is labeled as counseling is diverse and wide-ranging. An analogy from the geography of the United States seems descriptive of the current status of counseling and its history.

A River Story

The Platte River, beginning in the Rocky Mountains, fed by melting snow, flowing through the prairies of Eastern Colorado and Nebraska, and finally merging with the mighty Missouri River has been described in its prairie version as a "mile wide and an inch deep." In all its forms, the Platte River has primarily been a nurturant river (Michener, 1974). It has been a site for camps of prairie Indians. As a guide for western migration it nourished the pioneers on the Oregon and Mormon Trails. It continues to supply irrigation water for farms and ranches and its underlying aquifer supplies water for the cities of Nebraska.

However, the further the Platte River gets from its source the less vigor it appears to have. Unlike its beginnings as a tumbling, vibrant mountain river, it widens and seems to be more a river of sand and sandbars than of water. One must be reminded that most of its water supply has been diverted upstream to fill irrigation and recreational lakes. Likewise, many of its contributory rivers have also been bled for irrigation purposes. One must remember that this mile-wide river has a channel, first on one side of the river, only to cut through the sand to the other side, which flows swiftly to its confluence with the Missouri. Like the downstream portion of the Platte River, the enterprise currently described as counseling is broad and sometimes meandering. The remaining portion of this chapter will examine the headwaters and upstream contributaries of counseling. In like manner, diverted resources and hidden channels will be described.

Historical Contributions

Vocational Guidance Movement

The mountain beginning of counseling was clearly the vocational guidance movement. This interesting and robust heritage, itself the product of diverse sources, grew from a period of social problems, but yet one that was characterized by optimism. Rockwell and Rothney stated that the "guidance movement was born in the swelter and confusion of protest, reform, utopian idealism, and defenses of the status quo which were rampant in the late nineteenth and early twentieth century" (1961, p. 349). The industrial revolution resulted in a concentration of the workforce, a demand for a skilled workforce, and uncertainty in the labor market. Subsequently, there was a growth in secondary school enrollment and a challenge to the relevance of a classical education for preparing a skilled workforce.

Brewer (1942) identified four social cues that led to the development of vocational guidance including: (a) the division of labor, (b) the growth of technology, (c) the extension of vocational education, and (d) the spread of democracy. From such, vocational guidance began as a movement by philanthropically minded citizens to improve the postschool vocational adjustments of boys and girls. People such as Frank Parsons at the Civic Service House in Boston and Jesse B. Davis in the schools of Detroit and Grand Rapids began to develop approaches to vocational guidance that allowed a person to study self and aptitudes and occupations and to make wise decisions based on this study. Vocational guidance was not only viewed as assisting the development of individuals, but was also seen as a means for achieving social goals.

The contribution of psychology to the vocational guidance movement was described by Brewer (1942) "the psychologists and their researches did not lead to the organization of a systematic plan for guidance; the plan came from the work of the publicist, the social worker, the teacher, the promoter of adult education" (p. 9) and "while the practice of vocational guidance has been greatly aided through the researches of the psychologists, in no sense can it be said that experimental or theoretical psychology contributed to its actual origin" (p. 9).

The importance of Frank Parsons' thinking as reflected in his 1908 book *Choosing a Profession,* must be emphasized. Whereas the need for studying an individual and prescribing a career had long been advocated, Parsons' emphasis on self-discovery and decisions is a legacy clearly reflected in counseling. Sources that document this early influence include books such as *History of Vocational Guidance* (Brewer, 1942) and *Social Reform and the Origin of Vocational Guidance* (Stephens, 1970) and articles such as "Some Social Ideas of Pioneers in the Guidance Movement" (Rockwell & Rothney, 1961) and "Transition: From Vocational Guidance to Counseling Psychology" (Super, 1955).

Psychological Testing

The next contributing source for counseling, as represented by the vocational guidance movement, was the great progress being made in psychological testing. Whereas vocational guidance has a history separate from psychology, the history of the testing movement is in many ways the history of psychology, at least for a significant period. First, the work of Alfred Binet on the measurement of intelligence provided the impetus for the development of measures of aptitudes and interests. Second, the process of classification in World War I developed a technology for matching recruits and military jobs. This technology provided a major resource for the vocational guidance movement.

The testing movement, obviously, was never totally subsumed by the guidance movement. However, the testing movement served to provide a conceptual strength and methodology to guidance. It also served to provide a formal tie between guidance and psychology. The strength of this tie has been a source of ongoing controversy for the identity of counseling.

Both counseling and clinical psychology have roots in the psychometric trend. Watkins (1983) differentiated the effects of the psychometric trend on counseling and clinical psychology. Whereas, "in the early years, the clinical psychologist was basically a psychological examiner, who administered intelligence and projective tests" (with this being the case until World War II), "psychometrics was incorporated into vocational guidance work" with the main purpose "not to assess the personality in depth; rather the counselor was interested first and foremost in interests and aptitudes'' (p. 77).

The adaptation of psychometric techniques by the vocational guidance movement provided a strong bridge to psychology. As Aubrey (1977) stated, ''the movement was largely devoid of philosophical or psychological underpinnings'' (p. 290) prior to this incorporation. Stone (1984) stated that the testing movement and

developments in trait and factor psychology provided the technologies that enabled guidance workers to conduct individual and job assessments. Moreover, such scientific methods helped transform guidance workers into psychologists, and established the respectability of vocational counseling. (p. 300)

Such a transformation was largely carried out at the University of Minnesota through the pioneering work of Donald Paterson and his colleagues and students, especially E. G. Williamson.

Mental Hygiene Movement

Just as the vocational guidance movement sprang from a period of intense social reform, reform of our mental health services was facilitated by Clifford Beers and his book *A Mind That Found Itself* (1908). Coinciding with the introduction of psychoanalytic theories to the United States at the turn of the century, (e.g., 1909 Psychology Conference at Clark University; Evans & Koelsch, 1985), the mental hygiene movement contributed to the acceptance and understanding of mental illness by our society. Although this influence was not immediate in counseling, it certainly had an indirect, and more recently a direct, impact through the inclusion of counseling/psychological services in the provision of health services.

The Psychotherapy Influence

Counseling from Parsons on was largely a process of providing information and assisting the client with rather direct decision making. Even though several, mostly imported, approaches to psychotherapy were part of psychiatry and psychology in the United States, these lacked the practical orientation required by vocational guidance counselors.

The impact of Carl Rogers and his book *Counseling and Psychotherapy* (1942), therefore cannot be underestimated. Not only did this approach pro-

vide a way to expand the focus of vocational guidance, it also provided a vehicle that later would take counseling far from its vocational guidance origin. Rogers' theoretical and practical approach was philosophically consistent with the goals of vocational guidance, was easily understood, and was easily taught.

Post—World War II: The Emergence of Counseling Psychology

Coming out of the Second World War was a profession, although not clearly defined, primarily concerned with educational-vocational issues, tied to psychology through the psychometric testing thread, and employing a client-centered methodology for communicating with clients. From these mountain beginnings and tributaries, the time was right for professional definition and continued lateral expansion.

Educational-vocational guidance had been introduced to the college-university campus before World War ll (Williamson, 1939).

The role of counseling (before 1945) was broadly defined as helping students remove a variety of obstacles or problems (e.g., personality, educational, occupational, financial, and health) so that students could maximally benefit from course instruction. (Heppner & Neal, 1983, p. 82)

It had also gained a foothold in the schools of the United States, also with a primary focus on educational/vocational guidance. Paralleling the widening of a river as it flows downstream this lateral expansion is described by Russo (1985) ''. . . the evolution of psychologic thought and practice has periodically grown to encompass new methodologies, clinical populations, or sites to practice . . .'' (p. 43).

Clinical psychology at the end of WWII largely used traditional psychological approaches characterized by work with deviant populations (Watkins, 1983). Thus, there was a clear and definite position in relation to developmental concerns, vocational/career issues, and problems of living not addressed by clinical psychology and for which counseling psychology emerged as a recognized specialization (Super, 1955).

Counseling psychology as a separate psychological specialty developed from the reorganization of the American Psychological Association during and following World War II. In an effort to bridge the gap between APA and the American Association for Applied Psychology, a merger of the two organizations resulted in a new structure of APA with the emergence of divisions. First designated the Division of Personnel Psychologists, it met officially as a charter division of APA titled the Division of Counseling and Guidance. Pepinsky stated that

the origins of counseling psychology are implied in these earlier titles. Most of the division's early leaders were university teachers and administrators, training and supervising others for activities that had become generally known as "student personnel work" in colleges and universities and as "guidance" in elementary and secondary schools. By 1946 the "counseling" of students in face-to-face interviews had come to be regarded as an essential part of both guidance and student personnel services. (1984, p. 119)

The final postwar movement in the transition from vocational guidance to counseling psychology resulted from an invitational meeting held at Northwestern University in 1951 called by C. Gilbert Wrenn. Based on reports prepared by early leaders (Edward S. Bordin, Francis P. Robinson, and Donald E. Super) the term *counseling psychology* was adopted and standards for the training of counseling psychologists were proposed (Super, 1955). In 1952, the division changed its title to the Division of Counseling Psychology. This explication of training standards and title change was partly in response to Veterans Administration's need for staff members to "help emotionally disturbed veterans to obtain and maintain suitably gainful employment outside the hospital" (Pepinsky, 1984, p. 119). Also in 1952, the VA announced two major positions: counseling psychologist (vocational), a doctoral-level position under VA's Division of Medicine and Neurology and counseling psychologist (VR & E), a subdoctoral position under the VA's Division of Vocational Rehabilitation and Education (Pepinsky, 1984).

Throughout this period conceptual development was solid (Whiteley, 1984). The founding of the *Journal of Counseling Psychology* in 1954, extensive writing on career development and vocational choice (e.g., Ginzberg, Ginsburg, Axelrad, & Herma, 1951; Super, 1953), further refinement of counseling uses for the Strong Vocational Interest Blank and the Minnesota Multiphasic Interest Inventory, and research on the practice of various theoretical orientations all have had lasting influence (Wrenn, 1954).

The transition to counseling psychology resulted in energy focused on increased standards and other professional issues. Counseling psychology was concerned with trying to define itself as a distinct specialization within psychology. As a result of this focus, a major opportunity was missed and diversion of a portion of the counseling stream occurred.

NDEA: A Missed Opportunity

In 1957 the Russians beat the United States into space and our national pride was wounded. In reaction, the National Defense Education Act (NDEA) of 1958 was passed. This act, in the name of national defense, was intended to identify young persons with exceptional talents, guide them into proper careers, and provide them with adequate opportunities for training. To accomplish this, major funds were allocated for the training of subdoctoral counselors to work in elementary and secondary schools.

Division 17, as representative of Counseling Psychology, remained relatively uninvolved in this entire process. Despite the warning of divisional presidents such as Ralph Berdie and Edward Shoben, no organized response from counseling psychology was effective in shaping legislative directions or becoming involved in the consequences. Wrenn (1980) described the outcomes of NDEA vis-à-vis counseling psychology as permitting the training of thousands of counselors at both the doctoral and master's level with many at the doctoral level clearly not being psychologists. Many colleges of education began or greatly expanded counseling programs during this period to take advantage of federal funding.

Perhaps the splitting of the profession between counseling psychology with its clear allegiance to doctoral level training and its roots in psychology and counselor education and counseling and guidance with its roots in education and multilevel training was unavoidable. Counseling psychology, as a developing specialty, was in no position to jeopardize its position within psychology[1] and the recognition by the VA system for which it had fought.

The 1960s

NDEA affected the size of programs training school counselors as well as the number of col-

---

[1]Note the continuing conflict within school psychology with its doctoral level (APA, Division 16) and its subdoctoral level (NASP) training standards and organizations.

leges of education involved in counselor training. It served as a springboard for continued program expansion.

The 1960s were a time of expansion in higher education. Increased enrollments from the baby boom resulted in the addition of faculty and student services. More doctoral level graduates were needed to fill new faculty lines, counseling centers grew, and community colleges were established throughout the nation. Counselors were needed at all levels to keep up with this expansion.

At the same time, training standards for school counselors were further developed to, in most cases, set the master's degree as the minimum level of preparation. Many of the counselors trained through the early NDEA institutes sought additional preparation and credentialing.

Also during this decade federal and state legislation, intended to provide greater services in the least restrictive environment, both mandated and funded greatly expanded community mental health services. Thus, counselors at all levels were again needed as this new domain was opened.

Social concerns about racial inequities, the physically handicapped, and the Vietnam War all came to the forefront in the 1960s. Our social/educational institutions were directly confronted by the challenges presented. Counselors and student personnel workers were seen as key problem solvers in working with the challenges presented by the disadvantaged and alienated.

Also in the 1960s, various theoretical perspectives served to give direction to the training and practice of counseling. The behavioral revolution in counseling (e.g., Krumboltz, 1966) pulled some counseling psychologists away from existing paradigms and further legitimized behavior science as a source for counseling procedures. Other counselors stayed away from behavioral science, choosing the more humanistic approach (e.g., Rogers, 1965). The human potential movement as a means for personal fulfillment and the exploration of potentialities also served to further separate some from counseling as a psychological specialty. For some, counseling became an experiential event not to be studied through acceptable scientific paradigms.

Counseling psychology was actively engaged during the 1960s in defining itself and strengthening its position as a psychological specialty. The Greyston Conference (Thompson & Super, 1984) served to assess the status of counseling psychology and to identify needs in relation to such issues

as research, the substantive base for counseling, and the professional roles of counselors. Whiteley (1984) states that an "important legacy of the previous . . . [efforts] . . . in counseling psychology's growth as an organized applied-scientific specialty was a much clearer definition of the central thrust of the profession" (p. 69). This is represented by the statement by Jordaan, Myers, Layton, and Morgan (1968), which identified three clear roles for the counseling psychologist; the remedial or rehabilitative, the preventive, and the educative and developmental.

The 1970s

Whereas in previous years psychology in general was concerned with differentiating itself as a field, freedom of choice legislation changed the movement. The push now became one to show that psychology could provide cost-effective, quality mental health services. Freedom of choice legislation was fostered nationwide to allow the consumer to choose from a variety of health service providers, including psychology.

Reimbursement for health service provision was primarily for remedial or rehabilitative services, however, and not for the preventive or educational. Counseling psychology was pulled closer to APA accreditation criteria, was more influenced by state licensure procedures, and was attracting students more and more interested in working with those clients/patients qualified for health services. This movement toward health service provision served to distance counseling psychology further from some other counseling specialties and further from educational institutions.

The expansion of employment opportunities in mental health agencies was accompanied by a restriction of opportunities in educational settings. As the baby boom passed through elementary/ secondary schools and then into institutions of higher education, the demand for new counselors and faculty in these institutions was greatly reduced. Training institutions and students interested in counseling careers began to train counselors for an ever widening array of roles and settings as previous employment opportunities declined.

Social concerns with women, cultural diversity, and the Vietnam veteran continued or began to influence counselor training. Not only was accessibility of ethnic and gender groups into counseling careers an issue, but counselors were forced to look at attitudes and practices in dealing with diverse client populations. Multicultural and women's issues increasingly became a legitimate focus for research by counseling psychologists.

Conceptual developments included the further refinement of behavioral techniques with the addition of cognitive domains (Ellis, 1969; Mahoney & Thoreson, 1974). Another line of research applied social psychological processes to counseling (Strong, 1968). Social psychology continues as a rich source for counseling research (see summaries by Corrigan, Dell, Lewis, & Schmidt, 1980; Heppner & Dixon, 1981). Whiteley (1984) characterized the theoretical and research literature of the early part of the 1970s as showing a "steady increase in sophistication and methodological rigor, though it lacked the originality of the theoretical formulations of the 1950s" (p. 81). Whiteley summarized the theoretical and research literature of the later 1970s and early 1980s as characterized by "consistent programmatic inquiries in psychometrics, student development, behavior change, vocational psychology, and career development and interventions" (p. 87).

Current Status

C. Gilbert Wrenn, in reviewing the current status of counseling psychology, stated, "The challenges to the profession are unmistakable. But I think, however, that anybody . . . would feel it was worth all the struggle we have been through over the past 30 or 40 years" (Whiteley, 1984, p. 87).

Counseling psychology stands as a clearly recognized specialization in psychology. In 1984, the executive committee of Division 17 approved the following definition of counseling psychology.

Counseling psychology is a specialty in the field of psychology whose practitioners help people improve their well-being, alleviate their distress, resolve their crises, and increase their ability to solve problems and make decisions. Counseling psychologists utilize scientific approaches in their development of solutions to the variety of human problems resulting from interactions of intrapersonal, interpersonal, and environmental forces. Counseling psychologists conduct research, apply interventions, and evaluate services in order to stimulate personal and group development, and prevent and remedy developmental, educational, health, organizational, social, and/or vocational problems. The specialty adheres to standards and ethics established by the American Psychological Association. (APA Division 17, 1985, p. 141)

It is not too difficult to look back upstream and see the sources for that definition.

The evolution of specialties in psychology parallels the specialization in other professions. Just as the apostle Paul was raised a devout Jew but became a zealous Christian, the founding fathers/mothers of any specialty were never trained in that specialty. They either were trained in a different area entirely or at a more general level. The earliest counselors were not trained as counselors, the first counseling psychologists were trained in other areas of psychology, and the first educational psychologists were typically trained as psychologists with no adjectival modifier. Increased specialization seemingly is the wave from the past into the future. Currently, the general label of counseling psychologist or educational psychologist is often inadequate, needing additional descriptors (e.g. marital and family emphasis or statistics and program evaluation emphasis) to adequately describe the professional.

How the specialties of counseling and educational psychology relate to one another is difficult to describe. The relationship in some situations is organizational in nature (e.g., both areas may be located in a college of education). The complimentarity of the two specialties on conceptual issues include: a) research—with theory development currently more emphasized in educational psychology and application of theory to the change process relatively more emphasized in counseling psychology, b) theory base—with educational psychology concerned with theories in learning, cognition, and problem solving that have direct relevance to the counseling process, and c) psychometrics—with educational psychology focusing on basic issues that may have relevance to the assessment techniques and tests used and developed by counselors. The conceptual divergence is appreciable as well; however, the growth of cognitive theories and approaches in counseling and educational psychology holds promise for some productive convergence.

The foci for application of counseling and educational psychology are also related in a complex manner. Historically, both specialties have been concerned with solving problems related to education. The applied field for educational psychology, in a sense, has been teacher training and the development of knowledge to influence what future teachers learn and ultimately do. The settings for counseling and counseling psychology are decreasingly in formal educational institutions. Counseling psychology, as distinct from guidance and counseling, has never had a major emphasis in

K–12 schools, although it has had an emphasis in higher education through the college student personnel areas.

There are still many challenges to the profession of counseling psychology. One tension that continues is that between psychology and education. Counseling programs are frequently located in colleges of education whereas others are located in departments of psychology. Colleges of education ask for relevance to college goals (usually teacher training), they frequently have large master's programs, and they are generally concerned with the preparation of school counselors. Colleges are increasingly faced with accountability issues both inside and outside the university. As universities are faced with declining resources, colleges of education are forced to respond to the university value of scholarship and research productivity. At the same time, they are held accountable for the condition of education in our nation's schools. Counseling psychology programs in colleges of education often assist colleges in meeting university goals (scholarship), but are less involved in contributing to college goals (teacher training). On the one hand, they are viewed as contributing strongly to accountability within the university, but perhaps less so to society demands for educational quality.

Another, perhaps more serious challenge, lies within the profession itself. Two commentaries from clinical psychology are especially pertinent. Peterson (1985), in reviewing the 20-year history of practitioner training (as opposed to the scientist-practitioner model), observed that few practitioner programs are in major research universities and that the "number of students enrolled in scientist-practitioner programs and the number enrolled in professional schools appear to be about equal" (p. 444). McFall (1985) stated that

psychology is under attack by a growing coalition of psychologists concerned almost exclusively with the professionalization of the mental health field. They are out to promote psychology as a cure-all, and are not about to allow the skeptical attitudes of research psychologists to slow them down. (p. 30)

This split within psychology over the importance of research training and professional practice is not as new to counseling psychology as perhaps to clinical psychology; the split between counseling psychology and non-psychological-based counseling has been discussed earlier in this chapter. This challenge, however, may create some strange alliances. Perhaps as Watkins (1985) and Levy (1984) suggest, clinical and counseling psychologists with certain professional goals may evolve into a human services psychology defined to include

all professional psychology specialties concerned with the promotion of human well-being through the acquisition and application of psychological knowledge concerned with the treatment and prevention of psychological and physical disorders (Levy, 1984, p. 490).

Where programs in counseling (or clinical) psychology with a strong commitment to the scientist-practitioner model will be if human services psychology merges is uncertain. Perhaps the scientist-practitioners within counseling psychology, clinical psychology, and school psychology will be forced into an alliance in response. The commitment to methodological inquiry as opposed to a nonresearch professional model may be a source of greater commonality than the current professional specialty designations.

Conclusion: A Return to the River

The mountain beginnings with the vocational guidance movement provided a strong impetus; this stream was fed by such sources as the testing/psychometric movement and the mental hygiene/ client-centered counseling influence. From these sources counseling psychology emerged. Many outstanding figures have been part of the historical voyage including: Frank Parsons, E. K. Strong, Jr., Donald G. Paterson, E. G. Williamson, C. Gilbert Wrenn, Sidney Pressey, John Darley, Donald Super, G. Frederic Kuder, Francis Robinson, Harold Pepinsky, Robert Hoppock, John Holland, Leona Tyler, Barbara Kirk, Cecil H. Patterson, Ralph Berdie, Edward Bordin, and Anne Roe.

Without question these historical figures, and many others, have provided the major conceptual and research leadership in vocational psychology/career development (e.g., Super, Roe, Holland, Tiedeman, Osipow, Dawis, Lofquist, Krumboltz). In addition, psychometric developments in relation to these theories have been extensive (e.g., Kuder Occupational Interest Inventory, Strong-Campbell Interest Inventory, Holland's-Vocational Preference Inventory, Crites'-Career Maturity Inventory, and Super's-Career Development Inventory). Counseling psychology has, and continues to be, tied to education through conceptual contributions in the vocational/career area benefitting not only counseling practice, but also related fields such as vocational education and career education. The work of counseling psychologists has also contributed greatly to college student personnel as a field (e.g., Williamson, Kirk, Wrenn, Clyde Parker, Harold Cottingham, Thomas Magoon, Robert Brown, Ursula Delworth). The study of counseling process, whether from a client-centered perspective or more recently from a social psychological perspective, has been a focus for counseling psychology. Additionally, counseling psychology has greatly contributed to the research literature in the training and supervision of psychotherapists.

The quality of university-based training programs in counseling psychology is stronger than it ever has been. The position of counseling psychology as a specialty in psychology is also better established than ever before. The challenges to counseling psychology, and psychology in general, from related, but less established areas are definite and increasing. How counseling psychology with its historical roots in social reform and its strengthened tie to psychology responds to the challenges of a complex society will determine its future. Its ability to address personal and social needs using psychological methods will guarantee the continued vitality of counseling psychology.

The Platte River is wide, but shallow. The strong, often hidden channels are hard to detect. A traveler on the river can easily lose the channel only to end up on a sandbar. The challenge is to keep in the channel. Human needs coupled with scientific methodology are the currents of progress.

References

APA Division 17 Executive Committee Meeting Minutes. (1985). *The Counseling Psychologist, 13*(1), 141.

APA Membership Register. (1984). Washington, DC: American Psychological Association.

Aubrey, R. F. (1977). Historical development of guidance and counseling and implications for the future. *Personnel and Guidance Journal, 55,* 288–295.

Beers, C. W. (1908). *A mind that found itself.* Garden City, NY: Longmans-Green.

Brewer, J. M. (1942). *History of vocational guidance: Origins and early development.* New York: Harper.

Committee on Accreditation. (1984). APA-accredited doctoral programs in professional psychology: 1984. *American Psychologist, 39*(12), 1466–1472.

Committee on Professional Standards. (1981). Specialty guidelines for the delivery of services. *American Psychologist, 36*(6), 639–681.

Corrigan, J. D., Dell, D. M., Lewis, K. N., & Schmidt, L. D. (1980). Counseling as a social influence process: A review

[Monograph]. *Journal of Counseling Psychology, 27,* 395–441.

Council for Accreditation of Counseling and Related Programs. (1984). Reported in the *Journal of Counseling and Development, 63*(6), 1985, 335.

Dowd, E. T. (1984). Counseling psychology. In R. J. Corsini (Ed.), *Encyclopedia of Psychology* (Vol. 1, pp. 301–303). New York: Wiley.

Ellis, A. (1971). A cognitive approach to behavior therapy. *International Journal of Psychiatry, 8,* 896–899.

Evans, R. B., & Koelsch, W. A. (1985). Psychoanalysis arrives in America: The 1909 Psychology Conference at Clarke University. *American Psychologist, 40*(8), 942–948.

Gelso, C. J. (1982). Editorial. *Journal of Counseling Psychology, 29*(1), 3–7.

Ginzberg, E. Z., Ginsburg, S. W., Axelrad, S., & Herma, J. L. (1951). *Occupational choice.* New York: Columbia University Press.

Heppner, P. P., & Dixon, D. N. (1981). A review of the interpersonal influence process in counseling. *Personnel and Guidance Journal, 59,* 542–550.

Heppner, P. P., & Neal, G. W. (1983). Holding up the mirror: Research on the roles and functions of counseling centers in higher education. *The Counseling Psychologist, 11*(1), 81–98.

Hollis, J. W., & Wantz, R. A. (1983). *Counselor preparation 1983–85: Programs, personnel, trends.* (5th Ed.) Muncie, IN: Accelerated Development.

Jordaan, J. P., Myers, R. A., Layton, W. C., & Morgan, H. H. (1968). *The Counseling Psychologist.* Washington, DC: American Psychological Association.

Krumboltz, J. D. (Ed.). (1966). *Revolution in counseling: Implications of behavioral science.* Boston, MA: Houghton Mifflin.

Levy, L. H. (1984). The metamorphosis of clinical psychology: Toward a new charter as human services psychology. *American Journal of Community Psychology, 39,* 486–494.

Mahoney, M. J., & Thoreson, C. E. (1974). *Self control: Power to the person.* Monterey, CA: Brooks/Cole.

McFall, R. M. (1985). Nonbehavioral training for behavioral clinicians. *The Behavior Therapist, 8,* 27–30.

Michener, J. A. (1974). *Centennial.* New York: Random.

National Commission for Excellence in Teacher Education. (1985). *A call for change in teacher education.* Washington D.C.: American Association of Colleges for Teacher Education.

Parsons, F. (1909). *Choosing a vocation.* Boston: Houghton Mifflin.

Pepinsky, H. B. (1984). History of counseling psychology. In R. J. Corsini (Ed.). *Encyclopedia of Psychology* (Vol. 2, pp. 118–121). New York: Wiley.

Peterson, D. R. (1985). Twenty years of practitioner training in psychology. *American Psychologist, 40*(4), 441–451.

Rockwell, P. J., Jr., & Rothney, J. W. M. (1961). Some social ideas of pioneers in the guidance movement. *Personnel and Guidance Journal, 40,* 349–354.

Rogers, C. R. (1942). *Counseling and psychotherapy.* Boston, MA: Houghton Mifflin.

Rogers, C. R. (1965). A humanistic conception of man. In R. E. Farson (Ed.), *Science and human affairs* (pp. 18–31). Palo Alto, CA: Science and Behavior Books.

Russo, D. C. (1985). Clinical training in behavioral health psychology. *The Behavior Therapist, 8,* 43–46.

Stephens, W. R. (1970). *Social reform and the origins of voca-*

tional guidance. Washington, DC: National Vocational Guidance Association.

Stone, G. L. (1984). Counseling. In R. J. Corsini (Ed.). *Encyclopedia of Psychology* (Vol. 7, pp. 300–301). New York: Wiley.

Strong, S. R. (1968). Counseling: An interpersonal influence process. *Journal of Counseling Psychology, 15,* 215–224.

Super, D. E. (1953). A theory of vocational development. *American Psychologist, 8,* 185–190.

Super, D. E. (1955). Transition: From vocational guidance to counseling psychology. *Journal of Counseling Psychology, 2,* 3–9.

Thompson, A. S., & Super, D. E. (Eds.). (1964). *The professional preparation of counseling psychologists: Report of the 1964 Greyston Conference*. New York: Teachers College, Columbia University.

Watkins, C. E., Jr. (1983). Counseling psychology versus clinical psychology: Further exploration on a theme or once more around the "identity" maypole with gusto. *The Counseling Psychologist, 11*(4), 76–92.

Watkins, C. E., Jr. (1985). Counseling psychology, clinical psychology, and human services psychology: Where the twain shall meet? *American Psychologist, 40*(9), 1054–1056.

Whiteley, J. M. (1984). Counseling psychology: A historical perspective. *The Counseling Psychologist, 12*(1), 3–109.

Williamson, E. G. (1939). *How to counsel students*. New York: McGraw-Hill.

Wrenn, C. G. (1954). Counseling methods. *Annual Review of Psychology, 5,* 337–356.

Wrenn, C. G. (1980). Birth and early childhood of a journal. In J. M. Whiteley (Ed.), *The history of counseling psychology* (pp. 41–46). Monterey, CA: Brooks/Cole.

CHAPTER 7

School Psychology

A DEVELOPMENTAL REPORT WITH SPECIAL ATTENTION TO EDUCATIONAL PSYCHOLOGY

Jack J. Kramer

Introduction

One does not need to be intimately involved in either school psychology or educational psychology to suspect that these two fields might share many common features. Upon inspection of only the names of the two disciplines a naive observer might inquire as to whether there could be any significant characteristics that distinguish the two disciplines. After all, the primary purpose of schools is education, and most formal education in our society does take place within schools. Thus, both school psychology and educational psychology must involve the study of the relationships among human behavior, educational processes, and the settings in which teaching and learning take place—and so it is. Not surprisingly, these common interests have resulted in numerous similarities within these disciplines. However, important differences remain between the disciplines and are evident upon closer inspection.

The primary purposes of this chapter are to trace the development of school psychology and to identify the nature and extent of the school psychology–educational psychology connection. That is,

to what extent has the evolution of school psychology been influenced by educational psychology and how much of school psychology's past can be traced to factors outside of educational psychology? In addition, this chapter explores the current school psychology–educational psychology relationship with an eye towards future developments.

In order to provide a context in which to compare school psychology and educational psychology, an overview of the historical development of school psychology will be presented. Similarities and differences between these disciplines are enumerated and finally, suggestions are offered for future cooperative endeavors that may serve to better both fields.

School Psychology: A Developmental Analysis

During the past few years numerous accounts of the history of school psychology have appeared in the literature (e.g., Fagan & Delugach, 1984; French, 1984; Grimley, 1985). Further, in a continuing series in The Journal of School Psychology, a number of distinguished school psychologists have detailed historical developments in school psychology (e.g., Bardon, 1981; Crissey,

Jack J. Kramer • Department of Educational Psychology, University of Nebraska, Lincoln, NE 68588-0345.

1983; Mullen, 1981; Newland, 1981; Perkins, 1984: Phillips, 1984; Porter, 1984; Reynolds, 1985; Sarason, 1983; Shaffer, 1984; Tindall, 1983). Taken collectively, these efforts provide a comprehensive review of school psychology's past. The current chapter borrows heavily from these previous efforts and provides but an overview of the many events and individuals that have shaped the development of the school psychological specialization. The following sections of this chapter outline three generally agreed on stages in the evolution of the delivery of psychological services in American schools and serve as a foundation for subsequent comparisons of school psychology and educational psychology.

The Itinerant Years

The evolution of psychology in the schools has been traced to earlier centuries when Greek philosophers debated the nature of man and universal laws of behavior (Tindall, 1979). Most others suggest school psychology's creation to have coincided with the child study movement and the association of psychology and the public schools that occurred at the turn of the last century (e.g., French, 1984; Slater, 1980). The laboratory clinic developed by Lightner Witmer at the University of Pennsylvania in 1896 often has been cited as the birthplace of school psychology and Witmer commonly is acknowledged as the founding father of both school and clinical psychology in America (Reynolds, Gutkin, Elliott, & Witt, 1984). Witmer's clinic, like others established around the turn of the century, was important in that it emphasized the delivery of psychological services to children. Furthermore, these clinics stressed teaching, service, and research as well as the importance of developing cooperative alliances between psychology and education. Professors Davidson and Benjamin provide an excellent review of the child study movement in an earlier chapter of this volume. Regardless of the century, decade, or year of its creation, it is clear that the merger of psychology and American schools has evolved in an interesting and somewhat controversial fashion.

It has been assummed that in the United States the title of "school psychologist" was first granted to Arnold Gesell in 1915 by the state of Connecticut (Bardon & Bennet, 1974; Fagan & Delugach, 1984). It is also clear that during the first quarter of this century there was a definite connection between the development of the mental testing movement and the provision of special services for the mentally retarded within and outside of the public schools (Bardon, 1982; Cutts, 1955). Indeed experimental and physiological psychologists sought to work in Chicago schools as early as 1899 (Slater, 1980). In the same year the Chicago Bureau of Child Study was established as the first psychoeducational clinic serving a public school district and offering formal training in school psychology (Tindall, 1979).

Guydish, Jackson, Zelhart, and Markley (1985) report that by 1920 school districts in 18 major cities were delivering psychological services to pupils. In many of these instances districts sought "Binet testers" capable of identifying those children least likely to profit from instruction. These testers were often trained as clinical psychologists and provided services to schools on a part-time basis. Meanwhile, in rural districts where financial constraints and distance from urban and university clinics were factors, efforts to provide psychological services in schools were infrequent, though occasionally reported (Kramer & Peters, 1986). Itinerant psychologists such as Arnold Gesell, T. Ernest Newland, Marie Skodak, and George Kelly "rode the circuits" in rural areas of the country, conducting psychological evaluations, academic assessments, and preschool screenings as well as engaging in consultation with parents and school personnel. During the 1930s field and extension clinics appeared in some areas, thereby providing rural areas with centrally located, yet available services.

Bardon (1981) refers to this early period (prior to 1944) as school psychology's "prehistory," because there was no formal professional organization to define issues or conduct discussions pertaining to psychological practitioners' and researchers' interests in providing positive benefits to children in schools. Bardon states that

although there were school psychological services in some urban and suburban school districts prior to 1944, the practice of psychology in the schools until about the end of World War II tended to reflect developments that were not closely related to a particular field of psychology or of education. (p. 199)

It is obvious from the early history that the practice of psychology in the schools was limited in scope and in significance. School districts that provided psychological services hired itinerant psychologists trained in clinical psychology, psychological services in most areas were a "one person" operation, and services usually consisted of the application of the new psychometric devices. However, itinerant services reported to have been established prior to WW II are on record, and to some extent serve as models for the effective delivery of services to contemporary schools. During this period schools were beginning to identify the potential benefits of providing psychological services to children and states were beginning to establish regulations for school practitioners. The stage was set for the emergence of the school psychology specialization.

The Move Toward Specialization

As noted above, prior to WW II psychology was being practiced in the schools, albeit infrequently. However, there was not a distinct, identifiable entity called school psychology. Others (e.g., Bardon & Bennett, 1974; Fagan, 1985; Reynolds *et al.*, 1984) have described some of the events within American psychology that have helped to provide school psychology with an identity, including: the creation of a number of graduate level school psychology training programs during the 1940s and 1950s, the establishment of Division 16 of the American Psychological Association (APA) in 1946, and the Thayer Conference in 1954 at which the first definitive statement related to the training and practice of school psychologists was drafted.

Although Fagan (1985) has suggested that at least two school psychology programs were in existence prior to 1940, it was not until the 1940s and the 1950s that graduate level school psychology training programs were firmly in place at institutions of higher learning. It is clear that during this early period there were no universally held assumptions that guided training program philosophy and curriculum. According to Reilly (1973) there were at least six different training models during the first quarter century (approximately 1940–1965) of graduate training in school psychology: (a) the clinical/medical model, (b) the psychoeducational model, (c) the educational programmer model, (d) the data-oriented problem solver model, (e) the social facilitation model, and (f) the preventative mental health model (see Brown, 1982; Reilly, 1973 for a more complete discussion of these models). Just as there had been a number of diverse influences on the emergence of school psychology, there continued to be different approaches to the training of school psychologists and diverse philosophies regarding the roles to be filled by school psychologists.

Although there is some debate as to when Division 16 was established as part of the American Psychological Association, it is clear that the Division was a part of the APA structure by 1946 (Reynolds *et al.*, 1984; Tindall, 1979). During the first 40 years of the century influences associated with the child study movement, the call for an increase in mental health services during the 1920s, the emergence of child guidance and extension clinics during the 1930s, and the explosion of interest in intelligence testing had served to focus the attention of a small group of psychologists on the delivery of psychological services to children and schools. Bardon (1981) has suggested, however, that although all of these influences were important, the true birth of school psychology came at the point in which the American Psychological Association and the American Association of Applied Psychology joined forces. A divisional structure was created within this new organization and, in spite of recommendations to the contrary (Doll, 1946), school psychology was included as a seperate division. This division

> brought together a small number of psychologists who, for the first time to my knowledge, used "school psychologist" as a rubric, a focal point, to think about the issues and problems faced by psychologists working in the schools or by those interested in the direct application of psychological knowledge and skills to the solution of problems of children in schools. (Bardon, 1981, p. 200)

In 1948 there were only 90 members of Division 16, however, the total swelled to 270 by 1951 (Newland, 1981) and currently stands at 2,261 (American Psychological Association, 1985).

Because of the lack of consensus regarding the appropriate role for school psychologists and because of shortage of trained school psychologists, T. Ernest Newland in 1952 suggested that leaders in school psychology meet to chart the future of the profession. In 1954 at the Hotel Thayer, West Point, New York, 48 individuals met to produce a definitive statement regarding the functions, qualifications, and training of school psychologists. Cutts (1955) summarized the conference in a volume entitled *School Psychologists at Mid-Century*. The conference participants drafted recommendations suggesting that school psychologists be involved in:

1. The assessment and interpretation of intellectual, social, and emotional development of children

2. Collaboration with other professionals in the identification of exceptional children and the development of remedial programs
3. The development of strategies to facilitate the learning and adjustment of all children
4. The initiation of research programs and the interpretation of research findings relevant to the solution of school problems
5. The diagnosis of educational and personal problems and the recommendation of programs for the resolution of these problems

During the conference it was agreed that there was a need for individuals trained at both the predoctoral and doctoral levels. Two years of study with a half-year internship was considered to be the minimal amount of training necessary to enter the profession. Doctoral programs were to consist of 4 years of advanced study with a 1-year internship. As a result of the Thayer Conference, school psychologists had, for the first time, reached consensus regarding standards of training and major functions for school psychologists. The Thayer Conference was a major milestone in the history of school psychology and did a great deal to enhance the reputation of those who were identified as school psychologists (Reynolds *et al.*, 1984).

At the time of the Thayer conference (Cutts, 1955) there appear to have been at least 28 institutions offering school psychology programs (Fagan, 1985). Approximately 10 of these offered doctoral training in school psychology. Most of these programs were housed in departments of psychology rather than schools/colleges or departments of education (White, 1963–1964), although the exact distribution is not known.

It is also interesting to note that in American society the postwar period was a time of social emphasis on achievement and emotional well being. These factors, combined with the emergence of a school psychological specialization and surging economic growth and opportunity, gave rise to the demand for more psychological services for children. In the years following the war there were, after all, more children in the schools and as the demand for more services rose, more school psychologists were hired. This in turn, led to state departments of education beginning to establish tighter controls on quality and accountability (Fagan, 1985).

Although all of the previously cited factors were important in the development of school psychol-

ogy, these events did not immediately change school psychological services from a "one person operation" in most school districts across the nation (Herron, Green, Guild, Smith, & Kantor, 1970). It is true, however, that school psychology was beginning to gain an identity as a specialty area in psychology and positioning itself for future collaborative efforts with public education.

Recent Developments

Not all school psychologists were pleased with the role of school psychology as one of many disciplines in generic psychology. Many school psychologists felt greater kinship with education than psychology. As a result of this dissatisfaction and the perceived need for an organization to represent practitioners, the National Association of School Psychologists (NASP) was formed in 1969. NASP's inception coincided with a rapid growth in the demand for school psychologists and today, NASP's membership is listed as 8,222 (or 3 and a half times that of Division 16 of APA) (NASP Membership Directory, 1985). Major differences in philosophy between NASP and APA center on whether: (a) school psychology is an independent profession or a part of generic psychology, and (b) school psychologists should be able to enter the profession at the sixth-year level (Educational Specialist degree) or at the doctoral level (Brown, 1979a, 1982). The debate continues between the proponents of each position and is an issue in state legislatures across the country.

Even more significant than the emergence of NASP on the recent development of school psychology have been judicial decisions pertaining to the constitutionality of testing, protecting individual and parental rights, and bias toward minority students. The impact of judicial decisions and the subsequent landmark legislation, Public Law 94-142, The Education for All Handicapped Children Act of 1975, is immeasurable. As a result of a number of judicial decisions (e.g., *Diana v. State Board of Education*, 1970; *Larry P. et al. v. Riles; PARC v. Pennslyvania*, 1971) as well as the aforementioned legislation, service delivery in schools has changed in both quantitative and qualitative aspects. In many areas where little or no psychological assistance to school children existed prior to 1975, services have expanded to become comprehensive (e.g., involving more than just IQ testing) and multidisciplinary (i.e., involving a variety of professionals representing different disciplines in the decision-making process) in nature. Since the introduction of P.L. 94-142 every handicapped student has been entitled to a "free, appropriate" education, which has therefore increased the number of students qualifying for and receiving special services. Handicapped students cannot receive services nor be placed in special services unless comprehensive psychoeducational evaluations have been completed. In almost all cases, these evaluations involve school psychologists.

Clearly, the nature and extent of psychological services in schools changed following the implementation of P.L. 94-142. States and school districts were required to develop plans detailing how schools that previously lacked psychological and special education services would, in a relatively short period of time, provide free, appropriate education for all handicapped children. It is clear that no other event prior or subsequent to the passage of P.L. 94-142 has had as much impact as has this legislation in guaranteeing the existence of psychological services in schools.

P.L. 94-142, and the manner in which individual states have interpreted this mandate, continues to have major impact on the practice of school psychology. For the most part, this impact has been positive and has resulted in the development of systems for providing psychological services to handicapped children and in the training of individuals to provide these services. The ramifications of this federal mandate have not, unfortunately, all been positive. Today, far too many school psychologists function in a limited, psychometric capacity in public schools. This role is not unlike the role performed by the early "Binet testers." The Education for All Handicapped Children Act cannot be blamed for the fact that school psychology's history is tied to the mental testing movement; however, the case can be made that P.L. 94-142 is the glue that has cemented (or perhaps, institutionalized) our role "as a tester, a number-getter, whose sole usefulness is his or her authority to remove a deviant youngster from a classroom" (Ysseldyke, 1978, p. 374). Dissatisfaction with this role has been evident for years; and today there is a growing consensus that the utilization of school psychologists in this manner is a wasted resource and that the time for the introduction of alternative delivery systems for the provision of psychological services in the schools is now. Research investigating the value of an increased emphasis on school psychologists serving as educational and psychological consultants in

schools (e.g., Conoley, 1980; Gutkin & Curtis, 1982) and the importance of serving all children within an ecological or systems approach to human behavior (e.g., Reynolds *et al.*, 1984) suggest that more productive and efficient models of school psychological services are available for implementation.

Clearly, there are a number of critical issues in need of resolution within school psychology in the mid 1980s. To believe otherwise would be to ignore major problems confronting the profession. Many of these problems are interrelated and have been mentioned above. They include, among others: (a) determination of whether school psychology will be identified as a specialization within generic psychology or as a separate discipline; (b) evaluation of whether school psychology will be best represented by APA, NASP, or whether continued coexistence of these national organizations is possible and productive; (c) resolution of the debate regarding the extent of training necessary for entry into the profession; and (d) delineation of alternative models for the delivery of psychological services in the schools.

No attempt will be made here to detail the nature of nor to suggest strategies for the resolution of these problems. These issues have been dealt with extensively elsewhere (e.g., Conoley, in press; Lambert, 1981; National School Psychology Inservice Training Network, 1984; Oakland, 1986; Reynolds, 1986) and a thorough treatment of the material is beyond the scope of this chapter. Suffice it to say that the manner in which school psychologists respond to these challenges will do much to determine the future role of psychologists in the schools and the very nature of school psychology.

The Nature and Extent of the School Psychology—Educational Psychology Connection

Similarities and Differences: A Historical Analysis

It is of interest to note that both school psychology and educational psychologys' origins are traced to the child study movement of the late 19th century (Davidson & Benjamin, this volume; French, 1984; Slater, 1980). According to Davidson and Benjamin's analysis "child study was seen as a natural bridge between the universities and the schools, a link that would aid in the acceptance of an educational psychology.'' In fact, the truth of the matter is that the child study movement gave rise to two educational psychology disciplines: school psychology and educational psychology (as well as perhaps, clinical psychology).

There is little information available, however, that would suggest that school psychology's development was tied to educational psychology in any substantive manner. That is, although educational psychology programs and departments preceded school psychology programs by more that two decades and even though both disciplines trace their historical roots to the child study movement, there is little evidence that these departments of educational psychology played a major role in the development of the school psychology specialization. Yes, throughout its development school psychology programs were occasionally housed in educational psychology departments, just as they were in departments of psychology, counseling psychology, school counseling, clinical psychology, developmental psychology, community psychology, special education, elementry education, administration, and school psychology (Brown, 1982). Yet there is little evidence that would suggest that factors or individuals from educational psychology were significant influences on the development of school psychology.

More often, school psychology has been conceptualized as an offshoot of clinical psychology. As indicated earlier in this chapter, during the 1930s psychological services often were provided to schools by individuals trained in specialities other than school psychology, most notably, clinical psychology. Clinical psychology had evolved in response to many of the same factors as had school psychology, primarily the need to identify and classify special needs children (Bardon, 1982). However, clinical psychologists served a variety of institutions of which schools were but one example. During World War II there was a need for individuals trained to provide services to individuals suffering from emotional and personality problems and clinical psychologists quickly moved to fill void. According to Bardon (1984), following the war

clinical psychology rapidly became the glamour speciality in psychology as it moved the practice of psychology from psychometric testing to diagnostic testing and on to the practice of psychotherapy. (p. 5)

Others have reviewed these events and suggested than rather that conceptualizing school psychology

as an offshoot of clinical psychology ''it seems nearer the truth to view school psychology as an offshoot of applied psychology which 'stayed at home,' while clinical psychology moved on to new neighborhoods'' (Harris, 1980, p. 15).

In either case, whether conceptualized as an offshoot of clinical or applied psychology, it is clear that school psychology evolved more in response to the need for applied psychologists in the schools, whereas educational psychology responded to the need for a data base to use in the application of psychology in the schools. These disciplines appear to have a similar intellectual history originating in the child study movement and continuing today as manifested in a commitment to applying psychology to education. However, the disciplines have diverged as they have responded to the need for practitioners and researchers knowledgeable in both psychology and education. According to Glover and Ronning (this volume) educational psychology developed in order to fill the need for a ''middleperson who applied the principles of psychology to education''. In educational psychology this application generally has involved the discovery of knowledge, that is, research. Those individuals who refer to themselves as educational psychologists typically have been researchers first. This is not meant in any way to deny the existence of many educational psychologists who have worked in applied settings, but rather an ordering of priorities within the educational psychology discipline. In contrast, it is clear that school psychology developed largely to fill the need of schools for a very specific set of applied skills.

Before moving on to an examination of the current relationship between educational psychology and school psychology, it is appropriate to note a series of events that appears to be characteristic of both disciplines. In their attempt to be a healthy mix of education and psychology, educational psychology and school psychology often have experienced a great deal of tension. This tension has often resulted in a great deal of internal debate as the disciplines struggle to form an identity. In educational psychology the debate has involved role definition (What do educational psychologists do?), professional affiliation (Do we identify with the APA or the American Educational Research Association?), extent of emphasis on research and/or practice (Should we emphasize basic research or practical research with direct application to education?), and a variety of other factors. If one were to substitute NASP for AERA in the previous statement, the analysis would be a good fit for the type of self-questioning that school psychology has engaged in since its inception. Obviously, the marriage that these disciplines have attempted to effect between education and psychology has not been without turmoil. The emergence of these disciplines as important influences in both education and psychology suggest, however, that there have been benefits to the education/psychology union as well as limitations. There is, however, no end in sight to the debate in either school psychology (see, for example, Bardon, 1979, 1985; Brown, 1979b; Trachtman, 1985) or educational psychology (see, for example, Roweton, 1976; Scandura *et al.*, 1978).

The Current Relationship

In the opening chapter to this volume Glover and Ronning provide a cogent summary of educational psychology as it exists today by describing, "who are educational psychologists." Their conclusions tell us not only about what educational psychology looks like today, but, when examined in light of data from school psychology, also provide evidence of the similarities and differences between educational psychology and school psychology as they exist in the mid-1980s.

It appears that for educational psychology the only major professional organization representing the interests of the specialization is Division 15 of the APA, although the representativeness of this group is questioned by Glover and Ronning. Clearly, there has been a different scenario for school psychology where both NASP and APA are strong voices (although with different messages) representing the interests of school psychologists. However, even in school psychology only about one half of all school psychologists belong to one or both of the two national organizations (Zins & Curtis, in press).

Both educational psychology and school psychology exist primarily as a graduate specialization. In both disciplines (educational/school) there are approximately three times as many nondoctoral (180/254) as doctoral (60/79) programs. Today, there are approximately 15,000 school psychologists with more than 250 training programs. Although the number of students in these programs has grown consistently since the inception of the profession, it also appears that the rate of growth has slowed or perhaps even plateaued (much as has the population at large) (Zins & Curtis, in press). These figures indicate that although there may be

more individuals who identify themselves as school psychologists as opposed to educational psychologists, a larger percentage of the latter are trained at the doctoral level. Furthermore, both disciplines are training fewer students than was once the case (Glover & Ronning, this volume; Zins & Curtis, in press).

Whereas educational psychology has no agreed upon standard of training, school psychology can look towards the training standards of both NASP and APA for guidance. The influence of these standards is apparent in that the profession has witnessed an increase in the number of programs accredited by both professional organizations during the past decade. (Technically, the National Council for Accreditation of Teacher Education is the vehicle for NASP accreditation.) Conoley (in press) has suggested that this trend will continue as NASP and APA exert influence on state departments of education and state boards of psychology to adopt the training standards of the respective organizations. This trend has had the effect of exerting pressure on training programs to fall in line and seek accreditation by these national organizations in order to insure that the training programs will be able to attract students and, more importantly, that graduates of these programs will be eligible for certification and licensure.

Finally, over the past two decades more school psychology programs have appeared within education academic units. In the past most graduate programs in school psychology were located in departments of psychology. More recently, Fagan (1985) found that school psychology training programs are almost evenly distributed between psychology (40%) and education (42%) academic units (with the remainder split among different academic and interdepartmental programs). The specific cause of this shift is unclear; however, the emergence of NASP with its focus on practitioners in the schools and the passage of P.L. 94-142 with its emphasis on special education are probably both significant factors. Whatever the reasons, the trend toward more school psychology programs in education would appear to present school psychology and educational psychology with unparalleled opportunities for interaction. Although the potential for interaction has always existed (e.g., many educational psychology programs are housed in departments of psychology as have been most school psychology programs), the increased proximity suggested by the data presented earlier should facilitate cooperation between the disciplines. Whether this potential is realized during the coming years remains to be seen. Some suggestions for increasing the likelihood of cooperative interaction are presented in the following section.

Summary and Conclusions: Maintaining the Diversity and Maximizing the Interaction

It is apparent that the diversity of developmental influences that have shaped the profession of school psychology has had a positive impact. As we move towards the 21st century it will be important for school psychology to maintain that same type of diversity.

Houtz (1985), in his analysis of the future of educational psychology, voiced similar sentiments when he stated that

educational psychology should continue as a discipline generally defined; a field of study concerned with conducting research into the problems of education. What may be a reasonable suggestion, however, is that individual educational psychology programs in universities and colleges, especially at the doctoral level, respond appropriately to the increasing specializations within the discipline. . . . Some schools and programs may find it desirable to remain research-oriented. Others may wish to become more service oriented, concentrating on teaching functions or contributions to local schools and community. Both types of "missions" are valuable. (p. 4)

Although it is true that school psychology will be more concerned with the delivery of psychological services than with research, the emphasis on balance and diversity is important. School psychology must continue to look to the fields of psychology, educational psychology, special education, counseling psychology, clinical psychology, as well as the many disciplines in regular education if it is to remain responsive to the changes that are sure to occur in psychology and education. One method of insuring that this vigilance occurs is for school psychology programs to continue to exist in the same departments (or in close proximity to) the previously cited disciplines. We can be sure that this type of balancing of diverse influences from education and psychology will cause tension within the field; however, in the final analysis, the potential benefits would seem to outweigh the problems.

It should also be clear from the analysis provided herein that although school psychology and educational psychology share many common char-

acteristics, there are many differences between the disciplines. As has been the case since its inception, educational psychology remains concerned primarily with the generation of knowledge and appears today to be focusing more on the theoretical rather than the practical side of its fence (Glover & Ronning, this volume). In contrast, school psychology has had a clear and consistent clinical focus and continues to move away from its reliance on assessment to concern for the whole child and the child's interaction with the school and family. Although there is little doubt that school psychology's history is more closely tied to disciplines other than educational psychology, there is clear evidence that there exists a great deal of untapped potential for interaction. It appears that this opportunity has developed as a result of the natural similarities in the fields rather than as a result of a concerted effort by professionals to bring the disciplines together.

In fact, very little has been written about the manner in which these two disciplines can cooperate for the betterment of both. When discussions have appeared in the literature (e.g., Bardon, 1983; Phillips, 1984) they generally have focused on the belief that educational psychology serves as the knowledge base for school psychology. Given educational psychology's emphasis on research, this is as it should be. In his 1983 analysis of doctoral study in school psychology, Jack Bardon suggested that to survive and thrive a discipline must have a base of "research and inquiry." He further suggested that school psychology should look to educational psychology for that base. Clearly there is no other discipline whose interests so closely parallel those of school psychology. It is suspected, however, that the impact that these disciplines have on each in the future will not (or at least should not) be unidirectional. School psychologists work, for the most part, in the schools. This regular and continual association with the schools may enable school psychology to assist educational psychology in the prioritizing of issues in need of research in the schools.

Further, during the last decade school psychology has moved more towards an ecological or systems perspective of human behavior (e.g., Reynolds et al., 1984) and this trend appears likely to continue in the future (Conoley, 1985). Although educational psychologists are undoubtedly concerned with the whole child, the discipline is often construed as a collection of learning, development, and measurement specialists (among others) with common interests in education. Educational psychology's association and collaboration with school psychology may well serve as a unifying force that assists educational psychology as it attempts to integrate the research from its component parts. School psychology can provide an important assist in the integration of educational research into meaningful information and ultimately, educational policy. In this manner these disciplines can cooperate to facilitate our understanding of the many influences impacting on children, parents, families, and education.

ACKNOWLEDGMENTS. The author gratefully acknowledges the contributions of a number of individuals who commented on earlier drafts of this paper, including the editors of this volume. Jane Close Conoley of the University of Nebraska-Lincoln provided many helpful suggestions regarding the early history and current status of school psychology. Her thoughts on the nature of the school psychology/educational psychology connection have influenced significantly the content of this chapter.

References

American Psychological Association (1985). Membership directory. Washington, DC: Author.

Bardon, J. I. (1979). Debate: Will the real school psychologist please stand up? I. How best to establish the identity of professional school psychology. *School Psychology Digest, 8,* 162–167.

Bardon, J. I. (1981). A personalized account of the development and status of school psychology. *Journal of School Psychology, 19,* 199–210.

Bardon, J. I. (1982). The psychology of school psychology. In C. R. Reynolds & T. B. Gutkin (Eds.), *The handbook of school psychology* (pp. 1–14). New York: Wiley.

Bardon, J. I. (1983). Psychology applied to education: A speciality in search of an identity. *American Psychologist, 38,* 185–196.

Bardon, J. I. (1985). Response to Trachtman's article. *School Psychology Review, 14,* 118–120.

Bardon, J. I., & Bennett, V. C. (1974). *School psychology.* Englewood Cliffs, NJ: Prentice Hall.

Brown, D. T. (1979a). Issues in accreditation, certification, and licensure. In G. D. Phye & D. J. Reschly (Eds.), *School psychology: Perspectives and issues* (pp. 49–82). New York: Academic Press.

Brown, D. T. (1979b). Debate: Will the real school psychologist please stand up? The drive for independence. *School Psychology Digest, 18,* 168–173.

Brown, D. T. (1982). Issues in the development of professional school psychology. In C. R. Reynolds and T. B. Gutkin (Eds.), *The handbook of school psychology* (pp. 14–23). New York: Wiley.

Conoley, J. C. (Ed.). (1980). *Consultation in schools: Theory, research, technology.* New York: Academic Press.

Conoley, J. C. (1985, August). *Schools and families: Theoretical and practical bridges.* Paper presented at the meeting of the American Psychological Association. Los Angeles, CA.

Conoley, J. C. (in press). "Dr. Future, We Presume," Said School Psychology. *Professional School Psychology.*

Crissey, M. S. (1983). School psychology: Reminiscences of earlier times. *Journal of School Psychology, 21,* 163–177.

Cutts, N. E. (Ed.). (1955). *School psychology at mid-century.* Washington, DC: American Psychological Association.

Diana v. State Board of Education, C-70 37 RFP, District Court for Northern California (February 1970).

Doll, E. A. (1946). The divisional structure of the A.P.A. *American Psychologist, 1,* 336–345.

Fagan, T. K. (1985). The quantitative growth of school psychology programs in the United States. *School Psychology Review, 14,* 121–124.

Fagan, T. K., & Delugach, F. J. (1984). Literary origins of the term "school psychologist." *School Psychology Review, 13,* 216–220.

French, J. L. (1984). On the conception, birth, and early development of school psychology: With special reference to Pennsylvania. *American Psychologist, 39,* 976–987.

Grimley, L. K. (Ed.). (1985). *Historical perspectives on school psychology.* Terre Haute, IN: Curriculum Research and Development Center, Indiana State Univesity.

Gutkin, T. B., & Curtis, M. S. (1982). School-based Consultation: Theory and techniques. In C. R. Reynolds & T. B. Gutkin (Eds.), *The handbook of school psychology* (pp. 796–828). New York: Wiley.

Guydish, J., Jackson, T. T., Zelhart, P. F., & Markley, R. P. (1985). George A. Kelly's contribution to early rural school psychology. *Journal of School Psychology, 23,* 297–304.

Harris, J. (1980). *The evolution of school psychology.* Unpublished manuscript.

Herron, W. G., Green, G., Guild, M., Smith, A., & Kantor, R. E. (1970). *Contemporary school psychology.* Scranton, PA: Intext Education Publishers.

Houtz, J. C. (1985). I still like being called an educational psychologist. *The School Psychologist, 40,* 1–4.

Kramer, J. J., & Peters, G. J. (1986). Service delivery to rural schools: Conceptual and logistical hurdles. In S. N. Elliott and J. C. Witt (Eds.), *The delivery of psychological services in schools: Concepts, processes, and issues* (pp. 203–225). Hillsdale, NJ: Erlbaum.

Lambert, N. M. (1981). School psychology training for the decades ahead, on rivers, streams, and creeks—currents and tributaries to the sea. *School Psychology Review, 10,* 194–205.

Larry, P. et al. v. Wilson Riles et al. United States District Court, Northern District of California, Case No. C-71-2770 RFP, 1972, 1974, 1979.

Mullen, F. A. (1981). School psychology in the U.S.A.: Reminiscences on its origin. *Journal of School Psychology, 19,* 103–119.

National Association of School Psychologists. (1985). *Membership Directory.* Kent, OH: Author.

National School Psychology Inservice Training Network. (1984). *School psychology: A blueprint for training and practice.* Minneapolis: Author.

Newland, T. E. (1981). School psychology: Observations and reminiscence. *Journal of School Psychology, 19,* 4–19.

Oakland, T. D. (1986). Professionalism within school psychology. *Professional School Psychology, 1,* 9–27.

PARC v. Commonwealth of Pennsylvania, 343 F. Supp. 279 (E.D. Pa 1972)

Perkins, K. J. (1984). On becoming a school psychologist: A semiautobiographical account. *Journal of School Psychology, 22,* 1–15.

Phillips, B. N. (1984). Reminiscences of things past. *Journal of School Psychology, 22,* 119–130.

Porter, R. B. (1984). The emerging role of school psychology. *Journal of School Psychology, 22,* 223–231.

Reilly, D. H. (1973). School psychology: View from the second generation. *Psychology in the Schools, 10,* 151–155.

Reynolds, C. R. (1986). The elusive professionalism of school psychology: Lessons from the past, portents for the future. *Professional School Psychology, 1,* 41–46.

Reynolds, C. R., Gutkin, T. B., Elliott, S. N., Witt, J. C. (1984). *School psychology: Essentials of theory and practice.* New York: Wiley & Sons.

Reynolds, M. C. (1985). The special education of a drummer. *Journal of School Psychology, 23,* 205–216.

Roweton, W. E. (1976). *Revitalizing educational psychology.* Chicago, IL: Nelson-Hall.

Sarason, S. B. (1983). School psychology: An autobiographical fragment. *Journal of School Psychology, 21,* 285–295.

Scandura, J. M., Frase, L. M., Gagne, R. M., Stolurow, K.,

Stolurow, L., & Groen, G. (1978). Current status and future directions of educational psychology as a discipline. *Educational Psychologist, 13,* 43–56.

Shaffer, M. B. (1984). It's the only dream I know. *Journal of School Psychology, 22,* 313–322.

Slater, R. (1980). The organizational origins of public school psychology. *Educational Studies, 11,* 1–11.

Tindall, R. H. (1979). School psychology: The development of a profession. In G. D. Phye & D. J. Reschly (Eds.), *School psychology: Perspectives and issues* (pp. 3–24). New York: Academic Press.

Tindall, R. H. (1983). I didn't aspire to be a school psychologist. *Journal of School Psychology, 21,* 79–89.

Trachtman, G. M. (1985). Repressers, sensitizers and the politics of school psychology. *School Psychology Review, 14,* 108–117.

White, M. A. (1963–1964). Graduate training in school psychology. *Journal of School Psychology, 2*(1), 34–42.

Ysseldyke, J. (1978). Who's calling the plays in school psychology. *Psychology in the Schools, 15,* 373–378.

Zins, J. E., & Curtis, M. J. (in press). Current status of professional training and practice: Implications for future directions. In T. R. Kratochwill (Ed.), *Advances in school psychology* (Vol. 6). Hillsdale, NJ: Lawrence Erlbaum.

CHAPTER 8

The Impact of Behaviorism on Educational Psychology

Thomas R. Kratochwill and Sidney W. Bijou

Introduction

Contemporary behavior modification in educational psychology can be traced to a philosophy of science called behaviorism that holds that psychology is the study of individual behavior in interaction with the environment. Behavior involves the total functioning of an individual as he or she interacts with the environment. The environment consists of the conditions, functionally and reciprocally defined, under which the species evolves (philogeny) and in which the individual develops (ontogeny) and functions. It should be emphasized that behavior analysis is not a theory, but rather a system that contains the following components:

1. It is tied to a philosophy that postulates that the subject matter of psychology is the continuous interaction between any behaving organism and physical and social observable objects and events.

2. It is a general theory in that its functionally defined laws relate to (a) the strengthening and weakening of environment–behavior relations (as in learning and development); (b) the evolution and devolution of behavior topographies (as in changes in abilities and skills); (c) the maintenance of behavior; and (d) the generalization, induction, or transfer of interactions.

3. It has a characteristic research methodology for investigating the behavior of an individual in relation to the specific events and setting factors: that constitute his or her environment (i.e., the single case research strategy).

4. It has an explicit procedure for relating basic and applied research and for practical applications (Bijou, 1979, p. 4).

Each of these features is elaborated in detail in the context of historical issues in the development of behaviorism. Specifically, we trace the philosophical, biological, and physiological origins of behaviorism, and focus on the development of the experimental analysis of behavior and applied behavior analysis because of their major impact on psychology and education. Special emphasis is placed on the relation of behaviorism and educational psychology. The roots of behaviorism lie in the experimental analysis of infrahuman behavior initially studied in laboratory settings (Skinner, 1938). Experimental analysis of behavior falls within the domain of behaviorism, which grew out of objectivism in psychology, and embraces experimental methodologies to study its subject matter. It was (and is) a methodological revolt in the development of the scientific study of psychology.

Thomas R. Kratochwill • Department of Educational Psychology, University of Wisconsin, Madison, WI 53706. Sidney W. Bijou • Department of Psychology and Special Education, University of Arizona, Tucson, AZ 85721.

Particularly impressive about behaviorism are the basic and applied research it has spawned as well as the controversy surrounding its basic tenents.

Philosophical, Biological, and Physiological Origins

Empiricist Roots

Although it is not possible to link behaviorism to a specific influence during ancient times, the empirist roots traced to such individuals as Aristotle, Descartes, Locke, Berkeley, and Hume are noteworthy. Aristotle's major contribution to psychology was his attempt to interpret human experience and behavior in concrete terms (Murphy, 1949). Of particular impact on later psychology was his argument that individuals remember events due to "contiguity, similarity, and contrast." This conceptualization set the stage for later empirical work on learning that was to be a major focus of behaviorism.

The behaviorism later supported by John B. Watson evolved from a philosophical tradition of objectivism espoused by René Descartes during the 17th century. Descartes argued for a dualistic conception of man, the brain as mediator of behavior, reflex as the unit of behavior, internal stimuli as determinants of body behavior, and internal capacities, such as innate ideas. Descartes' account of involuntary action became known as the *reflex arc*. The reflex arc was said to account for all behavior of animals and involuntary behavior of humans (Schwartz, 1978). These notions were further developed by associationist philosophers to be discussed in the following.

Associationism (and with it, British Empiricism) was concerned with discovery of the laws of the mind (Schwartz, 1978). John Locke, a follower of Hobbes, is credited with developing an empirical psychology. Hobbes viewed voluntary action as a feature of the mind, but in contrast to Descartes he posited that activities of the mind could be explained by mechanical laws. Locke suggested that complex ideas are created by combining simple ideas, a kind of mental chemistry. In fact, he noted that mental life could be reduced to association of ideas. Murphy (1949) noted:

Locke's greatest contribution to psychology thus lay in making explicit the possibilities of a theory of association which should start with the data of experience and work out the laws governing the interconnections and sequences among experiences. The concern of associationism had, of course, been apparent in the work of Hobbes, which in turn went back to Aristotle. But Locke's lucid exposition of the implications of empiricism, and of the possibility, through analysis, of clearly understanding the origin and organization of ideas, gave the empirical approach an appealing and challenging quality which greatly contributed to its strength and influence. (p. 29)

George Berkeley can be regarded as one of the founders of association psychology. He argued, in contrast to Locke, that there are no qualities in experience except those that are subjective. In effect, he argued that there is no world other than that experienced through sensations, and therefore experience was a property of the soul. David Hume, on the other hand, held that experience was the primary force of association and a "soul" was not necessary in analyzing experience.

Associationist School

Although Berkeley and Hume set the stage for associationism, Hartley launched what may be called a psychological *system* (Murphy, 1949). Unlike his predecessors, he created a hypothetical physiological basis for the associational perspective, speculating, for example, on the physical basis for memory or memory sequences.

James Mill and John Stuart Mill were to have major influence in the development of associationism. James Mill adopted the position that mental life can be reduced to sensory particles and suggested that complex emotional states could be reduced to more simple sensory activities. This extreme view was tempered by John Stuart Mill's position that the mind was an active rather than a passive entity. Nevertheless, he argued that sensations could be combined like chemical elements (i.e., sensations combined to form compound ideas).

The last two great defenders of associationism were Alexander Bain and Herbert Spencer. Bain, who incorporated a great deal of biological research into his writings, contributed to behaviorism by his work on learning and habit. He conceptualized learning in terms of "(1) random movements, (2) retention of acts which bring pleasant results, and elimination of those bringing unpleasant results, and (3) fixation through repetition" (Murphy, 1949, p. 106).

Spencer, a contemporary of Darwin, elaborated on the development of the mind, claiming that the mind develops and gains substance through adaptation to diverse environments. He suggested that organisms engage in random activity and that some of these activities result in pleasurable consequences, which eventually promoted the selection of activities that preceded them, a principle that later became the law of effect (Schwartz, 1978).

Conditioning Research in Russia

Three Russian scientists, Ivan M. Sechenov, Ivan P. Pavlov, and Vadimir M. Bechterev, contributed substantially to behaviorism primarily through their mechanistic interpretations of subjective processes and overt behavior of infrahuman organisms (Kazdin, 1978). Although all three men were involved in experimental neurophysiology, their work ultimately became part of the domain of psychology, namely, the use of an experimental methodology that emphasized objective research procedures.

Sechenov (1829–1905).   Sechenov has been regarded as the father of Russian physiology because he introduced experimental methods into physiological investigation. His interest in psychology, which he regarded as an inexact science, led him to introduce more objective measurement into psychological research. For example, he argued that all behavior is reflexive, that the initial cause of human action lies outside man, and suggested that the experimental methods employed by physiologists were also appropriate for psychologists.

Within the context of his contributions to behaviorism, two features are salient (Kazdin, 1978). First, in emphasizing that the methodology used in physiology was appropriate for psychology, Sechenov helped to bring more rigor to psychological research at that time. Second, in emphasizing the role of reflexes and learning in behavior, he focused psychology's efforts on understanding behavior in relation to the environment.

Pavlov (1849–1936).   Pavlov's research followed in the tradition of Sechenov, but has gained more recognition. As part of his investigation of the functions of the alimentary canal, he demonstrated that certain reflexes could be conditioned. Later, he limited his work to the salivary reflex in dogs. Pavlov documented the nature of the conditioned reflex by repeatedly pairing a stimulus that elicited a reflex reaction (labeled an unconditioned stimulus) with a neutral stimulus that did not (labeled a conditioned or reinforcing stimulus). Among the more famous of his experiments was the conditioning of dogs to salivate at the sound of a tone. In the experiment an unconditioned stimulus (e.g., diluted acid on the dog's tongue) was observed to be slow in eliciting drops of saliva (unconditioned response). The conditional stimulus (i.e., a tone) was sounded a certain number of times and was followed each time by the acid. In test trials, the tone was sounded but was not followed by the acid. When the dog began to salivate, Pavlov counted the number of drops of saliva, which he considered as the strength of the conditioned reflex.

Like Sechenov, Pavlov promoted the use of objective experimental methods in the studying of conditioning. Moreover, his work went beyond this contribution; he elucidated a number of processes associated with conditioning, including extinction, generalization, and differentiation.

His major contribution to behaviorism lies in his research methodology (Johnston & Pennypacker, 1980). Pavlov (1927) wrote:

In the course of a detailed investigation into the activities of the digestive glands, I had to inquire into the so-called psychic secretion of some of the glands, a task which I attempted in conjunction with a collaborator. As a result of this investigation an unqualified conviction of the futility of subjective methods of inquiry was firmly stamped upon my mind. It became clear that the only satisfactory solution of the problem lay in an experimental investigation by strictly objective methods. For this purpose I started to record all the external stimuli falling on the animal at the time its reflex reaction was manifested (in this particular case the secretion of saliva), at the same time recording all changes in the reaction of the animal. (p. 5)

Bechterev (1857–1927).   In the same tradition as Sechenov and Pavlov, Bechterev used objective methods to study psychological processes. However, when the experimental findings of Pavlov and Bechterev did not show agreement, Pavlov attacked him on the discrepancies in print (Fancher, 1979). Bechterev is credited with developing reflexology, which involved the investigation of response patterns and association reflexes, and with making two major contributions to the behavioral movement (Kazdin, 1978). First, he furthered the position that external behavior was the only suitable area for scientific study. Second, he discussed a wide range of topics, including various psychiatric disorders and treatment. It should be mentioned that Pavlov also attempted to relate conditioning to psychiatric disturbances in individuals (Pavlov, 1932).

Learning Research in the United States

Edward L. Thorndike (1874–1949).   Thorndike, working in the associationistic tradition, made major contributions to animal learning. His work differed from that of the Russian physiologists, particularly Pavlov and Bechtenev, who studied the relation between conditioned and unconditional stimuli and reflexive responses. Thorndike focused on the acquisition of responses, such as how cats, dogs, and chickens learned means of escape from puzzle boxes. Thorndike recorded the number of trials required for a hungry animal to escape from a puzzle box or pen to obtain food. He viewed his area of investigation as *instrumental learning* in that the animal's learned responses were instrumental in getting it to the sources of food.

Thorndike hypothesized that through repeated trial-and-error learning, certain connections between stimuli and responses are strengthened or weakened by the consequences of behavior. He invoked two principles—the Law of Effect, and the Law of Exercise—to account for this kind of learning (Thorndike, 1911). Although Thorndike's laws of learning were later modified by other investigations (i.e., the law of effect was revised to conform with new findings and the law of exercise was found to be unnecessary), he made important methodological contributions and showed the importance of consequences of voluntary behavior.

Whereas Thorndike's contribution to behaviorism is noteworthy, his work influenced more the development of the field that became known as educational psychology, a term that he succeeded in spreading through the quotations in his text *Educational Psychology* in 1903. Thorndike emphasized the scientific approach in his test. As he stated in the preface to his 1903 text, *Educational Psychology,*

This book attempts to apply to a number of educational problems the methods of expert science. I have therefore paid no attention to speculative opinions and very little attention to the conclusions of students who present data in so rough and incomplete a form that accurate quantitative treatment is impossible. (1903, p. v.)

Thorndike also carried the position over to a lead article in the first issue of the *Journal of Educational Psychology.*

The introduction of the scientific method in educational psychology may have had a positive influence on the field, but it could not be said that the field was saved through Thorndike's influence. Grinder (1982) noted:

Emphasis on methodology led educational psychology to the brink of scientific respectability, but this approach has brought

neither unity within educational psychology nor integration with other disciplines. A divisive fissure runs through the entire history of the discipline. Educational psychologists have never agreed upon who they are or what they are about. Their history is marked, on the one hand, by struggles with metaphysicians and philosophers for academic esteem and, on the other, by an increasingly restrictive methodological posture in respect to social engineering and applied psychology. Thorndike performed a pivotal role in the sequence of frays. He led the vanguard that helped purge metaphysics from educational psychology, and he set in motion a rush of educational research that even now continues to accelerate. But the methodological trajectory on which he launched it was so narrow that the danger today of educational psychology passing into oblivion is more real than apparent. (p. 357)

Although Thorndike overcame some of the problems of educational psychology of his time (e.g., he attacked the child study movement, specified laws of learning), he fell short of establishing any unity in the field of educational psychology for several reasons (Grinder, 1982). To begin with, Thorndike maintained a metaphysical position in that he contended that many behaviors were instinctive. This was in dramatic contrast to Watson (see discussion in next section).[1] Second, his emphasis on learning research led to a de-emphasis of the broader problems facing education and consequently, may have led to a gap between research and the practice of education (see also Jackson, 1981).

John B. Watson (1878–1958).   Watson was the undisputed leader of behaviorism when it made its appearance in America. In order to understand the context for Watson's contributions, it is necessary to consider the functionalist school that dominated American psychology at the time of his graduate training at the University of Chicago. This school of psychology, associated with the work of John Dewey, James Angell, and Harvey Carr, among others, focused on treating psychological processes as functions, in the context of Herbert Spencer's philosophy and Charles Darwin's theory of evolution. Primarily interested in functions related to adaptive behavior, they concerned themselves with all the activities of an organism. Although functionalism developed, in part, as a reaction to structuralism, both schools employed introspection as an experimental method of investigation. Despite his functionalist-type training, Watson was influenced greatly by a movement al-

---

[1]Thorndike was rejected as a behaviorist by Watson (1919) because some of his learning formulations included hypothetical states or components of consciousness (Kazdin, 1978).

ready gaining momentum in psychology called objectivism,[2] which de-emphasized private experiences and advocated more objective methods in experimental work.

In 1913, Watson presented his first published statement in an article entitled "Psychology as the Behaviorist Views It." He noted:

> Psychology as the behaviorist views it is a purely objective experimental branch of natural science. Its theoretical goal is the prediction and control of behavior. Introspection forms no essential part of its methods, nor its scientific value of its data dependent upon the readiness with which they lend themselves to interpretation in terms of consciousness. The behaviorist, in his efforts to get a unitary scheme of animal response, recognizes the dividing line between man and brute. The behavior of man, with all of its refinement and complexity, forms only a part of the behaviorist's total scheme of investigation. (Watson, 1913, p. 158)

Watson's behaviorism had two main characteristics that distinguished it from structuralism and functionalism (Bijou, 1985). First, Watson argued that psychologists should discard mentalistic concepts that characterized these schools, and should favor a stimulus and response formulation, an approach that eventually became known as "S–R psychology." Second, he maintained that the goal of psychology should be to predict and control behavior rather than explore consciousness through the method of introspection.

Watson is also well known for his research on the conditioning of human emotions, and his work in that area is noteworthy for at least two reasons (Kazdin, 1978): (a) he demonstrated that the emotions could be studied by objective methods, and (b) he showed that emotional problems (e.g., disturbing fears) might be treated by objective conditioning techniques.

A classic study, often surrounded by controversy, was reported by Watson and Rayner (1920), while Watson was at Johns Hopkins University. The study dealt with three major issues: (a) whether an infant could be conditioned to fear an animal that was presented simultaneously with a fear arousing sound, (b) whether this fear could be transferred to other animals or objects, and (c) to know how long such fears would persist. At the age of approximately 9 months, an infant named Albert was tested to determine whether he feared

live animals (e.g., a rat, a rabbit, a dog) and certain objects (e.g., cotton, human mask, burning newspaper). Although no fear reaction was observed during testing, Albert did display a fear reaction when a steel bar behind his back was struck with a hammer. Watson and Rayner then presented a white rat to Albert followed by the loud sound of a hammer hitting a steel bar whenever he touched the animal. Following seven pairings of reaching for the rat and loud noise, Albert responded by crying and avoiding the rat when it was presented even without a loud noise. Watson presented the loud noise contingent upon Albert's reaching for the animal, thereby following the instrumental or operant paradigm rather than the Pavlovian model in which conditioned and unconditioned stimuli are paired. Yet Watson and Rayner's research is usually referred to as Pavlovian or classical conditioning.

A test of generalization was conducted by presenting the rat, a set of familiar wooden blocks, a rabbit, a short-haired dog, a seal-skin coat, a package of white cotton, and a bearded Santa Claus mask, and in addition, Watson and two assistants bowed their heads before him so that he could touch their hair. The researchers reported that Albert showed a strong fear response to the rat, rabbit, dog, and seal-skin coat, a somewhat negative response to the mask and Watson's hair, and only a mild fear response to the package of cotton. He presumably played freely with the wooden blocks, and with Watson's assistants' hair.

After 5 days, Albert was reconditioned to the rat and an attempt was also made to condition him directly to fear the previously presented rabbit and dog. He showed only a slight negative reaction to the rat, dog, and rabbit. Thereafter, the rat was again paired with a loud noise. Unfortunately, the dog began to bark at Albert during this period, thus confounding the experiment.

Watson and Rayner subsequently conducted a series of tests to determine whether Albert would show a fear reaction to the Santa Claus mask, seal-skin coat, the rat, the rabbit, and the dog. Although he made contact with the coat and the rabbit, he showed some ambivalence. At this point, the experiment was concluded because Albert's mother removed him from the hospital setting.

This study and the conclusions aroused considerable controversy. (The original accounts of the experiment have apparently been distorted in introductory textbooks and even in the behavior modification literature.) Harris (1979), for example, con-

---

[2]Several individuals had earlier written books that either minimized or rejected the study of consciousness in psychology (e.g., McDougall, 1905, 1909; Pillsbury, 1911; Meyer, 1911).

cludes that a critical reading of Watson and Rayner's (1920) study reveals little evidence that Albert ever developed a fear response or rat phobia, or even that the animals evoked any fear reactions during the experiment itself. However, the more serious problem with the investigation appears to be difficulties in replicating the work (e.g., Bregman, 1934; English, 1929). For example, Bregman (1934) was unsuccessful in her attempts to condition infants to fear wooden and cloth objects using aversive sound as an unconditioned stimulus. Differences in procedures might account for the discrepency.

Watson's theory, too, has been the target of criticism, even among other behaviorists, such as those aligned with the neobehavioristic (S–R) theory (e.g., Eysenck, 1979, 1982). Among the more salient criticisms include the following (Eysenck, 1982, pp. 213–216):

1. The Watson and Rayner (1920) study is based on a single case, and thus, coupled with the failures to replicate do not form a solid base for the rather large theory based upon it.
2. Phobias are not as simple as Watson seemed to postulate. Watson accepted the assumption of equipotentiality (i.e., one CS is as good as another in producing conditional responses).
3. Watson assumed that various disorders start with a single traumatic conditioning event (or with a series of similar events of this nature). Yet, disorders such as phobias may occur without one traumatic UCS.
4. Watson's theory cannot explain the development of problems when the conditions of the laboratory are not met, as in real life settings.
5. Extinction occurs with phobias, and Watson seems to have assumed that early conditioned reactions will occur throughout life.
6. There is often a failure to observe the expected extinction of the unreinforced CS, and an incremental (enhancement) effect is found such that the unreinforced CS produces more anxiety (CR) with successive presentations of the CS.
7. Physical pain or restraint (UCS), prominent in Watson's theory, may play little or no part in producing fear or anxiety, such as in adult disorders. Thus, the theory may have little to offer for understanding adults.

Watson's contributions to education and educational psychology have been considered negligible by some scholars. With regard to education, Travers (1983, p. 430) notes:

Watson wanted teachers to view children as empty black boxes, such that the outputs could be controlled by the inputs. This was an unacceptable philosophical position in the 1930s, when educators were becoming concerned with the thoughts of children and how they viewed the educational experiences provided for them. It was an age in which education was centered on the child as a self-devoted and self-energized system. The black-box conception of the pupil had no place within the prevailing educational philosophy.

On the topic of educational psychology, Travers (1983, p. 30) writes:

The contemporaries of Watson in educational psychology who might have sponsored his course, viewed him only as a man of unreasonable excesses. It must have been known to Judd at Chicago, but Judd's writings completely ignored the existence of Watson. Thorndike also ignored Watson, though one summer Watson lectured at Teachers College, but Thorndike was in no mood to strike up a friendship with Watson. Watson was never an easy man to relate to, except on his terms.

Although Travers minimizes Watson's contributions, behaviorism at the time could be best viewed as a cultural expression (Krasner, 1982). Although behaviorism was already well in progress moving toward objectivism (Kazdin, 1978), Watson combined elements of behaviorism into a social movement and gave it a new momentum.

Moreover, although a number of uncertainties surround the initial study, the experiment opened up a new area of investigation and promoted future work on conditioning, exemplified by the work of Mary Cover Jones (1924a, b) who extended the procedures of Watson and Rayner's to eliminate fear reactions in children. Jones' (1975) research was recognized as seminal to the development of behavior therapy at the First Temple University Conference in Behavior therapy and Behavior Modification, titled "Behavior Therapy—50 Years of Progress." The conference was held in Philadelphia, November, 1974.

Although Watson's contributions indeed set the stage for theoretical and empirical investigations within the behavioral school, they nonetheless generated much criticism. Most controversial was his position that mental states and processes (the major focus of structuralism) could not be investigated in the domain of science because they were not publicly observable. His belief that all psychological phenomena are determined by observable or potentially observable conditions also aroused criticism. And finally, Watson's philosophical reductionism, characterized by explaining psychological interactions in terms of physiological activities, was looked upon unfavorably by those who advocated a natural science approach. Despite these problems and criticisms, Watson's point of view was a major force in shifting psychology from the study of consciousness and subjectivism to materialism and objectivism (Bijou, 1985).

The Vienna Circle. Over the two decades following Watson's work, the behavioral perspective as a system of psychology did not take hold. Nevertheless, some important philosophical developments were occurring that would revive the movement. A group of philosophers of science, the Vienna Circle, prompted this renaissance (Travers, 1983). The individuals affiliated with this group, which included Rudolf Carnap, Herbert Feigl, Gustav Bergmann, and Kurt Gödel, met in Vienna during the 1920s to discuss issues related to the language of science and scientific methodology. Bergmann was to have a decided influence on Kenneth W. Spence at the University of Iowa, a leading proponent of Hullian behaviorism during the 1930s and 1940s. Spence, in turn, later influenced the work of Sidney W. Bijou.

According to Travers (1983) the Vienna Circle emphasized primarily logical positivism, scientific empiricism, neopositivism, and the unity-of-science movement. The movement was characterized as follows:

A basic concept of the Vienna Circle philosophy was that all statements, to be meaningful, had to be reducible to empirical statements, that is, to statements in which the terms pertained to verifiable observations. The statements of a science had to be verified from publicly observable data. The concept of the unity of science was introduced through the idea that all the statements involved in the scientific, social, and historical disciplines could be reduced to statements involving physical observations of the real world. The views expressed by the members of the Vienna Circle in their writings were at a sophisticated level. (Travers, 1983, p. 432)

This movement not only helped to move science toward more operational and reproducible concepts, but also had a positive impact on education in that colleges and schools of education were forced to reevaluate vague and nonobjective variables then being investigated. In fact, the operational specification of independent and dependent variables had a positive impact on curriculum design and evaluation of student outcomes, a feature that characterizes contemporary behavior modification in education.

Neobehaviorism

Following the work of the early behaviorists, a number of American psychologists, including Edwin R. Guthrie, Edward C. Tolman, Clark L. Hull, Kenneth W. Spence, O. Hobart Mowrer, and B. F. Skinner formulated various neobehavioral learning theories. Unlike their predecessors in psychology, most of the neobehavioral scholars developed essentially "mini" theories that were circumspect and restricted in focus and content (Bijou, 1985). Skinner's work, however, devel-

oped and expanded into a system of psychology that has had a major impact on educational psychology.

Edwin R. Guthrie (1886–1959). Guthrie, who remained closest to Watson's position and is best known for his contiguous conditioning concept (1952), contended that learning occurs through the pairing of a stimulus and response. Thus, a response performed in a given situation under given conditions will likely be repeated in that situation. Guthrie claimed that rewards did not strengthen connections learned through pairing a stimulus and response but that responses were important because they change the stimuli so that new responses are not associated with previous stimuli. This aspect of the theory has been refuted because it has been demonstrated that consequences (reinforcement or punishment) do indeed alter the strength of a response class.

Edward C. Tolman (1896–1961). Tolman is best known for his *Purposive Behaviorism* (1932). Maintaining that all behavior was purposive or goal directed, his position was a contrast to that of Watsonian behaviorists who avoided goal-mediated constructs. Tolman also created intervening variables to account for processes that occurred between the stimulus and response. Moreover, he argued that organisms learn meanings and develop cognitions during learning stimulus–response connections, and that goal attainment leads to confirmation of the goal expectation. Rewards played a more minor role in this process than in Thorndike's position in that they were purported to assist in confirming experiences that the goal was reached.

Clark L. Hull (1884–1952). Hull is best known for his hypothetic-deductive approach to a theory of behavior (1951). In one way, Hull's work was similar to Tolman's because both used intervening variables in a stimulus–response learning framework. Among the more important aspects of Hull's intervening variables were habit strength and drive. Habit strength was the strength of the stimulus response connection that was learned through reinforcement, drive was conceptualized as reinforcement that became functional during some arousal state, such as hunger. Actually, Hull's system was quite complex and was often presented in a mathematical formulation. Another significant contribution of Hull's was his synthesis and extension of the work of Pavlov and Thorndike. Drive reduction was invoked to explain the role of reinforcement and conditioned responses in the two systems, respectively. Kenneth W. Spence

(1907–1967) worked in close collaboration with Hull and published a number of formulations that synthesized their work (cf. 1956).

O. Hobart Mowrer (1907–1982). Mowrer developed a two-factor theory of learning in an attempt to integrate the work of Pavlov and Thorndike (Mowrer, 1947, 1960). He contended that Hull's drive reduction theory could not account for complex learning, especially the learning of emotions, nor could drive reduction account for avoidance learning, especially under punishment conditions. He argued, moreover, that punishment could strengthen learning, a view that disagreed with Thorndike's, which stated that, through the law of effect, punishing consequences stamped out responses, but resulted in no learning. Mowrer also maintained that learning to avoid aversive events contributed to the avoidance behavior, something that was not accounted for by the Pavlovian conditioning paradigm.

In contrast to previous work among behaviorists, Mowrer proposed a two-factor theory of learning: sign learning and solution learning. Sign learning included the conditioning of involuntary responses of organs, glands, and emotions. Solution learning involved the problem-solving responses that were acquired in drive reduction and demonstrated in the performance to reduce drives. Mowrer (1960) later revised his two-factor theory to incorporate acquisition and avoidance of fear within the sign-learning paradigm. Although Mowrer made contributions to learning theory (i.e., combining conditioning and trial-and-error learning to explain avoidance behavior), his work probably has had greatest impact on psychopathology and psychotherapy based on his original two-factor theory (Kazdin, 1978).

Perspectives on Early Behaviorists

Watson launched a behavioristic model that promoted objective measurement of overt behavior. Nevertheless, his paradigm, as well as those of the Russian researchers, was considered inadequate as an explanation of learning, or at least incomplete. The neobehaviorists extended the understanding of basic learning processes by developing alternative principles to explain observable responses. There were many similarities among the theories of Hull, Guthrie, and Tolman, and some (e.g., Schwartz, 1978) have regarded them more alike than different. Although the roles of Guthrie, Tolman, Hull, Spence, and Mowrer should not be minimized in

terms of their influence on learning theory and the development of educational psychology as a profession, their main contribution was to learning theory and subsequent research in behavior modification. In this sense their contributions set the stage for accelerated development of that field. But it is the work of one neobehaviorist, B. F. Skinner, that has influenced profoundly basic and applied research and practice in the field of educational psychology.

Operant Conditioning and Development of the Experimental Analysis of Behavior: B. F. Skinner

B. F. Skinner (1904) has made and continues to make major contributions to diverse areas of the social sciences, most notably to education and psychology. His original theory has evolved into a system of psychology that encompasses a philosophy of science (radical or root behaviorism), a theory of behavior (experimental analysis of behavior), a research methodology (single-case designs), and a wide range of applications through the experimental analysis of behavior and applied behavior analysis (a subdivision of behavior modification).

Skinner's radical behaviorism differs from Watson's classical behaviorism in two salient dimensions (Bijou, 1985). Skinner's view is that covert, implicit, or private events can be studied by acceptable scientific procedures, and that psychology should promote the functional analysis of the environment's (stimuli) influence on behavior (responses), without resorting to reductionism. This contrasts with Watson's mechanistic notion that an individual's behavior, defined physiologically, is examined through its interactions with the environment, also defined in physical terms.

Skinner's early work (1935, 1937, 1938), like Hull's and Mowrer's, examined the relationship between the learning paradigms of Pavlov and Thorndike. He concluded that there are two types of responses and conditioning. Responses are classified as respondents that are elicited and as operants that are emitted (i.e., no eliciting stimulus is identified). Conditioning is classified as either Type S or Type R. Type S conditioning involves the conditioning of respondent behavior wherein the conditioned stimulus is paired with the unconditioned stimulus and eventually elicits the conditioned response (i.e., Pavlovian or classical conditioning). On the other hand, the Type R procedure refers to the conditioning of operant behavior wherein a consequent stimulus strengthens a class of behavior or subsequent similar occasions, a formulation similar to Thorndike's instrumental learning.

Experimental Analysis of Behavior

Skinner's major contribution is termed the "experimental analysis of behavior." Within this framework the investigator demonstrates functional relations between behavior and various environmental stimuli. These functional relationships are investigated within a natural science orientation. Some writers recognize Skinner as the founder of the natural science approach to the study of behavior as an independent discipline (Johnston & Pennypacker, 1980). In *The Behavior of Organisms* (1938) Skinner notes:

When a science of behavior had once rid itself of psychic fictions, it faced these alternatives: either it might leave their places empty and proceed to deal with its data directly, or it might make replacements. The whole weight of habit and tradition lay on the side of replacement. The altogether too obvious alternative to a mental science was a natural science, and that was the choice made by a non-mentalistic psychology. The possibility of a directly-descriptive science of behavior and its peculiar advantages have received little attention. (p. 4)

Espousing this natural science viewpoint, Skinner became well-known for his rejection of hypothetical accounts of behavior, and especially rejection of cognitive states or processes in accounting for observed behavior. In this regard, several characteristics of the experimental analysis of human behavior distinguish it from other approaches to psychology (Johnston & Pennypacker, 1980; Kazdin, 1978).

Objective Description. Central to the science of behavior is objective description of observable past and present events without resorting to nonobservable constructs. Skinner was especially concerned with the practice of using hypothetical constructs to explain learning and suggested that theoretical accounts with hypothetical constructs were inadequate for the future development of a science of behavior. Indeed, Skinner argued that faulty theory is an outgrowth of not understanding the basic subject matter under investigation and he favored the inductive rather than the deductive method of theory construction advocated by the philosophers of the Vienna Circle.

Measurement Paradigm. The basic measurement employed in the experimental analysis of behavior includes standard and absolute units anchored to the amount of a physical property being measured. For example, Skinner (1953b) emphasized the frequency or rate of responding because it could be used to predict and even control behavior.

Skinner, as well as other early behaviorists, embraced a measurement system that has been labeled idemnotic, which stands in sharp contrast to vaganotic measurement used in other areas of the social sciences (Johnston & Pennypacker, 1980). *Vaganotic* measurement involves the development of scales and units of measurement based on the variability in a set of scores or measures in a specified population.

In educational psychology, the use of vaganotic measurement, known as norm-referenced measurement, is predominant, and is represented especially by academic, intellectual, and psychological tests. To illustrate, IQ tests are developed on the basis of items thought to represent the construct of intelligence and are administered to large numbers of students to develop norm groups at different age levels. The mean and standard deviation are determined and assigned values on an equal interval scale (e.g., T-scores, Z-scores). As noted by Johnston and Pennypacker (1980), vaganotic measurement provides a way for defining phenomena into existence (e.g., intelligence is developed and defined as the basis of scores on IQ tests). Moreover, different tests that purport to measure the same construct often use different scales and norms; consequently one is not sure what it is that is being measured.

Idemnotic measurement, on the other hand, employs standard and absolute units as the data base. The meaning of scores in idemnotic measurement, like the meaning of scores on criterion-referenced tests (Glaser, 1971), can be established prior to and separate from the actual measurement operations (see following).

Experimental Datum. In concert with the use of objective data and absolute unit-based measurement, Skinner (1953a) argued for the use of frequency (or rate) of responses to establish a scientific basis for the understanding of behavior. The advantages of frequency measures were that they were regarded as an extremely orderly datum, were easily reproduced, contained an immediate referent to the individual, provided a continuous measure of behavior, lent themselves to "automatic experimentation" (i.e., automated electrical or electronic apparatus), and provided a basis for the concept of a probability of action (Skinner, 1953b, p. 77).

Especially important in the use of frequency data was the ease of graphing responses as a cumulative record that provided an ongoing record of the dependent variables (behavior) in experimentation. From the graph the investigator could usually inspect patterns of the data to examine the influence of various independent variables (stimuli).

Establishing Functional Relations. At the heart of the experimental analysis of behavior is the identification of the functional relationship between behavior and environmental events. The behavioral researcher demonstrates experimental control over certain environmental variables so that any observed changes in behavior can be attributed to the manipulated variable and not to other variables. As noted earlier, repeated measures (frequencies) of the behavior are gathered over time to determine the reliability of the functional relation. In this process uncontrolled sources of variability are examined and attempts are made to control the variance, rather than to treat it statistically as error. Moreover, the researcher is interested in establishing the generality of the functional relationship across individuals in interactions with similar situations, rather than groups of subjects.

Methodology. As noted earlier, the experimental analysis of behavior is concerned with the study of individuals. Working from this paradigm, the unit of measurement is a response class of an individual monitored over time. Single subject designs are employed to demonstrate a functional relationship. A class of procedures called "intrasubject replication designs" (Sidman, 1960) was developed by workers in the field. These designs schedule a replication of the independent variable on various dependent variables. The most common designs include the replication design, in which baseline and experimental performances are repeated, and designs for comparing the effects of two or more variables, or for comparing the effects across individuals and situations.

The designs originally used by Skinner and others working within the experimental analysis paradigms benefitted from considerable scientific visibility through the publication of Sidman's now classic *Tactics of Scientific Research* (1960). The text represented the first major work to outline research strategies within this approach. Since that time, many other texts describing single-subject

research methods have appeared (e.g., Barlow & Hersen, 1984; Hersen & Barlow, 1976; Johnston & Pennypacker, 1980; Kazdin, 1982; Kratochwill, 1978; Tawney & Gast, 1984).

Operant Conditioning

Skinner refined and elaborated the basic principles of operant conditioning and helped to elucidate the factors that contriubted to understanding the variables that influence the conditioning process. A discussion of operant responses and the principles of operant conditioning will illustrate how these areas set the stage for the development of applied behavior analysis and specific contributions to educational psychology.

Operant Responses. As noted above, Skinner focused his research on operant behavior, that is, behavior that operates directly on the environment. In his early research on free-operant responding, animals were placed in an experimental chamber equipped with a lever that could produce a consequence when pressed. Various schedules of reinforcement were then examined, and identical schedules were compared across different species. An important feature of the experimental work by Skinner and others was that operant responding involved not a single response but a class of functionally similar responses, that is to say, the data for analysis are the number of bar presses and not the almost infinite number of ways in which an animal can press the bar.

Principles of Operant Conditioning. Skinner articulated the principles of operant conditioning that described the relations between operant behavior and the functional environment, or the environment that affects it (e.g., Skinner, 1953a). Table 1 presents a summary of the basic principles of operant conditioning. It must be emphasized that these are the most basic principles, and that there are many other details (e.g., positive and negative reinforcement, schedules of reinforcement, etc.).

During the 1950s the basic principles of operant conditioning were being investigated in animal laboratories using mostly rats and pigeons. The generalizability of operant principles was first recognized at the conceptual, and later at the empirical level. Skinner extended his operant conditioning principles into a description of a utopian society in *Walden Two* (1948), to the operation of social institutions (government and law, religion, psychotherapy, economics, and education) in *Science and Human Behavior* (1953a), and to an anal-

Table 1. Summary of Basic Principles of Operant Conditioning

Principle	Characteristic procedure or operation	Effect on behavior
Reinforcement	Presentation or removal of an event after a response	Increases the frequency of the response
Punishment	Presentation or removal of an event after a response	Decreases the frequency of the response
Extinction	Ceasing presentation of a reinforcing event after a response	Decreases the frequency of the previously reinforced response
Stimulus control and discrimination training	Reinforcing the response in the presence of one stimulus (S_D) but not in the presence of another (S^Δ)	Increases the frequency of the response in the present of the S_D and decreases the frequency of the response in the presence of the S^Δ

Source: Adapted from Kazdin, A. E. (1978). *History of behavior modification: Experimental foundations of contemporary research* (p. 100). Baltimore, MD: University Park Press.

ysis of language behavior in *Verbal Behavior* (1957). Likewise, Keller and Schoenfeld (1950) indicated that operant principles were soon to contribute greatly to the scientific understanding of human behavior.

We now turn our attention to some of the early developments in the extension of operant conditioning to human behavior in psychology and education.

Development of Applied Behavior Analysis

During the 1950s, behavioral research began to take on a definite, applied bent: humans were included as subjects, socially meaningful responses were studied, and much discussion ensued regarding the practical significance of the experimental results. Understandably, this early work was tinged with a laboratory flavor because the techniques of the laboratory were used to control independent variables and to measure dependent variables.

The expansion of operant research, made practical application of operant principles inevitable, not only in the United States but in other countries as well. This work was later to be incorporated within the rubric of behavior modification. Dissatisfied with psychoanalysis and the treatment approaches associated with that school, Joseph Wolpe and his co-workers in South Africa were beginning treatment research on adult psychopathology based on the Hullian model of learning theory. At approximately the same time, Hans J.

Eysenck and his associates in the Maudsley Hospital in London, England, also began a similar Hullian-type research program applying learning principles to the treatment of disturbed (neurotic) adults. These investigators likewise rejected psychoanalysis as a treatment approach and like the South African group, embraced Hull's learning theory. The rejection of psychoanalysis, as well as the disease model and associated constructs, represented a common theme in the development of behavior therapy and behavior modification, including the then relatively newly emerging field of applied behavior analysis (Kazdin, 1979).

The extension of operant research to psychopathology in adults included work by Skinner and O. R. Lindsley (e.g., Lindsley, 1960; Skinner, 1954a; Skinner, Solomon, & Lindsley, 1953; Skinner, Solomon, Lindsley, & Richards, 1954). Although these contributions to the field were of great significance, our emphasis here is the application of behavior principles to educational settings. (The interested reader may wish to read Kazdin, 1978, for an overview of the early applications of applied behavior analysis to mental health and psychotherapy.)

Teaching Machines and Programmed Instruction

Whereas Sidney J. Pressey (1926, 1927) is generally credited with introducing the teaching machine, it was Skinner who stimulated interest in the use of programming devices for educational purposes. Skinner had already presented possible applications of operant conditioning principles for use in education (Skinner, 1953a), but his *Harvard Educational Review* article entitled "The Science of Learning and the Art of Teaching" (1954b), was more explicit and described how operant principles could be used for instructional purposes. Skinner noted at the time that traditional teaching strategies provide aversive rather than positive consequences for learning and fail to sequence curriculum material so as to maximize learning.

As an alternative to traditional teaching procedures, Skinner (1954b) recommended that teaching machines be used to individualize instruction, including the arrangement of the curriculum materials and contingencies surrounding learning. In effect, instruction could be programmed by taking into account the following considerations (Ausubel & Robinson, 1969, p. 325–326):

(a) The instructional goal would be defined in concrete behavioral terms.
(b) The task to be learned would be broken down into a smaller number of subtasks.
(c) Each frame or item of the program would require the student to make an observable response.
(d) The student would be provided immediate feedback.

Although teaching machines and programmed instruction became active areas of research (e.g., the *Journal of Programmed Instruction* was founded in 1962) and an increasing number of edited volumes were devoted to work in the area (e.g., Lumsdaine & Glaser, 1960, 1965), most of the research eventually was carried on outside the scope of the operant paradigm. Nevertheless, the concept has continued throughout Skinner's writings on American education. In a recent *American Psychologist* article, Skinner (1984) presented his views under the title, "The Shame of American Education." His proposed solutions will be familiar to those who are acquainted with Skinner's early work on teaching machines and programmed instruction. Among the solutions (e.g., "Be clear what is to be taught," "Teach first things first," and "Stop making all students advance at the same rate", pp. 950–951), Skinner (1984) recommended the following:

Program the subject matter. The heart of the teaching machine, call it what you will, is the programming of instruction—an advance not mentioned in any of the reports I have cited. Standard texts are designed to be read by the student, who will then discuss what they say with a teacher or take a test to see how much has been learned. Material prepared for individual study is different. It first induces students to say or do the things they are to learn to say or do. Their behavior is thus "primed" in the

sense of being brought out for the first time. Until the behavior has acquired more strength, it may need to be prompted. Primes and prompts must then be carefully "vanished" until the behavior occurs without help. At that point the reinforcing consequences of being right are most effective in building and sustaining an enduring repertoire. (p. 951)

Skinner (1984) suggests that most current problems in education could be solved if students had the opportunity to learn twice as much in the same time frame with the same degree of effort. Commenting on the country's unhappy state over education he writes:

Everyone is unhappy about education, but what is wrong? Let us look at a series of questions and answers rather like the series of propositions that logicians call a *sorites*:
1. Are students at fault when they do not learn? No, they have not been well taught.
2. Are teachers then at fault? No, they have not been properly taught to teach.
3. Are schools of education and teacher's colleges then at fault? No, they have not been given a theory of behavior that leads to effective teaching.
4. Are behavioral sciences then at fault? No, a culture too strongly committed to the view that a technology of behavior is a threat to freedom and dignity is not supporting the right behavioral sciences.
5. Is our culture then at fault? But what is the next step? Let us review the sorites again and ask what can be done. Shall we:
1. Punish students who do not learn by flunking them?
2. Punish teachers who do not teach well by discharging them?
3. Punish schools of education which do not teach teaching well by disbanding them?
4. Punish behavioral science by refusing to support it?
5. Punish the culture that refuses to support behavioral science? But you cannot punish a culture. A culture is punished by its failure or by other cultures which take its place in a continually evolving process. (p. 953)

Operant Conditioning with Children

Sidney W. Bijou. At approximately the same time that Skinner and Lindsley were involved in operant research on adult psychiatric individuals, Bijou was applying operant principles in the study of children. Because we were both at the same university several years ago, the first author availed himself of the opportunity and pleasure of conducting an interview with the second author. When we were invited to write this chapter, we decided to include the interview so that readers could have an upclose and personal perspective of the field of behavior modification. The following section is that interview with Bijou, updated somewhat, which took place on April 12, 1979 at the University of Arizona, Tucson, Arizona.

DR. KRATOCHWILL: Sid, I'd like to thank you for sharing your thoughts about behavioral psychology. There is a variety of theories of child development which have evolved over the years. Your work has been affiliated with the behavioral model. How does this approach to child development differ from another major theoretical approach, the cognitive position?

DR. BIJOU: The main difference between the behavioral and the cognitive approach to child development is in the definition of the subject matter. In the behavioral approach, the subject matter is the interaction between a total functioning individual and the environment, with all terms functionally and reciprocally defined. Human development, from this perspective, consists of progressive changes in the relationships between a biologically maturing individual and the successive social, physical, and organismic environment. In the cognitive approach, the focus is on the progressive changes in some mental construct. Changes in behavior–environment interactions are observed and measured in research only insofar as they throw light on the nature of inner, hypothetical events. In sum, the behavioral approach eschews nonobservable hypothetical concepts; the cognitive approach embraces them as the essence for study. This distinction often leads to the erroneous conclusion that behaviorists are not interested in that part of a human interaction that is not observable. Behaviorists are interested in all aspects of an individual's psychological life but study them by objective means and in terms of empirically derived constructs.

DR. KRATOCHWILL: What would be an example of a hypothetical construct in a cognitive position and how would that contrast with the behavioral approach that you're talking about?

DR. BIJOU: Cognitive structures, cognitive processes, and information processing are some well-known examples of hypothetical constructs. Such concepts are created to account for perceiving, thinking, knowing, remembering, feeling, and so on. In contrast, the behavioral perspective demands that interactions involving the behavior of an individual, the current stimulus situation, and the setting conditions (context) all be functionally and reciprocally defined. More specifically, the way a person behaves in a specific situation is a function of his or her history of interactions in similar situations and the current stimulus conditions. Take thinking as an example. To cognitivists, thinking involves hypothetical cognitive processes (sometimes fictitiously linked with brain activity) which in some way bring together past experiences and the demands of the current situation. To behaviorists, thinking is a series of interactions between implicit responses and substitute stimuli, beginning and ending in a situation that requires thinking behavior as part of an adjustive response. In other words, thinking generates from a situation in which an individual cannot make an adjustive response without first engaging in certain precurrent activities such as rearranging the context of the problem.

DR. KRATOCHWILL: Sid, what is the functional analysis of child behavior and development? Could you elaborate on what that means in contemporary behavioral psychology?

DR. BIJOU: The best description of a functional analysis of child behavior and development that I know of appears in a paperback book I wrote with Don Baer, *Behavior analysis of child development*, published by Prentice Hall in 1978. In essence, the view is that psychological behavior evolves from interactions between the behavior of an individual and the environment. Hence, a child's development depends on the specific ways in which past and present events transform him or her from a state of complete helplessness into one of relative independence. In behavior analysis, the child is conceptualized as a unique biological structure having the capacity for activities characteristic of his or her specie, including linguistic behavior, who is always in a symbiotic relationship with stimuli that constitute his or her environment. The environment is conceptualized functionally as internal and external stimuli and setting conditions that interact with an individual. The unit of study is not the child, but the child in interaction with the environment.

A child is genetically endowed to make adjustments both to situations that involve the pairing of antecedent stimuli (respondent interactions) and the pairing of behavior and consequent stimuli (operant interactions). Principles derived from research are used to account for how a child acquires, maintains, and generalizes simple (fear of water) and complex (creative behavior) respondent and operant capacities that make up his or her personality. Personality development goes through three stages: foundational, in which the motor and linguistic equipment is established; basic, in which the fundamentals of the personality are laid down; and societal, in which patterns of general social behavior are incorporated into the personality of the individual. As you can see, the functional analysis of child development concerns itself thoroughly and completely with the behavior of individuals in interactions with his or her environment. It is the psychology of the individual.

DR. KRATOCHWILL: Sid, you first came into contact with B. F. Skinner at the University of Minnesota in 1940 and again with him in 1946 at Indiana University. How did Skinner influence your thinking and what effect did this have on your own personal work?

DR. BIJOU: My first contact with Skinner was during a visit to his laboratory at the University of Minnesota in 1940 when he was studying the behavior of rats. At the time, I was a graduate student of Kenneth Spence's at the University of Iowa and my purpose in going to Minnesota was to see the apparatus that Stuart Cook had used to study experimental neurosis in rats. I was interested in Cook's procedure and findings as background material for a doctoral study I was about to launch on the role of conflict in producing experimental neurosis in rats, using the Pavlovian model of constraining the animal to a fixed position.

So I decided that while I was at Minnesota, I'd stop in to see Skinner and learn something about his research. I was particularly curious because in Spence's learning and conditioning course I learned that Skinner, one of the neobehaviorists, had been using nontraditional learning terms such as respondent and operant conditioning, and was presenting his data, not on graphs with discrete points, but on graphs with cumulated values and pips to indicate reinforcements.

When I got to his laboratory, I was amazed to see that his apparatus was entirely mechanized. He had a large number of rats, each responding separately in his own experimental chamber. Bar-pressing responses were mechanically recorded so that means and central tendencies were automatically shown on a large display. My amazement stemmed from the fact that at Iowa the faculty and graduate students were conducting animal studies on small groups of subjects (Lindquist's influence) and time and errors were taken on each animal's performance in a variety of large and cumbersome mazes.

In 1945, Skinner went to Indiana University as chairman of the department of psychology. Soon after, at the recommendation of Kenneth Spence, Skinner invited me to head up the newly formed clinical program. He wanted someone with both clinical and experimental training who would be willing to emphasize in the training program experimental psychopathology rather than psychometrics, projective tests, and psychoanalysis. We were successful in instituting a graduate program in psychopathology with an experimental orientation, despite the fact that the clinic staff had a traditional clinical bent.

Although I worked in the clinical setup, I continued my research on experimental neurosis and extended it to include problems of conflict in accordance with Neal Miller's model of approach and avoidance gradients. Skinner, too, continued his research, working with graduate students among whom were Norman Guttman and William Estes. Skinner was now studying the behavior of individual animals. His apparatus was equipped with circuitry systems to present and withdraw antecedent and consequent stimuli and to record bar presses on cumulative, ink-on-paper recorders.

Skinner never directly attempted to influence my research. When I commented one day that I wasn't getting the results I had anticipated, he merely remarked with a smile that "the animal is always right."

At one time at Indiana, Skinner and Kantor presented jointly a lively and memorable seminar. There was also a graduate student and faculty seminar on the views of Skinner, Kantor, and Hull. Having been trained by Spence, I of course sided with the Hullians and had great fun ridiculing the inductive approach to theory construction. However, Kantor, with his probing questions about the place of physicalism, reductionism, and hypothetical constructs in behavior theory, began to plant seeds of doubt about the efficacy of Hull's approach to a science of psychology.

In 1947, I left Indiana to go to the University of Washington as Director of the Institute of Child Development, and Skinner left for Harvard. Now I had an opportunity to establish a research program with children and began by studying children in doll play situations, as did Robert Sears, one of Hull's outstanding students. The procedure consisted of placing a preschool child in a playroom with a family constellation of dolls and doll furniture, and an observer recording the child's interactions with the pieces. Data were analyzed in terms of the child's actions toward the dolls and doll furniture and interpreted in psychoanalytic concepts of personality traits, needs, and like. There was no control over the stimuli to which the child was exposed since he or she could do as each pleased with the material; there was no objective recording of the child's responses; and the interpretation of findings was based on concepts far removed from the interactions observed.

Having come from several years of experience in laboratory research with infrahuman subjects, I was terribly disillusioned about the possibility of doing sound research in child development based on the Sears' conception of applying Hull's system to the study of children's behavior.

At that point, I decided to study child behavior in the mode of operant research with infrahuman subjects. To do this, I had to be fully acquainted with Skinner's approach. Fortunately, his *Science and human behavior* (1953) had just become available to help me with that task. I devised an apparatus that automatically presented antecedent (lights and sounds) and consequent stimuli (trinkets or goodies) and tallied responses (dropping a ball, pressing a lever, or pushing a button) on a Gerbrand cumulative recorder so that I could study simple schedules of reinforcement which had close relationships with the then current research in animal operant laboratories. I also equipped a traveling laboratory (a reconstructed mobile home) so that I could have the same space and equipment for all the research, whether conducted at the Institute or at several other nursery schools in Seattle.

So you see that Skinner's influence was not so much personal and direct as that my acquaintance with him and his work at Indiana pointed the way to a new direction in research with children. I must also credit Spence for training me as an experimental psychologist, and Kantor for helping me to evaluate Hull's hypothetical approach to theory construction.

DR. KRATOCHWILL: Despite the fact that behavior modification has made a tremendous impact on psychological and educational practice, some individuals have been critical of its influence. For example, some people note that behavior modification is too powerful, some say its too mechanistic and antihumanistic, and there are even some who say that it's too simplistic in accounting for the richness of human performance and behavior. What are your thoughts on some of these issues?

DR. BIJOU: There are indeed many critics of the behavioral approach. Let me deal with the criticisms you mentioned. The first—that behavior modification is too powerful—means to me that behavior modification techniques practiced by untrained people could produce harmful rather than beneficial results. This is a criticism not of the approach but of the laxity of governmental, professional, and educational agencies in setting inadequate standards for practitioners who hold themselves out as qualified to apply behavior principles. Applications of the principles of any branch of the natural sciences have often led to abuses or self-serving ends by untrained and unethical persons. Society seeks to reduce or eliminate instances of malpractice by establishing qualification standards. When requirements and standards are established for those wishing to apply behavior modification to educational or clinical settings, both the frequency of misuse and the frequency of criticisms will be reduced greatly.

The second criticism—behavior modification is mechanistic and antihumanistic—denotes a misunderstanding of the nature of contemporary behaviorism. Watsonian or classical behaviorism certainly is mechanistic, with its concept of the passive individual and active environment and the telephone switchboard metaphor. Contemporary cognitive psychology is also mechanistic in that the human being is viewed as a computer with stimulus input, throughput (information processing), and response output. But behavior modification is not based on a mechanistic model; it is based on a functional, reciprocally related, interactional model. That is to say, behavior is analyzed in terms of a person's interactional history and the current situation. The environment can only be understood in terms of his or her past interactions under similar circumstances. Modern behaviorism views both the person and the environment as being active from prenatal viability to death.

The antihumanistic criticism is no doubt voiced by those who misperceive the nature of the natural sciences and their application. They seem to believe that behavioral educators and mental health practitioners are more intent on furthering the science of psychology than on enhancing the education, development, and welfare of pupils and clients. This is an erroneous conception. The only objective of the well-trained and ethical practitioner is to blend his or her knowledge of behavior principles and an existing situation so as to help an individual learn and develop. Behind the practicing behaviorists, working in universities, institutes, and laboratories are two groups of researchers: those interested in applying well-documented behavioral principles to practical, everyday problems, and those seeking new knowledge about the nature of psychological interactions.

DR. KRATOCHWILL: I have one final question. What are some of your thoughts on the future development of behavioral psychology? What is the outlook?

DR. BIJOU: I believe that behavioral psychology, as an integral part of psychology, will expand and change in accordance with findings in research and reevaluations of its basic assumptions, that is, its philosophy. During the past 65 years, its growth has been marked by vicissitudes. High points have been associated with Watson, Hull, and Skinner: low points with the surge of other views of psychology as science, such as those of Freud, Rogers, Lewin, Piaget, Maslow, and Bruner.

It's my belief that behavioral psychology is destined to have a long and fruitful life because its concepts and principles are made up of empirically established behavior–environment relationships that have evolved gradually and carefully through laboratory research throughout its history. When these concepts and principles are properly applied to practical problems, they have worked, the reason being that they are, after all, replications of demonstrated natural phenomena.

I further believe that the kinds of problems that are studied in the future will shift. Basic behavioral research to date has emphasized relationships that have direct effects on the environment, such as operant behavior. Although behaviorists will continue to work on these relationships, they will devote more attention to language behavior, which I consider to be the key to understanding much of human behavior. This trend is already underway. Investigators will probably also focus more on long-range interactions involving cognitive or knowing behavior, thinking and creative behavior, and feeling reactions. There is reason to expect that applied behavioral research in the future will be more concerned with complex educational and social treatment programs, with the processes in self-control, and with the role of feelings, attitudes, and knowledge on effective behavior.

I'm confident that those who anticipate that behaviorism will soon pass as another fad in psychology will be disappointed. Judging from the trends in the history of modern psychology, behavioral psychology is very likely to remain as that part of psychology that is concerned with a natural science approach to the understanding of the individual.

DR. KRATOCHWILL: Thank you, Sid.

Extensions of Applied Behavior Analysis to Educational Settings

In the late 1950s and 1960s a number of operant researchers extended their work to applied settings with an emphasis on the clinical treatment of disturbed children and adults. Although this early work unquestionly greatly influenced educational psychology and, specifically, treatment approaches in school psychology, we do not include these extensive contributions here because they have been covered adequately elsewhere (See Kazdin, 1978, 1982 for a review.) We focus, rather, on the application of behavioral principles to specific educational concerns.

During this period Bijou was working with normal and retarded children at the Institute of Child Development at the University of Washington. In collaboration with Bijou, Donald M. Baer began research with children on imitation and a number of contingencies including punishment, escape, and avoidance using simple responses such as bar pressing. Baer (1962) also extended this basic work to an analysis of thumb sucking in five-year-old children.

At Arizona State University in the early 1960s Arthur W. Staats demonstrated that operant principles could be applied to clinical and educational problems. Although he was interested primarily in the application of behavior principles with psychiatric clients, he also did research on teaching reading to young children. In laboratory settings, Staats conducted a series of investigations in which marbles, as generalized conditioned reinforcers (tokens), were delivered contingent upon correct reading responses. Later, the marbles were exchanged for toys, pennies, edibles, and the like. In an extended series of investigations that included normal, retarded, culturally deprived, and disturbed children, Staats showed that by using behavioral techniques, various academic skills (e.g., reading, writing, arithmetic) could be improved (e.g., Staats, 1968, Staats & Butterfield, 1965; Staats, Staats, Schulz, Wolf, 1962; Staats, Minke, Finley, Wolf, & Brooks, 1964; Staats, Minke, Goodwin, & Lindeen, 1967; Staats, Minke, & Butts, 1970).

As Bijou continued his laboratory research with normal and retarded children, he realized that an experimental classroom at the Rainer School, a state residential school for handicapped clients, would be an excellent setting in which to study ways of improving the reading, writing, and arith-

metic of retarded children. He proceeded to establish an experimental classroom at the school, and asked Montrose M. Wolf, who had worked with Staats at Arizona State University and was now (1962) a member of the Institute staff, to work with him on this special project. A token system of reinforcement was set up in which the tokens were check marks that could be traded for activities, money, prizes, and edibles. Jay C. Birnbrauer, who received behavioral training at Indiana University established carefully graded programs in reading, writing, and arithmetic. Research at the school indicated that academic tool subjects, as well as social behavior, could be greatly improved through effective programming, systematic monitoring of progress and a token reinforcement system (Bijou, Birnbrauer, Kidder, & Tague, 1966; Birnbrauer, Bijou, Wolf, & Kidder, 1965). Meanwhile, at the University of Washington, research was underway on developing social skills and decreasing problem behaviors, such as aggressiveness, shyness, operant crying, etc. (e.g., Harris, Johnston, Kelly, & Wolf, 1964; Harris, Wolf, & Baer, 1964; Hart, Allan, Buell, Harris, & Wolf, 1964; Johnston, Kelly, Harris, & Wolf, 1966; Sloane, Johnston, & Bijou, 1967). These wide-ranging efforts, combined with other work by these investigators, established the basis for an effective technology for teaching and treating young handicapped children.

In 1965 Bijou left the University of Washington to join the psychology faculty at the University of Illinois at Urbana-Champaign, where he established the Child Behavior Laboratory to continue his research with exceptional children. Wesley Becker, whose interest lay in the application of operant techniques in classroom settings, was also at Illinois at the time. Becker and his students later demonstrated that praise, tokens, and other interventions could be readily applied to managing the behavior of children in the classroom (Becker, Madsen, Arnold, & Thomas, 1967).

At the same time that Bijou went to the University of Illinois, Baer moved to the University of Kansas, where he was instrumental in recruiting other behavioral researchers. Among whom were Montrose M. Wolf, Todd R. Risley, James A. Sherman, Barbara C. Etzel, and Judith M. Le Blanc. Others who eventually joined the faculty include Vance Hall, Betty Hart, William Hopkins, Keith Miller, Donald Bushell, and K. Eileen Allen.

With this staff, all of whom had at one time been

associated with the University of Washington, he was successful in establishing what has become one of the outstanding centers for research in applied behavior analysis.

Professional Developments in Behaviorism

A clearer picture of the growing influence of behaviorism is reflected in the professional developments that occurred in the field. Of utmost importance was the emergence of associations to bring together individuals interested in basic and applied behavioral research that lent momentum to the advancement of the behavioral approach.

Developments in Basic Research

In the 1940s a small group of faculty and students from Columbia and Indiana Universities, spearheaded by Keller, Skinner, and others, met occasionally to discuss topics regarding the experimental analysis of behavior. A more formal meeting of the expanding membership was held at Indiana University in 1946, and subsequently, meetings were held annually in conjunction with meetings of the American Psychological Association (APA).

Initially, this group affiliated with the APA Division of Experimental Psychology (Division 3) where operant conditioning represented a subinterest in the larger domain of experimental psychology. In 1964, in order to have more presentation time in the APA annual program and to have a voice in the APA Council of Representatives, they formed their own division, the Division of the Experimental Analysis of Behavior (Division 25).

Representation in the APA was only one area of concern in the broader context of the psychological political arena. As research on operant conditioning proliferated during the 1950s, it became apparent that publication outlets were limited. Researchers encountered difficulty in getting articles published because their research did not fit into the mainstream of experimental investigation, which was characterized by group designs, large samples, and reliance on statistical analysis. In contrast, operant researchers relied on single subject designs, ($n = 1$) with a limited number of subjects for replications, and visual analysis of graphic displays. To provide a publication outlet, leaders in the field formed the Society for the Experimental Analysis of Behavior (SEAB), which began pub-

lication of the *Journal of the Experimental Analysis of Behavior* (JEAB) in 1958, with Charles B. Ferster as the first editor.

Developments in Applied Research

The extension of operant research into applied areas led to a need for another kind of journal because JEAB was concerned primarily with publishing reports of basic animal research. In 1968, 10 years after the founding of JEAB, the society established the *Journal of Applied Behavior Analysis* (JABA) as a publication outlet for applied research. Montrose M. Wolf was its first editor and Donald M. Baer was the associate editor. Although many other journals now publish this type of research, JABA has remained the primary publication outlet. On its masthead was the following:

The Journal of Applied Behavior Analysis is primarily for the original publication of reports of experimental research involving applications of the analysis of behavior to problems of social importance. It will also publish technical articles relevant to such research and discussion of issues arising from behavioral applications. (JABA, 1968, p. i)

In a feature article in JABA's first issue, Baer, Wolf, and Risley (1968) elucidated how applied behavior analysis differed from the more traditional experimental analysis of behavior. They stated:

Thus, the evaluation of a study which purports to be an applied behavior analysis is somewhat different than the evaluation of a similar laboratory analysis. Obviously, the study must be *applied, behavioral,* and *analytic;* in addition, it should be *technological, conceptually systematic,* and *effective,* and it should display some generality. (p. 92)

Spread of Behavior Modification Organizations

Behavior modification began to expand in scope during the 1960s and 1970s. Interest groups representing different areas of research, focus, and orientation formed three major organizations: the Association for the Advancement of Behavior Therapy (AABT),[3] the Behavior Therapy and Research Society (BTRS), and the Midwestern Association of Behavior Analysis (MABA), which subsequently became the Association for Behavior Analysis (ABA), An International Organization.

The AABT was formed in 1966 as a multi-

---

[3]The original name was Association for Advancement of Behavior Therapies, but this was changed to ''Therapy'' in 1969.

disciplinary group to represent the research and practice interests of behavior therapists. After a few years of publishing a newsletter, a journal, *Behavior Therapy,* was started, although it still puts out its newsletter, *The Behavior Therapist,* which also includes a few empirical studies and conceptual pieces. Here again, the group initially held annual meetings in conjunction with APA, but now holds an independent national meeting, and occasionally a special international meeting.

In 1970, in order to organize a professional group of behavior therapists, Joseph Wolpe formed the BTRS, which promotes research on behavior therapy and fosters information exchange through *The Journal of Behavior Therapy and Experimental Psychiatry.* Wolpe serves as the editor, and L. J. Reyna as associate editor of this interdisciplinary journal. The society meets in conjunction with the annual convention of American Psychiatric Association.

Table 2. Major Conferences in the United States on Behavior Modification

Conferences	Date of inception/state
Association for Advancement of Behavior Therapy (originally held in conjunction with APA annual meeting)	(1968)
Conference on Behavior Analysis in Education	(1968, KS)
Southern California Conference on Behavior Modification	(1969, CA)
Brockton Symposium on Behavior Modification	(1971, MA)
National Behavior Modification Conference	(1971, CO)
National Conference on Behavior Research and Technology in Higher Education	(1973, GA)
Temple University Conference on Behavior Therapy and Behavior Modification	(1974, PA)
Drake Conference on Professional Issues in Behavior Analysis	(1974, IA)
Midwestern Association of Behavior Analysis in 1978 became the Association for Behavior Analysis	(1974, IL)

Source: Adapted from Kazdin (1978, p. 199).

Table 3. International Conferences on Behavior Modification

Conference	Date of inception/location
Banff/International Conference	(1969, Alberta, Canada)
Annual International Symposium on Behavior Modification	(1970, Mexico)
Conference on Behavior Modification	(1970, New Brunswick, Canada)
European Conference on Behavior Modification	(1971)
Latin American Congress on Behavior Analysis	(1973, Mexico)
Mexican Congress on Behavior Analysis	(1974, Mexico)
International Symposium of Applied Behavior Analysis	(1981, Mexico City)

Source: Adapted from Kazdin (1978, p. 200).

The MABA, organized in 1974 as a protest against the limited time that the Midwestern Psychological Association (MPA) allowed for single subject research reports, originally met at the time of MPA conventions. In 1978, MABA changed its name to the Association for Behavior Analysis to indicate its national and international character, began to publish the *Behavior Analyst,* and holds independent annual meetings in various parts of the country.

Because of these and other organizational developments, a growing number of behavioral-type conferences and conventions now take place both in the United States and around the world. Table 2 lists some of those originating and held in the United States over the past 15 years. Among behavior modification groups and societies in existence abroad are those in England, France, West Germany, The Netherlands, Sweden, Israel, Japan, Italy, Mexico, Peru, Australia, Venezuela, Uruguay, Belgium, and South Africa. Conferences have taken place in a number of these and other countries (see Table 3). As behavior modification grew in popularity, journals devoted to the publication of research and theory proliferated. Table 4 displays a chronological listing. It should be emphasized that this list represents only the major

Table 4. Major Journals Devoted to Publishing Papers on Research and Theory in Behavior Modification

Journal	Date of inception
Journal of the Experimental Analysis of Behavior (Basic Research)	1958
Behavior Research and Therapy	1963
Journal of Applied Behavior Analysis	1968
Behavior Therapy	1970
Journal of Behavior Therapy and Experimental Psychiatry	1970
Behaviorism	1972
Journal of Personalized Instruction	1976
Behavior Modification	1977
The Behavior Analyst	1977
Education and Treatment of Children	1977
Behavior Analysis Newsletters: An International Journal	1981

journals. Many other journals in psychology and education publish original research and/or conceptual papers in behavior modification.

Concluding Perspectives

The Impact of Behaviorism

To summarize the contributions of behaviorism to educational psychology is difficult for several reasons. To begin with, the movement has been intertwined with other movements and developments in psychology and education (Travers, 1983). For example, Skinner has had a great impact on the programmed instruction movement, but this area has also developed within education somewhat independently of its historical roots and is usually not viewed as a part of contemporary behavior modification (Lumsdaine & Glaser, 1960). Similarly, many behavior management and consultation strategies used in educational settings represent a hybrid combination of behavioral and other techniques that are not part of the behavioral approach.

Second, it is useful to distinguish behaviorism as a scientific and technological discipline from the dissemination and applications of the research and technology. Kazdin (1981a) notes:

Within the scientific and technological discipline, several questions remain to be investigated to increase the overall understanding of existing practices and to extend their effectiveness. However, even at this point in time, remarkable advances have been achieved in identifying techniques and applications that improve student and teacher behaviors. A major limitation in applying behavior modification in education pertains to dissemination and extension of the existing techniques to a large number of settings likely to profit from their use. The dissemination and implementation problems pertain to the social and political action that is required following development of an effective technology. As yet, behavioral techniques have not been implemented on a large scale outside of the context of research programs, even though applications have strongly attested to their efficacy. . . . Hence, although major questions remain within the field of behavior modification, perhaps even larger questions exist for society at large regarding the failure to act on existing advances. (p. 52)

Some individuals have pointed to a number of dimensions of the impact of behaviorism, but imply that these impacts have been largely negative. While acknowledging the merits of precise, functional definitions for education, Travers (1983) has noted that the type of specification associated with the approach often led to ludicrous applications. Moreover, he noted that reinforcement was used in ways that grossly oversimplified actual situations (e.g., picking children up when they cry may reduce crying rather than increase crying, as might be expected from the operant paradigm).

The superficial application of behavioral principles has also been used to illustrate the limitations of behavior analysis in general. For example, Farnham-Diggory (1981), responding to Kazdin's (1981a) review of the contributions of behavior modification to education, pointed to several personal anecdotes where misguided or incomplete applications were apparent. Farnham-Diggory (1981) argued that behavioral technology lends itself to serious abuse in the educational field.

I am left with this question, then: Why are behavior modifiers unwilling or unable to do the rigorous homework demanded by their own system? What reinforcements are shaping up a preference for easy facsimiles and for superficial analytical strategies? Is it better to give the *appearance* of being a hard scientist than to do the work of actually becoming one? Why is it better? Are the people who are attracted to the behavior modification field just a little lazier, or a little less bright than the people attracted to hard science? Or are they mostly interested in management, period—in getting control over children for sheer power's sake? If they really want to help children learn, then why are they so quick to avoid the hard work of understanding what learning—especially their own learning—really involves? (p. 59–60)

In a rejoinder, Kazdin (1981b) raised the issue of whether or not certain ''applications'' of classroom management techniques noted by Farnham-Diggory can be called behavior modification. More importantly, Kazdin drew attention to the potential abuse that surrounds any approach used in educational settings and the criteria that might be invoked to evaluate interventions, behavioral or otherwise. The views held by Travers and Farnham-Diggory confuse philosophical issues, basic and applied research, and applications.

It must be remembered that positive and negative contingencies were used in education long before behavior modification emerged as a major movement (Kazdin, 1978, 1981a; Ulman & Klem, 1975). In fact, one of the contributions of applied behavior analysts has been to refine application of contingencies and to evaluate systematically various teaching techniques and procedures (Bijou, 1985).

Applications

The applications of behavior modification to education are extensive and have been reviewed in detail elsewhere (e.g., Bijou & Ruiz, 1981; Catania & Brigham, 1978; Etzel, LeBlanc, & Baer, 1977; Kazdin, 1977, 1978, 1980, 1981a; Klein, Hapkiewicz, & Roden, 1973). (Also, the reader is referred to Williams, this volume, for an overview of current research in classroom behavior management.) Our purpose is not to duplicate this literature, but to provide a context from which behaviorism has evolved. We shall limit our discussion to the application of single concepts and principles to pupil achievement and adjustment, and to the application of multiple concepts and principles to whole areas of education. Finally, we present some examples of the application of behaviorism to educational psychology.

Applications of Single Concepts and Principles. Most of the attention in research and application of behavioral principles has been devoted to specific aspects of pupil learning and adjustment. Because a good share of the early experimental work was based on operant studies of infrahuman organisms, research has tended to focus on the conditions that follow specific behaviors, academic and social. Among the techniques investigated were positive reinforcement (e.g., praise, attention, privileges, feedback, tokens), punishment techniques (e.g., verbal reprimands, timeout, response cost, positive practice); self-control procedures (self-monitoring, self-reinforcement),

and group-based contingencies, peer reinforcement, and schedules of reinforcement, such as differential reinforcement of other behaviors and differential reinforcement of low and high rates of responding. These procedures have been used with various behaviors, including classroom management problems with normal children (Becker, Madsen, Arnold, & Thomas, 1967) as well as with a wide range of special education areas such as, mental retardation, emotional disturbance, learning disabilities, deaf, blind, and physically handicapped, autism, speech, and language problems (Kazdin & Craighead, 1973).

Although the subject of contingencies of reinforcement has received much attention, the conditions that precede academic and social behavior (e.g., sequencing of curriculum materials, providing instructions, and prompting correct responses) has been somewhat neglected. However, areas such as programmed instruction and teaching machines have been incorporated into a number of educational settings, as for example, the sequencing of elementary-level reading and arithmetic for exceptional children and programmed hierarchies for teaching mentally retarded children a variety of skills (e.g., self-help, language, gross and fine motor coordination, social behavior, preacademic and academic subjects, and occupational and vocational skills).

Application of Multiple Concepts and Principles to Areas of Education. Some educational programs have been based entirely on behavioral concepts and principles. These programs have dealt mainly with preschool education for handicapped children, elementary education for socially disadvantaged children, and teaching at the college level.

Preschool Education and Parent Training Programs. Research on educating young handicapped children has consisted of intervention in the preschool setting (centerbased) and in the home environment with the mother serving as the teacher or therapist (homebased).

In training children in skills and knowledge, the centerbased programs have emphasized the following (Bijou, 1985):

1. Criterion-referenced measures to determine entry levels for basic programs
2. Instructional programs focusing on a wide range of self-help, language, cognitive, and social skills
3. Behaviorally based teaching techniques

4. Development of measures for monitoring progress in instructional programs
5. Procedures for modifying or changing instructional programs and teaching procedures to maximize progress
6. Procedures for encouraging effective parental involvement

At the preschool level research has included all kinds of children: normal, mentally retarded, physically handicapped, and behavior disordered. In assessing the success of various programs, at least two factors have emerged that promote positive educational outcomes: parent participation, and individualization of instruction.

Research on home-based preschool education for handicapped children has produced parent training models that have been adapted widely in the United States and in several other countries including Canada, England, Peru, France, and Japan (Dangel & Polster, 1984). The Portage Project model developed by Shearer and Shearer (1972) is an example. Here, a trained teacher makes periodic visits (usually once a week) to the home of a preschool handicapped child and instructs the mother or father in ways that will enhance their child's development. Diagnostic evaluation by a criterion-referenced checklist is used to establish the beginning points in the instructional program (baseline). The teacher follows a curriculum guide that is implemented easily in graded tasks in motor, self-help, social, linguistic, and cognitive skills. He or she determines what tasks are to be taught and teaches the parent techniques to be used in the teaching process. The mother carries out the assignments and keeps records of the child's responses. Progress is measured by the number of units the child has mastered since the beginning of training. On the average, handicapped children participating in the program have been shown to make the kind of gains usually associated with normal rather than handicapped children (Revill & Blunder, 1979; Shearer & Shearer, 1976) and the parents tend to express satisfaction with their involvement (Reville & Blunder, 1977).

Programs for Socially Disadvantaged Children. In 1969, two large scale behavior modification programs, the Direct Instruction Model and the Behavior Analysis Model, were carried out with socially disadvantaged children as part of the Follow Through program sponsored by the United States Office of Education (Abt Associates, 1976, 1977). This project can be considered preventive in that the children participating were socially disadvantaged and were considered to be at high risk for school achievement (Jason, Durlak, & Holton-Walker, 1984). The Direct Instruction Model developed by Wesley C. Becker, Siegfried Engelmann, Douglas W. Carnine and others at the University of Oregon used a curriculum of graded sequences in reading, arithmetic, and language, that was taught under relatively standardized conditions. For example, children in groups of 5 to 10 were required to respond to questions and instructions in unison, with the teachers using prompts and reinforcers to help them to progress through the material. The curriculum, named DISTAR, involved a task analysis of specific skills and the teaching of these skills, with the ultimate objective of having the children learn the basic concepts in the tool subjects (Becker & Englemann, 1978a).

Although there is controversy surrounding the evaluation (cf. *Harvard Educational Review,* 1978), an assessment of all the teaching approaches at the end of third grade revealed that the Direct Instruction Model resulted in the greatest advances in academic skills and knowledge. In addition, the children scored higher on *cognitive* and *affective* tests than those participating in the other projects. Follow-up evaluations 2 years later, when the children reached the fifth and sixth grades, indicated that they continued to make satisfactory progress compared to the controls, but that their academic progress declined somewhat when compared to national norms (Becker & Engelmann, 1978). Becker and Gersten (1982) recommended that the Direct Instruction programs also be used with older children to facilitate academic progress.

The Behavior Analysis Model was based in large part on the work of Donald Bushell of the University of Kansas. Unlike the made-to-order Direct Instruction materials, the curriculum for the Behavior Analysis Model was pieced together from commercially prepared materials. This approach emphasized the role of contingencies of reinforcement in the teaching of basic academic skills. As an example, tokens earned were paired with praise, and could be exchanged for games, art projects, stories, playground activities, singing, and other academic activities (Bushell, 1978). Children were taught in small groups and academic progress was monitored through token earnings. Parents were encouraged to participate in the program by serving as teacher aides and were taught how to monitor child behavior and manage contingencies of reinforcement. An evaluation of the Behavior Analysis Model (see Bushell, 1978; Stallings, 1975) indicated that the children in the program were achieving at a much higher level than children in the regular school programs. Academic gains made by the children were still apparent 2 years after the program had ended, as were in the Direct Instruction Model.

Since the termination, psychologists and educators at the University of Oregon have developed new instructional materials and have refined the instructional procedures used in the Direct Instruction Model (Carnine & Silbert, 1979; Engelmann & Carnine, 1982; Silbert, Carnine, & Stein, 1981) and the Model is now being used in a variety of educational settings throughout the country. In 1974 the Oregon group established the Association for Direct Instruction, which publishes the *ADI News*.

Programs for Delinquent and Predelinquent Adolescents. Some large scale programs have focused on development of social and academic skills in delinquent and predelinquent adolescents. One such program called Achievement Place, was developed by Montrose M. Wolf and his associates (e.g., Fixsen, Phillips, & Wolf, 1972, 1973; Phillips, Fixen, & Wolf, 1972). The Achievement Place model is based on a program in which a small number of youths live in a home that is managed by "teaching parents". While a major focus of the program has been on the development of prosocial behavior, a substantial component relates to school attendance, homework grades, and related academic performance. Some studies have documented the effectiveness of the program on specific social and academic skills (e.g., Fixsen *et al.*, 1972, 1973; Kifer, Lewis, Green & Phillips, 1974; Minken *et al.*, 1976; Phillips *et al.*, 1971).

The program is based on a rather elaborate token/point program with a monitoring component. Each youth receives a card that includes a written specification of target behaviors, performance criteria, and exchange rate. Points are exchanged for various back up reinforcers and eventually are faded out.

College Teaching. Many of the applications of behavior modification to education have centered on children. Yet at least one rather unique application, termed the Personalized System of Instruction (PSI), focuses on college teaching. While at Columbia University, Fred S. Keller (1968) collaborated with J. Gilmour Sherman in the United States, and with Rodolfo Azzi and Carolina M.

Bori of Brazil, on research in college instruction at the University of Brasilia to develop the PSI approach.

PSI emphasizes teaching for mastery of subject matter rather than passing conventional essay or objective-type examinations. It is typical of traditional instruction in large college and university classes for students to listen to lectures and take examinations that are graded on the so-called curve. In contrast, the PSI presents carefully prepared assignments from standard textbooks or accompanying materials together with prepared supplements, study questions, instructions, and self-quizzes that the student completes at his or her own pace. When a student believes that he or she has mastered a unit of material he or she takes an examination, which is on a one-to-one basis and evaluated by a trained monitor. Each student progresses through the units of the course until the final objectives are mastered.

There are both small (Lloyd, 1978) and large scale applications of PSI (e.g., Elkins, 1975; Mallott, Hartlep, Keenan, & Michael, 1972; Pennypacker, Heckler, & Pennypacker, 1978). Students taking courses under the PSI system generally do well and often express a preference for it over traditional courses (e.g., Lloyd, 1978). Unfortunately, like some of the other methods and procedures discussed in this chapter, the PSI has not been adopted widely even though data strongly support its beneficial effects on learning (Sherman, 1981).

Example Applications to Educational Psychology. Several specific applications of behaviorism to educational psychology can be noted. To begin with, most master's and doctoral-level training programs include at least one course devoted to behavioral theory or application. In the latter case students often enroll in courses in which they receive training in behavior modification procedures for classroom management. In the former case students routinely take courses in learning theory. Both intermediate and advanced courses include sections devoted to behaviorism. Most introductory educational psychology texts include content that reviews theory and application of behavior analysis and at least one introductory text has been based in part on a behavioral approach (e.g., Lahey & Johnson, 1978).

A second, and related, example application of behaviorism to educational psychology occurs in courses offered to undergraduate students receiving their psychology training within educational psychology departments. Ash and Love-Clark (1985) conducted an historical analysis of the content of educational psychology textbooks from 1954–1983. Topics related to pragmatic concerns of teachers increased. For example, the topic "Classroom Management and Interaction" increased 75% from 1954–1964 and 1965–1975 and 100% from 1965–1975 to 1976–1983. Clearly, classroom management techniques and procedures extend beyond behavior modification; however, a major component of classroom management techniques involve or have evolved from applied behavior analysis. Recognition of the advances for practitioners that have occurred with behaviorism were noted by the ad hoc committee on the "Current Status and Future Directions of Educational Psychology as a Discipline" (Scandura *et al.*, 1978), and especially the principles of reinforcement.

Whereas considerable integration of behaviorism into preservice education has occurred within university and college environments, there has also been a clear development of behavioral techniques for school professionals. In fact, a rather large and growing research literature reveals that teachers have been trained successfully in a wide variety of behavior management skills as well as in the principles of behavior on which those techniques have been based (Allen & Forman, 1984; Anderson & Kratochwill, in press). Behavioral principles have been integrated into training packages used in these research studies.

Another major contribution of behaviorism to educational psychology and in particular, its closely affiliated disciplines of school psychology and special education, relates to advances in assessment of student behavior. Many traditional assessment practices involve a norm-referenced models in which individual student performance is compared to relative student performance in the norm group. In contrast, behavioral assessment involves a paradigm in which student performance is measured in absolute rather than relative terms and measurement occurs continuously throughout the assessment process (Cancelli & Kratochwill, 1981). The contributors of the behavioral assessment paradigm can be observed in numerous areas of special education, such as in work with learning disabled students (Ysseldyke & Thorlow, 1984) and severely handicapped learners (Strain, Sainto, & Maheady, 1984). Behavioral assessment also appears to be making a major impact on school psychology practice with the National Association of School Psychologists sponsoring a professional development publication devoted to behavioral assessment (Alessi & Kaye, 1983).

Another area of the impact of behaviorism on educational psychology is in the area of research methodology. As noted earlier in the chapter, a basic but not exclusive methodology of behaviorism involves single-case applied behavior analysis research design. Most introductory educational research textbooks now include a section devoted to single-case research designs. Perhaps the most significant contribution of this aspect of behavior analysis research methodology is the emphasis placed on replication during the research process (Shaver, 1979).

Summary

Behaviorism is a philosophy of science that holds that psychology is the study of individual behavior in interaction with the environment. Behavior analysis is linked to a philosophy that postulates that the subject matter of psychology is the continuous interaction between a behaving organism and physial and social observable objects and events. It is also a general theory that contains functionally defined laws. Its characteristic research methodology is a single-case research design. Finally, it has an explicit procedure for relating basic and applied research.

In the chapter we provided an overview of the philosophical, biological, and psysiological origins of behaviorism. Specifically, we reviewed the empiricist roots of behaviorism, the associationist school, conditioning research in Russia, learning research in the United States, and the neobehaviorists. We also traced the development of operant conditioning and research in the experimental analysis of behavior with a special emphasis on the contributions of B. F. Skinner. The characteristics of the experimental analysis of behavior and operant conditioning were described and we traced the development of applied behavior analysis. Within the professional arena, we also traced the developments in basic and applied research and documented the spread of behavior modification organizations.

In the final section of the chapter we presented our perspectives on the impact of behaviorism on educational psychology and reviewed some examples of applied applications of behavioral programs.

ACKNOWLEDGMENTS. The authors express their thanks to the editors, Elizabeth M. Goetz, and Maribeth Gettinger, for their thoughtful comments on the manuscript. The authors also express appreciation to Ms. Karen Kraemer for her assistance in word processing the manuscript.

References

Abt Associates. (1976). *Education as experimentation: A planned variation model* (Vol. III). Cambridge, MA: Author.

Abt Associates. (1977). *Education as experimentation: A planned variation model* (Vol. IV). Cambridge, MA: Author.

Alessi, G. J., & Kaye, J. H. (1983). *Behavior assessment for school psychologists*. Kent, OH: National Associates of School Psychologists.

Allen, C. T., & Forman, S. G. (1984). Efficacy of methods of training teachers in behavior modification. *School Psychology Review, 13,* 26–32.

Anderson, T. K., & Kratochwill, T. R. (in press). Dissemination of behavioral procedures in the schools: Issues in training. In J. C. Witt, S. N. Elliott, & F. M. Gresham (Eds.), *Handbook of behavior therapy in education*. New York: Plenum Press.

Ash, M. J., & Love-Clark, P. (1985). An historical analysis of the content of educational psychology textbooks: 1954–1983. *Educational Psychologist, 20,* 47–55.

Ausbel, D. P., & Robinson, F. G. (1969). *School learning*. New York: Holt, Rinehart & Winston.

Baer, D. M. (1962). Laboratory control of thumbsucking by withdrawal and representation of reinforcement. *Journal of the Experimental Analysis of Behavior, 5,* 525–528.

Baer, D. M., Wolf, M. M., & Risley, T. R. (1968). Some current dimensions of applied behavior analysis. *Journal of Applied Behavior Analysis, 1,* 91–97.

Barlow, D. H., & Hersen, M. (1984). *Single case experimental designs: Strategies for studying behavior change* (2nd ed.). New York: Pergamon Press.

Becker, W. C., & Carnine, D. W. (1980). Direct instruction: An effective approach to educational intervention with the disadvantaged and low performers. In B. B. Lahey & A. E. Kazdin (Eds.), *Advances in clinical child psychology* (Vol. 3, pp. 429–473). New York: Plenum Press.

Becker, W. C., & Englemann, S. (1978a). Systems for basic instruction: Theory and applications. In A. C. Catania & T. A. Brigham (Eds.), *Handbook of applied behavior analysis: Social and instructional processes* (pp. 325–377). New York: Irvington.

Becker, W. C., & Engelmann, S. (1978b). *Analysis of achievement data on six cohorts of low-income children from 20 school districts in the University of Oregon Direct Instruction Follow Through Model* (Technical Report 78-1). Eugene, OR: University of Oregon.

Becker, W. C., & Gersten, R. (1982). A follow-up of follow-through: The later effects of the direct instruction model on children in fifth and sixth grades. *American Educational Research Journal, 19,* 75–92.

Becker, W. C., Madsen, C. H., Jr., Arnold, C., & Thomas, D. R. (1967). The contingent use of teacher attention and praise in reducing classroom behavior problems. *Journal of Special Education, 1,* 287–307.

Bijou, S. W. (1979). Some clarifications on the meaning of a behavior analysis of child development. *The Psychological Record, 29,* 3–13.

Bijou, S. W. (1985). Behaviorism. In *International encyclopedia of education: Research and studies* (pp. 444–451). New York: Pergamon Press.

Bijou, S. W., & Baer, S. W. (1978). *Behavior analysis of child development*. Englewood Cliffs, NJ: Prentice Hall.

Bijou, S. W., Birnbrauer, J. S., Kidder, J. D., & Tague, C. (1966). Programmed instruction as an approach to the teaching of reading, writing, and arithmetic to retarded children. *Psychological Record, 16,* 505–522.

Bijou, S. W., & Ruiz, R. (Eds.). (1981). *Behavior modification: Contributions to education*. Hillsdale, NJ: Lawrence Erlbaum Association.

Birnbrauer, J. S., Bijou, S. W., Wolf, M. M., & Kidder, J. D. (1965). Programmed instruction in the classroom. In L. P. Ullmann & L. Krasner (Eds.), *Case studies in behavior modification* (pp. 358–363). New York: Holt, Rinehart, & Winston.

Bregman, E. O. (1934). An attempt to modify the emotional attitudes of infants by the conditioned response technique. *The Pedagogical Seminary and Journal of Genetic Psychology, 45,* 169–198.

Bushell, D., Jr. (1978). An engineering approach to the elementary classroom: The Behavior Analysis Follow Through Project. In A. C. Catania & T. A. Brigham (Eds.), *Handbook of applied behavior analysis: Social and instructional processes* (pp. 525–563). New York: Irvington.

Cancelli, A. A., & Kratochwill, T. R. (1981). Advances in criterion-referenced assessment. In T. R. Kratochwill (Ed.), *Advances in school psychology* (Vol. 1, pp. 217–254). Hillsdale, NJ: Erlbaum.

Carnine, D., & Silbert, J. (1979). *Direct instruction reading*. Columbus, OH: Merrill.

Catania, A. E., & Brigham, T. A. (Eds.). (1978). *Handbook of applied behavior analysis: Social and instructional processes*. New York: Irvington.

Dangel, R. F., & Polster, R. A. (Eds.) (1984). *Parent training: Foundations of research and practice*. New York: Guilford.

Deitz, S. M. (1982). Defining applied behavior analysis: An historical analogy. *The Behavior Analyst, 5,* 53–64.

Elkins, F. S. (1975). A description of a strategy for implementing a system approach to instruction on a campus-wide basis. In J. M. Johnston (Ed.), *Behavior research and technology in higher education*. Springfield, IL: Charles C Thomas.

Engelmann, S., & Carnine, D. (1982). *Theory of instruction: Principles and applications*. New York: Irvington Publishers, Inc.

English, H. B. (1929). The cases of the conditioned fear response. *Journal of Abnormal Social Psychology, 24,* 221–225.

Etzel, B. C., LeBlanc, J. M., & Baer, D. M. (Eds.). (1977). *New developments in behavioral research: Theory, method, and application. In honor of Sidney W. Bijou*. Hillsdale, NJ: Erlbaum.

Eysenck, H. J. (1979). The conditioning model of neurosis. *The Behavioral and Brain Sciences, 2,* 155–199.

Eysenck, H. J. (1982). Neobehavioristic (S–R) theory. In G. T. Wilson & C. M. Franks (Eds.), *Contemporary behavior therapy: Conceptual and empirical foundations* (pp. 205–276). New York: Guilford.

Fancher, R. E. (1979). *Pioneers of psychology.* New York: W. W. Norton.

Farnham-Diggory, S. (1981). But how do we shape up rigorous behavioral analysts? *Developmental Review, 1,* 58–60.

Fixsen, D. L., Phillips, E. L., & Wolf, M. M. (1972). Achievement place: The reliability of self-reporting and peer-reporting and their effects on behavior. *Journal of Applied Behavior Analysis, 5,* 19–30.

Fixsen, D. L., Phillips, E. L., & Wolf, M. M. (1973). Achievement place: Experiments in self-government with pre-delinquents. *Journal of Applied Behavior Analysis, 6,* 31–47.

Glaser, R. (1971). A criterion-referenced test. In W. J. Pophem (Ed.), *Criterion-referenced measurement: An introduction.* Englewood Cliffs, NJ: Educational Technology Publications. nology Publications.

Grinder, R. E. (1982). The "new" science of education: Educational psychology in search of mission. In F. H. Farley & U. J. Gordon (Eds.), *Psychology and education: The state of the union* (pp. 364–366). Berkely, CA: McCutchan.

Guthrie, E. R. (1952). *The psychology of learning* (rev. ed.), New York: Harper.

Harris, B. (1979). Whatever happened to Little Albert? *American Psychologist, 34,* 151–160.

Harris, F. R., Johnston, M. K., Kelley, C. S., & Wolf, M. M. (1964). Effects of positive social reinforcement on regressed crawling of a nursery school child. *Journal of Educational Psychology, 55,* 35–41.

Harris, F. R., Wolf, M. M., & Baer, D. M. (1964). Effects of adult social reinforcement on child behavior. *Young Children, 20,* 8–17.

Hart, B. M., Allen, K. E., Buell, J. S., Harris, F. R., & Wolf, M. M. (1964). Effects of social reinforcement on operant crying. *Journal of Experimental Child Psychology, 1,* 145–153.

Hersen, M., & Barlow, D. H. (1976). *Single case experimental designs: Strategies for studying behavior change.* New York: Pergamon Press.

Hull, C. L. (1951). *Essentials of behavior.* New Haven, CT: Yale University Press.

Jackson, P. W. (1981). The promise of educational psychology. In F. H. Farley & U. J. Gordon (Eds.), *Psychology and education: The state of the union* (pp. 389–405). Berkeley, CA: McCutchen.

Jason, L. A., Durlak, J. A., & Holton-Walker, E. (1984). *Prevention of child problems in the schools.* In M. C. Roberts & L. Peterson (Eds.), *Prevention of problems in childhood: Psychological research and applications* (pp. 311–341). New York: Wiley.

Johnston, J. M., & Pennypacker, H. S. (1980). *Strategies and tactics of human behavioral research.* Hillsdale, NJ: Erlbaum.

Johnston, M. K., Kelley, C. S., Harris, F. R., & Wolf, M. M. (1966). An application of reinforcement principles to development of motor skills of a young child. *Child Development, 37,* 379–387.

Jones, M. C. (1924a). A laboratory study of fear: The case of Peter. *Pedagogical Seminary and Journal of Genetic Psychology, 6,* 181–187.

Jones, M. C. (1924b). The elimination of children's fears. *Journal of Experimental Psychology, 7,* 382–390.

Jones, M. C. (1975). A 1924 pioneer looks at behavior therapy. *Journal of Behavior Therapy and Experimental Psychiatry, 6,* 181–187.

Kazdin, A. E. (1977). *The token economy: A review and evaluation.* New York: Plenum Press.

Kazdin, A. E. (1978). *History of behavior modification: Experimental foundations of contemporary research.* Baltimore, MD: University Park Press.

Kazdin, A. E. (1979). Fictions, factions, and functions of behavior therapy. *Behavior Therapy, 10,* 629–654.

Kazdin, A. E. (1980). *Behavior modification in applied settings* (2nd ed.). Homewood, IL: Dorsey.

Kazdin, A. E. (1981a). Behavior modification in education: Contributions and limitations. *Developmental Review, 1,* 34–57.

Kazdin, A. E. (1981b). Uses and abuses of behavior modification in education: A rejoinder. *Developmental Review, 1,* 61–62.

Kazdin, A. E. (1982). *Single-case research designs: Methods for clinical and applied settings.* New York: Oxford University Press.

Kazdin, A. E., & Craighead, W. E. (1973). Behavior modification in special education. In L. Mann & D. A. Sabatino (Eds.), *The first review of special education* (Vol. 2, pp. 51–102). Philadelphia, PA: Buttonwood Farms.

Keller, F. S. (1968). Good-bye teacher. *Journal of Applied Behavior Analysis, 1.* 79–89.

Keller, F. S., & Schoenfeld, W. N. (1950). *Principles of psychology: A systematic text in the science of behavior.* New York: Appleton-Century-Crofts.

Kifer, R. E., Lewis, M. A., Green, D. R., & Phillips, E. L. (1974). Training predelinquent youths and their parents to negotiate conflict situations. *Journal of Applied Behavior Analysis, 7,* 357–364.

Klein, R. D., Hapkiewicz, W. G., & Roden, A. H. (Eds.) (1973). *Behavior modification in educational settings.* Springfield, IL: Charles C Thomas.

Krasner, L. (1982). Behavior therapy: On roots, contexts, and growth. In G. T. Wilson & C. M. Franks (Eds.), *Contemporary behavior therapy: Conceptual and empirical foundations* (pp. 11–62). New York: Guilford.

Kratochwill, T. R. (Ed.). (1978). *Single subject research: Strategies for evaluating change.* New York: Academic Press.

Lahey, B. B., & Johnson, M. S. (1978). *Psychology and instruction.* Glenview, IL: Scott Foresman.

Lindsley, O. R. (1960). Characteristics of the behavior of chronic psychotics as revealed by free-operant conditioning methods. *Diseases of the Nervous System, Monograph Supplement, 21,* 66–78.

Lloyd, K. E. (1978). Behavior analysis and technology in higher education. In A. D. Catania & T. A. Brigham (Eds.), *Handbook of applied behavior analysis: Social and instructional processes* (pp. 482–521). New York: Irvington.

Lumsdaine, A. A., & Glaser, R. (Eds.) (1960). *Teaching machines and programed learning, Vol. II: A source book.* Washington, DC: National Education Association.

Lumsdaine, A. A., & Glaser, R. (Eds.). (1965). *Teaching machines and programed learning, Vol. II: Data and directions.* Washington, DC: National Education Association.

Malott, R. W., Hartlep, P. A., Keenan, M., & Michael, J. (1972). Groundwork for a student-centered experimental college. *Educational Technology, 12,* 61.

McDougall, W. (1905). *Physiological psychology.* London: J. M. Dent & Sons.

McDougall, W. (1909). *An introduction to social psychology.* Boston, MA: J. W. Luce.

Meyer, M. F. (1911). *The fundamental laws of human behavior: Lectures on the foundations of any mental or social science.* Boston, MA: Badger.

Mowrer, O. H. (1947). On the dual nature of learning—a reinterpretation of "conditioning" and "problem solving." *Harvard Educational Review, 17,* 102–148.

Mowrer, O. H. (1960). *Learning theory and behavior.* New York: Wiley.

Murphy, G. (1949). *Historical introduction to modern psychology.* New York: Harcourt, Brace, & World.

Pavlov, I. P. (1927). *Conditional reflexes* (G. Aurap, trans.). London: Oxford University Press.

Pavlov, I. P. (1932). Neurosis in man and animals. *Journal of the American Medical Association, 99,* 1012–1013.

Pennypacker, H. S., Heckler, J. B., & Pennypacker, S. F. (1978). A university-wide system of personalized instruction: The personalized learning center. In A. C. Catania & T. A. Brigham (Eds.), *Handbook of applied behavior analysis: Social and instructional processes* (pp. 584–602). New York: Irvington.

Phillips, E. L., Phillips, E. A., Fixsen, D. L., & Wolf, M. M. (1971). Achievement place: Modification of the behaviors of pre-delinquent boys within a token economy. *Journal of Applied and Behavior Analysis, 4,* 45–59.

Phillips, E. L., Phillips, E. A., Wolf, M. M., & Fixsen, D. L. (1973). Achievement place: Development of the elected manager system. *Journal of Applied Behavior Analyses, 6,* 541–561.

Pillsbury, W. B. (1911). *The essentials of psychology.* New York: Macmillan.

Pressey, S. L. (1926). A simple apparatus which gives tests and scores—and teaches. *School and Society, 23,* 373–376.

Pressey, S. L. (1927). A machine for automatic teaching of drill material. *School and Society, 25,* 549–552.

Revill, S., & Blunden, R. (1977). *Home training of preschool children with developmental delay: Report of the development and evaluation of the Portage Service in South Glamorgan.* Unpublished manuscript, Department of Health and Social Security and the Welsh Office.

Revill, S., & Blunden, R. (1979). A home training service for preschool developmentally handicapped children. *Behavior Research and Therapy, 17,* 207–214.

Ribes, E. (1977). Relationship among behavior theory, experimental research, and behavior modification techniques. *The Psychological Record, 27,* 417–424.

Ruggles, T. R., & LeBlanc, J. M. (1982). Behavior analysis procedures in classroom teaching. In A. S. Bellack, M. Hersen, & A. E. Kazdin (Eds.), *International Handbook of Behavior Modification and Therapy* (pp. 959–996). New York: Plenum Press.

Scandura, J. M., Frase, L. T., Gagne, R., Stolurow, K., Stolurow, L., & Groen, G. (1978). Current status and future directions of educational psychology as a discipline. *Educational Psychologist, 13,* 43–56.

Schwartz, B. (1978). *Psychology of learning and behavior.* New York: W. W. Norton.

Shaver, J. P. (1979). The productivity of educational research and the applied-basic research distinction. *Educational Researcher, 8,* 3–9.

Shearer, M. S., & Shearer, D. E. (1972). The Portage Project: A model for early childhood education. *Exceptional Children, 38,* 210–217.

Shearer, M. S., & Shearer, D. E. (1976). The Portage Project: A model for early childhood intervention. In T. D. Tjossem (Ed.), *Interventions strategies for high risk infants and young children* (pp. 335–350). Baltimore, MD: University Press.

Sherman, J. G. (1981). Do the data count? In S. W. Bijou & R. Ruiz (Eds.), *Behavior modification: Contributions to education* (pp. 281–289). Hillsdale, NJ: Erlbaum.

Sidman, M. (1960). *Tactics of scientific research: Evaluating experimental data in psychology.* New York: Basic Books.

Silbert, J., Carnine, D., & Stein, M. (1981). *Direct instruction mathematics.* Columbus, OH: Merrill.

Skinner, B. F. (1935). Two types of conditioned reflex and a pseudo type. *Journal of General Psychology, 12,* 66–77.

Skinner, B. F. (1937). Two types of conditioned reflex: A reply to Konorski and Miller. *Journal of General Psychology, 16,* 272–279.

Skinner, B. F. (1938). *The behavior of organisms: An experimental analysis.* New York: Appleton-Century.

Skinner, B. F. (1948). *Walden two.* New York: Macmillan.

Skinner, B. F. (1953a). *Science and human behavior.* New York: Macmillan.

Skinner, B. F. (1953b). Some contributions of an experimental analysis of behavior to psychology as a whole. *American Psychologist, 8,* 69–78.

Skinner, B. F. (1954a). A new method for the experimental analysis of the behavior of psychotic patients. *Journal of Nervous and Mental Disease, 120,* 403–506.

Skinner, B. F. (1954b). The science of learning and the art of teaching. *Harvard Educational Review, 24,* 86–97.

Skinner, B. F. (1957). *Verbal behavior.* New York: Appleton-Century-Crofts.

Skinner, B. F. (1984). The shame of American education. *American Psychologist, 39,* 947–954.

Skinner, B. F., Solomon, H. C., & Lindsley, O. R. (1953, November). *Studies in behavior therapy,* Metropolitan State Hospital, Waltham, Massachusetts, Status Report I.

Skinner, B. F., Solomon, H. C., Lindsley, O. R., & Richards, M. E. (1954, May). *Studies in behavior therapy,* Metropolitan State Hospital, Waltham, Massachusetts, Status Report II.

Sloane, H. N., Jr., Johnston, M. K., & Bijou, S. W. (1967). Successive modification of aggressive behavior and aggressive fantasy play by management of contingencies. *Journal of Child Psychology & Psychiatry, 8,* 217–226.

Spence, K. W. (1956). *Behavior therapy and conditioning.* New Haven, CT: Yale University Press.

Staats, A. W. (1968). *Learning, language and cognition: Theory, research, and method for the study of human behavior and its development.* New York: Holt, Rinehart & Winston.

Staats, A. W., & Butterfield, W. H. (1965). Treatment of nonreading in a culturally deprived juvenile delinquent. An application of reinforcement principles. *Child Development, 36,* 925–942.

Staats, A. W., Staats, C. K., Schutz, R. E., & Wolf, M. (1962). The conditioning of textual responses using "extrinsic" reinforcers. *Journal of the Experimental Analysis of Behavior, 5,* 33–40.

Staats, A. W., Finley, J. R., Minke, K. A., & Wolf, M. (1964). Reinforcement variables in the control of unit reading responses. *Journal of the Experimental Analysis of Behavior, 7,* 139–149.

Staats, A. W., Minke, K. A., Finley, J. R., Wolf, M., & Brooks, L. O. (1964). A reinforcer system and experimental procedure for the laboratory study of reading acquisition. *Child Development, 35,* 209–231.

Staats, A. W., Minke, K. A., Goodwin, W., & Landeen, J.

(1967). Cognitive behavior modification: ''Motivated learning'' reading treatment with subprofessional therapy-technicians. *Behavior Research and Therapy, 5,* 283–299.

Staats, A. W., Minke, K. A., & Butts, P. (1970). A token-reinforcement remedial reading program administered by black therapy-technicians to problem black children. *Behavior Therapy, 1,* 331–353.

Stallings, J. (1975). Implementation and child effects of teaching practices in Follow Through classrooms. *Monographs of the Society for Research in Child Development, 40* (7–8 Serial No. 163).

Strain, P. S., Sainto, D. M., & Maheady, L. (1984). Toward a functional assessment of severely handicapped learners. *Educational Psychologist, 19,* 180–187.

Tawney, J. W., & Gast, D. L. (1984). *Single subject research designs in special education.* Columbus, OH; Merrill.

Thorndike, E. L. (1911). *Animal intelligence: Experimental Studies.* New York: Macmillan.

Tolman, E. C. (1932). *Purposive behavior in animals and men.* New York: Century.

Travers, R. M. W. (1983). *How research has changed American schools: A history from 1984 to the present.* Kalamazoo, MI: Mython Press.

Ulman, J. D., & Klem, J. L. (1975). Communication. *Journal of Applied Behavior Analysis, 8,* 210.

Watson, J. B. (1913). Psychology as the behaviorist views it. *Psychological Review, 20,* 158–177.

Watson, J. B. (1919). *Psychology from the standpoint of a behaviorist.* Philadelphia, PA: J. B. Lippincott.

Watson, J. B., & Rayner, R. (1920). Conditioned emotional reactions. *Journal of Experimental Psychology, 3,* 1–14.

Ysseldyke, J. E., & Thurlow, M. L. (1984). Assessment practices in special education: Adequacy and appropriateness. *Educational Psychologist, 9,* 123–136.

CHAPTER 9

Humanistic Psychology

THEORY, POSTULATES, AND IMPLICATIONS FOR EDUCATIONAL PROCESSES

Don E. Hamachek

Prologue

The two primary objectives of this chapter are to examine the theoretical framework and basic postulates of humanistic psychology, and to discuss ways in which humanistic principles may contribute positively to approaches for enhancing teaching processes and learning outcomes. En route, we will survey the philosophical roots that have nourished humanistic psychology's embryonic beginnings and early development. In addition, we will sample the views of some of the primary contributors associated with this stance in order to better understand the theoretical-philosophical blueprint that has guided the evolvement of humanistic approaches within the larger arena of educational psychology.

It may be important to point out that, although I feel comfortable and at ease with humanistic approaches and emphases, whether in educational or counseling settings, I do not see myself as being rigidly humanistic. For example, I frequently find myself deliberately reinforcing positively certain

responses I would like to see more of in my students, as do my behavioristically inclined colleagues, or searching for possible unconscious motivations behind certain behaviors as do my psychoanalytical friends, or exploring ways to modify a person's thinking about certain issues in order to change his or her feelings about those issues, as do my more cognitively slanted associates.

Humanistic psychology, with its focused attention on the purely human dimensions involved in teaching and learning, can be and has been of enormous value in helping to understand complex classroom dynamics in terms of subjective feelings, individual perceptions, and self-concept variables. During the past 30 years or so, it has grown from being just another point of view to a sanctioned and respected discipline within psychological and educational circles. For whatever else contemporary humanistic psychology may be, it is more than a dressed-up version of the phenomenological-existential movement that has had a long history in Europe and in Western thought. In relation to schooling, it means more than saying to students, "Be free, grow, expand, follow your feelings, do what you want, be yourself." And it is more than a poetic accounting and description of a person's dreams, feelings, and experiences.

Don E. Hamachek • Department of Counseling, Educational Psychology, and Special Education, College of Education, Michigan State University, East Lansing, MI 48824-1034.

Which, for openers, leads us to ask an important question.

What Is Humanistic Psychology?

We need first of all to acknowledge the fact that there is no single position that is identifiable as *the* humanistic psychology approach. Unlike other areas of psychology—for example, personality, physiological, experimental, or abnormal psychology, humanistic psychology is not so much a specific content area as it is an attitude or outlook about how to think about psychology, how to use it, and how to apply our knowledge about it to solving human problems and enhancing human existence on a day-to-day basis. Charlotte Buhler (1971), one of the pioneers of the humanistic movement, has observed that one of the most generally agreed on aspects of humanistic psychology is that it strives to "find access to the study and understanding of the person as a whole" (p. 378). The emphasis on perceiving each individual as an integrated whole, rather than fragmented into different "selves" unrelated to each other, is a central, key feature of this position. It is a point of view that looks at behavior not as isolated, unrelated happenings, but as connected outer reflections of people's deeper feelings and images of themselves.

In an effort to understand self-image dynamics more fully, humanistic psychology has also endeavored to develop a body of scientific knowledge about human behavior that is guided primarily by a conception of how a person views him or herself rather than through the study of lower animal forms. The idea of deriving principles of human behavior and learning through the study of rats, monkeys, pigeons, and other animals is uncongenial to growing numbers of psychologists who feel that the way to understand human behavior is to study, of all things, human behavior. In the broadest sense of the word, this is what humanistic psychology is all about. It enables us to concentrate on the study of human meanings, human understandings, and human experiences involved in growth, teaching, and learning.

A humanistic psychology, then, is one that makes humans and the human condition the center of attention. It is a psychological framework that focuses on how persons, in a social context, are influenced by their self-perceptions and guided by the personal meanings they attach to their experiences. It is a point of view that centers not so much on persons' instinctual drives, but on their conscious choices; not so much on their responses to external stimuli, but on their replies to internal needs; not so much on their past experiences, but on their current circumstances; not so much on "life conditions" *per se,* but on their perceptions of those conditions. Hence, the emphasis is on the subjective qualities of human experience, the personal meaning of an experience to persons, rather than on their objective, observable responses.

A brief overview of part of the "Articles of Association" (Shaffer, 1978) formulated by the American Association of Humanistic Psychology gives us a good idea of the range of research and theoretical interests embraced by this frame of reference:

> Humanistic psychology . . . stands for the respect for the worth of persons, respect for differences of approach, open-mindedness as to acceptable methods, and interest in exploration of new aspects of behavior. . . . it is concerned with topics having little place in existing theories or systems: e.g., love, creativity, self, . . . self-actualization, higher values, being, becoming . . . meaning, fair play, transcendental experience, peak experience, courage, and related concepts. (p. 2)

All in all, humanistic psychology is a point of view that looks at human behavior not only through the eyes of an outsider, but through the eyes of the person doing the behaving. It is a psychology searching to understand what goes on inside us—our needs, wants, desires, feelings, values, and unique ways of perceiving and understanding that cause us to behave the way we do. In an everyday sense, it is the psychology concerned friends use as they wonder why we may seem "so troubled"; in a clinical sense, it is what therapists use as they probe for the deeper meanings behind what subjective experiences mean to the client; in an educational way, it is what teachers practice as they help students to see the personal relevancy in what they are learning.

Early Humanism: Parent of the Humanistic Spirit

The tap root of humanistic psychology extends into the distant past, back as far as to the Middle Ages, when a philosophy known as humanism was born, and to the Renaissance, a time when humanism grew in scope and stature. Beginning as a social attitude and growing into a philosophical position, humanism began in 15th century western Europe as a reaction against, and protest to, a firmly entrenched ecclesiastic and scholastic authority (Richardson, 1971). Early humanists differed on many issues from scholastic philosophers of the church, the most important, no doubt, being the humanists' emphasis on the freedom of individuals to arrive at their own opinions through independent critical thinking and an emphasis on the natural world rather than the spiritual world. In Barron's (1979) view, humanism

sought to express in common language and everyday real images the feelings of the ordinary person. It did not scorn learning or art, but it did reject the abstract, the pedantic, the rigid. . . . It embraced reason [and an] . . . enlightened rationalism [that] distinguished it from superstition and anarchy alike. (pp. 5–6)

It is no surprise to note that the basic idea undergirding the philosophy of humanism is one that asserts the dignity and worth of each individual and the right of each person to arrive at some level of self-realization through reason and rational thought. The Renaissance, the Reformation, science, and democratic government, along with an emphasis on the free pursuit of knowledge, the development of the intellect, and opposition to dogmatic authority are all outgrowths and expressions of early humanism.

Humanistic Psychology is a natural outgrowth of the repudiative, questioning spirit that has been so characteristic of humanism over the centuries. Just as early humanism developed as a protest against the narrow, thought-restricting, authority-oriented religious dogma of its time—the dogma, for example, behind the inquisition and eventual exile and imprisonment of Galileo, who dared suggest that the earth was not the center of the universe—so, too, has contemporary humanistic psychology evolved as a protest against certain psychological dogmas of its time.

Emergence of the Humanistic Orientation as Psychology's "Third Force"

For the first 50 years or so of the 20th century, psychological thinking, practice, and research was largely dominated by two major forces—behaviorism and psychoanalysis. Both of these giants-to-be emerged at about the same time early in the century, and for essentially the same reasons, namely, in reaction to what was seen as psychology's excessive preoccupation with consciousness and introspection (Matson, 1971).

Stressing the importance of environmental determinants, behavioristic psychology focused its attention on outer experience, overt behavior, action and reaction, and offered the point of view, supported by its theory and findings from research with animals, that people are conditioned, by virtue of the rewards and punishments to which they are exposed, to turn out (behave, respond, grow, act) in certain ways (Lundin, 1983; Skinner, 1968). No statement reflects more powerfully the essence of this point of view than the words of one of behaviorism's early leaders, John B. Watson (1926), who said,

Give me the child and my world to bring it up in and I'll make it crawl or walk; I'll make it climb and use its hands in constructing buildings of stone or wood; I'll make it a thief, a gunman, or a dope fiend. The possibility of shaping in any direction is almost endless. (p. 35)

Although not all modern-day behaviorists would agree that Watson could do all he promised to do, there would nonetheless be substantial agreement that behavior can be dramatically altered, shaped, controlled, and manipulated through the use of appropriate reinforcements. Behaviorism's contemporary leader, B. F. Skinner (1971), has underscored this point of view with his idea that human freedom and dignity is really a myth, a misconception we nourish by failing to see that all behavior is subject to the controlling influences of environment. Indeed, Skinner's (1948) novel, *Walden Two,* is a fictional accounting of how an ideal society, filled with happy and contributory people, can be created by correctly manipulating external rewards and punishments.

Psychoanalysis, the second major force of the 20th century, was less interested in the external stimuli that produced the responses, and more interested in the unconscious motivations and internal instincts that propelled the behavior (Giovacchini, 1983; Hall, 1954). This view of behavior, particularly as it was articulated by Freud (1937/1964) promoted the idea that people were very much creatures of instincts classified under two general headings: life instincts and death instincts. Life instincts are those concerned primarily with individual survival and racial propagation. Basic drives, energized by the ubiquitous Freudian libido, such as hunger, thirst, or sex would fall in this category. The concept of death instincts, or, as Freud sometimes called them, the destructive instincts, were deep reflections of the basic pessimism built into psychoanalytic thinking about the human condition. For example, Freud (1930/1961) himself expressed the idea that

men are not gentle, friendly creatures wishing for love, who simply defend themselves if they are attacked, but . . . a powerful measure of desire for aggressiveness has to be reckoned as part of their genetic endowment. The result is that their neighbor is to them not only a possible helper or sexual object, but also a temptation to gratify their aggressiveness . . . to seize his possessions, to humiliate him, to cause him pain. (pp. 85–86)

Add to this Freud's (1937/1964) idea that "even before the ego exists, its subsequent lines of development, tendencies and reactions are already determined" (pp. 343–344), and you have a brief overview of the core ingredients of psychoanalysis: psychogenetically determined instincts, an emphasis on unconscious motivation, and a basically gloomy view of humankind.

Between the environmental determinism of behaviorism and the biological determinism of psychoanalysis, any sort of view of the person as a whole, complete, intraconnected individual was all but squeezed out of psychology by the 1950s. Both of these major forces made significant and powerful contributions to our understanding of humankind. However, as reported by Berelson and Steiner (1964) in their massive review of 1,045 scientific findings, our understanding of human behavior that emerged to that point in time was "incomplete." In their words:

Indeed, as one reviews this set of findings, he may well be impressed by another omission more striking still. As one lives life or observes it around him (or within himself) . . . he sees a richness that somehow has fallen through the present screen of the behavioral sciences. This book, for example, has rather little to say about the central human concerns: nobility, moral courage, ethical torments, the delicate relation of father and son or of the marriage state, life's way of corrupting innocence, the rightness or wrongness of acts, evil, happiness, love and hate, death, even sex. (p. 666)

Humanistic psychology is a reaction against this state of affairs. It is a countermovement against the sort of reductionistic thinking in psychology that compartmentalized human behavior into responses and instincts, and in the process largely overlooked what it was that made a human being "human" in the first place. Thus, humanistic psychology

emerged as a "third force" alongside behaviorism and psychoanalysis not so much as a new psychology, but as a new orientation to psychology. It was, as described by Abraham Maslow (1969), father of the humanistic movement, "a larger superordinate structure" (p. 724) that could accomodate behaviorism, psychoanalysis, and other positions in psychology. When we consider that a significant aspect of humanistic psychology grows directly out of the holistic theories of Kurt Goldstein (1939) and Fritz Perls (1969), who both stressed the idea that humans function as organized wholes and are best understood within the interactive context of the person and the environment, rather than just one or the other, it is not difficult to see why the humanistic position easily encompasses other points of view.

Actually, the emergence of humanistic psychology was a slow and gradual process, one that started in about the middle 1950s and has been growing ever since. In a sense, humanistic psychology started out as modern humanism addressed to the construction and defense of a concept of humankind comprised of people as creative beings, capable of self-determination, purpose, and intention, who are controlled not by outside or unconscious forces, but by their own values and choices.

Specific Milestones in the Evolution of Contemporary Humanistic Psychology

Given the rapid acceleration of the humanistic movement since the mid 1950s, may find it helpful to see a somewhat consolidated overview of those events and happenings that reflect its modern development.

1. Highly significant publications, each in its own way promoting and espousing a humanistic orientation, began to appear, including Abraham Maslow's *Motivation and Personality* (1954), Gordon Allport's *Becoming* (1955), Clark Moustakas' *The Self* (1956), and Gardner Murphy's *Human Potentialities* (1958).

2. Reflecting the international scope of the movement, an English psychologist, John Cohen, published his book, *Humanistic Psychology* in 1958.

3. The *Journal of Humanistic Psychology* was founded in 1961, edited by A. J. Sutich.

4. In 1962, the American Association for Humanistic Psychology was organized and formed.

5. Also in 1962, the Esalen Institute was organized in Big Sur, California by Michael Murphy

and Richard Price, who founded it for the purpose of investigating the full range of human potential within what they hoped to be an open, non-doctrinaire, "humanistic" atmosphere of free exploration.

6. James F. T. Bugental (1963) presented what amounted to the first official "position paper" on humanistic psychology in the United States, in which he asserted (referring to humanistic psychology): "We are returning to what psychology still seems to mean to the average, intelligent layman, that is, the functioning and experience of the whole human being" (p. 566).

7. The first graduate program in humanistic psychology was started at Sonoma State College (California) in 1963.

8. Books with specific humanistic themes and emphases began to appear in the mid 1960s. Prominent examples include: *Humanistic Viewpoints in Psychology,* edited by Frank T. Severin (1965) and *Challenges in Humanistic Psychology,* edited by James F. T. Bugental (1967). In addition to these professionally targeted volumes, books aimed at the public at large began to appear that focused on affective states, intrapersonal feelings, and ways to improve interpersonal modes of expression. Prominent examples include, *Please Touch* by Jane Howard (1970), *Turning On* by Rasa Gustaitis (1969), and *Joy: Expanding Human Awareness* by William Schutz (1967).

9. In 1970, a new subdivision called the Division of Humanistic Psychology (Division 32) was created within the American Psychological Association. In addition, the American Association for Humanistic Psychology expanded into an international organization, the Association for Humanistic Psychology, which held its first international conference in Holland in 1970.

10. From the early 1960s through the 1970s, the highly publicized, so-called human potential movement grew and blossomed. Stressing, as it did, intra- and interpersonal outcomes, such as knowing oneself, knowing others, self-disclosure, authenticity, and discovering one's "true potential," this movement was a natural outgrowth of humanistic ideals related to personal development. An earmark of the human potential movement was what Carl Rogers (1970) referred to as the *encounter group,* which he felt served as a powerful medium in which people could have meaningful and important opportunities for self–other exploration. Tomkins (1976) has provided a simple and direct definition of what an encounter group is all about:

"A way of achieving personal growth through the exploration of feelings among people gathered together for that purpose" (p. 30). Although different kinds of group encounter techniques, methods, and emphases grew out of the human potential movement (see, for example, Back, 1972; Bebout, 1973; Bindrum, 1968; Bugental, 1965; Burton, 1969; Egan, 1970; Jourard, 1971; McGrath, 1984: Peris, 1969; Schutz, 1967), the intent was essentially the same: a focus on subjective feelings, inner awareness, and personal learning, outcomes that have implications for educational methods designed to blend cognitive gains and affective involvement. Publications such as *Learning Together and Alone: Cooperation, Competition, and Individualization* (Johnson & Johnson, 1975), *A Humanistic Psychology of Education* and *Group Processes in the Classroom* (Schmuck & Schmuck, 1974, 1983) are excellent examples of contemporary efforts to extend humanistically oriented group approaches to classroom settings. As a movement, the human potential idea is alive and well in our contemporary mode of psychology and education, but in a quieter, less flamboyant, and more mature way. In today's world, journalists are doing less to sensationalize its methods, which have become less extreme and more moderate, and educational psychologists and social psychologists are doing more to study its outcomes.

The human potential movement as an outgrowth of humanistic thinking is not all that surprising, particularly when considered in light of the deeper influences of phenomenology and existentialism, an idea we turn to next.

Contributions of Existential Psychology and Phenomenology

Because humanistic psychology, phenomenology, and existential psychology are frequently used in the same breath by persons discussing humanistic viewpoints, it may help us to be clearer about the theoretical structure and philosophical roots of humanistic psychology by briefly examining how existentialism and phenomenology are historically connected to the emergence of humanistic views in psychology.

Let's begin with existentialism. This is basically a 20th-century philosophy that stresses each person's responsibility for determining his or her own fate. It is an introspective philosophy that focuses on intrapersonal conditions such as awareness, personal contingency, and freedom to choose from among alternatives for behaving. Indeed, the existential outlook maintains that a person's essence (being, behavior, personality, ''self'') is *created* by his or her choices. As existentialist Jean-Paul Sartre once put it: ''I *am* my choices.'' Within this framework, each individual is seen as having absolute freedom. In fact, even refusing to choose represents a personal choice. Thus, the criteria for behavior are within the individual, which, in effect, makes each person the architect of his or her fate. The pillars of the existential position have been stated in the form of three propositions (Morris, 1966):

1. I am a *choosing* agent, unable to avoid choosing my way through life.
2. I am a *free* agent, absolutely free to set my goals for life.
3. I am a *responsible* agent, personally accountable for my free choices as they are revealed in how I live my life.

A central tenet of existentialism is the idea that humans struggle to transcend themselves—to reach beyond themselves—always oriented to their possibilities. Further, there is the idea in existential thought that humans are capable of what Morris (1954) has called ''dynamic self-consciousness.'' That is, not only can people think but they can also think about (criticize and correct) their thinking, not only can people feel, but they can have feelings about their feelings. We are not only conscious, we are self-conscious.

Phenomenology is a related philosophical position within the humanistic framework and represents a view that asserts that reality lies not in the event, but in the phenomenon, which is to say, an individual's *perception* of the event. Because, by definition, a phenomenon is ''that which is known through the senses and immediate experience,'' you can see why perceptions play such a key role in determining what is and what is not real (true, valid, authentic) for a given individual.

Snygg and Combs (1949) took this basic phenomenological idea and creatively developed a new frame of reference for studying and understanding behavior, which has been variously called phenomenological or perceptual psychology. From this point of view, they suggested that the proper subject matter for psychological study was the individual's phenomenal field, that is, ''the universe of naive experience in which each individual lives, the everyday situation of self and surroundings, which each person takes to be reality'' (p. 15). In describing this phenomenological position, Combs and Snygg (1959) have written that

this approach seeks to understand the behavior of the individual from his point of view. It attempts to observe people, not as they seem to outsiders, but as they seem to themselves. People do not behave solely because of external forces to which they are exposed. People behave as they do in consequence to how things seem to them. (p. 11)

From a phenomenological point of view the idea is that each person behaves in a manner consistent with his or her *perceptual field,* which is a more or less fluid organization of personal meanings existing for each individual at any given instant in time. The concept of perceptual field has been variously called one's private or personal world, one's psychological field or life space, or one's phenomenal field. Rogers (1951) has observed that a person responds to his or her field ''as it is experienced or perceived. This perceptual field is, for the individual, reality'' (p. 483). In other words, people respond not to an ''objective'' environment, but to the environment as they perceive and understand it. For each person, it is reality no matter how much he or she may distort and personalize it. If, for instance, a person walking across the front of a room filled with people suddenly heard giggles and laughter, he might very well feel self-conscious, awkward, and even embarrassed. From an objective point of view, they may have been laughing at a funny story someone had just told. However, this is really immaterial to our embarrassed friend, so far as his reaction is concerned. His awkward feelings can only be understood by recognizing that the stimulus to which he was responding was his own subjective perception that they were laughing at him. From the point of view of phenomenological or perceptual psychology, we are best able to understand human behavior by taking into account the individual's subjective interpretation of stimuli. Seymour Epstein (1980) has taken this idea even further by postulating that people's subjective perceptions are the basis for the development of an implicit theory of reality, which then serves as an emotional lens through which the world is perceived and interpreted. (More will be said about this idea later.)

Phenomenology is difficult to define with precision. It is an old term, now stewing in its own metaphysical juices, that allows for so much individuality that there could be almost as many phenomenologies as there are phenomenologists. The reason for this is probably because the essential concern is with meaning, and meanings can vary extensively.

To summarize, we could say that the emphasis of existential psychology is on personal choice, freedom, and responsibility, whereas with phenomenological psychology the emphasis is on our perceptions, personal meanings, and subjective experiences. Inasmuch as humanistic psychology is an orientation that focuses on human interests and values, a person's capacity to make conscious choices, and one's self-perceptions, you can see that the incorporation of existential and phenomenological ideas into this system is a natural blending and synthesis of overlapping concerns and views regarding human behavior.

As humanistic psychology has grown and matured, it has developed its own basic postulates about the nature of human behavior, something to which we now turn our attention.

Basic Humanistic Views about Human Behavior

When the American Association for Humanistic Psychology was first formed in 1962, one of its primary goals, as described by its first president, James T. Bugental (1967), was "The preparation of a complete description of what it means to be alive as a human being" (p. 7). In another source, Bugental (1965 pp. 11–12) offered five basic postulates of human behavior from a humanistic perspective, which help to give additional meaning to this point of view.

1. *Man, as man, supercedes the sum of his parts.* This is very much a reflection of humanistic psychology's "holistic" emphasis. Humans are no more viewed as a collection of unconscious motivations or responses to stimuli than Rachmaninov's Second Piano Concerto is viewed simply as the summation of musical notes that went into its composition.

2. *Man has his being in a human context.* The unique nature of the human condition is expressed in relationships with other people, and in this sense humanistic psychology is concerned with each person's potential in an interpersonal context; hence, the popularity of the human potential movement with its emphasis on encounter group activities.

3. *Man is aware.* This suggests that, whatever the degree of consciousness, people are aware of themselves and their existence. That is, how persons behave in the present is related to what happened in their past, and this is connected to their hopes for the future.

4. *Man has choice.* We see here both the influence of existential thought and the early humanist emphasis on the freedom of individuals to make their own decisions. This concept underscores the idea of personal awareness, a mental state that leads to choice, a process that enables people to become active participants, rather than passive bystanders, in their own lives.

5. *Man is intentional.* A person's intent is reflected in his or her choices. That is, people intend through having purpose, through valuing, and through seeking meaning in their lives. It is through this "conscious deliberateness," as it might be called, that each individual structures a personal identity that distinguishes him or her from all others.

A common thread that weaves its way through these five basic humanistic concepts is what we might call an emphasis on holistic self-development consciously determined. What one becomes is what one *chooses* to become, which is a far cry from being the product of instinctual drives or the outcome of conditioned responses. Three key terms commonly associated with humanistic positions are "self-actualization," "self-fulfillment," and "self-realization." There are different points of view—not necessarily exclusive of each other—within the humanistic movement about how to achieve these states: for Erikson (1980) it is via the route of positive resolution of conflicts associated with different psychosocial stages; for Jourard (1971) it is through disclosing oneself to others; for Rogers (1961) it is through learning to trust one's own judgments and inner feelings; for Maslow (1954) it is by satisfying lower needs so one is freer to reach for the higher ones; for White (1959) it would be the development of competency. Although there are these different emphases within the humanistic movement, the common feature that connects them is the idea, as expressed by Buhler (1971), that "humanistic psychologists see the goal of life as using your life to accomplish something you believe in, be it self-development or other values. From this they expect a fulfillment towards which people determine themselves" (p. 381). Thus, the emphasis on self-understanding in order to make better choices about how to go about the business of living a creative and fulfilling life is a dominant conceptual theme in humanistic psychology. Indeed, the whole concept of the self is an important one, an idea we turn to next.

Role of the Self in Humanistic Thinking

With so much emphasis on how people perceive themselves, on personal meanings, values, choices, subjective experiences, and perceptions, it seems only natural that the idea of self, or self-concept, should end up being a focal point for studying and understanding behavior in a humanistic framework. Although the idea of the self was first introduced in the late 19th century by William James (1890) in his brilliant chapter, "The Consciousness of Self," the self as a theoretical construct of any stature, and its use in psychological thought, all but disappeared as the tides of behaviorism and psychoanalysis swept the shores of psychological thinking during the first 40 years of the century. Behaviorists viewed the self as being too "internal" and hence too unobservable to be of much value, and psychoanalytic thinkers considered it to be too conscious and hence too subject to distortion to be believed.

Since the 1950s, however, the idea of the self as the central core of the person has emerged as a kind of unifying principle of personality for psychologists and educators (Hamachek, 1987). As Combs (1981) has described it:

Perhaps the most important single contribution of humanistic psychology over the past 30 years has been the recognition of the crucial importance of the self-concept to every aspect of human growth and behavior. A person's image or beliefs of self are a vital part of his or her every activity. People behave in terms of what they believe to be true about themselves. People who believe they can, do; people who believe they cannot, avoid confrontation. . . . Student self-concepts control what students learn. (p. 447)

The self occupies a central seat of importance in humanistic psychology because it underscores the phenomenological idea that it is how people perceive themselves and the world in which they live that determines their intrapsychic feelings and interpersonal behaviors. A self-concept point of view allows for the opportunity to consider self-perception as the intervening variable between the stimulus and the response. Rather than it being a S–R world, one that some feel negates the person, it becomes an S–P–R (Stimulus –*Person* – Response) world, one that others feel elevates the person, whereas at the same time establishing a frame of reference for explaining why responses may vary from one individual to another even though stimulus conditions are the same.

Humanistic psychology's emphasis on the self as the mantlepiece of its theoretical framework is a natural outgrowth of the importance given to an individual's conscious, subjective experiences, which then serve as major routes to understanding the meaning of life, living, and learning from that person's point of view. The self as it is referred to here is internal; it is that part of each person of which he or she is conscious, an idea I think Jersild (1952) has described as well as anyone:

The self is a person's total subjective environment. It is a distinctive center of experience and significance. The self constitutes a person's inner world as distinguished from the "outer world" consisting of all other people and things (p. 9).

Humanistically oriented psychologists and social psychologists have described and studied the self from a variety of theoretical slants over the years. For example, there has been the "material, social, spiritual self" of James (1890); the "looking-glass self" of Cooley (1902); the "socially formed self" of Mead (1934); the self reflecting one's "inner nature" or "essential nature" of Fromm (1941, 1947), Maslow (1970), and Moustakas (1956); the self that is the "individual as known to the individual" of Raimey (1948) and Rogers (1951); the self that is the organizational core for self-consistency of Lecky (1945); the "self-system" of Sullivan (1947); the "inferred self" of Hilgard (1949); the "phenomenal" or "nonphenomenal" self of Snygg and Combs (1949); the "proprium" of Allport (1955); the "authentic" or "inauthentic" self of Seeman (1966); the "judging" self, "identity" self, and "behavior" self (Fitts *et al.*, 1971); the "inner" and "outer" self of Franks and Marolla (1976); the "categorical" self of Lewis and Brooks-Gunn (1981); and the helix-like "evolving self" of Kegan (1982).

The idea of the self as a legitimate conceptual construct in the humanistic system has been enormously enhanced in recent years by Epstein's (1973, 1980) integrative cognitive theory of self-concept, which, as an integrative synthesis of existing self-theories, psychoanalysis, behavioral approaches, and other cognitive theories, offers the point of view that self-concept is actually a *self-theory,* one that individuals unwittingly develop because they need it to lead their lives. As described by Epstein, a person's self theory—that is, assumptions about what he or she is like—interacts with a person's world theory, which are assumptions about what the world is like. To-gether, these two theories, unconsciously derived, constitute a person's *implicit theory of reality,* the purpose of which is to assimilate experiential data, maintain a favorable pleasure–pain balance, and optimize self-esteem. Defense mechanisms—de-nial, projection, rationalization, etc.—are used not only to defend one's theory of reality and self-esteem by fending off unacceptable impulses, as stressed by psychoanalysis, but also to maintain the consistency and unity of a person's self-sys-tem, as stressed by self-theorists. In addition, Ep-stein's (1980) theory has built into it the idea "that behind almost every emotion there is a hidden cog-nition" (p. 109), which suggests that it is how we think about or interpret events, not the events themselves, that determine the emotions we feel. This particular aspect of the theory incorporates nicely some of the more cognitive approaches to behavior such as those of Beck (1976), Ellis (1962), and Meichenbaum (1974), each of which stresses the idea that the way to encourage people to change maladaptive emotional states or negative self-images is to teach them to change their ways of thinking.

Self-concept, then, is not just a route for know-ing a person more deeply from the inside out, but a door for helping people change for the better from the outside in, an idea quite compatible with hu-manistic approaches to teaching and learning.

Major Contributors to the Growth of Humanistic Psychology

As humanistic psychology has grown as a the-oretical discipline to stand as a legitimate "third force" next to psychoanalytic and behavioristic psychology, certain key persons have been instru-mental in assisting it from its philosophical womb. The input of Charlotte Buhler, James Bugental, Donald Snygg and Arthur Combs has already been mentioned. The contributions of Abraham Maslow in the mid-1950s were particularly important to the growth of humanistic psychology because of his ground-breaking emphasis on the need for a psy-chology that focused on human potentials and not just human deficiencies. At a time when the field of psychology was preoccupied with the id and super ego, with stimuli and responses, Maslow (1954) was suggesting that psychologists turn their attention to questions that reflected a more positive approach to psychology, such as:

How do people learn to be wise, mature, kind, to have good taste, to be inventive . . . to seek the truth, to know the beau-tiful, and genuine?

[What do people learn] from unique experiences, from tragedy, marriage, having children, success . . . falling in love, being ill, death?

Why does so much of educational psychology concern itself with means, i.e., grades, degrees, credits, diplomas, rather than with ends, i.e., wisdom, understanding, good judgment, good taste?

[What do we know about] the affective side of love and friend-ship, the satisfactions and pleasures that they bring?

How do people get to be unlike each other instead of like each other? (pp. 364–377)

Gordon Allport (1955) was another strong sup-porter of humanistic psychology because, as he saw it:

Some [views of human behavior] are based largely upon the behavior of sick and anxious people or upon the antics of cap-tive and desperate rats. Fewer theories have derived from the study of healthy human beings, those who strive not so much to preserve life as to make it worth living. Thus we find many studies of criminals, few of law-abiders; many of fear, few of courage; more on hostility than affiliation; much in the blind-ness of man, but little on his vision; much on his past, little on his outreaching into the future. (p. 18)

Humanistic approaches to education have had an effective and persuasive outlet in the work and writing of Carl Rogers, who, aside from influenc-ing how some counselors counsel, has had a con-siderable impact on how some teachers teach. Rogers has always had a fundamental concern with the idea of human freedom and has committed his life to developing a theoretical framework that al-lows teachers and counselors alike to establish the sort of emotional climate that enables students or clients to actively and freely seek the necessary personal meanings that make learning possible. Rogers' ideas have been important ones because they have emphasized the relationship aspect in-volved in teaching and learning, that tenuous, elu-sive connection between student and teacher, the content of which makes learning exciting and meaningful or dull and impersonal. In Rogers' (1969) judgment, "Learning which takes place 'from the neck up' [and which] does not involve feelings or personal meanings [has] no relevance for the whole person" (p. 4). Unfortunately, Rogers' ideas can be easily misinterpreted, some-thing to be explored more fully in the discussion of teaching and learning in a humanistic context.

The seven contributors mentioned up to this

point are by no means exhaustive. Other names that could be added include: Alfred Adler (1939) and his ideas about "social interest"; Erich Fromm (1941) and his views about the development of "social character"; Karen Horney (1937) and her concepts of "basic anxiety" and "neurotic needs"; Gardner Murphy (1947) and his "biosocial" approach; Henry Murray (1938) and his theory of "personology." I have limited this to the earlier contributors and to those who were primarily theorists because it is from their writings and research that contemporary humanistic psychology has taken its substance and shaped its form.

Some Common Criticisms of Humanistic Psychology

As with all viewpoints in the broad field of science, when any particular viewpoint grows beyond being just one person's idea to a more widely discussed—if not accepted—point of view, it becomes the object of intense critical scrutiny. Those friendly to its tenets are critical in hopes of strengthening its deficiencies and making it stronger, whereas those antagonistic to its offerings do so in hopes of weakening it further. Humanistic psychology is no exception. It has had (and has) its critics, who, when listened to, may help to provide a balanced perspective. Three major criticisms are frequently heard:

1. In the first place, humanistic psychology has been criticized because it is too vague in the sense that the concepts used are ambiguous and subject to individual interpretation (Child, 1973). *Authenticity,* a favorite concept among humanistically inclined psychologist and educators, is a good example. Critics wonder how it is possible to recognize an "authentic" person or an "authentic" act. A person described as a "fully functioning" individual or a student engaged in a "real and meaningful learning experience" would be examples of other vague concepts. The bothersome part of this is that it is difficult to verify conceptual conclusions in the usual ways. "How," ask the critics, "can we verify or confirm the existence of an authentic person or a fully functioning individual or a real and meaningful learning experience? How can we go beyond the subjectivity involved in deciding what, for example, is 'authentic'?" This, of course, leads to problems in accumulating objectively verified knowledge. The critics wonder,

"How can we objectify 'real' learning when what is 'real' is so subjectively determined? That is, what is real for one student may be unreal to another. How do we know whom to believe?"

2. A second major criticism of humanistic psychology is that it seems like too much common sense and too little like science. Michael Wertheimer (1978), one of its harshest critics, has said that

it has the earmarks of a burgeoning religion. . . . It is capturing the allegiance of many innocents who don't have the sense to ask for evidence that the magic treatments, experiences or encounters do indeed result in the idyllic consequences they are supposed to. Uncritical testimonials take the place of hardnosed data. (p. 744)

The idea behind this seems to be humanistic approaches are sometimes viewed as derivatives of a naive type of phenomenology, which, translated, means that there is more to understanding human behavior than a study of conscious processes may allow us to observe. M. Brewster Smith (1950), for example, notes that

such a psychology of consciousness has an element of commonsense appeal. . . . It does make sense to the layman; it accords with what he is ready and able to recognize in himself. . . . Because it overstates its claims, however, it may tend to promote the state of affairs away from which we have been striving—every man his own psychologist. (p. 517)

I suppose we might quarrel with whether it is such a bad idea to work in the direction of helping persons to be their own psychologists—I see virtue in that, not evil—but the fact remains it is a criticism worth considering for its moderating effect. As far as being too little science, I suspect there may be some truth in that, particularly for those whose allegiance with humanistic psychology is governed less by systematically gathered data and empirical searching and more by subjective impressions and personal conclusions. The scientific method is valued highly within the mainstream of the humanistic movement. Maslow (1968a) himself has vigorously stated: "Only science can progress." Indeed, he went on to say that "Science is the only way we have of shoving truth down the reluctant throat" (p. v).

3. Still a third criticism leveled at the humanistic position is what Child (1973) calls a "trend toward sentimentality." From the critics' point of view, this means that there is more to understanding human behavior than that which is embodied in simple religious optimism or in emphasizing the

power of positive thinking or stressing the infinite capacity of the human will to achieve good. Or, as Wertheimer (1978) has expressed it, "A humanistic background can be a source of inspiration, and of perspective, but it should not be seen as a license for vague or vapid thought" (p. 744).

All in all, critics of humanistic psychology view it as being too "soft," not rigorous enough to encourage the sort of tough, objective scientific investigations necessary to render it more than a "commonsense" psychology. Now we may agree that humanistic psychology is neither theoretically nor philosophically inclined to be "tough" and coldly "objective" in the usual sense, but that does not excuse us from being as rigorous as possible in defining humanistic psychology as a psychological system, researching its premises, and operationalizing its applications.

Strengths and Virtues of the Humanistic Position

As we have just seen, the humanistic movement is by no means flawless, nor is it accepted by all. In fact, even among some who value its contributions, it has not won easy acceptance. For example, Madsen (1971), whose major work has been the comparative study of psychological theories, wrote:

After some doubts and ambivalent attitudes toward humanistic psychology, I am now convinced that it represents a new and broader philosophy of science, and that humanistic psychology shares in a "revolution" in the philosophy of science with other philosophical trends of European origin. (p. 1)

A particular strength, or perhaps virtue, of humanistic psychology is that it reflects what seems to be an enduring and universal human value—at least among the free countries of the world: a regard for individual choice and responsibility. Indeed, even in authoritarian systems individuals are expected to be responsible for whatever limited aspects of their lives remain within their choice. The respect for individual initiative and freedom is best illustrated by the quest of contemporary Americans for more personally satisfying ways of life. Their protests against an increasingly hi-tech computerized society are due not just to the specific frustrations of feelings dehumanized, but also to the more general sense that more and more automation and electronic accounting is incompatible

with each person's importance and value as a unique center of awareness and freedom.

A humanistically oriented psychology has the advantage and virtue of helping people to stay in touch with what it means to feel and live and think and behave as human beings. It lends itself easily and readily to general discussions or probing analyses of personal ideals, of fulfillment, of self-actualization, and of authenticity and what it means to be real. Child (1973) suggests that perhaps the most persuasive virtue of humanistic psychology is the "intuitive rightness" of the model. By this he does not mean absolute correctness, but rather that the humanistic model is one that "agrees with most people's intuitive impression of what it is like to be a human being, and that this agreement is one important item of positive evidence for the scientific value of the model" (p. 18).

Another strength of the humanistic position is that it offers a flexible framework within which to observe and study behavior. It is an open rather than a closed system. Humanistic psychology used properly is not a psychology that says feelings are more important than thinking or that personal perceptions are more crucial than observable behavior. It is, or at least should be, a psychology that considers the total person in a total environment of interpersonal relationships and intrapersonal feelings. A common distortion of the humanistic position is one which says, in effect: "Your feelings and personal values are more important than anything else and so long as I can accept you for where you are and where you want to go then I will have done my best for you as a teacher (or friend, spouse, parent, or what have you)." Humanistic psychologists and educators who promote this latter position are as inflexibly myopic in denying the importance of external conditions as are extreme behaviorists who berate the significance of internal feelings or psychoanalytic thinkers who negate the significance of conscious motivation. A balanced humanistic psychology starts with a simple, but profound assumption: both the inner person and the outer world are important in influencing the final form in which behavior is expressed and feelings are felt. Along this line, Epstein (1980) has noted:

It is obviously necessary to take into account both objective and subjective reality. If orderliness is to be demonstrated in human behavior, it will be necessary to understand the mediating process by which people transform data from the objective world into their subjective world of experience. This is a critical problem for personality theory, and perhaps for all of psychology. (p. 121)

Up to this point we have examined humanistic psychology's historical roots, surveyed its theoretical and philosophical framework, and examined some of its strengths and weaknesses. The next step is to see how this framework has been and can be translated into strategies and practices that may enhance teaching and learning.

Beginnings of the Humanistic Movement in Education

In some ways, what is now referred to as humanistic education goes back as far as the 1920s and 1930s when progressive education became the focus of national attention. Even then, there was a concern about the possible dangers of compartmentalizing students into unconnected cognitive and affective fragments, and about the lack of effort to teach the whole child. In some circles it became known as the child-centered movement and flourished largely within university schools and elite private schools. Although the movement served to sensitize educators and psychologists to the human relationships aspects of teaching and to the importance of the affective domain when considering learning outcomes, its influence was more on the order of a light breeze rustling some leaves than it was of a strong wind shaking the trees. First and foremost, in those earlier days, subject matter was important and then came the student. Humanistic voices were heard, but not much listened to.

By the 1950s and early 1960s, there were signs of change. Thousands of veterans of World War II had either returned to or resumed their education, thousands more babies were born in the 1950s who were beginning their schooling, and increasingly more attention was paid to what was happening in classrooms across the nation. America had begun its space race with the Russians during the Sputnik era of the 1950s and, as part of the political fallout of that race, more and more stress was placed on the importance of schooling, particularly its math–science curriculum. Consequently, there was great emphasis on learning, but, in the minds of some, too little emphasis was given to understanding the learner.

This began to change as a chorus of humanistically oriented educators, psychologists, and social critics raised their voices and their pens to protest what they saw as education's lack of concern for the student. Carl Rogers (1959), suggested that if students in school, like a client in therapy, were given more voice and choice about what went into their education, they will "wish to learn, want to grow, seek to find out, hope to master, desire to create" (p. 234). A. S. Neill (1960), who was probably the first of the modern-day humanistic educators, built an entire school (Summerhill) around the idea that "a child is innately wise and realistic. If left to himself, without adult suggestion of any kind, he will develop as far as he is capable of developing" (p. 4). These writings were followed by the stinging commentaries of Goodman's (1964) *Compulsary Miseducation,* Holt's (1964) *How Children Fail,* and Kozol's (1967) *Death at an Early Age: The Destruction of the Hearts and Minds of Negro Children in the Boston Public Schools.* The titles speak for themselves. Not long after, these books were followed by *Schools Without Failure* (Glasser, 1969), written by a psychiatrist talking about why success is so important and how to go about helping students achieve it, and Rogers' (1969) *Freedom to Learn,* a book devoted to ideas, techniques, and approaches for making teaching more relevant and learning more meaningful within a humanistic framework.

Confluence of Humanistic and Cognitive Psychology

As humanistically inclined psychologists and educators in the 1960s and 1970s were arguing in behalf of educating the whole child, of bringing into fairer balance the affective and cognitive aspects of the teaching–learning process, modern cognitive psychology evolved into sharper focus as interest was renewed in understanding behavior generally, and learning specifically, more from the inside out rather than so exclusively from the outside in. The time was ripe for a resurgence of interest in how and why cognitive functioning went on the way it did, particularly when considered in light of how learning could be influenced by one's unique perceptions and understandings of a learning situation. If we can agree, as stated earlier, that humanistic psychology is more on the order of a new orientation to psychology than it is a new psychology unto itself, then it is easy to see how cognitive psychology fits comfortably under the humanistic umbrella. For example, both humanistic psychology and cognitive psychology acknowledge the existence of each person's "phe-nomenological reality," the idea that people behave in a way that is consistent with how things seem to them (Snygg & Combs, 1949), and both have been heavily influenced by holistic theory (Goldstein, 1939), gestalt theories (Perls, 1969; Wertheimer, 1950), and by field theory (Lewin, 1935), each of which have contributed to the general idea that people behave, learn, perceive, in other words, function, as organized wholes and not as compartmentalized segments.

Led by psychologists Jerome Bruner (1960, 1966), and David Ausubel (1960, 1963), cognitive psychology became a more clearly defined part of the contemporary scene with the 1967 publication of Ulrich Neisser's *Cognitive Psychology*. Looking back, we can see that humanistic psychology, coming into its own in the mid-1950s, established a theoretical-philosophical beachhead that focused on the whole person, that highlighted the importance of conscious processes, that gave psychological respectability to the constructs *self* and *self-concept*, and that underscored the importance of being sensitive to personal and interpersonal aspects of schooling. In the early 1960s, cognitive psychology emerged as a parallel current, but with a specific interest in the sort of conscious perceptual-mental processing that goes on when people seek to understand a situation from their own unique point of view. Whereas humanistic psychology focuses more on the affective and interpersonal components that influence the overall educational experience, cognitive psychology attends more to information processing and cognitive development factors that influence learning outcomes. Along this line, Wittrock has observed that

a cognitive model emphasizes the active and constructive role of the learner. . . . Learners often construct meaning and create their own reality, rather than respond automatically to the sensory qualities of their environments. (1979, p. 5)

We can see in this quote the overlapping interest that humanistic and cognitive psychology have in the idea of the learner being an active participant in the learning process, as opposed to being simply a passive receiver; we can also see the overlapping attention given to the idea that meaning and reality are the products of one's own point of view, not someone else's. Exactly how one goes about the business of converting perceptions into personal meaning (learning) is a problem that contemporary cognitive psychology is addressing in an offshoot of cognitive theory termed information processing. By using computers to simulate less complex human learning processes, significant gains have been made in formulating models of human information processing (Bower & Hilgard, 1981, pp. 315–453).

It is not within the scope of this chapter to do a detailed historical/contemporary analysis of cognitive psychology, but it is important to recognize the confluency of its aims and purposes with humanistic leanings and thrusts. Running as parallel currents in the same stream of holistic and phenomenological thinking, each with its own eddys of interest, humanistic and cognitive emphases have converged to have an enormous influence on teaching-learning activities at all levels of education. Although in the remainder of this chapter I will be discussing humanistic implications and applications within educational psychology, I want to make it clear that much of this discussion applies equally well to what has been called cognitive psychology. Both are interested in perceptions, personal meanings, and learning within a holistic framework—humanistic psychology emphasizing more the affective and interpersonal dimensions of this framework and cognitive psychology emphasizing more of the cognitive and information processing components.

Implications of the Humanistic Movement for Educational Processes

From a humanistic slant, the major goals of education are to help develop the individuality of persons, to assist individuals in recognizing themselves as unique human beings, and to help students actualize their potentialities. These are broad goals and probably no more or no less than what any teacher would want regardless of his or her view of human behavior. Actually, the difference lies not so much in the goals, but in the means for achieving them. I think Maslow (1968b) stated the difference most clearly when he wrote:

We are now being confronted with a choice between two extremely different, almost mutually exclusive conceptions of learning. [One] is what I want to call for the sake of contrast and confrontation, *extrinsic learning* i.e., learning of the outside, learning of the impersonal, of arbitrary associations, of arbitrary conditioning, that is, of arbitrary . . . meanings and responses. In this kind of learning, most often it is not the person himself who decides, but rather a teacher or an experimenter who says, "I will use a buzzer," "I will use a bell," "I will use a red light," and most important, "I will reinforce this or that." In this sense, learning is extrinsic to the learner, extrinsic to the personality and is extrinsic also in the sense of collecting associations, conditionings, habits or modes of action. It is as if these were possessions which the learner accumulates in the same way that he accumulates keys or coins and puts them in his pocket. They have little or nothing to do with the actualization or growth of the peculiar, idiosyncratic kind of person he is. (p. 691)

This does not mean that extrinsic learning and the conditions that promote it are unimportant. It means, rather, that the emphasis is on intrinsic learning and those conditions that foster it.

A major implication for educational processes growing from this point of view is the emphasis on helping students decide for themselves who they are and what they want to be. The further implications are that students can decide for themselves, that they have conscious minds that enable them to make choices, and that through their capacity to make choices they can at least have a chance at developing the sense of self necessary for productive, actualizing lives. (You may recognize the influence of existential psychology here.) In other words, a meaningful educational experience (external) can assist a student toward finding out what is already in him or her (internal) that can be refined and developed further.

Another major implication growing from humanistic approaches to education is the idea that in order to enhance teaching effectiveness it is necessary to understand students from their point of view. This is consistent with a truism growing out of perceptual psychology that holds that people behave in terms of what is believed to be true about reality as it is perceived (see Combs & Snygg, 1959). If teachers hope to be as effective as they can be as teachers, then it would be helpful for them to attempt to see the world as students see it, accept it as truth for them, and not to force them into changing. This does not mean that teachers should not challenge what students believe or avoid presenting them with alternatives, it only suggests that to maximize teaching effectiveness teachers are advised to start where the student's perceptions are and not where their own happen to be at the moment.

Humanistic education starts with the idea that students are different, and it strives to help students become more like themselves and less like each other. Another significant implication emerging from this point of view is that good teaching is best done through a process of helping students explore and understand the personal meanings that are inherent in all their experiences. Indeed, humanistic psychology stresses the idea that adequate persons are, among other factors, the products of strong personal values. Efforts to include value clarification exercises in teacher preparation programs and public education reflect the growing response to the importance of recognizing how personal values influence behavior (Howe & Howe, 1975; Simon, Howe, & Kirschenbaum, 1972).

Sometimes students get the idea that how they feel and what they think is not very important compared to what they know about scientific and objective facts. From a humanistic point of view, *over*emphasizing narrowly scientific and impersonally objective learning tends to inhibit the development of personal meanings. Indeed, an overemphasis of the purely subjective or purely objective violates the basic concern humanistic psychology has for the education of the *total* person. In *Perceiving, Behaving, and Becoming*, a pamphlet now regarded as a classic statement of the humanistic position in education, the implication here was nicely stated by Combs (1962):

Many students perceive school as a place where one is forced to do things which have little pertinence to life as he experiences it. Education must be concerned with the values, beliefs, convictions and doubts of students. These realities as perceived by an individual are just as important, if not more so, as the so-called objective facts. This does not mean that factual materials are not useful in making sound value judgments or in formulating constructive social policies, but rather that an overemphasis on the scientific and the objective impedes self-fulfillment. Facts have no value in themselves alone. It is only as facts find their way into human organization of convictions, beliefs, frames of reference and attitudes that they come to fruition in intelligent behavior. (pp. 68–69)

The question remains, how can the philosophical tenets and theoretical framework of humanistic psychology be translated into meaningful principles for teaching practices and learning experiences?

Toward Facilitating Teaching and Learning within a Humanistic Framework

Humanistic psychology does not offer a formalized theory of instruction. It tends to take a holistic rather than atomistic approach to the study and understanding of teaching and learning. More specifically, it is an approach that seeks to understand behavior—inside the classroom and out—within an everyday living context of perceptions, personal meanings, and relationship variables rather than within the more laboratory-oriented paradigm of operant conditioning, reinforcement schedules, S–R bonds, and the like. This does not mean that operant conditioning does not go on or that reinforcement schedules never occur, or that S–R bonds do not exist. These things do go on and do exist as classroom realities. The reason we do not hear much about these phenomena when teaching and learning are discussed within a humanistic framework is that they are primarily ways to make things happen and to explain how they happen from an outsider's point of view. I think that most humanistically oriented psychologists and educators would probably agree that many of the behavioristic principles (reinforcement schedules, contingency contracting, and other behavioral modification approaches) that are used to enhance learning do work and can be beneficial (see, for example, Bower & Hilgard, 1981, pp. 169–296; Hill, 1982; Hulse, Egeth, & Deese, 1980, chaps. 2–8). The issue is not whether approaches of this sort have value—they do—or whether or not teachers should use them—good teachers tend to use many different approaches—but, rather, where teachers choose to put their emphasis. Teachers can choose to emphasize those events and experiences that are external to students or to emphasize those instructional components that are more internal. As a general rule, in practice this means that humanistically inclined teachers are somewhat more focused on understanding students' internal perceptions than they are with manipulating the students' external environments; they tend to be more involved with the discovery of subjective, personal meanings to explore further than they are with looking for objective, observable behaviors to reinforce; they tend to be somewhat more concerned with questions related to how to have good relationships than they are with questions associated with how to give good rewards, although none of these aspects of a teaching-learning environment is entirely independent of the others.

The emphasis a person chooses is not necessarily an either-or issue. That is, humanistic teachers or psychologists are not necessarily either subjective or objective, manipulative or understanding, cognitively focused or feeling oriented. Emphasis of one approach does not automatically mean exclusion of the other(s). What it does mean, however, is that instruction will very likely be done in a somewhat different manner, with somewhat different goals, and will be described in somewhat different ways depending on where the emphasis is placed. We may understand these differences more clearly by examining two variables that, when considered within the humanistic framework described in this chapter, are components of the teaching-learning situation that humanistically oriented teachers acknowledge as crucial aspects of the overall educational experience, those being: (a) relationship variables and (b) climate variables. The research I will discuss in relation to each of these two components is not necessarily research done by persons who would call themselves humanistic, nor are the findings of that research applicable only to "humanistic" classrooms. Rather, it is a sampling of research findings that identify and exemplify those elements of classroom life that underscore basic humanistic concerns: interpersonal relationships, personal perceptions, overall climate factors, self-concept and so forth.

Teacher–Student Relationship Variables Are Important

For humanistically inclined teachers, good teaching begins with a good relationship between student and teacher. It is the emotional medium through which information is conveyed, expectations are communicated, and feelings are transmitted. It is the connection between teacher and student that, for better or worse, can affect a teacher's teaching and a learner's learning.

In almost all discussions about the importance of teacher–student relationships, an inevitable question is raised: "Does attention to relationship variables actually help students *learn* more?" The evidence does not allow us to say that students always learn more in classrooms where teachers pay greater attention to the quality of interpersonal relationships, feelings, and personal perceptions, but it does allow for the conclusion that students learn at least as much and, in addition, usually feel better not only about what they have learned, but about themselves. Rogers (1969), for instance, summarized his review of research related to the nature of a teacher's relationship to students by noting:

We may say with a certain degree of assurance, that attitudes I have endeavored to describe are not only effective in facilitating a deeper learning and understanding of self . . . but that these attitudes characterize teachers who are regarded as effective teachers, and that the students of these teachers *learn more,* [italics added] even of a conventional curriculum, than do students of teachers who are lacking in these areas. (p. 119)

Reviews of process-product research related to teacher behaviors and student outcomes by Dunkin and Biddle (1974), Good, Biddle, and Brophy (1975), Hamachek (1985, chap. 10), and Rosenshine and Furst (1973) have identified a cluster of teacher behaviors and characteristics that have been most frequently associated with positive teacher–student relationships and a greater likelihood of high student achievement: flexibility in style and approach; clarity; variability in teaching methods: enthusiasm; indirectness (questioning rather than lecturing, frequent use of student-to-student interactions); allowing enough time for students to learn the material; frequent use of praise, but delivered contingently and to specific students for specific contributions; use of multiple levels of questions or cognitive discourse (as opposed to relying only on one level of discourse); interpersonal warmth and involvement. These are some of the major teacher behaviors that contribute to positive teacher–student relationships and high student achievement. Most of these findings are derived from correlational rather than experimental studies, so it would not be accurate to claim they are *causative* factors in making for positive teacher–student relationships or high student achievement. However, the consistency with which they are found in study after study would suggest that relationship variables are an important aspect of students' achievements in school and attitudes about school.

The power of teacher–student relationships is nicely illustrated in the results of a study reported by Pedersen, Faucher, and Eaton (1978). In the process of looking at the long-term outcomes of 59 adults who had all attended a single school in a poor neighborhood, one bit of information kept popping up: among the individuals being studied, those who had a particular first-grade teacher (called "Miss A" in the study) were more likely to show I.Q. increases during elementary school, got better grades, finished more years of schooling, and were more successful as adults. Not a single one of Miss A's students whom Pedersen was able to contact for interview (44 others were interviewed who had other first-grade teachers) was in the lowest level of adult success defined in this study, despite the fact that most of the children in Miss A's classes came from poor families, many minority families. In all ways, race, religion, intelligence, and economic status, Miss A's pupils were similar to their schoolmates. The reason for the differences was Miss A herself. She believed that all of her students could learn, conveyed that message strongly to them, and got involved in the lives of her students in ways personally meaningful to them.

In the course of his research, Pedersen asked all his subjects to name as many of their elementary-school teachers as they could. Everyone who had Miss A remembered her. Most of those who had other first grade teachers could not remember their teacher's names. Four of the subjects said Miss A was their first-grade teacher when, in fact, records showed she was not. Pedersen ascribed this to "wishful thinking."

Although this is only one study, and with a small number of subjects, the results are consistent with the research mentioned earlier in this section. Teachers with good rapport, high but reasonable expectations, and sound teaching skills can make a big difference for the better. As Pedersen and his colleagues put it:

If children are fortunate enough to begin their schooling with an optimistic teacher who expects them to do well and who teaches them basic skills needed for academic success, they are likely to perform better than those exposed to a teacher who conveys a discouraging, self-defeating outlook. (p. 11)

There is no magic in this, no Eastern mysticism. Being sensitive to relationship variables does not mean that a humanistically tilted teacher gives up thinking in favor of feeling or that academic standards are lowered. It does suggest, however, the value of striving for a more reasonable balance between emotional processes and academic outcomes so that teachers do not end up overstressing production and performance (externals) to the exclusion of attitudes and feelings (internals).

Classroom relationships between teachers and students do not work in just one direction. Teacher–student relationships are more clearly two-way streets than we may have thought. For example, Brophy and Good (1974) have made the point that "students influence teacher behavior at the same time that their own behavior is being influenced by the teacher" (p. viii). Apparently, teacher–student relationships are reciprocal and mutually reinforcing. Individual differences in students make differential impressions upon teachers, which, in turn, trigger a cyclical process of differential teacher behaviors and attitudes that begin to affect teacher–student interaction patterns and student learning. Attention to relationship variables can help us understand these phenomena more clearly. Humanistically oriented teachers seem inclined to do this and, in that way, stay in touch with interpersonal emotional processes while keeping academic goals squarely in sight.

Considered Crucial: Classroom Climate and Its Impact

Whether in first grade, twelfth grade, or graduate school, the composition of every classroom is made up of a miniature, transient society with its own members, rules, organizational structure, social order, and hierarchy of authority. Just as each person develops unique characteristics, so, too, does each classroom. Indeed, it would not be going too far to say that each class develops its own personality, which for better or for worse, is the collective blend of the individual personalities within it. I have noted, for instance, in classes of my own that one class can be somewhat quiet and withdrawn, whereas a second is outgoing and assertive; still another can be cold and detached, whereas a fourth is warm and receptive. The kind of personality a class develops is not a chance happening. It is, rather, the outgrowth of student–student and teacher–student relationships that, together, give a classroom's evolving personality both form and substance. As Anderson's (1982) monumental review of school climate research suggests, there has been increasing interest and research in recent years in how a school's or classroom's climate can affect, among other things, such factors as achievement, disciplinary problems, student aspirations, satisfaction with school, and self–other attitudes.

Every class has, as it were, a social-emotional-intellectual climate that can make a crucial difference in how students perform academically and how they feel about themselves personally. After reviewing the climate characteristics of instructionally effective schools, Lezotte (1981) stated:

Two conclusions about the role of school climate seem to be well grounded in research. First, school climate appears to be a contributing factor, along with other factors, in forecasting the level of effectiveness of the school. Second, school climate research is sufficiently compelling and ought to be considered as one aspect of any school initiative. (p. 30)

Brookover *et al.* (1978) found that climate variables were clearly a factor in affecting achievement outcomes of over 8,000 students in 68 different elementary schools, and Anderson (1970) found that climate factors influence not only how much is learned, but how long the learning lasts.

How a class functions and the kind of personality it reflects depend to a very large extent on the teacher and the sort of personal style that is projected in his or her everyday behavior. However we look at it, the teacher occupies a central position as leader of the class. How a class behaves as a group or feels about itself depends to a large extent on how the teacher handles his or her role. The now classic White and Lippitt (1968) studies of the effects of different social climates on group behavior demonstrate well how behavior is affected by climate variables. In earlier research, Anderson, Brewer, and Reed (1946) found that classroom climates were very much influenced by certain teacher behaviors. For instance, where teachers relied largely on dominating techniques, there were more signs of interpersonal conflict. Tension was a major climate variable. On the other hand, where more cooperative working methods were used, spontaneity and social contributions were more frequent. Cooperativeness was a major climate variable. Moreover, it was noted that the longer a class was with a teacher who encouraged a cooperative climate, the more likely it was that there would be increases in contributory and spontaneous behaviors. In addition, it was noted that when a class changed to a more dominating teacher, students' reflected more interpersonal conflict in their behavior.

Relationship and climate variables make a difference. They are among those very human factors that either enhance a total learning experience or interfere with it. The qualities of a positive or negative relationship cannot be seen, but the consequences of it can be. A tense or cooperative climate is not directly observable, but it is something that is felt and sensed. All in all, climate variables and relationship variables seem to be outgrowths of those very human transactions that constitute the phenomenological reality of every classroom at every level of education. It would be neither accurate nor fair to say that only teachers who call themselves ''humanistic'' pay attention to the two variables we have examined. One does not have to be a humanistic teacher in order to use humanistic principles, anymore than one has to be a psychologist in order to use psychological principles.

Implications for Educational Psychology

In the broad sense, educational psychology is a discipline that studies the use and application of psychological principles in schools generally and classroom settings specifically. There has been, I feel, some confusion about how, exactly, humanistic psychology fits into the total educational psychology scheme of things. Some say it does not fit at all. Others say that it is a legitimate division within the overall domain of educational psychology. Part of the confusion, I feel, resides in misunderstandings about what a so-called humanistically oriented teacher does, and also in how humanistic principles can be applied in classroom settings. I realize that this is only one person's point of view and that there may be different opinions, and with that in mind I would like to offer some ideas, first of all, about what applications of humanistic principles to educational psychology do not mean, and then turn to an examination of what they do mean.

What Humanistic Applications to Educational Psychology Do Not Mean

Inasmuch as humanistic approaches to educational matters include ideas that take into account such matters as the importance of personal choice, relationship variables, private perceptions, individual meanings, the value of an emotionally healthy classroom climate, and the like, it seems only natural to conclude (erroneously) that, to be an effective humanistic teacher, one needs simply to be a warm, open, friendly person who is more of a facilitator than a teacher. An example of this view is found in Kolesnik's (1975) book, *Humanism and/or Behaviorism in Education,* in which the humanistic teacher is described as the kind who "is first and foremost a warm, friendly, sympathetic, understanding, sensitive human being who loves her students and has a genuine desire to help them" (p. 46). The behavioristically inclined teacher, however, is described quite differently: "It is not enough for a [behavioristic] teacher to be a 'warm, friendly person.' She must be a skilled technician, a behavioral engineer" (p. 83). In addition, the behavioristic teacher "believes that learning involves a certain amount of hard work and discipline. She expects her students to work hard and she works hard herself" (p. 111). Observations of this sort reflect, I think, popular misconceptions of the all too ubiquitous idea that

suggests humanistic teachers have only to be warm, friendly, and loving, and create an essentially permissive classroom climate in order to promote learning and positive self–other attitudes. Were it only that easy. Nowhere do we find A. H. Maslow or Carl Rogers, or Arthur Combs or Gordon Allport declaring: "Expecting your students to work hard is not all that important, because the thing that really matters is being a warm and friendly person." Indeed, research by Rutter, Maughan, Mortimore, Ouston, and Smith (1979) involving a study of 1,400 students in 12 secondary schools in central London showed that some of the major characteristics of successful teachers (those with well-behaved classes and high achievement) were that they did more active and direct teaching, they were less casual about letting classes out early, they gave more homework, and they put more emphasis on academic performance. Successful teachers, far from being harsh, detached, nonhumanistic, authoritarian martinets, more frequently encouraged their students, put good work on the bulletin boards, and made themselves available for students to consult them about problems of a personal sort. Strong evidence, it would appear, for the idea that high warmth and involvement, when combined with high expectations and standards, can produce positive results.

Humanistic applications to education do not mean that teachers are passive in setting limits, establishing standards, or permissive about expectations for either achievement or behavior. Valuable lessons can be learned from Summerhill (A. S. Neill's totally "free" school in Suffolk, England) in this regard. On the basis of in-depth interviews with 50 former Summerhill students, Bernstein (1968) found that attending a school with an atmosphere of total freedom (students take what they want, come to class when they want) was not so inspiring as it may seem. One student, for instance, who had attended Summerhill for 10 years, confessed that classes were rather "humdrum" and that it was rather easy to be led astray by new students who did little or no studying. In fact, he went on to state that procrastination was an attitude one could easily pick up at Summerhill. The disenchantment with the lack of academic emphasis was further evidenced in the fact that only 3 of 11 parents—all former Summerhill students—sent their own children to Summerhill! The 3 parents who did send their children to Summerhill took them out before age 13, almost wholly because of their convictions that not enough emphasis was placed upon the academic side of learning.

Somewhere between too much freedom and too much control there is a fulcrum point that allows us to balance and weigh the advantages of student choice and teacher guidance. The bulk of learning research, not to mention good old common sense, suggests that the best way to encourage motivation and learning is to blend a student's choices, interests, with a teacher's guidance, direction, and experience. There is little question but that the Summerhill philosophy is appealing. It does, after all, seem to make good sense to allow students to study only those subjects and topics that have intrinsic value because then the problem of extrinsic motivation is eliminated altogether. However, it is the rare and fortunate student who is able and willing to put together fragmented bits of information if left entirely to his or her own cunning and devices. There is a fine line between allowing students to have choices and abandoning them to those choices. Humanistic teaching does not necessarily mean leaving students with unstructured choices (although at times that may be appropriate), but presenting them with *guided alternatives.*

An important footnote we might add to this is that when students do pretty much what they want to do, they may seldom be stretched beyond the safety of their own choices. I say ''safety'' of their own choices because there is evidence to indicate that when individuals do only what they choose to do, they feel less successful and competent, even if they succeed at what they choose to do, than those who accomplish a task that they did not choose and that represents another person's expectations. Luginbuhl (1972) has noted, for example, that if individuals succeed at a problem they chose from a number of problems, their feelings of success may be blunted by the knowledge that they influenced the situation to make the success more possible. This suggests that it may not be wise for a teacher to permit students to have their own way (e.g., choose the number or kind of books to read or the kind of paper to write, etc.) all of the time. Living up to a teacher's expectations (e.g., writing a report on an assigned topic, getting it done and in on time) can be another way students can feel successful and thereby add to their feelings of competence and self-esteem.

What Humanistic Applications to Educational Psychology Do Mean

Emphasizing, as they do, such factors as perceptions, personal meaning, and subjective views, humanistic applications within the larger domain of educational psychology no doubt can mean different things to different people. The following ideas suggest what humanistic approaches to educational processes mean to me.

1. Humanistic applications to teaching and learning keep in mind that students bring their total selves to class. They bring heads that think and feel. They bring values that help them to filter selectively what they see and hear, and they bring attitudinal sets and learning styles that render each student unique and different from all the rest. Humanistic teachers do not only start out with the idea that students are different, but they recognize that students may still be different at the end of an academic experience. Indeed, they may even applaud that fact. They recognize that because students may have the same learning experience—in terms of exposure to similar ideas and content—that this is no guarantee that they will use, interpret, or feel in similar ways about the experience, or learn the same thing from it.

2. Humanistic applications to education recognize that not only must teachers thoroughly understand their subject matter and make wise use of research-demonstrated principles of motivation and learning, but that understanding themselves and making wise use of the self as an important teaching aid is a very good idea. Effective teachers recognize that it is not only what they say that is important, but how it is said, both of which influence and are influenced by relationship and climate variables. I have expanded this idea of teacher self-understanding at greater length elsewhere (Hamachek, 1985, pp. 333–358).

3. Humanistic applications to teaching and learning emphasize the here and now. This is simply a way to help students be tuned into current reality and contemporary experiences. For example, in an educational psychology class, rather than talking about individual differences that may exist ''out there'' in a hypothetical classroom with hypothetical students, would it be possible to discuss the individual differences in *this* classroom, with *these* students? Rather than only lecturing on the differential consequences of different group climates, would it be possible to examine and discuss the group climate of this classroom at this time? Rather than merely discussing ways to evaluate and grade students ''you may teach someday,'' would it be possible to discuss the grading and evaluation that is going on in this and other classes at this time during this term or semester? This leads to a fourth idea.

4. Humanistic applications strive to create expe-

riences that involve thinking and feelings. One good way to avoid feeling and encourage just cognitive processing is to stay in discussions that are primarily there-and-then oriented. It is easy enough to involve students in abstract discussions about the group dynamics of a White-Lippitt study or even of a hypothetical class, but perhaps it might be more meaningful in a more personal way to blend thinking and feeling in a here-and-now experience. An example may illustrate my meaning. Take the group dynamics topic. A way to approach this is actually to create different "climates" by role playing different leadership styles. One way to do this is to bring a series of questions to class (the sorts of questions that easily arouse opinions—e.g., "Should class attendance be mandatory?" "Should grading be abolished?" and so forth) and then to passively, nondirectively wonder if anyone would like to discuss them. Usually, there is a good bit of searching for leadership that goes on and lots of rambling discussion. And then, after 10 or 15 minutes—depending on the time you have— you can move subtly into a more democratically run classroom by asking for suggestions for what to discuss, giving feedback, synthesizing responses and, in general, create a "we" feeling. From this you gradually move into a more dictatorial and authoritarian mode by asserting more and more of your own views in forceful, even intolerant ways. Depending on how skillfully you are able to role play the laissez-faire, democratic, and authoritarian styles, your students will experience for themselves the feelings associated with differential classroom climates. Now students have not only something to think about, but an affective framework within which a more cognitive structure can fit. They can see for themselves that different students respond in different ways to different classroom climates and leadership styles. The ways to enact ideas in order to combine cognition and affect are practically endless.

5. Humanistic applications to teaching and learning do mean that teachers work at being prepared, knowledgeable persons who are actively involved in the total educational process. Teachers who are essentially nondirective and who see themselves more as facilitators than as teachers, and who, within this context, feel that students should do most, if not all, of their own planning and decision making are not necessarily humanistic teachers.

6. Humanistic applications to educate strive to personalize teaching and learning so as to encour-age a here-and-now involvement with thinking and feelings in a human process of people-to-people transactions. Encouraging students to speak for themselves rather than for others is one of the things a teacher can do to help create a learning climate that is a dynamic blend of cognition and affect. For example, rather than students saying something like: "When you study the effects of teacher understanding it makes you aware of aspects in yourself you might improve," they are encouraged to "own" their statements and speak only for themselves; for example: "I think that my study of the effects of teacher self-understanding has made me aware of aspects in myself that I might improve."

7. Humanistic applications to teaching and learning do mean being flexibile. By far, the single most repeated adjective in research literature describing good, or effective teachers is "flexibility" (Hamachek, 1969). If I am interpreting the literature correctly, this does not mean flexibility only within activities and emphases that are clearly humanistically oriented to begin with—for example, allowing students to have choices, encouraging students to study what interests them, giving students more freedom, and so on. There are many students who, by virtue of past experience and/or personal inclination prefer more structure, direction, and active teacher guidance. Consider, for example, some responses that Hunt and Sullivan (1974) received from a group of high school students who were asked: "What do you think is the best way for you to learn?"

I like rigid rules and a pattern set down.
I like a teacher standing up there and telling us what to do.
I think I need to be pushed a bit in order to learn.
I need that crack on the back.
I have to be told it has to be done, and if not, I won't do it. (p. 244)

Teachers aligning themselves with humanistic views who believe that their primary responsibility is that of creating the sort of unconditionally accepting climate that allows students to choose freely may not have rigid or authoritarian attitudes, but they are no less dogmatic than those who believe that the traffic flow of learning should always be determined by the teacher. Rogers (1969) has addressed this issue in the following way:

It does not seem reasonable to impose freedom on anyone who does not desire it. Consequently, it seems wise, if it is at all possible, that when a group is offered the freedom to learn on their own responsibility, there should also be provisions for those who do not wish or desire this freedom and prefer to be instructed and guided. (p. 134)

Truly humanistic teachers are not intellectually myopic. They are—or can be—total teachers, in the deepest sense of that word. That is, they are able to do what they have to do to meet the demands of the moment. They can be firm and evaluative when necessary (able to say "No!" or "You can do better than that" and mean it) or accepting and permissive (able to say "I really like what you've done" or "Do it your way" and mean that, too) when appropriate.

Epilogue

This chapter has explored the historical roots, philosophical influences, and psychological implications of a humanistically oriented approach to understanding behavior and using this understanding in a teaching-learning context. Humanistic psychology can trace its beginnings as far back as the Middle Ages and the Reformation when a philosophy known as Humanism emerged as an expression of protest against the powerful ecclesiastic and scholastic authority of the times. Just as Humanism developed as a protest against the narrow, authority-oriented religious dogma of its time, so, too, did contemporary humanistic psychology evolve as a protest against certain psychological dogmas of its time. Hence, humanistic psychology grew into what was called a "third force," not so much to be a new psychology, but a new orientation to psychology. Influenced, as it was (and is) by existential psychology's emphasis on personal choice, freedom, and responsibility, and by phenomenological psychology's emphasis on perceptions, personal meanings, and subjective experiences, humanistic psychology has been a congenial host for ideas about human behavior that go beyond the S–R bonds of behaviorism and the instinctual forces of psychoanalysis. With the leadership of Allport, Bugental, Buhler, Maslow, and Rogers, to name a few, it has become permissable to talk about the self, self-concept, and conscious, self-determined choices as being important aspects of the human condition. Rather than focusing on just those conditions outside the person (the stimuli) or those psychic states inside the person of which one was unaware (the unconscious), humanistic psychology offers a legitimate way to focus on the person from that person's own point of view. Perceptions, including one's own self-perceptions, are now allowed into the arena of psychological thought and research.

Implications for educational practices growing out of the humanistic movement have been slow, but generally positive. However, when carried to extremes, humanistic principles translated to the level of classroom practices sometimes offer too little by way of structure and organization and sometimes expect too little in terms of student output and achievement.

Cognitive psychology has been an important part of the overall humanistic movement in educational psychology. Both of these streams of thought have been influenced by holistic, gestalt, and field theories and both acknowledge the idea that, to fully understand teaching-learning processes, it is necessary to consider two conceptual aspects of classroom life: (a) the idea that teachers and students behave in accordance with their own phenomenological reality, which means that they will behave in a manner consistent with how things seem to them, and (b) that people tend to perceive, behave, learn, and function as organized wholes, not as compartmentalized segments. Cognitive psychology differs from humanistic psychology primarily in terms of its focus. Whereas educational psychologists with more of a humanistic bent concentrate on the affective and interpersonal components that impact the overall educational experience, educational psychologists with more of a cognitive leaning pay particular attention to cognitive development and information processing factors that influence learning outcomes.

The overall impact of humanistic psychology on the field of educational psychology has been one, I think, of sensitization; that is, sensitizing researchers, teacher educators, curriculum planners, and textbook writers to the importance of knowing more about, being more alert to, and researching more thoroughly all components of the total teaching-learning experience, particularly those that involve interpersonal relationships and intrapersonal feelings, such as self-concept variables and self-esteem considerations, climate factors, and perceptual modes moderating students' receptivity to new learning (input), capacity for acquisition of learning (processing), and motivation for continued learning (output).

Humanistic approaches to teaching, learning, and research do not have a lock on how these things should be done. They are approaches that say, simply: if one wants to understand the whole process, do not just look at one part of it. Everything is connected; hence, the holistic emphasis. Life in one corner of the classroom affects, to some extent, life in all other corners. It is not just what the teacher does that matters, but it is also how the teacher is perceived doing what he or she does. All in all, humanistic psychology is a theoretical umbrella under which can be found a framework and a language for understanding the inner person and for teaching in such a way as to enhance the integration of cognitive processes and affective outcomes.

References

Adler, A. (1939). *Social Interest.* New York: Putnam.

Allport, G. W. (1955). *Becoming: Basic considerations for a psychology of personality.* New Haven, CT: Yale University Press.

Anderson, C. S. (1982). The search for school climate: A review of research. *Review of Educational Research, 52,* 368–420.

Anderson, G. (1970). Effects of classroom social climate on individual learning. *American Educational Research Journal, 7,* 135–152.

Anderson, H. M., Brewer, J. E., & Reed, M. R. (1946). Studies of teachers' classroom personalities, II. *Applied Psychology Monographs* (Monograph No. 46).

Ausubel, D. P. (1960). The use of advance organizers in the learning and retention of meaningful verbal material. *Journal of educational psychology, 51,* 267–272.

Ausubel, D. P. (1963). *The psychology of meaningful verbal material.* New York: Grune & Stratton.

Back, K. W. (1972). *Beyond words: The study of sensitivity training and the encounter movement.* New York: Russell Sage Foundation.

Barron, F. (1979). *The shaping of personality: Conflict, choice, and growth.* New York: Harper & Row.

Bebout, J. A. (1973). A study of group encounter in higher education. *Educational Technology, 13,* 63–67.

Beck, A. T. (1976). *Cognitive therapy and the emotional disorders.* New York: International Universities Press.

Berelson, B., & Steiner, G. A. (1964). *Human behavior: An inventory of scientific findings.* New York: Harcourt, Brace & World.

Bernstein, E. (1968, fall). Summerhill: A follow-up study of its students. *Journal of Humanistic Psychology,* pp. 123–136.

Bindrum, P. A. (1968). A report on a nude marathon. *Psychotherapy: Theory, Research, and Practice, 5,* 180–188.

Bower, G. H., & Hilgard, E. R. (1981). *Theories of learning* (5th ed.). Englewood Cliffs, NJ: Prentice-Hall.

Brookover, W. B., Schweitzer, J. H., Schneider, J. M., Beady, C. H., Flood, P. A., & Wisenbaker, J. M. (1978). Elementary school social climate and school achievement. *American Educational Research Journal, 15,* 301–318.

Brophy, J. E., & Good, T. L. (1974). *Teacher-student relationships: Causes and consequences.* New York: Holt, Rinehart & Winston.

Bruner, J. (1960). *The process of education.* Cambridge, MA: Harvard University Press.

Bruner, J. (1966). *Toward a theory of instruction.* Cambridge, MA: Harvard University Press.

Bugental, J. F. T. (1963). Humanistic psychology: A new breakthrough. *American Psychologist, 18,* 563–567.

Bugental, J. F. T. (1965). *The search for authenticity: An existential-analytic approach to psychotherapy.* New York: Holt, Rinehart & Winston.

Bugental, J. F. T. (1967). *Challenges of humanistic psychology.* New York: McGraw-Hill.

Buhler, C. (1971). Basic theoretical concepts of humanistic psychology. *American Psychologist, 21,* 378–386.

Burton, A. (Ed.). (1969). *Encounter.* San Francisco: Jossey Bass.

Child, I. L. (1973). *Humanistic psychology and the research tradition: Their several virtues.* New York: Wiley.

Cooley, C. H. (1902). *Human Nature and the Social Order.* New York: Charles Scribner's Sons.

Combs, A. W. (1962). Perceiving and becoming. In *Perceiving, Behaving, and Becoming* (pp. 65–82). Association for Supervision and Curriculum Development Yearbook, Washington, DC: National Education Association.

Combs, A. W. (1981, February). Humanistic education: Too tender for a tough world? *Phi Delta Kappan,* pp. 446–449.

Combs, A. W., & Snygg, D. (1959). *Individual behavior* (rev. ed.). New York: Harper & Row.

Dunkin, M. S., & Biddle, B. J. (1974). *The study of teaching.* New York: Holt, Rinehart & Winston.

Egan, G. (1970). *Encounter: Group processes for interpersonal growth.* Monterey, CA: Brooks/Cole.

Ellis, A. (1962). *Reason and emotion in psychotherapy.* New York: Lyle Stuart.

Epstein, S. (1973). The self-concept revisited, or a theory of a theory. *American Psychologist, 28,* 404–416.

Epstein, S. (1980). The self-concept: A review and the proposal of an integrated theory of personality. In E. Staub (Ed.), *Personality: Basic aspects and current research* (pp. 81–132). Englewood Cliffs, NJ: Prentice-Hall.

Erikson, E. (1980). *Identity and the life cycle.* New York: Norton. (Originally published 1959).

Fitts, W., Adams, J., Radford, F., Richard, W., Thomas, B., & Thompson, W. (1971). *The self concept and self actualization.* Nashville, TN: Counselor Recordings and Tests.

Franks, D., & Marolla, J. (1976). Efficacious action and social approval as interacting dimensions of self-esteem: Formulation through construct validation. *Sociometry, 39,* 324–341.

Freud, S. (1964). Civilization and its discontents. In *Standard edition* (Vol. 21). London: Hogarth. (First German edition published 1930).

Freud, S. (1964). Analysis terminable and interminable. In *Standard edition* (Vol. 23). London: Hogarth Press. (First German edition published 1937).

Fromm, E. (1941). *Escape from freedom.* New York: Rinehart.

Fromm, E. (1947). *Man for himself.* New York: Rinehart.

Giovacchini, P. L. (1983). Psychoanalysis. In R. S. Corsini & A. S. Marsella (Eds.), *Personality Theories, research, and assessment* (pp. 25–68). Itasca, IL: Pencock.

Glasser, W. L. (1969). *Schools without failure.* New York: Harper & Row.

Goldstein, K. (1939). *The organism.* New York: American Book Co.

Good, T. L., Biddle, B. J., & Brophy, J. E. (1975). *Teachers make a difference.* New York: Holt, Rinehart & Winston.

Goodman, P. (1964). *Compulsary miseducation.* New York: Horizon Press.

Gustaitis, R. (1969). *Turning on.* New York: Macmillan.

Hall, C. S. (1954). *A primer of Freudian psychology.* New York: New American Library.

Hamachek, D. E. (1969). Characteristics of good teachers and implications for teacher education. *Phi Delta Kappan, 50,* 341–345.

Hamachek, D. E. (1985). *Psychology in teaching, learning, and growth* (3rd ed.). Boston, MA: Allyn & Bacon.

Hamachek, D. E. (1985). The self's development and ego growth: Conceptual analysis and implications for counselors. *Journal of Counseling and Development, 64,* 136–142.

Hamachek, D. E. (1987). *Encounters with the self* (3rd ed.). New York: Holt, Rinehart & Winston.

Hilgard, E. R. (1949). Human motives in the concept of the self. *American Psychologist, 4,* 374–382.

Hill, W. F. (1982). *Principles of learning: A handbook of applications.* Palo Alto, CA: Mayfield.

Holt, J. (1964). How children fail. New York: Pitman.

Horney, K. (1937). *Neurotic personality of our time.* New York: Norton.

Howard, J. (1970). *Please touch: A guided tour of the human potential movement.* New York: McGraw-Hill.

Howe, L. W., & Howe, M. (1975). *Personalizing education: Values clarification and beyond.* New York: Hart.

Hulse, S. H., Egeth, M., & Deese, J. (1980). *The psychology of learning.* New York: McGraw-Hill.

Hunt, D. E., & Sullivan, E. V. (1974). *Between Psychology and Education.* Hinsdale, IL: Dryden.

James, W. (1890). *Principles of psychology.* (Vol. 1). New York: Henry Holt.

Jersild, A. T. (1952). *In search of self.* New York: Bureau of Publications, Columbia University.

Johnson, D. W., & Johnson, R. (1975). *Learning together and alone: Cooperation, competition, and individualization.* Englewood Cliffs, NJ: Prentice-Hall.

Jourard, S. M. (1971). *The transparent self.* New York: Van Nostrand Reinhold.

Kegan, R. (1982). *The evolving self: Problem and processes in human development.* Cambridge, MA: Harvard University Press.

Kolesnik, W. B. (1975). *Humanism and/or behaviorism in education.* Boston, MA: Allyn & Bacon.

Kozol, J. (1967). *Death at an early age: The destruction of the hearts and minds of Negro children in the Boston public schools.* Boston, MA: Houghton Mifflin.

Lecky, P. (1945). *Self-consistency: A theory of personality.* New York: Island Press.

Lewin, K. (1935). *A dynamic theory of personality.* New York: McGraw-Hill.

Lewis, M., & Brooks-Gunn, J. (1981). The self as social knowledge. In M. D. Lynch, A. A. Norem-Hebeisen, & K. J. Gergen (Eds.), *Self-concept: Advances in theory and research* (pp. 101–118). Cambridge, MA: Ballinger.

Lezotte, L. W. (1981). Climate characteristics in instructionally effective schools. *Impact on Instructional Improvement, 16,* 26–31 (New York State Association for Supervision and Curriculum Development)

Luginbuhl, J. E. R. (1972). Role of choice and outcome of feelings of success and estimates of ability. *Journal of Personality and Social Psychology, 22,* 121–127.

Lundin, R. W. (1983). Learning theories: Operant reinforcement and social learning theories of B. F. Skinner and Albert Bandura. In R. J. Corsini & A. J. Marsella (Eds.), *Person-* ality theories, research, and assessment (pp. 287–330). Itasca, IL: Peacock.

Madsen, K. B. (1971). Humanistic psychology and the philosophy of science. *Journal of Humanistic Psychology, 11,* 1–10.

Maslow, A. H. (1954). *Motivation and personality.* New York: Harper.

Maslow, A. H. (1968a). *Toward a psychology of being* (2nd ed.). Princeton, NJ: D. Van Nostrand.

Maslow, A. H. (1968b). Some educational implications of humanistic psychologies. *Harvard Educational Review, 38,* 685–696.

Maslow, A. H. (1969). Toward a humanistic biology. *American Psychologist, 24,* 724–735.

Maslow, A. H. (1970). *Motivation and personality* (2nd ed.). New York: Harper & Row.

Matson, F. W. (1971). Humanistic theory: The third revolution in psychology. In T. C. Greening (Ed.), *Existential Humanistic Psychology* (pp. 44–56). Belmont, CA: Brooks/Cole.

Mead, G. H. (1934). *Mind, self, and society.* Chicago, IL: University of Chicago Press.

Meichenbaum, D. H. (1974). *Cognitive behavior modification.* Morristown, NJ: General Learning Press.

Mead, G. H. (1934). *Mind, self, and society.* Chicago, IL: University of Chicago Press.

McGrath, J. E. (1984). *Groups: Interaction and performance.* Englewood Cliffs, NJ: Prentice-Hall.

Morris, V. C. (1954). Existentialism and education. *Educational Theory, 4,* 252–253.

Morris, V. C. (1966). *Existentialism and education.* New York: Harper & Row.

Moustakas, C. E. (Ed.). (1956). *The self: Explorations in personal growth.* New York: Harper.

Murphy, G. (1947). *Personality: A biosocial approach to origins and structures.* New York: Harper.

Murphy, G. (1958). *Human potentialities.* New York: Basic Books.

Murray, H. A., & Collaborators. (1938). *Explorations in personality.* New York: Oxford.

Neill, A. S. (1960). *Summerhill: A radical approach to child rearing.* New York: Hart.

Neisser, U. (1967). *Cognitive psychology.* New York: Appleton-Century-Crofts.

Pederson, E., Faucher, T., & Eaton, W. W. (1978). A new perspective on the effects of first grade teachers on children's subsequent adult status. *Harvard Educational Review, 48,* 1–31.

Perls, F. S. (1969). *Gestalt therapy verbatim.* New York: Bantam.

Perls, F., Hefferline, R., & Goodman, P. (1958). *Gestalt therapy: Excitement and growth in human personality.* New York: Random House.

Raimey, V. C. (1948). Self-reference in counseling interviews. *Journal of Consulting Psychology, 12,* 153–163.

Richardson, W. J. (1971). Humanism and existential psychology. In T. C. Greening (Ed.), *Existential humanistic psychology* (pp. 123–133). Belmont, CA: Brooks/Cole.

Rogers, C. R. (1951). *Client-centered therapy.* Boston, MA: Houghton-Mifflin.

Rogers, C. R. (1959). Significant learning: In therapy and education. *Educational Leadership, 16,* 232–242.

Rogers, C. R. (1961). *On becoming a person.* Boston: Houghton Mifflin.

Rogers, C. R. (1969). *Freedom to learn.* Columbus, OH: Merrill.

Rogers, C. R. (1970). *Carl Rogers on encounter groups.* New York: Harper & Row.

Rosenshine, B., & Furst, N. (1973). The use of divert observation to study teaching. In R. Travers (Ed.), *Second handbook of research on teaching* (pp. 122–183). Chicago, IL: Rand McNally.

Rutter, M., Maughan, B., Mortimore, P., Ouston, J., & Smith, A. (1979). *Fifteen thousand hours: Secondary schools and their effects on children.* Cambridge, MA: Harvard University Press.

Schmuck, R. A., & Schmuck, P. A. (1974). *A humanistic psychology of education: Making the school everybody's business.* Palo Alto, CA: National Press Books.

Schmuck, R. A., & Schmuck, P. A. (1983). *Group processes in the classroom* (4th ed.). Dubuque, IA: Brown.

Schutz, W. C. (1967). *Joy: Expanding human awareness.* New York: Grove Press.

Seeman, M. (1966). Status and identity: The problem of inauthenticity. *Pacific Sociological Review, 9,* 67–73.

Severin, F. T. (Ed.). (1965). *Humanistic viewpoints in psychology: A book of readings.* New York: McGraw-Hill.

Shaffer, J. B. P. (1978). *Humanistic psychology.* Englewood Cliffs, NJ: Prentice-Hall.

Simon, S. B., Howe, L. W., & Kirschenbaum, H. (1972). *Values clarification.* New York: Hart.

Skinner, B. F. (1948). *Walden two.* New York: Macmillen.

Skinner, B. F. (1968). *The Technology of Teaching.* New York: Appleton-Century-Crofts.

Skinner, B. F. (1971). *Beyond freedom and dignity.* New York: Knopf.

Smith, M. B. (1950). The phenomenological approach to personality theory: Some critical remarks. *The Journal of Abnormal & Social Psychology, 45,* 516–522.

Snygg, D., & Combs, A. W. (1949). *Individual behavior: A new frame of reference for psychology.* New York: Harper.

Sullivan, H. S. (1947). *Conceptions of modern psychiatry: The first William Alanson White Memorial Lectures.* Washington, DC: The William Alanson White Foundation.

Tomkins, C. (1976, January). Profiles: New paradigms. *The New Yorker,* pp. 30–51.

Watson, J. B. (1926). *The ways of behaviorism.* New York: Harper.

Wertheimer, M. (1950). Laws of organization in perceptual forms. In W. D. Ellis (Ed.), *A source book of gestalt psychology* (pp. 71–88). New York: Humanistics Press.

Wertheimer, M. (1978). Humanistic psychology and the humane and tough-minded psychologist. *American Psychologist, 33,* 739–745.

White, R., & Lippitt, R. (1968). Leader behavior and member reaction in three social climates. In D. Cartwright & A. Zander (Eds.). *Group dynamics* (3rd ed., pp. 318–335). New York: Harper & Row.

White, R. W. (1959). Motivation reconsidered: The concept of competence. *Psychological Review, 66,* 297–333.

Wittrock, R. C. (1979). The cognitive movement in instruction. *Educational researcher, 8,* 5–11.

CHAPTER 10

A History of Instructional Design and Its Impact on Educational Psychology

Walter Dick

The term *instructional design* has only come into use in education in the past decade. It refers to the process of systematically applying instructional theory and empirical findings to the planning of instruction. It is applied educational psychology in the best sense of the term. There is a clear focus on an instructional goal that represents what the learner will be able to do when the instruction is completed, the present skills of the learner, and how instruction will take place.

The term *instructional design* was preceded by the term *educational technology,* which is widely used to represent several approaches to instruction. Educational technology has been defined by many as having two fundamental components: (a) a hardware or media component that is used to deliver instruction and (b) a process component that indicates how instruction will be prepared for delivery via some medium. Instructional design is the term used to describe the process component. Its relationship with educational technology indicates the historical and conceptual relationship between the process of designing instruction and innovative instructional delivery methods.

Walter Dick • Department of Educational Research, Florida State University, Tallahassee, FL 32306.

This chapter traces the historical development from World War II of what has come to be called instructional design, and assesses its impact on the field of educational psychology. The chapter concludes with a prognosis of the future directions of this field. The position is taken that instructional design is not only a process for designing instruction, but also a field of academic study that has been pioneered by educational psychologists and continues to be of great importance to those who are committed to improving human learning and performance.

The Beginnings of Instructional Design—World War II to 1958

It is impossible to identify a single meeting, journal article, text, or similar product that launched the field of instructional design. Many writers begin their description of the field with a narrative about Skinner's early work with programmed instruction. When the programmed instruction movement began in the late fifties, there was already a receptive environment for any innovation in the area of human learning that could be applied in the classroom. This interest had been building since the second Word War.

Conversations with pioneers in the field, Robert Gagné (personal communication, April, 1984) and Leslie Briggs (personal communication, April, 1984), indicate that a number of psychologists were influenced by the training demands made by World War II and the corresponding lack of relevant research and experience that could be drawn upon from the field of psychology. After the war these training problems continued to be of interest to many psychologists.

The Air Force set up a number of research centers beginning in 1944 to investigate methods not only for selecting personnel for the service but also for effectively training pilots, navigators, and other crewmen. John Flanagan, who had directed one of the Air Force research centers, established the American Institutes for Research (AIR) as a nonprofit behavioral sciences research company in 1947. AIR continued the tradition of research in pilot selection, human factors engineering, and training.

In the decade from 1948 until 1958, major developments were under way that prepared the training world for Skinner's contributions. One set of activities was the continuing research on the use of media in training. The Navy funded research in the use of films and television, and various agencies became interested in the use of a wide range of training aids such as tape/slides, overhead transparencies, simulators, and eventually, teaching machines. At a conference in 1959 in which much of this research was summarized, Melton (1959) concluded that the presentations clearly indicated the futility of trying to identify the "best" medium, and that researchers were going to have to relate the specific characteristics of the task to be learned to the characteristics of the media available to teach it. From the point of view of those involved in military research, the summative comparison of media was no longer a significant issue.

Another important development during this decade was the issuance of weapons systems regulations. In effect, the military would no longer merely purchase equipment but rather would consider the operator and operational environment in which the equipment would operate—the entire system. It became a major task to forecast job requirements and to derive selection and training requirements. Some of the initial task analyses, which later were to become so important to the field of instructional design, were conducted by Miller (1962) for the Air Force. The process of considering training as a system was taking shape in the military in the late fifties and resulted, in part, in a book titled *Psychological Principles of System Development,* which was edited by Robert Gagné (1962b). The authors of the chapters in this book drew heavily on their military research and development experiences of the fifties.

A third area of eventual interest to instructional designers was testing and evaluation. The concern over the problems of personnel selection continued after World War II and the Korean War. In addition to the testing of intellectual capabilities, the assessment of psychomotor and perceptual skills was greatly increased. Overall there was an emphasis on norming instruments in order to select and classify soldiers appropriately.

There was little distinction between research and evaluation at this time. The terms tended to be used synonymously. Experimental designs that involved no-treatment control groups were the typical means of determining which of several approaches was best. Psychometrically designed, norm-referenced tests often served as a measure of the dependent variable. Often an innovative approach to instruction was compared in such studies to "traditional" instruction that had been in place for many years.

It should be noted that these early events that eventually culminated in the field of instructional design occurred almost entirely in a military context under the direction of researchers who had been trained in experimental psychology and who had a primary interest in applied human learning. Very few academic institutions were active in this type of research and training. Pennsylvania State University conducted research on films for the military, and Indiana University and the University of Southern California developed outstanding graduate programs in educational technology with an emphasis on media production. However, the predominant thrust of educational psychology programs was to train preservice teachers and to conduct research that, unfortunately, did not transfer easily to the classroom context. Skinner's work was to change all this.

The Late Fifties—Sputnik and Programmed Instruction

The year 1958 is a demarcation point in the early history of instructional design. In that year two important events occurred. The first was the launching of Sputnik by the Russians. This earth-orbiting satellite signaled not only the beginning of a space race but also a revitalization of our national interest in the quality of mathematics and science instruction in the public schools. The second event of significance to the field of instructional design was the publication of Skinner's second major paper on programmed instruction (Skinner, 1958). This paper, along with the research produced in his Harvard laboratory, stimulated widespread interest in both research and development in applied human learning. The impact of Sputnik on the curriculum tended to be somewhat transitory whereas that of programmed instruction has been enduring.

As a result of Sputnik, the federal government, through the National Science Foundation and United States Office of Education, became involved in improving instruction through the sponsorship of large curriculum development projects. The purpose of these projects was to teach "good" science and "good" mathematics through the use of up-to-date texts written by the most prestigious scientists. Major projects in physics, chemistry, and biology were undertaken along with numerous ones in modern mathematics. In most cases the model was the same. A well-known scientiest recruited other scientists and support personnel to write new materials. These were published and sold to the schools with little regard for the evaluation of the curriculum being sold.

At the beginning of the decade of the sixties, the new curriculum development movement and the programmed instruction movement proceeded, with rare exception, on separate paths. However, as problems began to occur with the use of the new curricula, the educational psychologists/ instructional designers of that time began to see their ideas being incorporated into the development of the new curricula. A number of the new concepts in instructional design, including hierarchical analysis and formative evaluation, were first applied within the curriculum development projects. The concepts themselves are described in some detail in the next major section of this chapter. The point to be noted here is that the post-Sputnik era was one in which federal funds became available for projects that eventually provided an opportunity to evaluate the emerging instructional design theories and procedures.

The other major development in 1958 was the publication of the paper titled "Teaching Machines" by Skinner (1958). Skinner was already well known in the academic community for his scientific analysis of behavior and especially his use of reinforcement to shape behavior. It is said that he became concerned when he found that the teaching techniques that he used so successfully in the laboratory were not applied in the public school classrooms. As he observed children being taught, he saw a number of problems that could be addressed through the use of programmed instruction. Skinner's fundamental approach was to identify the desired behavior, then to create situations in which successive approximations of the behavior would occur and be reinforced. This would increase the probability that the same response would occur in the same circumstances in the future.

When this approach was applied to the creation of instructional materials for students, the result was a *linear* text. All students read the text from beginning to end, but in contrast to regular texts, programmed instruction contained small steps, or frames. Each frame contained information followed by a question that required a response from the learner. This response could be compared with the correct answer, that usually appeared on the back of the page. The student proceeded from frame to frame making successively more complex responses to successively more difficult questions. The goal was to minimize student errors in their study of the text. Upon its completion, it was assumed that the student had acquired the desired behaviors. The basic characteristics of programmed instruction were the use of small units or steps in the instructional process, the requirement for a constructed response from the student, and the provision of immediate feedback to answers as a form of positive reinforcement. Students studied the text at their own pace; this was not a group-learning approach.

What has been described is both the theory and the format of programmed instruction. When incorporated in the design of actual instruction, it did not always work well. To the Skinnerians' credit and to the long-term benefit of instructional design, they tried to find out why the instruction did not work. A number of techniques were employed, especially an analysis of the errors made on each frame, to locate and correct problems. Programmed instruction materials were tried out on small numbers of students and revised until they reached the desired level of effectiveness.

The Skinnerian form of linear instruction was soon criticized for not taking into consideration individual differences among learners. As a result, writers started using branching techniques based on learners' responses to multiple choice questions. Norman Crowder is generally credited with the development of this technique; however, Sidney Pressey did research with a multiple-choice teaching machine in the thirties. This work was largely ignored at that time. A number of research studies indicated that Skinner's teaching machine, (a box designed to expose the programmed instruction text to the learner one frame at a time), was not really required for students to learn. They could proceed through the instruction without the machine.

When, in the mid-sixties, researchers began to investigate the viability of computers to deliver instruction, most drew upon the programmed instruction approach, both linear and branching, as the method to use in preparing instruction for the computer. Therefore, although the pure Skinnerian programmed instruction text never gained widespread use in public education, the process that was used to prepare the text and the general concept of self-paced individualized instruction were to serve as foundations for the instructional design movement. A variety of self-paced courses were created and implemented in the curricula of schools and colleges, as well as in industry (see, for example, Moore, Mahan & Ritts, 1969). It is difficult to identify a major figure in the early history of instructional design who was not influenced to some extent by the Skinnerian approach to classroom (as opposed to laboratory) learning.

The continuing influence of this early work in programmed instruction on the subsequent development of the field of instructional design will be apparent in the sections that follow. Davies (1971) has provided an excellent description of the changing or expanding emphases that occurred throughout the sixties. For example, the initial approach of breaking behavior down into small steps was enlarged to include, eventually, behavioral objectives, task analysis, content analysis, job analysis, and needs assessment. The evaluation of instruction was expanded to include several phases of instructional tryouts and revisions, that became known as both developmental testing and formative evaluation.

There is one other result of the programmed instruction movement that deserves consideration, namely the production of a product that could be sold for a profit. Although in the past the measurement-oriented educational psychologist had worked with private companies, this was a new experience for many learning-oriented educational psychologists. Companies were formed and contracts let to produce and sell programmed texts.

This experience provided the educational psychologist with much more knowledge of the social, political, and economic aspects of the instructional process as it is undertaken in the public schools. More and more educational psychologists became aware of the discrepancy between their laboratory approach to investigating the human learning process and the conditions that prevail in a typical classroom. This sparked new interest in classroom relevant research and even the establishment of a journal, *Contemporary Educational Psychology,* which specializes in the publication of studies that have been conducted under classroom conditions. The long-term effect, whether it was in public education or military and industrial training, was to draw the educational psychologist/instructional designer into a team of specialists all of whom were concerned with instructional effectiveness. Soon media specialists and managers, evaluators and teachers, would team up with the instructional designer to collectively develop instructional systems. With the advent of programmed instruction, the educational psychologist was no longer necessarily isolated in the halls of ivy.

The Conceptual Revolution of the Sixties

Most of the major components of the instructional design process emerged in the decade of the 1960s. Spurred on by the Russians' success in space and funded by a variety of new federal programs in the United States Office of Education, the National Science Foundation, and the research arms of the military, researchers developed and documented new procedures for improving instruction. The names associated with this era are still quite familiar: Gagné, Briggs, Glaser, Mager, Cronbach, Scriven, and Carroll. It is important to examine their contributions because they were incorporated into the systems approach to instructional design in the 1970s. The major contributions of these men and others during the 1960s are described in the following.

One of the most significant and pervasive concepts that emerged from the programmed instruction movement was that of the behavioral objective. Mager (1962, 1984) indicated the necessity of specifying exactly what it is that learners were to be able to do when they completed their instruction. In its simplest form, this was a shift from telling about what the teacher was to accomplish to what the student was to accomplish. If the programmed instruction writer was going to shape learners' behavior, it was imperative to know what that behavior was to be.

Mager's now famous behavioral objective had to include not only a statement about the behavior of the learner but also the conditions under which the behavior would occur and the criteria that would be used to judge if the behavior was acceptable. The necessity of using such behavioral objectives stirred great controversy throughout the sixties, especially from subject-matter educators who objected to expressing the outcomes of instruction in such simplistic terms.

Many questions about objectives also surfaced, among the most significant of which were: Where do objectives come from and What do I do with them after I have them? These questions were answered by subsequent developments in the field. Some argued that objectives should be based on an analysis of what must be learned. What the student must learn with regard to intellectual skills were identified via a learning hierarchy. Gagné (1962a) hypothesized that in order to master a complex intellectual skill, the learner must first master certain prerequisite skills. But what were these specific prerequisites? They are those skills that are identified when the researcher asks the question, What does the learner have to know or be able to do in order to learn this new skill? The answer to this question is a listing of one or more subordinate skills. The question is repeated for each of these until the learning hierarchy has been developed. Each of the subordinate skills can be converted into a specific objective that a student must master on the way to mastery of the terminal objective. The hierarchical analysis technique remains the primary method of identifying the subordinate skills required in intellectual skills instruction.

One answer to the question, What do you do with objectives, was to test them. In 1963 Glaser published his article on the necessity for criterion-referenced testing. Glaser, who was heavily involved in research in programmed instruction, found that although such instruction was being designed to teach very specific behaviors, often the test instruments did not assess those same behaviors. He was extremely critical of the norm-referenced approach to testing—an approach that seemed to put more of a premium on the comparison of students than on an assessment of their individual ability to achieve the objectives of the instruction.

Glaser essentially emphasized two points in his article. The first, which Mager also indicated, was the necessity of making clear the criterion for successful performance. His second point was that the test items must measure the behavior described in the objective. It is this second aspect of criterion-referenced testing that was so important to subsequent developments in the field that it resulted in the term *objective-referenced* testing, that is, testing that directly reflects the behaviors described in a set of objectives.

The idea of criterion-referenced testing (CRT) and its seeming attack on the traditions of norm-referenced measurement, did not go by unnoticed. Articles soon appeared noting the limitations of CRT and the continuing importance of the norm-referenced approach (see Ebel, 1978, and Popham, 1978). In particular, it was noted that objective-referenced tests could be used to rank order learners (which is usually done with norm-referenced tests), and that some norm-referenced instruments, such as competitive selection tests, do have an important role to play in education. The primary point of CRT for instructional design was that it is necessary to have assessment instruments that identify what students have learned from their instruction and what they have not learned. Rank ordering students by test scores did not tell the designer what was wrong with the instruction or how it could be improved.

By the mid-sixties the programmed instruction writer, who by now had gone beyond the strictly linear progression of frames advocated by Skinner, was using various branching approaches as proposed by Crowder. The designer was also contemplating the computer as a delivery mechanism. But the writer/designer still either depended upon the Skinnerian approach to designing instruction, or developed a somewhat idiosyncratic approach based on psychological literature. Then, in 1965, Gagné published *The Conditions of Learning,* which provided the broad theoretical underpinnings that many instructional designers are still using.

Gagné first emphasized that there are five domains of learning, each of which has a different set of conditions for instructing the learner. He indicated that these domains include verbal information, intellectual skills, psychomotor skills, attitudes, and cognitive strategies. A particularly important distinction was made between verbal information, which is essentially the recall of facts, and intellectual skills, which require the cognitive manipulation of symbolic information. In his first edition, Gagné said little about cognitive strategies except to note that they seem to be skills that indicate how we go about learning and are themselves learnable. (Twenty years later, the area of learning strategies is of great importance to both instructional designers and educational psychologists.)

In *Conditions of Learning,* Gagné indicated that there are nine basic elements in teaching any objective. These "events of instruction," as he termed them, are generic components that should be considered when any instruction is developed. The inclusion or exclusion of any event depends on the sophistication level of the learner and the nature of the content. Briefly, Gagné indicated that first the learner's attention must be obtained. It is then possible to inform the learner of what will be learned, and thus to motivate him or her. Then the designer must insure that the learner has the prerequisite skills, as identified by a learning hierarchy, which are required to begin instruction.

The learner is now ready to receive a direct indication of what is to be learned and to receive guidance in how to perform the skill. Practice, with response sensitive feedback, is then provided. The learner is tested to insure that the skill has been mastered, and additional instruction to facilitate retention and transfer is provided when appropriate.

Gagné and Briggs (1979) subsequently elaborated on the various events of instruction as they vary according to the various domains of learning. They also stressed the hierarchy of skills within the intellectual skills domain, that is, that the subordinate intellectual skills for problem solving are principles. To learn principles one must first learn defined concepts, which in turn are dependent on concrete concepts. Each type of intellectual skill requires a slightly different approach within the events of instruction.

Another critical component that played a prominent role in the sixties was evaluation. Up until this time evaluation tended to be equated with research, and therefore the tools of the researcher were applied to the evaluation process. This meant the use of experimental designs to determine which of two innovations was better or, more typically, if an innovation was better than the ubiquitous traditional approach. All this began to change with the use of what Scriven (1967) called formative evaluation. This term was used to identify the process of collecting data and information in order to improve instruction. Scriven had observed that only

after much of the new science curriculum of the sixties was published and in the schools was it realized that many students had serious problems in the use of the materials. Why was this not discovered until it was too late to make changes? Scriven said that evaluation had to be undertaken *while* the instruction was being developed in order to determine what parts were working and what parts were not. Those parts that were not working should be revised until they did work. This type of formative evaluation was in sharp contrast to summative evaluation, which was used after an instructional innovation was complete to determine its comparative or absolute value or worth.

Actually, Scriven's concern with the evaluation process was related in part to earlier work by Cronbach (1963), which pointed out the wholesome use of evaluation to improve courses. The actual operationalization of the concept of formative evaluation was most influenced by Markle (1967) who, under the label of developmental testing, described the phases of evaluation that were employed by programmed instruction writers. Markle's work is reflected in the subsequent writings of Baker and Alkin (1974) and Dick (1977). The formative evaluation process usually includes three phases. The first is one in which the writer/designer goes through the instruction on a one-to-one basis with several representative students for the purpose of discovering problem areas. Revisions are made and the instruction is tried out with a larger number of learners. The designer then makes another set of revisions based on the data collected from this evaluation, and then a field trial and final revision are conducted.

In the formative evaluation process, the data-collection process is focused primarily, but not exclusively, on the learner. Performance data are collected not only on a posttest but also on a pretest and on any practice activities in the materials. Student comments about the instruction, learning time, and responses to specific attitude items are all used to identify where problems are located and how they can be revised. This process of formative evaluation was extremely important in the entire instructional design process, which came to be conceived in the 1970s as a system with a self-correcting mechanism.

Several other trends began in the sixties that should be noted because of their subsequent influence on the field of instructional design. The first trend was to begin implementing systems of instruction, or at least to try to apply the ideas that have been presented here to real-world instruction. Glaser developed Individually Prescribed Instruction (IPI), whereas Keller (1968) was developing the Personalized System of Instruction to introduce the use of student tutors into self-paced courses that required students to master successive unit tests. Bloom (see Block, 1971) developed a system of mastery learning in which students studied self-instructional materials in order to master specific skills. Students were tested periodically to determine if they were ready to progress or were in need of remedial instruction. As another example, Flanagan established Project PLAN, which involved computer analysis of student tests in order to write prescriptions for remediation or enrichment. All of these models were distinctly different from traditional classroom instruction in which the teacher was the primary instructional delivery medium. With the new approaches the teacher had a new role as manager and motivator. Variations on these self-pacing, mastery learning approaches have continued to be used to a moderate extent ever since their first introduction in the sixties.

Another important thrust at this same time was the research being undertaken on the uses of computers in education. As large mainframe systems were installed at major universities and research organizations, researchers began to examine their role in the instructional process. Direct, interactive use was investigated in terms of computer-assisted instruction that included tutorial, and drill and practice approaches. Computer managed instruction, such as Project PLAN, involved off-line instruction with on-line testing and record keeping (see, for example, Dick & Gallagher, 1972). As will be noted later, the preparation of instruction for delivery via computer started a trend that was not to really blossom until the eighties.

Finally, the theoretical models of instruction that were published had important influences on the field. For example, Carroll's (1963) Model of School Learning incorporated key factors that were believed to influence the learning process. Variables such as quality of instruction and time spent on instruction (in proportion to that which was needed) were considered. It was apparent from Carroll's model that learning was not the function of any single variable but the result of the interaction of a great many factors.

The other set of models that began appearing in the sixties was referred to as systems models. These were further attempts to put together the various processes that had been developed more or less independently in the sixties. The integration of these parts is described in the next section.

From Instructional Design to Instructional Systems in the Seventies

For instructional design, the decade of the 1970s can best be represented as the decade of the systems approach. Banathay (1968) has described the systems approach as the application of the systems viewpoint of thinking to human endeavors. The systems viewpoint means that instructional systems are

assemblages of parts that are designed and built by man into organized wholes for the attainment of specific purposes. The purpose of a system is realized through processes in which interacting components of the system engage in order to produce a predetermined output. (p. 12)

Banathy also indicates that each system receives its purpose and support from a larger, encompassing system (a suprasystem), and its output must satisfy the suprasystem.

Heinich (1970) has emphasized the systems approach as the integrating concept that pulls together the design, development, implementation, evaluation, and management of instruction. Heinich pointed out that as early as 1956 Hoban (1956) proposed a systems approach as the technique to employ to manage the learning process. Other noted researchers, including Finn (1956) and Carpenter (1960) have come to view the systems approach as *the* process to use in designing and implementing instructional systems.

Gagné (1962b) furthered the idea that there were basic psychological principles that can be applied to system development. Gagné's book included chapters on human functions, computers, human tasks and equipment design, and an early report on task description and analysis.

Glaser (1965) was one of the first to apply the system concept directly to the design and development process. He proposed a very basic five-step model: formulate objectives, diagnose learner strengths and weaknesses, deliver instruction, evaluate instruction, and revise instruction. It was the concept of revising instruction that was synonymous with Scriven's formative evaluation and the systems approach component of a feedback loop. A system is always self-monitoring in order

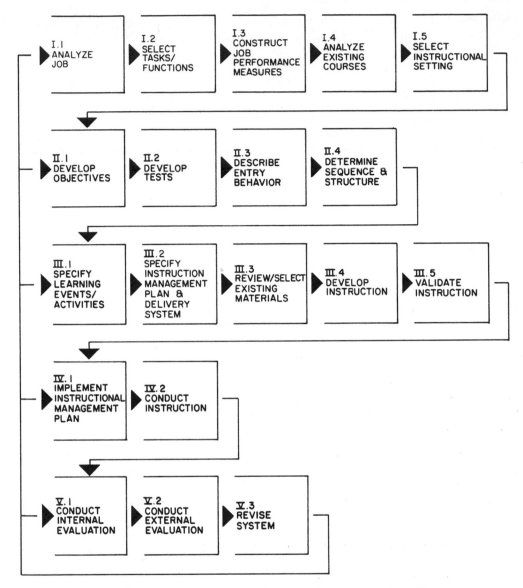

Figure 1. Instructional Systems Development model (Branson *et al.*, 1975).

to adjust its product to meet the needs of the suprastructure. If the systems approach were to be applied to instruction, the feedback loop had to be implemented and the instruction revised until it worked effectively.

Following the publication in 1968 of Banathy's important book, *Instructional Systems*, there were a number of systems approach models developed in the 1970s. It is important to review these models because it is clear that they include the major concepts and techniques that were developed in the 1960s. They also reflect the strong influence of systems thinking in the 1970s, and they encompass the major concepts of the instructional design field in the 1980s.

One of the best known of the models is the Instructional Systems Development (ISD) model. It was developed and extensively documented by Branson *et al.* (1975) under contract to the Navy. This 20-step model (see Figure 1) was adopted by all military services as the set of procedures to be used for developing instruction. The model emphasized job analysis as the starting point of designing instruction and the use of internal and external evaluations as sources of data to revise instruction. This model of the instructional design process has had a critically important impact on the conceptualization, if not the actual development, of instruction in the military.

One of the systems approach models that drew on the research of the 1960s and was published in the 1970s was that developed by Dick and Carey (1978, 1985). This model, shown in Figure 2, has only half as many components as that of Branson *et al.* (1975). The Dick and Carey model was developed as a practical approach for novice instructional designers. The steps in the model are described briefly in the following in order that the reader may understand the flow of the process as the designer proceeds from an identified need for instruction to the development of products and procedures that effectively meet that need.

Identifying an Instructional Goal. The first step in the model is determining what students are to be able to do when they have completed the instruction. The definition of the instructional goal may be derived from a list of goals, from a needs assessment with regard to a particular curriculum, from practical experience with learning difficulties of students in the classroom, from the analysis of the performance of someone who is already doing a job, or from some other requirement for new instruction.

Conducting an Instructional Analysis. After identifying the instructional goal, the designer determines what type of learning is required of the student. The goal is then analyzed to identify the subordinate skills that must be learned. This process will result in a chart or diagram that depicts these skills and shows the relationship among them.

Identifying Entry Behaviors and Characteristics. In addition to identifying the subordinate skills and procedural steps that must be included in the instruction, the designer identifies the specific skills students must have prior to beginning instruction. This is not a listing of all the things learners can do, but an identification of the specific skills they must be able to perform in order to begin. It is also important to identify any specific characteristics of the learners that may be important considerations in the design of the instructional activities.

Writing Performance Objectives. Based on the instructional analysis and the statement of entry behaviors, the designer writes specific statements of what the learners will be able to do when they complete the instruction. These statements, which are derived from the skills identified in the instructional analysis, identify the skills to be learned, the conditions under which the skills must be performed, and the criteria for successful performance.

Developing Criterion-Referenced Test Items. The designer then develops assessment items based on the objectives and measures the learner's ability to achieve the behavior described in the objectives. Major emphasis is placed on testing the specific kind of behavior described in the objectives.

Developing an Instructional Strategy. Given the groundwork established in the five preceding steps, the designer identifies a plan for presenting the instruction to the learners. The plan includes an indication of the preferred media to be used to achieve the terminal objective. The strategy will include sections on preinstructional activities, presentation of information, practice and feedback, testing, and follow-through activities. The strategy will be based on current outcomes of learning research, current knowledge of the learning process, content to be taught, and the characteristics of the learners who will use the materials. These features are used to develop or select materials or to develop a strategy for interactive classroom instruction.

Developing and Selecting Instruction. In this step the designer uses the instructional strategy to produce (or select) the instruction. This typically includes a learner's manual, instructional materials, tests, and an instructor's guide. The decision to develop original materials will depend on what is taught, the availability of existing relevant materials, and the amount of resources available for development.

Designing and Conducting the Formative Evaluation. Following the completion of a draft of the instruction, the designer conducts a series of evaluations to collect data to determine how to improve the instruction. The three types of formative evaluation are referred to as one-to-one evaluation, small-group evaluation, and field evaluation. Each type of evaluation provides the designer with a different type of information that can be used to improve the instruction. Similar techniques can be applied to the formative evaluation of classroom instruction.

Revising Instruction. The final step in the systematic design process is to revise the instruction. Data from the formative evaluation are summarized and interpreted to identify difficulties experienced by learners in achieving the objectives and to relate these difficulties to specific instructional deficiencies in the instruction. The line in Figure 2, labeled "Revising Instruction," indicates that the data from a formative evaluation are not simply used to revise the instruction itself but are used to reexamine the validity of the instructional analysis and the assumptions about the entry behaviors and characteristics of the learners. It is necessary to reexamine statements of performance objectives and test items in light of performance data. The instructional strategy is reviewed and all relevant changes are incorporated into the instruction.

Conducting Summative Evaluation. The dotted line in Figure 2 indicates that, although summative evaluation is the culminating evaluation of the effectiveness of instruction, it generally is not a part of the design process. It is an evaluation of the absolute and/or relative value or worth of the instruction, and occurs only after the instruction has been formatively evaluated and sufficiently revised to meet the standards of the designer. Because the summative evaluation usually does not involve the designer of the instruction, but does involve an independent evaluator, this component is not considered an integral part of the instructional design process *per se*.

These steps are generally characteristic of the many systems models that appeared in the seventies. An article by Andrews and Goodson (1980) contains conclusive evidence that the seventies was the decade of the systems approach. In their article they identify no less than 40 systems approach models that appeared in the literature, all but four of which were published in the 1970s. The fact that the authors found 40 documented models clearly indicates that there is no single systems approach model. However, the authors found a great deal of similarity in the components of the 40 models. The authors identified 14 generic tasks, which are described in Table 1.

Current Status of Instructional Design

It is almost impossible to define precisely the boundaries of an academic discipline, and instructional design is not an exception. There have been several readily identifiable trends in recent years in the field that have increased its complexity. Four

Table 1. Fourteen Common Tasks in Model Development

Task number	Definition
1.	Formulation of broad goals and detailed subgoals stated in observable terms
2.	Development of pretests and posttests that match goals and subgoals
3.	Analysis of goals and subgoals for types of skills/learning required
4.	Sequencing of goals and subgoals to facilitate learning
5.	Characterization of learner population "as to age, grade level, past learning history, special aptitudes or disabilities, and, not least, estimated attainment of current and prerequisite goals"
6.	Formulation of instructional strategy to match subject-matter and learner requirements
7.	Selection of media to implement strategies
8.	Development of instruction based on strategies
9.	Empirical tryout of courseware with learner population, diagnosis of failures, and revision of instruction based on diagnosis
10.	Development of materials and procedures for installing, maintaining, and periodically up-dating the instructional program
11.	Assessment of need, problem identification, occupational analysis, competence, or training requirements
12.	Consideration of alternative solutions to instruction
13.	Formulation of system and environmental descriptions and identification of constraints
14.	Determine cost of instructional programs

Source: Adapted from Andrews, D., & Goodson, L. H., 1981.

influences are of particular note: systems design, cognitive psychology, media, and computers.

Systems Design. The original work of Skinner and Gagné focused on the application of psychological principles to the design of classroom instruction. As more and more systems thinking was applied to the process, emphasis on the total design of instruction increased, that is, on the design of training systems. This expansion resulted in greater emphasis on the role of needs assessment (Kaufman & English, 1979) and job analysis, as well as summative evaluation of the completed product (Branson *et al.*, 1975).

The whole field of instructional design is now referred to by some as instructional systems design, which includes a host of skills related to project design, budgeting, and personnel management. Cost comparisons and quality control have become more important factors as the original instructional design concepts have been put to use in various real world environments. In essence, instructional design may be considered the major component within a larger framework of instructional systems design, which includes management and communications concerns as well as the psychology of instruction.

Cognitive Psychology. The second contemporary influence on the field of instructional design is that of cognitive psychology. Cognitive psychology, with its definite systems perspective, has been the dominant trend in the field of psychology in the last 20 years. How has it influenced instructional design? It would appear that to date there has been only a small impact. Some influences, however, are apparent. For example, Gagné (1985) has related the external events of instruction (those events that the designer can manipulate) to their corresponding internal events. The internal events are explained in terms of a cognitive input-process-output model of the learning process. In essence, Gagné has bridged the behavioristic and cognitive approaches with his events of instruction.

One of the most important contributions of cognitive psychology, as it has been translated in the field of instructional design, is the approach to task analysis. Both Scandura (1983) and P. Merrill (1978, 1980) have described task analysis techniques relating to each of the cognitive steps that the learner must take to execute a skill. These authors emphasize that as the stimulus situation changes, the learner must be able to elaborate on the use of the skill in a variety of different ways. This type of analysis is somewhat different from,

but not incompatible with, the hierarchical approach developed by Gagné.

Another contribution of cognitive psychology is the concept of the schema as a representation of how knowledge is stored in memory. Instructional designers who have become interested in the use of computers in instruction, and especially those who are investigating the role of artificial intelligence in the design of courseware, have used the schema as a way of organizing the knowledge data base of the artificial intelligence system. This may prove to be a very productive line of research in the future.

Media. Another influence on the field of instructional design is the growing complexity of the media available for inclusion in an instructional system. Early research, such as that by Carpenter and Greenhill at Penn State, compared the teaching effectiveness of such media as radio, films, television, and programmed instruction with printed or teacher-delivered instruction. Now, computer-controlled video-disc systems can provide video motion, quality audio, colorful graphics, and letter-perfect text—any of which can be used to provide instruction directly tailored to the needs of the learner.

The impact of new technology has been to put the mystique back into the design and development process. This has occurred because the theory of instructional design has simply not kept pace with the electronic capabilities available to even the most novice designers. Although Reiser and Gagné (1983) have provided a very systematic and practical approach to selecting the medium for instruction, the research data seem to indicate that except for the most extreme of circumstances, the selection of a particular medium has little influence on the quality of learning that occurs. The net result is that the instructional designer is charged with the responsibility for developing "good" instruction, with no more guidelines as to what good instruction is than the basic instructional design principles that have been available for some time.

Computers. The impact of computers must be dealt with separately because of the magnitude of their influence on the field of instructional design. In the 1960s, it appeared that computers would be one more medium that the designer could select for inclusion in an instructional system. Although research indicated that "computers could teach," the critics were quick to point out that the costs, in terms of dollars per student hour of use, were prohibitive. This argument nearly won the day as most computer manufacturers, excepting

Control Data, withdrew from the field. For all practical purposes, the use of computers in instruction was nearly extinct by the late seventies. However, the development of the microcomputer completely turned around this trend. These new systems put the power of the multimillion dollar mainframe in the hands of any designer who could afford a computer that cost several thousand dollars.

The computer is now *the* medium for the instructional designer. It has the ability to control all other media and thus is the ideal vehicle for delivering mediated instruction. Nearly every instructional designer takes one or more courses in his or her training program in the use of computers in instruction. Some go on to make this an almost exclusive area of specialization.

There is increasing interest in the role that the computer can play in the total instructional design process. Consideration is being given to what steps in the instructional design process could conceivably be done by a computer in order to reduce the cost of the design of instruction. Can, for example, the computer be programmed to do a task analysis or to generate objective-referenced test items? Although very little has been accomplished to date, this is an extremely promising area for the future.

In summary, the field of instructional design has been expanded to take on what Banathy has called a systems view. When the instructional process is viewed as a system, all aspects of the system must be attended to: its design, development, implementation, management, and evaluation. The field of cognitive psychology is just beginning to influence the instructional design process, although theory has not been able to keep up with the development of electronic media. The computer has become the predominant medium for the designer as its availability increases almost exponentially.

The Instructional Designer: 1960 and 1987

It is of interest to examine who, in 1987, is an instructional designer, how he or she was trained, and where he or she works. These questions will be examined first in terms of the designer's 1960 counterpart.

In 1960 no one referred to him or herself as an instructional designer. Typically an instructional designer was an educational psychologist, media specialist, or training specialist. Some preferred the term *educational technologist*. But the people who were designing instruction using Skinnerian principles were likely to be psychologists who wrote programmed instruction units on introductory psychology topics, and did research on its effectiveness with college sophomores. As faculty or graduate students in psychology departments, they were trained in the basic core knowledge of experimental and clinical psychology, tended to have a definite behavioral view, and were expert in research and analysis methodology.

By 1965, some academics had decided to apply their new technology in industry. They formed new companies or joined special divisions of large companies that specialized in the writing and selling of programmed instruction materials and teaching machines. For a number of reasons, most of these ventures did not last into the 1970s. The largest client of most of these companies was the military. The public schools dabbled with teaching machines but never committed themselves to the use of programmed instruction, nor did they tend to hire people who had the skills required to write and develop such instruction. Nor did publishing companies rush to hire the instructional designer of the sixties. They tended to stay with the team of a subject-matter expert and an editor.

The instructional designers of 1987 tend to be quite different from those of 1960. At the present time, there are a number of major universities offering graduate degrees—both the masters and the doctorate—in instructional design. These include Arizona State, Brigham Young, Florida State, Indiana, Southern California, and Syracuse; there is also an excellent master's program at San Diego State.

The students entering these programs are no longer interested solely in psychology and applied human learning. Although some psychology students have entered these programs, they are outnumbered by former public school teachers, social workers, artists, media specialists, music educators, military personnel, and home economists. The field of instructional design now draws its students from the entire range of undergraduate majors. In any given program, the students will often vary in age from 21 to 50, with many students seeking either a second profession or new skills to add to their present ones. In effect, the instructional designer of the eighties is trained in a professional school as opposed to the designer of the sixties who was trained in an Arts and Sciences environment.

The curriculum of the designer trained in the eighties is very different from that used to prepare the professor who is doing the instructing. Many of those who are instructional design professors were trained in psychology departments. They are now teaching topics that were not in their curriculum: needs assessment, criterion-referenced testing, computer-assisted instruction, formative evaluation, program planning and budgeting, dissemination and diffusion, and interpersonal skills. The designer of the eighties typically finds that the curriculum at the master's level includes very little traditional learning theory and a lot of hands-on experience in designing instruction. Most programs require an internship experience with an instructional design project so that upon graduation the designer is ready to join an instructional design team.

The doctoral programs in instructional design emphasize more of the traditional research and theory skills as well as provide for the exercise of management and interpersonal skills in additional internships. The dissertation studies often use experimental designs to investigate various instructional strategies, but students are also beginning to broaden the scope of the dissertation study to include cost-benefit analyses, the development of new methodologies, and the application of known technologies to novel situations. Recent articles by Briggs (1982, 1984b) describe a full range of dissertation studies which have been undertaken by instructional design students.

It is probably fair to say that there is a greater diversity in the skills and interests of the designers of 1987 than those of 1960. The designers of 1960 tended to share a common academic heritage and had quite similar skills and interests. Those of 1987 come from a great variety of academic backgrounds and have a wider range of options in their academic training. The continuum is anchored at one end by the designer who is primarily interested in the application of psychological theory (usually cognitive theory) to the design of instruction, and at the other end by the designer who basically wants to become a manager in an instructional design group. The former student will find employment in a university, whereas the latter will undoubtedly find a position in industry.

Neither of the prototype students described above is likely to have been trained in a psychology department. All of the programs listed earlier are housed in schools and colleges of education. Some are directly associated with educational psy-

chology programs (such as Florida State) while others are much more closely related to media or educational technology programs and have little contact with the educational psychology program.

One other aspect of these programs should be noted—the enrollment of international students. Whereas nearly all United States graduate programs have experienced an increase in international student enrollments in recent years, such enrollments in instructional design programs has been impressive. Much of this interest has been generated by projects sponsored by government agencies, (e.g., the Agency for International Development), that have employed systematic instructional design techniques in a number of third world countries (see, for example, Morgan & Chadwick, 1971). As a result, students in those countries want to attend United States institutions that teach these skills. Many have returned to their countries to begin to play leadership roles in directing educational development activities. Some observers believe that the next breakthroughs in the use of instructional systems design techniques to solve significant educational problems will come from third world nations that have no economically acceptable alternative but to investigate these approaches.

The employment opportunities for the instructional designer of the eighties far exceed those available in the sixties. For the Ph.D. graduate there is an increasing number of faculty positions at major universities in instructional design programs. Positions are also available in traditional education departments of curriculum and instruction, and in educational technology or media departments. Some companies are eager to hire the instructional design Ph.D. who has leadership experience. Positions are available for working with in-house training development teams or with teams that contract their instructional design expertise to other companies.

The master's graduate can find employment with any number of companies or military agencies. In these positions, the new designer almost always joins a team of designers, subject-matter experts, evaluators. media specialists, and a manager. The new designer must learn about the company, its approach to instructional design, and its approach to the client—whether the client be an internal group for whom training services are being provided, or another company or government agency.

Thus, the instructional designer of the eighties is

quite different in many ways from the programmed instruction writer of the sixties who was trained in psychology. The new designer may come from one of many areas in education, from the military, or a third world nation. Graduate training is targeted on the wide variety of skills and knowledge required of a successful master's or doctoral graduate. Positions are available in both academic and the private sector, and designers soon find themselves playing a variety of roles in these institutions.

The Current Impact of Instructional Design on Educational Psychology

Previous sections of this chapter have presented some of the historical background to, and the current status of, the field of instructional design. Educational psychologists have significantly influenced the early development of this new field of applied human learning. It is fair now to examine the extent to which the emerging field of instructional design has had an impact on educational psychology. In order to determine this impact, the *Journal of Educational Psychology* and four educational psychology textbooks were analyzed to identify the extent to which studies relevant to instructional designers are being reported and the extent to which instructional design concepts are being included in the textbooks.

Analysis of the Journal of Educational Psychology. The *Journal of Educational Psychology* (JEP) was chosen as the collection of research articles most representative of the research being conducted in the field of educational psychology. The questions posed were: Are there papers being published in JEP that are of interest and relevance to the instructional designer? and Do the studies that are of interest employ systematic instructional de-

sign procedures in the development of the instructional materials used in the study?

The reason for asking if articles published in JEP are of interest to instructional designers was an attempt to determine if researchers with an instructional systems orientation are publishing in the most influential journal in the field and are thus influencing the overall direction of the field. If articles were found, then the question could be raised about the use of instructional design techniques in the conduct of the studies.

In order to determine the extent to which articles were of interest to instructional designers, this writer reviewed all the articles in JEP in a recent year, 1983 (volume 75). Abstracts of the 83 articles for that year were carefully read to identify those articles that dealt directly or indirectly with the major components of the systems approach to instructional design as presented earlier in Figure 2. The review of the abstracts was similar to the process typically used by a journal reader who scans each article to decide if it is relevant to his or her personal interests. Each article was rated by this writer as of direct interest to an instructional designer, of some interest, or of no direct interest. The results, by issue and total, are shown in Table 2.

The table indicates that over 25% of the articles appeared to be of direct interest to an instructional designer, and that an additional 10% held some interest. Although these data must reflect, by the nature of the way they were generated, the perspective of this writer, it is probable that the totals that would be obtained by other instructional designers would be similar.

What kinds of articles were of no direct interest? Two major types of studies can be identified. The first are those studies related to teacher characteristics and their interaction with student characteristics. Instructional designers have tended to

Table 2. Articles in Volume 75 of JEP Rated for Their Interest to Instructional Designers

Rating of articles	Issue						Total	Percentage of total
	1	2	3	4	5	6		
Number of articles of direct interest	4	4	5	4	2	3	22	27
Number of articles of some interest	1	2	4	2	0	1	10	12
Number of articles of no interest	11	7	4	9	12	8	51	61
Total number of articles	16	13	13	15	14	12	83	100

deemphasize the role of the teacher and particularly the personality and style of the teacher. Designers prefer to emphasize the concept of a system of instruction, of which a teacher or instructor is one component. The instructional materials tend to be of greater interest than the vehicle for delivering the instruction.

The second type of study of little interest to the designer were those that examined individual differences in learners. Although factors such as race and sex are of concern to some psychologists, the instructional designer tends to interpret the trait–treatment interaction data as having minimal impact on instructional design. In essence, the designer tends to produce an instructional system that will serve the largest possible percentage of students, with the remaining students receiving special individualized help. The exception to this position is the growing interest in the use of computers in delivering instruction. The computer is an ideal device for tailoring instruction relevant to individual differences. The individual difference of greatest demonstrated importance to the instructional designer is the amount and type of knowledge the learner has when he or she begins instruction.

What kinds of articles in Volume 75 are of great interest to the instructional designer? The great majority are those having implications for the instructional strategy the designer might use. For example, a number of studies that reflect a cognitive psychology orientation examine various ways to influence the level at which information is processed and the effect of this on recall. Others demonstrate how the learner's perspective influences what is recalled. New studies on the use of repetition, discussion, and elaboration are of interest, as are those studies that examine the format of the instruction in terms of the effectiveness of headings and underlining.

Also of major interest to the designer are articles that examine the general effectiveness of CAI, comparisons of radio and TV presentations, and the function of learning time in mastery learning. There is also a continuing interest in studies about the effects of reinforcers and test feedback on subsequent performance.

After identifying 22 studies of interest, this writer further examined them using Briggs's (1984a) criteria for culture four studies. Culture four studies are those that have the following characteristics:

1. The researcher classifies the type of learning outcome being studied and provides objectives and test items for checking the classification.

2. The instructional passages used in the research studies are similar in length to textbook chapters and are real curriculum topics.

3. The materials have been systematically designed and formatively evaluated.

4. The tests require students to classify examples and nonexamples of the concepts taught or apply the rules that have been taught.

Briggs argues that in order for research studies to be relevant to the instructional designer, the studies must not only reflect an appropriate experimental design but also appropriate instructional design. Those studies not meeting the criteria listed above, such as those employing nonsense syllables or 300-word passages for stimuli, are of only limited value to the instructional designer.

The 22 studies that were rated of direct interest to instructional designers were each evaluated using the criteria listed by Briggs. The extent to which the studies met the criteria had to be inferred in many cases on the basis of what was said (or not said) in the article. For example, an article was judged as meeting the criterion even if objectives and test items were not included as long as there was a clear description of the desired type of learning outcome and an assessment method that was appropriate for the outcome. It was also assumed that if there was no description of how a learning passage, such as an essay or a story, was developed, then it was not systematically designed.

Because of space limitations, the entire set of data from the analysis of the articles will not be shown here. However, very clear trends were evident when the 22 studies were analyzed. With regard to Brigg's first criterion, only one of the 22 studies made reference to a specific taxonomy of learning outcomes. However, all but three of the remainder did make it clear what type of performance was required of the learner and, with regard to criterion four, did use appropriate assessment instruments. A great majority of the studies assessed recall (what Bloom would call knowledge and Gagné would call verbal information), by asking students to write down everything they could remember from what they had read. Several studies were targeted on problem solving and used appropriate problem-solving tasks.

The criterion on which there was the greatest variability was the length of the instruction. Briggs had suggested using curriculum materials about the length of one chapter. Sixty-eight percent of the studies met this criterion. However, some of the studies reported findings based on instructional (or reading) passages of only 150 to 500 words. In some cases it was necessary to estimate the number of pages covered or number of minutes spent studying.

Of interest was the fact that none of the researchers reported the use of systematic instructional design techniques to develop instructional interventions. A number of researchers selected existing topic stories or topic presentations thought to be of interest to the students. In several cases it was necessary to develop original materials. The formats used in these studies appear to be quite reasonable, but there were no descriptions of the use of formative evaluation and revision. Several researchers did indicate that pilot studies had been conducted but they resulted in procedural improvements, not instructional improvements.

In summary, the analysis of the 22 articles classified as being of interest to an instructional designer indicated that the typical researcher starts with an interest in a process such as recall or problem solving, and develops appropriate assessment instruments. There is no reference to a specific learning taxonomy. The materials included in the instructional intervention are often selected from existing texts and modified to reflect the independent variable. The content is often science or math, or a prose passage that might be studied in a literature course. Although most of the materials are of sufficient length, 1000 words or more, they are not systematically designed and formatively evaluated before they are used in the study. None of the 22 investigations met all four of the criteria listed by Briggs. However, 55% did meet three of the four criteria.

Examination of Undergraduate Educational Psychology Textbooks.   It was of interest to determine the extent to which undergraduate educational psychology textbooks include instructional design concepts and procedures. It may be argued that collectively these texts define the basic elements of the field. Thus, if instructional design is making an impact, the major concepts and procedures from the field should be included in these texts.

In order to conduct the analysis, four texts in current use, which are listed below by authors, publishers, and years of publication, were selected (complete titles are provided in the references for this chapter).

1. Reilly and Lewis, Macmillan (1983)
2. Biehler and Snowman, Houghton Mifflin (1982)
3. Gage and Berliner, Houghton Mifflin (1984)
4. Woolfolk and McCune-Nicolich, Prentice-Hall (1984)

These books were chosen because of their immediate availability to the writer. Although the selection was not random, there is no reason to believe that the sample is biased. None of the texts is used by the writer to teach educational psychology.

The texts were analyzed by first preparing a list of key words, such as *behavioral objectives* and *formative evaluation,* that tend to be associated with the field of instructional systems. A list of 11 terms with relevant synonyms was generated. Then the table of contents of each book was reviewed to determine whether any of the concepts was included. As a more thorough check, the index of each text was examined for the inclusion of these terms or their synonyms. Listed as follows are the terms that were used and the percentage of texts that included each term in either the table of contents or the index.

In terms of the specific textbooks, the percentage of terms that could be located varied from 36% in Biehler and Snowman to 73% in Reilly and Lewis. The overall percentage was just over 50%.

The data with regard to the presence of instructional design concepts in educational psychology textbooks are somewhat ambiguous. From the positive point of view, it is quite clear that all concepts but one are represented in one or more texts and that, on the average, each text includes about half the terms.

However, a closer examination of how the concepts are taught tends to indicate that they are not being presented systematically. None of the texts describes the systems approach to designing instruction or indicates the possible role of the teacher as an instructional designer. Although learning domains and hierarchies and events of instruction are mentioned, it is often in the context of a general description of Gagné's work and not as part of an instructional strategy to be employed by the reader of the text. Although there is no doubt that goals and objectives are thoroughly described, the link to criterion-referenced testing and instructional strategies tends to be missing. Even the references to formative evaluation are in terms of test-

Instructional design concepts	Percentage of texts that include the concepts
a. needs assessment	0
b. goals	100
c. objectives—instructional, educational, or behavioral	100
d. criterion-/objective-referenced tests	75
e. learning outcomes stated as skill domains	75
f. learning hierarchies	50
g. events of instruction	25
h. media selection	25
i. formative evaluation	100
j. individualized instruction, mastery learning	75

ing students in mastery learning situations rather than the revision of replicable instruction.

The impact of instructional design on textbooks in the field of educational psychology is barely apparent at the present time. Although some of the prominent concepts are included, the texts do not present the systematic approach to instruction advocated by instructional designers.

A Comparison of the Current Orientations of Educational Psychology and Instructional Design

The review of the educational psychology textbooks and JEP provided an opportunity to compare the current content and orientation of the field to that of instructional design. Although there certainly are differences in the texts, they share a great deal of similarity.

The texts seem to focus on human development, especially as it relates to cognitive development. This leads to a consideration of various developmental and learning theories. Individual differences in learners are described in terms of IQ, race, sex, and personality. The texts then turn to teaching strategies, including concern for motivation, delivery of instruction, managing instruction, and discipline. The final topic in most texts tends to be testing, with consideration given to both standardized testing and teacher-made tests. Although the texts often suggest activities for the students, their enormity strongly implies an instructional orientation in which it is more impor-

tant for the students to know about something than to do something.

The coverage of the educational psychology texts differs to a great extent from the usual emphases in the field of instructional design. The field of instructional design is concerned with models of the process of designing instruction. The models take into consideration what is known from learning theory and empirical research. The emphasis is on the "doing" aspects of instruction. Instructional strategies focus on the events of instruction and their relation to desired learning outcomes. There is much more interest in individual similarities than in individual differences in learners. Standardized tests are of little interest to the designer. Testing is viewed from a criterion-referenced perspective in order to relate objectives to instruction and to assessment. No texts were found that presented the concepts of instructional design in a unified way.

By contrast, there is a distinct lack of consideration of the general area of human development by instructional designers. This signals a major difference in the orientation of the two fields. For example, educational psychology has traditionally included research on students in the public schools, and texts in educational psychology are typically written for students who plan to become public school teachers. Whereas instructional designers share these interests, their perspective is much broader. Generic instructional designers may find themselves involved with any type of learning outcome, to be taught in any type of learning environment, to any type of individual. Therefore, the training of the designer does not focus on childhood and adolescent development, but assumes that the designer will become knowledgeable about the target population and the learning environment for which the instruction will be designed. Similarly, instructional design texts are written for a wide range of readers, not just preservice teachers.

In summary, it appears from the review of research and texts that educational psychology and instructional design are complementary. Educational psychology is providing the theoretical background and empirical research base being applied by instructional designers. Educational psychology texts tend to be knowledge-oriented whereas texts in instructional design teach practical skills. A number of educational psychology research articles report investigations of learning processes that can be adapted by the instructional designer. Educational psychology serves as a conceptual bridge between the parent field of psychology and instructional design (see Wildman & Burton, 1981), just as many of the early contributors to the field of instructional design were trained as psychologists and functioned as educational psychologists.

Summary

The future of instructional design will be enhanced to the extent that educational psychologists understand the conceptual orientation of the instructional designer and the types of knowledge that will further the design and development of instructional systems.

Banathy (1968) has described what he calls the systems view of education, which is held by most instructional designers and includes sine qua non a systems approach to designing instructional systems. The greater the extent to which educational psychologists share this view of instruction, the greater will be their contribution to instructional design.

One indication of the extent to which the systems view of education will influence educational psychologists is the degree to which research articles meet the criteria expressed by Briggs (1984a) for culture four studies. Studies that use systematically designed instruction of significant length will enhance the relevance of the results to the instructional designer. The systems approach model (as shown, for example, in Figure 2) is one means of conceptualizing research that will be of value to instructional designers. The more that is

known about the components in the process and their interrelationships, the more effective the model will be.

As viewed in the mid-eighties, the field of instructional design appears to be maturing. It has its own journal, *The Journal of Instructional Development,* and instructional designers are substantial contributors to several related journals. Teacher education and training are evolving in ways which reflect instructional design concepts. Instructional design is now being influenced by the current developments in electronic technology and management. Nevertheless, the roots of the instructional design discipline are in the field of educational psychology, and it may be anticipated that designers will continue to draw upon it for new ideas and approaches to the learning process.

In an earlier article, this author has argued that instructional design should be considered neo-educational psychology (Dick, 1978). Regardless of the terminology, all those in this field will be served well by the integration of the major components of each approach, and each will be weakened to the extent that it ignores the contributions of the other.

References

Andrews, D. H., & Goodsen, L. A. (1981). A comparative analysis of models of instructional design. *Journal of Instructional Development, 3*(4), 2–15.

Baker, E. L., & Alkin, M. C. (1983). Formative evaluation of instructional development. *AV Communication Review, 21,* 389–418.

Banathy, B. H. (1968). *Instructional systems.* Belmont, CA: Fearon.

Biehler, R. F., & Snowman, J. (1982). *Psychology applied to teaching* (4th ed.). Boston, MA: Houghton Mifflin.

Block, J. H. (Ed.). (1971). *Mastery learning: Theory and practice.* New York: Holt, Rinehart & Winston.

Branson, R. K., Rayner, G. I., Cox, L. J., Furman, J. P., King, F. J., & Hannum, W. H. (1975). *Interservice procedures for instructional systems development.* Ft. Monroe, VA: US Army Training and Doctrine Command.

Briggs, L. J. (1982). A comment on the training of students in instructional systems design. *Educational Technology, 22*(8), 25–27.

Briggs, L. J. (1984a). Trying to straddle four research cultures. *Educational Technology, 24*(8), 33–34.

Briggs, L. J. (1984b). Rules for doing a valuable dissertation in instructional design. *Educational Technology, 24*(11), 32–33.

Carpenter, C. R. (1960). Approaches to promising areas of research in the field of instructional television. In *New teaching aids for the American classroom.* Stanford, CA: Institute for Communications Research, Stanford University.

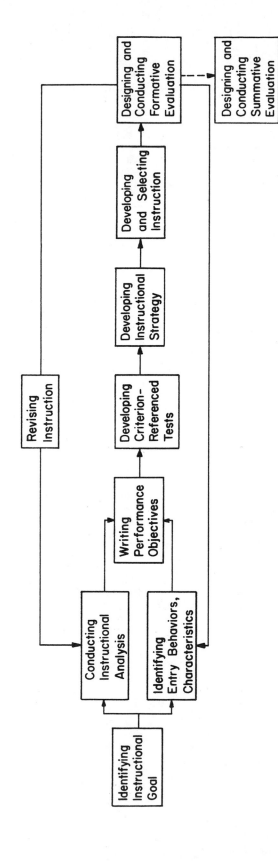

Figure 2. Systems Approach Model for Designing Instruction (Dick & Carey, 1985).

Carroll, J. B. (1963). A model of school learning. *Teachers College Record, 64,* 528–543.

Cronbach, L. J. (1963). Course improvement through evaluation. *Teachers College Record, 64,* 672–683.

Davies, J. K. (1971). *The management of learning.* New York: McGraw Hill. 3–18.

Dick, W. (1977). Formative evaluation. In L. J. Briggs (Ed.), *Instructional design: Principles and applications* (pp. 311–333). Englewood Cliffs, NJ: Educational Technology Publications.

Dick, W. (1978). The educational psychologist as instructional designer. *Contemporary Educational Psychology, 3,* 265–271.

Dick, W., & Carey, L. M. (1978). *The systematic design of instruction.* Glenview, IL: Scott, Foresman.

Dick, W., Carey, L. M. (1985). *The systematic design of instruction* (2nd ed.). Glenview, IL: Scott, Foresman.

Dick, W., & Gallagher, P. (1972). Systems concepts and computer-managed instruction: An implementation and validation study. *Educational Technology, 12*(2), 33–39.

Ebel, R. L. (1978). The case for norm-referenced measurements. *Educational Researcher, 7*(11), 3–5.

Finn, J. D. (1956). AV development and the concept of systems. *Teaching Tools, 3*(1), 63–64.

Gage, N. L., & Berliner, D. C. (1984). *Educational psychology* (3rd ed.). Boston, MA: Houghton Mifflin.

Gagné, R. M. (1962a). The acquisition of knowledge. *Psychological Review, 69,* 355–365.

Gagné, R. M. (Ed.). (1962b). *Psychological principles in system development.* New York: Holt, Rinehart & Winston.

Gagné, R. M. (1965). *The conditions of learning.* New York: Holt, Rinehart & Winston.

Gagné, R. M. (1985). *The conditions of learning* (4th ed.). New York: Holt, Rinehart & Winston.

Gagné, R. M., & Briggs, L. J. (1979). *Principles of instructional design* (2nd ed.). New York: Holt, Rinehart & Winston.

Glaser, R. L. (1963). Instructional technology and the measurement of learning outcomes: Some questions. *American Psychologist, 18,* 519–521.

Glaser, R. (1965). Toward a behavioral science base for instructional design. In R. Glaser (Ed.), *Teaching machines and programmed learning, II.* Washington, DC: National Education Association.

Heinich, R. (1970). *Technology and the management of instruction.* Washington, DC: Association for Educational Communications and Technology.

Hoban, C. F. (1956). *A systems approach to audiovisual communications.* Keynote address at the 2nd Lake Okoboji Audiovisual Leadership Conference, Iowa City, IA: State University of Iowa.

Kaufman, R., & English, F. W. (1979). *Needs assessment: Concepts and applications.* Englewood Cliffs, NJ: Educational Technology Publications.

Keller, F. S. (1968). Goodbye teacher. *Journal of Applied Behavioral Analysis, 1,* 1–6.

Mager, R. F. (1962). *Preparing instructional objectives.* Belmont, CA: Pitman Learning. (Rev. 2nd ed., 1984)

Markle, S. M. (1967). Empirical testing of programs. In P. C. Lange (Ed.), *Programmed instruction.* The Sixty-sixth Yearbook of the National Society for the Study of Education (pp. 104–140). Chicago, IL: University of Chicago Press.

Melton, A. W. (1959). Summing up: Comment towards the future. In G. Finch (Ed.), *Educational and training media—A symposium* (pp. 196–206). Washington, DC: National Academy of Sciences-National Research Council.

Merrill, P. F. (1978). Hierarchical and information processing task analysis: A comparison. *Journal of Instructional Development, 1*(2), 35–40.

Merrill, P. F. (1980). Analysis of a procedural task. *NSPI Journal, 19*(1), 11–15.

Miller, R. B. (1962). Task description and analysis. In R. M. Gagné (Ed.), *Psychological principles in system development* (pp. 187–230). New York: Holt, Rinehart & Winston.

Moore, J. W., Mahan, J. M., & Ritts, C. A. (1969). Continuous progress concept of instruction with university students. *Psychological Reports, 25,* 887–892.

Morgan, R. M., & Chadwick, C. (Eds.). (1971). *Systems analysis for educational change: The Republic of Korea.* (Contract AID/ea-120-Korea). Tallahassee, FL: The Florida State University.

Popham, W. J. (1978). The case for criterion-referenced measurements. *Educational Researcher, 7*(11), 6–10.

Reilly, R. R., & Lewis, E. L. (1983). *Educational psychology: Applications for classroom learning and instruction.* New York: Macmillan.

Reiser, R. A., & Gagné, R. M. (1983). *Selecting media for instruction.* Englewood Cliffs, NJ: Educational Technology Publications.

Scandura, J. M. (1983). Instructional strategies based on the structured learning theory. In C. Reigeluth (Ed.), *Instructional design theories and models: An overview of their current status* (pp. 213–246). Hillsdale, NJ: Laurence Erlbaum Assoc.

Scriven, M. (1967). The methodology of evaluation. In R. Tyler, R. M. Gagné, & M. Scriven (Eds.), *Perspectives of curriculum evaluation* (pp. 39–83). Chicago, IL: Rand McNally.

Skinner, B. F. (1958). Teaching machines. *Science, 128,* 969–977.

Wildman, T. M., & Burton, J. K. (1981). Integrating learning theory and instructional design. *Journal of Instructional Development, 4*(3), 5–14.

Woolfolk, A. E., & McCune-Nicholich, L. (1984). *Educational psychology for teachers* (2nd ed.). Englewood Cliffs, NJ: Prentice-Hall.

CHAPTER 11

The Cognitive Movement and Education

Francis J. Di Vesta

Although education remains dominated by behavioristic principles, a steadily increasing influence of cognitive science is apparent. The research literature is abundant with articles that are concerned with cognitive development, thinking and problem-solving, cognitive learning strategies and skills, and cognitively based instructional designs. The cognitive influence is finding its way into the teaching of specific subjects, particularly reading, but in mathematics, science, and social studies as well.

With these developments a level of maturity has been reached such that issues are being raised about the differences between experts and novices and the implications of these differences for curriculum development; whether results from verbal learning studies can be applied to learning from text; about the relation between what the learner knows and what he or she comprehends from text; whether information is processed in linear step-by-step fashion through the information processing system or whether some alternative model is a better descriptor; the relation between teaching knowledges and strategies; whether the traditional methods of educational measurement make sense

in terms of our knowledge about educational goals, such as comprehension, understanding, the ability to solve problems, and so on. The relation of these issues to education is apparent. The prospects of the potential their solutions hold for the improvement of education is exciting.

In the present chapter I have attempted to develop a sketch of the cognitive movement emphasizing its development from Wundt's time to the present. The contributions of various disciplines are represented because cognitive science in education has been influenced by all branches of psychology, including, of course, the important work of Piaget, computer simulation of learning, studies of artificial intelligence, and the recent work of psycholinguists, in addition to the contributions of such influential educators as Dewey, Ausubel, and Gagné. The historical maze is a complicated one, but I have tried to convey a sense of continuity that I see as inherent in the course of the developing science and its applications to our understanding of cognition to education. This objective required touching on numerous facets of the field that the reader might use as a base for further study. Some topics have, of necessity, not been included or have been touched on only sketchily, not by neglect but because of space limitations; some topics had to be given priority over others.

Although the study of cognition is beginning to have a major influence on education and instruc-

Francis J. Di Vesta • Division of Counseling and Educational Psychology, Pennsylvania State University, University Park, PA 16802.

tion, its full impact has yet to be felt. The reasons are readily apparent. The aim of cognitive science is to understand how people think and comprehend; how they learn and remember; and how they solve problems and come to be creative. There can be no more complex research than that of humans attempting to understand the workings of the human mind. Underlying these and other concerns of similar complexity is that of understanding how people understand.

The Nature of Understanding

Understanding occurs when a person can relate new information (perceptual, linguistic, and semantic) to a categorical structure (grouping, classification, spatial, maps, and the like) (Deese, 1969). Information can be acquired without understanding, of course. It can be learned by rote—by sheer repetition. But such knowledge is relatively inert. Often it is unrecognized in a similar form only a few months after it has been learned. On the other hand, domain content or domain procedures that are understood have been assimilated into the person's knowledge structures. As a consequence, such knowledge is capable of being activated: that is, of signaling interpretation, of being used and recognized in paraphrase, and of activating related knowledge for other generative processes (Wittrock, 1974, 1978) including problem solving and prediction. These are but a few reasons for stating that understanding is as much a fundamental educational objective as it is a fundamental concern of the cognitive scientist.

Understanding is a highly complex and idiosyncratic experience. It involves perceiving, attending, interpreting, making inferences, and predicting. Individual differences in any one of these processes, for a given situation, may have profound effects on achievement and retrieval. In brief, the cognitive view is concerned with how incoming information (the input) is processed by the learner, and with what results.

The study of human thought establishes peculiar problems requiring highly elaborate and sophisticated theories to understand it. The cognitive scientist requires special constructs to explain what is happening while one reads or does problems in arithmetic and new ways of representing what the learner does while studying (e.g., flow charts to illustrate sequences of decisions and resulting states) or what differences exist between the knowledge structures of experts and novices (e.g., representations of concepts and relational links among them). Further, new types of measures are being invented. In addition, measures that had been in use previously are being rediscovered and are being put to new uses in order to infer what is happening in the thinking process. Among these measures are chronometric measures (e.g., latency or reaction time measures), protocol analyses, eye fixations, and data from computer simulations of human problem solving.

Education: Two Philosophies

An educator's theory of thinking clearly dictates what is done in his or her classroom. Different views, of course, lead to different instructional practices and to different outcomes that are considered acceptable (see Geddis, 1982). Educators' and psychologists' conceptions of thinking have been influenced by two main currents of philosophy, empiricism and rationalism.

Empiricism

The empiricist tradition in psychology is represented, at least in part, by Aristotle's basic view of associationism, but the view has been enhanced by numerous experiments, greater precision, and attention to such processes as motivation, reinforcement, punishment, and transfer. Nevertheless, the orientation was consolidated into a form indicating that knowledge consists of *copying* elements from the world into a sensory store in a mechanistic way. Sense impressions were the basis for all knowledge: larger components (abstractions) were developed through associative links, and complex knowledge could be reduced to component elements.

The extreme behavioral position, representing empiricism, assumed that teaching procedures could directly affect the pupil's achievement. The student was conceptualized as a receptacle capable (or incapable) of profiting from experience. Instruction emphasized drill and practice, rote rehearsal, shaping errorless learning, and sheer transmission of content as reasonable educational practices and goals. Precise, verbatim recall of facts was measured as a legitimate outcome. The use of strategies involved in learning, such as attending, encoding, retrieving, or transfering information to problem-solving situations were expected of students but were left for them to accomplish to the best of their ability. The aim was to refine the teaching method to produce a uniformly acceptable behavioral outcome. As new technologies were introduced, whether in the form of slide projectors, recorders, movies, television, teaching machines, or the computer, they were examined for their possible potential in the transmittal of information—although interest in sheer transmittal of information was typically denied (see e.g., Skinner, 1984). The behavioral tradition has been an enduring one, with many important contributions to education. Nevertheless, the philosophical view that instruction directly affects learning and that all students should receive the same input has the intrinsic weakness of viewing the learner as a passive recipient of instruction, regardless of how active or interactive the teaching situation might be, because the influence of the learner-as-processor is ignored.

Rationalism

The creativity of the mind, though neglected in modern empiricism, had been proposed by Plato through Socrates' demonstration that Meno's slave boy had a seemingly unknown capacity or knowledge. In this anecdote the inventor of the Socratic dialogue successfully directs the boy to prove that the square twice as large as a given square has a side equal to the diagonal of the given square. The Socratic dialogue was based on clever use of questions to lead the boy to arrive intuitively at the correct solution. Socrates' conclusion was that materials were not newly learned but that learners are only led to discover what was already stored in their minds. Nevertheless, as Skinner (1984) correctly notes, Socrates recognized that the boy would not be able to solve further problems automatically, without considerable additional experience.

Almost two thousand years following Plato the emphasis on reasoning, interpretation, and comprehension was to come in a formal distinction from empiricism in the philosophy of Immanuel Kant (1781). He proposed the innateness of certain mental activities that operate on experience in specifiable ways to impose organization and interpretation on ambiguous inputs. Memory was not to be considered as a copy of elements but as a consequence of interpretation or transformation. What is remembered are the structures or categories. New learning was assumed to take place by assimilation of the new input into existing categories. Even ideas that seem to be purely associative are structured in the sense that they are linked by a meaningful relation.

Linguists (e.g., Lenneberg, 1967) have also demonstrated that innate language structures permit the child to employ extremely complex language rules (grammatical, syntactical, phonological, etc.) at a very early age and that the general nature of these rules appear to be universal. Studies on perceptual organization and organization of movement have similar qualities. Very young infants learn depth perception, react to distorted faces (nose and eyes displaced, for example) with surprise, and move away from an object that seems to be following a path that will hit them but merely trace with their eyes the path of an object moving in a way that will not hit the child.

These observations are but a few that describe the characteristics of the rationalists' position; observations that are difficult to explain via the empiricists' viewpoint. The value of a psychological science that does not consider the nature of human minds, the enormously complicated operations that can be performed, the interpretations that people make, or the function and qualities of understanding has been questioned by psychologists (e.g., Deese, 1969). According to Deese (1969), understanding is not a behavior but a process of assimilating content into existing categories or structures, "modes of human thought into which we may cast our ideas" (Deese, 1969, p. 319). These categorical structures consist at least of grouping, classification, and spatial (scaling and mapping, for example) representation.

The cognitive stance places the learner in an active role. Given the same teaching method, the rationalist's perspective implies that students of "equal intellectual ability" and motivation do not receive the same instruction, even when inputs are standardized. Each student emerges with a different ability to apply the content, a different interpretation, or an otherwise different understanding of what was "taught." The teaching method, by whatever criterion one uses, can only have an indirect influence on what the pupil learns, through the processes it induces the learner to employ. The learner, having a central role and being in a highly active mode attempts to make sense out of the content being studied, making assumptions about what has to be learned, and imposing expectations on what should be done to achieve these expectations. If any facet of the learner's cognitive processing is bypassed in curriculum development and instruction, understanding about how it affects learning will be, at best, limited.

The Transition from Philosophy to Educational Psychology

Cognitive orientations were introduced to 20th century psychology through Wilhelm Wundt, who is more often known merely as the founder of the first psychological laboratory at Leipzig in 1879. Blumenthal (1970) must be credited with bringing attention to the importance of Wundt's voluminous (and almost uninterpretable) work for a cognitive approach to psychology and psycholinguistics. Wundt's psychology was to have an influence on such figures as Huey and Judd.

Wundt: The First Psychologist

Wundt saw cognition as an active, creative process aimed at providing structure to experiences. Attention (apperception) was an active state determined by subjective factors, such as innate mental structures, motivation, memories, and affect. External features (environmental inputs) were secondary and organized principally by associationistic principles, such as continuity and intensity of stimuli. Both thought (logic) and the input worked in parallel fashion. The primary feature of apperception was the identification of psychological relations in an experience, the making sense of the experience, and the finding of logical connections. Wundt's concern was with the nature of understanding; the assimilation of the experience into the knowledge structures one already had.

From Wundt's perspective, psychological contrasts were important for increasing the precision of understanding (i.e., by pitting opposites against one another and by varying contexts). Is a cardinal a bird? a clergyman? a color? a ball player? A speaker may creatively monitor his utterances through self-correcting statements, "let me say it this way," or, "compare this with the opposite side of the picture." In dialectics and the Socratic dialogue, one arrives at a conclusion by the tortured twisting, pulling, and pitting of one idea against another until the underlying abstraction has been identified. In Wundt's terms, the consequences of these processes are "creative resul-

tants." Intentional cognitive activity goes beyond itself, that is, beyond specific components. What becomes stored in memory are the creations of the learner, who logically derives an organization or rule rather than a mere collection of attributes or examples. The new organization (rule or principle) has different properties from the elements comprising it (compare this statement with findings from studies of experts and novices later in this chapter).

In Wundt's writings, the beginning of the study of the components of cognition can be observed: the important role of learner as an active processor of information; the role of intention and organization on the selecting and structuring function of attention; the creativity of the outcomes of assimilating new information into existing knowledge; and a definition of outcomes of learning in terms of rules and principles or other structures rather than the mere accumulation of facts and instances. There was even an anticipation of the capacity of short-term memory in his finding that the apperception span—span of clear consciousness—was about six or seven items (Blumenthal, 1970, p. 14). The theory that learners transformed input (to achieve creative resultants) is to be found in some form in most theories since Wundt's time (e.g., Freud's defense mechanisms; the Gestaltist's configurations; Piaget's structures; the neobehaviorist's distinction between nominal and effective stimuli, and the cognitivist's emphasis on encoding).

Huey: The Psychology of Reading

Following Wundt, the cognitive movement quickly turned to educational problems, one of the most important of which was the nature of reading. To understand the reading process would be to understand much of cognitive activity. One of the outstanding figures in this movement was E. B. Huey, who is known to most readers for his classic book *The Psychology and Pedagogy of Reading* (Huey, 1908/1968). It remains an important text in reading behavior today and is widely cited. Huey studied with G. S. Hall, who, after receiving his doctorate with William James, had gone to study with Wundt. It is not, therefore, surprising that Huey's work had a highly cognitive tone.

Huey's book is full of the basics of cognition, and cognitive psychology, well based on substantial experimental evidence. He emphasized the role of meaning, that is, of prior knowledge in perception in reading, by his phrase "meaning leads," which means that what the person brings to a listening or reading situation determines the fluency with which one reads or listens, the prediction of words or ideas yet to come, and the integration of the ideas into a wholistic impression.

Cognitive factors were found in many facets of reading. Most of the mechanical features of reading reflect, to some degree, the meaningful knowledge of readers: the number of letters tachistoscopically presented (at 100 ms exposure) that can be read is around four or five when they are presented in random order. If they comprise a meaningful word, 10 to 15 letters are "recognized." Creative synthesis, described by Wundt, is reflected in the fact that disfigured words (words with displaced letters, incorrect letters, or mutilated words) are recognized as correctly spelled words (making proofreading difficult). With regressive eye movements and the shifting of the eyes to lines forward of the focal point, input might create problems if one did not consider parallel (cognitive) processing. When viewed in serial order, the sequence of words would be a scrambled hodgepodge, yet it is never recognized as such by the reader. Similarly, the eye–voice span becomes extended as the meaningfulness of the text increases.

These ideas about cognition in reading were eventually to lead to the configuration or wholeword approach; an attempt to teach reading without directing attention to the constituents of words or phrases, such as the regularities of phonetics or of the roots of words. Unfortunately, in attempts to make immediate applications of new research findings, the configuration approach was misapplied. Although mature fluent readers do construct meanings from text fragments, beginning readers still must become skilled in decoding or word identification, and the decoding process should become automatic. To achieve this end phonetic regularities can be taught or the linguistic method can be employed to have the child recognize regularities (Blumenthal, 1970, pp. 170–171).

Despite disagreement about the order in which reading processes should be taught, general evidence supports Blumenthal's statement that although considerable variation in teaching methods exists, most children do learn to read and often do so without instruction. It is clear that the time devoted to the phonics or linguistic components of reading relative to time spent on comprehension may be disproportionate in some reading programs.

Classical Gestalt Theories: Problem Solving

The years of 1925 to 1950 saw the development of grand theories that proposed to integrate all known facts around the main theme of describing, predicting, and controlling learning and behavior. Among these theories was a class of cognitive theories that dealt with the organization of perceptions and knowledge and with the thinking process in general. They were the classical Gestalt theories, the Field-Gestalt theories, and expectancy theories that developed out of opposition to the behavioristic (empiricist) tradition, then represented primarily by Thorndike. The classical Gestalt theory dealt with such laws of perception as proximity, similarity, figure–ground relationships, and good direction for the formation of structures (patterns or configurations).

The construct of structure was extended to rote memory and meaningful learning (understanding) by Katona (1942). To demonstrate the importance of structural organization in memory, tasks were devised that could be acquired either mechanically (without understanding) or by use of meaningful rules depending on the extent to which the structure in the stimulus was perceived, as in, for example, ELIBOMOTUA (automobile) or 137153163127 (2n + 1). Subjects who were given hints such as, "changing the order or looking for a rule might be helpful" remembered the material more accurately than those who had not been given hints. If they found the rule for a given type of task they were also able to transfer it to other tasks of a similar type. Meaningful learning, as described by Katona, aids understanding because contact is made between the new content and what the learner already knows. Through this process the new material has the advantage of being partially learned because it has been related to representations of prior experience.

Another contribution of Gestalt psychology was oriented around problem solving (Wertheimer, 1959). Problems could be solved if the proper cognitive structure could be identified. Sometimes the structure would appear suddenly and the solution would become immediately apparent—that is, the solution was insightful. At other times the structure might have to be discovered or sought after, but, for school problems, blind solutions or simply seeking the right answers was to be avoided. Wertheimer claimed that many school problems were "solved" by simple application of given rules and without seeing the relations or structures represented in these rules; that is, the student did not know how a higher-order solution was obtained. For example, young Gauss, who while still in elementary school was said to have discovered (perhaps insightfully?) the higher-order structures involved in adding a series of numbers such as 1 to 100. The average student might have solved the problem by the simple algorithmn of consecutively adding each number to the previous sum.

The lessons taught by the Gestaltists emphasized the need to avoid mechanical learning and to aim for discovery or understanding. In retrospect, one finds hints of the importance of the learner's knowledge structures for acquiring and using new information. Problem solving itself involves an understanding of the problem statement, of the knowledge structures underlying a given problem and of sophisticated (higher-order) strategies for solution. No one of these requirements, by itself, is a sufficient condition for successful meaningful learning or problem solving. Instruction should be designed to contribute to identifying meaningful arrangements. These considerations in designing instruction are again reemerging in such issues as (a) what the balance of instruction in content and strategies should be; and (b) whether learning strategies are generalizable across a variety of subject-matter areas (de Bono, 1985) or whether they are domain specific. In general, these issues, including the need for evidence about what strategies learners use at various stages of learning and the extent to which they can be learned, (taught), modified, or made more efficient are important issues for both psychologists and educators.

The Current Cognitive Movement

The learner as an active participant in the learning process has been emphasized in such terms as selective attention, processor of information, learning as a generative process, reconstruction in memory, and active retrieval. Similar metaphors are used in computer simulation studies of information processing and in studies of artificial intelligence. Investigators of artificial intelligence and behavioral scientists often borrow similar terms from one another to explain the behavior they are investigating. The metaphors of decision trees, subgoals, information mapping, and top-down processing are shared by both groups.

Underlying the assumptions of the learner as an active processor is another assumption that there is no one set of generalized learning laws with each

law applying to all domains. For example, even the meaning of a single sentence or the importance of a sentence to the reader changes drastically when the context within which it is embedded changes (Bransford & Johnson, 1973).

The Contextualist-Constructivist Position

The contextualist-constructivist position (Hoffman & Nead, 1983; Jenkins, 1979, 1980; Pepper, 1942) is a convenient way of summarizing most of the current emphases of the cognitive movement. The emphasis is on the total instructional event of which the learner is a part. The situational demands, the characteristics of the learner, the task demands, the purposes of the learner, and so on *interact* to determine the quality and texture of an event, such as a teaching or learning episode. They determine the context of learning that influences the construction of representations that are the outcomes of the instructional episode. Because human behavior is highly adaptive, the behavior measured in a given experiment (or instructional unit) reflects a model of perceiving and performing a given task in specific ways; change the task but slightly and performance may change radically. The measure reflects the use of a given strategy for a particular learning event (Jenkins, 1980). A familiar example comes from research on clustering (Bousfield, 1953; Bousfield & Sedgewick, 1944; Bousfield, Esterson, & Whitmarsh, 1958) in list-learning studies (Jenkins, 1974). Although the task of recalling a list is the same and the items in the list are the same for two treatment groups, the structure of the total event is changed by orienting instructions to select an appropriate modifier for each word versus instructions to identify a rhyming word for the words in the list. As a consequence, recall and clustering are higher for the first set of conditions than for the second. The nature of the event (the learner's attention, interests, beliefs, intentions and purposes, the actual task requirements, the interactional and social context, the learner's changes in the requirements, or perceptions of the situation) comprises its context and contributes to the strategies selected and therefore to what is recalled. As a result, learners recall more of the overall quality of the instructional event. Orienting tasks that emphasize specific content results in fragile recall and difficult retrieval. The effect of the nature or quality of an event seems to be more durable and robust (Jenkins, 1980).

Context, therefore, affects the way an event is experienced, which in turn determines (generates) the criteria for what representation is to be constructed for proper understanding (van Dijk & Kintsch, 1983). Bransford and Johnson (1973), for example, presented subjects a passage describing a series of actions taking place in a city. Different groups of subjects received different titles (orienting tasks) for the essay. One orienting task titled the passage as a "Space trip to an inhabited planet"; a second title was "Watching a parade from the fourth floor." The third sentence in the passage referred to "The landing was gentle. . ." This sentence was recalled more frequently by the first group than by the second group. Some learners in the second group said they had noted the sentence but shrugged it off as irrelevant and forgot it. Differences in perception and world views can also be seen to have an effect in the case of one student who transferred the parade from the city to the airport because of lack of accomodations and invented a celebrity whose plane landed during the course of the parade and other related events. By changing the event slightly the learner accomodated the anomalous event nicely. Simple isolated sentences are insufficient for comprehension without consideration of the context, the learner's purposes, and the learner's knowledge (see, for example, Anderson, Reynolds, Schallert, & Goetz, 1977). The constructivist aspect of the contextualist position is reflected in Jenkins' (1980) statement:

What the learner is trying to do interacts with and overrides the structure of the event or, where the structure is a familiar one and can be performed only in certain ways, a particular event may override the (learner's) efforts to achieving specific memory. (Jenkins, 1980, p. 231)

Results such as those described above imply that several considerations are important, if one is to understand a learner's test performance, including:

1. *The learner's characteristics.* These are individual aspects of the learner's knowledge, aptitudes, purposes, motivations, etc.

2. *The learner's activities during the course of studying.* These include attention to details or specifics, strategies for approaching the learning task, and other ways of adapting to the requirements of the task. Is this a memory task? Will I be taking a multiple choice or essay test? Is this a problem with a definite solution?

3. *The teacher's activities and teaching methods.* The sequencing of assignments, the use of recitation or questioning, the kind of media used, or the interaction of teacher and students or among students may have important effects on the way lessons are processed by the learner.

4. *The criterial measure employed.* The criterial measure may or may not provide information about what the learner knows. For example, a recognition test may yield high scores but tell only that the learner has some information available. It tells little about how the information has been processed, how accessible it might be for later retrieval, whether the information can be used in a problem situation, or whether the information has any durability in terms of resistance to interference. From the student's view point, expectations about the kind of measure to be used can affect strategies used in studying.

These four facets of concern comprise Jenkins' (1980) tetrahedral model. They have been illustrated by him for examining experimental data, by Bransford (1979) for general educational concerns, and by Brown, Campione, and Day (1981) for learning to learn. Another illustration, summarizing research on advance organizers, may be found in Figure 1 of this chapter. The implementation of the tetrahedral model does not demand the instructional designer and curriculum constructor to take all variables into account simultaneously (Jenkins, 1974). It does indicate, however, that one should not treat a given curriculum, instructional method, or evaluation technique as though the other variables did not exist.

Many processes contribute to learning in the classroom. These include orienting instructions, advice given, what the learner perceives as important, background knowledge, comprehension of the task, strategies for making inferences, and procedural skills brought to bear on the task, to name but a few concerns. To investigate the effects of a teaching method, to attempt to teach via a teaching method, or to develop a piece of software for a given lesson without considering pupil perceptions (for example) about how to process the information is to invite disaster by failing to understand the contributions of the learner. Without considering inference, for example, the teacher-designer may be baffled by the learner's questions, interpretations, or test performance that reflect the transformations of a learning event by the student. (It is not a rare event for teachers to ask their students, "Where in the world do you get your interpretations?")

To eliminate some of the complexity imposed by the tetrahedral model, Jenkins (1974, p. 794) suggests that such questions as the following should be asked:

What kind of analysis of memory (or other mental process) will be useful to you for the objectives, or purposes of a learning event? What kinds of learning events (e.g., concepts, strategies, and so on) are of concern?

When these are specified other factors such as contextual arrangements, textures that support experiences, strands that interrelate aspects of experience, and so on, may be considered in turn.

Information Processing

The constructivist's position places considerable emphasis on the learner's role and responsibility for learning. The learner characteristics and learner activities comprise two important facets of the tetrahedral model. Learner characteristics include all characteristics that set limits on what can be learned. They include abilities, intentions, knowledge, purposes and so on (Bransford, 1979). To summarize characteristics related to learning to learn one might include knowledge (metacognitions) related to what one has to do to bypass memory limitations, to activate available knowledge, or to reason by analogy (Brown *et al.,* 1981). A first consideration in these matters is the nature of the information-processing system, its phases and how the limitations of each phase may be accomodated by control mechanisms.

The System

Information processing models typically assume a system that processes, in sequential fashion, information from the time of the input to the time of storage in secondary or long-term memory. The basic mechanisms consist of the sensory registers (apparently one for each sense), the short-term memory, and the long-term memory. Some investigators have hypothesized a working memory to account for the dynamic aspects of understanding and reasoning whereby information stored in long-term memory is retrieved to aid in reworking input and forming new structures or relations.

The three-stage system assumes that all people have the same mechanisms but that individual differences exist in the capacity of one or more parts or in the way each is used. Each part has internal limitations but these limitations can be influenced by favorable use of control systems.

The Control Systems

The sensory registers take in immense amounts of information but hold it only briefly (milliseconds). There is too much information to attend to in the short period available; some has to be selected out. The control system here is selective attention. It determines what is sufficiently important to be channeled to the short-term store. Short-term memory has its limitations too, because it can only handle six or seven chunks of information and then only for several seconds. However, there are two control processes for short-term memory: one is repetition and the other is chunking. Neither affects the capacity directly. Maintenance rehearsal, for example, may be employed to retain information until it is no longer needed. If it is important or usable it can be made meaningful by elaborative rehearsal during which the information is related to existing knowledge structures thereby forming chunks. A chunk, by definition, varies in the amount of information it can hold: The sequence of letters in *bkj* may be three chunks but the same number of letters in *cow,* for a fluent reader, is one chunk. The expression $(a + b)^2$ may be one chunk to a teacher of mathematics, but it might be six chunks to a beginning algebra student. A chunk is a complex pattern of node-link associations and it becomes so through increased knowledge, frequent practice, and experience.

Craik and Lockhart (1972) claimed that either short-term or long-term memory resulted from the way the material was processed. Maintenance processing could be used to maintain the processing at a particular level, leaving behind it memory that was primarily phonological or sensory (shallow processing). Elaborative rehearsal facilitates long-term memory by linking new material into existing schemata, thereby making it meaningful and more easily retrieved. Since the early studies there have been many criticisms of the original levels of processing approach. Morris, Bransford, and Franks (1977), for example, suggest the notion of transfer-appropriate processing, implying that facilitation of recall is determined by the congruity between the way the material is processed and the means by which retention is assessed. This notion is implicit, in Tulving's (Tulving, 1979; Tulving & Thomson, 1973) encoding specificity principle. (Also see the section on elaboration.)

Information in short-term memory is probably the basis of "being conscious" about an event (Norman, 1982). When information is in short-term memory and working memory, there is considerable flexibility with what can be done with it. The information can be used as a cue to retrieve other information from long-term memory, it can be elaborated, it can be used to form images, it is used in thinking, it can be structured to be placed in long-term or secondary memory, or if nothing is done with it, it can be discarded.

What is done with the information in short-term (and working) memory has profound consequences for the value of that information at some later time since it either is forgotten, is stored as an isolated piece of information, or becomes integrated within some part of the framework of the schemata in long-term memory. It is from the long-term memory that information is retrieved at some later time. Though the capacity of long-term memory is apparently immense, retrieval from it is more sluggish than from the short-term memory. Accordingly, it is not surprising that learners differ in the extent to which information is retrievable, even in simple tasks (Posner, Boies, Eichelman, & Taylor, 1969). For example, when given two tasks, one of determining whether the letters in the pair aa or in the pair AA are physically identical or are the same letters, learners in the first task must only match the two letters; in the second task they must, additionally, compare information in working memory with their knowledge about letters taken from the long-term store. Learners who perform poorly on a test of verbal ability take longer on the second (same-letter) task than do learners who perform well on the test. The difference for one of the comparisons is not great (less than 100 milliseconds). However, these data imply that where many such decisions must be made in brief periods of time, as in reading and writing, the reader or writer may have difficulty in comprehending because the whole process is slowed down. The slow reader, for example, may have to reread text to get its meaning, may seem to ponder over phrases for unknown reasons or may lose interest because he keeps falling behind in the amount read.

Working Memory

Why a model of working memory? We need a model to deal with an obvious fact about memory, that is, while working on problems or making decisions, we retain information for longer periods than the short-term memory will allow. We have to account for a temporary storage that allows information to be held and manipulated while it is being processed. We can leave a problem or decision and come back to it an hour later or contemplate its solution while carrying out other tasks. Working memory is neither as short as short-term memory nor as remote as long-term memory but is situationally determined for the immediate environment. It contains the elements of the decision, of the situation, and the context that occur at a given time. It provides a "flow" to our perceptions. A sudden flash of light is not seen typically as a surprising element but, depending upon the context, it might be recognized as a lightning bolt or a sudden burning out of a light bulb.

Bower (1975) describes the functions of working memory as (a) providing the context for perception, (b) serving a "holding function for later retrieval," (c) keeping a running account of immediately prior events that provide a reasonable context for occuring events, (d) observing deviations in naturally occuring events (or in games such as chess) so that necessary adjustments can be made in the knowledge or procedural systems, and (e) initiating and implementing plans for a given task within a given context.

The Schemata: Knowledge Base for Assimilation and Retrieval

The information-processing system does not function *in vacuo*. New material is processed in terms of knowledge held by the learner, that is, knowledge structures. The importance of schematic knowledge is succinctly summarized in a phrase attributed to Pasteur to the effect that "discovery favors the prepared mind." This statement is a declaration of the assumption that higher-order processes such as problem solving and creativity depend on highly integrated knowledge structures. The contents of long-term memory affect what we attend to and may in some instances negate the need for all but a few fragments of the input to interpret a given situation. We may, for example, hear the first note or two of a melody and know what is to follow. We may read a few words and recognize it as a full-blown phrase or passage. "To be . . ." is easily completed by most learners. Very frequently we may impatiently and impolitely complete a phrase or sentence for speaker with whom we are conversing. Not surprisingly, good readers are better able to use contextual and other higher-order constraints in text than are poor readers—they are better top-down processors (Perfetti & Roth, 1981). The effects of schemata on such conceptually driven (top-down) processing are reflected in perceptual processing, making inferences, predicting, and the like. These processes, of course, also depend on the input for guidance (data-driven processing). When dealing with unfamiliar material, there is more dependence on data-driven guidance; when an unfamiliar word or phrase in a text is encountered higher-order comprehension skills are preempted by lower-order skills until the meaning of the word or phrase is clarified.

The term *schema* was used very early in contemporary cognitive psychology by Bartlett (1932), who spoke of its role in understanding in a frequently used citation that the "organism turns around on its own schemata and to reconstruct them afresh" (p. 206) in an "effort after meaning" (p. 45). Bartlett is cited in numerous studies of memory, especially those dealing with reconstruction, in order to illustrate the point that learners rarely recall verbatim information. Rather, they recall the gist of information or some paraphrased version of what was encountered. The learner has "an overmastering tendency to get a general impression of the whole and, on the basis of this, he constructs the probable detail" (Bartlett, 1932, p. 206).

Schemata were also employed by Piaget to refer to knowledge content and organization (knowledge structures) of learners at various levels of development. Ausubel's cognitive structures were closely related to current definitions of schemata. He considered cognitive structures so important that he was prompted to write (Ausubel, 1968),

If I had to reduce all of educational psychology to just one principle, I would say this: The most important single factor influencing learning is what the learner already knows. Ascertain this and teach (her)him accordingly. (p. vi)

Knowledge, then, becomes organized, probably in packets comprised of ideas from several content areas (Norman & Rumelhart, 1975; Norman, 1982). Schemata are but frames to be filled with descriptions (instantiations) and may be embedded in other schemata (Rumelhart & Ortony, 1977). They are represented in memory in a form (such as hierarchies or complex networks) that can be used independently of, or in conjunction with, other schemata. Current descriptions of this organization

come from many different approaches in psychology and from computer studies of artificial intelligence. These organizing structures have been variously referred to as schemata (Rumelhart & Ortony, 1977), as frames (Minsky, 1975), or as scripts (Schank & Abelson, 1977). It is impossible to describe each of these concepts in any detail here. However, all share some common dimensions: there are central conceptual components called "nodes." Around these nodes are various relationships that may include features, properties, functions, links with other declarative knowledge (concepts, facts), procedures for accessing the information, uses, and a host of other relationships that may be specified. The relations in these node-link expressions may take the form of agent, object, location, or time, for example (Fillmore, 1968). Or, they may be expressed in terms of subordinate or superordinate exemplars, functions, and properties of exemplars in hierarchical organizations.

The critical feature of such theories is that knowledge consists of ideas linked by relations. These can be further linked into hierarchies but probably not as a vast network of interrelated ideas (van Dijk & Kintsch, 1983). Ideas and relations around nodes can be densely or loosely "packed." They can have many "routes" emanating from them or few. They may be weakly linked, making them available but difficult to access, or strongly linked, making them automatically accessible and capable of excitation or spreading activation (Collins & Loftus, 1975).

The characteristics of schematic networks allow access to an idea(s) by a number of different routes, and activation of one idea (e.g., by priming) may activate others closely linked to it. Typically, activated information appears to be retrievable. Schemata, whether hierarchically organized or comprised of overlapping or embedded subsets, are never complete. There are always voids to be filled; ideas to be linked to other ideas; concepts to be elaborated; and modifications of properties by which concepts are identified. These necessities characterize learning. In short, the schemata provide the basis for the assimilation of new information (R. C. Anderson, 1977; Norman, 1982).

Schemata are highly individualistic because they contain a record of individualized experiences, records that are declarative representations of knowledge. In principle, the network encompasses all that the person knows, believes, and feels about himself, other persons, events and information in episodic, semantic, and affective terms. It encompasses all that one knows about how to keep things in memory, how to solve problems, how to get from one place to another, (metacognitions, images, cognitive maps) and so on. The schemata are flexible in the sense that one schema may substitute for another and they are context sensitive in the sense that a selected schema may depend on the conditions under which the input occurs (Rumelhart & Norman, 1981). In brief, schemata comprise the learner's theory of the world, his or her world view; schemata direct perceptual organization and the process that provides samples of the present environment for information; this information, in turn, further modifies the schematic knowledge (Neisser, 1976).

The Schemata and Inference

Much of top-down processing consists of making inferences. Text inferences range from certainty, (necessary consequences of text), to plausible, and to possible plausibility (van Dijk & Kintsch, 1983). Typically, inferences are used to bridge gaps in information or to elaborate information. The kinds of inferences that are made depend on how information is represented in the schemata and how it is accessed. The following assumptions seem consistent with existing data: (a) knowledge is represented in the form of schemata, networks, frames, or scripts; (b) these representations may consist of propositional, spatial, semantic, procedural or other relationships; (c) relevant information is stored separately so that it is retrievable, but it may also be interconnected, to a greater or lesser degree, with other information about the concepts; (d) the greater the interconnection the greater the likelihood that activating one source may activate other sources linked to it: (e) much of this information may be organized hierarchically; (f) under the proper conditions (e.g., priming, context, etc.) any of the forms of representations may be accessed; (g) what is accessed determines the inferences that are made; and (h) people have bases for comparing information accessed with information given to determine the validity of the inference as well as for judging their confidence in the validity of the judgment.

In summary, students come to the classroom with a great amount of information integrated in some fashion. How much information and how it is organized is obviously a source of individual differences. This information is employed in building new representation of new material and may become a part of those representations; they enter into selective attention, into monitoring task demands, into developing expectations about reasonable outcomes, and so on. Thus, the kinds of representations that are to be constructed or generated by the student require understanding and careful monitoring by instructors. If the prototype of the outcome is not defined by the teacher, the student will define his or her own. As Driver (1973) indicates, the belief system that students use in school settings for passing examinations may never be related to the way the information learned is to be used in every day settings.

Facilitating Understanding by External Aids

Educators have always had a concern for the nature of the materials used in the presentation of content. During the past decade, increasing attention has been paid to characterizing how variables associated with teaching input affect learning, retention and later application (transfer) of what has been learned; in particular, attention has been given to the cognitive facets of how the learner's processing can be guided or directed by the teacher's efforts (e.g., see Mayer, 1984).

Repetition

As with mechanical (rote) learning, repetition and drill have low priority as a teaching strategy. However, it is frequently used in educational settings through the use of exercises or other forms of repeated trials. Unfortunately, sheer repetition, keeping all other variables controlled, seems to have little effect on learning, at least in list learning. On the other hand, educators, who are continually confronted with the importance of on-task time, often turn to drill and practice with the idea that anything that engages learners will promote achievement. Very often the relation between time expended, the nature of the processes employed while on task, and the probable outcomes are left undefined.

Despite the concern that instructors may favor drill and repetition, these strategies may have their place in the accretion phase of learning (see Table 1 of this chapter) for making certain kinds of infor-

Table 1. Characteristics of Three Modes of Learning

Mode	General characteristic	Attributes of the student's knowledge structures	Learning strategy	Testing	Interference from related topics	Transfer to related topics
Accretion	Adding to the amount of knowledge, traditional verbal learning.	Accumulation of knowledge according to existing KMs (Knowledge module)	Study, probably using mnemonic systems and good depth of processing.	Factual tests short answers, multiple choice Basic recall and recognition tests	High	Low
Restructuring	Insight. Feeling of understanding material that was previously disorganized Often accompanied by "oh," or "aha."	New structures for KMs are formed	Thought, teaching by example, analogy, metaphor. Socratic dialogue	Conceptual tests Questions that require inference or problem solving	Medium	High
Tuning	Making existing KMs more efficient. No new knowledge or structures, but refinement of current skills	The parameters of KMs are adjusted for maximum efficiency. Special cases are directly encoded.	Practice	Speed, smoothness. Performance under stress or pressure.	Low	Of general knowledge, high. Of specific (tuned) knowledge, very low.

Source: Norman, D. A. (1978). Notes toward a psychology of human learning. In A. M. Lesgold, J. W. Pelligrino, S. D. Fokkema, & R. Glaser (Eds.), *Cognitive, psychology and instruction* (p. 44). New York: Plenum Press.

mation readily available (e.g., multiplication tables). In the later stages (tuning) practice and repetition may be useful for enhancing compilation, unitization, and automatization of the subparts of a cognitive skill (Neves & Anderson, 1981). There is also some evidence (Mayer, 1983) that for the acquisition of declarative knowledge, repetition has effects not only on how much is learned but also on the structure of what is learned. These effects depend on the mental resources devoted to the rehearsal process (Naveh-Benjamin & Jonides, 1984). Verbatim recall falls sharply with the number of repetitions whereas recall of conceptual principles and performance on creative problem-solving increases (Mayer, 1983). In a meaningful learning task (such as learning a scientific principle), the learner may acquire a conceptual framework or schema. Mayer (1983) suggests that the encoding process during repetition should provide for (a) refocusing from formal facts to ideas that fit the framework within which the facts are presented, (b) reorganizing the ideas into the learner's schemata rather than allowing the learner to blindly accept the presented organization of informa-

LEARNER CHARACTERISTICS

Experienced (−)
Inexperienced (+)
Rich set of subsuming knowledge (−)
Low ability (+)

LEARNER STRATEGIES

Good encoders (good encoding strategies) (−)
Shallow processors (+)
Depth limit processors (+)
Tendency toward premature closure (+)
Rote memorization (+)
Repetition (+)

EVALUATION

Fails to measure transfer (−)
Far transfer (+)
Retention of details (−)
Near transfer (−)
Conceptual generalizations (+)
Retention of conceptual information (+)

MATERIALS

Type of AO-Concrete models (+)
Type of AO-Higher Order Rules (+)
Type of AO-Main Themes (+)
Type of AO-Factual prequestions (−)
Type of AO-Summaries (−)
Type of AO-Outlines (−)
Type of AO-Directions to pay attention (−)
Well structured text materials (−)
Poorly oriented or poorly integrated text (+)
Integrated text (−)
Familiar text (−)
Spiral or well-organized text (−)
Post AO (−)
Pre AO (+)

Figure 1. When advance organizers may have an influence. (Plus indicates possible favorable influence; minus indicates possible little, no, or negative influence.). Based on Mayer (1979a,b).

tion, and (c) rewording so as to use familiar terminology and sentence structures rather than allowing the learner to recall text materials verbatim.

Advance Organizers

As the name implies, advance organizers are placed before the material to be learned (Ausubel, 1968). They are advantageous provided that the material is potentially meaningful to the learner (i.e., the learner has the background necessary to understand the material as it is presented), that the learner is motivated to learn the material in a meaningful way, that the learner attends to the critical points in the material, and that the learner actively uses the structure provided as a context.

Advance organizers may not have a positive in-

fluence on learning or retention if the learner already has the appropriate conceptual organization, if the sequence of content is such that the structures can be easily implied, or if the learner's existing learning strategies effectively relate new learning to old learning (Ausubel, Novak, & Hanesian, 1978; Mayer, 1979a,b).

To illustrate the use of the tetrahedral model (Jenkins, 1980) as a conceptual base for organizing such findings, the conditions under which advance organizers may be effective are summarized in Figure 1. Although there seems to be evidence for each of the variables indicated, the reader is cautioned against overgeneralizing the information in the table. Furthermore, many of these variables are certain to interact in an instructional setting. Thus, for example, where appropriate knowledge structures are present, the advance organizer may function to bind the new material to existing structures, or, for learners who have appropriate knowledge but inadequate strategies, the advance organizers may serve as a mapping device.

Organization

The organization of materials is a powerful variable in learning. Among other outcomes, it affects the interconnectedness of events from which inferences might be made, it affects the logical flow of ideas, and it affects the context, thereby influencing the processing required by the learner. Because these variables affect the way the content is structured by the learner, organization may significantly affect learning outcomes.

The imposition of external organization of input on clustering was demonstrated initially by free recall of a randomly presented set of words selected from four categories (e.g., animals, furniture, musical instruments, etc.) (Bousfield, 1953). The free-recall testing procedure permitted the learner to recall the words in any order. Bousfield noted that the words were recalled in clusters of words belonging to the same category. Similar results were found by Jenkins and Russell (1952) who used pairs of words with high associative connections (e.g., table, chair) in their list. Upon free recall the subjects produced associated words together. External organization may also be imposed by presenting items in blocks, representing examples of subcategories of a hierarchy. For example, the superordinate, minerals, encompasses stones and metals at one level, the adjective pair precious-common at a lower level, followed by specific examples of each at the object level. Upon free recall of the blocked material more was retained than on the randomly presented items (Bower, Clark, Lesgold, & Winzenz, 1969). Obviously, the effectiveness of external organization depends on the learner's knowledge of the categories used.

Not only can organization be externally imposed on inputs but learners tend to impose their own organization on events, such as words that are unrelated. Subjective organization was noted by Tulving (1962), who observed that learners tended to use the same organization of items on successive free-recall trials, that the organization increased with repetition, and that the degree of organization was positively correlated with performance based on the number of items recalled.

Even though learners appear to have inherent tendencies to pattern, or to find patterns in their environment, the patterns to be identified can be given more definitive direction by using external organization. Needed is a description of what conceptual categories are required for understanding information in a subject-matter domain and what conceptual categories are held at the same time by the learner. The emerging area of studies of experts and novices is beginning to shed some insights on this very important problem.

Incidental Cues to Organization

Interestingly, learners are sensitive to any number of implicit cues, of which the instructor may be unaware, and may base their organization on these cues even though they may not be meaningful. For example, students will copy into their notes (and in some study guides are told of this technique) almost anything an instructor writes on the black board. Further, if novel information is presented in blocks (followed by short pauses), learners will attempt to use the block as an organizing cue, imposing any number of hypothetically possible organization bases, such as alphabetical (real or implied) order, lengths of words, or concreteness (Reitman & Reuter, 1980). This again illustrates that if what is to be acquired is not carefully defined by the instructor, students will identify their own (often highly naive) rules for signals of what is important. With further experience and achievement in a content area, the imposed organization will be made on more meaningful bases. Nevertheless, whatever the status of the learner and whatever organizational scheme is used by the instructor, the information as presented will rarely coincide perfectly with the information as transformed.

Organization by Scripts

The more recent developments on organization involve studies of how connected discourse is organized. One way of organizing such material is in the form of a narrative following a script (i.e., a huge schema) representation of *setting, theme, plot,* and *resolution*. When a narrative is based on this organization the story is easily followed and understood. Disrupt this organization, and the recall drops accordingly (Thorndyke, 1977). Other studies have shown, however, that when learners are given a story in which the paragraphs are scrambled they will take more time to study the paragraphs than when they receive them in logical order. However, at the time of recall learners reorganize the elements into their correct order, retaining the same amount of information from the narrative as do control subjects (Kintsch, Mandel, & Kozminsky, 1977).

The importance of organization has been shown in Meyer's (1975) studies. Readers, for example, tend to employ the ready-made organization presented in a text. They pay more attention to the higher-order (main ideas) structures within a passage and recall more of them. Their reactions to lower-order content (details) are less predictable and tend to have less durability. These few points have as much implication for writing as for reading. Thus, a writer who wants an idea to be remembered will place that idea high in the structure of the text passage and will provide a tightly knit structure supporting comparative or other relations rather than the mere listing of attributes to provide coherence among higher-order and lower-order structures.

Scripts, as relatively stable integrations of packets of information (both procedural and declarative), apparently exist for many types of commonly experienced events. They may include going on a trip, attending a lecture, and going to a physician's office, among many others (Bower, Black, & Turner, 1979).

Signaling

Signals to the reader of important content to be acquired may be incorporated into textual, lecture, or other forms of presentation. The use of headings, outlines, statements of what is to follow, italicized words, notations of causes and effects, summary statements, or simply indicating such things as the number of points to consider or what will be covered can function as signals (Meyer, 1975). Signals are typically embedded in text as pointers to the reader but are unrelated to the content, for example, "one cause was . . . ," "to summarize . . . ," "a frequent result of these reactions is . . . ," "three points to consider are . . . ," and so on. Signals that emphasize the top levels of the organization and content of the passage typically lead to better retention of the content. Because of the direction given to the activity induced in the learner they facilitate problem solving and inference (Loman & Mayer, 1983). In general, signals function to call the student's attention to the structure

of the text and to help students integrate the content into a cohesive framework.

Contexts

The provision of contexts in texts helps to define the schemata activated (Di Vesta, 1958). In general, contexts play a crucial role in establishing frames that alter or transform the meaning of an event (Neisser, 1976). The role of context in memory has been demonstrated in the encoding specificity principle (Tulving & Thomson, 1973) and in a number of other areas ranging from memory to artificial intelligence (Minsky, 1975) to influencing the outcomes of social events (Goffman, 1974). Bransford (1979) has provided ample evidence to demonstrate that providing a title for an ambiguous passage not only improves comprehensibility of the passage but also facilitates memory, probably through activation of the appropriate schemata thereby allowing assimilation of the new information.

The same word may take on different meanings, may be instantiated differently (i.e., may activate different schema) by the context in which it is embedded. In one study (Anderson & Ortony, 1975) when subjects were given the sentence "The container held the cola" learners tended to recognize "bottle" rather than "container" on a posttest. As another example, the sentence, "The container held the apples," the subjects instantiated "basket" for "container." Thus, although "container" is appropriate at the surface structure of the sentence, the semantic meanings (representations) of "container" are "basket" for apples and "bottles" for cola. Such results imply that in retrieval, associative links provide for activating other conceptual nodes closely linked (related) to the one presented initially. For these purposes declarative knowledge must be both available and accessible.

Context, then, appears to have its affects on activation of schemata, on instantiation of words and concepts, on reconstruction, and on spreading activation. But, in addition, information learned in one context may be irretrievable in another context (Riccio, Richardson, & Ebner, 1984), that is, it may become context dependent, or context bound (Tulving & Thomson, 1973). Even mood may comprise a part of the context affecting memory (Bower, 1981). To be useful, information must be available for a variety of situations. Decontextualization then seems to be an important educational goal. One means by which it can be achieved is by varying the context in which a given principle or its exemplars are employed (Nitsch, 1978; Di Vesta & Peverly, 1984). For example, the principle of refraction applies equally well to aiming a BB gun at a target under water, to understanding the colors produced by a prism, or to understanding the properties of lenses.

Cognitive Skills and Control Processes

Compensations for the limitations of the information processing system are eventually developed through continuous elaborations of schemata and by the strategies the learner employs. Together with schematic knowledge, cognitive skills can be used to make meaningful structures of information that, because of chunking or patterning, can be handled more efficiently than numerous small bits of information that might comprise the structure. Cognitive skills can be used by the learner to construct or generate what for the learner is new knowledge (i. e., new understandings) by combining known information with new inputs from the environment or with other known information. Chase and Ericsson (1981) report, for example, the "phenomenal" feat of an expert on track records, who was able to recall 80 digits by linking clusters of digits to various running records (e.g., "that was close to a record" "that was a slow time—"). Thus, cognitive skills not only enter into encoding and storage but they also affect the retrieval of information once it has been stored. Like expert mnemonists, people are good at recalling textual materials with which they are familiar and have had much practice (Chase & Simon, 1973). The beginning of a chunk should lead to (should prime) recalling the remainder (Kintsch, 1982).

The Executive: A Macrocontrol System

The executive is constructed as a metaphor to represent an overall global plan of alternative decisions and their consequences for a given situation or situations (Miller, Galanter, & Pribram, 1960: Neisser, 1976). The contents of working memory may comprise some of that which is included under the metaphor of executive control. These include metacognitions, planning, monitoring comprehension and procedural sequences, selective attention, self-regulation in the use of strategies,

and the like (see Brown *et al.*, 1983 and the section on metacognition in this chapter). One does not start a day by blindly responding to hundreds of stimuli or enter into a problem-solving situation without initiating a plan for proceeding in order to achieve certain goals, regardless of how naive these plans might seem. The executive determines what subgoals are to be achieved, and monitors behaviors to determine the extent to which the subgoals are being achieved, whether a new plan of attack may be required, what changes in the overall plan might be made, and whether the plan is completed or whether it should be aborted and replaced with a new one. There is direction to executive montoring but it does not rigidly constrain the execution of the plan. Rather, it is dynamic, subject to change with added information and changing inputs. Strategies are employed for implementing decisions called for by each step in the plan, including the decisions that have to be made, the choices or alternatives available, and their possible consequences.

The executive control system is critical to the cognitive processing system and serves as its general monitor. It is fed by the inputs in the situation: schematic, situational, contextual, and production plans. It will supervise processing in short-term memory, activate and actualize needed episodic and more general semantic knowledge, provide the higher-order information into which the lower-order information must fit, coordinate the strategies, decide which information from short-term memory should be moved to episodic memory, activate the relevant situation models in episodic memory, and guide effective search of relevant information in long-term memory. The control system guarantees that all strategies are geared toward producing information, such as semantic representations (but also pragmatic and other interactional and contextual representations) that is "consistent with the goals of understanding" (van Dijk & Kintsch, 1983, p. 12).

Development of Cognitive Skills

In the study of development of rules used by children, Siegler and his associates (Siegler, 1983, p. 264) assumed that five generalizations accounted for the emergence of processes by which problems are solved by young children. Three of the generalizations deal with knowledge children have: (a) the rule for making judgments is the basic representation of knowledge; (b) there are premastery rules, garnered from across a wide range of situations, arranged according to their accuracy for prediction across those situations; and (c) similar reasoning principles tend to be used across many different situations when conceptual knowledge is sparse—reasoning principles become more diverse with increases (greater differentiation) in conceptual knowledge. Two of the generalizations relate to metacognitions regarding the adequacy of rules for given situations: (d) the most adequate learning situation is one that involves conflict in the sense that a given experience demonstrates that a rule is inadequate for some newly encountered situation; and (e) when the inadequacy of their rules become known, children turn more to encoding strategies (taking several dimensions into account) in order to obtain higher-level rules and organizations of knowledge.

The U-Shaped Curve

Changes in knowing what to encode seem to trace a U-shaped curve (Richards & Siegler, 1981; Strauss, 1982) for rules in a number of domains. For example, children initially learn irregular verbs (e.g., bought) correctly because they are experienced more frequently; then they learn the "ed" ending rule for forming the past tense of regular verbs and simultaneously incorrectly overgeneralize this rule to irregular verbs (thus, boughted, comed); and in later stages of development, children relearn the correct use of the past tense inflection for irregular verbs (Slobin, 1971).

Norman (1982) cautiously concludes that abrupt changes in outcomes may be attributable to changes in the cognitive skills of mature learners as well. As all psychology students know, learning curves for experiments on telegraphy by Bryan and Harter (1899) resulted in continuing improvement followed by a plateau and followed again by another period of increasing gains, thereby reflecting a U-shaped curve. In another study (Ruger, 1910, as cited in Norman, 1982), subjects solved the heart-and-arrow mechanical puzzle. The time per trial decreased rapidly from the 1st to 15th trial, with slight decrease from the 15th to 75th trial. However, on the 75th trial there was a dramatic increase in time taken (about 6 times longer than on the previous trial) followed by a precipitous increase in efficiency from there on. Norman (1982) also describes the course of learning programming strategies and notes that after several more or less time-consuming attempts at certain

steps in the procedure the student has a flash of insight and says, "Of course, that makes sense." What appears to be happening in all of these situations whether in language, telegraphy, solving mechanical puzzles, or learning programming skills corresponds to Siegler's view that the learner acquires a new representation of the knowledge needed and more efficient strategy for accessing that knowledge and using it. This is the change that transforms a person who is knowledgeable about a task to one who is an expert, a change that Rumelhart and Norman (1981) ascribe to the tuning phase (see Table 1).

Metacognition

The knowledge a learner has and can relate (state) about existing strategies may be the initial step in arriving at effective use of strategies in attending, learning, remembering, and retrieving information (Flavell, 1979). Cognitions about strategies that are generalizable across many subject-matter domains have been labeled metacognitions. They exist, at different levels of sophistication, at all age levels. A 3-year-old may hold an object or stare fixedly at it when instructed to remember it. Eight- and eleven-year-old children take more time to read anomalous sentences, reflecting the knowledge that to unravel the meaning of the sentence the reader must spend more time on it. However, the ability to verbalize the difficulties encountered increases with age; a greater percentage of 11-year-olds than 5-year-olds said that they felt something was wrong with the way the passage was written (Harris, Kruithof, Terwoght & Visser, 1981). Interestingly, more of the younger children were unable to indicate why they spent more time on the anomalous sentence.

Although young children understand some of their information-processing skills, awareness of the relevant processes increases over the school years. Metacognitions for thinking, remembering, how to react to social-personal problems and how to solve problems in subject-matter areas are illustrations. On the other hand, existing curricula make little provision for the learning of metacognitions or of strategies.

Metacognition in school tasks involves knowing about such procedural skills as planning, checking, evaluating, and self regulating the use of the skill (Flavell, 1979). Good learners conduct these processes automatically (Armbruster & Brown, 1984). Fluent reading, for example, runs off smoothly when comprehension creates no problem. When comprehension hits a snag, the fluent reader engages in conscious deliberation. Poor learners may not know the strategies or if they do they are unable to use them to monitor the learning activity or may be unable to use them automatically. However, they can be taught to do so by direct instruction (see Brown *et al.*, 1981, for examples).

As Brown *et al.* (1981) indicate, metacognitive training is really a new term for an old idea (i.e., learning to learn). A host of outstanding early educators and psychologists including Dewey, Thorndike, and Judd spoke about the importance of students' knowledge of procedures for problem solving and transfer.

Less well known is the fact that Binet did not intend his scale to be employed for classifying people into categories. Rather, he, too, intended its purpose to be a basis for selecting pupils who might benefit from a program designed to enhance the pupil's capacity to learn and to assimilate instruction: "in a word they must learn how to learn" (Binet, 1916, p. 257).

Harlow's (1949) studies of learning sets are often referred to as studies in learning to learn. Upon repetition of variations of problems that required similar strategies (e.g., selecting the middle-sized objects), learners would acquire the rule for solving the problem by eliminating such irrelevant attributes (error factors) as position, color, or brightness of the objects, and by attending only to the relevant attributes that were reinforced.

Unfortunately, as important as metacognition is, the term has become a catchall. However, it can be delimited somewhat to a learner's awareness about what skills or strategies are useful or detrimental for performing, understanding, comprehending, or reasoning about particular tasks, given the learner's knowledge about her advantages or limitations in capacity, knowledge, motivations, or other characteristics. "One of the real advances spurred by the interest in metacognition is the revived concern for mechanisms of change (Brown *et al.*, 1983, p. 126). Some means for implementing change are discussed in subsequent sections below.

Illustrative Cognitive Strategies

The identification of metacognitions, strategies, and procedural skills is an outcome of the current cognitive movement marked by the now classic studies of Bruner, Goodnow, and Austin (1956) who identified focusing, scanning, and gambling strategies in learning concepts. The evidence implies that these and other strategies used by the learner can be effectively directed by the instructor. For example, if precise elaboration is useful to the learner then textual input can be elaborated, and the techniques of making precise elaborations can be taught along with why the approach is useful, and how its effectiveness can be evaluated.

Imagery

Studies in which students are instructed to employ imagery (Bower, 1970, 1972, 1973) support the view that one kind of cognitive process is the ability to employ spatial orientation in thinking. In addition, orienting instructions to employ imagery have been shown to affect recall, thereby tempting investigators to advocate their use for enhancing recall. However, imagery may be effective mainly for the recall of ideas that have spatial features or for those ideas on which spatial features can be imposed as a model (e.g., as in the three-term problems). If these conditions do not exist, imagery instructions may be effective merely because they make additional processing demands on the learner.

Much of the current work advocating the training of strategies for educational purposes began with training in imagery (e.g., Dansereau, 1978; Weinstein, 1978; Wood, 1967). Many of the studies using imagery instructions have used concrete words for which there is an imageable (e.g., pictorial) counterpart. In one example for teaching the Spanish equivalents for English words the learner might imagine, or be shown a picture of a duck with a pot on its head in order to recall the Spanish word "pato" for the English word "duck". In this example, an acoustic link is formed by the image of the pot and a perceptual link is formed by the picture of the duck (thus, pato is pronounced pot-oh and it is the equivalent for the word duck). Teacher-prepared (imposed) images seem to be more effective than learner-prepared (induced) images, especially for young children and for abstract words because of the difficulty young children may have in generating appropriate images or because of the difficulty that learners in general may have for generating images of abstract materials. Imagery can also be used for complex text learning of passages that contain many concrete relations such as the sentence "People in this culture make clothes out of palm leaves'' (Kulhavy & Swenson, 1975). In this use of imagery, the elaborations contribute to the learning of thematic (interactive) relations rather than simply the learning of links within phrases or between words.

The use of imagery is a basic form of elaboration and may be limited to more or less concrete materials. Whether its use for abstract relations is practical or possible for the average learner appears to be an unsettled question at the present. Nevertheless, it may be a functionally useful device for some basic elaborations employed in working memory.

Mnemonic Aids

Closely related to imagery instructions as an elaborative device are mnemonic aids, such as the pegword system, method of loci, the hook method, and so on. They involve making links between a stored linearly ordered representation (one is a bun, ten is a hen) or a maplike system of a familiar layout (such as the floor plan of a familiar house) to which the to-be-learned items are linked in some meaningful way. Retrieval occurs by accessing the newly learned material through reversing the process. That is, the unitized sentence formed initially through association with an object in the pegword system or with a location in the method of loci is recalled.

The initial experimental studies on imagery and mnemonic aids were necessary to establish that such processing had a favorable influence on memory. They emphasized the importance of linking the input to what was already known, even though the ''already known'' was an artificial system (such as the pegword or method-of-loci systems). However, the practical utility of extending simple imaginal productions beyond word-recognition and serial learning applications seems limited at best. In a criticism of the method of loci, Quintilian, an ancient educator, commented that

for the purpose of getting a real grasp of what we have written under the various heads, division and artistic structure will be of great value, . . . they are practically the only means of ensuring an accurate remembrance of what we have merely thought out. For correct division will be an absolute safeguard against error in the order of our speech, since there are certain points not merely in the distribution of the various questions in our speech but, also in their development, . . . which naturally come first, second, and third and so on, while the connection will be so obvious that nothing can be omitted or inserted without the fact of the omission or insertion being obvious. (Quintilian, 1922, XI, ii, 36–38)

Quintilian's criticism is a reminder that a useful mnemonic strategy should provide the framework of an organizational plan that could be entered at any point. Such plans would provide routes to a number of different meaningful relations and would help access information closely related to that location. It would also permit the possibility of accessing information located further away from the access node by systematically following the appropriate routes (spreading activation).

Reasoning by Analogy

The use of analogies may be a common way people apply knowledge from one subject-matter domain to another and involves the mapping of a new, perhaps abstract, schema on a familiar one. For example, cricket may be understood by most Americans if it is compared to baseball (Hayes & Tierney, 1982). The study of fractions is often begun with a comparison of cutting a whole pie into halves, quarters, eighths, and so on. Analogies of this sort provide a basis for bringing appropriate declarative and procedural knowledge into activation. Rumelhart and Norman (1981) indicate that the appropriate use of analogies in instruction would have these characteristics (p. 358):

(a) The starting point would be a domain with which the student is very familiar and in which he understands the reasoning procedures.
(b) The target domain (new learning) and the source domain (schematic knowledge) should be as similar as possible in their underlying dimensions or attributes and in their natural operations. What are appropriate (or inappropriate) dimensions should be commonly shared by both.

An ultimate outcome of reasoning by analogy should be a family of schemata for a given domain. Each schema within the family (a) would have its own context dependencies to determine what procedures or knowledge are applicable to a target domain and (b) would provide alternate conceptualizations of the target domain. Any analogy, though helpful, has its limitations and will not be useful in all applications (e.g., how does one multiply a quarter by an eighth of a piece of pie?) of the new information.

Elaborations

In a sense, imagery, mnemonic aids, and analogies all share the characteristic of requiring some form of elaboration; perhaps elaboration is one of the most important of the cognitive skills, *provided elaborations are precise.* Elaborative processes require extensions of an idea by linking it to something the learner already knows, whether the linkage is provided by the learner herself or by the teacher. Whatever elaborations are made by a learner must depend on his or her own schemata (Mayer, 1980). Without training, students may produce very idiosyncratic, artificial, or context-bound extensions. For example, the typical elaborations for remembering the spaces and lines of the treble clef or the aids for remembering the planets closest to or farthest from the earth are effective but have no utility beyond these very limited purposes. These kinds of elaborations have a purpose in some kinds of training, for example, in assembling parts of objects or in running through an aircraft take-off checklist, but they contribute little to understanding or comprehension. Indeed, in many instances, there is no need for them to do so. Under these circumstances artificial elaborations have a positive effect on the learner's achievement because such instructions influence attention and simplify the encoding of temporal relations so that more cognitive capacity can be employed for understanding. However, unqualified instructions to elaborate (e.g., when learners are told simply ''to elaborate'') yield erratic, unpredictable outcomes. If students' elaborations do not coincide with objectives to be tested, the content may be irretrievable in a new context although it may be retrievable when the original learning context (provided in the subjective elaboration) is reinstated (Barnett, Di Vesta, & Rogozinski, 1981; Tulving & Thompson, 1973).

Imprecise elaborations have little or no effect on recall over that obtained by unelaborated sentences (Bransford, 1979; Bransford *et al.*, 1982). Precise elaborations, on the other hand, clarify relations necessary for understanding, thereby making the material meaningful and allowing for applications to a variety of situations. For example, (Bransford *et al.*, 1982) the idea that ''arteries have thick walls, are flexible, and have no valves'' can be learned arbitrarily. Although recognizable on a later test, the learning may not be applicable to other situations by the learner.

An elaboration such as ''arteries are like water hoses which are thick walled, can be twisted and turned, and have no valves'' can help in the retrieval of the original statement (provided one remembers ''hoses'') but, again, may have little additional transfer advantage. Elaborations that are precise, on the other hand, are effective for recall

and for transfer because they facilitate understanding as in the elaboration, ''arteries are thick walled to accomodate to forceful surges of blood from the pumping of the heart, they are flexible to allow for contraction and dilation resulting in the valve like functions.'' Good learners in elementary school tend to make more precise elaborations than do poor learners; they are more effective at engaging background information; are better at drawing inferences; can use text structure better; and know more about elaboration and other strategies. Nevertheless, poor learners do profit from training in making elaborations.

Text materials can also be elaborated for effective use by the learner. Bradshaw and Anderson (1982) found that integrated, highly elaborated statements in terms of cause–effect relations were better recalled than unelaborated or large poorly elaborated statements. These results are attributed to the formation of elaborate, tightly knit links (integrated units) among nodes, (i.e., relevant associative links), in declarative knowledge (J. R. Anderson, 1983; Collins & Loftus, 1975), thereby facilitating activation (accessibility) of that knowledge at retrieval.

Cognitive Skills Training

Strategies amenable to training also include outlining, notetaking, underlining, self-questioning, and summarizing procedures. All, including imagery of concrete materials, have some beneficial effect on processing for recall. On the other hand, they may result in outcomes with limited transfer value unless they result in highly meaningful and integrated organizations of ideas. To be useful, any training program should result in cognitive skills that are durable (long lasting), accessible (retrievable), flexible, and generalizable (transferable or decontextualized). Of most importance, they should become autonomous to permit the use of the learner's resources for acquisition of packets of information represented in instructional objectives.

Brown *et al.* (1981) understate the issue in their comment that

rote recall though valuable, is not the only desirable outcome of learning activities. Often we want to enhance students' ability to understand the significance of the material they are learning rather than to recall it. (p. 14)

Their research, designed to train learners to understand the significance of learning strategies, demonstrated that self-control training was clearly the procedure of choice. The children were taught how to use the combination of (a) knowledge about a strategy, (b) employment of the strategy, (c) monitoring the use of the strategy, (d) checking the results of the strategy, and (e) evaluating the results of the strategy (i.e., why the strategy is useful). Not only was this procedure more effective than a blind training or modeling procedure for transfer to other situations but after a year these children had also improved upon the strategies taught them.

In a related study, Brown and Day (1983) taught college students to use summarization rules with similar results. The procedure of using rules plus self-management plus training in how to control the use of the rules for summarization was more effective than either self-management only, rules for summarization only, or rules plus self-management (but employing the combination of the two by whatever means the student cared to use). Paris and his colleagues (Paris *et al.*, 1982) developed a curriculum program oriented toward instruction in comprehension strategies, comprehension monitoring, and related metacognitions. Unlike other programs, theirs was a lengthy one, comprising a 20-week course for third- and fifth-grade children. It required step-by-step use of procedures and intensive involvement by pupils and teachers. On several measures of comprehension, students in the curriculum program excelled over those in a control group by a wide margin. The results were still found on tests nearly a year later.

Gordon and Pearson (1983) provided guided practice in making inferences by using a four stage model: (a) asking a question, (b) answering the question, (c) identifying evidence to support the answer, and (d) providing a rationale for why the evidence supported the answer. In the first phase of training, the teacher modeled all four stages. In the second stage, the teacher posed the question and gave the answer, then the students gave the evidence and the rationale. In the third phase, the teacher posed the question and identified relevant evidence whereas students answered the questions and gave the rationale. In the final stage, students did all phases.

The studies by Paris, Gordon and Pearson, and Brown, Campione and Day share the essential characteristic of providing for the gradual release of responsibility for using the strategy to the student. They proceed from modeling (all teacher responsibility) to guided practice (gradually releas-ing responsibility to the pupil) to eventually turning all responsibility over to the student (Pearson & Gallagher, 1983).

Recognizing the complexity of the variables involved in the Socratic method, Collins (1977) has devised at least a partial analysis of some of the rules that teachers use in helping pupils make inferences in what has been described as the "Socratic Tutor." In initiating a problem such as, "What factors are influential in the growing of rice?," the student might be asked, "Can they grow rice in Florida?" After a series of questions, based on 24 rules, the procedure culminates in the student's summarization of the relevant factors and consequences of a general rule for the problem (e. g., of the factors involved in growing rice). The procedure works extremely well for a number of problems and does draw on the learner's prior knowledge. The theoretical orientation provides a framework by which computers might be employed for teaching causal dependencies about geography, social studies, and other subject-matter areas.

The Psychology of School Subjects

The cognitive psychology of school subjects is beginning to reemerge in the basic skills of reading, writing, and arithmetic as well as in physics, computers, social studies, and other subject matter areas. An important outcome is that instruction in these content areas seems to have similar underlying principles for procedural skills. They do differ, however, in the kinds of declarative knowledge that contribute to and become embedded in a given procedure, thereby limiting the degree to which a procedure is generalizable from one domain to another.

Reading and Writing

The psychology of reading emphasizes decoding and comprehension skills. There is agreement that decoding skills must be learned before the young reader can become too concerned with comprehension. Eventually, decoding skills should become automatic so as not to interfere with fluent reading. Comprehension of narratives can be increased by teaching children the underlying scripts of narratives (Brooks & Dansereau, 1983: Singer & Donlan, 1982). Other techniques for enhancing comprehension are described in Professor Andre's chapter.

The expert writer has many characteristics in common with the fluent reader (Scardamalia, Bereiter, & Boelean, 1982). He or she has a good knowledge base, recognizes the need for revision, uses a variety of notation systems, knows that ideas will change, reorganizes and revises, spends time on planning, and the like. The novice writer writes full sentences, puts down ideas in their formal order, may make a few notes, uses only minor revisions and spends little time on planning. Novices tend to recall content through direct access whereas experts use different levels of representation. Instruction can be implemented by tracing through the stages of planning, selecting ideas, expanding on ideas, employing various forms of representation, changing the order of ideas, and conveying intention. Making skills such as spelling, punctuation, and paragraph organization automatic allows more time for the writer to consider the composition of ideas. Thus automaticity of relevant basic skills is fundamental to reading and writing. But just as declarative (schematic) knowledge is essential to reading, so is it fundamental to writing. Without the appropriate knowledge, relevant details that provide cohesion are omitted.

Mathematics

One of the earlier studies that examined the teaching of mathematics was conducted by Brownell and Moser (1949). They used a two-by-two design to study methods for teaching subtraction: decomposition and equal additions comprised one factor and rote (mechanical) versus meaningful (explaining the logic) methods of teaching comprised the second factor. On an immediate test, meaningful teaching (generally) was the best procedure. On a delayed test that included transfer items, the decomposition method taught in meaningful fashion produced the highest scores for transfer and flexibility of use. The equal additions method produced poor transfer scores even when used meaningfully. Teachers indicated that the children did not understand it as well despite efforts to explain the logic behind the method. Thus, a teaching method is effective only to the extent that it conforms to the learner's schemata and induces the learner to process the information in given ways.

Skills in computation that aid comprehension of the concepts involved may eventually become au-tomatic. Furthermore, given instruction in certain computational skills, children will tend to invent their own variations of arithmetic operations. As indicated earlier in this chapter, sometimes these variations are more sophisticated ones than those that had been taught (Groen & Resnick, 1977). Nevertheless, children will often invent rules that, although shortcuts, are not applicable to a variety of situations or may produce erroneous outcomes. Recognizing this possibility, Brown and Burton (1978) developed debugging programs to diagnose difficulties children might be experiencing in subtraction by identifying the rules they were using (e.g., whether they were "borrowing" correctly or whether they are using a incorrect rule, such as subtracting whichever number is smaller from the larger number in a column). These studies again illustrate that whatever is taught may undergo reconstruction by the learner to result in idiosyncratic rules or organization of information.

Science

In the teaching of science, similar results are obtained. The young child's schemata for concepts such as "living" or "minerals" or "insects" may contain small amounts of information that are loosely but clearly organized, though usually at a superficial level, such as a prototype (e.g., any small crawling thing is a bug). With instruction and experience not only are more details of declarative knowledge available, but the organization of the details takes on more sophisticated semantic characteristics (i. e., in the form of underlying rules and patterns) (Chi, Feltovich, & Glaser, 1981).

These several illustrations of developments in subject-matter domains indicate that other areas too will be investigated for instructional implications. In each subject-matter area, it is important to know how experts and novices differ in *what* they know and *how they use* what they know.

Implications for Teaching Cognitive Skills

Behaviors are not random responses to the environment, nor are children's errors. Treating errors by drill and practice may be a futile or highly inefficient enterprise when one recognizes that errors are reflections of the learner's attempts to bring consistency into one's world view. Errors should be perceived as reflections of the rule the pupil is using (i.e., of the child's understanding)

(Strauss, 1982), thereby providing the basis for training in a cognitive skill appropriate to a given subject-matter domain. The extent or explicitness of cognitive skill training should be matched to the severity of the learning problems, that is, the zone of proximal development, which Vygotsky (1978) defines as

the distance between the actual developmental level as determined by independent problem-solving, and the level of potential development as determined through problem-solving under adult guidance or in collaboration with more capable peers. (p. 86)

Expertise: Procedural Knowledge and Declarative Knowledge

Procedural knowledge is a primary ingredient of cognitive skills and may be characterized simply as "knowing how." Its separation from declarative knowledge (knowing that) is for discussion purposes only. One assumption is that declarative knowledge is embedded in procedural knowledge, or that knowledge of how (procedural knowledge) is used to produce knowledge that (declarative knowledge) (Rumelhart & Norman, 1981). The schemata are comprised of declarative knowledge (i.e., facts, or, more technically, basic units of meaning consisting of arguments linked by relations) interspersed with procedural knowledge, that is, with "If-then" statements (e.g., IF I am to study for a multiple choice test THEN I must study to recognize details) (J. R. Anderson, 1980).

Experts have more complicated arrangements of declarative and procedural knowledge than do novices, a point to be discussed further below. Estimates of the time it takes to achieve expertise (the "right" combination of declarative and procedural knowledge) range from 5000 hours (Norman, 1978) to perhaps 10 years (J. R. Anderson, 1980, p. 235, based on a personal communication with T. R. Hayes). During that period, the person acquires the semantic, conceptual, and production foundations related to understanding a subject-matter domain. In the course of acquiring this knowledge, fragments of the procedures are garnered and accumulated to become part of the schemata. The phases required for useable learning as described by Norman (1978) are summarized in Table 1, showing characteristics of the learning modes, related teaching methods, and applicable testing modes.

An important difference between the novice and the expert, whether in reading, writing, reasoning, or some other skill is that proceduralization, put to the service of a broader function, becomes a part of higher-order productions. Ultimately, the proceduralization becomes systematized and automatic (Neves & Anderson, 1981). The novice's working memory is overloaded by the need to pay attention to the problem, the knowledge that must be dealt with, and the procedures to be followed. With expertise, attention to surface structures are supplanted by attention to the deep structures implied by the surface cues (Chi *et al.*, 1981). Simple relations are replaced by higher-order relations. To the novice, the Tower of Hanoi puzzle is a perplexing problem; many people give up before really trying to solve the six disc version. But, through "learning by doing" (Anzai & Simon, 1979), the powerful recursive pyramid subgoal strategy makes the problem solution apparent and elegantly simple (Wickelgren, 1974).

The ability to ask questions is closely linked to one's schematic knowledge and to competence in an activity. One of my students made the insightful remark that "It is useless to interject the question, 'Do you understand?' into a lecture, when we don't know what we are to understand." This is essentially the point made by Miyake and Norman (1979) who found that experts asked more questions with difficult tasks in the domain of their competence (computer programming) whereas novices asked more questions on easy tasks. There were no differences in self-generation of questions on tasks where neither group excelled.

The development of the characteristics of expertise is closely related to amount of declarative knowledge. A young child's representation of a class of dinosaurs with which she was familiar was at a higher-order structural level than of a less familiar class (Chi & Koeske, 1983). Similarly, 10-year-old experts in chess recall chess position patterns better than do novice adults, just as adult master chess players remember pieces in patterned plays better than do adult novices. Thus, retrieval depends on the linkage between nodes in schematic structures that are characteristic of experts.

In the course of acquiring expertise, some declarative knowledge gets subsumed or embedded within procedural knowledge. It is often the case that to recall how to spell a word we may want to write it out; to describe where the keys are on a typewriter a skilled typist may have to "tap-out" the letters to aid recall. Jenkins (1980, p. 233) illustrates the automatic functioning of higher order perceptual skills by describing a TV commentator's narration of a diver's performance in one of the competition trials. Just after the trial an expert is invited to comment on the performance. The expert's reply is that the dive was not a clean one because the diver failed to get his hands positioned fully behind his head as was required for good form. The slow motion replay confirmed this observation, although it was not at all apparent to the other observers of the original performance. Jenkins (1980) spells out several questions that provide insight into the nature and complexity of procedural skill and their interdependence with schemata in expertise,

Did the expert actually see that hand position in real time? Or does the expert know the consequences of the failure so that he automatically deduces the defect occurred? Or does the expert have a template or gestalt against which the total performance is judged and against which the defect stands out? We do not know. It is clear, however, that what is available to the expert is not available to us under the same time constraints. (Jenkins, 1980, p. 233)

Although procedural knowledge is being given considerable research attention at this writing, there are different opinions regarding its importance relative to knowledge representation in the thinking process. Chi, Glaser, and Rees (1981) state the issue well. On the one hand, problem representations would include experience in school-related knowledge domains that subsume general ways of solving problems. Under these circumstances, novices and experts might have the same declarative knowledge about a given task but the expert would excel in such procedural skills as problem representation, use of means–ends analyses, subgoal analyses to describe the problem space, and the like. However, it is relatively impossible to develop domain-free, general problem-solving strategies. All such programs involve some forms of representations that are typical of knowledge in a given content area (Glaser, 1984).

On the other hand, a knowledge based orientation would imply deemphasizing instruction in general processing skills in relation to instruction on the ways knowledge in a given domain could be structured, ways to recognize whether the information needed is available and ways of manipulating knowledge. Chi *et al.* (1981), for example, note that novices' knowledge representations of an inclined plane are comprised of its surface characteristics (plane, incline, length, height, existence or nonexistence of friction, and so on) expressed in terms of key words. The expert on the other hand, tends to represent the same problem primarily in terms of the principles of mechanics (e.g., force laws for acceleration and equilibrium) and their applications, and secondarily on surface characteristics. Less successful novices are less (or not) knowledgeable about physics, and do not know when to use the knowledge they have. As a result, they are prevented from making useful inferences that would help them to solve problems.

The two positions are not incompatible. They differ primarily in regard to whether instructional emphasis should be placed on general processing (learning-to-learn) skills or on procedural knowledge within the context of a given knowledge domain. The former orientation would imply that these skills should be taught in decontextualized form (de Bono, 1985) without regard to specific knowledge. Although some claims have been made for the efficacy of this procedure and it has been widely adopted, the supportive research data have not been forthcoming. The latter position would imply that investigators must understand the nature of differences between novices' and experts' knowledge representations, and the order in which levels of expertise appear. On these bases, recommendations for instruction would be made. Rather than teaching general problem-solution procedures in isolation, the curriculum would be oriented toward teaching problem solving by methods that incorporate procedural and declarative knowledge for a given subject-matter domain.

Motivation

Any instructional program gives at least some concern to motivation, a complex construct (Norman, 1981). The simple external input–output model is insufficient because of the interpretations given by the learner. For example, a learner may desire to learn a computer language but be unwilling to put forth the effort to learn it. The achievement of reward has affective outcomes, but when the reward indicates some knowledge of progress it also provides some information (Langley & Simon, 1981). Knowledge of progress on the other hand may affect the learner's self-evaluation or some cognition about what caused success (or failure), either of which may affect efforts in the future. Praise has always been considered to be a positive form of feedback, yet when given to an individual for tasks that other students perform easily, it may be interpreted by the recipient as a sign of lack of ability (''She's praising me for succeeding at this easy task because I generally don't do as well as the others.'' Or, ''He's surprised at the fact that I succeeded'').

Norman (1981) summarizes the status of the motivation construct, thus,

motivation . . . result[s] from a combination of things, from one's fundamental knowledge and goal structures, partially from emotional variables, and partially from decisions about the application of mental resources . . . there is not a single phenomenon of motivation. . . . Rather . . . a complex of things, some biological, some cultural, some emotional, some the results of conscious goals and intentions, others subconscious. Motivation is indeed important, worthy of serious study, and a major determiner of behavior. . . . It seems, however, to be a derived issue, composed of different aspects of belief systems, emotion, consciousness, learning, memory and skill. (Norman, 1981, p. 290)

One commonly accepted theory of emotion illustrates that the evaluation of an emotion contains a cognitive component. If, as they are presumed to be, bodily reactions are similar in pleasant (e.g., excitement) and unpleasant (e.g., fear) states, the sequence appears to be (a) the experienced input; (b) the resulting behavior (including bodily reactions; (c) a cognitive evaluation of one's behavior; and (d) the final evaluation of the affect (Schacter & Singer, 1962).

Affect and Information

These same concerns were voiced by McKeachie in his Presidential Address to the APA (McKeachie, 1976). However, the tone was optimistic since progress is being made, although, perhaps, not at the pace currently found in the study of the intellectual cognitive processes. McKeachie indicates that the two aspects of a reward are affective and informational. Extrinsic rewards may diminish the intrinsic motivation (Lepper & Greene, 1975) but are sometimes necessary in the early stages of learning to maintain the student's interest until the proper affective structures have been constructed. Underlying this tendency are the interpretations of the meaning placed on the reward. Knowledge of results has an effect only if it conveys information, the learner wants to improve, and the learner has some better alternatives by which the improvement can be made (R. L. Thorndike, as cited in McKeachie, 1976, and based on a conference presentation). The need to

improve, that is, the need for competence has had an enduring place in studies of motivation and is implied in McClelland's (1965) ''need for achievement.''

A common complaint that underscores the emotional facet of motivation is that low achieving students, or those who merely perceive that they are low achieving, have feelings of inadequacy. In the extreme form, this takes on the character of learned helplessness. Under proper training conditions, where responsibility is gradually turned over to pupils, low-achieving students who realize that they can perform tasks successfully and with good results, who learn to control their own learning activities, such as making precise elaboration successfully, are excited over the outcome (Franks *et al.*, 1982). The consequence is an increased belief in their own potential as students. Helping pupils to learn to learn thus has positive effects not only on the self-control of strategies but on changes in motivation, and, incidentally, on the teacher's positive perception of the pupil's potential (Brown *et al.*, 1981).

Curiosity

Early studies on epistemic curiosity (Berlyne, 1960) clearly involved cognitions but, probably because of the period in which the construct was proposed, interpretations were made in a behavioristic framework. However, Berlyne's studies and those of other investigators did involve motivation aroused by cognitive factors, usually due to a discrepancy or conflict of ideas and the resolution of these conflicts. This was the essence of Piaget's construct of equilibration and disequilibration, of Festinger's (1964) cognitive dissonance, Suchman's (1966) incongruity, and the discrepancy between the present state and the goal state used in computer simulations of problem solving as well as in cybernetic models of learning.

Attribution

Attributions for one's successes or failures are significant for understanding classroom motivations (Weiner, 1979; Weiner, Graham, Taylor, & Meyer, 1983). The common attributions for achievement are classified in terms of their locus (external or internal), stability (stable or unstable), and controllability (controllable or uncontrollable). Specific attributions within this classification that have been investigated most frequently are immediate effort (controllable, unstable, and internal), ability (uncontrollable, stable, and internal), task difficulty (uncontrollable, stable, and external) and luck (uncontrollable, unstable, and external). Each of these attributions is accompanied by cognitive and affective interpretations. For example, the affective reaction to the attribution of effort is increased pride (following success) or increased shame (following failure); the cognitive reaction is an expectation of possible change in the future depending on the amount of effort expended. Affective reactions to ability, another internal attribution, are the same but the cognitive reaction (because ability is a stable characteristic) is an expectation of similar performance in the future.

Some attributions, such as learned helplessness, are general to a variety of situations (''I can't do it'' or ''I'm just an inadequate person, I always make mistakes''). Other attributions may be more specific, whether for subject-matter areas, social interaction or athletics (''I'm just no good at math'' or ''I could never do well at any sport''). A wide variety of emotions are associated in varying degrees with causal attributions. Success attributed to ability, for example, is associated with the affect of competence and confidence, whereas for attributions of lack of ability following failure the affect is a feeling of incompetence.

The investigations on attributions have led to detailed analyses of the loci of motivations and the consequences in highly interactive situations such as classrooms. They hold considerable promise for understanding the complex role of cognitions in social learning situations and for the control of those cognitions to enhance performance (e.g., Diener & Dweck, 1978; Dweck, 1975). The theory provides a framework involving the temporal sequence of (a) information about the outcome of performance, (b) how the learner perceives those outcomes, (c) inferences concerning the locus of causality, (d) affectivity associated with cognitions about the outcomes, and (e) cognitive expectations about future performance. However, research is needed to examine the usefulness of changing metacognitions regarding the perceptions and interpretations of performance outcomes and of teaching strategies and self-management strategies that compensate for lack of abilities or other processing limitations (Corno & Mandinach, 1983).

''Learning takes place in interpersonal contexts with peers, the teacher, and the family as part of the social context of the learner'' (Weiner et al., 1983, p. 122). These contexts contribute to the world view of the learner and provide the bases for understanding the dynamic consequences of behavior.

Summary

The current cognitive movement has mustered an impressive array of research interests and capabilities from the fields of psychology, computer science, and education. Judging by the number and nature of journal publications it is apparent that the problems being addressed by all sides are more oriented toward and applicable to education than at any other time in the past century.

The movement's most distant antecedents clearly reside in the prescience heritage from the ancient orators and philosophers. The experimental study of cognition probably is to be dated around the turn of the present century. However, the attention given to the subject was typically sporadic and short-lived, giving ground to the rising popularity of behaviorism sparked by the works of Thorndike, Watson, and so on. The most direct historical roots of the current movement that endured were, in the main, offshoots of the contributions of the Field-Gestalt-Expectancy tradition, although their progress too was interrupted by emergence of the popular behaviorism of Skinner and Hull.

Major transitions to the cognitive orientation in education were to be found in the fifties and sixties in the works of Piaget, Ausubel, and Bruner. Bruner's (Bruner et al., 1956) initial research on concept-learning strategies was probably the formal forerunner of the recent research (e.g. O'Neil, 1978; Anderson, 1981) thrust on learning strategies and cognitive skills. Ausubel's (1966) subsumption theory, with its emphasis on meaningful learning, on cognitive structures, and on assimilation of new information into existing knowledge structures, has within it clear antecedents of the current research on schema theory. Inherent in Piaget's (Flavell, 1963) developmental epistemology were the elements of operational knowledge, schemes, and processing mechanisms including assimilation, accomodation, and equilibration.

Despite these substantial contributions the precipitating force firing the current burgeoning pace of involvement was the paradigm shift (Kuhn, 1962) accompanied by Chomsky's (1957a) criticism of behavioristic approaches to the study of language, and his book on syntactic structures (Chomsky, 1957b), in which the constructive processes of transformational grammar were emphasized.

The research summarized in this chapter reflects the influence of these several historical antecedents on changes that might be expected in education. Instruction can no longer be viewed as a one-way communication of an authority who transmits knowledge in a form that can be reiterated upon demand by all students. Nor can teaching be viewed as control by some expert who plans a curriculum that dictates precise outcomes for all students, who knows the precise organization of content that will be applicable to all contexts and outcomes, or who tests achievement by a teacher-made or standardized test without consideration of how that test is related to the student's engagement in the learning task. From the cognitive view, instruction is a two-way communication in which the student plays an important role in what is learned even when the teaching situation seems to be controlled completely by the teacher. The student, to a greater or lesser degree, constructs the encoded representations that are stored in memory on the bases of his or her knowledge structures, procedural skills, and expectations about their abilities and about what goals are to be achieved. Differences in achievement among learners are therefore inevitable and likely to be highly idiosyncratic. What they learn depends on their knowledge structures and how that knowledge is represented, on the amount of effort and time they are willing to devote to making the new knowledge meaningful and useable, and on the way the information is processed, that is, what strategies are used.

Although research on the character and influence of cognitive motivations on learning has not kept pace with research on the cognitive facets of information processing, it is apparent that this will be a new research thrust in the coming decade. It is quite apparent from existing research, some of which has been reviewed here, that motivations do have their effects through emotional and cognitive components. Anxieties have worry and emotionality components. They are often context dependent (e.g., test anxiety or state anxiety). Attributions for failure and success may be accompanied by shame or pride (emotionality) and by expectations for probable success or failure in the future (cognitions). Some needs may be physiologically based, but there are also efficacy motives (e.g., need for achievement, competency

motivations) that seem to be related to cognitive achievements.

The foregoing view of the learner as playing a central, constructive role in learning takes the teacher out of the role of authoritative controller of the learning-teaching situation and into the role of a manager-director who guides the student in understanding what needs to be learned, how to process information for representations that apply to different contexts and purposes, and how to use general and specific strategies and cognitive skills.

Other implications of the cognitive movement apply to test constructors who must be sensitive to the effects of the contexts employed in the testing situations, the effects of the kinds of tests used in determining student expectations that, in turn, determine what strategies for learning are used and what representations are constructed during the learning tasks, and how errors on tests may reflect more than sheer lack of specific facts (e.g., in identifying bugs in the use of rules). For instructional designers the cognitive movement has already produced implications for innumerable practical applications. Although the guidelines are not completely spelled out, some can be used cautiously, including the use of orienting instructions, the use of advance organizers, the use of signaling devices, and the importance of different forms of discourse organization. In different combinations they can be used to manage the kinds of processes pupils will use in learning and, as a consequence, to guide the kinds of outcomes desired. There is a growing armamentarium of programs for teaching cognitive skills and strategies. The effectiveness of what learners construct from a given teaching situation may depend as much on the awareness and use of these strategies (metacognitions) as on other parts of the curriculum.

It is apparent that the current cognitive movement, rather than seeking the general all-encompassing laws for controlling and predicting behavior, as did the earlier grand theories of learning, is directed toward miniature models of specific facets of cognition, such as models of discourse analysis, models of comprehension, ways of aiding understanding and meaningful learning, the nature of the schemata, the memory system, the development of cognitive skills, and the like. A decade ago in an earlier description (Di Vesta, 1974) of the potential of the cognitive movement for education, it appeared sufficient to develop themes about knowledge structures, attending, and processing. Since that time, the new insights that have been attained about thinking and understanding are impressive, indeed. Each new issue of a journal contains one or more articles that have a bearing, perhaps in only a small way, on better understanding the nature of learning and teaching. The literature relating cognitive psychology to education has become extremely complex. The nature of learning and teaching for understanding is influenced by a number of contexts and its generality or specificity across contexts is becoming better understood. The next 10 years are certain to bring even more exciting developments than did the past decade.

References

Anderson, J. R. (1980). *Cognitive psychology and its implications.* San Francisco: W. H. Freeman.

Anderson, J. R. (1983). A spreading activation theory of memory. *Journal of Verbal Learning and Verbal Behavior, 22,* 267–295.

Anderson, R. C. (1977). The notion of schemata and the educational enterprise. In R. C. Anderson, R. J. Spiro, & W. E. Montague (Eds.), *Schooling and the acquisition of knowledge* (pp. 415–431). Hillsdale, NJ: Erlbaum.

Anderson, R. C., & Ortony, A. (1975). On putting apples into bottles—A problem of polysemy. *Cognitive Psychology, 7,* 167–180.

Anderson, R. C., Reynolds, R. E., Schallert, D. L., & Goetz, E. T. (1977). Frameworks for comprehending discourse. *American Educational Research Journal, 14,* 367–382.

Anzai, Y., & Simon, H. A. (1979). The theory of learning by doing. *Psychological Review, 86,* 124–160.

Ausubel, D. P. (1968). *Educational psychology: A cognitive view.* New York: Holt, Rinehart & Winston.

Ausubel, D. P., Novak, J. D., & Hanesian, H. (1978). *Educational psychology: A cognitive view* (2nd ed.). New York: Holt, Rinehart and Winston.

Barnett, J. E., Di Vesta, F. J., & Rogozinski, J. T. (1981). What is learned in note taking? *Journal of Educational Psychology, 73,* 181–192.

Bartlett, F. C. (1932). *Remembering.* Cambridge: Cambridge University Press.

Berlyne, D. E. (1960). *Conflict, arousal, and curiosity.* New York: McGraw-Hill.

Binet, A. (1916). The development of intelligence in children (The Binet-Simon Scale). (Translated from articles in *L'Année Psychologique* from 1905, 1908, and 1911 by Elizabeth S. Kite.) Baltimore, MD: William & Wilkins.

Blumenthal, A. L. (1970). *Language and psychology, historical aspects of psycholinguistics.* New York: Wiley.

Bousfield, W. A. (1953). The occurrences of clustering in the recall of randomly arranged associates. *Journal of General Psychology, 49,* 229–240.

Bousfield, W. A., & Sedgewick, C. H. W. (1944). An experimental analysis of sequences of restricted verbal associative responses. *Journal of General Psychology, 30,* 149–165.

Bousfield, W. A., Esterson, J., & Whitmarsh, G. A. (1958). A study of developmental changes in conceptual and perceptual associative clustering. *The Journal of Genetic Psychology, 92,* 95–102.

Bower, G. H. (1970). Analysis of a mnemonic device. *American Psychologist, 58,* 496–510.

Bower, G. H. (1972). Mental imagery and associative learning. In L. Gregg (Ed.), *Cognition in learning and memory* (pp. 51–88). New York: Wiley.

Bower, G. H. (1973, October). How to . . . uh . . . remember! *Psychology Today,* pp. 63–70.

Bower, G. H. (1975). Cognitive psychology: An introduction. In W. K. Estes (Ed.), *Handbook of Learning and Cognitive Processes. Vol. 1. Introduction to Concepts and Issues* (pp. 25–80). NY: Erlbaum.

Bower, G. H. (1981). Mood and memory. *American Psychologist, 36,* 129–148.

Bower, G. H., Clark, M. C., Lesgold, A. M., & Winzenz, D. (1969). Hierarchical retrieval schemes in recall of categorized word lists. *Journal of Verbal Learning and Verbal Behavior, 8,* 323–343.

Bower, G. H., Black, J. B., & Turner, T. J. (1979). Scripts in memory for text. *Cognitive Psychology, 11,* 177–220.

Bradshaw, G. L., & Anderson, J. R. (1982). Elaborative encoding as an explanation of levels of processing. *Journal of Verbal Behavior and Verbal Learning, 21,* 165–174.

Bransford, J. D. (1979). *Human cognition: Learning, understanding, and remembering.* Belmont, CA: Wadsworth.

Bransford, J. D., & Johnson, M. K. (1973). Conceptual prerequisites for understanding: Some investigations of comprehension and recall. *Journal of Verbal Learning and Verbal Behavior, 11,* 717–726.

Bransford, J. D., Stein, B. S., Vye, N. J., Franks, J. J., Auble, P. M., Mezynski, K. J., & Perfetto, G. A. (1982). Differences in approaches to learning: An overview. *Journal of Experimental Psychology: General, 111*(4), 390–398.

Brooks, L. W., & Dansereau, D. F. (1983). Effects of structural schema training and text organization on expository prose processing. *Journal of Educational Psychology, 75,* 811–820.

Brown, A. L., & Day, J. D. (1983). Macrorules for summarizing texts: The development of expertise. *Journal of Verbal Learning and Verbal Behavior, 22,* 1–14.

Brown, A. L., Campione, J. C., & Day, J. D. (1981). Learning to learn: On training students to learn from texts. *Educational Research, 10,* 14–21.

Brown, A. L., Bransford, J. D., Ferrara, R. A., & Campione, J. C. (1983). Learning, remembering, and understanding. In P. H. Mussen (Ed.), *Handbook of Child Psychology.* (Formerly, *Carmichael's manual of child psychology.*) (Vol. 3, pp. 77–166). New York: Wiley.

Brown, J. S., & Burton, R. (1978). Diagnostic models for procedural bugs in basic mathematics skills. *Cognitive Science, 2,* 155–192.

Brownell, W. A., & Moser, H. E. (1949). *Meaningful versus mechanical learning: A study in grade III subtraction. Duke University Research Studies in Education.* No. 8. Durham, NC: Duke University Press.

Bruner, J. S., Goodnow, J. J., & Austin, S. A. (1956). *A study of thinking.* New York: Wiley.

Bryan, W. L., & Harter, N. (1899). Studies of the acquisition of a hierarchy of habits. *Psychological Review, 6,* 325–345.

Chase, W. G., & Ericsson, K. A. (1981). Skilled memory. In J. R. Anderson (Ed.), *Cognitive skills and their acquisition.* Hillsdale, NJ: Erlbaum.

Chase, W. G., & Simon, H. A. (1973). Perception in chess. *Cognitive Psychology, 4,* 55–81.

Chi, M. T. H., Feltovich, J., & Glaser, R. (1981). Categorization and representation of physics problems by experts and novices. *Cognitive Science, 5,* 121–152.

Chi, M. T. H., & Koeske, R. D. (1983). Network representations of knowledge base: Exploring a child's knowledge and memory performance of dinosaurs. *Developmental Psychology, 19,* 29–39.

Chi, M. T. H., & Rees, E. T. (1983). A learning framework for development. In M. T. H. Chi (Ed.) *Trends in memory development research.* In J. A. Meacham (Series Ed.), *Contributions to human development, 9,* 71–107. (New York: Karger-Basel.)

Chi, M. T. H., Glaser, R., & Rees, E. (1981). *Expertise in problem-solving.* (Tech. Rep. No. 5). Pittsburgh, PA: University of Pittsburgh, Learning Research and Development Center.

Chomsky, N. (1957a). Review of B. F. Skinner's *Verbal Behavior. Language, 35,* 26–58.

Chomsky, N. (1957b). *Syntactic structures.* The Hague: Mouton.

Cicero (1959). *De Oratore, I, II* (E. W. Sutton, Trans.). Cambridge, MA: Harvard University Press.

Collins, A. (1977). Processes in acquiring knowledge. In R. C. Anderson, R. Spiro, & W. E. Montague (Eds.), *Schooling and the acquisition of knowledge* (pp. 339–364). Hillsdale, NJ: Erlbaum.

Collins, A. M., & Loftus, E. F. (1975). A spreading activation theory of semantic processing. *Journal of Verbal Learning and Verbal Behavior, 8,* 240–247.

Corno, L., & Mandinach, E. B. (1983). The role of cognitive engagement in classroom learning and motivation. *Educational Psychologist, 18*(2), 88–108.

Craik, F. I. M., & Lockhart, R. S. (1972). Levels of processing: A framework for memory research. *Journal of Verbal Learning and Verbal Behavior, 11,* 671–684.

Dansereau, D. (1978). The development of a learning strategies curriculum. In H. F. O'Neil, Jr. (Ed.), *Learning strategies* (pp. 1–29). New York: Academic Press.

de Bono, E. (1985). The CoRT thinking program. In J. W. Segal, S. F. Chipman, & R. Glaser (Eds.), *Thinking and learning skills. Vol. 1. Relating instruction to research* (pp. 363–388). Hillsdale, NJ: Erlbaum.

Deese, J. (1969). Behavior and fact. *American Psychologist, 24,* 515–523.

Diener, C., & Dweck, C. S. (1978). An analysis of learned helplessness: Continuous feedback in performance, strategy, and achievement cognitions following failure. *Journal of Personality and Social Psychology, 36,* 451–462.

Di Vesta, F. J. (1958). The effects of sets induced by labeling on the modification of attitudes. *Journal of Personality, 26,* 379–387.

Di Vesta, F. J. (1974). Cognitive structures and symbolic processes. *Teachers College Record, 75,* 357–370.

Di Vesta, F. J., & Peverly, S. T. (1984). The effects of encoding variability, processing activity and rule-examples sequence on the transfer of conceptual rules. *Journal of Educational Psychology, 76*(1), 108–119.

Driver, R. P. (1973). *The representation of conceptual frameworks in young adolescent physics students.* Unpublished doctoral dissertation, University of Illinois at Urbana-Champaign.

Dweck, C. W. (1975). The role of expectations and attributions in the alleviation of learned helplessness. *Journal of Personality and Social Psychology, 31,* 674–685.

Festinger, L. (1964). *Conflict, decision, and dissonance.* Stanford, CA: Stanford University Press.

Fillmore, C. J. (1968). The case for case. In E. Bach & R. T. Harms (Eds.), *Universals of linguistic theory* (pp. 1–89). New York: Holt, Rinehart, & Winston.

Flavell, J. H. (1963). *The developmental psychology of Jean Piaget.* Princeton, NJ: Van Nostrand.

Flavell, J. H. (1979). Metacognition and cognitive monitoring. *American Psychologist, 34,* 906–911.

Franks, J. J., Vye, N. J., Auble, P. M., Mezynski, K. J., Perfetto, G. A., Bransford, J. D., Stein, B. S., & Little, J. (1982). Learning from explicit versus implicit texts. *Journal of Experimental Psychology: General, 111,* 414–422.

Geddis, A. N. (1982). Teaching: A study in evidence. *The Journal of Mind and Behavior, 3*(4), 363–373.

Glaser, R. (1984). Education and thinking: The role of knowledge. *American Psychologist, 39,* 93–104.

Goffman, E. (1974). *Frame analysis.* Cambridge, MA: Harvard University Press.

Gordon, C., & Pearson, P. D. (1983). *The effects of instruction in metacomprehension and inferencing on children's comprehension abilities* (Tech. Report No. 269). Urbana, IL: University of Illinois, Center for the Study of Reading.

Groen, G., & Resnick, L. B. (1977). Can preschool children invent algorithms? *Journal of Educational Psychology, 69*(6), 645–652.

Harlow, H. F. (1949). The formation of learning sets. *Psychological Review, 56,* 51–65.

Harris, P. L., Kruithof, A., Terwogt, M. M., & Visser, P. (1981). Children's awareness of textual anomaly. *Journal of Experimental Child Psychology, 31,* 212–230.

Hayes, D. A., & Tierney, R. J. (1982). Developing reader's knowledge through analogy. *Reading Research Quarterly, 17,* 256–280.

Hoffman, R. R., & Nead, J. M. (1983). General contextualism, ecological science, and cognitive research. *The Journal of Mind and Behavior, 4,* 507–560.

Huey, E. B. (1968). *The psychology and pedagogy of reading.* Cambridge, MA: M.I.T. Press. (Original work published 1908)

Jenkins, J. J. (1974). Remember that old theory of memory?! Well, forget it! *American Psychologist, 29,* 785–795.

Jenkins, J. J. (1979). Four points to remember: A tetrahedral model. In L. S. Cermak & F. I. M. Craik (Eds.), *Levels of processing in human memory* (pp. 429–446). Hillsdale, NJ: Erlbaum.

Jenkins, J. J. (1980). Can we have a fruitful cognitive psychology? In H. E. Howe, (Ed.), *Nebraska Symposium of Motivation,* Lincoln, NE: University of Nebraska Press.

Jenkins, J. J., & Russell, W. A. (1952). Associative clustering during recall. *Journal of Abnormal and Social Psychology, 52,* 818–821.

Kant, I. (1781). *Kritik der reinen Vernunft [Critique of pure reason].* Leipzig: P. Reclam.

Katona, G. (1942). *Organizing and memorizing.* New York: Columbia University Press.

Kintsch, W. (1982). Memory for text. In A. Flammer & W. Kintsch (Eds.), *Text processing.* Amsterdam: North-Holland.

Kintsch, W., Mandel, T. S., & Kozminsky, E. (1977). Summarizing scrambled stories. *Memory & Cognition, 5,* 547–552.

Kuhn, T. S. (1962). *The structure of scientific revolutions.* Chicago, IL: University of Chicago Press.

Kulhavy, R. W., & Swenson, I. (1975). Imagery instruction and the comprehension of text. *British Journal of Educational Psychology, 45,* 47–51.

Langley, P., & Simon, H. A. (1981). The central role of learning in cognition. In J. R. Anderson (Ed.), *Cognitive skills and their acquisition* (pp. 361–380). Hillsdale, NJ: Erlbaum.

Lenneberg, E. H. (1967). *Biological foundations of language.* New York: Wiley.

Lepper, M. R., & Greene, D. (1975). Turning play into work: Effects of adult surveillance, and extrinsic rewards on children's intrinsic motivation. *Journal of Personality and Social Psychology, 31,* 479–486.

Levin, J. R., Pressley, M., McCormick, C. B., Miller, G. E., & Shriberg, L. K. (1979). Assessing the classroom potential of the keyword method. *Journal of Educational Psychology, 71,* 583–594.

Loman, N. L., & Mayer, R. E. (1983). Signaling techniques that increase the understandability of expository prose. *Journal of Educational Psychology, 75*(3), 402–412.

Mayer, R. E. (1979a). Can advance organizers influence meaningful learning? *Review of Educational Research, 40,* 371–383.

Mayer, R. E. (1979b). Twenty years of research on advance organizers: Assimilation theory is still the best predictor of results. *Instructional Science, 8,* 133–167.

Mayer, R. E. (1980). Elaboration techniques that increase the meaningfulness of technical text: An experimental test of the learning strategy hypothesis. *Journal of Educational Psychology, 72,* 770–784.

Mayer, R. E. (1983). Can you repeat that? Qualitative effects of repetition and advance organizers on learning from science prose. *Journal of Educational Psychology, 75*(1), 40–49.

Mayer, R. E. (1984). Aids to text comprehension. *Educational Psychologist, 19*(1), 30–42.

McClelland, D. C. (1965). Toward a theory of motive acquisition. *American Psychologist, 20,* 321–333.

McKeachie, W. J. (1976). Psychology in America's bicentennial year. *American Psychologist, 31*(12), 819–833.

Meyer, B. J. F. (1975). *The organization of prose and its effects on memory.* New York: American Elsevier. Amsterdam: North-Holland.

Miller, G. A., Galanter, E., & Pribram, K. H. (1960). *Plans and the structure of behavior.* New York: Holt, Rinehart & Winston.

Minsky, M. (1975). A framework for representing knowledge. In P. H. Winston (Ed.), *The psychology of computer vision.* New York: McGraw-Hill.

Miyake, N., & Norman, D. A. (1979). To ask a question, one must know enough to know what is not known. *Journal of Verbal Learning and Verbal Behavior, 18,* 357–384.

Morris, C. D., Bransford, J. D., & Franks, J. J. (1977). Levels of processing versus transfer appropriate processing. *Journal of Verbal Learning and Verbal Behavior, 16,* 519–533.

Naveh-Benjamin, M., & Jonides, J. (1984). Cognitive load and maintenance rehearsal. *Journal of Verbal Learning and Verbal Behavior, 23,* 494–507.

Neisser, V. (1976). *Cognition and reality.* San Francisco: W. H. Freeman.

Neves, D. M., & Anderson, J. R. (1981). Knowledge compilation: Mechanisms for the automatization of cognitive skills. In J. R. Anderson, (Ed.), *Cognitive skills and their acquisition* (pp. 57–84). Hillsdale, NJ: Erlbaum.

Nitsch, K. E. (1978). Structuring decontextualized forms of knowledge (Doctoral dissertation, Vanderbilt University, 1977). *Dissertation Abstracts International, 38,* 3479B–3968B.

Norman, D. A. (1978). Notes toward a psychology of human learning. In A. M. Lesgold, J. W. Pelligrino, S. D. Fokkema, & R. Glaser (Eds.), *Cognitive psychology and instruction* (pp. 39–48). New York: Plenum Press.

Norman, D. E. (1981). Twelve issues for cognitive science. In D. E. Norman (Ed.), *Perspectives in cognitive science.* Hillsdale, NJ: Erlbaum.

Norman, D. A. (1982). *Learning and memory.* San Francisco: W. H. Freeman.

Norman, D. A., & Rumelhart, D. W. (1975). *Explorations in cognition.* San Francisco: Freeman.

Paris, S. C., Lipson, M. Y., Cross, D. R., Jacobs, J. E., De Britto, A. M., & Oka, E. R. (1982, April). *Metacognition and reading comprehension.* Research colloquium presented at the annual meeting of the International Reading Association, Chicago, IL.

Pearson, P. D., & Gallagher, M. C. (1983). *The instruction of reading comprehension* (Tech. Report No. 297). Urbana, IL: Center for the Study of Reading. Reading Education Reports.

Pepper, S. C. (1942). *World hypotheses: A study in evidence.* Berkeley, CA: University of California Press.

Perfetti, C. A., & Roth, S. (1981). Some of the interactive processes in reading and their role in reading. In A. Lesgold & C. Perfetti (Eds.), *Interactive processes in reading.* Hillsdale, NJ: Erlbaum.

Posner, J., Boies, W., Eichelman, W., & Taylor, R. (1969). Retention of visual and name codes of single letters. *Journal of Experimental Psychology Monographs, 79*(1, Pt. 2).

Quintilian. (1922). *The Institutio Oratoria, Vol. 4.* (With an English translation by H. E. Butler, M. A.). Cambridge, MA: Harvard University Press.

Reitman, J. S., & Rueter, H. H. (1980). Organization revealed by recall orders and confirmed by pauses. *Cognitive Psychology, 12,* 554–581.

Riccio, D. C., Richardson, R., & Ebner, D. L. (1984). Memory retrieval deficits based upon altered contextual cues: A paradox. *Psychological Review, 96,* 152–165.

Richards, D. D., & Siegler, R. S. (1981). Very young children's acquisition of systematic problem-solving strategies. *Child Development, 52,* 1318–1321.

Ruger, H. A. (1910). The psychology of efficiency. *Archives of Psychology, 19,* 15.

Rumelhart, D. E., & Ortony, A. (1977). Representation of knowledge. In R. C. Anderson, R. J. Spiro, & W. E. Montague (Eds.), *Schooling and the acquisition of knowledge.* Hillsdale, NJ: Erlbaum.

Rumelhart, D. E., & Norman, D. A. (1981). Analogical processes in reasoning. In J. R. Anderson (Ed.), *Cognitive skills and their acquisition* (pp. 335–359). Hillsdale, NJ: Erlbaum.

Scardamalia, M., Bereiter, C., & Boelean, H. (1982). The role of productive factors in writing ability. In M. Nystrand (Ed.), *What writers know: The language, process, and structure of written discourse* (67–95). New York: Wiley.

Schachter, S., & Singer, J. (1962). Cognitive, social and physiological determinants of emotional state. *Psychological Review, 69,* 379–399.

Schank, R. C., & Abelson, R. P. (1977). *Scripts, plans, goals, and understanding.* Hillsdale, NJ: Erlbaum.

Siegler, R. S. (1983). How knowledge influences learning. *American Scientist, 71,* 631–638.

Singer, H., & Donlan, D. (1982). Active comprehension: Problem-solving schema with question generation for comprehension of complex short-stories. *Reading Research Quarterly, 17*, 166–186.

Skinner, B. F. (1984). The shame of American education. *American Psychologist, 39*, 947–954.

Slobin, D. I. (Ed.). (1971). *The ontogenesis of grammar.* New York: Holt, Rinehart, & Winston.

Suchman, J. R. (1966). A model for the analysis of inquiry. In H. J. Klausmeier, & C. W. Harris (Eds.), *Analyses of concept learning* (pp. 177–187). New York: Academic Press.

Thorndyke, P. (1977). Cognitive structures in comprehension and memory of narrative discourse. *Cognitive Psychology, 9*, 77–110.

Tulving, E. (1962). Subjective organization in free-recall of "unrelated" words. *Psychological Review, 69*, 344–354.

Tulving, E. (1979). Relation between encoding specificity and levels of processing. In L. S. Cermak & F. I. M. Craik (Eds.), *Levels of processing in human memory* (pp. 405–428). Hillsdale, NJ: Erlbaum.

Tulving, E., & Thomson, D. M. (1973). Encoding specificity and retrieval processes in episodic memory. *Psychological Review, 80*, 352–373.

van Dijk, T. A., & Kintsch, W. (1983). *Strategies of discourse comprehension.* New York: Academic Press.

Vygotsky, L. S. (1978). *Mind and society: The development of higher psychological processes* (M. Cole, V. John-Steiner, S. Scribner, & E. Bouberman, Eds. & Trans.). Cambridge, MA: Harvard University Press.

Weiner, B. (1979). A theory of motivation for some classroom experiences. *Journal of Educational Psychology, 71*, 3–25.

Weiner, B., Graham, S., Taylor, S. E., & Meyer, W. (1983). Social cognition in the classroom. *Educational Psychologist, 18*(2), 109–124.

Weinstein, C. E. (1978). Elaboration skills as a learning strategy. In H. F. O'Neil, Jr. (Ed.), *Learning strategies* (pp. 31–56). New York: Academic Press.

Wertheimer, M. (1959). *Productive thinking.* New York: Harper & Row.

Wickelgren, W. A. (1974). *How to solve problems.* San Francisco: W. H. Freeman.

Wittrock, M. C. (1974). Learning as a generative process. *Educational Psychologist, 1*, 87–95.

Wittrock, M. C. (1978). The cognitive movement in instruction. *Educational Psychologist, 13*, 15–29.

Wood, G. (1967). Mnemonic systems in recall. *Journal of Educational Psychology, 58*(6), 1–27.

PART III

Current Issues and Future Directions

Describing all of the areas of interest to contemporary educational psychology may be an impossibility because of its diverse nature. In this section, we have organized a set of representative state-of-the-art chapters that deal with important areas of research in educational psychology. The coverage is not all-inclusive, nor is it meant to be. Instead, what we have done is include topics that seem to be of particular interest to a majority of educational psychologists in the late 1980s.

CHAPTER 12

Program Evaluation

AGENDAS FOR DISCUSSION OF ISSUES AND FOR FUTURE RESEARCH

Robert D. Brown

Students of all ages and levels make evaluation judgments everyday about their teachers and courses. These judgments are informal and are probably based most often on likes and degrees of satisfaction. Parents, educators, and legislators often want more formal evaluations and will want information on how much students learned and how cost-efficient was the curricula or program innovation. Whether the judgments are being made by students or legislators, the evaluations can be complex and there will be divergent views of what kind of evaluation information is needed and how it should be used.

This chapter enumerates and examines perennial issues in evaluation. They range from defining what is evaluation to questions of whether or not evaluation is a profession. After a discussion of these issues, the same questions are reexamined from a research perspective. What research is needed to provide further insights into these issues? The chapter provides readers with two parallel agendas, one for discussing perennial and current issues and one for determining a research program for the future.

Historical Perspective

Evaluation can be traced to the beginning of time. The Book of Genesis states that God created heaven and earth and on the sixth day looked upon what he created and called it "good." This has been cited as the first evaluation act (Patton, 1981), and would make evaluation one of the oldest concepts of humankind, an idea in existence as long as life itself. By now the concept should have been fully dissected and analyzed without the remotest possibility of any subtle nuances being unexplored. Has this in fact happened?

The consensus is that evaluation, as it is practiced today, evolved from the testing movement prior to and after World War I and the continued growth of testing and subsequent curriculum innovations after World War II (Merwin, 1969). Evaluation in this century has been intimately associated with developments in educational psychology and measurements and educational innovations in America. New questions about how students learn, how to measure what they learn, and how to provide better learning experiences led directly to new conceptualizations about program evaluation.

Merwin (1969) suggested that though the testing movement focused primarily on individual students or groups of students rather than programs,

Robert D. Brown • Department of Educational Psychology, University of Nebraska, Lincoln, NE 68588-0641.

testing programs led to changes in educational programs as well. Haggerty (1918) described a survey of school officials that indicated schools made changes, not only in classification of students, as a result of testing programs, but also in school organization and methods of instruction. As objective tests increased in usage, so did their use in assessing teaching effectiveness (Reavis, 1938). The relationship between testing in the schools and program evaluation continues into this decade, as results of standardized testing programs lead to national, state, and local attention being focused on the worth and effectiveness of school instructional programs.

Changes in the school curriculum motivated by new societal needs and pressures or by new learning theories also played an integral role in the development of evaluation. Smith and Tyler (1942) described how decisions to add new courses in effective study skills and critical thinking prompted the development of new tests and a rethinking about the purposes of evaluation. In discussing the role of evaluation, Smith and Tyler (1942) recognized multiple purposes for evaluation, including providing feedback to different audiences and serving a public relations function. They also noted the complexity of evaluation that sought to measure content that was often vague and that reflected value judgments about what the schools should be teaching.

Ralph Tyler is considered to be the founder of evaluation in the modern era. His influence was instrumental in prompting educators to think more broadly than using standardized tests as a sole evaluation tool. His focus on operationalizing objectives and assessing outcomes provided a foundation for educational theorists and practitioners for many years (Tyler, 1950).

Until the mid-1960s, and still sometimes today, however, evaluation and specific measurement concepts were seen as identical. The behavioral braggadocio that "What cannot be measured, does not exist," restricted the range of outcomes open to investigation by program evaluators. This prompted Scates (1947) to lament that the literature in education did not recognize the subjective origin of evaluation and thus evaluation had become a slave to "objectivity." Scates' (1947) distinction, that measurement examines the *amount* of something whereas evaluation considers the *appropriateness* of that something, echoed through the next two decades and continues to merit discussion.

In the 1960s, major influences on evaluation were perhaps more political than educational in origin and their effects are still being felt. Government funded educational programs during the Great Society and the War on Poverty period from the mid-1960s and through the 1970s provided the need, rationale, and funds for evaluations. The government required evidence of program implementation and effects. Evaluation now had a broader audience than school superintendents and school boards: elected public officials at the national level debated the relative merits of educational programs and demanded evaluation information. Evaluators began to examine their role in providing information for decisions, assessing the political and social climate in which evaluations were conducted, and to question the effectiveness of evaluation methodologies (Scriven, 1967; Stake, 1967; Stufflebeam, 1971).

Evaluation flourished through the 1970s and professional organizations (Evaluation Network, Evaluation Research Society) devoted exclusively to evaluation were founded. Graduate programs began to offer courses and specialties in program evaluation and a few educational psychologists began to identify themselves as "program evaluators."

Today, though federal and state budget cuts limit the expansion of evaluation activities, evaluation continues to move steadily toward professionalism. The two major professional organizations have held joint national meetings for several years and have recently merged. Several professional journals (*Evaluation in Planning and Policy Analysis, Evaluation Review, Studies Educational Evaluation*) and an annual publication of evaluation studies (*Evaluation Studies Annual*) are nearing a decade of publication.

Parallel to the increased funding of national and state programs in community mental health and other health services has been increased interest by psychologists, sociologists, political scientists, and other professionals in program evaluation. This has resulted in books and journals devoted to evaluation in specific areas, such as the health services. An informal content analysis of these publications suggests that as each new discipline or professional area becomes concerned about evaluation, the same evaluation issues arise in nearly the same order.

From this brief historical profile, it is apparent that program evaluation owes a significant share of its origin and growth to educational psychology and measurement. The initial focus of learning theories and measurement on how individual students

239

and then groups of students learn provided instruments and data for use in evaluating the effectiveness of educational programs. Assessing and providing for individual differences among learners provided the rationale for society and its politicians to initiate programs to meet the unique educational needs of students and society's needs for other services. At times, the narrow focus of educational measurement and its obsession with objectivity restricted the range of outcomes and effects evaluators needed to and, indeed, now do explore. Today, evaluation's span is broader than education and educational measurement, but a significant percentage of its clientele, its professional heritage, and its academic core remains in education, educational psychology, and educational measurement.

This chapter presents and discusses current issues and research needs that reflect the priorities and judgments of the author. Although others may be concerned about different issues or priorities, the agenda of this chapter should provide both the novice and the knowledgeable with ideas about how evaluation might progress in the next decade.

An Issue Agenda

The issues in evaluation are perennial questions that have confronted evaluation as long as it has existed and promise to be raised again with new nuances as each new generation of evaluators confront new evaluation contexts. As one storyteller suggests, even God's evaluation of creation was questioned by Lucifer who inquired about the criteria used for God's judgment and whether or not God was the appropriate person to pass judgment because of God's personal involvement with the project (Patton, 1981). These questions are equally important today. Five major issues and their implications are discussed in the following pages: (a) What is evaluation and what is its purpose? (b) How should evaluations be conducted? (c) Who are the clients and audiences for evaluation information? (d) How should evaluation information be used? and (e) Is evaluation a profession?

What Is Evaluation and What Is Its Purpose?

Although efforts have been made to develop a consensus or synthesis of the definition and purpose of evaluation (House, 1980), there is no definitive categorization acceptable to all evaluators.

Unlike academic disciplines such as biology, which most will accept as the study of the origin, history, and characteristics of plants and animals, and unlike other professions such as the practice of medicine, which most will accept as treating and preventing disease, a precise and singular statement on the purpose of evaluation remains elusive. Perhaps a closer scrutiny of biology and medicine, however, would find microbiologists describing themselves quite differently from other biologists and practitioners of holistic medicine portraying the nature and practice of medicine differently from their colleagues.

To illustrate the variety of definitions available, six definitions or purpose statements are described. Each could be further refined but collectively they include most of the major efforts to define evaluation and describe its purpose.

1. *Evaluation is assessment of whether or not a program has met its objectives* (Tyler, 1950). The primary tasks of the evaluator, according to this definition, are determining a program's objectives, phrasing the objectives in behavioral and therefore measurable form, assessing program outcomes and comparing the hoped-for objectives with the measured outcomes. Few would question that this approach to evaluation had a significant impact on program planning and program evaluation for many years. Teachers preparing daily lesson plans and fund seekers for federal grants have become practiced experts at writing behavioral objectives.

Evaluators adhering to this purpose of evaluation will press hard for what some writers characterize as ''pre-ordained'' objectives (Guba, 1979). Assessment strategies focus on objective measurement of behavioral outcomes. The process encourages program developers to think ahead and to be specific about program objectives. Critics maintain that this process molds evaluation into a lock-step sequence and potential positive and negative side effects of a program are less likely to be assessed and taken into account in the evaluation process (Guba, 1979).

2. *Evaluation involves providing information for decision making* (Alkin, 1969: Stufflebeam, 1971). This approach recognizes that the context of most, if not all, evaluation involves a decision about a program. Program planners and funders hope to use evaluation information to make decisions about whether or not to modify, continue, or discontinue the program being evaluated. The efforts of the evaluator following this approach focus on determining who are the decision makers and the decisions they must make. The evaluator

must determine what information is wanted and needed by the decision maker and ensure that the data collected will pertain to the decisions that must be made.

There are few strong critics of this perspective on evaluation, but many have commented on the complexities of aiding decision makers. Determining who are the real decision makers in a particular evaluation context is not always easy. The decision making process itself remains somewhat of a mystery despite efforts to reduce it to mathematical logic (Thompson, 1982) or a sociopsychological formula (Janis & Mann, 1977). Adherents to this approach often assume that decision making is entirely a rational and systematic process, which can be disillusioning for the evaluator when it is not.

3. *Evaluation is the assessment of merit or worth* (Scriven, 1967). This definition comes closest to the root meaning of evaluation—the assessment of value. In contrast to the credo of the measurement heritage of many early evaluators, which demands objectivity and a value-free perspective, this definition recognizes that value judgments are an inherent part of evaluation. Full recognition of evaluation as determining the worth of a program is likely to compel the evaluator to take a broader perspective than evaluators who focus exclusively on determining whether outcomes match objectives or whether data match decision makers' information needs. Ultimate worth, for the evaluator, is not necessarily accomplishing the funder's or program director's objectives. Instead, worth is based on social utility (Worthen & Sanders, 1973). This implies that the goals of a program, as well as the outcomes, are appropriate fodder for the evaluator's cannon. The most effective program in meeting program objectives or the most rational decision about how to improve a program may be irrelevant if the program's objectives are not worthwhile (valued). At the same time, a program can have worth, even though it is not accomplishing its stated objectives because its side effects are positive and have social utility.

By a dictionary definition the *evaluator* is the determiner of value or worth, however, in practice, the professional evaluator is more often the collector of information than the decision maker. This raises questions as to who is to determine worth and what is the relationship of the evaluator to this person or persons. This issue has not been resolved. If the evaluator is solely a provider of information, then a more accurate job title would be "evaluation technician."

4. *Evaluation is description.* This approach suggests that an evaluator can help evaluation audiences arrive at useful insights through descriptions of programs or portrayals of what goes on in programs (Guba & Lincoln, 1981; Stake, 1975). Providing decision makers with real or vicarious experiences through narrative reports, films, or portrayals of program outcomes gives them a sense of the program and a perspective on its accomplishments. Evaluators adhering to this definition or purpose will rarely be in a position to have all or key evaluation clients participate in the program themselves (e.g., a fifth-grade art workshop, a recreation program for the mentally retarded) so data collection and summaries remain important. Evaluators need to be as concerned about sampling procedures and representativeness as much as the experimental researcher, but perhaps the nature of the data and most certainly the presentation format will differ from those of the experimental researcher.

Descriptive evaluations may be most helpful for a human service program or when the program's process and what happens to program participants are vital information. When the focus of client concerns is on outcomes, when the client already knows what happens during the program, or when a straightforward, simple answer is needed, a descriptive evaluation may be inappropriate.

5. *Evaluation focuses on examination of programs for the purpose of improving them* (Cronbach *et al.*, 1980). This approach has both practical and philosophical roots. Its philosophical ties are closer to those emphasizing the importance of description in evaluation than to those suggesting that evaluation involves determination of worth. Generalizability is seen as elusive. The approach also recognizes that few programs are discontinued because of evaluation data that are focused on outcomes; often decisions about program continuance and termination are based on political and/or cost determinations. Those suggesting that evaluation should focus on program improvement believe that political and cost considerations should be left to other experts or consultants. The evaluator should focus on determining ways to improve the program.

Critics of this focus (Nilsson & Hogben, 1983) believe that focusing on improvement denies the value of rational thinking and judgment in life, the sciences, and for evaluation. Some programs are "bad," and some evaluations are "bad." It is evaluations' province, according to these critics, to provide information for making these judgments.

6. *Evaluation is persuasion.* House's (1977) argument that evaluation is persuasion is perhaps less a distinctive definition than a philosophical orientation. Nevertheless, acceptance of this orientation could have a significant effect on how the evaluator approaches an evaluation task. House suggests that most scientific reports, no matter how objectively presented, are in fact attempts to persuade the reader to accept or reject a theory or a research outcome. Even use of statistical models for decision making assumes a trust in probability theory. The persuasive use of evaluation has also been considered by others (Leviton & Hughes, 1981; Patton, 1978; Weiss, 1977b), usually from the perspective of attempting to get the client to attend to the implications of evaluation findings.

Viewing evaluation as persuasion or attempting to persuade clients to use evaluation information are not traditional postures for many educational researchers. Research methodology attempts to avoid exaggeration and polemical arguments in favor of objective and largely neutral presentations. The data are expected to speak for themselves.

Evaluators who see persuasion as an important dimension of evaluation may be concerned about credibility and utility more than other evaluators, however no empirical evidence supports this view. In any case, such evaluators would probably have a broader conceptualization of their role than adherents of an experimental approach. Viewing evaluation as persuasion is not a comfortable philosophical or methodological stance for all evaluators.

Implications and Commentary

During the 1960s and 1970s an evaluation theorist could not be in fashion without proposing a new model or approach to evaluation. Proliferation of definitions and approaches emulated the population explosion. Evaluators vied for attention and sometimes seemed to compete for the composer of the most radical definition.

Not a definition *per se,* but worthy of special comment is the continuing discussion of what evaluation is *not.* A significant portion of the evaluation community distinguishes evaluation from research, as research is traditionally defined (e.g., usually the experimental model) (Patton, 1978; Worthen & Sanders, 1973). The purpose of research is usually characterized as discovering truth

or developing theory, whereas for many, evaluation is seen to have more utilitarian purposes. What makes this distinction more fuzzy is that despite different purposes evaluation and research may employ similar methodologies.

Nevertheless, the proposed definitions serve a useful purpose by expanding the concept of evaluation by extending its boundaries. Several of the definitions and models are aligned by nature, philosophy, or orientation with distinctive methodologies. So, acceptance, rejection, or emphasis on one or more of the meanings and purposes of evaluation conceivably could affect a practicing evaluator in ways such as (a) how objectives are treated, (b) who is consulted in an evaluation or considered to be the client, (c) how worth is defined and determined, and, perhaps most importantly, (d) the evaluator's role and function. Is the evaluator a technician who collects data and reports it, a consultant who interacts closely throughout the evaluation process with clients, or a judge who assesses the worth or merit of a program? Or, is the evaluator all (or none) of these?

Although debates on definitions flourish at professional meetings, the practice of evaluation has gone on. Evaluation practitioners are perhaps more eclectic and also more conservative than evaluation theorists. Clients would be expected to be even more pragmatic. Two questions remain: (a) Have the broadened definitions of evaluation had an impact on how practitioners conduct evaluations? and (b) What are client reactions to the different concepts of evaluations? Have their expectations changed?

At this time, no synthesis of definitions or purposes has been broadly accepted. Major efforts to distinguish evaluation from traditional research have had some impact but each new class of researchers/evaluators continues to learn the differences. Furthermore, not every new entrant accepts the distinctions as worthy or valid. Currently, it seems that the multiple definitions and purposes are being accepted, that evaluation is and will remain a pluralistic field. Theorists may stick close to brand name definitions of evaluations whereas practitioners remain more eclectic and satisfied with a generic product.

How Should Evaluations Be Conducted?

Models or approaches to evaluation have mushroomed in the past 20 years. Each new theorist seems compelled to propose a new model, methodology, or approach. As the value of evaluation is recognized by other academic disciplines, old evaluation models are rediscovered or refurbished with new and catchy acronyms. Today, education, psychology, sociology, business, political science, social work, medical education, and other academic subjects all have their own evaluation theories, often derived from each other and then propounded as unique models or approaches.

Six methodological approaches to evaluation are described and discussed briefly in the next few pages: experimental, quasi-experimental, naturalistic inquiry and case studies, issue and decision-oriented evaluations, goal-free evaluation, and metaphorical models. This discussion is not intended to be comprehensive but instead illustrative of methodological issues. Its complexity may explain the confusion of neophyte evaluators and their clients.

Experimental   The work of Campbell and Stanley (1963) and Campbell (1969) literally served as "the bible" for educational and psychological researchers for nearly 20 years. The necessity for a true experimental design, employing random selection and assignment and a control group continues to serve as the epitome for many researchers conducting evaluations. Program effectiveness can be determined by assigning persons randomly to the program group or to a no-program alternate group and comparing them on objective outcome measures. Alternate designs may help control for pretesting effects or help abate fears of sampling error. These designs assume that manipulation of program participants is in control of the evaluator. They often are most applicable to highly controlled pilot studies. As a result, such designs often have stronger internal than external validity.

Quasi-Experimental.   Many evaluation settings do not permit random selection of participants nor random assignment of participants to a program or no program group. Experimenters in education and evaluators in general must often assess impact on participants who self-selected a program or were assigned to a program based on specific criteria. Designs that enhance the credibility of conclusions have also been codified and proposed as useful for evaluations (Campbell & Stanley, 1963; Cook & Campbell, 1976). These designs are usually stronger in external validity than internal validity.

Unfortunately, naive researchers and clients often ignore the prefix *quasi* and give greater credence to the validity of the studies because of inclusion of the word *experimental*. The paradox is that for some designs and in some circumstances, the quasi-experimental approach may not only be more practical but also more generalizable than "true experimental" designs.

Naturalistic Inquiry and Case Studies.   The experimental and quasi-experimental approaches to evaluation appear to emulate the methodologies of the physical sciences and focus on objective, measurable outcomes. In contrast, the naturalistic and case-study approaches to evaluation model their techniques after anthropological and similar social science models (Welch, 1981). Manipulation is viewed as obtrusive and to be avoided and instead the focus is often on the subjective perceptions of participants. Descriptions of what happens are of primary importance and generalization is of less importance. Sometimes the value of generalization or its possibility is denied. The goal of the evaluator is to provide a description of what happens during a program and how participants feel and behave in the process and as a result of the program (Patton, 1980).

This methodology can be time-consuming and costly. Its results are of little use to a client who wants a quick answer to questions about products and outcomes. Case studies can, however, provide data that are descriptively rich and highly communicative.

Issue and Decision-Oriented Evaluation.   The motivation to conduct an evaluation is often derived from need to make decisions. A program has to be cut because of budget limitations. Which one should it be? A program has been piloted, should it be fully implemented or not? Someone must make a decision about dropping, maintaining, or expanding a program (Stufflebeam, 1971). In this evaluation context, (as in most others) there are two sides to the question, that is, there is an issue involved (Rippey, 1973). There will be protagonists and antagonists. Sometimes the underlying issue is not even related to the apparent decision that must be made. Whether a middle-management person keeps the same title or same office space as result of a program innovation may be as much an issue influencing program decisions as whether or not the evaluation indicates the program is helping participants or not. It is important for the evaluator to determine the decisions and issues involved and focus the methodology and data collection on the issues, sometimes to the exclusion of outcome data (Stake, 1975).

This approach requires the evaluator to have extraordinary consultative skills. The evaluator needs to be a conflict resolver and to understand how people make decisions. Not all evaluators have these talents and not all clients want to entrust conflicts in their organization to a third party, the evaluator.

Goal-Free Evaluation. Educators have been strongly influenced by behavioral scientists in stressing the value of clearly specifying behavioral objectives before a program is implemented. Evaluators have been equally influenced. Time and technique limitations often force the evaluator to narrow the scope of an evaluation and concentrate on assessing and comparing stated objectives to measured objectives. This process may result in bias and a failure to observe and record unintended side effects, good or bad (Scriven, 1972). Goal-free evaluation (Scriven, 1973) calls for the evaluator to enter the evaluation completely unaware of a program's goals and to attempt to assess all possible outcomes. Ideally, measures of all possible outcomes would be available to compare to participant needs and stated objectives. The program would be judged on the merits of its outcomes, not solely the match of stated objectives to measured outcomes.

The novelty of this approach may attract or repel the evaluation client. Because it usually requires a goal-based evaluation as well, it can be costly. The goal-free approach may help remove one source of bias. The question is whether or not and under what circumstances the approach is justified?

Metaphorical Models Poets use metaphors to help us understand much about the human condition. Evaluators have attempted to directly apply the implications of metaphors to evaluation strategies and techniques (Smith, 1981; Smith, 1982). The use of a judicial approach ranging from hearings to trials has been scrutinized and used (Wolf, 1979) as has the approach of investigative reporting (Guba, 1981). Art (Gephart, 1981) and art criticism (Eisner, 1981) have also been suggested as helpful metaphors for evaluation. In addition, photography has been used as a metaphor for conceptualizing evaluation and has also been employed to gather and report evaluation data (Brown, Petersen, & Sanstead, 1980).

The closer metaphors come to helping develop an understanding of the natural human process of evaluating, the greater their promise for utility to the evaluation practitioner and client. If applied literally to program evaluation, the metaphoric evaluator risks being seen as ludicrous. Not all metaphors, however, have to be put to use to have value. They can help by simply affecting how people think when designing or receiving an evaluation.

Implications and Commentary

Efforts to synthesize the models/approaches continue. Among the efforts to put them into a framework have been those that characterized the approaches as: (a) descriptive, decision oriented, or judgmentally based (Worthen & Sanders, 1973), (b) preordinate or emergent in design and objectives (Guba, 1979), (3) question or value oriented (Stufflebeam & Webster, 1980), (4) utilitarian or liberal (House, 1980), and quantitative or qualitative (Lynch, 1983). Examination of these efforts suggests that any comprehensive classification schema will have to be at least three-dimensional. No categorization or synthesis has been broadly accepted.

Although there is some question of whether or not these approaches to evaluation are true models (Borich, 1983; Stake, 1981), there is little doubt that strict adherence to one or the other approaches will have a significant impact on how an evaluator perceives his or her role and perhaps on how the evaluation is conducted. True and precise models might provide the evaluator more structure and a more consistent relationship between philosophy, approach, style, and techniques than do the multitude of approaches. Nevertheless, evaluators professing support for one approach contrasted to another might be expected to differ in ways, some of which will be described below.

1. *Goal Development and Assessment.* The goal-based evaluator interacts differently with administrators and staff than does a goal-free evaluator. The goal-based evaluator probably works more closely with administrators and staff in developing operational definitions of goals and determining how program components relate to expected outcomes. The goal-free evaluator, on the other hand, has minimal contact with the administrators and staff, especially about goals.

2. *Use of Control Groups.* Evaluators applying an experimental design approach would prefer to have complete control in selecting the sample and determining who participates in the program and who does not. Randomization would be the hoped-for participant selection process. This approach would probably also affect the size of the sample recommended by the evaluator. An evaluator using

a naturalistic inquiry approach, in contrast, might not only prefer but actually seek out an intact group participating in the program to be evaluated.

3. *Type of Information Collected and Assessment Techniques.* Whether the focus is on outcomes (Scriven, 1967), values (Guba & Lincoln, 1982), or cost-benefit information (Thompson, 1980), will affect not only what information the evaluator collects but also how it is collected and interpreted.

4. *Roles and Functions of the Evaluator.* If the evaluator's role is to provide information for a decision that will determine whether the program is continued or dropped, evaluator interactions with the staff will be different than if the role is to provide information designed to help improve the program. This distinction will probably not only affect how the evaluator behaves but how he or she is perceived by the administrator and staff. If the evaluator sees evaluation as a sociopsychological process, greater attention will probably be given to staff perceptions and to values and motivations of funders and key stakeholders than for an evaluator who sees decision making primarily as a rational process. The sociopolitical approach to evaluation will attend more to organizational structures, noting how the organization processes information and how it makes decisions (Litto, 1983).

5. *Needed Skills for the Evaluator.* An important distinction among the approaches is the type of consultation skills needed by the evaluator. An evaluator who focuses on measured outcomes will need to have a strong background in measurement, research design, and statistics. On the other hand, an evaluator who focuses on the values of participants or in determining the effect of decisions on participants will need to be highly effective in working with groups of people from diverse backgrounds. In some instances, the evaluator may need good conflict resolution skills (Rippey, 1973).

The most effective evaluator adapts evaluation approaches to the needs and parameters of the particular evaluation setting. It is unlikely that any one approach is appropriate for all settings, even if it were safe to assume that the evaluator had full control of the purpose and techniques of the evaluation.

There is no doubt that the diversity of approaches available to evaluators has had an impact on the development of the field as a profession. The more radical approaches serve to put neophyte evaluators into culture shock, which can be the stimulus for thinking anew about basic issues. At the same time, however, the diversity has been divisive. Developers of standards for the profession (Joint Committee, 1981) sometimes have had to placate warring factions by providing double standards, for example, criteria for accuracy for naturalistic studies versus experimental (quantitative) evaluations. These can be confusing to consumers.

There are implications as well for training programs. Program evaluators today are likely to walk out the door of most any building on a college campus: the psychology building, the political science building, the college of education building, or even the anthropology building. Career ladders to being a professional evaluator are likely to hang out the window of any academic department on campus.

Who Are the Clients and Audiences for Evaluation?

The evaluation client is usually the person or group who commissioned the evaluation. The evaluation audience typically includes the client and perhaps others who may influence or be affected by the decision. When the evaluation focuses on the client's needs, the communication process between the evaluator and the client can be reasonably straightforward. Reports for other audiences can be adapted from the major report to the client.

If, however, the interests of those participating in the program being evaluated and those ultimately affected by decisions made about the program are considered, the identification of the real client or significant audiences becomes more complex. The political and psychosociological nature of evaluation as well as ethical considerations readily raise issues about who is entitled to what information about a program evaluation.

One approach to determining potential audiences has been to identify those who are considered stakeholders in the program or the evaluation (Guba & Lincoln, 1981). In an educational context, the stakeholders may include parents, teachers, students, taxpayers, administrators, and school board members. In some instances this might be everyone in town! The extent of individual or group investment and interest will vary with how much impact the program and/or a decision about the program will have on them. Parents might be strongly interested in how a new sex education program will be taught to their children and what affect it will have on children's behavior. Teachers may be concerned about how much work will be involved in preparing the new program, students might be concerned about whether the classes will be co-ed and whether there will be academic credit or not. Taxpayers may be concerned that this program will necessitate hiring additional staff and thus become a budget item, and administrators and school board members will probably be concerned about what parents, teachers and the taxpayers think. Who, then, is the client and who are the audiences for evaluation information about this new sex education program? To whom is the evaluator obligated for a full report of relevant evaluation information?

A determination of the appropriate audience and client has implications for how evaluation is conducted. If the evaluator waits until the evaluation is completed to consider who should get copies of the report, chances are the evaluation report will be less relevant and less well received than if the relevant audiences were involved in the initial phases of the evaluation. The evaluator needs to determine the questions of interest to the stakeholders to determine what the major evaluation issues and questions will be. These questions will have an effect on the sources of data, the number of evaluation reports, and how the reports are presented or written. A federally funded project may require a quite different formal report to the funding agency than is needed for the local school board. The evaluation questions and data needed could be the same although this might not necessarily be true.

Implications and Commentary

Ethical and legal determinations about who owns the evaluation data and has access to it have not been completely resolved but they certainly can become questions causing consternation to evaluators. What are the obligations of the evaluator when a school superintendent, for example, releases only a part of an evaluation report to the public? Does the evaluator have the right or obligation to protest this act or to release other information?

As with other issues examined thus far, the question of who is the appropriate audience is affected by other issues and in turn affects the response to the others. In politically controversial evaluations, a judicial approach or a descriptive approach may serve to make the information accessible to relevant stakeholders. A goal-free evaluation might be most appropriate when concern focuses on bias, a case-study approach when participant perceptions are important.

A courageous and perhaps a financially independent evaluator is required to attend conscientiously to the needs and interests of all potential stakeholders, especially when their views may differ from the client paying for the evaluation. Standards and ethical guidelines may be insufficient to motivate the evaluator to take extraordinary action. More thinking and research is needed to help the evaluator determine when and how to communicate with diverse audiences.

How Should Evaluation Information Be Used?

Questions about how evaluation information should be used have been asked since the first evaluation. It is quite likely that Lucifer did not agree when God passed judgment on his creation and called it, "Good," and neither the world nor evaluation has been the same since (Patton, 1981). More recently, evaluators have been concerned about whether evaluation information ever helps administrators or government officers make decisions (Guba, 1969; Weiss, 1977a).

The experienced and sophisticated evaluator may be angry and chagrined when one of his or her evaluation reports gathers dust on a shelf, but hardly surprised. The relatively few studies of the use of evaluation information often conclude that direct use of evaluation information as the final determining point about whether to maintain, expand, or drop a program seldom occurs (Davis & Salasin, 1975).

Several questions related to the use of evaluation reports are being discussed among evaluators. Major questions for the next decade include: (a) What is use? How is it defined? (b) How does use relate to decision making? and (c) What is the evaluator's role in ensuring use?

Definitions of Use. The most customary definition of use implies direct and immediate influence on decisions made about a program. It assumes a rational and straightforward relationship between data and recommendations and between recommendations and program decisions. Such a definition permits relating decisions to expand, reduce, or terminate a program directly to an evaluation report's recommendations. Or, it should be possible to find actions taken and decisions made as a result of evaluator recommendations. When this definition of evaluation is used to study utilization, however, it is not easy to find evaluations that have been used (Davis & Salasin, 1975).

At first, the lack of use of evaluations to influence decision making was discouraging to evaluators. Experiential knowledge and the early investigations of use seemed to agree that evaluation reports and evaluator recommendations were not being used. This eventually led to a reexamination of what use is. Two things have happened as a result of this reexamination. First, evaluation use is no longer viewed as simplistically as it was earlier and second, use is now more broadly defined.

Evaluation can aid decision making in ways other than providing prescriptive recommendations for decision makers and information useful for decision makers can include material other than test or outcome data or statistical findings. Descriptive portrayals that provide audiences with deeper insights into the characteristics of a program's clientele, the issues a program staff faces, and the nature of program activities may in some cases be many times more useful to decision makers than are statistical analyses. Thus, if an evaluation takes on characteristics different from a traditional research study with hypotheses, operational definitions, precise measurements, and decisions based on the significance level of statistical testing, then use will also take on different characteristics. As evaluators found that the scientific paradigm, particularly an experimental model, was not always appropriate for conducting successful evaluations, they moved to more global and often naturalistic methodologies, which in turn provided different information intended for different uses.

Leviton and Hughes (1981) provided a helpful framework for thinking about use when they identified three kinds of use: *instrumental use,* in which direct relationships are apparent between the evaluation and decision making; *conceptual use,* in which information influences a person's thinking about an issue; and *persuasive use,* in which attempts to convince others are made with evaluation evidence. These three are now viewed as legitimate and sometimes sufficient uses for evaluation.

Decision Making and Evaluation. Evaluators often behave as if decision making is entirely a rational process and that rational decisions will be based on evaluative data. From this perspective, all the evaluator has to do to ensure use of evaluation information is to collect relevant information and pass it on. As noted earlier, this has not been successful. Realistically, evaluation is a political and social activity (Braskamp & Brown, 1980; Weiss, 1972). It occurs in an arena filled with power struggles and conflicting social relationships. Decisions are sometimes made about programs because someone has more power than someone else or because of friendships or other personal relationships. This means that evaluation findings are sometimes used selectively to support predetermined decisions and sometimes ignored entirely.

Besides political and social implications, there are also individual and group psychological perspectives that influence information processing during decision making. Janis and Mann (1977) presented a model for examining how fear of personal loss (job or status) and belief in a right solution interact to affect when and how a person uses information to make decisions. The application of this model in research or decision making in evaluation contexts (Brown, Newman, & Rivers, 1984) suggests that decision making in evaluation settings is complex. Amount of personal risk, available time, and characteristics of the evaluation setting interact to affect how decision makers process evaluation information (Newman, Brown, Rivers, & Glock, 1983).

Responsibility for Use. Is it the evaluator's responsibility to see that evaluation information is used or is it the client's? No one argues that the evaluator has *no* responsibility for the use of the evaluation information, so at first glance there is no issue, only a matter of degree. If, however, evaluation processes and evaluation reports are studied in detail and clients interviewed regarding the evaluation's worth, the conclusion might be drawn that some evaluators behave as if they have no responsibility for use. Evaluations are sometimes carried out with little consultation with program administrators or staff; reports are late, and in some cases communicated in a specialized language understandable for only by the evaluator's colleagues but not necessarily by the clients.

Professors teaching research and evaluation courses need to make consultation and communication skills important components of their courses and degree programs. Successful evaluators ask the right questions, use the appropriate methodology, and report results in an understandable manner to interested audiences. Unfortunately, many graduate programs provide little training in asking the right questions or reporting results in a meaningful fashion. Knowing how to express null hypotheses or how to summarize results for a journal article are not sufficient communication skills for an evaluator.

Once an evaluator accepts the responsibility for conducting an appropriate evaluation and reports it in an understandable manner, what is the evaluator's responsibility for seeing that the evaluation information is used? This is an issue that is not resolvable by easy prescription. Most evaluators would agree that the report should be understandable, a few less might agree that the evaluator must see that it is read carefully, a smaller number might agree that it is the evaluator's responsibility to have the report considered when a decision is made, and there would probably be a small core who would agree that the decision made should be influenced directly by the evaluation report.

Implications and Commentary

How evaluation use is defined and considerations of who is responsible (and to what degree) to ensure appropriate use of evaluation information affect the evaluator's role and activities. As Patton (1978) suggests, considerations about use need to begin at the same time the evaluation begins and not wait until the data are collected and analyzed. Optimal use occurs when the right evaluation questions are asked and the relevant data collected. These are decisions that should be made when an evaluation begins.

The issues illuminated by pursuit of how decisions are made and how evaluation data are processed and used by decision makers include considerations of the activity and roles of the evaluator. If political power, social relationships, and cost data, for example, are critical influences on an educational program, should the evaluator be responsible for collecting data related to these dimensions? Should the evaluator be restricted or restrict her or himself to educational outcome data when it is clear that other facets will be equally and sometimes more important? If so, what training background and skills does the typical evaluator have to justify or support exploration of these broader criteria for decision making?

If use of evaluation information is more complex than a straightforward relationship between outcome data and the decision, what responsibility does the evaluator have for understanding this process and operating accordingly? Should the evaluator or some member of an evaluation team be sufficiently skilled in consulting with decision makers to be able to work closely with them in how best to process the information? If evaluators assume a major role in assuring evaluation information use they need training and experience in related consultative skills including assessment of decision making by individuals and organizations and communication skills. It is time for training programs to consider these issues and their curricular implications.

Should Evaluation Become a Profession?

The accoutrements of an occupation that becomes a profession usually include standards, ethical codes for practice, accreditation guidelines for training programs, and certification of licensing of professionals. There has been movement in program evaluation in recent years in the development of standards and there has been discussion of certification (Evaluation Research Society, 1981; Joint Committee, 1981; Rossi, 1982). Some see certification or licensing as essential for the protection of the public, others believe the diversity of evaluation settings and potential formats mitigates against accreditation of programs or licensing of evaluators. These discussions raise, however, related and important issues: (a) how should evaluations be evaluated? (b) how should evaluators be trained? and (c) should evaluators be licensed?

Evaluating Evaluations. The concept of meta-evaluation, evaluation of evaluations (Stufflebeam, 1974), necessitates clarification of what constitutes a good evaluation and who determines what is good. Does a good evaluation adequately measure all of the program's objectives and compare the program's accomplishments with its objectives? Or, does a good evaluation meet the needs of the clients? Are these criteria mutually exclusive and if not, how are the criteria weighted? Describing a good evaluation could vary depending on the evaluator's orientation as well as the client's needs. Among the standards are accuracy and utility. These, though, will also have different meanings for evaluators using different models or approaches. Studies employing experimental research designs will have different expectations for control of extraneous variables, for example, than will those using naturalistic observation as a primary methodology. One set of standards has different criteria for accuracy for quantitative and qualitative evaluations (Joint Committee, 1981). This may be helpful, but who decides and what criteria are used to decide that an evaluation should include more or less quantitative or qualitative data?

The usefulness of an evaluation also can be variously defined as noted earlier in this chapter. Who decides whether the criteria for usefulness should be a direct relationship between data and a decision (instrumental use) or making the client more aware of the options available (conceptual use)? On the surface, the utility of evaluation information seems to be a logical criterion on which to judge the quality of an evaluation. But little in evaluation is that straightforward (Sheinfeld & Lord, 1981).

The validity of evaluation designs has not yet been subjected to the intense analysis or paradigm construction that experimental designs have seen (Lindval & Nitleo, 1981). The evaluation counterpart to the Campbell and Stanley (1963) classic of research designs does not exist.

Should evaluation move toward professionalism, much more discussion on procedures and policies related to peer reviews and even consumer reviews will be necessary. As a minimum, evaluators should be obligated to make clients aware of their orientation and style through the sharing of past evaluation products and clientele references. At least clients will be forewarned, if not fully knowledgeable, of what to expect.

Training Evaluators. Initially, in the emergence of evaluation as a professional and perhaps specialized activity, evaluators came out of the research molds of educational psychology. They were trained as experimental researchers with knowledge of measurement principles and statistical skills. This training paradigm remains important for a significant proportion of evaluators. However, as evaluation has become increasingly recognized as a political activity occurring in a social context, research skills alone have proven inadequate. Also, as different paradigms (e.g., naturalistic inquiry) gained prominence so has the need for evaluators to be knowledgeable and skilled in a variety of approaches to data collection. Efforts to outline the requisite training needs and competencies are broadening. For the most part, however, they still focus extensively on the core skills found among traditional experimental researchers but with the ability to apply the principles to a field setting (Sechrest, 1980).

If evaluators work closely with clients and systems and evaluation decisions are recognized as taking place and being influenced by a large array of political, social, and psychological dimensions, then evaluators need knowledge and skills in other areas than the traditional research paradigm. They will need an understanding of decision theory, cost-effectiveness, cost-benefit analysis, organizational theory, political theory, and perhaps even personality theory. Essential as well will be the ability to integrate these bodies of knowledge and apply them directly as a consultant to a specific evaluation context.

Where is the evaluator to obtain this knowledge and gain these experiences? Should it be course work in a variety of disciplines such as economics, political science, psychology, or anthropology? Should it be from specialty seminars within educational psychology? What level of traditional statistical and measurement competencies are needed?— Should the evaluator know enough to *do* or to *seek* consultation in sophisticated statistical methods? Similar concerns could be raised regarding continuing education needs.

Implications and Commentary

Development of standards, consideration of accreditation for training programs and certification of evaluators requires careful consideration of the purpose behind these efforts. The ultimate goal is protection of the public through measures that ensure the best possible evaluation. Professional groups risk taking on the characteristics of protective guilds for their members. Restricting membership to only those who are like them and excluding others can be motivated by the need to keep membership low so that demand for services remains constant. Consumer rights and interests are particularly important in evaluation. The purpose, as well as the content of standards, ethical statements, and other guidelines needs to be continually scrutinized to ensure that they serve the best interests of the public (Stufflebeam, 1980).

Evaluation, as it matures, needs to avoid the gulf that has sometimes arisen between the academician and the practitioner (e.g., psychology, education). Just how this can be avoided remains an agenda item for the future.

Summary

The issues enumerated are not new and are unlikely to be resolved in the next decade. Questions about purpose, methods, and usage prevail throughout the infancy and the mature years of a discipline. Such issues were discussed nearly two decades ago by Merwin (1969) and remain current issues for the field (Nevo, 1983). Even the answers may not change through the decades, though it seems that the pluralistic nature of evaluation as to its purpose, methods, and potential use has expanded or at least been fleshed out during the past 15 years. It is important, nevertheless, that the questions continue to be asked because each new generation of evaluators needs to confront and respond to them in the context of the world at that moment. New technologies, new discoveries, and current social and political realities may suggest variations on the appropriate responses.

A Research Agenda

Questions such as, What is evaluation?, How should it be conducted?, and How should it be used?, arise continually even in more mature professions, such as medicine and law. But because they are perennial issues does not mean they can be shrugged off as irresolvable or relegated to sideshows at professional meetings. Systematic research can illuminate the issues, enhance the understanding of their nuances, and perhaps provide guidance in specific circumstances. If research does not provide answers, at least evaluators will have a better understanding of what they are getting into, even though they might not know much more about how to get out of it. This section examines and illustrates research questions relevant to the issues enumerated in the previous section. It proposes a research agenda for evaluation for the next decade that focuses on (a) the purpose of evaluation, (b) methods of evaluation, (c) determining clients and audiences, (d) enhancing the usefulness of evaluations, and (e) professional issues. As in the discussion of evaluation issues, this agenda is intended to be illustrative and provocative rather than comprehensive.

Purpose of Evaluation

Most of the possible purposes of evaluation have been delineated, though there will probably always be efforts to redefine evaluation and describe its purposes. The distinctions between traditional research and its purposes and evaluation and its purposes needs to be continually made. It might be useful if authors resisted juxtaposing the words *evaluation* and *research* in the expression *evaluation research*. This implies that evaluation activities are one kind of research rather than a dis-

tinct activity. Even though there can be extensive overlap in methodology, some may question whether evaluation is one kind of research or if research is one kind of evaluation. Undoubtedly, there are and will continue to be different opinions regarding the nature and purpose of evaluation and debate and discussion will continue, though it may be of more interest to academicians than to practicing evaluators.

Research needs in this area include determining the implications of acceptance or rejection of different definitions and purposes of evaluation, assessing how people who commission and use evaluation define the purpose of evaluation, and examining the nature of evaluation activity as a cognitive process.

There are times, given specific social and political contexts, when an evaluation is requested solely for the purpose of determining whether or not program objectives were met. There are also times when descriptions of program events and processes are most appropriate for helping clients make decisions. The purpose of the evaluation should be related to the needs of the client and the context of the evaluation at least as much as by the philosophy of the evaluator. Evaluators should adapt their approaches and methodologies to the evaluative question, not adapt the question to their methodology. Research is needed to determine when the purposes of evaluation should vary and what the implications of different evaluation definitions are.

Descriptive research is needed to determine how persons who commission evaluations, conduct evaluations, and use evaluations, operationally define them and their purpose. What images come to mind for the evaluation practitioner and the client when the word *evaluation* or *evaluator* is considered? For the lay public, the word *scientist* may be associated with adjectives such as *crazy* or *impractical*. For others, the image may be brilliant or a life-saver. What images and adjectives come to mind related to ''evaluator?'' Is evaluation viewed as helpful or harmful; positive or negative? Answers to these questions will provide the field of evaluation with a perspective on what consumers think of evaluation and what educational activities might be necessary to provide the public with an appropriate and useful definition of the field.

It would be helpful to have descriptive and naturalistic studies of the antecedents and correlates of clients', and consumers', perceptions of evaluation. Simulation studies suggest that occupational roles (Braskamp, Brown, & Newman, 1980), perceived need for evaluation (Brown, Newman, & Rivers, 1980), and personality characteristics such as locus of control (Newman, Brown, & Braskamp, 1983) are related to an evaluation audience's reaction to and use of evaluation information. A more thorough examination of how background characteristics of clients and audiences interact with the evaluation context to affect attitudes and behaviors is a necessary step to understanding how people define and react to evaluations.

Methods and Process of Evaluation

The many different approaches to models of evaluation have largely been derived from personal whim or insights from past successes and failures. Empirical research on what approach works best for a particular evaluation client is sparse, if not nonexistent. Research is needed to determine what methods are now in use, what occurs during the evaluation process, what are the potentialities of team approaches, what effectiveness is and how effectiveness can be measured.

Current Methods. Models proposed or described in textbooks, journal articles, and at professional meetings often are portrayed in pristine terms. The evaluation models available to the practitioner vary in the degree to which they provide explicit step-by-step instructions, so it is possible that applications of the same approach to the same evaluation problem by two different evaluators will result in two different and perhaps unrecognizable evaluations. A straightforward, but important research question is what methods *are* being used by evaluators.

It is quite possible that experienced evaluators who possess profound differences in orientation may interact with clients and prepare highly similar reports. This possibility, however, has not been examined. Descriptive research is needed to portray what evaluators of differing views do when they conduct an evaluation.

Evaluation Process. Closely aligned to research questions about practicing evaluators' theoretical orientations and professional practices is the need to examine the evaluation process. How do evaluators communicate and interact with clients when determining evaluation questions, methodologies, and reports? Descriptive research would be helpful for providing baseline information on how often evaluators meet with administrators, what staff levels they involve in determining data needs, and what kinds of informal as well as formal contacts they actually seek with clients and staff (Roecks, 1983). These are examples of questions about which there is much prescriptive guidance in "how to" evaluation manuals but about which there is little empirical data. There are theories, there are prescriptions, and there are anecdotes, but there are few data.

Evaluator Skills and Team Approaches. The effective evaluator is often portrayed as a highly effective consultant, a professional who can communicate with clients effectively so that their information needs and decision styles are integrated in considerations of the evaluation process (Braskamp & Brown, 1980). This requires a person who has strong interpersonal skills as well as measurement and analytical skills. Evaluators also need to understand how organizations process information and make decisions (Torres & Braskamp, 1982). Decision making in organizations is influenced by factors broader than those influencing individuals. Particularly important are the dynamics of what part of the organization makes decisions about specific programs and what staff are affected by the decisions (Braskamp, 1982). Team approaches to conducting evaluations are not new, but there is little empirical evidence of what constitutes the characteristics of successful evaluators, much less what should be the professional backgrounds appropriate for evaluation teams.

Although some research has been done on the characteristics of successful evaluations (Boruch & Cordray, 1980), more is needed on the characteristics of the successful evaluator. What are the characteristics of successful evaluators who are staff members within an organization? What are successful external evaluators like? How do they compare in characteristics and styles? Like the earlier suggestion about possible commanlities among evaluations conducted using supposedly different theoretical orientations, it is possible that successful evaluators may have skills and characteristics in common that transcend training and theoretical differences.

Definitions of and Measurement of Effectiveness. Effectiveness of educational programs can be defined in many different ways. Is an effective program one in which people learn? Is satisfaction important? Is long-term learning more critical than short-term? What about program elements, such as staff satisfaction and efficiency? Oversimplified definitions of effectiveness will no longer suffice (Mohr, 1982) nor will over-simplified measures of effectiveness (Baugher, 1981), if evaluation is to increase its worth to decision makers.

With the ubiquitous computer, more refined and complex statistical procedures and analyses (e.g., path analysis, meta-analysis, & multi-dimensional scaling) for assessing effectiveness and displaying data (e.g., charts and graphs) are becoming readily available and accessible to program evaluators. Progress in these techniques, however, will probably continue to be a generation away from the evaluator in the field and perhaps two generations away from the understanding of clients and evaluation audiences. It is difficult to estimate, however, whether in this context a generation represents 20 years or 20 months.

Of at least parallel importance is effort to determine how best to communicate the results of sophisticated methodologies and statistics to the unsophisticated client. There is evidence that suggests that references to probability levels as compared to percentages and different presentation styles is enough to evoke different reactions in evaluation audiences (Brown & Newman, 1982; Thompson, Brown, & Fergason, 1981). What happens when these same audiences are exposed to much more complex methodologies? If evaluators are not careful, it is possible they could have rich and complex analyses readily available but lose the clients and audiences who find that such analyses result in only more inconclusive results. It is also possible that more separation will occur between the professional evaluator and the client in the language and information used to communicate findings. Or, will technology (e.g., charts and graphs) make communication easier?

Determining Clients and Audiences

Three basic research needs stand out regarding clients and audiences. The first is how to determine who are the important clients and audiences and the second is designing strategies for getting clients and audiences involved in the evaluation process. Third, the field needs to take a long-term view of educating future clients and audiences.

How does an evaluator best determine who are the real clients and the real audiences for an evaluation? Even though it is a simple question with perhaps a straightforward and accurate answer, few evaluators probably ask anyone directly, "Who is it that will ultimately decide the fate of this program I am being asked to evaluate?" The bromide, "Determine who the decision makers are," is probably more often than not going to be interpreted by the evaluator to be the person who commissions or pays for the evaluation. This means the evaluator is often working through an intermediary rather than directly with the decision makers. Evaluators need to recognize the importance of knowing the needs and intents of the ultimate decision maker(s) if their evaluation efforts are to have the fullest utility.

Descriptive and experimental research could provide useful information in understanding how successful evaluators operate and what consultative techniques are helpful in determining the needs of their clients. Studies by Alkin and his colleagues have come closest to determining the path that evaluation questions and information take as they are processed by an organization (Alkin, Daillak, & White, 1979).

Knowing who asks for what information, when, where, and how within an organization is vital background information for an evaluator trying to fathom who the decision makers are and what their evaluation questions are. Research on what environmental mapping procedure would be appropriate—knowing the organizational chart, tracing past information use, finding out who makes decisions or has a voice in decisions—in different organizational contexts could be useful to evaluators.

Determining stakeholders who are not decision makers but who would be affected by program decisions is not any easier. Besides the obvious impact on the client, program staff, and participants, the evaluator may be hard pressed (and not sufficiently motivated) to look at different or broader impacts. It would be fruitful to determine ways an evaluator might react to unanticipated program impact or to the identification of unexpected stakeholders as well as ways to predict who the potential stakeholders might be. Politicians often leak potential policy changes or actions to determine what the voter reaction might be. Is there a way evaluators might leak potential evaluation findings or program decisions to determine who will be affected and respond?

Enhancing the Usefulness of Evaluations

Most of the suggestions for future research and possible directions for the profession focus on educating the public about the purposes, methods, and potential usefulness of evaluation. This educational process, if successful, should result in more useful and used evaluations. If those who commission evaluations are more knowledgeable from the beginning of a project about what evaluation is and what it can and cannot do, the resulting evaluations should come closer to meeting consumer expectations and perhaps their needs as well (Brown *et al.*, 1980). Having an educated and critical consumer would go far toward ensuring the good use of evaluations.

Nevertheless, research specifically aimed at studying utilization merits continued attention and time. Knowledge is not the sole rationale for many decisions that are made in life so it should not be surprising to find the same is true for evaluation. Knowledge alone about what evaluation is and what it can do to assist decision makers is not a guarantee that this knowledge will be used to influence the decision. Therefore, a parallel research program, which examines how and why people process evaluation information the way they do, can grow out of other educational programs to increase people's understanding of evaluation and in turn can feed the insights derived from research into the educational program.

There are several research topics that have been studied during the past decade that need continued efforts and several topics that need initial examination. These include: (a) theoretical frameworks for examination of use, (b) descriptive research on how and in what situation evaluation information is used, (c) descriptive research on the styles, methods, and characteristics of effective evaluators, and (d) experimental studies to test the validity of utilization theories and their descriptive and practical utility.

Theoretical Frameworks. The contributions of theories derived from a variety of disciplines hold promise for understanding the use of evaluation information theory. Attribution theory (McGuire, 1969) has provided the framework for several studies of the relationship between evaluator characteristics and how audiences use evaluations (Braskamp, Brown, & Newman, 1982). Evaluator characteristics such as gender, job title, field of study, and educational level have thus far been shown to affect how evaluation audiences process evaluation information (Braskamp *et al.*, 1982).

Communication theory (Newman *et al.*, 1980) suggests that characteristics of the evaluation audience and characteristics of the evaluation message play a role in how evaluation information is used. Whether the evaluation audiences are made up of administrators or staff, their areas of expertise and personality characteristics are related to how they respond to evaluation information and evaluation situations. How an evaluation report is written and presented also determines how information in the report is processed and accepted (Braskamp *et al.*, 1980; Brown, Braskamp, & Newman, 1978). The communication paradigm holds further promise for explorations of how evaluation information is processed. The message mode (written or oral) has been unexplored as an important variable as has the formality (formal or informal) of the message. Several evaluation theorists (e.g., Alkin, 1980; Patton, 1978) suggest that much of an evaluation's impact is made through informal communication processes rather than formal written reports. This process needs continued study through naturalistic inquiry approaches as well as controlled experimentation.

Though evaluation has been defined for some time as an aid to decision making (Stufflebeam, 1971), there has been little research in the evaluation field on how decision-making theory helps an understanding of how evaluations are used. O'Reilly (1981) examined the research on decision making in organizations and concluded that organizations are goal-directed and evaluation information is viewed as only one component that influences the decision about a program. Decision making is described as an interactive process where politics and power hold as much weight as information. Evaluators need to recognize that some information will be viewed as helpful to some within an organization but also be viewed by others as threatening.

The conflict model (Janis & Mann, 1977) served as the conceptual model for examining decision making in an evaluation context (Brown, Newman, & Rivers, 1984) and for several empirical studies in educational settings (Newman, Brown, Rivers, & Glock, 1983; Pflum & Brown, 1984). As the model predicts, evaluation audiences respond differently to the same information when the evaluation context contains different professional or personal risk levels and when the content varies. These situational factors influence decisions, what information is desired, and who the decision makers want to consult.

As with attribution and communication theories, decision-making theories provide excellent frameworks for exploring other concerns and issues in evaluation. Decision making by groups versus individuals is an important but relatively unexplored topic in evaluation utilization. How decision makers assign weight or differing values to different kinds of information would also merit exploration. How expert opinion versus informed opinion of colleagues is processed and weighted in the decision-making process is another important question.

Each of these theoretical issues is worth exploring independently as are other theoretical questions. However, a metatheory or at least a multitheoretical approach might organize such efforts. How can these theories be integrated to provide an overall framework for studying and understanding the use of evaluation information for decision making? The breadth of variables these models provide for research studies is almost unlimited, which is of immediate value for the researcher. The practitioner, however, may ultimately face a confusing and complex list of important variables (e.g., report style, characteristics of audience, decision-maker style), which may be difficult to sort out for the evaluation task at hand. An appropriate integration of the theories and their empirical support might provide the practitioner with heuristics helpful to the everyday practice of evaluation.

Descriptive Research on Use. One of the best methods for finding out how evaluations are used is to observe how evaluation information is processed in real life settings. How do administrators interact with evaluators? What information do they seek out? What kind of time (amount and quality) do decision makers spend on reading and processing formal reports? How much and what kind of evaluation information is processed in informal settings (over coffee, in informal teacher meetings, phone conversations with school board members)? Answers to these questions and others will provide valuable insights into how decision makers and evaluation audiences now process evaluation information and how the process might be improved. Participant observation, use of logs, and other forms of naturalistic inquiry (Alkin *et al.*, 1979) are tools particularly appropriate to these questions.

Experimental Research to Test Theories. Experimental research usually necessitates control of key variables and manipulation of at least one variable as well as precise measurement of outcomes. These conditions are extremely difficult to overlay on an evaluation project, much less to employ for studying evaluation use. One research strategy has been to use simulations to ex-

amine specific variables involved in information use in evaluations (Braskamp *et al.*, 1982). This methodology permits the experimenter to control systematically the nature of the evaluation information (content, length, style), the source of information (ascribe the information variously to evaluators of different background, training, gender), and other contextual variables such as the amount of time to make a decision (Pflum *et al.*, 1984). Through intensive study of evaluation audiences or decision makers, the researcher can examine the relationship of audience characteristics to how information is processed and used.

Experimental simulations provide helpful information in two ways. First, the closer the simulation is to real life the more likely the findings are to have direct relevance to actual evaluations. Simulations can come close to real life by employing real evaluation problems and by using real decision makers as subjects. Although there are no known studies where pressure and risk have been induced other than through role playing, participants do get involved in the role playing situations (Braskamp *et al.*, 1982). In good simulations it is doubtful that participants behave or respond radically differently from their behavior in real evaluations, albeit even modest differences may profoundly influence the results and implications.

At a minimum, however, simulation studies provide clues as to what might or could happen. If the amount of jargon in a simulated evaluation report has an impact on an experimental sample, this at least suggests that it is possible that a jargon-loaded evaluation report might affect a real evaluation audience. Knowing this and relating it to attribution theory and communication models may provide clues as to what to be wary of when conducting evaluations or studying evaluations in a natural setting.

There has been a modest debate regarding which methodology is most appropriate for studying utilization in evaluation (Alkin, 1980). Fortunately, it does not appear that these discussions have led to crystallization of viewpoints. Much is to be learned from a multifaceted approach to studying utilization. Naturalistic and experimental paradigms should complement each other. Controlled experimentation in simulations or experimental manipulation in the field can provide excellent opportunities to test out theoretical propositions derived from speculations from other fields or from field observations. Naturalistic inquiries can lead both to new theoretical formulations and to validation of existing theories. It may also provide insights into what specific contextual variables affect evaluation use.

The realm of questions open to researchers from the theoretical speculations based on attribution, decision making, or communication theory is almost boundless and could easily provide an academic career for many researchers for the next decade. It is important to recognize that the overall efforts continue to move back and forth along a continuum that extends from simulations to experimentation in real life environments. It is, perhaps, unimportant whether or not this movement is made by the same researchers, but it is important that the same theoretical principles be tested in the full range of the continuum.

Creative researchers should find it possible to move beyond experimental simulations in studying some of the same variables. In some applied settings, for example, it may be possible for evaluators to produce two different reports (varying in content or style) and randomly distributing them to decision makers and audiences for review with perhaps eventually all getting both reports but in a different order. Judicial evaluation formats could be used for one component of an evaluation project but not others or for a randomly selected portion of the evaluation audience. A randomly selected portion of the decision makers and audience could be provided with an educational experience on how best to process and use evaluation information and their deliberations and recommendations compared with those who do not receive such training. These manipulations will necessitate careful planning and demand the cooperation of participants but the questions are too important to be left unanswered. If the creativity of evaluators in proposing new evaluation models was matched by creative research designs on utilization, understanding of evaluation utilization could be many strides ahead.

Descriptive Research on Successful Evaluators. The evaluator is an important link in the evaluation process. Technical reports and presentations are important, but it is possible that the persona of the evaluator may be more critical to the success of an evaluation than professional evaluators would like to think. The skilled surgeon might be successful in saving lives through intricate surgical techniques and superb mastery of operation room techniques without having a bed-side manner, but not necessarily the general practitioner. Is the same true in the field of evaluation? The computer analyst may not need exceptional

interpersonal skills to be successful if he or she can provide the results of a sophisticated statistical analysis. But can the evaluator who must work closely with clients and audiences succeed without some measure of interpersonal skills? Evaluation is often viewed as an onerous task at best for the client and for those whose program is being evaluated. At worst, it is viewed as a costly, worthless, and threatening process.

Must a good evaluator also have a good project-side manner comparable to the physician's bedside manner? A stereotypical portrayal of an evaluator might be of a cold, objective, and bloodless person. Program administrators may fear the potential ruthlessness of the evaluator and may even fear fairness. What an administrator wants is help, support, and a pat on the back. The traditional stance between many administrators and evaluators is based on antagonism. Weiss (1972) has suggested that administrators and evaluators may be natural enemies. Can research verify this and provide clues as to how to overcome it?

The premise of adversarial roles needs examination from several perspectives. Taking into consideration the evaluation context, a formative evaluation may provide the evaluator with more opportunity to work closely with administrators and staff and thus be perceived as less threatening than in a summative evaluation context where there may be decisions about the ultimate worth and survival of the program. In the formative context, the evaluator is explicitly charged with collecting data that will help improve the program. In the summative context, the evaluator is collecting data that may result in the termination of the program. It follows that trust, openness, and cooperation may be easier to obtain in a formative evaluation than in a summative evaluation. Aloofness may, in fact, be a more appropriate stance in a summative evaluation context.

Communication and interpersonal styles may provide a framework for examination of evaluator characteristics and professional activities as they interact with the administrator's style to effect the usefulness and impact of evaluation information. For example, is an evaluator who is seen as nurturant more effective in providing negative feedback to a program administrator than an evaluator who is less nurturant? Gender might be a related variable and perhaps an independent one. How do male administrators react to negative or positive evaluative information when it is provided by a female evaluator? How do female administrators respond to male or female program evaluators?

Descriptive research needs a theoretical base to establish a focus for examining the characteristics of evaluators whose reports and information are used most effectively by clients. Along with expertise and attractiveness, other skills and characteristics, such as empathy and nurturance, may be worth examining.

Professional Issues

Issues related to professional growth and maturity of evaluation may be less open to empirical investigation than others. Research may provide perspectives but not solutions. Nevertheless, research can illuminate several professional issues in the next decade.

Evaluators need to take a long-term view and recognize that future clients are now in grade school, high school, or undergraduates in college. Will these students have to wait until they are in graduate programs before they are exposed to the rudiments of evaluation? Or, must lay persons wait until they are evaluation clients to learn about the process? Basic texts for undergraduate education courses are beginning to include short sections on evaluation; this represents a start, but the educational process must begin even sooner.

In educating future generations about the role and usefulness of evaluation, it is essential that this be a participatory educational process and not a passive learning experience. Having fifth graders memorize three definitions for evaluation will not enhance their future effectiveness as commissioners or consumers of evaluations. But having the students participate as program evaluators and as decision makers holds promise for future generations to have a fuller understanding of potential usefulness of program evaluation as well as its nuances. Research and evaluation programs are needed to examine the effectiveness of evaluation training programs for the wide spectrum of publics and audiences, including adolescents as well as persons in career positions in education or the human service fields.

Evaluation of training programs for evaluators should not be neglected. What is the appropriate proportion of class-to-field work experiences for the fledgling evaluator? What levels of supervision should be provided and when? Are there, for example, developmental stages in training evaluators that would provide guidance for curriculum development and program planning for individual stu-

dents? Similar research questions need to be considered relative to the continuing education needs of evaluators.

Conclusion

Two themes have been pervasive throughout this discussion of current issues in evaluation and illustration of potential research topics: (a) the growing interdisciplinary nature of evaluation and its methodology; and (b) the need to educate clients and audiences about the purpose and roles for evaluation. The issues have been debated long and hard and should continue to be debated. However, the pluralistic nature of evaluation as a multimethod, multidisciplinary activity needs to be accepted as well as the consequent implications for the practitioner and for training programs. More research that attempts to integrate theories from several disciplines and apply them to the evaluation process will enrich what is known about how to use evaluation information.

Evaluation is said to be a natural human activity, but this is no reason for failing to subject the process to empirical research using a variety of research methodologies. Thinking, eating, and sleeping are also natural human activities, but few would deny the value of studying these processes in detail.

Perhaps word of mouth is the best advertisement and the best education for evaluation clients. But the public becomes cynical towards professions that limit personal freedom, communicate almost entirely in technical jargon, and fail to police their ranks. Evaluators of the next decade are in a position of becoming public advocates rather than public adversaries. How honestly and directly they confront the issues enumerated in this chapter and how diligently they pursue related research agendas will largely determine how the public views evaluation in the next decade.

The recent merger of the Evaluation Network and the Evaluation Research Society into the American Evaluation Association and the increasing concern with ethical issues in evaluation (Bunda, 1985: Kirkhart, 1985: and Smith, 1985) are good behavioral indicators of growing maturity in this important application of educational psychology. Perhaps when the final Judgment Day arrives, God will look on this evaluation professions and call it ''Good.'' Probably even then someone will question the criteria and ask for a meta-evaluation.

References

Alkin, M. C. (1969). Evaluation theory and development. *Evaluation Comment, 2,* 2–7.

Alkin, M. C. (1980). Naturalistic study of evaluation utilization. In L. A. Braskamp & R. D. Brown (Eds.), *New directions for program evaluation utilization of evaluative information* (pp. 19–28). San Francisco, CA: Jossey-Bass.

Alkin, M. C., Daillak, R., & White, P. (1979). *Using evaluations: Does evaluation make a difference?* Beverly Hills, CA: Sage.

Baugher, D. (1981). *Measuring effectiveness* San Francisco: Jossey-Bass.

Borich, G. D. (1983). Evaluation models: A question of purpose not terminology. *Educational Evaluation and Policy Analysis, 5*(1), 61–63.

Boruch, F. R., & Cordray, D. S. (1980). *An appraisal of educational program evaluations: Federal, state, and local agencies.* Evanston, IL: Northwestern Unversity.

Braskamp, L. A. (1982). Evaluation systems are more than information systems. In R. Wilson (Ed.), *New directions for higher education: Designing academic program reviews* (pp. 55–66). San Francisco: Jossey-Bass.

Braskamp, L. A., & Brown, R. D. (Eds.). (1980). *New directions for program evaluation utilization of evaluative information* San Francisco, CA: Jossey-Bass.

Braskamp, L. A., Brown, R. D., Newman, D. L. (1980). Credibility of a local educational evaluation report: Author source and client characteristics. *American Educational Research Journal, 15,* 441–450.

Braskamp, L. A., Brown, R. D., & Newman, D. L. (1982). Studying evaluation utilization through simulation. *Evaluation Review, 6*(1), 114–126.

Brown, R. D., & Newman, D. L. (1982). An investigation of the effects of different data presentation formats and order of arguments in a simulated adversary evaluation. *Educational Evaluation and Policy Analysis, 4*(2), 197–204.

Brown, R. D., Braskamp, L. A., & Newman, D. L. (1978). Evaluator credibility and acceptance as a function of report styles: Do jargon and data make a difference? *Evaluation Quarterly, 2,* 331–341.

Brown, R. D., Newman, D. L., & Rivers, L. S. (1980). Perceived need for evaluation as an influence on evaluation's impact on decision making. *Educational Evaluation and Policy Analysis, 2*(1), 67–72.

Brown, R. D., Petersen, C. H., & Sanstead, M. (1980). Photographic evaluation: The use of the camera as an evaluation tool for student affairs. *Journal of College Student Personnel, 21*(6), 558–563.

Brown, R. D., Newman, D. L., & Rivers, L. S. (1984). Decision making theory and evaluation. *Educational Evaluation and Policy Analysis, 6*(4), 393–400.

Bunda, M. A. (1985). Alternative systems of ethics and their application to education and evaluation. *Evaluation and Program Planning, 8,* 25–36.

Campbell, D. T. (1969). Reforms as experiments. *American Psychologist, 24,* 409–429.

Campbell, D. T., & Stanley, J. (1963). *Experimental & quasi-experimental designs for research* Chicago, IL: Rand McNally.

Cook, T. D., & Campbell, D. T. (1976). The design and conduct of quasi-experiments and true experiments in field settings. In M. D. Dunnette (Ed.), *Handbook of industrial and organizational psychology* (pp. 223–326). Chicago: Rand McNally.

Cronbach, L. J., Ambron, S. R., Dronbusch, S. M., Hess, R. D., Hornik, R. C., Phillips, D. C., Walker, D. E., & Weiner, S. S. (1980). *Toward reform of program evaluation.* San Francisco: Jossey-Bass.

Davis, H. R., & Salasin, S. E. (1975). The utilization of evaluation. In E. L. Struening & M. Guttentag (Eds.), *Handbook of evaluation research.* Beverly Hills, CA: Sage.

Eisner, E. (1981). On the differences between scientific and artistic approaches to qualitative research. *Educational Researcher, 10*(4), 5–9.

Evaluation Research Society. (1981). *Standards for program evaluation.* Potomac, MD: Author.

Gephart, W. (1981). Watercolor painting. In N. Smith (Ed.). *Metaphors for evaluation* (pp. 247–272). Beverly Hills, CA: Sage.

Guba, E. G. (1969). The failure of educational evaluation. *Educational Technology, 9,* 29–38.

Guba, E. G. (1979). *Toward a methodology of naturalistic inquiry in educational evaluation.* Los Angeles, CA: UCLA Center for the Study of Evaluation.

Guba, E. G. (1981). Investigative reporting. In N. Smith (Eds.), *Metaphors for evaluation* (pp. 67–86). Beverly Hills. CA: Sage.

Guba, E. G., & Lincoln, Y. S. (1981). *Effective evaluation.* San Francisco, CA: Jossey-Bass.

Guba, E. G., & Lincoln, Y. S. (1982). The place of values in needs assessment. *Educational Evaluation and Policy Analysis, 4*(3), 311–320.

Haggerty, M. E. (1918). Specific uses of measurement in the solution of school problems. *The measurement of educational products.* Seventeenth Yearbook. National Society for the Study of Education. Part II. Bloomington, IL: Public School Publishing Co.

House, E. R. (1977). *The logic of evaluative argument.* CSE Monograph Series. Los Angeles, CA: University of California, Los Angeles.

House, E. R. (1980). *Evaluating with validity.* Beverly Hills, CA: Sage.

Janis, I. L., Mann. (1977). *Decision-making.* New York, NY: The Free Press.

Joint Committee on Standards for Educational Evaluation. (1981). *Standards for evaluations of educational programs, projects and materials.* New York: NY: McGraw-Hill.

Kirkhart, K. E. (1985). Analyzing mental health evaluations: Moral and ethical dimensions. *Evaluation and Program Planning, 8,* 13–23.

Leviton, L. A., & Hughes, E. F. X. (1981). Research on utilization. *Evaluation review, 5*(4), 525–548.

Lindvall, C. M., & Nitleo, A. J. (1981). Basic considerations in assessing the validity of evaluation designs. *Educational Evaluation and Policy Analysis, 3*(4), 49–68.

Litto, L. S. (1983). Revisiting the roles of organizational effectiveness in educational evaluation. *Educational Evaluation and Policy Analysis, 5*(3), 367–378.

Lynch, K. B. (1983). Qualitative and quantitative evaluation: Two terms in search of a meaning. *Educational Evaluation and Policy Analysis, 5*(4), 461–464.

McGuire, W. J. (1969). The nature of attitudes and attitude change. In G. Lindzey & E. Aronson (Eds.), *The handbook of social psychology* (pp. 136–314). Reading, MA: Addison-Wesley.

Merwin, J. C. (1969). Historical review of changing concepts of evaluation. In R. W. Tyler (Ed.), *Education Evaluation: New Roles, New Means. The sixty-eighth yearbook of the national society for the study of education* (pp. 6–25). Part II. Chicago, IL: University of Chicago Press.

Mohr, L. B. (1982). *Explaining organizational behavior.* San Francisco, CA: Jossey-Bass.

Newman, D. L., Brown, R. D., & Braskamp, L. A. (1980). Communication theory as a paradigm for studying evaluation use. In L. A. Braskamp & R. D. Brown (Eds.), *New directions for program evaluation utilization of evaluative information.* San Francisco: Jossey-Bass.

Newman, D. L., Brown, R. D., & Rivers, L. S. (1983). Locus of control and evaluation use: Does sense of control affect information needs and decision making? *Studies in Educational Evaluation, 9,* 77–88.

Newman, D. L., Brown, R. D., Rivers, L. S., & Glock, R. F. (1983). School boards' and administrators' use of evaluation information: Influencing factors. *Evaluation Review, 7*(1), 110–125.

Nevo, D. (1983). The conceptualization of educational evaluation: An analytical review of the literature. *Review of Educational Research, 53*(1), 117–128.

Nilsson, N., & Hogben, D. (1983). Metaevaluation. In E. R. House (Ed.) *Philosophy of evaluation* (pp. 83–98). San Francisco: Jossey-Bass.

O'Reilly, C. III (1981). Evaluation information and decision making in organizations: Some constraints on the utilization of evaluation research. In A. Bank & R. C. Williams (Eds.), *Evaluation in school districts: Organizational perspectives.* CSE Monograph Series in Evaluation No. 10. Los Angeles: Center for the Study of Evaluation.

Patton, M. Q. (1978). *Utilization focused evaluation.* Beverly Hills, CA: Sage.

Patton, M. Q. (1980). *Qualitative evaluation methods.* Beverly Hills, CA: Sage.

Patton, M. Q. (1981). *Creative evaluation.* Beverly Hills, CA: Sage.

Pflum, G., & Brown, R. D. (1984). The effects of conflict, quality, and time on small group information use and behavior in evaluative decision making situations. *Evaluation and Program Planning, 7,* 35–43.

Reavis, W. C. (1938). Contributions of research to educational administration. *The scientific movement in education.* Thirty-seventh yearbook of the National Society for the Study of Education, Part II. Bloomington, IL: Public School Publishing Co.

Rippey, R. M. (Ed.). (1973). *Studies in transactional evaluation.* Berkeley, CA: McCutchan.

Roecks, A. L. (1983). How much evaluator time is spent working with program staff? *Evaluation News, 4*(2), 69.

Rossi, P. H. (1982). *Standards for evaluation practice.* San Francisco: Jossey-Bass.

Scates, D. E. (1947). Fifty years of objective measurement and research in education. *Journal of Educational Research, 41*(4), 241–264.

Scriven, M. (1967). Methodology of evaluation. *American Educational research association monograph series on curriculum evaluation.* Chicago, IL: Rand McNally.

Scriven, M. (1972). Prose and cons about goal-free evaluation. *Evaluation Comment, 3*(4), 1–3.

Scriven, M. (1973). Goal-free evaluation. In E. R. House (Ed.), *School evaluation: The politics and process* (pp. 319–328). Berkeley, CA: McCutchan.

Sechrest, L. (1981). *Training program evaluators.* San Francisco: Jossey-Bass.

Sheinfeld, S. N., & Lord, G. L. (1981). The ethics of evaluation researchers: An exploration of value choices. *Evaluation Review, 5*(3), 377–391.

Smith, E. R., & Tyler, R. W. (1942). *Appraising and recording student progress.* New York: Harper & Brothers.

Smith, N. L. (Ed.). (1981). *Metaphors for evaluation: Sources of new methods.* Beverly Hills, CA: Sage.

Smith, N. L. (1982). *Field assessments of innovative evaluation methods.* San Francisco: Jossey-Bass.

Smith, N. L. (1985). Some characteristics of moral problems in evaluation practice. *Evaluation and Program Planning, 8,* 5–11.

Stake, R. E. (1967). The countenance of educational evaluation. *Teacher's College Record, 68,* 523–540.

Stake, R. E. (Ed.). (1975). *Evaluating the arts in education: A responsive approach.* Columbus, OH: Menull.

Stake, R. E. (1981). Persuasions, not models. *Educational Evaluation and policy analysis, 3*(1), 83–84.

Stuffelbeam, D. L. (1974). *Meta-evaluation.* (Occasional Paper No. 3), Kalamazoo, MI: Western Michigan University.

Stufflebeam, D. L. (1980). Standards research, and training: Three priorities for professionalizing educational evaluation. In W. W. Welch (Ed.), *Educational evaluation: Recent progress, future needs* (pp. 37–49). Minneapolis, MN: Minnesota Research and Evaluation Center.

Stuffelbeam, D. L., Foley, J., Gephart, W. J., Guba, E. G., Hammond, R. I., Meneman, H. O., & Provus, M. M. (1971). *Educational evaluation and decision making.* Itasca, IL: Peacock.

Stuffelbeam, D. L., & Webster, W. J. (1980). An analysis of alternative approaches to evaluation. *Educational Evaluation and Policy Analysis, 2*(1), 5–20.

Thompson, M. (1980). *Benefit-cost analysis for program evaluation* Beverly Hills, CA: Sage.

Thompson, M. (1982). *Decision analysis for program evaluation* Cambridge, MA: Ballinger.

Thompson, P., Brown, R. D., & Fergason, J. (1981). The impact of evaluation report styles on evaluation audiences: Jargon and data do make a difference. *Evaluation Review, 5*(2), 269–279.

Torres, R. T., & Braskamp, L. A. (1982). *What is the value of evaluation?* Paper presented at Evaluation Network/Evaluation Research Society, Baltimore, MD.

Tyler, R. W. (1950). *Basic principles of curriculum and instruction* Chicago, IL: University of Chicago Press.

Weiss, C. H. (Ed.). (1972). *Evaluating action programs.* Boston, MA: Allyn & Bacon.

Weiss, C. H. (1977a). Research for policy's sake: The enlightenment function of social research. *Policy Analysis, 3*(4), 531–545.

Weiss, C. H. (Ed.). (1977b). *Using social research in public policy making.* Lexington, MI: Lexington Brooks.

Welch, W. W. (Ed.). (1981). *Case study methodology in educational evaluation* Minneapolis, MN: Minnesota Research and Evaluation Center.

Wolf, R. L. (1979). The use of judicial evaluation methods in the formation of educational policy. *Educational Evaluation and Policy Analysis, 1,* 19–28.

Worthen, B. R., & Sanders, J. R. (1973). *Educational evaluation: Theory and practice* Belmont, CA: Wadsworth.

CHAPTER 13

Processes in Reading Comprehension and the Teaching of Comprehension

Thomas Andre

Readin, and writin, and ritmetic,
all to the tune of the hickory stick.

The hickory stick may be gone (mostly), but reading remains the backbone of education. As the most important of the troika of fundamental educational subjects, reading has been of great interest to educational and cognitive psychology since their very beginnings. That interest in reading continues and is especially strong currently. Both past and present educational cognitive psychologists have and are contributing much to our understanding of reading processes.

Why is reading of such great interest to educational psychologists? It is difficult to discuss this question without seeming obvious. Historically, teaching people to read and write has been a fundamental goal of education and the mark of the educated person has been literacy. Reading forms the basis of much of the rest of education; to learn science, mathematics, history, philosophy, or driver education, students must read. Students who have difficulty reading also have difficulty in other subject matters. Reading also forms the basis of most informal adult education; to learn to do new

things, adults read. Even when we take into account the influence of television, reading is the medium of the ongoing communicative dialogue of a free and democratic society. Reading also involves a complex cognitive performance; understanding reading has profound implications for understanding learning in all subject matters. For all of these reasons, it is natural that educational psychologists whose goals are to improve educational practice have often studied reading.

This chapter is about reading comprehension. Its major purpose is to provide an overview of current work in reading comprehension for students and practictioners of educational psychology. The chapter briefly describes the historical role of educational psychologists in reading research in order to fit the current work into a historical perspective, but the focus and emphasis is on current work. Current work on reading comprehension is very extensive; it includes work by computer/cognitive scientists and psychologists into computer models of language perception and comprehension, by experimental psychologists in how individuals comprehend, learn, and remember textual material, by linguists on the linguistic cues that signal different

Thomas Andre • Department of Psychology, Iowa State University, Ames, IA 50011.

acts of comprehension, and by instructionally oriented researchers into the ways and means of improving the learning of reading comprehension in schools. No single chapter can hope to review all of the work that is currently underway. In order to reduce the problem of scope to manageable proportions, this chapter is organized around a view of reading comprehension that currently predominates in the field. We will call this view the schema-theoretic perspective, though it is discussed by a variety of names in the literature (story grammars, script theory, frame theory, etc). The chapter is divided into four major sections that deal with different aspects of current work related to the schema-theoretic view.

Section 1 discusses some of the historical work on reading and reading comprehension. This section has two purposes: (a) to demonstrate that research on reading has traditionally been a part of educational psychology since its earliest beginnings and (b) to indicate that many of the fundamental ideas of the schema-theoretic perspective were anticipated by earlier students of reading comprehension. The point is not to show that current views offer nothing new; they do, most importantly a precision and clarity unavailable in previous accounts. Rather, the point is to demonstrate that when educational psychologists have thought profoundly about the nature of reading comprehension, a number of themes, important in current theory, have repeatedly been discussed. In my view, this historical overview suggests that, though the terminology may change, there has been a fundamental unity about some major themes among scientists who have theorized about reading comprehension.

Section 2 discusses models of the reading process. A great deal of exciting work in reading comprehension is concerned with developing an adequate theoretical model of the comprehension processes. My view is that, although no adequate model has yet been completed, considerable progress towards the outline of an effective model has been made. This section attempts to show that models of the reading process have changed from models that emphasize the role of decoding the message of text to models that emphasize the interaction of the reader's previous knowledge with the text in order to construct meaning. The schema-theoretic view captures the interactive position very well. To demonstrate why a schema-theoretic view is necessary, this second section reviews earlier models, points out their weaknesses, and then

comprehensively discusses schema-theoretic models by presenting three examples in some depth. By the end of this section, I hope the reader will have appreciated why schema-theoretic models are important and will have an understanding of their fundamental features.

Section 3 focuses on current empirical research in reading comprehension that is consistent with the schema-theoretic perspective. Again, no attempt was made to review comprehensively all current work on reading comprehension; instead, four currently active areas are discussed. Several criteria contributed to the inclusion of these areas. Each of the areas discussed involved more theoretically oriented basic research (as opposed to directly instructional research, discussed in Section 4) that was consistent with the schema-theoretic view, illustrated important components of the reading process according to that view, and were areas in which I was interested and had some familiarity. The four areas discussed are (a) the role of syntactical factors in comprehension, (b) the problem and role of metaphor in comprehension, (c) the role of elaboration in improving comprehension, and (d) the role of metacognitive schemata in comprehension.

Section 4 is concerned with the teaching of comprehension. If the goal of educational psychology is to improve educational practice, then it is important to discuss implications of psychological research for pedagogy. This section has two conceptual parts; the first part reviews the current status of comprehension teaching and finds it lacking, especially when viewed from a schema-theoretic position. The second part focuses on current research on improving the teaching of comprehension that has been generated from the schema-theoretic position. In my view, one of the exciting aspects of the schema-theoretic position is that it has important implications for the teaching of comprehension skills.

There are numerous issues related to reading comprehension that this chapter slights, both for reasons of space and the competence of the author. The issue of how to assess reading comprehension is not covered. This issue is an important one because the procedures used to assess comprehension represent the operational definition of comprehension in any given study and because the testing of reading comprehension has been an important part of the history of educational psychology. With respect to assessment, my basic position is that comprehension is a complex cognitive process that can manifest itself behaviorally in a variety of ways. There are a number of valid ways to assess comprehension that reflect different aspects of the comprehension process. In this chapter, I have basically accepted whatever assessment procedure the authors of the studies discussed herein used as a measure of reading comprehension. The reader interested in assessment is refered to Johnston (1985). In addition, the chapter does not deal with the visual layout of text and the effects of differing visual arrangements on comprehension. This is an important area of research that is receiving much contemporary interest (see Jonassen, 1984; Wright, 1977). A related issue, that of readability, is also not discussed (see Klare, 1985). I have also paid little direct attention to the word perception and decoding processes. Obviously, there can be no comprehension unless the visual code of written language is broken by the reader. However, such comprehension of visual forms is not what is usually meant by reading comprehension. These perceptual aspects of reading are discussed only in the schema-theoretic view of reading I present in this chapter, which envisions the process of letter/word perception as operating similarly to the processes involved in the comprehension of meaning. The reader interested in such perceptual processes is refered to relevant chapters in Pearson (1985).

The Concept of Schemata. I have used the concept of schemata a number of times in this introduction. Although the idea of schemata is discussed more completely below, a preliminary description may make the following more comprehensible. According to the schema-theoretic perspective, the reader's knowledge store is organized into schemata. *Schemata* are knowledge structures that have a number of properties. They actively search the current perceptual and consciousness stream for conditions that satisfy them; they have labeled relationships to other schemata (including schemata that serve as slots and defaults for themselves), and they have a production or task activity component (Andre, 1986). The schema-theoretic perspective basically argues that reading consists of a process by which text cues serve to activate schemata; from the knowledge represented in such schemata, the reader constructs a meaning for a communication. Thus reading (and language comprehension generally) is dependent on the reader's prior knowledge and experience. The schemata involved in reading comprehension are of two types; the first type involves the knowledge and activities involved in particular language pro-

cessing skills. R. C. Anderson, Pichert, and Shirey (1983) suggest this type captures "knowledge of the discourse-level conventions of text" and refer to them as textual schemata. I will call them text processing or discourse processing schemata because that label captures their function more precisely. The second type of schemata embodies knowledge of the substance of text, the concepts, principles, rules, scripts, paradigms, etc., that represent our knowledge of the world. R. C. Anderson *et al.* (1983) refer to these as content schemata. Elsewhere (Andre, 1986), I have argued the schema theory provides a unifying theme for conceptualizing the goals of learning and what is learned in education. In that paper, I argued the goals of education are to promote the acquisition of schemata in various subject matters. Because the basic form of a schema is the same regardless of subject matter, procedures that facilitate acquistion of schemata are similar across different subject matters. If my arguments have validity, then the discussion in this chapter has implications beyond the teaching of reading comprehension. Schema theory has relevance for all areas of formal and informal education and should be of interest to educational psychologists regardless of their particular domain of expertise.

Educational Psychology and the Study of Reading: A Brief Historical Overview

This section owes much to excellent papers by Spache (1956/1958) and Venezky (1985), which provide a good overview of the history of psychological research in reading comprehension. Another important source is a book by Smith (1934) that provides a historical analysis of American reading instruction and the factors that led to changes in reading instruction.

Psychological studies of reading processes began in Wundt's laboratory as part of the very earliest studies of human cognition and learning (Venezky, 1985). The earliest studies focused more on physiological and perceptual factors in reading (Spache, 1956/1958; Venesky, 1985). Psychologists with an interest in the practical problems of education began to study reading in schools before the turn of the century. Reading comprehension was a topic of early interest and a number of studies were carried out attempting to measure reading comprehension and to relate reading comprehension to factors such as the rate of reading and to silent and oral reading. Reading was seen as a tool of the mind and understanding what was read was the essential component of reading.

This orientation is present in Huey's 1908 book *The Psychology and Pedagogy of Reading*. Huey provided an impressive review of the psychological work on reading that had been conducted to that date and drew many implications for pedagogical practice. Huey argued strongly for an educational psychology in which psychologists examined school learning and attempted to improve educational practice. He believed that approach had benefits for both psychology as a science and education as a practical discipline. He suggested that the study of school subjects offered psychology "modes of mental and physiological functioning which furnish to psychology problems fruitful to psychology's own purposes" (1908, p. ix). This theme has been repeated by current psychologists who have pursued studies of educational tasks (e.g., Simon, 1984). Huey also argued that educational psychology would offer "great service . . . to psychology and education, by . . . organization and concentration of data concerning the various school subjects" (1908, p x). In his book, Huey discussed physiological and perceptual processes in reading, the relationship of reading rate to comprehension, the history of reading and education, educational issues such as when to teach reading, the implications of home or school teaching of reading, what sorts of reading should be encouraged, and the ergonometrics of print.

With respect to reading comprehension, Huey argued that comprehension was an active process in which the reader constructed meaning from ideas present in the reader's mind. His views anticipated many ideas that have been developed more explicitly in current theories. In a chapter on interpretation of material read, Huey discussed a particularly interesting introspective study that illustrated his views on comprehension. Adult readers read text that had been cut apart and pasted on cardboard slips and introspected about the ideas the words produced as they read. The texts were presented either in random or normal text order. When the words were presented in a random order, only vague and general ideas were aroused by the text. When the words were presented in the text order, each word aroused images that were detailed and specific to the ongoing context of the story. The subjects also reported a "forward push" to complete the details as words emerged. Readers also reported feelings of "fulfillment or disappointment of expectation" as newly exposed words confirmed or disconfirmed the expectations the readers had developed. Although Huey did not present this explicitly, his subject's descriptions are consistent with the idea that reading comprehension involves the active construction of a structure in the mind that is built following the directions of the text but whose raw materials are the ideas already present in the mind of the reader. Those ideas allow the reader to build a structure that contains more detail than is present in the text itself and lead to expectations on the part of the reader as to what will come next (Huey's forward push).

Other early educational psychologists displayed an interest in reading comprehension processes and emphasized the role of the reader's previous knowledge and thought processes in comprehending. For example, Thorndike (1917) likened reading comprehension to reasoning and problem solving and argued that "reading is a very elaborate procedure, involving a weighing of each of many elements in a sentence, their organization in the proper relations one to another, the selection of certain of their connotations and the rejection of others, and the cooperation of many forces to determine final response." The concerns of early educational psychologists for promoting reading comprehension was a factor in their research comparing silent and oral reading and their support for a silent reading program emphasizing comprehension. The support of early psychological reading researchers contributed to a change in school reading programs from being oral reading programs to being silent reading programs (Spache, 1956/1958; Smith, 1936).

According to Spache (1956/1958), during the 1910s and 1920s, research on reading comprehension led to two generalizations. In my view these generalizations anticipated aspects of the schema-theoretic view; (a) comprehension is an active process "dependent upon the extent and richness of the meaning vocabulary of the reader and his reading backgrounds" (Spache, 1956/1958, p. 12); (b) "training in comprehension really involved the promotion of critical thinking—the making of judgements, the drawing of inferences, and the formulations of conclusions based upon many sources" (1956/1958, p 12).

After the 1920s, research on the cognitive processes involved in reading comprehension declined. Venesky (1985) argued that this decline was caused by the influence of the testing movement and the advent of behaviorism, both of which shifted attention away from the direct study of cognitive processes. Venesky reported that few studies of comprehension were done. In this period there were isolated instances of research relevant to comprehension, such as Bartlett's work on memory for stories (1932), additional work on errors in comprehension that built on Thorndike's study (Touton & Berry, 1931) and work on learning from prose (reviewed by Welborn and English, 1937), but there was no sustained attack on reading comprehension. An analysis of the content of educational psychology texts during this period supports Venesky's position. Thorndike's 1925 *Educational Psychology: Briefer Course* makes only brief reference to reading in a discussion of the conditions of improvement. Jordan (1933) focuses on the role of the interest value of material read and a discussion of how associative principles relate to the teaching of reading. Pressey (1933) does not contain a reference to reading. Cronbach (1954, 1963), in a major educational psychology textbook of the 1950s and 1960s discusses the teaching of reading, reading tests, and phonemic analysis, but makes no mention of reading comprehension.

A few writers during the period did discuss reading comprehension. For example, Gray (1933), in a book that described a study of how to improve reading achievement in elementary schools, discussed procedures for improving reading comprehension. Gates (1935) discussed reasons for and diagnoses of comprehension difficulties. McKee (1948), in a textbook on teaching reading, presented a view that is remarkably contemporary. He argued that reading comprehension consists not of gaining the meaning of text, but rather the construction, by the reader, of a meaningful representation based on the readers existing knowledge. In McKee's own words:

No reader gets meaning from the printed page . . . When you as a reader identify or recognize a word or groups of words, your observing of that symbol stimulates you to recall or to construct the meaning for which the symbol stands. . . . the meaning you arrive at is recalled or built by your mind rather than given to you by the print. . . . Thus you read, not only with your eyes, but with your experiences, with what you have seen, heard, done, tasted, smelled, felt, and with what has happened to you, with your emotions, including your hopes and fears, your likes and dislikes; with your prejudices and your ideals; with your observations and the conclusions you have drawn from them. (McKee, 1948, pp. 59–61)

As we shall see, these views of reading comprehension and the generalizations discussed earlier are part of the fundamental doctrine of contemporary theories of reading comprehension. The next section provides an overview of current models of reading comprehension.

Models of Reading Comprehension

A layperson's view of the reading comprehension process would suggest that words have definite meanings as given by their dictionary definitions and/or associations with other words or responses. Comprehension would consist of concatenation of the definitions/associations as the words occur in sentences. Language, written or spoken, would have definite meaning and the process of comprehension would involve decoding the meaning of the text. Initial information processing models of reading began with such a relatively unsophisticated view and attempted to describe the processes by which written language was perceived, formed into words, sentences, and comprehended. Such models emphasize what are called *bottom up* or *data-driven* models of comprehension (Rumelhart, 1977; Rumelhart & McClelland, 1981).

This view of reading is inadequate. Reading and language comprehension involve more than a simple transformation of the language in a communication. Readers have expectations about the nature of a communication that activate knowledge structures that serve to fill in missing details of messages and lead readers to make particular kinds of inferences from messages. In other words, rather than simply constructing a meaning from the elements of a message, readers use organized prior knowledge to comprehend a message. The use of prior knowledge structures in comprehension is called *top-down or conceptually driven processing* (Rumelhart, 1977; Rumelhart & McClelland, 1981). The idea of top-down processing is not new; that the comprehension of meaning in presented information occurs as a result of top-down as opposed to bottom-up processing was a basic message the Gestalt psychologists tried to communicate. The alternative perceptions of the famous goblet/faces figure occur not because the elements of the figure give rise to two different interpretations, but because we have learned two knowledge structures (called ''gestalts'' by the Gestalt psychologists, but currently labeled schemata) that can be applied to give meaning to the visual figure. As noted previously, the idea that prior knowledge was essential in reading was also present in the work of early educational psychologists.

Rumelhart (1977) and Adams and Collins (1977) argued that neither top-down nor bottom-up models could account for the data on comprehension. Instead they proposed an *interactive* view of reading and listening comprehension. In this view, both data driven and relatively automatic processes and relatively conscious conceptually driven processes are involved in reading and comprehension. In this section, I discuss examples of sophisticated bottom-up, top-down, and interactive models of comprehension. My goal is to allow the reader to gain an appreciation of the features of such models and to demonstrate why an interactive view is necessary.

Bottom-Up, Data Driven Models

An example of a well thought out bottom-up model of comprehension is provided by Gough (1973). Gough attempted to develop a detailed model of events that occur in the first second of reading a sentence; he recognized that his model would be flawed in particulars, but argued that the general form of the model would hold up. Gough's model was a major contribution because it organized many of the known facts of reading into a coherent and testable whole.

In the model, Gough argued for a strict bottom-up model in which the reader *plodded* "through a sentence, letter by letter, word by word" (p. 354). Processing began with an eye fixation of 250 milliseconds and a saccadic movement taking 10 to 23 milliseconds, followed by a second fixation, another saccade, and so on. Gough estimated that during the fixation an *icon* consisting of a set of visual features not yet identified as letters was formed. This icon was formed in approximately 50 milleseconds and contained features of 15 to 20 letters. Once the icon was formed, letter identification began to occur, proceeding serially from left to right, at a pace that Gough estimated to be 10 to 20 milliseconds per letter. Assuming that the icon endured 250 milliseconds and three fixations per second, Gough computed a possible reading rate of over 300 words per minute; a value well in the normal range of reading rates. This estimate is important because one criticism of bottom-up models is that sequential processing would take too long to accomodate typical reading rates.

The next stage in the model was the formation of a mapping between letters and "systematic phonemes" that provide the sound of the language. Systematic phonemes should not be thought about as pronounced words, but rather, the mental representations that may lead to pronounced words. From these systematic phonemes, the "lexical entries" or words of a sentence are recognized. Again, the recognition process is serial and proceeds from left to right. The recognized words are then entered into a storage buffer Gough identified as primary memory (short-term memory). The items in primary memory have access to the phonological, syntactic, and semantic information possessed by the words they represent. Gough makes no assumption that the items are stored in a phonological form in primary memory. The words in primary memory are operated on by integrative processes that construct the meaning of the sentence. Gough believes that understood sentences are transferred to secondary memory (long-term memory) although he does not argue this point. His model makes no assumption about what happens to understood sentences except that they are transferred to the "Place Where Sentences Go When They Are Understood."

Critique of Bottom-Up Models. Gough's model rested on a number of assumptions he believed to be supported by empirical findings. For example, because of the serial nature of letter identification and the assumption that word recognition could not occur until all letters in a word had been identified, Gough's model predicts that letters in nonword strings should be recognized just as quickly as letters in words. Gough reports a result by Scharf, Zamansky, and Brightbill (1966) as support for this assumption. Several other studies, (e.g., Adams, 1979; McClelland, 1976; Reicher, 1969) however, demonstrate results inconsistent with the assumption. In a commentary on Gough's model, Brewer (1973) points out several classical arguments against bottom-up models of the type proposed by Gough based on work by Cattell (1885, 1886a, 1886b, 1947). According to Brewer, Cattell's work raised four major objections against pure bottom-up models: "(a) Words in prose passages can be read almost as fast as lists of letters. (b) The immediate visual apprehension span for letters in prose is much greater than for random letters. (c) Latencies to initiate pronunciation of words are shorter than those for letters. (d) Visual recognition threshold for words are lower than the thresholds for letters," (Brewer,

1973, p. 359). In addition Brewer argued that (a) readout of letters from the icon does not seem to be serial (Eriksen & Spencer, 1969; Haber 1970) as Gough assumed, (b) the strict translation of letters to systematic phonemes as proposed by Gough cannot be entirely accurate or else homophones could not be distinguished, and (c) the strict translation of words to meaning without influence of prior words in a sentence seems to contradict conscious experience as in sentences such as *We could see that the dumbbell was painted dark blue, even though the weight lifter said it was light.* (adapted from Brewer, 1973). Brewer concludes that these arguments require top-down processes in models of reading.

Top-Down, Conceptually Driven Models

Top-down or conceptually driven models emphasize the role of previously acquired knowledge in the reading process. Rather than depicting reading as consisting of a careful analysis of text to determine meaning, top-down models hold that the readers' expectations about the text and his or her previous knowledge about the subject matter being communicated control the comprehension process. Text or spoken language does not have meaning in a top-down model, rather language serves as a cue for the reader/listener to construct meaning.

No model of reading is strictly a top-down model. Obviously if communication occurs, there is some connection between a writer's intention; the written language; and the meaning the reader constructs. At some level there must be a relationship between text and comprehension; in other words, some degree of bottom-up processing is posited in every model. Models vary however, in the degree to which they emphasize top-down processes. Some models place most of the "action" in top-down processes. A good example of top-down models is Goodman's psycholinguistic theory of reading.

Goodman's Psycholinguistic Guessing Game. Goodman's work originated in studies of the errors that children make in oral reading. He worked in a relatively naturalistic setting, asking children to read complete stories, at a reading level slightly difficult for them. Analysis of children's miscues (oral reading errors) suggested to Goodman that reading was controlled primarily by psycholinguistic processes that led the reader to predict the content of the upcoming text and to use the text only as a means of confirming or disconfirm-

ing predictions. For this reason, Goodman, in his most famous paper, called reading a psycholinguistic guessing game (Goodman, 1982a).

According to the Goodman model, the reading process consists of four cycles of operation: optical, perceptual, syntactic, and meaning. The optical cycle begins the process by picking up graphic cues, perceptual and syntactical processes provide analysis of the graphic input and begin the process of constructing meaning. If the four cycles were strictly sequential, Goodman's model would be a bottom-up, data driven model. Instead, Goodman holds that as soon as the reader begins to construct some meaning, the reading system (the brain, in Goodman's words, 1982b, p. 13) strives for meaning by using minimal graphic/perceptual/syntactic information to make predictions about the nature of the upcoming input and feeding those predictions downward into the perceptual system for confirmation. There are 5 basic processes in the predictive reading process: (a) Recognition-initiation—this process is the start of reading. Written text is recognized; (b) Prediction—on the basis of what the brain predicts the text is about (its meaning), the brain predicts what upcoming stimulation will be like; (c) Confirmation—the actual input is verified against the predictions; (d) Correction—if discrepancy is found, the brain seeks additional input to correct the mistake; and (e) Termination—reading is finished when goals are achieved or it seems likely that they will not be achieved (1982, p. 13).

At any given time in reading, the learner may make miscues or errors. Such errors are not random, but occur because of the application of the same psycholinguistic processes used in successful reading. Some of the psycholinguistic reasons miscues occur are (a) misperception of the graphic cues because perception depends on stimulus input and what the reader is expecting to see; (b) inability to process—either because of lack of proficiency or degraded input (bad handwriting), the graphic information is difficult to handle; (c) inference of a different deep structure than that intended by the author because of different language rules and ambiguity in the surface structure leading to alternative deep structure interpretations; (d) an inability of the reader to construct meaning because of a lack of relevant prior experience or concepts; and (e) choice of alternative syntactical/phonological rules to produce oral surface structure. These reasons for miscues reveal important features of Goodman's model. Reason (e) implies that oral reading proceeds from graphic to meaning rather than proceeding from graphic to sound to meaning. That is, what the reader says while reading aloud is not a one-for-one mapping of written word to oral word. Rather, the reader encodes or constructs the meaning of the message and then uses his or her normal speaking procedures to say that meaning. Reason (d) suggests that meaning is dependent on and constructed from relevant known concepts on the part of the reader, a theme that is echoed in schema-based theories discussed in the following.

Goodman's and his colleagues' (Goodman, 1982c; Goodman & Goodman, 1982) analysis of errors indicated that errors that preserved meaning were not corrected and errors that interfered with meaning led to rereading and correction. Goodman and Goodman (1982) provided an example. In reading a phrase *the old apple tree* in a context in which *the big old apple tree* had been previously mentioned, a child reader left out "old" and did not correct this miscue. Goodman and Goodman correctly pointed out that this omission did not change meaning and that the change was consistent with the linguistic rule to drop descriptive adjectives for a definite noun in a known context. In a later sentence, the child misread *the* for *she*. This change did lead to a meaning change and the child noted and corrected the error.

Critique of Goodman's Theory. Goodman's theory has strong and weak points. Among its strengths is that in its emphasis on top-down processes it anticipated many of the prime features of current interactive theories. A variety of lines of evidence to be discussed later make it clear that a pure bottom-up approach to comprehension fails to take into account the necessary contribution of the reader's previous knowledge. Goodman's emphasis on the role of prior syntactic and semantic knowledge in making predictions about the text is generally consistent with many results. Because of its origins, the theory has some intuitive appeal in its explanation of errors or miscues in oral reading and the notion that errors represent an important source of information about reading is an important one (Adams, 1980; Leu, 1982).

The theory seems to me to be weak in two areas. First of all, it overemphasizes the role of top-down processes. For example, the theory predicts that good readers should make less use of graphic information and more use of contextual information than weak readers. This does not seem to be the

case (Leu, 1982). The second, and perhaps more important problem, is that the model is not very specific. For example, one possible prediction from the theory is that readers should be able to guess at the next words in typical text. Typically, readers are unable to do so (Balota, Pollatsek, & Rayner, 1985), a finding apparently inconsistent with the model. Of course, this inconsistency assumes that the predictions made by readers are conscious and Goodman is not clear that such predictions are in the reader's conscious awareness. In fact, even though the authors are quite critical of Goodman, if conscious guessing is not assumed, the Balota *et al.* study reported evidence that could be considered as consistent with Goodman's theory.

Subjects read text on a computer screen while their eye movements were monitored. In sentences that highly constrained at least one word, the target word sometimes changed during the saccade that would have fixated it. Thus, sometimes the parafoveal information acquired before the saccade began was consistent with the information received as the target word was fixated and sometimes it was not. Results consistent with the Goodman model were that the target word was more likely to be skipped over (not fixated) when it was highly constrained by the sentence context and when the parafoveal information received from the target word was consistent with the context. In addition, if the subject fixated the target word, fixation duration was less if the target word was the highly constrained word.

These seem like effects Goodman would predict, but one cannot be sure given the looseness of this model. From the viewpoint of a theorist attempting to capture all the details of the reading process, Goodman's theory represents a set of relatively general statements about processes in reading rather than being a precise description of the processes involved. The statements may provide guidance for the designer of a precise model, but they are fuzzy enough (in the sense of designating a fuzzy set) to cover a range of possible interpretations. For example, is the prediction that Goodman refers to a conscious prediction made by the subject or is it an expectation that the reading system automatically generates and uses to guide its analysis of foveal input? If the latter, what are the processes by which this expectation is generated and confirmed? It is answers to questions such as these upon which precise tests of the theory would need to be based. To be fair to Goodman, it does not seem that his purpose was to develop a precisely detailed theory of reading. Rather, his theory developed in the context of providing a description of reading processes that would account for miscues in oral reading and that would guide instruction in the reading process. His theory has the value that it pointed out the importance of top-down processes in reading at a time when the need for such processes were not well understood.

Interactive Models of Reading

Because pure top-down models have difficulty in accounting for variations in the input from previously acquired structures and bottom-up models have difficulty in accounting for the effects of previous knowledge on reading comprehension processes, numerous models in which top-down and bottom-up processes interact to produce comprehension have been proposed. I will discuss three of them, the Rummelhart (1977)/Rummelhart and McClelland (1981) model, the van Dijk and Kintsch (1978) model, and the Adams and Collins (1979) schema-theoretic view.

The Rummelhart and McClelland Model. The Rummelhart and McClelland (1981) model focuses on the way in which letter perception is influenced by context; but the principles described are believed to be general for the situation in which any higher-order knowledge structures interact with lower-order structures. The model makes use of the cascade theory proposed by McClelland (1979). The model assumes that the reader brings to reading a set of expectations and knowledge structures that contain information about orthographic and phonological regularities, syntactical rules, world knowledge, etc. This information exists in an interactive network in which lower-order structures can activate higher-order structures and vice versa. There are nodes in the network for individual letters, for individual words, and presumably for higher-order concepts, and rules, etc. Each node varies in its state of activation between a resting level and a threshold level. When threshold is reached, the node is fully activated and the system claims detection of that node (e.g., letter, word, etc). The important aspect of this feature of the model is that a node can receive partial activation that increases its activation state towards threshold. Connections occur between nodes at the same level and at different levels and connections can be excitatory or

inhibitory. Stimulation along an inhibitory connection would decrease the activation state of the node. As the reader begins to process the visual features of the letters in words, the nodes for letters that contain those features are partially activated. Partial activation spreads through these letter nodes to nodes for words that contain those letters in those positions. In turn, the partial activation of the word nodes sends activation back into the letter perception process offering constraints on the selection of letters. When the letters are a word or fall into a pattern for words, for example, a pronounceable nonword, this constraint from the word level serves to facilitate the perception of letters. When the context is not a word, there is no facilitation.

Let us see how the model would work in an actual example. Suppose the letter contains a middle horizontal line. Detection of this feature would activate nodes for A, H, P and other letters with a middle horizontal line. Inhibitory connections would decrease the activation level for words without middle horizontal lines. Simultaneously, the activation from these letters up to the word level would partially activate words containing letters with middle horizontal lines in those positions of the word. The partial activation of these words would be reflected back into the letter perception process, increasing the probability of detecting other letters that would fit the constraints of those words and decreasing the probability of detecting letters that would not fit those words. If the presented word were THIS, initial activation of the middle horizontal word feature should increase the activation level of H and A in the second position. Words such as THAT, THIS and TALL should receive momentary increases in activation level as well. Words such as LIFT and SOFT, should receive decreases in activation level. The increase in activation level of THAT, THIS, and TALL is reflected back into the letter processes level increasing the activation of T in the first position, H or A in the second position, T or S or L in the final position. As more letter features are processed, the activation level of letters and words change dynamically until THIS is recognized.

The foregoing is an oversimplified account of the model and the reader is referred to McClelland and Rumelhart (1980) and Rumelhart and McClelland (1980, 1981) for a more complete account. McClelland (1979) provides a technical description of cascade theory. Rumelhart and

McClelland (1981) demonstrate that the model can account for a number of the facts of letter perception and can dynamically adjust to changes in stimulus situations much as human perceivers do.

What does this detailed account of letter/word perception have to do with the process of reading comprehension? The point argued by Rumelhart and McClelland is that the basic principles of the model—interacting nodes that vary between a resting state and an activated state, dynamic spread of activation within and between levels, and inhibitory and excitatory connections—can be applied to the issue of reading comprehension. In Rumelhart's view, comprehension consists of applying world knowledge schemata to linguistic input so as to account for the input (Rumelhart, 1980; Rumelhart & Ortony, 1977). Rumelhart (1980) provides the following description of the operation of schemata in the comprehension process.

> Some event occurs at the sensory system . . . this event ''automatically'' activates certain ''low-level'' schemata (. . . called feature detectors). These . . . in turn, activate (in a data-driven fashion) certain . . . ''higher level'' schemata . . . of which they are constituents. These . . . schemata . . . then initiate conceptually driven processing by activating the subschemata not already activated in an attempt to evaluate . . . goodness of fit. (Rumelhart, 1980, p. 42)

This description is basically similar to the description of interacting levels of schemata previously described for letter perception.

Kinstch and van Dijk Model. The Rumelhart-McClelland model focuses on the letter/word perception process. A model with similar features that focuses on comprehension has been proposed by Kinstch and van Dijk (1978; van Dijk & Kintsch, 1983). The model is based on earlier work by Kintsch (1974), who had proposed a model of the representation of meaning. Kintsch's and van Dijk's model assumes a letter–word perception process that works along the general lines of a cascade theory model as proposed by Rumelhart and McClelland (1981).

The model begins with the analysis of text into a set of propositions based on the surface structure of a text. Each proposition represents one clause of a text. This analysis is based on the use of strategic propositional schemata that analyze text into overlearned role components such as actor, action, object etc. As these elementary propositions are analyzed, they begin to activate a set of strategic schemata concerned with *local coherence*. These local coherence schemata relate sentences on the basis of repetition of components of the sentences, syn-

tactic cues such as explicit connectives and clause ordering, and also schematic knowledge from long-term memory about the topic being discussed. Like the interactive word/letter recognition models discussed earlier, Kintsch's and van Dijk's model assumes that the comprehension process is not sequential. Processing for local coherence operates in parallel with the processing involved in the propositional analysis of clauses. In addition to processing for local coherence, a set of *macrostrategies* is applied to the set of interrelated propositions developed by the local coherence analysis. These macrostrategies lead to the development of a set of *macropropositions* that capture the gist or theme of the text. Again, macrostrategic processing occurs in parallel with lower levels of processing. In Kintsch's and van Dijk's words:

> it is plausible that with a minimum of textual information from the first propositions, the language user will make guesses about such a topic. These guesses will be sustained by various kinds of information, such as titles, thematic words, thematic first sentences, knowledge about possible ensuing global events or actions, and information for the context. (1983, p. 16)

The processing of macrostructure is facilitated when the text possesses a *superstructure,* a structure based on an overlearned schemata for organizing the elements of the text. Kintsch and van Dijk give as examples story scripts and the structure of psychological research articles. Superstructure facilitates comprehension by acting as a top-down device that allows subsequent elements at lower levels to be fit into the structure.

This description presents the general outline of the Kintsch and van Dijk model. Kintsch and van Dijk (1978) proposed a specific model to accomplish the tasks described in the general outline. In the specific model, text is analyzed into a text base using the propositional scheme proposed by Kintsch (1974). The propositions consist of the substance words of the sentence organized into relationships. For example, the sentence, *The subjects were 20 female students,* yields the following propositional list: subjects (STUDENT, SUBJECT); (FEMALE, STUDENT); (NUMBER, SUBJECT, TWENTY); (adapted from Kintsch, 1974, pp. 18–19).

The propositions are written in all caps and in parentheses. Each proposition consists of a first term called the predicator and one or more subsequent terms called arguments. The arguments assert something about the predicator or give some information about it. Kintsch (1974) specified rules that can be used to construct the propositional text base and Kintsch and van Dijk (1978) claimed that the process is reliable, although no reliability data were provided.

In a long text, processing limitations of the mental system prevent analysis of the entire text at once. Hence, the propositional analysis works cyclically. During each cycle, n(i) items are processed and s(i) propositions are selected to be maintained in a short term memory buffer [n(i) is variable; i indexes the cycle s<n]. These s(i) items are available for relating the next n(i) propositions to the previous propositions. The model looks for coherence between the propositions on the basis of overlap between the words/concepts in the propositions and constructs a coherent text base that represents the text. If the n(i+1) set of propositions contains overlap with the n(i) set of propositions, then the new set is accepted as coherent with the previous. If the new set does not contain overlap, the model engages in a reprocessing of the text to find coherence. This reprocessing is demanding in terms of conscious attention and the comprehension process is difficult when coherence is not obvious. With reasonably written texts, however, the propositional and coherence analyses are relatively automatic processes that demand little conscious attention (system resources).

During each cycle, each processed proposition has probability p of being stored in and becoming retrievable from long-term memory. Because some propositions are stored in the short-term buffer and reprocessed with the subsequent set, these propositions have multiple chances of being stored in long-term memory given by the probability $1 - (1 - p)\char`^k$ where k is the number of times processed. Differences in the probabilities of recall of different propositions represents one source of empirical tests for the model. The overall schema activated when a text is read determines the reader's goals and purposes while reading the text. As propositions are processed they are classified as relevant or irrelevant to the schema. Relevant propositions are included in a macrostructure for the text. The macrostructure provides the gist of the text.

The model provides reasonably accurate predictions of actual behavior. Kintsch and van Dijk (1978) found that estimates for the model fit actual recall data well at 1-month and 3-month retention intervals. Propositions for which the model predicted better recall were recalled more accurately. The model was less accurate on an immediate recall task, however. As predicted by the model,

variations in text that were designed to make the rhetorical structure of text more or less apparent influenced the kinds of questions students could answer from a text (van Dijk & Kintsch, 1983; Experiments 5a and 5b). Again predicted, students given higher-order knowledge structures as a context for reading a passage fragment were more likely to generate continuation sentences that were congruent with the knowledge structure and inconsistent with local sentence constraints. Students not given a knowledge structure context generated continuation sentences based on sentence constraints (van Dijk & Kintsch, 1983, Experiments 6). Words from the same macrostructure produce strong priming effects even when the student must infer the macrostructure (van Dijk & Kintsch, 1983, Experiments 2). All these findings are consistent with the model. Of course, any model as complex as the Kintsch-van Dijk model must be evaluated on the basis of many empirical studies. It is likely that the specific model will prove incorrect in details but that reasonable modifications consistent with the overall approach can be found to handle aberrant data.

The Schema-Theoretic View: A General Theoretical Perspective

The van Dijk-Kintsch and Rumelhart-McClelland models fit into the general class of what have been called schema-theoretic models by Adams and Collins (1977). I have used the term *schemata* (singular: schema) several times without examining it in depth. As conceptualized in the schema-theoretic viewpoint, schemata are mental structures that contain the essential aspects of our knowledge of a particular concept or activity. They have been likened to scripts (Rumelhart, 1980; Schank & Abelson, 1975), theories (Rumelhart, 1980), programmed computer procedures (subroutines) (Rumelhart, 1980), and parsers (Rumelhart, 1980). Rumelhart (1980) argues that schemata have the following features:

1. Schemata have variables, 2. schemata can embed in each other, 3. schemata can represent knowledge at all levels of abstraction, 4. schemata represent knowledge rather than definitions, 5. schemata are active processes, and 6. schemata are recognition devices whose processing is aimed at the evaluation of the goodness of fit of the data being processed. (1980, pp. 40–41)

Andre (1984a, b, 1986) has argued that schemata contain a recognition component that determines if they apply to particular input, a set of labeled connections to other schemata in memory, and a production component that carries out the activity of the schemata. The production component can be as simple as a naming function (e.g., input X is a dog) or it can be a complex series of activities (e.g., solving a quadratic equation). Our knowledge store consists of a network of more general to more specific schemata.

The schema-theoretic viewpoint proposed by Adams and Collins can serve as a general theoretical umbrella under which most current cognitive models of comprehension are nested. The schema-theoretic viewpoint contains several fundamental assumptions about comprehension. First of all, Adams and Collins assume that spoken or written language does not carry meaning. Rather, language consists of a set of instructions that lead the reader/listener to construct particular meanings based upon the reader/listener's previously stored schemata (knowledge). The construction of the message is guided by the principle that all of the input language must be "accounted for" or "mapped against some schema, and all aspects of that schema must be compatible with the input." (Adams & Collins, 1977; p. 8). Processing is both bottom-up and top-down as in the Rumelhart-McClelland and Kintsch-van Dijk models. The comprehension system is also bounded by the fact that the reader has a central limited capacity processor, is goal directed (has a motivational system) and has an executive or operating system schema that allocates limited processing resources to various tasks depending upon motivational constraints.

Schemata have at least 6 major functions in reading comprehension and learning (R. C. Anderson, 1984; Anderson & Pearson, 1985; Bransford, 1984). Schemata:

1. Provide ideational scaffolding for assimilating text information
2. Facilitate selective allocation of attention
3. Enable inferential elaboration
4. Allow orderly searches of memory
5. Facilitate editing and summarizing
6. Permit inferential reconstruction (Anderson, 1984; p. 248)

In operation, the schema-theoretic view works similarly to the Rumelhart-McClelland and Kintsch-van Dijk models. The reader begins to read text with particular schemata activated by the context and expectations. These schemata exist at the orthographic, phonological, syntactic, semantic, and world knowledge levels. As the reader begins to process text, schemata at various levels are partially activated as components are detected. The activation of the schemata serves to guide further processing as components consistent with schemata are searched for. As ideas are identified, they are fit into their "slots" in the schemata (ideational scaffolding). The message does not contain all the ideas that are part of the reader's comprehension. The message is fleshed out through elaborative inferences based on the reader's existing knowledge. Schemata produce this inferential elaboration by including details that are part of the reader's world knowledge, but may not be included in the communication. For example, in a story involving getting objects from a grocery store, the reader is likely to infer unmentioned details such as cash registers, conveyer belt counters, and sackers. In addition to content-specific schemata, readers also employ knowledge about language and how to comprehend in the process of comprehension. Such knowledge has been referred to as metacognitive or comprehension monitoring schemata. The role of metacognition in comprehension is discussed later.

Empirical Support for the Schema-Theoretic View

Many studies provide support for the general schema-theoretic model. R. C. Anderson *et al.* (1976) studied the elaborative inferencing process that they called instantiation and demonstrated that readers transform general terms in a text into a more specific instantiation on the basis of general schemata applied to the text. The *woman was outstanding in the theater* is transformed into the "actress was outstanding in the theater." The more specific instantiation (actress) serves as a better retrieval cue for the predicate than the actually presented term (woman).

When readers have schemata to apply to a text, they are more likely to understand and remember the text, to recall and/or misremember details consistent with the applied schemata (Anderson & Pichert, 1978; R. C. Anderson & Shifrin; 1980; R. C. Anderson *et al.*, 1984; Bransford & Franks, 1971; Bransford & Johnson, 1972; Bransford, Barclay, & Franks 1972; Dooling & Lachman, 1971; Pichert & Anderson, 1977; Reynolds, Schwartz, & Esposito, 1982; Spiro, 1977, 1980; Vosniadou & Ortony, 1983). For example, Steffensen, Joag-

Dev, and Anderson (1979) had Asian Indian and American students read letters about an American and an Indian marriage. The presumption was that the students would have different marriage schemata based on their different cultures. Consistent with a schema-theoretic view, in recalls of the letters the students took less time to read passages consistent with their schema, made misinterpretations of the other culture's wedding that were consistent with their own culture's schema, and made more elaborations with their own culture's letter. Additional research consistent with the schema-theoretic perspective is discussed in the following.

Dimensions of Comprehension Models

The schema-theoretic perspective is best viewed not as a specific model of reading comprehension, but as a set of constraining features of a class of models. Models that fit into the schema-theoretic perspective will emphasize the interaction of top-down and bottom-up processing and the role of previous knowledge in determining comprehension of text. It is beyond the scope of this chapter to provide an intensive review of such models. However, De Beaugrande (1981) has provided a description of 16 dimensions along which various models of reading vary. His dimensions are useful in that they help to provide a basis for comparison of models and for understanding features of particular models. De Beaugrande's dimensions include:

1. *Processor Contributions*. This is the top-down/bottom-up dimension. In top-down models, the processor contributes much to the comprehension processes. In bottom-up models, the processor contributes little. In interactive models, both types of processing occur.

2. *Memory Storage*. To the extent that comprehension is reflected in retention, what is the nature of the reading–memory interaction? Based on Royer (1977), De Beaugrande argued that the three main viewpoints are that memory contains only abstracted features of the text (abstractive approach); that the memory trace is based on an integration of previous knowledge and new information (the constructive approach); and that the memory trace is reprocessed and reorganized after the new information is stored (reconstructive approach).

3. *Utilization*. The extent to which a processor analyzes presented materials. In some models, the processor pays minimal attention to input. In others, input information is exhaustively analyzed.

4. *Automatization*. This is the degree to which automatic (nonattention or nonresource demanding, Shiffrin & Schneider, 1977) processes are used in the model and the extent to which conscious control can operate on proposed automatic processes.

5. *Decomposition*. This is the extent to which the model breaks down text elements into "primitives."

6. *Processing depth*. Models differ in the extent to which variations in processing task influence comprehension and retention.

7. *Scale*. This refers to the extent to which the model processes for comprehension only within a local context (understand a word or sentence) or the extent to which comprehension involves the formation of summary or gist statements that cut across sentence boundaries.

8. *Power*. Power is the extent to which the model's processes can apply to a variety of situations and occurrences.

9. *Modularity versus interaction*. This dimension refers to the extent to which each level of language is processed separately (phonemes processed before graphemes, syntax before semantics) or the extent to which these processes are integrated and exchange information.

10. *Serial versus Parallel Processing*. In serial processing, each step in an operation is completed before the next is begun. In parallel processing, operations can occur in parallel. Although it seems likely that human processing occurs in parallel, the issue is difficult to resolve. Models vary in the extent to which they involve parallel or serial processing.

11. *Freedom*. This dimension refers to the extent to which the features of the model are changeable to account for individual and situational differences.

12. *Openness versus Closedness*. Is the model limited to dealing only with the issues it was designed to handle or can it easily be modified without changing the fundamental features of the model?

13. *Logical versus Procedural Adequacy*. Logical adequacy is the ability of a model to handle difficulties and obstacles without breaking down. Logical adequacy refers to the ability to handle constraints of logic; procedural adequacy is the ability to handle actual human operations. These two adequacies may take different priorities for different model designers.

14. *Learning*. This dimension refers to the abil-

ity of the model to change its behavior as it deals with a new task.

15. *Typology of Materials*. This refers to the ability of the model to handle different types of materials, such as narrative or expository prose. Models differ in their ability to adapt to different types of material.

16. *Status of Programming*. This criterion involves the extent to which the model is actualized as a computer program. Designers vary in the extent to which they rely on computer programming as a way of precisely specifying models.

These dimensions are conceptually distinct, but may be correlated in actual proposed models. For example, the modularity-interactive distinction seems to be correlated with the processor contribution dimension. Models that emphasize a heavy processor contribution (much top-down processing) tend to be interactive, not modular. However, this is not a necessary feature of such models.

De Beaugrande discusses how these dimensions apply to several models. Most of the more recent psychological models adopt an interactive position with a heavy component of top-down processing involved in comprehension. Most hold that memory storage of read material can involve constructive and reconstructive processes. Most involve at least some interaction between processes and most strive for procedural adequacy. These positions represent a current consensus among cognitive scientists about the general nature of reading comprehension models. Within this consensus, models vary in the way in which they specifically accomplish particular tasks. Although the "ultimate" model is not yet available, the theorizing/model building activity has already yielded important implications for the analysis of reading difficulties and reading instruction. Some of these implications are discussed below.

Issues in Reading Comprehension Research

As the previous discussion has indicated, the schema-theoretic perspective offers a overarching umbrella for research and conceptualizations about reading comprehension. According to the schema-theoretic view, two types of schemata are involved in the reading comprehension process; these were termed content schemata and process schemata. *Content schemata* involve the schemata invoked by linguistic terms and phrases. Thus content schemata include the schemata that represent particular words as well as more inclusive schemata such as story scripts. *Process schemata* involve the schemata that represent the rules of linguistic processing. Process schemata include syntactical and semantic combinatorial rules or processes and metacognitive/strategic rules and processes. In this section, I examine some currently active areas of reading comprehension research that involve aspects of the role of schemata in the comprehension process. The inclusion of areas of research is based on several factors. One is my view that the area is related to the schema-theoretic prespective. That view is mine and is not necessarily shared by all active researchers in the area. A second factor was my impression that the area is currently active and productive; this factor involves a judgment that discussion of the area was necessary to complete the overview this chapter represents and that the discussion would be of general interest to educational psychologists. Four broad areas are discussed: (a) the role of syntactical schemata in comprehension, (b) the problem and role of metaphor in comprehension, (c) the role of elaboration in facilitating comprehension, and (d) the role of metacognitive factors in comprehension. The purpose of the discussion is to provide the reader with a sense of the nature of current research in the area and to indicate how the research relates to the schema-theorectic perspective. One important area is not discussed: research on letter/word recognition. This area was discussed at some length in the discussion of Rumelhart's and Gough's models above.

Syntactical Factors in Comprehension

Basic Findings. Syntactical processes contrast with semantic processes in that the former are concerned with the rules by which surface combinations of words can be formed or parsed to communicate or apprehend ideas or propositions whereas semantic processes deal with the permissible relationships among concepts or propositions and their relationship to knowledge in general. According to the schema-theorectic perspective, knowledge of syntactical rules is represented by a set of schemata that are activated by particular linguistic constructions. Knowledge of syntax is of obvious importance in an understanding of comprehension; it is the use of syntactical schemata that permits us to comprehend the equivalence between active and passive voice constructions, for example.

Syntax has been studied from a linguistic or a psychological perspective. Although there is no inherent reason why these traditions are different, the current American linguistic perspective attempts to provide a description of the rules of language relying on "purely" linguistic factors (linguistic *competence*) without much concern for psychological factors that may also contribute to actual linguistic *performance* (Morgan & Sellner, 1980). Psychologists (and artificial intelligence researchers) typically have been more concerned with developing models that reflect linguistic performance. When syntax is studied by linguists, what emerges are theories that describe the rules that determine the well-formedness of sentences and discourse, but which are typically insufficient to account for behavior. When psychologists study syntax, what emerges are models that describe the language behavior of language users in typical or prescribed situations. Such models may lack sensitivity to the subtleties of contemporary linguistic distinctions.

Initial linguistic theories of syntax emphasized the analysis of surface structure of sentences into components on the basis of phrase-structure grammars (Huggins & Adams; 1980). Theories based only on surface structure features proved inadequate because they could not distinguish between sentences that had identical surface structures but different underlying patterns of meaning. Chomsky (1957, 1965) proposed a transformational generative grammar in which linguistic communications produced by a speaker/writer emerged from a pattern of underlying "deep" propositions that were changed into a surface structure through the application of a series of transformational rules. A listener/reader applied similar transformational rules in reverse to ascertain the communicative intent. From a linguistic perspective, the transformational grammars were successful in accounting for much of English syntax (Huggins & Adams, 1980).

A number of empirical studies demonstrate that syntactical factors influence perception and retention of sentences. For example, it is generally the case that the greater the number of transformations a surface sentence must undergo to be parsed into deep structure, the more difficult the sentence is to understand and verify (McMahon, 1963; Miller, 1962), although for particular kinds of deletion transformations, the reverse is true (Fodor & Gar-

rett, 1966). The syntactical breakdown of sentences into clauses seems to have a psychological reality. For example, Martin (1970) found that subjects' intuitive organization of sentence components parallel clause breaks. When subjects are asked to judge the position of clicks heard while simultaneously listening to a sentence, the clicks tend to migrate to clause boundaries (Garrett, Bever, & Fodor, 1966). The underlying deep structure as opposed to the surface structure seems to determine where clicks are mislocated (Bever, Lackner, & Kirk, 1969). The occurrence of a clause boundary seems to signal the transformation of the surface structure of the clause into underlying meaning (Jarvella, 1971; Kleinman, 1975).

Syntax across Sentences. Syntactical factors also play a role in comprehension across sentences. Understanding of language requires that meanings be coordinated across sentence boundaries. One set of syntactical rules that must be acquired is that involved in the comprehension of anaphoric references. Anaphora refers to pronouns, some definite nouns, and other linguistic structures that involve reference from one "idea" in one sentence to a second sentence. For example, consider the following sentence pairs:

A. *The boy holding the stick attacked the girl. He hit her with it.*
B. *Fred can program Apple computers in assembly language. Will can too.*
C. *The two 10-year-old boys went fishing. The boat tipped over and the rods were lost.*

In each of these sentence pairs, something in the second sentence refers to an entity in the first sentence. Comprehension of the second sentence must involve being able to connect the element in the second sentence with the appropriate entity in the first sentence. For example, in pair A, there are three anaphoric references involving the three pronouns. In pair B, there is an unstated referent called an ellipsed verb phrase. The "entity" that Will can do is "program Apple computers." The boat in pair C is a definite noun phrase that requires an anaphoric referent to "the boat the boys went fishing in." This latter referent must be inferred in order to understand the two sentences. When the text implicitly or explicitly provides cues to the referent, comprehension is facilitated (Sanford & Garrod, 1981).

The issue of anaphoric reference is a critical one for an adequate theory of comprehension. Webber

(1980) demonstrated that anaphoric reference in English (and presumably other languages) is a complex process involving reference to many different types of referents and that the ability to understand anaphoric referents requires "complex cognitive abilities on the part of any understander." Anaphoric references in spoken or written language occur in a variety of relatively simple and more complex multisentence linguistic expressions. Such situations include "pronouns, proverbs, some definite noun phrases, and ellipses" (Webber, 1980, p 141). An important task is to describe the linguistic situations that permit anaphoric reference and the rules (schemata) readers use to understand anaphoric reference. This task is far from complete.

Given that the ability to understand anaphoric references involves the acquisition of complex linguistic skills, a reasonable prediction is that acquisition of such skills would develop slowly as children mature in language competence. This expectation is confirmed by available research, the ability to understand anaphora increases with age (Bormuth, Manning, Carr, & Pearson, 1970; Chipman & de Dardel, 1974; Lesgold, 1974; Rickek, 1976–1977; Tanz 1977). Unfortunately, this research may have been based on an incomplete conception of anaphora. The researchers seem to have assumed that the referent for anaphoric reference was another explicit text element. Webber (1980) has argued that this assumption was mistaken. In particular, she argues that anaphoric reference is not to specific text elements but to underlying meaning referents. She argues further that there are two basic classes of anaphoric reference, one based on syntactical considerations and one based on semantic considerations. This is similar to a distinction made by Sanford and Garrod (1982) between text-based and situation-based anaphora. With respect to the development of anaphoric comprehension, Webber argues that the available research does not permit us to determine if children initially "understand" anaphora by reference to explicit text elements and later shift to understanding by reference to underlying discourse structures.

The problem of reference is an important one in a model of text comprehension. Although some forms of references are signaled by syntactic cues, it seems likely that, as Webber suggests, a complete solution of reference must also make use of schemata in long-term memory to resolve reference (this is called pragmatics by linguists, see Morgan & Green, 1980, for a discussion). For example, the connections in the previous example between boat and rods in Example C seem to be based on a fishing schema. How the ability to understand anaphoric reference develops, what are the nature of the schemata involved in anaphoric reference, and how can the development of these schemata be best facilitated in educational situations are issues that have not been examined deeply by educational psychologists involved in reading comprehension. Explorations of these issues represent an important direction for future research.

Metaphor and Comprehension

One central issue in comprehension and in theories/models of comprehension is that of metaphor. The problem with metaphors is that they use concepts in a nonliteral sense. This same problem occurs in other rhetorical devices, such as nonliteral similes and analogies, and I will not try to deal with the distinctions between these terms. Roughly speaking, a simile is a comparison with a stated "like" or "as" (*Your beauty is like a flower);* a metaphor is an attribution of the sum of properties of one entity to another in a nonobvious or nontypical way (*The tires formed castle walls in the snow);* and an analogy is a comparison between relationships (*Night is to day as death is to birth).* I will use the term *metaphor* as a generic term to cover all such devices in this discussion. The fundamental comprehension issue with metaphor is determining how a concept, when used in a nontypical sense, can be understood (Ortony, 1980).

Ortony (1980) described three classes of theories about metaphors. The substitution view is that metaphors are dispensable literary devices. The comparison view is that a metaphor is an implied comparison and that an obvious similarity between the compared terms must be available if the metaphor is to be understood. The interactive view is that the interaction of terms in the metaphor produces a new concept. Ortony finds each of these views inadequate on grounds that are too complex to discuss here. He has, however, (1979) proposed a theory of the understanding of metaphor that was based on a modification of Tversky's model of similarity. Basically, the theory holds that each of the entities compared in a metaphor have a set of characteristics that are more or less salient in the context in which they are presented.

In my view, these characteristics can be understood as components of the schemata invoked by the terms of the metaphor. For example, in this metaphor, *books are horses for children's intelligence,* each of the substance words invokes a schema, which have particular default characteristics. Ortony argues that when the same characteristics of both entities are salient, a literal and not a metaphorical similarity statement has been made (*A bicycle tire is like a motorcycle tire.*). When the salient characteristics of the second term are low salient characteristics of the first term, a metaphorical similarity statement is made. (This could be a simile, metaphor, or an analogy, depending on its rhetorical form, e.g., *A harmonious class is a symphony. Her hair was a well tended lawn.*) When the compared terms do not match except on low salient characteristics of both, an anomolous or ineffective metaphor is created, (e.g., *Children are like picture frames.*) An interesting case is when high salient characteristics of the first term match low salient characteristics of the second term, in such cases dull and ineffective metaphors are created. Ortony (1979) uses this example: *Sleeping pills are like sermons* (p. 165). This is a much less effective metaphorical statement than the reversed *Sermons are like sleeping pills,* although the latter is now hackneyed. I think Ortony's model can be better understood if it is described from the perspective of schema theory. Recall that a schema is an entity that actively searches for elements in our perceptual input stream that will activate the schema. A metaphor can be considered to be an instruction to a comprehender to activate a particular schema and use it to process a particular set of input characteristics when that schema would not normally be used. For example, my earlier horse metaphor can be interpreted as an instruction to use the horse schema to process the book and intelligence schemata. To carry out the instruction, the reader would have to ask, how can the elements (characteristics) of the intelligence and books schemata be made to fit into slots of the horse schemata.

Ortony (1979) went on to describe the factors that contribute to the salience of entity characteristics. These details are too complex for the space available here. However, Ortony's model provides an interesting approach to the problem of understanding metaphors. Some support for the model was provided in a study by Baldwin, Luce, and Readence (1982). They found that fifth graders' ability to comprehend metaphors were strongly correlated with the ability to identify sali-

ent characteristics of the component terms. Providing students with attribute cuing facilitated understanding. Considerably more substantiation is needed, but Ortony's model does provide an account subject to empirical verification.

Research on the understanding of metaphors has developed along three separate lines. One line of research has examined the development of metaphorical understanding. A second line of research has examined metaphorical understanding in adults. A third line of research has examined the use of metaphors in improving educational communications.

Developmental Research on Metaphor. Developmental research on metaphors has examined the ability of children of different ages to use and explain metaphors. An excellent review of the research is provided in Ortony, Reynolds, and Arter (1978). In general, the research indicates that the ability to understand metaphors increases with age (Asch & Nerlove, 1960; Billow, 1975; Demorest, Silberstein, Gardner, & Winner, 1983). However, Ortony, Reynolds, *et al.* (1978) point out that the research confounds other types of knowledge (vocabulary world knowledge) that increase with age with metaphorical ability. Hence, the performance differences among ages may be attributed to factors besides metaphorical ability. Some evidence that children can process metaphors at young ages is provided by a study by Gentner (1977) that asked children aged 4 to 5 and college students to map elements of faces onto inanimate objects, a task that is metaphorical in nature. Both the children and the college students did well with the task and Gentner concluded that metaphorical ability is available to young children. Similarly, Vosniadou and Ortony (1983) found evidence for rudimentary metaphoric ability in 4-year-olds. Similar conclusions using a different paradigm were provided by Honeck, Sowry, and Voegtle (1978). Whatever the age that children can comprehend some forms of metaphors, it seems clear that there is growth in the ability to comprehend metaphors with age. Using a paradigm that answers many of Ortony's criticisms, Nippold, Leonard, and Kall (1984) found that 9-year-olds understood metaphors better than 7-year-olds even when the underlying key words and semantic features of the concepts were known to the students. Finally, when children are given formal instruction in metaphor use, their ability to use and understand metaphorical language increases (Horne, 1966; Pollio & Pollio, 1974).

Adult Studies of Metaphor Comprehension. Verbrugge and McCarrell (1977) applied the notion of encoding specificity to a model of metaphor comprehension. They argued that a metaphor is understood when the reader infers the unexpressed connection between the topic and the comparative term. If that is the case, the encoding specificity principle suggests that a statement of the connection should be a good retrieval cue for the original sentences. This hypothesis was supported and demonstrated to provide a more sufficient explanation of the findings than three alternative competing hypotheses. Ortony, Reynolds, *et al.,* (1978) however suggested that the Verbrugge and McCarrall study supported three major conclusions. Adults easily and consistently comprehend metaphors. Metaphor comprehension involved an implicit comparison between the topic and the comparative term, and comprehension of the metaphor emphasizes particular attributes of the topic at the expense of other attributes.

Osborn and Ehninger (cited in Reinsch, 1971) suggested that metaphorical processing occurs in three stages: error, puzzlement-recoil, and resolution. The error stage occurs when readers attempt to understand a metaphorical statement literally. The inability to produce literal comprehension then produces puzzlement, and reprocessing in a non-literal way leads to resolution. These three stages seem to suggest that literal processing of metaphors occurs before an attempt to process metaphorically occurs. Brewer, Harris, and Brewer (cited in Ortony, Reynolds, 1978 *et al.*) proposed and tested a similar model. Their data supported the notion that literal processing is attempted before metaphorical processing.

Conflicting evidence however, was presented by Glucksberg, Gildea, and Bookin (1982). In their study, students were presented with literally false statements that could either be metaphorically true or false (e.g., *Administrators are plumbers. Watermelons are yellow paint).* The first could be metaphorically true; both administrators and plumbers could be considered to deal with unsavory tasks. The latter does not seem to me to have a compelling metaphorical interpretation. Glucksberg *et al.* reasoned that if literal interpretation is first attempted subjects should be able to state equally quickly that both metaphorically true and metaphorically false statements are literally false. Reactions times, however, were longer for metaphorically true statements. Glucksberg *et al.* argued these results implied simultaneous processing of both metaphorical and literal meaning. Results supporting that notion were also presented by Ortony, Schallert, Reynolds, and Antos (1978). Their data suggested that the order of processing may be dependent on the context in which metaphors are presented. In their study, when a sufficiently detailed context was presented permitting the evocation of a schema that would account for the metaphor, time to comprehend the metaphorical statement was equivalent to the time to comprehend a literal statement. When an insufficiently detailed context was presented, metaphorical statements took longer to comprehend. In a related fashion, Gildea and Glucksberg (1983) examined the role of three types of context on the comprehension of metaphors. All three types of context facilitated comprehension compared to no context. The authors suggested that the results supported a notion that both literal and nonliteral understanding involves the automatic use of general discourse-processing strategies. Finally, Pollio, Fabrizi, Sills, and Smith (1984), using a sentence coding task in which subjects coded sentences in one of several categories, found that metaphoric comprehension did not take longer than literal comprehension.

The results of research on children and adults suggest that understanding of metaphor is a typical linguistic task that develops as children grow in linguistic competence. Ortony (1975, 1976) has argued that metaphor represents a basic means by which humans understand. If this is true and if the schema-theoretic view of metaphorical understanding has some validity, then the issue of metaphor is a critical one for educational psychologists interested in the role of comprehension in instruction. Stated in schematic-theoretic terms, the basic proposition I am arguing is that much of human understanding consists of processing the elements of one situation through the constraints of a second known schemata. When the first situation is a known schema, the comparison of schemata is a typical linguistic metaphor. When the first situation is a relatively new experience for the individual then the processing the new experience through the known schema provides a means of understanding the new experience. There are two cases of interest. First, if the new experience fits the known schema very well, then what occurs is recognition of an example of a concept. (e.g., this new perceptual experience is a *cow;* by denying me access to the information my boss treated me *unfairly;* The known schema in each sentence is italicized). Second, if the new experience fits the known schema only partially well, so that there are significant descrepancies in the goodness of fit, then the metaphorical processing leads to the development of an initial representation of the new experience. This initial representation can be modified and developed with subsequent experience into a new schema.

This latter point suggests that one way new schemata develop is by an initial metaphorical representation based on a previously acquired schema. It should be noted that this conceptualization is very similar to Piagetian notions of the growth of schemata based on assimilation, accomodation, and elaboration, and also to Ausubel's ideas about comparative organizers. One implication of this conceptualization is that the provision of metaphor or other figurative language within instructional materials and communications may facilitate acquisition of new schemata. This position has been argued by several researchers and some empirical research supports this hypothesis. This research is discussed in the following section.

Metaphor and The Facilitation of Learning

As noted earlier, Ortony (1980) has argued that metaphorical language plays an important role in learning and discovery. In support, he mentioned anecdotal evidence collected by Hadamard (1949) that supports the role of metaphor in scientific discovery. Further, several recent empirical studies have supported the importance of metaphors in communicating new ideas. For example, Mayer (1975) found that providing analogical models for computer programming functions facilitated the learning of programming by low ability students. Later, Mayer (1980) taught students a file-management computer language employing either metaphorical or nonmetaphorical instruction. Students who received metaphorical instruction that compared the operations in the language of typical office functions were better able to solve new problems in the language. Similarly, Royer and Cable (1975), Royer and Perkins (1977) and Perkins (1978) demonstrated that having students read a concrete analogical passage prior to reading an abstract text facilitated learning of the abstract material. In a related study, Arter (1976, cited in Ortony, 1980) had students read a passage about Bigfoot. Half the students read a passage containing metaphorical descriptions; half read a passage

containing parallel literal descriptions. Students who received the metaphorical version learned more. Similarly, Pearson, Raphael, Te Paske and Hyser (1979) found that children were better able to remember metaphorical descriptions than their literal equivalents. Likewise, Reynolds and Schwartz (1983) found that gist recall of passages containing metaphorical conclusion statements was superior to gist recall of the same passages containing literal concluding statements. A similar result is reported by Reynolds (1985, personal communication). In that latter study, gist, but not verbatim, recall of passages was facilitated by metaphor summary statements. All of these findings are consistent with the schema-theoretic conceptualization of metaphor I presented earlier.

Reading Comprehension and Elaboration

The level- or depth-of-processing hypothesis proposed by Craik and Lockhart (1972) and Jacoby and Craik (1979) has been extended to the learning and comprehension of prose. Originally developed in the context of word-list studies, the hypothesis was an alternative to multiple memory structure models, such as Atkinson and Shiffren's (1968), and basically held that verbal input could be analyzed at any of several levels ranging from basic low-level perceptual features to high-level construction of a mental representation of semantic meaning. The memorability of input increased as it was processed to a greater depth (or higher level).

Because text is composed of words and similarly contains many levels that may be analyzed, orthographic, phonemic, syntactic, semantic, and schematic, etc., it seems clear that a depth-of-processing model could be developed for text as well as for word-list studies. A number of authors (J. R. Anderson & Reder, 1979; R. C. Anderson, 1972; Reder, 1980; Schallert, 1976) have proposed such extensions and have argued that the degree to which readers relate information presented in text to information existing in memory and draw inferences on the material influences the comprehension and memorability of the presented information. Such models of text learning have been called elaboration models.

Although these views developed somewhat independently, in my view there are strong parallels between elaboration models and the schema-theoretic view of reading. Both views assume that text is processed at a variety of levels; importantly, both views argue that information already existing in the reader's memory is used to understand and draw inferences from the information presented in text; and the two views have generated some similar research studies. Theorists from the two perspectives have referenced similar studies (compare the references in Reder, 1980, and Anderson & Pearson, 1985). Finally, Reder (1980) called her final model a script-elaboration model and documented its relationship to schema-theoretic conceptions. My point is that elaboration models fit within the general perspective that I have called the schema-theoretic view. In this section, I discuss some of the research carried out from the elaboration perspective. I have two purposes in this discussion. First, this chapter attempts to provide an overview of some currently active areas of research in reading comprehension; the elaboration research represents an important tradition within that area. Second, because of the strong similarities between the elaboration and schema-theoretic views, I believe that research consistent with the elaboration view is also consistent with the schema-theoretic perspective.

Empirical Support for the Elaboration Perspective. Numerous studies support the elaboration position. For example, Schallert (1976) had subjects read ambiguous passages in either a context that biased a particular interpretation or did not. Subjects were led to process at either a low level, by counting four letter words, or at a semantic level by rating the degree of ambiguity. Analysis of recall indicated that subjects who received a disambiguating context and processed at a deep level were more likely to recall details consistent with the context. Brown, Smiley, Day, Townsend, and Lawton (1977) reported similar results. Children at several grade levels read a passage about a primitive tribe that was said to be either Eskimos or desert dwellers. Later, the children read a second passage about a boy in the tribe; recalls indicated that intepretations of ambiguous sentences and intrusions were consistent with the biasing interpretation. Older children displayed the elaborative effect more strongly. Reder (1979) demonstrated that the speed of judging the plausibility of statements related to a story that had been read was related to the number of elaborations made. Wagner and Rohwer (1981) similarly reported a developmental trend in inferential elaboration. In that study, preadolescents displayed less elaboration than did late adolescents, but only when the text did not explicitly support inferential elaboration. When statements were added to the text to

make the required inferences more explicit, the differences between the groups were reduced because the younger students were now able to make many of the elaborations.

The similarity of these findings to the results of studies of perspective taking on a story or passage should be noted. The reader will recall that the theme or perspective taken by a reader influences the details that the reader recalls from a story (Pichert & Anderson, 1977). It is a reasonable contention that the elaborations made by the reader as he or she attempts to comprehend the text are influenced by the general perspective taken. R. C. Anderson, Pichert, and Shirey (1983) propose this basic conclusion from research on story perspectives; "First, readers make inferences consistent with their schemata. Second, they recall more text information important to their schemata." (R. C. Anderson *et al.*, 1983, p 271). These authors go on to demonstrate that a perspective introduced prior to reading a passage influences the encoding given to a passage. The conclusion seems clear that both the elaboration and schema-theoretic lines of research provide very consistent and complementary results.

Adjunct Questions, Elaboration, and Comprehension. If elaborative processing of material facilitates its comprehension and retention, it is a natural instructional activity to attempt to influence students to make more effective elaborations. One line of research has focused on the role of leading students to engage in elaborative processing by asking questions about the material or by directing students to engage in particular activities while reading. When students are asked factual questions about particular items of information in a passage, they are more likely to remember that information (R. C. Anderson & Biddle, 1975; Andre, 1979, in press; Rickards, 1979). This effect is well known and could be predicted from a variety of theoretical perspectives.

More directly relevant to schema theory and the elaboration position are studies that have examined the effects of different levels of questions on learning and retention. For example, Andre (1981), Andre and Sola (1976), and Andre and Womack (1978) compared the effect of verbatim and paraphrased instructional questions on a posttest requiring encoding of the underlying meaning of passage propositions. The elaboration position would predict that paraphrased questions during instruction would be more effective because they would induce a greater depth of semantic encoding. As predicted, students who received adjunct questions performed better. The effects of paraphrasing were also examined by Pio and Andre (1981). In that study, some groups of students were led to paraphrase highlighted statements in text whereas other groups did not paraphrase. The paraphrasing groups performed better on the posttest. Similar findings were reported by Glover, Plake, Roberts, Zimmer, and Palmere (1981). In that study, students were led to paraphrase paragraphs, make logical extension statements, study model statements, or define key words while reading a passage. The students who paraphrased or made logical extension statements while studying recalled more ideas from the passage. Later Glover, Bruning, and Plake (1982) had college students read paragraphs containing scrambled or nonscrambled summary sentences. They argued that the scrambled summary sentences would lead to a more distinctive encoding that would enhance recall. This prediction was confirmed. In addition, subjects who paraphrased scrambled summary statements recalled both more idea units from the summary sentences and also more idea units from the paragraphs those statements summarized. Both of these results are consistent with the idea that activities that increase the elaborative processing of text will lead to better comprehension and recall. Glover, Plake, and Zimmer (1982) reported similar results. In a related study, Palmere, Benton, Glover, and Ronning (1983) had students read passages in which the main idea sentences were supported by zero to three supporting sentences. Across four experiments recall of the main idea sentences improved with the number of supporting details presented. In a fifth experiment, Palmere *et al.* had students respond to zero to three adjunct questions about the supporting details. Recall of main ideas improved as more questions about supporting details were answered. The requirement of answering questions seemed to increase the effectiveness of having more supporting details.

The role of adjunct questions in increasing elaborative processing and comprehension has also been examined in the context of studying the acquisition of concepts from text. When students read text that contains new concepts, they are typically presented with a concept description and an example or two. It is a reasonable hypothesis that students asked to engage in the elaborative processing necessary to recognize a new example of the concept will learn the concept better than students who are merely asking questions that require

simple factual recall. This use of adjunct questions has been tested in a variety of experiments. For example, Watts and Anderson (1971) reported that students given application adjunct questions were better able to use the concepts in a transfer situation than students given factual questions. Although this manipulation has produced somewhat inconsistent results (Andre, 1979; Andre, Mueller, Womack, Smid, & Tuttle, 1980), the inconsistencies were probably related to variations in the procedural details of the studies.

For example, Andre and Reiher (1983) suggested that the delay between passage study and the criterion test may be related to the effect of adjunct application questions. In that study this hypothesis was confirmed. Adjunct application questions, as compared with adjunct factual questions, facilitated transfer to new applications of the same concepts only after a delay between passage study and test. With an immediate test, no differences were found.

Another procedural variation that may influence the results of adjunct questions studies is the number of questions asked. Most studies have used only one adjunct question per concept. Tennyson and Rothen (1977) found that several application questions per concept were needed in order to produce reliable transfer of the concept to new applications. Similarly, Mayer (1980) found that adjunct questions demanding elaboration and application facilitated the learning of programming skills.

Recent studies of adjunct questions have employed the schema-theoretic view in the design of the questions. Pearson and Johnson (1978) proposed a tripartite taxonomy of questions based on schema theory. *Text explicit questions* simply required repetition of information presented explicitly in the text. *Text implicit questions* required an inference from information presented in the text. *Schema inference questions* required the students to relate text material to previous knowledge in a way that activated a schema for understanding the text. Several researchers have used the Pearson and Johnson model (or related models) to generate adjunct questions for research on reading comprehension and learning. Wixson (1983a), for example, had fifth grade students answer either text explicit, text implicit, or schema inference questions while reading. After a week, subjects recalled the experimental passages. Students who answered inference questions produced more propositions in their recall than students who answered text explicit questions. Further, the nature of the recalls were different between the text implicit and schema inference groups. Schema inference students produced more extrapassage propositions in their recalls; text implicit students produced more intrapassage connecting propositions. Similar results were also reported by Wixson (1983b, 1984) and Kormos (1983), who found that text implicit and schema inference adjunct questions led to more inference propositions in recall. In a follow-up analysis, Kormos (1984) found that the type of adjunct question interacted with the type of story schema. The third graders found it easier to generate schema inferences with a story based on a conversational schema, but found it difficult to generate inferences based on a problem-solution schema. These results suggest that, as predicted by schema theory, students must possess the requisite schemata before questions based on those schemata can be effective as instructional adjuncts to prompt appropriate elaborations and inferences. In another series of adjunct-questions studies based on the Pearson-Johnson taxonomy (summarized in Raphael, 1984), Raphael and her co-workers have demonstrataed that the ability to answer inference questions increases with grade level and with intellectual ability. In addition, students can be trained to answer questions of the three types. The training effects of these studies are discussed more completely in the section below on comprehension instruction.[1]

---

[1] The value of the adjunct questions research for practical learning situations has been questioned (T. H. Anderson, 1980; Duchastel, 1983). The point of these criticisms is that the constraints of the typical adjunct questions research are not ecologically valid and cannot be extended to the classroom situation. Although I agree that adjunct questions research has used procedures that do not match those of some typical classroom, I am not sure that this fact invalidates the questions research. First of all, most of the adjunct questions research was not designed to be directly applicable to classrooms, but was designed to reveal processes that operate when students answer questions about material they have read. Extensions to the classroom would have to be based on the theoretical generalizations that evolve, not on a mindless application of the research procedures employed. In addition, there are many educational situations that parallel important features of the adjunct questions research. For example, elementary school students receive a lesson and then complete workbook exercises on it; high school or college students receive a lecture in math or biology and then complete a homework assignment on that lesson. I would expect that the adjunct questions research should be relevant in those situations. Although such research does not yet exist, I believe it offers a promising field for future research.

Metacognitive Components of Reading

Metacognition refers to the cognitive processes we employ to control our own cognitive processes. Metacognitive processes are conscious and involve choice. They contrast with more automatic cognitive processes that seem to occur below our level of consciousness and operate without direct attention (Brown, 1980; Baker & Brown, 1985). As noted above, from the schema-theoretic perspective, metacognitive skills fall within the class of textual or text-processing schemata as opposed to the class of content schemata. Research on the role of metacognitive schemata in reading comprehension represents a very active and fruitful area of research. The sense of what is meant by metacognitive schemata in reading comprehension is best gained by describing how they would operate in reading.

For adults who are reading a relatively easy text, such as a novel, the cognitive processes involved in reading operate pretty much automatically. Such readers do not consciously try to construct the meaning of sentences, paragraphs, and the like, rather the novel's action flows relatively easily. Only if something unusual happened, for example, a printer's error that omitted part of a sentence, will the normal reading flow be interrupted. Then the reader will try to make sense out of the confusing part. Brown (1980) and Woods (1980) refer to the normal reading state as the "automatic pilot state," to the unusual event that interferes with the normal flow as a "triggering event," and to attempts to figure out what is wrong as a "debugging state." The activities of the debugging state are metacognitive activities. Other metacognitive activities involve planning how to read the chapter and conscious reviewing and summarizing. Brown (1980) lists the following among metacognitive activities involved in reading:

1. Clarifying the purposes of reading, . . . understanding the task demands
2. Identifying the important aspects of the message
3. Allocating attention so that concentration can be focused on major content.
4. Monitoring ongoing activities to determine whether comprehension is occurring.
5. Engaging in review and self-interrogations to determine whether goals are being achieved
6. Taking corrective action when failures in comprehension are detected
7. Recovering from disruptions and distractions—and many more deliberate, planful activities that render reading an efficient information-gathering activity. (p. 456)

Items 5 to 7 are sometimes referred to as comprehension monitoring strategies. Comprehension monitoring involves ascertaining the status of one's understanding, detecting difficulties in comprehension, and carrying out activities to increase understanding when difficulties arise. Brown (1984) quotes some interesting examples of young readers' failure to engage in adequate monitoring.

I stare real hard at the page, blink my eyes and then open them . . . cross my fingers that it will be right here. (pointing to head). . . . I read the first line of every paragraph. (Brown, 1984, p. 3)

There is considerable evidence that children have difficulty in carrying out metacognitive activities/comprehension monitoring and that metacognitive skills improve with development (Brown, 1975, 1978, 1980; Brown & Lawton, 1977; Brown & Smiley, 1978; Brown, Campione, & Barclay, 1978). Many of the difficulties involve detection of inconsistencies or missing information. For example, Markman (1975, 1977) found that children as old as sixth graders were unable to determine what was wrong with incomprehensible paragraphs without aid and to perceive difficulties with incomprehensible instructions for a game. In a related finding Robinson and Robinson (1976a, b) reported similar findings and indicated that young children often perceived the difficulty in comprehension to be their fault rather than the fault of the message even when the message was very confused. Patterson, O'Brien, Kister, Carter, and Kotinis (1981) also obtained similar results, but by videotaping the children, found nonverbal evidence that the children reacted to weak communications. Similarly, Markman (1979) found that third, fifth, and sixth grade students had difficulty detecting both explicit and implicit inconsistencies in a series of short essays. Part but not all of the problem had to do with ability to recall the text. In a second study designed to minimize the influence of differential recall, Markman found that 6th graders but not 3rd graders, improved on detecting inconsistency. Markman and Gorin (1981) also found that 8- and 10-year-old students had difficulty detecting errors in truth (external inconsistency) and in logic (internal inconsistency). However, errors in truth were easier to detect than were logic errors and 10-year-olds were influenced by sets to respond to one type of error or the other. Sensitivity to inconsistency and other text difficulties also varies with ability—good readers are more sensitive to problems than are poor readers (Canney & Winograd, 1979; Owings, Petersen, Bransford, Morris, & Stein, 1980).

A number of other metacognitive skills develop with age. For example, young elementary school children have difficulty knowing what they already know and do not exhibit the tip-of-the-tongue phenomenon until the middle school years (Brown, 1980, Brown & Lawton, 1977; Wellman, 1977). Elementary school children also do not understand what they need to know in order to perform a task. For example, Brown and Campione (1977) presented children with a multitrial free recall task and asked the children to select half the items for study on each trial. After Grade 3, students used the strategy of selecting items they had missed for more study; but prior to that age level, items seemed to be selected randomly. Further, they have difficulty distinguishing between hard and easy learning tasks (Brown, 1978, 1980). In this vein, Kreutzer, Leonard, and Flavell (1975) reported that prior to Grade 5 children are not aware that reporting the gist of a story in their own words is easier than reporting verbatim recall. Children also have difficulty selecting the main idea of passages, but performance varies with difficulty of the passage, ability of the subject, and age (Brown, 1980).

All of these skills or behaviors involve the effective use of metacognitive strategies. In an excellent review of comprehension monitoring research, Wagoner (1983) concludes that there is typical developmental trend in the acquisition of comprehension monitoring. Young children have difficulty recognizing and verbalizing comprehension problems. Truth problems and problems involving main ideas are detected at earlier ages than logic problems or problems involving minor details. As children get older, a set to detect problems can influence detection favorably. Good readers at all ages are more likely to detect comprehension difficulties than poor readers. Taken as a whole, it seems that problems in reading often involve a lack of needed skills in the detection and remediation of comprehension difficulties. A natural hypothesis that derives from this research is that more direct instruction in comprehension skills can facilitate reading performance. In the next section, I examine some reasons for weaknesses in comprehension skills and discuss instructional research designed to improve such skills.

Teaching Reading Comprehension Skills

Because a primary purpose of teaching reading in the schools is to allow students to use reading to understand new information, it may seem a truism that students would be taught comprehension skills. Unfortunately, several recent studies indicate that the direct teaching of comprehension is not a common event in reading programs. Instead, the teaching of comprehension seems to be indirect, as students complete activities designed to provide opportunities to practice comprehension skills. In this section, I discuss research on the current status of comprehension instruction and then discuss research motivated by a schema-theoretic perspective that attempts to provide more direct comprehension instruction.

Jenkins and Pany (1980) and Rosenschine (1980) reviewed the comprehension instruction practices of common reading programs. The most common instructional tools for teaching reading are basal reader series. Basal series contain (a) teacher's manual with relatively explicit directions for using the basal reader, (b) collections of stories and selections (the books seen by children), and (c) workbooks designed to provide individual practice activities for students. Approximately 95% of elementary school children use a basal reader series on all or most of their school days (Jenkins & Pany, 1980). Rosenschine (1980) collected the descriptions of comprehension skills presumably taught by five different commonly used basal reader programs. Although different publishers may give skills different names, there are important commonalities across the programs in identified skills. Moreover, these skill names are clearly related to important aspects of reading comprehension. Individuals who can comprehend what they read are able to "paraphrase and summarize"; show "empathy" by recognizing "character's emotions and traits"; and are able to interpret negative, passive voice, and right branching sentences. Note that in the schema-theoretic view such skills represent text processing schemata activated in reading comprehension.

Such lists of skills are descriptions of behavior that competent readers are able to perform. The lists can be extended by making the task description more specific. For example, V. Anderson (1976), cited in Rosenschine, provides this description of the subskills in learning from context:

- Contrast clues such as those provided by "but" and "also"
- Description clues such as "is," "is like," and "was"
- Synonym or antonym clues
- Summary clues
- Clues provided by tone, setting, and mode
- Clues provided by words in a series
- Clues derived from the main idea and supporting details
- Prepositional clues
- Clues derived from cause and effect pattern of sentence meaning.

(Rosenschine, 1980, p. 540)

As Rosenschine points out, if all aspects of reading are analyzed to this level, then the number of skills or subskills involved in reading is very large.

Regardless of the number of skills identified, the way in which such skills are presented in reading programs may be more important. Jenkins and Pany (1980) analyzed the activities provided in the Ginn, Economy, and Scott-Foresman series. The number of activities allocated to a particular skill varied considerably between series. A similar finding is reported by Armbruster, Stevens, and Rosenschine (1977), who reported that between-basal series correlations in the number of exercises for a particular skill ranged from −.08 to .43. Jenkins and Pany found that instruction in these skills across three series consisted mainly of a teacher-led discussions of a skill being taught followed by workbook practice. Jenkins and Pany also examined the Distar reading series, a behaviorally based series developed partly in conjunction with the Follow Through project. This series programs teacher behavior more explicitly than do the basal series, is explicit in teaching rules for carrying out skills, and provides for a more demanding criterion of mastery.

In another analysis of reading series, Durkin (1981) examined comprehension instruction practices in five basal teaching manuals. Durkin distinguished between direct expository instruction on comprehension and indirect instruction in which students are either told about a topic without it being explained or are given practice on the topic without adequate explanation. Durkin's basic findings were that instances of direct instruction in comprehension were a relatively infrequent part of the instruction suggested by the manuals. Durkin also classified suggestions for teaching in the manuals as instances of direct instruction, application, practice, review of instruction, preparation, and assessment. Of 12,370 suggestions for instruction classified, 500 or 4% were instances of direct instruction.[2]

Durkin included any suggestion for direct instruction, no matter how brief or imprecise, in the category of instruction. So a suggestion to "review that a comma suggests that a reader should pause" (Durkin, 1981, p. 523) was included in the instruction category. In the application category were activities that involved teacher-led use of a skill. Usually, the manuals did not include specific directions to the teacher on how to provide instruction in this context. Typically, the manuals led teachers to use the application activity more as a group assessment device than as a direct instruction procedure.

Durkin (1981) concluded that basal manuals do not lead teachers to provide sufficient attention to comprehension training. In her view, basal reading series provide insufficient direct instruction in comprehension and the instruction that is provided is often directed to the more easily identified and learned comprehension skills. Much of the instruction is concentrated on recognizing graphic comprehension signals, signal words, and within-sentence comprehension cues; little direct instruction is directed to between sentence and schemata-based inferential training. Durkin believed this emphasis is misplaced. In general, Durkin concluded that basal series devote too much attention to assessment and practice and not enough to direct instruction.

If the manuals and basal series were modified in practice by teachers so as to include more direct instruction and explanation, then Durkin's analysis might be somewhat academic. Unfortunately, an earlier study by Durkin (1979) suggested that teachers follow manuals very closely and provide relatively little direct comprehension instruction. Durkin (1979) and her coworkers observed 7500 minutes of reading and social studies instruction in 24 different schools in 13 districts in Grades 3 to 6.

Approximately 28 minutes went to direct comprehension instruction. If all of categories that might possibly involve some comprehension instruction are included, about 456 minuted (6.3%) of the classroom time involved direct instruction in comprehension. No instances of direct instruction in comprehension were observed during social studies activities. More detailed analyses were made of 12 fourth grades in three different schools. By Durkin's count, out of 2174 minutes of instruction observed, 4 minutes involved direct comprehension instruction.

Particularly interesting is the fact that no instances of application of comprehension rules materials instructed about were observed. A reasonable instructional procedure would involve presenting a comprehension rule, then giving students practice in using the rule. As noted, Durkin did not observe this procedure being followed. Instead, teachers seemed to provide a brief bit of comprehension instruction and then shifted to an unrelated exercise. If comprehension was not taught, what was? The categories of activities in the reading period with the largest proportion of time devoted to them were assessment of comprehension, noninstruction, transition, and listening to oral reading. These accounted for 48.6% of reading time. Durkin characterized the role of the teacher as that of " 'mentioners,' assignment givers and checkers, and interrogators." Because there was a heavy reliance on workbooks and ditto sheets, Durkin suggested that "do what is easy" was a prime force motivating these instructors. She argued that a much more explicit instruction in comprehension skills is needed. Durkin's conclusions are buttressed by the results of a study by Osborn (1984). During observations of 90 reading periods involving 45 teachers in Grades 1 through 6, a heavy reliance on prepared publishers' materials and workbooks was noted.

The heavy reliance on workbooks and ditto sheets found by Durkin and Osborn might be appropriate if such practice exercise provided meaningful guided experience that led students to develop comprehension skills. Osborn (1984) has reviewed workbooks from several series and has questionned the value of many of the exercises. According to her review, workbooks frequently contain: (a) irrelevant activities, (b) vocabulary in the directions that is not exact or is inconsistent with other parts of the lesson, (c) confusing directions, and/or (e) inaccurate directions. Osborn

[2]Examining Durkin's descriptions of the categories, it is possible, though not necessary, that direct instruction occurred in the categories of review, application, and preparation. If all instances of these categories were included then 42% of the suggestions may have led to some direct instruction. In my view, the 4% figure probably underestimates the amount of direct instruction implied by the manuals, but the 42% figure would be a gross overestimate of the amount of direct instruction. Durkin's conclusion that basal teaching manuals provide for relatively little direct instruction in comprehension skills is fundamentally sound.

marshalls an impressive array of bad examples to illustrate her claims and suggests that the examples she selects are not isolated instances but are at least typical of a substantial proportion of workbook exercises.

My favorite bad example is based on a lesson that presumably teaches students to discriminate fiction from nonfiction (Example 7, p. 65). Although the class instruction discussed fiction and nonfiction, the workbook instructions asked the students to classify each of four paragraphs as "real" or "not real," an inconsistency in language that Osborn points out. A more important objection may be that all four of the paragraphs are probably fiction. Two are fantasy fiction; that is, they involve violations of the natural rules of this universe. The other two selections do not involve obvious violations, but a reader has no way of knowing whether they are fiction or are descriptive reports of the actual behavior of real characters. Are they real or not real? Is realistic fiction real? In my view, such an exercise must teach mis-comprehension rather than comprehension.

Taken as a whole, these studies of the characteristics of reading instruction, basal readers, and workbooks paint a disappointing view of the state of reading comprehension instruction. Comprehension instruction consists mostly of being asked to accomplish comprehension tasks, sometimes after being told briefly about the task, sometimes without any real direction. What this suggests is that for most children, learning to comprehend written language is a discovery learning task. From a variety of presented examples, terms, and workbook exercises, students draw some impressions of what is to understand about what they read. For some students, the process probably works reasonably well. These students probably have higher ability and are able to carry out relatively independently the necessary inductive reasoning to discover the skills. Alternatively, they may have received extensive modeling from reading activities carried out in the home. Other students, particularly hard to teach students, probably fail to do the necessary discovery and instead discover alternative coping strategies that may satisfy the teacher, but that do not involve advancement in comprehension ability.

It is possible to argue that discovery learning may be a necessary component of comprehension instruction. Discovery learning usually takes longer than direct instruction, but may lead to better transfer and the ability to acquire skills more quickly in a new related situation (Andre, 1986). There are probably more skills involved in reading comprehension than can be taught directly in the time provided in school for teaching reading and so, some amount of discovery learning is probably necessary. In a study that demonstrates that discovery learning does occur, Meyer (1984) examined the reading instruction practices in a school district that had made substantial gains in standardized reading tests scores over a 20-year period. She observed no direct reading comprehension instruction statements by teachers in the first three grades. Instead, the pattern of in-class questions used by teachers changed over the three grades. As grade level increased, the percentage of factual (text explicit) questions decreased, and the frequency of text implicit and schema inference questions increased. Meyer argued that students acquired comprehension skills in a process of modeling and discovery from the types of questions asked about readings by teachers. A similar pattern of indirect learning of comprehension skills from the types of questions asked by teachers was reported by Morrow (1984).

Whereas such studies suggest that indirect or discovery learning of comprehension skills does occur, the analyses of reading instruction presented earlier suggest that the time allocated for direct comprehension instruction is insufficient. Clearly there are many students who fail to acquire adequate comprehension skills. Moreover, research is accumulating that indicates that comprehension skills can be directly taught and generalized to new reading situations.

Instruction in Reading Comprehension Skills

Training in comprehension skills has focused on identifying skill areas that a schema-theoretic view suggests are important in the reading process and in providing students with instruction in such skills. From a schema-theoretic view, these skills are text processing schemata. This section will discuss training studies in five main areas: recognizing main ideas, summarization, making inferences, detecting inconsistencies, and the use of background knowledge in comprehension.

Recognizing Main Ideas. The ability to identify main ideas in paragraphs and passages is often identified as an important skill in comprehension (Rosenschine, 1984). Most basal readers provide students with many opportunities to practice identifying main ideas, but provide little direct instruction on how to identify main ideas (Hare & Milligan, 1984). Not surprisingly, many students also experience difficulty in identifying main ideas.

Identification of main ideas is influenced by features of the text. For example, easier vocabulary and reading levels facilitate identification (Barrett & Otto, 1969), as does the number of supporting details provided (Mohr, Glover, & Ronning, 1984). The presence of an explicit topic sentence also helps main idea identification (Bridge, Belmore, Moskow, Cohen, & Matthews, 1984); but instructional texts often do not contain explicit statements of main ideas (Braddock, 1974; Baumann & Serra, 1984).

Readers do differ in their sensitivity to main ideas. Kimmel and MacGinitie (1984) compared groups of fifth and sixth graders matched on ability on their comprehension of paragraphs deductively (main idea first) and inductively (main idea last) structured. Students with difficulty identifying the main idea in inductively structured paragraphs seemed to be following a perserverative reading strategy in which they seemed unable to reformulate their conception of the main idea of the paragraph as additional sentences were read.

Baumann (1984) examined the effectiveness of direct instruction paradigms for teaching main idea comprehension. The experimental groups received direct training on explicit strategies to identify the main ideas in paragraphs. One control group received massed practice on basal reader type exercises for identifying main ideas. A second control group completed word learning exercises. The direct training groups performed much better than the basal and word exercise control groups on a posttest that asked the students to generate or identify main ideas in paragraphs. The improvement occurred on paragraphs with and without explicit topic sentences. Taylor and Beach (1984), in a study discussed more completely in the following, also found that direct training facilitated the ability to generate main idea sentences.

Summarization. The ability to summarize or provide the gist of a text is an important comprehension skill related to finding and expressing main ideas. Winograd (1984) examined the difficulties students have in summarizing text. His subjects consisted of 80 eighth graders and 40 adults. The subjects were divided into good and poor reading groups. The good and poor readers did not differ in their understanding of the summarization task demands. As other studies had found previously (Dunn, Mathews, & Bieger, 1979; Eamon, 1978; Meyer, Brandt, & Bluth, 1980), poor readers were less sensitive to important elements of the text than were good readers. Sensitivity to importance contributed significantly to performance even when differences in IQ and decoding ability were statistically removed from the regression. In addition, as had been reported by Brown and Day (1980) and Day (1980), good readers could use summarization transformations better than could poor readers.

Day (1980) trained students to use Kintsch and van Dijk's rules for summarizing narratives (taken from the model discussed earlier). There were four treatments that successively built on each other. The fourth treatment contained elements of the three simpler treatments and led to the best performance. Hare and Borchardt (1984) used similar summarization transformation rules to provide direct instruction in summarization to 22 low-income, minority high school students. Both inductive and deductive training procedures were used. The instruction occurred over three 2-hour sessions. The deductive and inductive training groups did not differ from each other, but did significantly outperform a control group on summarization efficiency and summarization rule usage. The experimental-control differences were maintained over a 2-week interval, but did not transfer to outlining tasks or to a main ideas task.

Several other studies support the efficacy of summarization training. King, Biggs, and Lipsky (1984) provided summarization training to college students in a developmental reading course. Summarization training improved ability to free recall passages and essay and objective test performance as compared to an untrained control group. Taylor (1982) trained students to attend to superordinate/subordinate relationships to produce summaries; trained students produced better summaries and comprehended novel passages better than did untrained students. Long and Aldersley (1982) used a networking procedure in which students constructed a network of interrelated concepts while reading. The training improved the students ability to summarize the gist of an instructional passage. Finally Armbruster (1979) used a similar networking or ''text mapping'' strategy that focused students' attention on key concepts in the passage; again comprehension and memory for passages improved as a result of training.

Structure and Previous Knowledge. Among the schemata readers may apply to passages are schemata that provide an organizing frame or format for a story. For example, a narrative story may be presented in a conversational frame or format or in a problem–solutions frame (Frederickson, 1981; Kormos, 1984). Knowledge of organizing schema for a particular passage can facilitate comprehension of a passage (Gourley, 1981). A number of studies have examined the effect of training students in such schemata. Bartlett (1978) trained junior high students in cause-effect, compare-contrast, description, and problem-solution schemata. Later, trained students recalled more of the important details from the passages they read than did untrained students. Fitzgerald and Spiegel (1983) trained average and below average fourth grade readers in the narrative structure of a story. A control group received training on dictionary usage. The instruction consisted of a short-term intensive phase and a longer-term review phase. The experimental group outperformed the control group on posttest comprehension measures. Taylor and Beach (1984) trained students to use hierarchical organizing principles for generating the structure of expository passages that did not follow a pre-established schema. Training facilitated both passage understanding and the writing of expository compositions. Barnett (1984) trained college students in the research report and journalism text structures. Instruction was provided either before reading the text or after reading the text. A control group received no instruction. Direct instruction in text structure provided before reading improved recall and recognition test scores on the passages.

Drawing Inferences. As discussed earlier in the section on adjunct questions, comprehending what one reads involves drawing inferences from what one reads. Two types of inferences are needed, text-based inferences in which inferences are drawn to fill in connections not explicitly stated in the text, and schema inferences, in which text information is related to background knowledge. As noted above, individuals who receive training in text- and schema-based inferencing and use known schemata to elaborate on text comprehend text more deeply and recall it better than individuals who process text more shallowly.

A number of studies have examined whether training students to use questions can facilitate comprehension. In an interesting study, Morrow (1984) examined the effects of providing training in answering questions to stories read to pre-

schoolers. There were four conditions; the three experimental conditions used Directed Reading Activity (DAR) with different types of questions. DAR consists of receiving prequestions, being read a story, then receiving and answering postquestions. The questions used in DAR defined the experimental groups. The traditional questions group received questions that asked about details (text explicit questions), required inferences (text inference questions), or asked critical questions. The story grammar group received questions about the general schematic framework of children's stories (eg., about setting, theme, episodes, or resolution). The combined condition received both types of question. A control condition received no questions. The posttest consisted of a transfer story about which students were asked traditional and story grammar questions. The basic result was that students learned to comprehend and acquire the kind of information from new stories, presented without any adjunct questions, that was required in the training stories. Carr, Dewitz, and Patberg (1983) employed three types of training with sixth graders: a structured overview to activate background knowledge, a cloze procedure designed to develop inferencing, and a self-monitoring checklist. One training group used the cloze procedure and the checklist, the second used the overview and cloze procedures. A control group received no training. The overview and cloze combination produced the greatest gains for below average readers on a posttest and on a delayed transfer test. Differences were not significant for above average readers. The authors speculated that the above average readers already possessed the necessary skills.

Raphael and her co-workers have conducted an extensive series of training studies involving the use the adjunct questions to train readers' inferencing skills. Raphael and Pearson (1982) trained high, average, and low ability sixth graders and average ability fourth and eighth graders in the differences between text explicit questions, text inference questions, and schema inference questions (the Pearson-Johnson taranomy) and how to answer them. The answer strategies were described as Right There (look for the answer right there in the text); Think and Search (think about what is needed and search different sentences in the text for it), and On My Own (find the answer in what you know on your own.) Training led to improved performance on new passages, but training interacted with ability. High ability students profited most from training on schema inference questions, whereas average and low ability students profited most from training on text explicit and text inference questions. Raphael and Wonnacott (1984) trained fourth grade teachers to use the taxonomy of questions to teach inferencing skills. The trained teachers then provided a week of intensive training to their students followed by 8 weeks of maintenance training. Training improved the ability of the students to draw inferences. The effects were greatest for low and average ability students. Raphael and McKinney (1983) provided inservices or inferences in reading to fifth and eighth grade teachers. The teachers then developed training programs for their students; the typical program consisted of 2 weeks of intensive training followed by a few weeks of one maintenance task a week. Again, training improved comprehension and inferencing for the low and average ability students.

Training in Detecting Inconsistencies. Comprehension monitoring involves taking remedial action when comprehension is unclear or when inconsistencies exist in the text. Younger and weaker readers typically have more difficulty in detecting and dealing with such inconsistencies (Garner, 1980, 1981; Markman, 1979; Winograd & Johnston, 1980). Grabe and Mann (1984) developed a series of computer-controlled reading activities presented in the guise of a Master Detective game. The subjects consisted of elementary and college students, the game consisted of two rounds of statements made by 10 "suspects" of a crime. During the first round 5 of the "suspects" gave inconsistent statements. During the second round only the "culprit" gave inconsistent statements. The students' job was to detect the culprit by determining which statements were inconsistent. One game was used as a pretest and a second as a posttest. Training consisted of playing four games designed to train students to identify the inconsistent statements. The trained group outperformed the control group on the posttest.

Reis and Spekman (1983) reported that middle grade students had more difficulty with text-based inconsistencies than they had with reader-based inconsistencies. In a second study, Reis and Spekman (1983, Study 2) provided short duration training on detecting inconsistencies to about half the students used in the first study. Training sessions lasted about 10 minutes and included direct instruction in the nature of inconsistencies and on comprehension monitoring skills. This direct instruction was followed by guided practice in which the student identified an inconsistency. Training facilitated performance in detecting reader-based, but not text-based inconsistencies.

Reciprocal Teaching: A More Comprehensive Comprehension Training Program

The instructional studies discussed earlier all represent relatively short-term studies that attempt to train a particular aspect of comprehension. A more comprehensive program has been proposed by Palincsar and Brown (1984). The Palincsar and Brown program attempts to teach four comprehension skills activities: summarizing (review), questioning, clarifying, and predicting. An interactive training procedure, called reciprocal teaching, is used to provide training. Because of its comprehensiveness and early success, I find this an exciting approach and describe it in some detail.

In the reciprocal teaching employed by Palincsar and Brown, the teacher and student take turns engaging in dialogue about the text. The teacher models comprehension activities and guides the student in engaging in comprehension activities. The teacher begins the lesson with a short discussion intended to activate relevant prior knowledge. The teacher and students then read a short selection silently. Then the teacher or student asks a question that might be asked by a test or a teacher. The teacher or student then summarizes the passage, identifies and clarifies any difficulties, and makes a prediction about future content. The discussion is embedded in a natural dialogue with students and teachers giving each other feedback (Palincsar & Brown, 1984, pp. 124–125). Initially the teacher spends more time modeling these skills and provides much feedback and guidance to the students as they used the skills; later in the training, the students assume more and more of an active role.

As used by Palincsar and Brown, the training program was extensive and the experimental design complex. All the students involved in the four experimental groups discussed in the following were below average in reading comprehension. Comparative assessments of average students were also made. Students met in the experimental group instead of with their normal reading group. Training consisted of 20 days of direct training followed by 5 days of maintenance assessment. A long-term follow up was given 8 weeks after the intervention. There were four groups involved in the study, the experimental Reciprocal Training group, a group that received training on locating information, a control group that received daily assessment activities but no training, and a control group that received the pre, post, and long-term assessments. Many different measures of reading comprehension were employed, including measures similar to the training activities and measures indicative of transfer to other content domains.

The results indicated that students in the reciprocal training group improved to about the level of average students on daily comprehension assignments. Students in the control groups did not. The improvement for the reciprocal training students generalized to social studies and science passages; performance for the control groups did not change. The reciprocal teaching students displayed improvements on transfer tests of summarizing predicting questions, and detecting incongruities; the control groups showed little or no change.

In a second study, two classroom teachers and two resource room teachers were trained to employ the reciprocal teaching intervention used in Experiment 1. The training procedures were the same as in Experiment 1. The subjects were seventh and eight grade pupils divided into four groups. All subjects were below average in reading. The design was a basic "AB" or time series with intervention design. No control groups were employed. All four groups of pupils showed improvement in daily assessment comprehension tasks, summarizing, predicting questions, and detecting incongruities.

Conclusions about Comprehension Training

Taken as a whole, the results of the training studies discussed in this section support the notion that the cognitive skills (text processing schemata) involved in comprehending text can be identified and taught to pupils. Teaching that consists of direct instruction in comprehension skills can be effective for helping students master such skills. The fact that direct instruction has been shown to be effective is important because research on current classroom practice suggests that comprehension instruction is indirect and occurs primarily as a kind of trial and error or discovery learning from extensive assessment exercises presented in classrooms. One common theme that was repeated in many of these studies was the notion that more able students may learn from the typical classroom procedures, but that less able students would find

difficulty in learning to comprehend from indirect instruction. This theme finds support in that fact that the direct instruction provided in many of the discussed studies was more effective for lower ability learners than for higher ability learners, although all students usually experience some benefit from direct instruction. Pearson and Gallagher (1983) reach similar conclusions in their review of training studies.

A second important feature of these training studies is that they have proceeded from a more complete theoretical base than many previous studies in reading. The studies have a foundation in the schema-theoretic view of reading, which holds that comprehension involves the interaction between text and previously acquired schemata, either in the form of content schemata and metacognitive strategic (text processing) schemata. The schema-theoretic view provides guidance in that analysis of differences between strong and weak comprehenders; in characterizing the comprehension skills to be taught, and in the design of training studies.

Pearson and Gallagher (1983) proposed a model of comprehension instruction that involves modeling of comprehension skills by the teacher and a gradual increase in student responsibility through practice guided by the teacher. This model is well represented in the reciprocal teaching method of Palincsar and Brown (1984). The Palincsar and Brown study is a particularly noteworthy instructional study. Unlike many of the other instructional studies, it involved a relatively long-term intervention occurring in a natural classroom setting. The gains made by students were impressive; students who had been considerably below average in comprehension were brought up to the level of average students on daily comprehension assessment activities. The gains also lasted over an 8-week interval and transferred to other subject matters. In addition, the second study demonstrated that it was possible to train typical teachers to employ the reciprocal teaching strategy and to effect similar gains. It should be noted that the Raphael studies shared this latter feature.

Summary and Conclusions

In this chapter, I have tried to present an overview of current issues in reading comprehension from a schema-theoretic viewpoint. The understanding of reading and language comprehension is critical for educational psychologists because reading and language lie at the heart of all instruction. Children who do not learn to read have difficulty in all of their formal education. In addition, because reading comprehension is intimately involved with the nature of and updating of the learner's knowledge store, the understanding of reading comprehension has implications for facilitating learning in all subject matters. This chapter has briefly presented early work in reading comprehension by educational psychologists, outlined some major current models of reading comprehension, discussed four currently active areas of research in reading comprehension, and discussed research on the teaching of comprehension.

Research by early educational psychologists revealed several important points about reading comprehension.

1. Reading is an active process involving drawing inferences, critical thinking, and problem solving.

2. In addition to knowledge of specific reading skills, the reader's prior knowledge of the world and his or her experience play a critical role in reading comprehension.

3. The meaning of a message is not in the text, but is generated in the mind of the reader through an interaction of the text and the reader's existing knowledge.

These points are fundamental to current models of reading comprehension. A review of current models of reading comprehension suggests that neither models that emphasize bottom-up (data driven) processes nor models that emphasize top-down (conceptually driven) processes can provide an adequate model of reading. Rather, models that emphasize the interaction of top-down and bottom-up processes are needed to provide an adequate description of reading comprehension. I have argued that the schema-theorectic perspective offers a convenient umbrella for developing an adequate theory of reading comprehension. The schema-theoretic perspective is not a complete theory or model, rather it is a set of generalizations about reading within which precise models of reading can be developed and tested.

According to the schema-theory the reader's existing knowledge is encoded in a network of mental structures called schemata. Schemata have the properties of being able to recognize when instances to which they apply occur, of relating to other schemata in memory through labeled associations, of taking on different values about aspects of themselves, of having default values that

used are when particular values, in a given situation, for that slot are missing, and of carrying out some sort of activity. Schemata may be perceptual or conceptual; examples of schemata would include our schemata for recognizing a face, and our schemata (or script) for going to a restaurant, burglarizing a house, conducting a psychology experiment, or doing a regression analysis. When individuals read, elements of the text lead to the activation of schemata according to the interactive cascade type model proposed by Rummelhart and McClelland (1981). The schemata are used to give a particularized interpretation to the text. This particular interpretation is generated by the construction of a representation in memory of the structure of the text in the way discussed by Kintsch and van Dijk (1983). The schemata used in reading comprehension are of two types: text-processing schemata embody knowledge of discourse structure and how to process language, content schemata embody knowledge of the world that is necesary to understanding. Text-processing schemata include relatively automatic schemata used by skilled readers (e.g., the schemata involved in recognizing grammatical equivalents) and consciously employed schemata that have been called metacognitive strategies.

This schema-theoretic perspective offers a convenient umbrella for conducting research on language comprehension. Knowledge of syntax is one class of the text-processing schemata involved in reading comprehension. The study of syntactical factors in comprehension by linguists has indicated a number of rules that must be built into adequate psychological models of comprehension. These include within- and between-sentence syntactical rules. The latter have received less attention and are less well understood than the former. Among the latter is the problem of anaphora. Research indicates that the ability to understand anaphoric reference increases with age; but current linguistic analysis suggests that the issues involved in anaphora have not been well conceptualized by psychological researchers.

Another issue with which an adequate theory of comprehension must deal is that of metaphor and figurative language. The difficulty with figurative language is that the schemata involved are used in nontypical ways. How, then, can what is meant be understood? Ortony (1979) suggested a plausible model that is consistent with the schema-theoretic perspective. In this paper, I have suggested that figurative language can be interpreted as an instruction to the reader to process the values of one schemata according to the constraints of a second schemata. For example, the statement, *The microwave is the jet plane of cooking,* is interpreted by examining the features of the schema *microwave* and seeing which of those can occupy the slots of the schema *jet plane.*

The issue of metaphor is of particular interest to educational psychologists. Ortony (1980) has argued that metaphor or figurative language may represent a basic way of understanding new knowledge. Research on metaphor has suggested that when students are provided with appropriate figurative language when being taught new schemata, they are more likely to learn meaningfully.

Research on the elaboration of prose has suggested that when students use existing schemata to develop more elaborate representations of the presented text, they are more likely to remember the information presented in the text. The details that are remembered are related to the schemata employed in processing the text, and the application of a different schemata after the text is read can lead to the recall of different details. Instructional manipulations, such as telling students to process for elaboration or asking questions that require more elaboration to answer, can lead to more effective learning by students. In addition, manipulations such as questions have been used to train students typically to process text more elaboratively and to draw inferences based on their existing schemata.

As part of learning to read, children acquire a number of schemata about reading that have been called metacognitive strategies. These strategies involve consciously applied skills used in reading, such as reviewing and summarizing, skimming for an overview before reading, etc. An important set of these metacognitive schemata are labeled comprehension monitoring strategies. These involve taking corrective action when comprehension failure is detected, reforming an interpretation when things do not make sense, etc. Children acquire these strategies slowly over the school years and good readers use such strategies more so than poor readers. When taught such strategies, children improve in reading comprehension.

Research on the teaching of reading comprehension reveals that the text-processing schemata involved in reading are not directly taught in most basal reading programs. Instead, children are provided with many assessment activities that test their use of such skills; children seem to learn what

the skills are indirectly, through a process of discovery learning. Because of the number of comprehension skills that must be taught, some discovery learning is probably necessary, but many children fail to make the necessary discovery and do not learn to read well. A number of research studies have shown that poor readers can be taught such skills and that, as a result, their reading improves. The schema-theoretic perspective is very useful in the design of reading programs because it identifies the skills (schemata) that must be taught. A quite exciting new teaching program has been proposed by Palincsar and Brown (1984) for the teaching of reading. The program is consistent with schema theory and uses direct instruction, modeling, and guided practice to train readers in the schemata necessary for effective reading.

References

Adams, M. J. (1979). Models of word recognition, *Cognitive Psychology, 11,* 133–176.

Adams, M. J., & Collins, A. (1977). *A schema-theoretic view of reading,* Champaign: University of Illinois, Technical Report No. 32, Center for the Study of Reading.

Adams, M. J., & Collins, A. (1979). A schema-theoretic view of reading. In R. O. Freedle (Ed.), *Discourse processing: Multidisciplinary perspectives* (pp. 486–502). Norwood, NJ: Ablex.

Adams, M. J. (1980). Failures to comprehend and levels of processing in reading. In R. Spiro, B. C. Bruce, W. F. Brewer, (Eds.), *Theoretical issues in reading comprehension* (pp. 11–28). Hillsdale, NJ: Erlbaum.

Anderson, J. R., & Reder, L. M. (1979). An elaborative processing explanation of depth of processing. In L. S. Cermak & F. I. M. Craik (Eds.), *Levels of processing and human memory* (pp. 230–257). Hillsdale, NJ: Erlbaum.

Anderson, R. C. (1972). How to construct achievement tests to assess comprehension. *Review of Educational Research, 42,* 145–170.

Anderson, R. C. (1984). Role of the reader's schema in comprehension, learning, and memory. In R. C. Anderson, J. Osborn, & R. J. Tierney, (Eds.), *Learning to read in American schools* (pp. 243–258), Hillsdale, NJ: Erlbaum.

Anderson, R. C., & Biddle, W. B. (1975). On asking people questions about what they are reading. In G. H. Bower (Ed.), *The psychology of learning and motivation, Vol. 9* (pp. 175–199). New York: Academic Press.

Anderson, R. C., & Pearson, P. D. (1985). A schema-theoretic view of basic processes in reading comprehension. In P. D. Pearson (Ed.), *Handbook of reading research* (pp. 255–292). New York: Longman.

Anderson, R. C., & Pichert, J. W. (1978). Recall of previously unrecallable information following a shift in perspective. *Journal of Verbal Learning and Verbal Behavior, 17,* 1–12.

Anderson, R. C., Pichert, J. W., & Shirey, L. L. (1983). Effects of the readers' schema at different points in time. *Journal of Educational Psychology, 75,* 271–279.

Anderson, R. C., & Shifrin, Z. (1980). The meaning of words

in context. In R. Spiro, B. C. Bruce, & W. F. Brewer (Eds.), *Theoretical issues in reading comprehension* (pp. 331–348). Hillsdale, NJ: Erlbaum.

Anderson, T. H. (1980). Study strategies and adjunct aids, In R. J. Spiro, B. C. Bruce, & W. F. Brewer (Eds.), *Theoretical issues in reading comprehension* (pp. 483–502). Hillsdale, NJ: Erlbaum.

Anderson, V. (1976). *Subskills in learning from context.* Unpublished paper, Toronto, Ontario: Ontario Institutes for Studies in Education.

Andre, T., & Sola, J. (1976). Imagery, verbatim and paraphrased questions and learning from prose. *Journal of Educational Psychology, 68,* 661–669.

Andre, T. (1979). On productive knowledge and levels of questions. *Review of Educational Research, 49,* 280–318.

Andre, T. (1981). The role of paraphrased adjunct questions in facilitating learning from prose. *Contemporary Educational Psychology, 6,* 22–27.

Andre, T. (1984, April). *Pedagogical control of cognitive processes involved in acquiring knowledge from instruction.* Paper presented at the annual meeting of the American Educational Research Association, New Orleans, LA.

Andre, T. (1984, October). *Designing instruction to better facilitate the learning of intellectual skills.* Paper presented at the annual meeting of the Midwestern Educational Research Association, Chicago, IL.

Andre, T. (1986a). Problem solving and education. In G. Phye & T. Andre (Eds.), *Cognitive classroom learning* (pp. 169–204). New York: Academic Press.

Andre, T. (1986b). Problem solving and education. In G. Phye & T. Andre (Eds.), *Cognitive classroom learning* (pp. 169–204). New York: Academic Press.

Andre, T. (in press). Recent research on using questions to facilitate learning: The state of the art, *Questioning Exchange.*

Andre, T., Mueller, C., Womack, S., Smid, K., & Tuttle, M. (1980). Adjunct application questions facilitate later application, or do they? *Journal of Educational Psychology, 72,* 533–543.

Andre, T., & Reiher, T. (1983, April). *Type of question, delay interval, and learning from prose.* Paper presented at the Annual Meeting of the American Educational Research Association, Montreal, Canada.

Andre, T., & Womack, S. (1978). Verbatim and paraphrased questions and learning from prose. *Journal of Educational Psychology, 70,* 796–802.

Armbruster, B. (1979). *An investigation of the effectiveness of ''Mapping'' text as a studying strategy of middle schools.* Unpublished doctoral dissertation, University of Illinois, Urbana.

Armbruster, B. B., Stevens, R. J., & Rosenschine, B. (1977). *Analyzing content coverage and emphasis: A study of three curricula and two tests* (Tech. Rep. N. 26). Urbana IL: Center for the Study of Reading, University of Illinois, March. (ERIC Document Reproduction Service No. ED 136-238).

Arter, J. L. (1976). *The effects of metaphor on reading comprehension.* Unpublished doctoral dissertation, University of Illinois, Urbana.

Asch, S., & Nerlove, H. (1960). The development of double function terms in children: An exploration study. In B. Kaplan & S. Wapner (Eds.), *Perspective in psychological theory* (pp. 302–327). New York: International University Press.

Atkinson, R. C., & Shiffrin, R. M. (1968). Human memory: A proposed system and its component processes. In K. Spence

& J. Spence (Eds.), *The psychology of learning and motivation, Vol 2,* New York: Academic Press.

Baldwin, R. S., Luce, T. S., & Readence, J. E. (1982). The impact of subschemata on metaphorical processing. *Reading Research Quarterly, 17,* 528–543.

Baker, L., & Brown, A. L. (1985). Metacognitive skills and reading, In P. D. Pearson (Ed.), *Handbook of reading research* (pp. 353–395). New York: Longman.

Balota, D. A., Pollatsek, A., & Rayner, K. (in press). The interaction of contextual constraints and parafoveal visual information in reading. *Cognitive Psychology.*

Barnett, J. E. (1984). Facilitating retention through instruction about text structure. *Journal of Reading Behavior, 16,* 113.

Barrett, T., & Otto, W. (1969). Elementary pupil's ability to conceptualize the main idea in reading. In R. C. Anderson, G. W. Faust, M. C. Roderick, D. J. Cunningham, & T. Andre, (Eds.), *Current research on instruction* (pp. 270–281). Englewood Cliffs, NJ: Prentice Hall.

Bartlett, B. J. (1978). *Top level structure as an organization strategy for recall of classroom tests.* Unpublished doctoral dissertation, Arizona State University, Tempe, Arizona.

Bartlett, F. C. (1932). *Remembering,* Cambridge, England: Cambridge University Press.

Baumann, J. F. (1984). The effectiveness of a direct instruction paradigm for teaching main idea comprehension. *Reading Research Quarterly, 14,* 93–112.

Baumann, J. F., & Serra, J. K., (1984). The frequency and placement of main ideas in children's social studies textbooks: A modified replication of Braddock's research on topic sentences. *Journal of Reading Behavior, 16,* 27–40.

Bever, T. G., Lackner, J. R., & Kirk, R. (1969). The underlying structures of sentences are the primary units of immediate speech processing. *Perception and Psychophysics, 5,* 225–231.

Billow, R. (1975). A cognitive developmental study of metaphor comprehension. *Developmental Psychology, 11,* 415–423.

Bormuth, J. R., Manning, J., Carr, L., & Pearson, D. (1970). Children's comprehension of between- and within-sentence syntactic structures. *Journal of Educational Psychology, 61,* 349–357.

Braddock, R. (1974). The frequency and placement of topic sentences in expository prose. *Research in the Teaching of English, 8,* 287–302.

Bransford, J. D. (1984). Schema activation and schema acquisition: Comments on Richard C. Anderson's Remarks. In R. C. Anderson, J. Osborn, & R. J. Tierney (Eds.), *Learning to read in American schools* (pp. 259–272). Hillsdale, NJ: Erlbaum.

Bransford, J. D., & Franks, J. J. (1971). The abstraction of linguistic ideas, *Cognitive Psychology, 2.,* 331–350.

Bransford, J. D., & Johnson, M. K. (1972). Contextual prerequisites for understanding: Some investigations of comprehension and recall. *Journal of Verbal Learning and Verbal Behavior, 11,* 717–726.

Bransford, J. D., Barclay, J. R., & Franks, J. J. (1972). Sentence memory: A constructive versus interpretive approach. *Cognitive Psychology, 2,* 193–209.

Brewer, W. F. (1973). Is reading a letter-by-letter process? A discussion of Gough's paper. In J. F. Kavanagh & I. G. Mattingly (Eds.), *Language by Ear and by Eye* (pp. 359–365). Cambridge, MA: M.I.T. Press.

Bridge, C. A., Belmore, S. M., Moskow, S. P., Cohen, S. S., & Matthews, P. D., (1984). Topicalization and memory for main ideas in prose, *Journal of Reading Behavior, 16,* 61–80.

Brown, A. L. (1975). The development of memory: Knowing, knowing about knowing, and knowing how to know. In H. W. Reese (Ed.), *Advances in child development and behavior* (Vol 10) (pp. 104–153). New York: Academic Press.

Brown, A. L. (1978). Knowing when, where, and how to remember: A problem in metacognition. In R. Glaser (Ed.), *Advances in instructional psychology* (pp. 77–166). Hillsdale, NJ: Erlbaum.

Brown, A. L. (1980). Metacognitive development and reading. In R. J. Spiro, B. C. Bruce, & W. F. Brewer (Eds.), *Theoretical issues in reading comprehension* (pp. 458–482). Hillsdale, NJ: Erlbaum.

Brown, A. L., & Day, J. D. (1980). *Strategies and knowledge for summarizing texts: The development of expertise.* Unpublished manuscript, University of Illinois.

Brown, A. L., & Lawton, S. C. (1977). The feeling of knowing experience in educable retarded children. *Developmental Psychology, 4,* 365–370.

Brown, A. L., & Smiley, S. S. (1978). The development of strategies for studying texts. *Child Development, 49,* 1076–1088.

Brown, A. L. Smiley, S. S., Day, J., Townsend, M., & Lawton, S. C. (1977). Intrusion of a thematic idea in children's recall of prose. *Child Development, 49,* 1454–1466.

Cattell, J. M. (1947). On the time required for recognizing and naming letters and words, pictures, and colors. In A. T. Poffenberger (Ed.). *James McKeen Cattell:* (Vol. 1, pp. 47–62). Lancaster, PA: Science Press.

Cattell, J. M. (1885). The inertia of the eye and brain. *Brain, 8,* 295–312.

Cattell, J. M. (1886a). The time taken up by cerebral operations. III. The perception-time. *Mind, 11,* 377–392.

Cattell, J. M. (1886b). The time taken up by cerebral operations. IV. The will-time. *Mind, II,* 524–534.

Carr, E. M., Dewitz, P., & Patberg, J. P. (1983). The effect of inference training on children's comprehension of expository text. *Journal of Reading Behavior, 15,* 1–18.

Chimpan, H., & de Dardel, C. (1974). Developmental study of the comprehension and production of the pronoun "it." *Journal of Psycholinguistic Research, 3,* 91–99.

Chomsky, N. (1957). *Syntactic structures.* The Hague: Mouton.

Chomsky, N. (1965). *Aspects of the theory of syntax.* Cambridge, MA: M.I.T. Press

Craik, F. I. M., & Lockhart, R. S. (1984). Levels of processing: a framework for memory research. *Journal of Verbal Learning and Verbal Behavior, 11,* 671–684.

Cronbach, L. J. (1954). *Educational Psychology,* New York: Harcourt, Brace, & World.

Cronbach, L. J. (1963). *Educational Psychology, Second Edition,* New York: Harcourt, Brace, & World.

Day, J. D. (1980). *Teaching summarization skills: A comparison of training methods.* Unpublished doctoral dissertation, University of Illinois, Urbana.

Demorest, A., Silberstein, L., Gardner, H., Winner, E. (1983). Telling it as it isn't: Children's understanding of figurative language. *British Journal of Developmental Psychology, 1*(2), 121–134.

de Beaugrande, R. (1981). Design criteria for process models of reading, *Reading Research Quarterly, 16,* 261–319.

Dooling, D. J., & Lachman, R. (1971). Effects of comprehension on retention of prose, *Journal of Experimental Psychology, 8,* 216–222.

Duchastel, P. C. (1983). Interpreting adjunct question research: processes and ecological validity. *Human Learning: Journal of Practical Research and Applications, 2,* 1–5.

Dunn, B. R., Mathews, S. R., II, & Bieger, G. (1979). *Individual differences in the recall of lower-level textual information* (Tech. Rep. No. 150). Urbana, IL: University of Illinois, Center for the Study of Reading (ERIC Document Reproduction Service No. ED 181 448).

Durkin, D. (1979). What classroom observations reveal about reading comprehension instruction. *Reading Research Quarterly, 14,* 481–534.

Durkin, D. (1981). Reading comprehension instruction in five basal reader series. *Reading Research Quarterly, 16,* 515–544.

Eamon, D. B. (1978). Selection and recall of topical information in prose by better and poorer readers. *Reading Research Quarterly, 14,* 244–257.

Eriksen, C. W., Pollack, M. D., & Montague, W. E., (1970). Implicit speech: Mechanism in perceptual encoding? *Journal of Experimental Psychology, 84,* 502–507.

Erikson, C. W., & Spencer, T. (1969). Rate of information processing in visual perception: Some results and methodological considerations. *Journal of Experimental Psychology Monograph 79* (2, Pt. 2).

Fitzgerald, J., & Spiegel, D. L. (1983). Enhancing children's reading comprehension through instruction in narrative structure. *Journal of Reading Behavior, 15,* 1–17.

Fodor, J. A., & Garrett, M. F. (1966). Competence and performance. In J. Lyons & R. Wales (Eds.), *Psycholinguistic papers.* Edinburgh: University of Edinburgh Press.

Fredericksen, C. H. (1981). Inferences in preschool children's conversations: a cognitive perspective. In J. Green & C. Wallat (Eds.), *Language and ethnography in educational settings.* Norwood, NJ: Ablex.

Garner, R. (1980). Monitoring of understanding: An investigation of good and poor readers' awareness of induced miscomprehension of text. *Journal of Reading Behavior, 13,* 215–222.

Garner, R. (1981). Monitoring of passage consistency among poor comprehenders: A preliminary test of the "piecemeal processing" explanation. *Journal of Educational Research, 74,* 159–162.

Garrett, M. F., Bever, T. G., & Fodor, J. A. (1966). The active use of grammar in speech perception. *Perception and Psychophysics, 1,* 30–32.

Gates, A. I. (1935). *The Improvement of Reading,* New York: Macmillan.

Gentner, D. (1977). On the development of metaphoric processing. *Child Development, 48,* 1034–1039.

Gerring, R. J., & Healy, A. F. (1983). Dual processes in metaphor understanding: Comprehension and appreciation. *Journal of Experimental Psychology: Learning, Memory, and Cognition, 9,* 667–675.

Gildea, P., & Gluckberg, S., (1983). On understanding metaphor: The role of context. *Journal of Verbal Learning and Verbal Behavior, 22,* 577–590.

Glover, J. A., Bruning, R. H., & Plake, B. S. (1982). Distinctiveness of encoding and recall of text materials. *Journal of Educational Psychology, 74,* 522–534.

Glover, J. A., Plake, B. S., Roberts, B. Zimmer, J. W., & Palmere, M. (1981). Distinctiveness of encoding: The effects of paraphrasing and drawing inferences on memory for prose. *Journal of Educational Psychology, 73,* 736–744.

Glover, J. A., Plake, B. S., & Zimmer, J. W. (1982). Distinctiveness of encoding and memory for learning tasks. *Journal of Educational Psychology, 740,* 189–198.

Glucksberg, S., Gildea, P., Bookin, H. B. (1982). On understanding nonliteral speech: Can people ignore metaphors? *Journal of Verbal Learning & Verbal Behavior, 21*(1), 85–98.

Goodman, K. S. (1982a). Reading: A psycholinguistic guessing game. In F. V. Gollasch (Ed.), *Language and literacy* (Vol. 1, pp. 19–31). Boston, MA: Routledge & Kegan Paul.

Goodman, K. S. (1982b). The reading process: Theory and practice. In F. V. Gollasch (Ed.), *Language and literacy,* (Vol. 1, pp. 33–43). Boston, MA: Routledge & Kegan Paul.

Goodman, K. S. (1982c). Miscues: Windows on the reading process. In F. V. Gollasch (Ed.), *Language and literacy* (Vol. 1, pp. 64–79). Boston, MA: Routledge & Kegan Paul.

Goodman, K. S., & Goodman, Y. M. (1982). Learning about psycholinguistic processes by analyzing oral reading. In F. V. Gollasch (Ed.), *Language and Literacy* (Vol. 1, pp. 149–168). Boston, MA: Routledge & Kegan Paul.

Gough, P. B. (1973). One second of reading, In J. F. Kavanagh & I. G. Mattingly (Eds.), *Language by ear and by eye.* Cambridge, MA: The M.I.T. Press.

Gourley, J. W. (1981). Discourse structure: Expectations of beginning readers and the readability of text. *Journal of Reading Behavior, 16,* 169–188.

Grabe, M. D. (1979). Reader imposed structure and prose retention. *Contemporary Educational Psychology, 4,* 162–171.

Grabe, M., & Mann, S. (1984). A technique for the assessment and training of comprehension monitoring skills. *Journal of Reading Behavior, 16,* 131–144.

Haber, R. N. (1970). How we remember what we see. *Scientific American, 222,* 104–112.

Hadamard, J. (1949). *An essay on the psychology of invention in the mathematical field.* Princeton, NJ: Princeton University Press.

Hare, V. C., & Borchardt, K. M. (1984). Direct instruction of summarization skills. *Reading Research Quarterly, 20,* 62–78.

Hare, V. C., & Milligan, B. (1984). Main idea identification: Instructional explanations in four basal reader series. *Journal of Reading Behavior, 16,* 169–203.

Honeck, R. P., Sowry, B. M., & Voegtle, L. (1978). Proverbial understanding in a pictorial context. *Child Development, 49,* 327–331.

Horne, R. N. (1966). A study of the use of figurative language by sixth grade children (Doctoral dissertation, University of Georgia, 1966). *Dissertation Abstracts International, 27,* 3367A. (University Microfilms No. 67-3, 555)

Huey, E. B. (1908). *The Psychology and Pedagogy of Reading,* New York: MacMillan.

Huggins, A. W. F., & Adams, M. J. (1980). Syntactic aspects of reading comprehension. In R. J. Spiro, B. C. Bruce, & W. F. Brewer (Eds.), *Theoretical issues in reading comprehension* (pp. 87–112). Hillsdale, NJ: Erlbaum.

Jacoby, L. L., & Craik, F. I. M. (1979). Effects of elaboration of processing at encoding and retrieval: Trace distinctiveness and recovery of initial context. In L. S. Cermak & F. I. M. Craik (Eds.), *Levels of processing and human memory* (pp. 141–169). Hillsdale, NJ: Erlbaum.

Jarvella, R. (1971). Syntactic processing of connected speech. *Journal of Verbal Learning and Verbal Behavior, 10,* 409–416.

Jenkins, J. R., & Pany, D. (1980). Teaching reading comprehension in the middle grades, In R. J. Spiro, B. C. Bruce,

& W. F. Brewer (Eds.), Theoretical issues in reading comprehension (pp. 555–574). Hillsdale, NJ: Erlbaum.

Jordan, A. M. (1933). *Educational psychology.* New York: Holt.

Johnston, P. H. (1985). Assessment in reading. In P. D. Pearson (Ed.), *Handbook of reading research,* (pp. 186–208). New York: Longman.

Jonassen, D. H. (Ed.). (1984). *The technology of text.* Englewood Cliffs, NJ: Educational Technology Publications.

Kimmel, S., & MacGinitie, W. H., (1984). Identifying children who use a preserverative text processing strategy. *Reading Research Quarterly, 14,* 162–172.

King, J. R., Biggs, S., & Lipsky, S., (1984). Students self-questioning and summarizing as reading study strategies. *Journal of Reading Behavior, 16,* 205–218.

Kintsch, W. (1974). *The representation of meaning in memory.* Hillsdale, NJ: Erlbaum.

Kintsch, W., & van Dijk, T. A., (1978). Toward a model of text comprehension and production. *Psychological Review, 85,* 363–394.

Klare, G. R. (1985). Readability. In P. D. Pearson (Ed.), *Handbook of reading research* (pp. 681–744). New York: Longman.

Kleinman, G. M. (1975). Speech recoding in reading. *Journal of Verbal Learning and Verbal Behavior, 14,* 323–339.

Kormos, L. (1983, April). *Individual differences in children's discourse comprehension under various questioning conditions.* Paper presented at the annual meeting of the American Educational Research Association, Montreal, Canada.

Kormos, L. (1984, April). *A discourse processing approach to children's question answering performance and its effects of recall of different passages.* Paper presented at the annual meeting of the American Educational Research Association, New Orleans, L.A.

Kreutzer, M. A., Leonard, C., Flavell, J. H. (1975). An interview study of children's knowledge about memory. *Monographs of the Society for research in Child Development, 40*(1, Serial No. 159).

Lesgold, A. (1974). Variability in children's comprehension of syntactic structures. *Journal of Educational Psychology, 66,* 333–338.

Leu, D. J. (1982). Oral reading error analysis: A critical review of research and application. *Reading Research Quarterly, 17,* 420–437.

Long, G. L., & Aldersley, S., (1982). Evaluation of a technique to enhance reading comprehension. *American Annals of the Deaf, 127,* 816–820.

Markman, E. M. (1979). Realizing that you don't understand: Elementary school children's awareness of inconsistencies. *Child Development, 50,* 643–655.

Martin, E. (1970). Toward an analysis of subjective phrase structure. *Psychological Bulletin, 74,* 153–166.

Mayer, R. E. (1975). Different problem solving competencies established in learning computer programming with and without meaningful models. *Journal of Educational Psychology, 67,* 725–734.

Mayer, R. E. (1980). Elaboration techniques that increase the meaningfulness of technical text: An experimental test of the learning strategy hypothesis. *Journal of Educational Psychology, 72,* 770–784.

McClelland, J. (1976). Preliminary letter identification in the perception of words and nonwords. *Journal of Experimental Psychology: Human Perception and Performance, 1,* 80–91.

McClelland, J. L. (1979). On the time relations of mental processes: An examination of systems of processes in cascade. *Psychological Review, 86,* 287–330.

McClelland, J. L., & Rumelhart, D. E. (1980). *An interactive activation model of the effect of context in perception, part I* (Chip Report 91). La Jolla, CA: Center for Human Information Processing.

McKee, P. (1948). *The teaching of reading.* Boston, MA: Houghton-Mifflin.

McMahon, L. (1963). *Grammatical analysis as a part of understanding a sentence.* Unpublished doctoral dissertation, Harvard University.

Meyer, B. J. F., Brandt, D. M., & Bluth, G. J. (1980). Use of top level structure in text: Key for reading comprehension of ninth-grade students. *Reading Research Quarterly, 16,* 72–103.

Meyer, L. A. (1984, April). *Teacher's comprehension questions: what functions might serve?* Paper presented at the Annual Meeting of the American Educational Research Association, New Orleans, LA.

Miller, G. A. (1962). Some psychological studies of grammar. *American Psychologist, 17,* 748–762

Mohr, P., Glover, J. A., & Ronning, R. R. (1984). The effect of related and unrelated details on the recall of major ideas in prose. *Journal of Reading Behavior, 16,* 97–108.

Morgan, J. L., & Green, G. M. (1980). Pragmatics and reading comprehension. In R. J. Spiro, B. C. Bruce, and W. F. Brewer (Eds.), *Theoretical issues in reading comprehension* (pp. 165–200). Hillsdale, NJ: Erlbaum.

Morgan, J. L., & Sellner, M. B. (1980). Discourse and linguistic theory. In R. J. Spiro, B. C. Bruce, & W. F. Brewer (Eds.), *Theoretical issues in reading comprehension* (pp. 165–200). Hillsdale, NJ: Erlbaum.

Morrow, L. M. (1984). *Reading stories to young children: effects of story structure and traditional questions strategies on comprehension.* Paper presented at the Annual Meeting of the American Educational Research Association, New Orleans, LA.

Nippold, M. A., Leonard, L. B., & Kail, R. (1984). Syntactic and conceptual factors in children's understanding of metaphors. *Journal of Speech & Hearing Research, 27*(2), 197–205.

Ortony, A. (1975). Why metaphors are necessary and not just nice. *Educational Theory, 25,* 53–69.

Ortony, A. (1976). On the nature and value of metaphor: A reply to my critics. *Educational Theory, 26,* 45–53.

Ortony, A. (1979). Beyond literal similarity. *Psychological Review, 86,* 161–180.

Ortony, A. (1980). Metaphor. In R. J. Spiro, B. C. Bruce, W. F. Brewer (Eds.), *Theoretical issues in reading comprehension.* Hillsdale, NJ: Erlbaum.

Ortony, A., Reynolds, R. E., & Arter, J. A. (1978). Metaphor: Theoretical and empirical research. *Psychological Bulletin, 85,* 919–943.

Ortony, A., Schallert, D. L., Reynolds, R. E., & Antos, S. J. (1978). Interpreting metaphors and idioms: Some effects of context on comprehension. *Journal of Verbal Learning and Verbal Behavior, 17,* 465–477.

Osborn, J. (1984). The purposes, uses, and contents of workbooks and some guidelines for publishers. In R. C. Anderson, J. Osborn, & R. J. Tierney (Eds.), *Learning to read in American schools.* Hillsdale, NJ: Erlbaum.

Palincsar, A. S., & Brown, A. L. (1984). Reciprocal teaching of comprehension-fostering and comprehension-monitoring activities. *Cognition and Instruction, 1,* 117–175.

Palmere, M., Benton, S. L., Glover, J. A., & Ronning, R. R. (1983). Elaboration and recall of main ideas in prose. *Journal of Educational Psychology, 750,* 898–907.

Park, O., & Tennyson, R. D. (1980). The adaptive design strategies for selecting number and presentation order of examples in coordinate concept acquisition. *Journal of Educational Psychology, 72,* 362–370.

Pearson, P. D. (1985). (Ed.). *Handbook of reading research.* New York: Longman.

Pearson, P. D., & Gallagher, M. C. (1983). The instruction of reading comprehension, *Contemporary Educational Psychology, 8,* 317–344.

Pearson, P. D., & Johnson, D. D. (1978). *Teaching reading coomprehension.* New York: Holt, Rinehart, Winston.

Pearson, P. D., Raphael, T., Te Paske, N., & Hyser, C. (1979). *The function of metaphor in children's recall of expository passages* (Tech. Rep. No. 131). Champaign, IL: University of Illinois, Center for the Study of Reading.

Perkins, M. R. (1978). *Measures of cognitive structure: Do they really assess learning at the level of comprehension?* Unpublished Ph.D. Dissertation, University of Massachusetts, Amherst, MA.

Pichert, J. W., & Anderson, R. C. (1977). Taking perspectives on a story. *Journal of Educational Psychology, 69,* 309–315.

Pio, C., & Andre, T. (1981, April). *Paraphrasing highlighted statements and learning from prose.* Paper presented at the Midwestern Educational Research Association Meeting, Los Angeles, CA.

Pollio, H. R., & Pollio, H. R. (1974). The development of figurative language in children. *Journal of Psycholinguistic Research, 3,* 185–201.

Pollio, H. R., Fabrizi, M. S., Sills, A., & Smith, M. K. (1984). Need metaphoric comprehension take longer than literal comprehension. *Journal of Psycholinguistic Research, 13,* 195–214.

Pressey, S. L. (1933). *Psychology and the new education,* New York: Harper and Brothers.

Raphael T. E. (1984). Teaching learners about sources of information for answering comprehension questions, *Journal of Reading, 27,* 303–311.

Raphael T. E., & McKinney, J., (1983). An examination of fifth and eighth grade children's question answering behavior: An instruction study in metacognition. *Journal of Reading Behavior, 15,* 67–86.

Raphael T. E., & Pearson, P. D. (1982). *The effects of metacognitive strategy awareness training on students' questions answering behavior* (Tech. Rep. No. 238). Urbana, IL: University of Illinois, Center for the Study of Reading.

Raphael, T. E., & Wonnacott, C. A. (1984). Heightening fourth grade students' sensitivity to sources of information for answering comprehension questions. *Reading Research Quarterly, 16,* 301–321.

Reder, L. M. (1979). The role of elaborations in memory for prose. *Cognitive Psychology, 11,* 221–234.

Reder, L. M. (1980). The role of elaboration in the comprehension and retention of prose: a critical review. *Review of Educational Research, 50,* 5–53.

Reicher, G. M. (1969). Perceptual recognition as a function of meaningfulness of stimulus material. *Journal of Experimental Psychology, 81,* 275–280.

Reinsch, N. (1971). An investigation of the effects of the metaphor and simile in persuasive discourse. *Speech Monographs, 38,* 142–145.

Reis, R., & Spekman, N. J., (1983). The detection of reader-based versus text-based inconsistencies and the effects of direct training on comprehension monitoring among upper-grade poor comprehenders. *Journal of Reading Behavior, 15*, 49–60.

Rickards, J. P. (1979). Adjunct postquestions in text: A critical review of methods and processes. *Review of Educational Research, 49*, 181–196.

Ricneck, M. (1976–77). Reading comprehension of anaphoric forms in varying linguistic contexts. *Reading Research Quarterly, 12*, 145–165.

Reynolds, R. E. (1985). *Metaphors in text: Implications for theories of prose learning.* Unpublished manuscript, University of Utah.

Reynolds, R. E., & Schwartz, R. M. (1983). Relation of metaphoric processing to comprehension and memory. *Journal of Educational Psychology, 75*, 450–459.

Reynolds, R. E., Schwartz, R. M., & Esposito, J. J. (1982). *The role of metaphor in prose comprehension* (Technical Report No. 259). Champaign, IL: University of Illinois, Center for the Study of Reading.

Rosenschine, B. V. (1980). Skill hierarchies in reading comprehension. In R. J. Spiro, B. C. Bruce, & W. F. Brewer (Eds.), Theoretical Issues in Reading Comprehension (pp. 535–554). Hillsdale, NJ: Erlbaum.

Royer, J. (1977). Remembering: Constructive or reconstructive? In R. C. Anderson, R. J. Spiro, & W. E. Montague (Eds.), *Schooling and the acquisition of knowledge* (pp. 167–174). Hillsdale, NJ: Erlbaum.

Royer, J. M., & Cable, G. W. (1975). Facilitated learning in connected discourse. *Journal of Educational Psychology, 67*, 116–123.

Royer, J. M., & Perkins, M. R. (1977). Facilitative transfer in prose learning over an extended time period. *Journal of Reading Behavior, 9*, 185—188.

Rumelhart, D. E. (1977). Towards an interactive model of reading, In S. Dornic (Ed.), *Attention and performance VI* (pp. 482–503). Hillsdale NJ: Erlbaum.

Rumelhart, D. E. (1980). Schemata: The building blocks of cognition. In R. J. Spiro, B. C. Bruce, & W. F. Brewer (Eds.), *Theoretical issues in Reading comprehension* (pp. 33–58). Hillsdale, NJ: Erlbaum.

Rumelhart, D. E., & McClelland, J. L. (1980). *An interactive activation model of the effect of context in perception, part II,* (Chip Report 95). La Jolla, CA: Center for Human Information Processing.

Rumelhart, D. E., & Mclelland, J. L. (1981). Interactive processing through spreading activation, In. A. M. Lesgold & C. A. Perfetti (Eds.), *Interactive processes in reading* (pp. 37–60). Hillsdale, NJ: Erlbaum.

Rumelhart, D. E., & Ortony, A. (1977). The representation of knowledge in memory. In R. C. Anderson, R. J. Spiro, & W. E. Montague, *Schooling and the acquisition of knowledge* (pp. 93–137). Hillsdale, NJ: Erlbaum.

Sanford, A. J., & Garrod, S. C. (1981). Bridging inferences and the extended domain of reference. In J. Long & A. Baddeley (Eds.), *Attention and performance IX.* Hillsdale, NJ: Erlbaum.

Sanford, A. J., & Garrod, S. C. (1982). Towards a processing account of reference. In A. Flammer & W. Kintsch (Eds.), Amsterdam: North-Holland. (p. 100–110).

Schallert, D. L. (1976). Improving memory for prose: The relationship between depth of processing and context. *Journal of Verbal Learning and Verbal Behavior, 15*, 621–631.

Scharf, B., Zamansky, H. S., & Brightbill, R. F. (1966). Word recognition with masking. *Perception and Psychophysics, 1*, 110–112.

Shiffrin, R. M., & Schneider, W. (1977). Controlled and automatic human information processing: II perceptual learning, automatic attending, and a general theory. *Psychological Review, 84*, 127–190.

Simon, H. A. (1984, Oct). *Talk presented at the Nobel Conference,* Gustafus Adolphus College, St. Peter, MN.

Smith, N. B. (1934). *American reading instruction.* New York: Silver Burdett.

Spache, G. D. (1956/1958) Psychological explanations of reading. In Causey O. S. (Ed.), *The reading teacher's reader.* (pp. 14–22), New York: Ronald Press.

Spiro, R. J. (1977). Remembering information from text: The "state of schema" Approach, In R. C. Anderson, R. J. Spiro, & W. E. Montague, *Schooling and the acquisition of knowledge* (pp. 137–165). Hillsdale, NJ: Erlbaum.

Spiro, R. J. (1980). Constructive processes in prose comprehension and recall. In R. J. Spiro, B. C. Bruce, & W. F. Brewer (Eds.), *Theoretical issues in reading comprehension* (pp. 245–278). Hillsdale, NJ: Erlbaum. (p. 245–278).

Steffensen, M. S., Joag-Dev, C., & Anderson, R. C. (1979). A cross cultural perspective on reading comprehension, *Reading Research Quarterly, 15*, 10–29.

Tanz, C. (1977). Learning how "it" works. *Journal of Child Language, 4*, 224–235.

Taylor, B. (1982). Text structure and children's comprehension and memory for expository material. *Journal of Educational Psychology, 74*, 323–340.

Taylor, B. M., & Beach, R. W. (1984). The effects of text structure instruction on middle-grade students' comprehension and production of expository text. *Reading Research Quarterly, 14*, 134–146.

Tennyson, R. D., & Rothen, W. (1977). Pretask and on-task adaptive design strategies for selecting number of instances in concept acquisition. *Journal of Educational Psychology, 69*, 586–592.

Thorndike, E. L (1917). Reading as reasoning: A study of mistakes in paragraph reading. *Journal of Educational Psychology, 8*, 323–332.

Thorndike, E. L. (1925). *Educational Psychology: Briefer Course,* New York: Teachers College, Columbia University.

Touton, F. C. & Berry, B. T. (1931). Reading comprehension at the junior college level. *California Quarterly of Secondary Education, 6*, 245–251.

van Dijk, T. A., & Kintsch, W., (1983) *Strategies of discourse comprehension.* New York: Academic Press.

Verbrugge, R. R., & McCarrell, N. S. (1977). Metaphoric comprehension: Studies in reminding and resembling. *Cognitive Psychology, 9*, 494–533.

Venezky, R. L. (1985). The history of reading research. In P. D. Pearson (Ed.), *Handbook of reading research* (3–39). New York: Longman.

Vosniadou, F. & Ortony A. (1983). *The influence of analogy in children's acquisition of new information from text: An exploratory study* (Technical Report No. 281). Champaign, IL: University of Illinois, Center for the Study of Reading.

Wagner, M., & Rohwer, W. D. Jr. (1981). Age differences in the elaboration of inferences from text. *Journal of Educational Psychology, 73*, 728–735.

Wagoner, S. A. (1983). *Comprehension monitoring: What it is and what we know about it. Reading Research Quarterly, 18,* 328–346.

Welborn, E. L., & English, H. (1937). Logical learning and retention: A general review of experiments with meaningful verbal materials. *Psychological Bulletin, 34,* 1–20.

Watts, G. H., & Anderson, R. C. (1971). Effects of three types of inserted questions on learning from prose. *Journal of Educational Psychology, 62,* 387–394.

Winograd, P. N. & Johnston, P. (1980). *Comprehension monitoring and the error dectection paradigm* (Technical Report Number 153). Urbana: University of Illinois, Center for the Study of Reading.

Winograd, P. N. (1984). Strategic difficulties in summarizing texts. *Reading Research Quarterly, 14,* 404–424.

Woods, W. A. (1980). Multiple theory formation in speech and reading. In R. J. Spiro, B. C. Bruce, & W. F. Brewer (Eds.). *Theoretical issues in reading comprehension* (pp. 59–86). Hillsdale, NJ: Erlbaum.

Wixson, K. K. (1983a). Questions about a text: What you ask about is what children learn. *Reading Teacher,* 287–293.

Wixson, K. K. (1983b). Postreading question-answer interactions and children's learning from text, *Journal of Educational Psychology, 30,* 413–423.

Wixson, K. K. (1984). Level of importance of postquestions and children's learning from text. *American Educational Research Journal, 21,* 419–434.

Wright, P. (1977). Presenting technical information: A survey of research findings. *Instructional Science, 6,* 93–134.

CHAPTER 14

Current Issues in Classroom Behavior Management

Robert L. Williams

Classroom management research, as described in this chapter, includes studies that systematically attempted to change or account for specific classroom behaviors, both academic and nonacademic. The inclusion of academic variables was considered appropriate because many conduct and disciplinary problems are attributable to academic difficulties. If educational psychology can broadly be construed as the application of psychological knowledge to the solution of educational problems, then classroom management surely resides near the heart of this discipline. Involving the management of both academic and nonacademic behaviors, classroom management research represents one of the most applied spheres of educational psychology.

The current chapter analyzes trends in classroom management research from 1980 to 1983. Trends related to types of participants, target behaviors, and treatment strategies are highlighted for this period. A final section of the chapter is devoted to an overall evaluation of the current and future status of classroom management research. The 186 research studies on which the chapter is based were selected from the following journals considered to be mainstream periodicals in either educational

psychology, school psychology, or applied behavior analysis: *Journal of Educational Psychology, Contemporary Educational Psychology, Educational Technology, American Educational Research Journal, Journal of School Psychology, Psychology in the Schools, School Psychology Review, Journal of Applied Behavior Analysis, Behavior Modification, Education and Treatment of Children,* and *Behavior Therapy.*

Types of Participants

Is classroom management research broadly based in subject types or is it skewed toward particular ages, grade levels, and psychological characteristics? The sampling distribution of the studies is heavily skewed toward the younger end of the age continuum. Subjects were identified by age level in 184 studies. Thirteen percent of these studies identified subjects in the 3–5 age range, 29% in the 6–8 age range, 28% in 9–11 age range, 15% in the 12–14 age range, 8% in the 15–17 age range, 5% in the 18–21 age range, and only 2% included subjects 22 and older.

Subjects were identified by grade level in 148 studies. Ten percent of these studies included participants in the preschool range, 22% in the K–3 grade range, 18% in the 4–5 grade range, 22% in the 6–8 grade range, 6% in the 9–12 grade range,

Robert L. Williams • Department of Educational and Counseling Psychology, University of Tennessee, Knoxville, TN 37916.

8% in the self-contained special classes or schools, 5% in resource rooms, and 9% in college. The grade distribution appears slightly less skewed than the age distribution.

Close to half the studies ($N = 91$, 49%) identified subjects by psychological categories. Of these 91 studies, 29% primarily included behaviorally disordered subjects, 19% educable mentally retarded (EMR) subjects, 15% learning disabled (LD) subjects, 15% average subjects, 13% trainable mentally retarded (TMR) subjects, 12% profoundly retarded subjects, 9% autistic subjects, 9% hyperactive subjects, 3% disadvantaged subjects, 3% hearing impaired subjects, 2% visually impaired subjects, 1% multiple physically handicapped subjects, and 1% gifted subjects. These data indicate that behaviorally disordered students were the most frequently identified subjects in classroom management research. Although academic variables were sometimes targeted with these students, they were mainly selected for inclusion in research studies because of their undesirable conduct in the classroom.

Target Behaviors

The three areas representing the principal targets of classroom management research were academic performance, negative behaviors, and appropriate process behaviors. Academic performance variables were used as targets 107 times, negative behaviors 72 times, and appropriate process behaviors 57 times. Other targets featured to lesser degrees were peer interaction (24 times), teacher behaviors (16 times), and self-management skills (11 times).

The 107 occurrences of academic dependent variables were distributed across the following categories: 25% general academic performance measures (e.g., unspecified test scores, GPA, and homework), 19% math indexes, 12% reading performance, 10% English skills, 7% general discrimination skills, 6% visual-spatial tasks, 5% spelling performance, 4% motor performance, 4% health-related measures, 2% social science skills, 2% problem-solving strategies, 2% class discussion skills, 1% science skills, 1% vocational skills, and 1% interviewing skills. These various academic performance indexes were favorably affected by treatment conditions in most instances.

Off-task behavior was the most popular negative target, representing 22% of the 72 occurrences of negative dependent variables. Disruptive behavior was featured in 21% of the 72 instances, autistic-like behaviors (e.g., bizarre verbal responses, self-stimulation, and stereotypic responses) in 17%, aggression in 17%, activity level in 6%, talking out in 3%, stealing in 1%, impulsive behavior in 1%, dropping out of school in 1%, tardiness in 1%, and unspecified negative behaviors in 10%. Again, these dependent variables proved consistently responsive to various treatment strategies.

On-task activity was by far the most commonly targeted appropriate behavior, being featured in 47% of the 57 occurrences of appropriate process behaviors. Emphasized to lesser degrees in this area were compliance with teacher requests (14%), attendance (12%), imitative behaviors (4%), study habits (2%), custodial activity (2%), task persistence (2%), information seeking (2%), and unspecified appropriate behaviors (16%). Once again, these targets were improved in essentially every case.

In the studies emphasizing peer interaction, general interaction among peers was targeted in 33% of the 24 cases, helping in 16%, cross-ethnic interaction in 13%, cross-ability interaction in 13%, sharing in 13%, cross-handicapped interaction in 8%, and perception of peer support in 4%. These peer dimensions were successfully changed in practically all of the reported instances.

In the 16 instances in which teacher behaviors were used as dependent variables, general behavior management skills were targeted 38% of the time, use of praise 19%, student ratings of teacher effectiveness 13%, teacher feedback 13%, teacher affection 6%, and teacher monitoring of student behavior 6%. Some improvement was reported in practically all cases where teacher variables were employed as targets.

In the 11 cases in which self-management skills were used as targets, self-verbalization was targeted 37% of the time, self-efficacy 27%, self-reinforcement 9%, self-assessment skills 9%, and general self-control skills 18%. These targets were among the most responsive of all dependent variables identified in this review.

Generalization effects across time, behaviors, settings, and/or participants were also often assessed in the studies surveyed. Seventy-five studies (40%) examined one or more types of generalization effects. In all, 89 demonstrations of generalization effects were reported. Generalization across time was demonstrated in 40% of these instances, across behaviors in 23%, across settings in 31%, and across participants in 7%. Of these four types, generalization across behaviors had the lowest success rate (83% of the times assessed). Contrast effects (the opposite of generalization) were evaluated far less frequently than generalization effects. Only 3 (less than 2%) of the 186 studies assessed contrast effects.

Treatment Strategies

This section provides an explanation of the various treatment strategies used with the participants and target behaviors previously described. These strategies are first grouped into two major categories: treatment components and treatment packages. The term *treatment components* refers to discrete manipulations used separately or in combination with other manipulations. Examples of treatment components are verbal approval, response cost, verbal reprimands, and ability grouping. The term *treatment packages* refers to intact combinations of variables. Examples are behavioral coaching, contingency contracting, compliance training, and token economics.

Treatment Components

Instructional Manipulations

Various aspects of the instructional process are often directly manipulated in classroom management research. The broad category of instructional manipulations ranked second in popularity only to reinforcement dimensions. Specifically, instructional treatment components were used 123 times in the 1980–1983 period. These instructional variables impacted a very wide range of both academic and nonacademic measures. Several of these components (e.g., ability grouping, expectancy training, fading) are discussed separately in this section, but instructional variables that received very limited and equivocal coverage in the literature (e.g., discrimination learning, instructional modality, task analysis, and verbal examples) were omitted from this discussion.

Ability Grouping. The concept of ability grouping was evaluated in only six studies included in this review. These studies suggest that heterogeneous grouping promotes a better interchange of academic information than does uniform grouping. Webb and Cullian (1983) report that a major way students help each other in group

situations is by answering peers' questions. This behavior is more likely to occur in heterogeneous than uniform groups (Webb, 1982a, b). Perhaps uniform grouping is more conducive to a competitive and unsupportive atmosphere than is a mixed grouping. When the cooperative versus competitive dimension is artificially controlled, ability grouping has no effect on achievement and cognitive reasoning strategies (Skon, Johnson, & Johnson, 1981).

In some cases, uniform ability grouping appears to promote a sense of cohesion among students from different ethic backgrounds. In one study, black and white students in an accelerated eighth grade track attended almost all of their classes together (Schofield & Francis, 1982). This arrangement produced much more cross-racial interaction than had been reported in earlier research and was especially efficacious in promoting cross-racial interaction among boys.

It has also been documented that instructional procedures tend to differ for high and low ability groups (Haskins, Walden, & Ramey, 1983). Students in high groups are more likely to work individually, whereas those in low groups are more likely to receive group instruction. Drill, error correction, control statements, direct instruction, and positive reinforcement are used more frequently with low than high groups. Not surprisingly, students in low groups are more disruptive and off-task than those in high groups.

Expectancy Training. Creating an expectancy of success is one avenue for inducing students to engage in those behaviors likely to lead to success. Seidner and Kirschenbaum (1981) embellished the impact of a study skills training program by informing undergraduates of the expected outcome of using those study techniques. Haynes and Johnson (1983) manipulated teacher and student expectation of college success by sending the teachers lists of students likely to improve their performance and some students letters indicating that they were likely to do well. Although high self-expectancy by itself was quite effective in increasing GPA, the combination of high teacher expectancy and high self-expectancy produced the greatest increment.

Fading. This strategy was used in only seven studies but with considerable success. As an example, Collins, Epstein, and Hannay (1981) evaluated the role of fading and feedback in teaching visual acuity skills to myopic college students. In one treatment condition, fading was accomplished by increasing the distance at which the visual stimuli were presented as the participants mastered each level. The feedback procedure provided confirmation that the participants' responses were correct. Various combinations of feedback and fading were evaluated in the study. Although both the fading and feedback conditions resulted in significantly more improvement than no treatment, the fading conditions were the most effective procedures for facilitating the visual acuity skills.

Feedback. This popular instructional variable was more frequently used in combination with other treatment components ($N = 34$) than as a singular treatment ($N = 16$). Although feedback was generally successful, it was judged to be exceptionally effective in 19 studies across a variety of dependent variables (e.g., writing, on-task activity, noise making, math performance, self-efficacy ratings, appropriate process, activity level, hearing aid use, peer interaction, underlining, discrimination tasks, and teacher praise) and subject types (e.g., elementary, college, and behavior problem students). It was most frequently reported as effective with elementary age students.

Both mechanical stimuli and verbal comments have been used to provide feedback. Sherman and Anderson (1980) used mechanical feedback to reduce nonattending behavior. Each participant was first seated at a table with a light box in front of him. Contingencies were arranged so the light would come on whenever the subject stopped attending to the assigned math task. This procedure was quite effective in reducing nonattending behavior both during and after treatment. LaRowe, Tucker, and McGuire (1980) used a similar feedback system to control noise level in a school lunchroom: a green light for acceptable noise level, a yellow light for noise approaching an unacceptable level, and a red light for unacceptable noise level.

Verbal feedback has been used to improve a variety of academic skills. As an example, an ingenious feedback system was developed by Glover, Zimmer, Filbeck, and Plake (1980) to help undergraduates acquire underlining skills. After the students underlined what they thought was the main idea in a passage, they peeled off a label to see what the experimenters considered to be the main idea. This feedback system was generally as effective as feedback plus points leading to grades in improving underlining skills and overall reading comprehension. The more precisely the positive feedback pinpoints the facilitative behaviors, the more likely those behaviors are to be strengthened (Koorland & Oseroff, 1980).

As one might expect, positive feedback can fundamentally affect expectations of success (Ballowe, Marlow, & Algozzine, 1981). On an initial task, students were told they were either correct or incorrect. Following this feedback, students were asked to rate how well they anticipated doing on the next task. Only those students receiving success feedback maintained their initially high expectations of success. Unfortunately, expectations of success were not highly related to performance on a novel and difficult task.

Teachers as well as students can be helped by feedback. For example, feedback has been very effective in helping teachers become more approving toward students (Gross & Ekstrand, 1983; Mace, Cancelli, & Manos, 1983). In Gross and Ekstrand's study, teacher praise was monitored through audio recordings of classroom interactions. In the initial phase of this study, frequency of teacher praise for the previous day was recorded on a wall chart in the classroom. In a feedback fading phase, the wall chart was removed and teachers were given direct feedback on randomly selected days about their use of praise. The feedback arrangement almost doubled teacher use of praise. The pace of teacher comments, the quality of teacher questions, and completion of evaluation forms have also proven highly modifiable through systematic feedback to teachers (Hundert, McMahon, & Kitcher, 1982; Tobin & Capie, 1982).

Instructional Games. One would think that a very effective way to promote on-task behavior, student achievement, and affinity for learning would be to combine game activities with instruction. However, this approach appeared in only two studies included in this review. Murphy, Hutchison, and Bailey (1983) found that organized games, such as rope jumping and foot racing, substantially reduced inappropriate (largely aggressive) playground behaviors. Kirby, Holborn, and Bushby (1981) used bingo cards to promote word identification skills in third grade students. Bingo cards with sight words were divided into several different boxes, and a center box was marked free. Correct identification of the sight words earned tokens that could be cashed in weekly for reinforcing activities. Playing several bingo games each day greatly increased the word identification skills of these third graders.

Interspersal Training. Two studies have investigated how variation in instructional tasks affects student performance (Dunlap & Koegel, 1980; Neef, Iwata, & Page, 1980). Dunlap and Koegel's study with autistic children compared the common method of presenting a single task throughout an instructional session with that of interspersing the task among a variety of other tasks from the subject's clinic curriculum. Correct responding declined in the constant task condition but improved and stabilized in the varied presentation. Neef *et al.* (1980) alternated new words with mastered words in teaching male disabled students word mastery skills. This interspersal arrangement was more effective than both baseline and a high density reinforcement system involving frequent approval for task related behavior.

Modeling. This revered concept from social learning theory continues to surface quite frequently in classroom management research. It is more commonly used in combination with other treatment components ($N = 18$) than as a singular treatment ($N = 4$). A good example of the instructional application of modeling is Schunk's (1981) cognitive-modeling treatment for teaching elementary students how to solve division problems. The students observed while an adult model verbalized aloud the strategies being used to arrive at the correct solutions. During a subsequent practice phase, the students received corrective modeling whenever they reached an impasse in working the problems. This treatment was effective in improving persistence, accuracy, and perceived efficacy in solving division problems.

Videotapes represent a powerful means of accomplishing modeling effects in the classroom. This approach was successfully used in teaching 4- and 5-year-olds how to deal with emergencies (Rosenbaum, Creedon, & Drabman, 1981). The children were exposed to a number of videotaped scenes of emergencies and nonemergencies, with an adult demonstrating what to do in each situation. Through this modeling procedure the children learned such skills as distinguishing emergencies from nonemergencies, reporting the number of people who appeared to be hurt, and determining whether an ambulance was needed. Murray and Epstein (1981) used a similar videotape approach in teaching toothbrushing skills to Head Start youngsters.

Modeling can also have a very adverse effect on student behavior. For example, an active model accelerated activity levels in hyperactive children (Copeland & Weissbrod, 1980). "Moral" stories that described inappropriate behaviors needing to

be changed actually increased negative behavior in a snack and clean-up situation (Lutzker, Crozier, & Lutzker, 1981). Thus, exposing children to examples of bad behaviors and the adverse consequences of those behaviors is likely to be counterproductive.

Prompting. This treatment component (included in 18 studies) was usually employed in combination with other treatment variables ($N = 14$). Although treatment effects were reported in most of the prompting studies, outstanding results were noted in only two instances. One of the more successful applications of this variable was the use of picture prompts to help moderately and severely retarded adolescents master complex vocational tasks (Wacker & Berg, 1983). A separate picture book was provided for each task, indicating the sequence of parts to be selected and how those parts fitted together. The picture prompts greatly increased the percentage of steps completed on vocational tasks and reduced the training time on novel tasks not involving picture prompts.

Task Difficulty. The difficulty level of a task (manipulated in two studies and highly effective in both) would logically seem to affect not only mastery of the task but disruptive behavior as well. This notion is based on the premise that tasks that over- or under-challenge the learner are likely to lead to off-task and disruptive activity. A study by Center, Dietz, and Kaufman (1982) provides some support for this notion. The criterion for a match between student ability and task difficulty was a success rate of 60% or above on a criterion-referenced test, whereas the criterion for a mismatch was 40% success or below. The matching procedure significantly reduced disruptive and other inappropriate behaviors.

Task Presentation. Teachers often attempt to improve student involvement in tasks by altering the way they present those tasks. The only comparison of presentation strategies was provided by Brophy, Rorkkemper, Rashid, and Goldberger (1983). Some tasks were begun with no presentation statement, others with negative statements about how boring and difficult the tasks were, and some with very positive statements about the challenging, useful, and interesting aspects of the tasks. Moving directly into the task without any presentation statement produced the highest level of task engagement. Negative presentation decreased student engagement but positive presentation did not raise it.

Testing. Do tests serve only as a convenient

vehicle for evaluating student learning or do they actually increase student learning? Two studies that manipulated testing conditions point to the latter. Halpin and Halpin (1982) compared the effects of studying for and taking a test over academic material with that of studying simply to learn. Subjects in the second condition were promised an "A" no matter what they actually made on the test in question. In fact, a subgroup in this second condition did not take the test at all. Six weeks following the treatment phase all subjects were administered an unannounced retention test. The combination of studying for and taking the initial test produced better performance on the initial test plus better retention 6 weeks later. Nungester and Duchastel (1982) compared the effects of taking a test over a small amount of material with that of spending equal time reviewing the material or going on to unrelated material. No feedback was provided subjects in the test group after the initial exam. On a later retention test, subjects who had taken the initial test did better than students in either of the other conditions.

Time Limits.   How much time teachers give students to perform a task surely affects how quickly and how well students do that task. The only recent study addressing this issue (Van Houten & Little, 1982) suggests that lowering time limits for performing academic tasks may increase not only the pace of work but accuracy as well. EMR adolescents were given math assignments under both a 5- and 20-minute time limit. The students completed almost as much work under the 5-minute limit as under the 20-minute limit and actually did slightly more accurate work under the 5-minute limit. Rather than simply producing rushed work, the shorter time limit apparently produced a higher level of task involvement—thus benefitting quality of work as well as quantity.

Response Delay Training. Another way time has been manipulated to promote academic performance is to impose a delay between an instructional stimulus and the child's response to that stimulus (Dyer, Christian, & Luce, 1982). The objective behind this strategy was to prevent the student from responding impulsively and perhaps incorrectly. The performance of autistic teenagers was evaluated under two conditions: (a) a no-response-delay condition in which the child was permitted to respond as soon as the discriminative stimulus was presented; (b) a response-delay condition in which a 3-second delay was imposed between the discriminative stimulus and the signal

for the child to respond. The subjects were taught such discriminations as right/left, his/her, and the functions of common objects. The results showed that the 3-second delay produced more correct responding than the no delay condition. Pilot testing, however, showed that a 6-second delay was too long. The delay apparently needs to be just long enough to require the child to consider carefully his or her answer but without forgetting the relevant stimuli.

Peer Control

Moderate attention is being given to the use of peers in classroom management. The 34 applications of peer control described in the selected studies usually resulted in adequate success and in about a third of the cases in exceptional success. Peer strategies have been used with such dependent variables as on-task behavior, math performance, peer interaction, reading performance, and disruptive activity. Peer control has most often been effective with elementary students categorized as slow learners and behavior problems.

Peer Controversy. Smith, Johnson, and Johnson (1981) attempted to evaluate the impact of controversy on the amount of information students accurately learned and the amount of additional information sought about the topic. Students in three conditions were first given both pro and con information about two controversial issues. Students in the controversy condition were divided into pro and con subgroups to argue for their respective views; those in the concurrence-seeking condition could study the issues any way they wished except arguing about them; and those in the individualistic condition were to study the materials without interacting with one another. The controversy condition was superior to the other conditions on both dependent variables.

Peer Cooperation.   Some form of peer cooperation was employed in eight studies, either as a singular treatment ($N = 5$) or as a part of a treatment package ($N = 3$). It was judged to be exceptionally effective in most of these studies. One study arranged for students to work under three types of goal structures: cooperative, competitive, and individualistic (Skon *et al.,* 1981). In the cooperative condition, the students worked together to complete one set of papers and were rewarded on the basis of the collective performance of group members. Students in the competitive condition worked alone and competed for first, second, and third places in their triad. Students in the individualistic condition neither cooperated nor competed. In this comparison, students in the cooperative condition perceived more peer support, used better strategies to complete their tasks, and indeed did better on their tasks than students in the other conditions.

Four other investigations by essentially the same research group indicate that cooperative learning can help students of very different backgrounds not only perform better but interact more effectively with one another. Johnson and Johnson (1981b) used cooperative groups with nonhandicapped and severely handicapped 4th graders to promote cross-handicapped interaction within the instructional setting, daily free time periods, and postexperimental problem situations with new peers. Armstrong, Johnson, and Balow (1981) used cooperative groups to increase achievement and interpersonal attraction between learning disabled and normal progress students. Similar manipulations have proven equally effective in promoting cross-ethnic interactions and attractions between minority and majority students (Johnson & Johnson, 1981a; Johnson, Johnson, Tiffany, & Zaidman, 1983).

A teacher need not employ cooperative groups continuously to get many of the benefits of this approach. In an investigation by Hertz-Lazarowitz, Sharan, and Steinberg (1980), experimental teachers used cooperative group learning at least 30% of the time, whereas control teachers employed whole-class instruction all the time. Students in the experimental classes proved more cooperative in judgments about distributing payoffs and also did better on learning tasks than students in control classes.

An obvious benefit of cooperative group learning is improved interaction among students. However, interaction can also be improved by training some peers to initiate interaction with other peers (Hendrickson, Strain, Tremblay, & Shores, 1982). Preschool peers were trained to exhibit three types of interaction toward target students: (a) play organizers, for example, "Let's play school;" (b) shares, for example, "Let's trade toys;" and (c) assists, for example, "Let me help you get on the merry-go-round." In one case a normal preschooler exhibited these behaviors toward withdrawn peers and in a second case a preschooler with a history of negative interactions did the initiating. The peer helpers were prompted, praised, and given stars and edibles for appropriate initia-

tions. In general, the target students reciprocated the initiations directed toward them.

Peer Feedback. Feedback from peers can be invaluable in assessing student behaviors. In one study the teacher assigned each student an explicit behavior goal, for example, "play more with friends during recess" (Ragland, Kerr, & Strain, 1981). To evaluate whether each student had attained his goal, the teacher called out each child's name and goal and then asked each of the other students whether the child had reached that goal the previous day. The other students had to provide examples to support their judgment of whether the child had achieved the goal. The teacher judged a goal to have been met if a majority of the students reported the goal as met. The authors report that independent observational data generally agreed with peer judgments and that the treatment strategy improved the targeted social behaviors. A second study by this same group of researchers separated the impact of simply assigning children goals from that of soliciting the peer judgments (Kerr, Strain, & Ragland, 1982). Goals by themselves had minimal impact on the target behaviors but the peer feedback system substantially improved social interaction.

Peer Modeling. Peer modeling was employed in seven studies, usually in combination with other treatments. As an example of this approach, Egel, Richman, and Koegel (1981) trained three normal functioning children from neighboring classrooms and a high functioning autistic youngster to serve as models for autistic children in a special education classroom. Models were approximately the same age as the participants. Models demonstrated how to perform discrimination tasks related to color, shape, on/under, and yes/no. Participants substantially improved their performance of these tasks by observing the models.

Peer Tutoring. Ten applications of peer tutoring were identified in the literature. These applications were evenly distributed across singular and combined treatments. A common peer tutoring arrangement was having older students tutor younger ones. Trovanto and Bucher (1980) used high achieving students from the 6th, 7th, and 8th grades to tutor second to fourth graders who were deficient in reading skills. Peer tutoring only and peer tutoring with home reinforcers were significantly superior to a control condition in improving oral reading accuracy and comprehension of the younger students.

Much of the research on peer tutoring indicates that both tutors and tutees benefit from this arrangement. Sharpley, Irvine, and Sharpley (1983) used fifth and sixth graders to tutor second graders in math. Both tutors and tutees improved significantly more in math performance than did comparable control subjects. Surprisingly, the tutors' preintervention math skills did not seem to affect the amount of progress made by tutees.

There is even some evidence that individuals may benefit more from tutoring than being tutored. Maher (1982) assigned socially and emotionally maladjusted adolescents to one of three treatment groups: (a) tutor an elementary school-aged EMR child; (b) receive tutoring from a nonhandicapped student in the high school; and (c) receive group counseling regarding academic problems. The students who served as tutors improved the most on measures of academic performance and significantly reduced their rate of absenteeism and disciplinary referrals.

Peer Management. Students implemented comprehensive behavior management procedures with peers in three of the studies reviewed. For example, McKenzie and Budd (1981) trained a 12-year-old student with emotional problems to work with an 11- and a 14-year-old who had displayed major behavior and learning problems. The tutor performed the following functions: (a) graded tutees' math problems; (b) provided praise and instructional feedback to tutees; and (c) awarded free time based on the tutees' math performance. The tutor was trained through modeling and praised after each session for appropriate use of behavior management strategies. The tutor was allowed to continue only if he maintained satisfactory progress in his own work.

Parent Interventions

Parents have played a very limited role in recent classroom management research. Only 11 different applications of parent involvement were identified in the literature.

Home-Based Reinforcers. One way that parents can facilitate classroom management is by making home-based reinforcers contingent on school-related behavior. This procedure was used in six studies and judged to be exceptionally effective in three instances. For example, Drew, Evans, Bostow, Geiger, and Drash (1982) had parents develop a list of privileges and rewards that their children found especially appealing. Children

could partake of the home-based privileges only if their daily report card from the teacher indicated that they had completed their math assignment with at least 76% accuracy. Both the quantity and accuracy of math performance immediately and significantly increased as a result of the home-based reinforcers. Among the home privileges that have proven especially useful with young children are playing outside, snacking, going swimming, watching ''Sesame Street,'' and having a friend over to play (Budd, Leibowitz, Riner, Mindell, & Goldfarb, 1981; Drew *et al.*, 1982).

Parent Tutoring. In the only study that evaluated parent tutoring, Gang and Poche (1982) trained three mothers (one a college graduate and two high school graduates) to tutor their 9-year-old sons in oral reading during summer vacation. The experiments employed a highly structured reading program that divided tutoring behavior into four categories: (a) presenting materials; (b) giving instructions; (c) correcting mistakes; and (d) timing and recording the child's performance. The mothers essentially exhibited no correct tutoring prior to training but remained above 90% correct after training. As a result of the summer tutoring, the children improved three times faster than their expected rate.

Teacher–Parent Communication. Apart from their roles as contingency managers and tutors, parents can provide some support for the instructional program simply through effective teacher–parent communication. A beginning point is for teachers to keep parents updated as to what is happening at school. Teacher communication in one study involved a single feedback note to parents that included the child's homework record, an evaluation of that record, the class's homework schedule, and an indication of the importance of homework (Lordeman & Winett, 1980). The teacher communication substantially increased homework submission, with the effectiveness lasting for about one marking period. Different forms of teacher feedback to parents, including daily report cards, daily letters, and daily phone calls have all proven successful in improving such dependent variables as class participation, homework completion, on-task behavior, attendance, and weekly GPAs (Trice, Parker, Furrow, & Iwata, 1983).

Parent communication to teachers (manipulated in two studies) may be as useful as teacher communication to parents. Gresham (1983) arranged for the parents of a mildly retarded student to send a note to school each day stating that the child did not commit a destructive act at home (e.g., fire setting, vandalizing, or attacking others). These notes became the basis of some powerful tangible reinforcement contingencies in the classroom. Even if the child brought a bad note, he was praised for bringing in the note but lost the more tangible reinforcers. Destructive acts at home dropped markedly both during and after the treatment phase. This study illustrates not only the importance of parent communication to the teacher but also how the teacher can support responsible student behavior at home.

Self-Administered Strategies

Students undoubtedly bring some characteristics to the classroom that affect the course of classroom management. The following student characteristics are among those receiving some attention in classroom management research: (1) Moral development—for example, middle school students at a preconventional level of moral development exhibit more unacceptable behavior in the classroom than those at higher levels of moral development (Bear & Richards, 1981). (b) Ability level—higher-ability students are more inclined to respond correctly to teacher questions than are lower-ability students, and teachers are more likely to respond positively to the correct responses of the higher-ability than of the lower-ability students (Gettinger, 1983). Despite these differences, lower-ability students are as likely to be on-task as higher ability. (c) Student effort—at least at the college level—has about the same impact on academic achievement as student aptitude (Grabe, 1982). (d) Stability of student behaviors—student responses gradually get worse over the course of the year with the greatest stability being near the middle of the year (Evertson & Veldman, 1981). (e) Student self-efficacy—students' perceptions of their academic skills are good predictors of their actual performance (Schunk, 1981). Feedback regarding ability is more likely to impact self-efficacy than feedback regarding effort (Schunk, 1983). (f) Student planning—monthly planning of study activity among college students is more related to high GPA than is daily planning (Kirschenbaum, Malett, Humphrey, & Tomarkin, 1982).

Although the variables described in the previous paragraph help to account for classroom behaviors, most of them may largely be beyond the teacher's control. The focus of this section, therefore, is on those student variables that can be impacted by teachers and that can help students assume a greater measure of responsibility for their classroom behaviors. Twenty-seven applications of these variables were identified in the literature reviewed.

Self-Instruction. Internal messages can serve both as cues and as consequences for overt behaviors. Self-talk has been one of the more popular self-management interventions in classroom management research, appearing in 10 of the studies reviewed—6 times as a singular treatment and 4 times in combination with other treatment variables. Virtually every time self-verbalization was used as a treatment strategy, it was judged to be highly effective. It has been used with elementary, slower-learning, college, and behavior problem students to improve on-task behavior, math performance, general academic achievement, accuracy of performance, aggression, and hyperactivity. The three types of self-instructions that have been the focus of research in this area are: (a) directions as to how to perform a task; (b) statements as to how to cope with mistakes; and (c) statements related to tuning out distractions. Burgio, Whitman, and Johnson (1980) used a combination of these procedures to reduce off-task behavior of EMR children.

Bryant and Budd (1982) have described how teachers can assist students in acquiring appropriate self-verbalizations. They had teachers fade overt instructions to a whispering level as the children began emitting overt self-instructions. The children then faded their own overt verbalizations by progressing to lip movements without sound and finally to self-instructions only at a covert level. Both this study and an investigation by Whitman and Johnston (1983) provide compelling evidence that focused self-instructions enhance the accuracy of student work.

Specific examples of self-instructions have been provided by Albion and Salzberg (1982). Substantially retarded students in a special education class improved their math performance by learning to make statements regarding their general approach to a task (e.g., "Work slowly," "Look at your own paper") and other more task-specific statements (e.g., "What is the largest number?" "Put a mark by the largest number"). As in other studies, prompts were used in training the children to engage in these self-verbalizations. Similar self-instructions have been effective in improving a variety of process and product behaviors (Forman,

1980; Kendall, 1982; Kendall & Zupman, 1981; Kim, 1980).

Self-Monitoring. The recording of one's own behavior was manipulated in 11 studies, usually with adequate success and with exceptional success in four instances. Self-monitoring is often used in evaluating the effectiveness of other self-management strategies (e.g., stimulus control, self-reinforcement), but can be used as a treatment strategy in and of itself. Workman, Helton, and Watson (1982) have demonstrated the potency of self-monitoring even with very young children. Through modeling, guided practice, and independent practice, a 4-year-old preschool male was trained to mark a sheet of paper if he was working on a teacher-assigned task when a kitchen timer went off at 5-minute intervals. This simple self-monitoring substantially increased the child's sustained schoolwork.

The impact of self-monitoring is somewhat related to what students are self-recording. Litrownik and Fretas (1980) contrasted the effects of four self-monitoring conditions on a bead stringing task. Retarded adolescents either recorded a positive aspect of their performance (finishing the task within the specified time), a negative aspect (not finishing the task), a neutral aspect (time when they strung), or no aspect. Although the four conditions did not differentially affect persistence at the task, recording a positive aspect of the task produced greater gains in task performance than recording a negative aspect. This finding is generally consistent with a large body of research in the self-management literature.

How effective is student assessment of behavior compared to teacher assessment of that behavior? Hallahan, Lloyd, Kneedler, and Marshall (1982) evaluated the math performance and on-task behavior of an 8-year-old learning disabled male under a self-assessment and a teacher-assessment condition. In the self-assessment phase, the student recorded whether he was paying attention whenever an audio recorder emitted quiet tones. In the teacher assessment phase, the teacher made the judgment as to whether the student was paying attention and instructed the subject as to what to record. The two conditions produced similar improvement in math performance but self-assessment was superior to teacher assessment in promoting on-task behavior.

The effectiveness of self-monitoring is sometimes contrasted with that of more traditional token procedures. Cohen, Polsgrove, Rieth, and Heinen

(1981) first trained underachieving students to self-record the frequency of their on-task and noise-making behaviors. Then, the students prepared behavioral graphs that were posted for all to see. Finally, they operated under a token system with tangible rewards. Although self-recording and graphing were somewhat more effective than baseline conditions, they were not nearly as effective as the token system.

Self-Reinforcement. Students can learn to reinforce their own behaviors in much the same way teachers reinforce those behaviors. Self-reinforcement can involve at least three operations: (a) self-selection of reinforcers; (b) self-determination of reinforcement contingencies; and (c) self-administration of reinforcers. These dimensions were at least moderately effective in six studies and highly effective in two of the studies.

One problem that has surfaced with self-reinforcement is a tendency of some students to set extremely lenient standards for themselves. Using a point system tied to free time and tangible rewards, Wall (1983) compared work completion rates under external and student determined reinforcement standards. The external standards required the students to increase their completion rates to receive substantial reinforcement. In the self-selection phase students were completely free to set their own reinforcement standards. Although both treatment conditions increased work completion rates over baseline, external standards proved significantly superior to self-standards. Students became increasingly lenient with the reinforcement standards during the self-selection phase and generally failed to imitate the external standards.

Dickerson and Creedon (1981) examined the impact of externally and self-selected standards when the standards were equated across conditions. Three conditions were employed: (a) student-selected standards for points leading to tangible payoffs; (b) externally selected standards with each subject yoked to a member of the student-selected group; and (c) a no contingency control condition. In contrast to Wall's findings, students in the self-selection group selected stringent reinforcement standards and performed at a significantly higher level than students in the external group.

Self-administration of reinforcement contingencies is often used as a sequel to external administration of contingencies. Gallant, Sargeant, and Van Houten's study (1980) with a bright 11-year-old illustrates this sequence of events. Following baseline, the student operated under externally administered contingencies in which the teacher checked his work and indicated whether he had earned access to a high priority science lab activity. In the subsequent phase, the student could go to the science lab whenever he had completed his work and felt that he had achieved the required accuracy. With the exception of a slight decrease in accuracy, the substantial improvement achieved in the external phase was generally maintained in the self-administration phase. Shapiro and Klein (1980) have also shown that improvement established in an external token system can be maintained through self-assessment and self-reinforcement.

Classroom Reinforcement Procedures

Reinforcement has received the most extensive attention of any general concept in classroom management research. Some aspect of this variable was manipulated 160 times in the recent literature.

Reinforcement Contingencies

Clarity of Contingencies. Witt and Adams (1980) demonstrated the importance of clear contingencies both in direct and vicarious reinforcement conditions. With a nontarget subject seated nearby, the target subject was either verbally approved without mention of what behavior was being approved (e.g., ''You're doing nicely'') or approved with clear specification of what was being approved (e.g., ''I like it when you play with your pencil,'' ''You are studying well''). Though both conditions increased the behavior being approved, the descriptive approval had a more decisive impact on the target and nontarget subject's behavior.

Group Contingencies. Although most classroom reinforcement systems operate on the basis of individual contingencies, group contingencies were used in 13 of the studies reviewed—usually in combination with other treatment conditions. These group contingencies consistently led to improvement in the target behaviors and in five instances to exceptional improvement.

One type of group contingency involves rewarding the class as a whole for meeting a particular standard. Bear and Richards (1980) studied the impact of awarding one minute of extra recess time for each one point improvement of first the weekly and then the daily class mean (compared to the baseline mean) in math and English. The group contingencies substantially improved both target behaviors, with the effect being more pronounced for math than English. In a similar vein, Allen, Gottselig, and Boylan (1982) used a kitchen timer and flip card system to award the class an additional minute of free time for every 5 minutes in which all students followed the class rules. Disruptive behavior dropped to a very low level during both math and language arts.

A number of group contingency studies have divided classes into teams. In some cases, all teams are competing against a common criterion. For example, in a study by Fishbein and Wasik (1981), a librarian awarded points several times during the period to teams whose members were all obeying the rules of good conduct in the library. To win, a team had to earn 75% of the possible points. A treatment phase with backup privileges (e.g., a special activity conducted by the classroom teacher) raised appropriate behaviors well above baseline whereas a phase with no backup privileges did not. Other studies (e.g., Saigh & Umar, 1983) have examined the effects of team contingencies involving interteam competition. In Saigh and Umar's study, the team with the fewest rule violations received a variety of rewards: official letters of commendation, extra recess time, victory tags, and a winner's chart. A number of disruptive behaviors were markedly reduced by the team competition.

McLaughlin (1981) contrasted the effects of individual and group contingencies on reading performance, negative peer comments, and pupil preferences for the two systems. In the individual phase, students earned points for accurate reading, hard work, and good behavior but lost points for disruptive and off-task behavior. In the group phase, points were contingent on the average reading performance in the class. In both conditions, a Friday activity period was used as the backup reward. A yoking system between the individual and group phase allowed for equivalence of point criteria under the two conditions. The group contingency was superior to the individual in promoting reading accuracy and the two were equally effective in reducing negative peer comments. Students expressed a slight preference for the group over the individual contingencies.

Reinforcement Sharing. A system very similar to group contingencies is one in which group rewards are based on the performance of a subset of students within the group. This reinforcement sharing contingency was reported in the literature to have been successfully applied six times, always in combination with other treatment variables. Swain, Allard, and Holborn (1982) used this contingency to promote immediate and long-term dental hygiene. Each day four students were randomly selected from each of two class teams to have their teeth checked for cleanness. The team with the cleanest teeth had all its names displayed on a winners' poster and all received "Scratch n' Sniff" stickers with positive comments on them.

Paine *et al.* (1982) used a reinforcement sharing arrangement to promote social skills. In this case the class as a whole earned extra recess privileges if the targeted student achieved a specified level of social interaction. Special peers were selected to interact with the target students and to model appropriate social interaction. The social skills emphasized were starting conversations, responding to others' conversation, maintaining conversation already under way, praising peers, and cooperating with peers. The combined package was quite effective in upgrading the targeted social skills.

How is the performance of specific students affected by the various types of contingencies? Speltz, Shimamuira, and McReynolds (1982) contrasted student math performance under individual, group, and reinforcement sharing contingencies. Although the contingencies were about equally effective for the group as a whole, two of four target students did their best work when they were identified before the task as the representative worker for the group (reinforcement sharing).

Functional Contingencies. A functional tie between the reinforcement delivery system and the target behavior could be expected to promote bonding between the two events. A study by Williams, Koegel, and Egel (1981) clearly illustrates one method for achieving this functional tie. In an arbitrary delivery phase, a correct response involving a hand movement was followed with an edible reward delivered to the mouth, whereas a correct response involving a specified movement of the mouth was followed with an edible delivered to the hand. In contrast, delivery of the reward was compatible with the target behavior in the functional phase (i.e., correct movement of the hand was followed by an edible being placed in the hand and correct movement of the mouth was followed by the edible being placed in the mouth). Rewards and target behaviors were held constant across the arbitrary and functional conditions. The functional delivery proved much superior to the arbitrary in promoting the target behaviors.

Dimensions of Reinforcement

Immediacy of Reinforcement. In two of the three studies in which the timing of reinforcement was manipulated, immediate reinforcement proved superior to delayed. For example, Mayhew and Anderson (1980) found that tokens provided during class sessions for on-task behavior were more effective than those provided during a videotape of the class sessions. Fowler and Baer (1981), however, found that behavior gains were generally comparable under an early (immediately after class) and a late feedback condition (end of the school day). In fact, performance gains generalized more readily to nontreatment settings under the late feedback condition.

Reinforcement Schedules. The seven studies that manipulated reinforcement schedules suggest that partial schedules are particularly useful in the regular classroom. Ollendick, Dailey, and Shapiro (1983), for example, found that intermittent praise was an effective adjunct to vicarious praise on a continuous schedule. In fact, children who observed others being praised on a continuous schedule and were themselves praised on an intermittent basis actually performed better than the children praised on a continuous schedule.

Laboratory research has shown that variable schedules of partial reinforcement are generally superior to fixed schedules in promoting permanency of behavior change. In a classroom setting, Van Houten and Nau (1980) compared fixed and variable schedules in which students earned checks for being attentive and not engaging in disruptive behavior. Checks were exchangeable for an opportunity to draw a prize from a grab bag. On the average, the two schedules required the same amount of appropriate behavior to earn checks. Attentive behavior was slightly higher, disruptive behavior was slightly lower, and behavior was more consistent under the variable than the fixed schedule.

Vicarious Reinforcement. Another dimension of reinforcement that affects the ease and scope of classroom management is vicarious reinforcement. The five studies addressing this issue indicate that a number of variables can affect the likelihood of vicarious reinforcement. Interaction among students is one important factor. Sharpley (1982) paired fourth graders on the basis of a prestudy writing test. Half of the subjects received direct rewards (e.g., written feedback, smiling faces, verbal praise, and a sweet edible) for good reproduction of alphabet letters and half did not. Some subjects could freely talk to each other after finishing each set of letters, whereas others were not permitted to talk. Although all the students responded favorably to direct rewards, only those students who were permitted to talk freely to peers evidenced the same performance under the vicarious as under the direct reinforcement condition. In fact, students in the no-talk condition showed no evidence of a vicarious reinforcement effect.

Vicarious rewards are also unlikely to be effective unless the subject is provided some direct reinforcement. Lancioni (1982) trained normal peers to use direct and vicarious rewards in tutoring mentally retarded age mates. Vicarious edibles and approval were effective after use of direct edibles and approval. Without some exposure to direct rewards, a child may actually evidence diminished performance under a vicarious reward condition (Ollendick *et al.*, 1983). Ollendick *et al.* found that a child might increase performance initially under a vicarious condition but then reach subbaseline levels if no direct rewards were given. Other researchers have found that vicarious praise is likely to be more useful in initiating behavior than in maintaining it (Boyd, Keilbaugh, & Axelrol, 1981).

Types of Reinforcers

Pre- and Postselection of Backup Reinforcers. Regardless of what privileges or rewards are used as backup reinforcers, does it make a difference whether the subject selects the reinforcing consequence before or after performing the target behavior? Kazdin and Geesey (1980) allowed primary age EMR boys either to pre- or post-select the backup reinforcers (e.g., special recess, free time, access to a highly valued toy, or selection of a small toy) in several different time periods during the day. Both approaches produced much higher levels of attentive behavior than did baseline, but the preselection of reinforcers was considerably more potent than postselection. Preselecting backup rewards may bring their controlling impact closer in time to the performance of target behaviors.

Reinforcer Variation. Rewards must be varied over time to maintain their reinforcement value. Egel (1981) used edible rewards for correct responses in working with developmentally disabled children. Each of three edibles was used for an extended number of trials in the constant reinforcement condition, but administered in random order across trials in the varied condition. Thus, each edible was used about the same number of times under the two conditions. Nonetheless, the two target behaviors both declined over time under the constant condition but increased and then stabilized under the varied condition.

Conditioned Reinforcers. Because teachers may not have access to many primary reinforcers in the classroom, they must develop efficient conditioned reinforcers. Although praise is itself a conditioned reinforcer, it can be used to develop other conditioned reinforcers. For example, Goetz, Ayala, Hatfield, Marshall, and Etzel (1983) paired an auditory click with praise (e.g., "The beeper tells me to thank you for picking up the blocks so well.") on either a fixed or variable interval schedule. After this pairing, the auditory stimulus alone maintained shorter pick-up time for the blocks. This study suggests that almost any kind of stimulus consistently paired with an event already reinforcing to students can come to serve as a conditioned reinforcer.

Verbal Approval. Perhaps the most readily available reinforcer in the classroom is teacher approval. Because praise is usually employed as a peripheral component in treatment packages (40 out of 43 times), its unique contribution to treatment packages is difficult to isolate. Although most treatment combinations involving approval were moderately effective, only about 25% of them proved highly effective.

The power of differential approval is graphically illustrated in a study by Buzas and Ayllon (1981). During a baseline condition, a tennis instructor demonstrated tennis strokes and then pointed out errors in student execution of those strokes. In a differential praise phase, the instructor's only feedback was praise for correct or near correct execution of components of strokes. The differential approval phase increased performance two to four times over baseline.

Grades. Perhaps the most readily available backup reinforcer in classroom token systems is grades. Nonetheless, this variable has received little isolated attention in the more recent classroom management research. In a study previously cited, Glover *et al.* (1980) compared a feedback alone phase (in which students contrasted what they had underlined with what the instructor had printed on the backing of a label) with a feedback plus points phase. Fractions of points were earned for correctly underlined words and lost for extraneously underlined words. Students were informed that points could be used to improve course grades. The researchers found no clear advantage for feedback plus points over feedback alone. However, it should be emphasized that the feedback system used in this study was immediate, efficient, and specific. Part of the potency of grades undoubtedly lies in their feedback value. When a subject is given efficient feedback regarding the performance of a valued behavior, grades may provide little added reinforcement. Smith, Schumaker, Schaeffer, and Sherman (1982) used contingent grades in a highly successful discussion skills package, but the grades appeared to carry a heavy feedback load in their study.

Tangible Reinforcers. Tangible payoffs continue to be frequently used in classroom management research (41 instances of tangible rewards in the literature reviewed). They usually come in the form of edibles or play objects and are often used in combination with social reinforcers (Russo, Cataldo, & Cushing, 1981). For example, in the Russo *et al.* study, small food items were used in combination with physical contact and verbal praise to strengthen compliance behavior in 3- to 5-year-olds. Tangible rewards should be especially effective with children for whom academic activities and other more natural consequences are not initially reinforcing.

Activity Reinforcers. A category of reinforcers at the disposal of almost every teacher is high priority activities. The 28 applications of this variable usually occurred in combination with other treatment components and consistently led to improvement in the dependent measures. In about 25% of the cases, outstanding improvement was noted. Increasingly, high priority *academic* activities are being used to strengthen other academic behaviors. Moreno and Hovell (1982) used access to a language laboratory to reinforce a 16-year-old Spanish-speaking student for answering a series of survival questions in English. The treatment increased the student's correct English answers from 40% to 85%. Gallant *et al.* (1980) made access to a highly preferred subject area (science lab activity) con-

tingent on accurately completing assignments in reading and math. This bright 11-year-old male's assignment completion and accuracy of performance were both greatly improved by the contingency.

Response Deprivation Hypothesis. According to the Premack reinforcement principle, any high-probability activity can be used to reinforce any lower-probability activity. Recent research on a notion called the "response deprivation hypothesis" has raised some questions about the general applicability of the Premack principle in classroom management. According to the response deprivation hypothesis, a contingent activity will exercise a reinforcing effect on a target behavior only if the contingency requires the subject to perform more of the target behavior than was present during baseline to preserve the same amount of the contingent activity that was present during baseline.

This response deprivation contingency is described by the equation $I/C > Oi/Oc$ in which I stands for the instrumental or target behavior and C stands for the contingent or reinforcing activity. The equation basically means that the required ratio between the instrumental and the contingent activity (I/C) must be greater than the observed ratio between those two behaviors during baseline (Oi/Oc) if C is truly to function as a reinforcer for I.

To illustrate this notion, let us assume that a student is observed to engage in 10 minutes of reading (which we will later designate as the instrumental activity) and 20 minutes of drawing (which we will later designate as the contingent activity) in a free field baseline setting. This student must then be required to engage in more than 10 minutes of reading (say 15 minutes) in order to engage in 20 minutes of drawing if the latter is to serve as a reinforcer for the former. Thus, the equation would be $15/20 > 10/20$. In this case, the student would be required to read 15 minutes before being allowed to draw 20 minutes. This contingency should increase the child's reading time above the baseline level.

Two studies indicate that instrumental responding increases only when a response deprivation contingency is present and never when it is absent (Konarski, Johnson, Crowell, & Whitman, 1980; Konarski, Crowell, Johnson, & Whitman, 1982). The response deprivation hypothesis holds even when the contingent activity is of lower probability than the instrumental activity. In the previous example, reading could be used as the contingent activity to increase drawing if the following contingency held: 25/10>20/10.

Techniques for Weakening Behaviors

Strategies for directly weakening behaviors continue to receive considerable attention in classroom management research. Such strategies were reported 52 times in the literature with adequate success noted in most instances. In about 40% of the cases, target behaviors were described as substantially changed.

Antecedent Exercise. Advocates of physical exercise have long contended that exercise can have an ameliorative impact on emotional stress. Bachman and Fuqua (1983) have explored the possibility of using exercise to reduce inappropriate behavior in the classroom. In a study with trainable mentally impaired students, these experimenters arranged for exercise (primarily jogging) to be the first daily activity. In general, the more intense and extensive the exercise, the greater the reduction in inappropriate vocalizations, repetitive movements, and off-task activity.

Medication. What is the comparative effectiveness of medication and environmental manipulations in improving student behavior? Pelham, Schnedler, Bologna, and Contreras (1980) compared three levels of Ritalin (placebo, .25 mg/kg, .75 mg/kg) to a behavior therapy package involving teacher and parent praising of good behavior, ignoring minor offenses, applying time out and response cost to more serious offenses, and awarding privileges and tangibles for completing academic work. The effectiveness of the behavioral intervention ranked between the effectiveness levels of .25 mg/kg and .75 mg/kg Ritalin prior to the behavioral treatment. Both dosage levels produced more on-task behavior after the behavioral therapy phase than before that phase. This interactive relationship between medication and behavior modification strategies has received additional support from Williamson, Calpin, Dilorenzo, Garris, and Petti's study (1981) on dexedrine and activity feedback.

Rapport, Murphy, and Bailey (1982) have provided a direct comparison between Ritalin and response cost in improving classroom behavior. Several dosages of Ritalin (5 to 20 mg/day) were contrasted with response cost backed up by free time. Although both treatments were effective in improving on-task behavior and daily assignment completion, response cost produced the greater improvement on both dimensions. For the two hyperactive boys used in this study, 15 mg. of Ritalin proved to be the optimal dosage—a dosage level slightly higher than that suggested in previous research.

Ignoring. Even though ignoring bad behavior has been a popular behavior modification strategy, it surfaced in only four studies in the recent literature and was mainly employed in combination with other procedures. As an example, Kindall, Workman, and Williams (1980) contrasted a praise-ignore combination with a praise-soft reprimand combination. A variety of appropriate behaviors were praised and disruptive behaviors were either ignored or privately reprimanded. Both treatment combinations were much superior to baseline, but the praise-soft reprimand combination produced more rapid improvement than praise-ignoring. However, the latter combination did produce better maintenance of treatment gains.

In-School Suspension. Highly disruptive children are sometimes removed from the regular classroom for one or more days to work in an isolation room. The students have virtually no contact with peers during this period and may even have lunch in the isolation room. An excellent evaluation of in-school suspension has been provided by Nau, Van Houten, and O'Neil (1981). The teacher, a multiple sclerosis victim confined to a wheel chair, had a large number of students in a small classroom. In one treatment condition, she posted feedback for each instance of disruptive behavior she observed. In a second condition, students receiving two reprimands for disruptive behavior were sent to the principal, who required them to work for one to three days in a large time-out room adjacent to his office. The order of these treatment conditions was counterbalanced in math and science classes. The publicly posted negative feedback was ineffective in both classes, but the in-school suspension was quite effective in reducing disruptive behavior in the two classes.

Response Cost. The most widely used procedure for weakening behavior (appearing in 14 studies and usually in combination with other treatment conditions) was response cost. Target behaviors were usually reported as improved by these treatment combinations, and exceptional improvement was noted in five cases.

Several different methods have been used for

administering response cost contingencies. Pace and Forman (1982) gave each second grader in their study a large envelope containing paper money. Students earned additional money for obeying class rules and lost money in varying amounts for breaking rules. Dollars accumulated by the end of the week could be traded in for inexpensive toys. Another example of a response cost procedure has been provided by Salend and Henry (1981), who taped strips of construction paper to the top of a second grader's desk. Each time he sought the teacher's attention, he had to give up one strip. Strips remaining at the end of the class period could be traded in for time with the teacher (e.g., having a coke with the teacher, helping the teacher clean the classroom, having lunch with the teacher). Similarly, Witt and Elliott (1982) arranged for slips of paper placed on students' desks to be taken away for rule violations. Slips remaining at the end of the study period could then be placed in a box for a lottery on Friday. Finally, Rapport, Murphy, and Bailey (1980) used a flip card method to deduct free-time credit whenever the target subject was observed to be off task. Each of these variations of response cost proved extremely effective in reducing the targeted behavior.

Verbal Reprimands. The nine studies that included some form of verbal reprimand suggest modest potential for this approach to weakening behavior. A study by Van Houten, Nau, MacKensie-Keating, Sameoto, and Colavecchia (1982) suggests some specific guidelines for delivering reprimands. They found that reprimands delivered in close proximity to the student, with eye contact, and with a firm grasp of the student's shoulders were more effective than verbal reprimands alone. Reprimanding one child also improved the disruptive behavior and academic performance for another student seated next to the reprimanded child.

Positive Practice Overcorrection. One way to weaken undesirable behavior is to require the student to practice behavior that is incompatible with the inappropriate behavior. This strategy was used in three studies as a singular treatment and once in combination with other treatment conditions. In most cases, marked improvement in the target behaviors was noted. Luiselli and Rice (1983) required primary age handicapped students to engage in 30 seconds of appropriate toy play whenever they acted inappropriately toward peers. Baseline assessment had shown an inverse relationship between toy play and bad behavior toward peers. The teacher used some physical prompting to get the students to play with the nearest toy whenever they began misbehaving toward peers. The treatment markedly reduced inappropriate peer interaction.

Positive practice overcorrection can also be applied to academic behaviors. In one study, the consequences for misspelling a word were to listen to the word pronounced by a teacher aide, pronounce the word correctly, say aloud each letter in the word, and write the word correctly (Ollendick, Matson, Esveldt-Dawson, & Shapiro, 1980). This sequence was repeated five times for each misspelled word. Pratt-Struthers and Struthers (1983) used a similar approach in helping students learn to spell consistently misspelled words from their creative writings.

Negative Preference Management. Three studies indicated that low priority behaviors can be used to weaken high probability behaviors even when the sets of behaviors are topographically dissimilar. Exercise has been the most frequently used low probability behavior in negative preference management (Dickie & Finegan, 1980; Luce & Hall, 1981; Luce, Delquadri, & Hall, 1980). Exercise may consist of running for a short distance, standing up and sitting on the floor 5 to 10 times, or running in place. The exercise contingency usually requires 30 seconds to 1 minute to apply and has been extremely effective in weakening a variety of bizarre and aggressive behaviors.

Differential Reinforcement of Low Rate of Responding (DRL). An excellent way to weaken behavior gradually without using aversive stimulation is the DRL schedule (employed in four studies reviewed). Under this schedule, the child is reinforced for exhibiting fewer and fewer instances of the target behavior. The first criterion for reinforcement is usually set just below the baseline level. When the first criterion level is attained, the criterion is reduced slightly further. Zwald and Gresham (1982) used this strategy to weaken teasing and name calling; Singh, Dawson, and Manning (1982) used it to reduce stereotypic responding; and Ratholz and Luce (1983) employed a DRL schedule in weakening off-task gazing and inappropriate vocalization.

Differential Reinforcement of Other Responses (DRO). Somewhat similar to the DRL approach is the reinforcement of any behavior other than the target response. This approach was used in three studies, two of which reported considerable success. Two versions of DRO have been used: (a) momentary DRO—subject is reinforced if the inappropriate response is not occurring at the end of a specified interval; (b) whole-interval DRO—subject is reinforced if the inappropriate behavior does not occur throughout the whole interval. Repp, Barton, and Brulle (1983) found that the whole-interval contingency was generally more effective than the momentary contingency. In fact, the momentary contingency was effective only if preceded by the whole-interval arrangement.

Treatment Packages

Far more treatment variables have been used in combination than as singular manipulations. Certain combinations appear with such regularity in the literature that they have come to be regarded almost as standardized treatment packages. Sixty-four applications of treatment packages were identified, with reasonable success reported in most instances and outstanding success in more than half the cases.

Behavioral Coaching. Recently, behavior modification techniques have been applied in the sports domain of school. Behavioral coaching was judged highly effective in three studies across a variety of sports such as tennis, ballet, football, gymnastics, and swimming. Although elementary students have been most frequently used in these studies, high school and college students have also been included. The behavioral coaching approach often includes instructions, descriptive feedback when a skill is performed correctly, and freezing when a skill is performed incorrectly. The freezing component has been particularly effective in improving skill execution. The moment skill execution begins to break down, the subject is stopped and instructed to hold that position while the instructor points out its maladaptive features and then models correct execution. The instructor may finally manually guide the subject through correct execution of the skill. The behavioral coaching package is often contrasted with a more standard coaching approach involving unsystematic modeling, instruction, and negative feedback. Fitterling and Ayllon (1983) found behavioral coaching far superior to standard coaching in teaching ballet skills. Allison and Ayllon (1980) have also documented the superiority of behavioral coaching over standard coaching in teaching football, gymnastics, and tennis skills. Koop and Martin (1983) used a variation of behavioral coaching in improving swimming skills.

Behavior Therapy. A few studies used the term *behavioral intervention* or *behavior therapy* to encompass a broad range of behavioral procedures. An excellent example is provided by Heaton and Safer (1982) whose junior high school behavioral program for multisuspended students included the following features: (a) contingency management, (b) small classes, (c) highly motivated teachers, (d) school-provided incentives for good behavior and academic effort, (e) behavioral counseling and contracting with the parents, and (f) parent-provided home incentives for good school reports. Although more of the treatment students entered high school than did a comparison control group, no difference was observed in the performance of the two groups after one year of high school.

Pelham *et al.* (1980) used a behavior therapy package that involved teacher and parent praising of good behavior, ignoring minor offenses, applying time out and response cost for more serious offenses, and using high priority activities and incentives to reward constructive behavior. Each student also received tutoring from a trained undergraduate. As noted earlier, the behavior therapy package in this particular study intensified the effects of medication on the children's classroom behavior.

Compliance Training. One of the immediate concerns of many teachers is how to get students to respond to their requests. Neef, Shafer, Egel, Cataldo, and Parrish (1983) arranged a series of steps to produce compliance with "do" and "don't" requests: (a) descriptive praise paired with tangibles and physical contact for compliance with one "do" request; (b) reinforcement for compliance with one "don't" request; and (c) variable ratio reinforcement for compliance with any "do" or "don't" request. This series of steps produced a high level of compliance with both types of requests. Russo *et al.* (1981) used similar treatment procedures in increasing the compliance of preschoolers who had generally been noncompliant to adult requests.

A naturalistic assessment of children's compliance with teacher requests and teachers' responses to student compliance has shown that students rated by teachers as being well-adjusted to school are more likely to comply with teacher commands than students judged to be poorly adjusted to school (Strain, Lambert, Kerr, Stagg, & Lenkner, 1983). High-rated students are more likely to receive positive feedback for compliance than the low rated, whereas low-rated students receive more positive feedback for noncompliance than do the high rated. Surprisingly, low-rated children are six times more likely than high rated to receive repeated commands following compliance.

Correspondence Training. Another way to get students to comply with teacher expectations is to solicit verbal commitments regarding the target behaviors. For example, the student may be asked to verbalize the specific components of a desired behavior and then whether he or she is going to exhibit that behavior. Nonverbal students can be asked to ''show me how you are going to . . . ''. Prompts, corrective feedback, positive feedback, and a changing criterion approach have been used as a part of the correspondence training package. Whitman, Scibak, Butler, Richter, and Johnson (1982) have found this package quite effective in changing such diverse behaviors as on-task responses, appropriate sitting posture, and out-of-seat activity.

Contracting. One of the more popular treatment packages in classroom management research is contracting. Five of the seven applications of contracting reported in the recent literature produced exceptional success. The facet of contracting that separates it from other treatment approaches is its emphasis on negotiated agreements. In one study, a contract defining the target behavior, contingencies, and rewards and punishment was negotiated by guidance personnel with a high school juvenile delinquent (Bizzis & Bradley-Johnson, 1981). Rewards included phone calls, letters, and recreational activity. The target behavior, school attendance, was improved so much by the contract that absences were completely eliminated the last 4 weeks of the school year. Similar contracting systems have been used to improve academic performance of adolescents in a special school program for dropouts (Kelley & Stokes, 1982) and to increase special students' participation in class activities (Kirschenbaum, Dielman, & Karoly, 1982).

Parents have proven to be useful participants in school-related contracts. Families of students with inconsistent performance records wrote and implemented contracts specifying rewards for teacher notification of acceptable school performance (Blechman, Kotanchik, & Taylor, 1981). Acceptable school performance was defined as a work level that equalled or exceeded their baseline mean. The contracting condition reduced the amount of scatter in the students' academic performance.

Direct Instruction. An instructional package that basically follows a behavior modification orientation is direct instruction (evaluated in four studies with considerable success reported each time). Gettinger's (1982) direct instruction model, which substantially reduced off-task behavior, typifies the components of this package: (a) teacher-directed instruction, (b) step-by-step learning, (c) group instruction, (d) mastery learning, (e) continuous practice, and (d) immediate, corrective feedback.

Carnine (1981) investigated the impact of two levels of direct instruction on language arts achievement and on-task behavior. Preschoolers were taught language skills from a commercial program with two different levels of direct instruction: (a) rapid pacing versus slow pacing, (b) frequent praise versus no praise, (c) clear signals versus no signals, and (d) regular, immediate corrections versus no corrections. High implementation of direct instruction components yielded considerably higher on-task behavior and language arts achievement than did the low implementation.

Another example of direct instruction is the Distar approach. In addition to the previously identified features of direct instruction, Distar involves a high frequency of unison group responses. The Distar package has been quite successful in improving standardized test scores, although these gains tend to diminish over time (Becker & Gersten, 1982).

Mastery learning is an approach usually subsumed in direct instruction packages. Under mastery learning students receive much corrective feedback and correct skill deficiencies before moving to higher skill levels. Arlin and Webster (1983) have provided evidence that students achieve at a higher level and retain skills better under mastery than nonmastery conditions. However, the mastery students devote greater amounts of time to learning than nonmastery students.

Discussion Skills Training. Development of discussion skills is a primary focus in many classrooms. One of the most direct attempts to develop and refine discussion skills has been provided by Smith *et al.* (1982). The rather elaborate package included two major phases, with one phase directed toward increasing the number of participants and a second toward improving the quality of participation. In the quantity phase, the teacher stated explicit rules for discussion, praised students for their contribution, paraphrased the students' comments orally or on the blackboard, pro-

315

vided an outline of discussion questions, gave students credit for participation, and publicly posted discussion grades. In the quality phase, providing reasons for statements, making comparisons between different points, and providing examples that supported statements were sequentially taught, recorded, and counted toward the students' grades. In a final phase, all members of a row received bonus points if each student made at least one contribution to the discussion. The percentage of students participating greatly increased in the quantity phase and each of the quality dimensions increased when it was targeted. The quality contingencies initially decreased percentage of participation until the group contingency was added.

Social Skills Training. Closely akin to the development of discussion skills is the development of general interactive skills. Coaching, modeling, rehearsal, and feedback have been used to teach learning disabled boys how to make eye contact and respond verbally to unfair criticisms, initiate interactions, give compliments, and request changes in behaviors (Berler, Gross, & Drabman, 1982). Although some of these skills were improved in the training situation, they did not generalize well to natural school settings.

One of the most publicized packages for teaching social skills is PREP (Preparation through Responsive Educational Programs). Students learn a body of cognitive information about behavior modification, social relationships, and careers. They also acquire specific social and study skills applicable to the classroom. One 5-year follow-up on PREP found consistently high academic performance and generally effective social behavior by students in this program (Filipczak, Archer, & Friedman, 1980).

Token Economy. The combination of conditioned reinforcers leading to backup reinforcers remains a viable approach in classroom management. In fact, the token economy package is by far the most popular treatment package in classroom management research (29 different applications). The token economy is probably the most consistently effective classroom management package reported in the literature. It has been highly effective with a variety of dependent variables (e.g., on-task behavior, math performance, self-efficacy ratings, discrimination skills, reading performance, disruptive activity, language arts performance, destructive behavior, attendance, work completion, stealing, and vocabulary development). Although its most frequent application has

been with elementary students, it has been used with secondary students, average students, slow learners, and behavior problem students.

The previously mentioned PREP package provides an excellent example of a classroom token economy. Contingencies focus on such targets as class attendance, assignments completed, and appropriate classroom behavior. Reinforcing events include tangibles, leisure activities, and social consequences. Backup reinforcers are available on both a daily and weekly basis. This program has been quite effective in improving such dependent measures as GPA, school attendance, and suspension time (Reese, Murphy, & Filipczak, 1981).

One of the most important dimensions of token economics is the mechanism for dispensing the conditioned reinforcers. In some cases, the conditioned reinforcement comes in the form of systematic feedback. In Cuvo and Riva's study (1980), a marker on a feedback board was moved forward for appropriate language responses and moved backward for incorrect responses. In most cases, points, stickers, and tokens are used as the conditioned reinforcers. When tokens are used, the teacher may choose to use different kinds of tokens to represent different levels of attainment or reward different target behaviors. Robinson, Newby, and Ganzell (1981) used four different colored tokens to reinforce four somewhat different skills.

One way to prevent dependency on a token system is to provide some way for students to earn their way off the system. Kazdin and Mascitelli (1980) followed a conventional token phase with an earn-off provision. Students were given the option of operating without the token system when they met the earn-off criterion. The earn-off provision produced higher levels of attentive behavior in this special education class than did the conventional token phase, presumably because students viewed being off the tokens as a sign of progress in the classroom.

Generalization Training. Some treatment packages have been designed to promote generalization of behavior change across time, settings, behaviors, and subjects. (Nine applications of generalization training were identified in the literature, with most reporting substantial success.) A popular strategy for promoting generalization across time is to thin the reinforcement schedule. Rosen and Rosen (1983) used this approach in reducing the stealing behavior of a child enrolled in a special education class. Materials appropriate for the child to have in his possession were marked with a green circle. He earned points for having only items with a green circle and lost points for having other materials in his possession. Initially the child's materials were checked every 15 minutes and token consequences were administered in combination with either descriptive praise or reprimands. During a subsequent thinning phase, the subject's materials were checked every 2 hours. In the followup phase, no markings or token contingencies were used. Stealing was substantially reduced both during the treatment phase and a one-month follow-up phase.

Anderson and Redd (1980) contrasted the effects of two instructional procedures (standard instruction and generalization training) on performance in a treatment and nontreatment setting. Standard instruction included several components of individualized remedial instruction (e.g., physical prompts, one-on-one tutoring, and continuous reinforcement schedules), whereas generalization training was directed toward increasing the similarity between the treatment setting and the regular classroom environment (e.g., fading of prompts, fading of tutoring, and thinning of reinforcement schedule). Both on-task behavior and reading performance were very high in the treatment setting, but both declined in the nontreatment setting following standard instruction. In contrast, generalization training produced as high a performance level in the nontreatment as in the treatment setting.

A treatment package for facilitating generalization across both settings and time has been described by Campbell and Stremel-Campbell (1982). After an initial training period in which correct verbalizations were prompted and continuously reinforced, a maintenance phase involving a variable ratio schedule with no prompts led to spontaneous use of correct verbalizations in a free-play setting and maintenance of the target behaviors over time.

Generalization across both settings and individuals has been demonstrated by Barton and Bevert (1981). These researchers focused on the physical sharing of play materials among preschoolers. The training program included instructions about sharing, peer modeling of sharing, rehearsal of sharing behaviors, and intermittent praise for sharing in play situations. Pairs of subjects trained to share in one group setting generalized that behavior to untrained group settings and increased the sharing of untrained subjects in those settings.

Self-management procedures have proven effective in promoting generalization across behaviors (Fantuzzo & Clement, 1981). Second grade boys noted for poor attention and bad behavior at school observed a confederate being either reinforced by a teacher or self-reinforced. Some subjects who observed the self-reinforcement had no opportunity to self-reinforce whereas others did have an opportunity. Changes in the target behavior (on-task vs. off-task) generalized to academic achievement, with the opportunity to self-reinforce producing the greater amount of response generalization.

The PREP package described earlier has been one of the most effective packages for promoting generalization (Filipczak *et al.* 1980; Reese & Filipczak, 1980). In the Reese and Filipczak study, tangible and activity reinforcers were gradually delayed as the children progressed through the school year. Also, a great many individual contracts were negotiated for students who either did not meet or exeeded the contingencies of the regular reinforcement system. PREP proved effective in producing generalization across settings, time, and behaviors.

Teacher Training Packages.   Five studies have examined interventions for changing teacher behaviors, with most reporting reasonable success. An illustrative sampling of target skills has been provided by Borg and Ascione (1982): questioning procedures, attentional cues, task-related prompts, involvement of peers, appropriate reprimands, suggestions for alternative behaviors, and different types of praise and rewards. Teachers trained to focus on specific target behaviors of students did better in acquiring these skills than those trained to focus on students' self-concept. The more the teachers used these skills, the better the classroom behaviors of their students.

Hundert (1982) has contrasted the effects of measurement training and programming training on teacher and student behavior. Measurement training emphasized setting objectives and measuring student progress objectively. Programming training emphasized the writing of behavior modification programs to deal with specific problems. In the latter training, teachers were taught to define problems in behavioral terms, identify teacher behaviors that might have contributed to specific problems, specify potential changes in teacher behavior, implement those changes, and evaluate the effects of those changes. Although measurement training had little effect on either teacher or student behavior, the programming training increased teachers' proficiency in writing and applying behavior modification procedures and students' level of classroom performance.

The generalized impact of training teachers to use behavioral strategies has been demonstrated by Mayer, Butterworth, Nafpaktitis, and Sulzer-Azaroff (1983). Teachers attended workshops dealing with a variety of behavioral approaches, all focusing on making school a more positive experience. Teacher use of praise and student classroom behavior were recorded, graphed, and shared with the teacher. Not only did teacher use of praise significantly increase and student off-task behavior significantly decrease, vandalism costs in the treatment schools also significantly decreased.

Evaluation of Classroom Management Research

Impact on Education. Researchers have generated a rich and extensive body of empirically based information about classroom management techniques. The research reviewed in this chapter represents only a small portion of what is actually available on the topic. Several educational journals that periodically publish classroom management research were not included in the present review. Additionally, the vast body of pre-1980 research greatly extends the base provided in this chapter.

The techniques and findings of classroom management research emanate from the same world in which the teacher functions—the classroom. The techniques described in this chapter were largely used by real teachers in real classrooms with real students. Thus, we are *not* faced with the problem of making the transition from the laboratory to the real world. Nonetheless, some teachers may question the appropriateness of certain behavior-management techniques with the types of students they serve. It is true that the bulk of contemporary classroom management research is directed toward special students, for example, behaviorally disordered, retarded, and learning-disabled students. Only about 15% of the selected studies primarily used subjects who would be considered average in terms of intellectual and other psychological characteristics.

To discredit the utility of classroom management techniques because they have been tested and refined with nonaverage youngsters would be to reach an unwarranted conclusion. Increasingly, all

teachers are having to deal with nonaverage students in their classrooms. Plus, the techniques that have proven effective with special students usually work quite well with average youngsters. In fact, over one third of the studies reviewed in this chapter included some average students in their samples.

Admittedly, a void does exist with respect to gifted students. Very little classroom management research has been directed toward students with exceptional intellectual and creative potential. Only seven studies even included above-average students in their samples. It remains to be demonstrated whether the techniques of classroom management would serve the needs of gifted students as well as those of problem and average students.

A characteristic that limited the general applicability of earlier classroom management research was its neglect of generalization effects. Very few of the early studies bothered to test whether treatment effects generalized across time, behaviors, settings, and students. However, classroom management research now gives far more attention to generalization. Approximately 40% of the studies included in this review assessed one or more types of generalization. Generalization across time, which would probably be the teacher's principal concern, was the most frequently assessed and demonstrated form of generalization in the recent literature.

Because of current reform in the training and evaluation of teachers, now may be the optimal time for classroom management researchers to take their skills and techniques to practitioners in the field. The technology of classroom management could become an integral part of the training and evaluation process. For this to happen, researchers must offer their services on the front end of educational reform. This assertive approach would permit researchers not only to introduce classroom management techniques into the training process but also to evaluate adequately how this training actually impacts teacher and student behaviors in the classroom. An after-the-fact involvement in the reform process would permit neither to occur.

The question of how best to train teachers in the techniques of classroom management is itself an empirical question. At this point, we can not precisely describe to what extent teachers apply systematic management techniques in their classrooms, or what training procedures best promote the application of these techniques. Only five of the studies included in this review evaluated interventions for changing teacher behaviors. These studies describe how teachers can be trained to use such simple tactics as defining classroom problems in behavioral terms, identifying teacher behaviors that may have contributed to the problems, specifying changes in teacher behavior that would likely correct the problems, implementing those changes, and evaluating the effects of the changes on the problem behaviors. Teachers' proficiency in applying behavior management procedures and students' level of classroom performance have been improved through these training programs.

How and when teachers are best trained to use classroom management procedures remain important research issues. It seems vital that trainers model the same procedures they are expecting teachers to use. In fact, the extent to which trainers employ effective management techniques in working with teachers may be the most critical predictor of the extent to which teachers employ similar techniques. On the issue of timing, it may be that inservice training would be far more effective than preservice training. Teacher trainees may not have the experiential base to give significant meaning to training in classroom management.

Impact on Educational Psychology. Where does classroom management research fit in the discipline of educational psychology? Perhaps the principal domain of educational psychology is academic learning. Within this research area, educational psychologists attempt to describe how learning occurs, evaluate potential for learning, and assess what has been learned. Classroom management research can impact the learning process in two ways: it can (a) create a classroom atmosphere conducive to academic learning; (b) provide the technology for actually teaching many academic skills in the classroom. Thus, classroom management represents educational psychology as practiced in one learning environment—the classroom.

Despite its potential for impacting educational psychology, classroom management research has not been emphasized in educational psychology journals. The bulk of the research on classroom management is being published in applied behavior analysis journals rather than in educational psychology journals. For example, the most prolific current publisher of classroom management research is the *Journal of Applied Behavior Analysis* (JABA). It published over twice as many classroom management articles as any other single journal during the 1980–83 period. Its studies included

participants from all age categories, all grade levels, and most of the major psychological classifications. The principal target behaviors addressed in JABA's research were academic performance, appropriate process behaviors, and negative process behaviors. Other applied behavior analysis journals that gave extensive attention to classroom management research during the 1980–83 period were *Behavior Modification, Education and Treatment of Children,* and *Behavior Therapy.*

The only educational psychology journal to publish a significant amount of classroom management research in the 1980–83 period is the *Journal of Educational Psychology* (JEP). However, in sharp contrast to the other major publishers of classroom management research, JEP published practically no operantly based research. This unfortunate arrangement means that JEP, APA's principal journal for educational psychologists, fails to reflect the primary approach to learning that characterizes classroom management research.

Adequacy of Research Base. It is not unusual for a characteristic to be a strength in one respect and a weakness in another. The packaging nature of much classroom management research may be one such characteristic. By using many treatment components in combination, studies in this area closely approximate the realities of the classroom. However, the packaging approach militates against precise cause–effect inferences. Research in this area could be greatly strengthened by more component analyses that isolate the contributions of specific treatment variables to treatment packages. Otherwise, widely used treatment packages may be replete with unnecessary, and even counterproductive, treatment manipulations.

The simplicity of most research designs in this area fosters understanding and application of research findings. The most used research designs in the 1980–83 period, reversal and multiple baseline designs, usually included no tests of statistical significance. The absence of sophisticated statistical tests makes the research much more palatable to the practitioner in the field. However, the criterion-by-inspection approach often makes it difficult to judge the magnitude of treatment effects. Researchers look for differences in level, slope, and variability from one phase to another, but simply "eye-balling" a data graph does not always provide a conclusive answer as to whether a change in level, slope, or variability embodies a treatment effect. The movement in the mid-1970s toward incorporating tests of statistical significance (e.g., time series analysis) into behavior modification designs has unfortunately gained little momentum in classroom management research.

Too much of current classroom management research is simply a replication of treatment effects firmly established before the 1980s. For example, token economy packages and the variables normally comprising these packages continue to dominate research in the 1980s. Unfortunately, much of this research on token economics basically duplicates what was already known about their effectiveness. More research is needed that would add precision to the technology of token economies and other standard classroom management procedures. Delivery systems for reinforcers, timing of reinforcers, scheduling of reinforcers, pre- and postselection of backup reinforcers, development of conditioned reinforcers, and the role of vicarious reinforcers are only a few of the treatment variables needing more varied and intricate technology.

Some treatment manipulations are woefully underrepresented in the current literature. Instructional variables, such as task analysis, task difficulty, task presentation, discrimination training, concept formation training, instructional examples, instructional modality, instructional games, direct instruction, and grading procedures are receiving negligible attention in the mainstream journals selected for this review. The whole area of self-administered strategies (e.g., self-verbalization, self-monitoring, self-reinforcement, and self-directed relaxation) has made few inroads into classroom management research. Thus, little attention has been devoted to teaching students to control their own emotions and behaviors in the classroom. Another area largely omitted from recent classroom management research is class rules, an area considered vital by practically all teachers. A treatment variable that has proven highly effective in clinical settings and appears to be a natural for the classroom setting is restitutional overcorrection. However, not a single study made use of this natural and potent procedure for weakening behaviors that produce damage or disarray in the classroom environment.

Whereas logistical refinement is certainly in order for classroom management research, research directed toward the testing of theoretical notions is even more imperative. For example, the response deprivation hypothesis represents a refreshing change of pace in the research literature. It provides the conceptual framework for testing specific hypotheses, some of which run counter to other notions, such as the Premack reinforcement principle. Research studies that provide differential predictions based on contrasting theoretical notions would be uniquely valuable in developing a rich conceptual framework for classroom management.

There is a similar lack of attention to developing and testing comprehensive conceptual models of classroom management. The conceptual model that dominates classroom management research is the operant approach of B. F. Skinner. Because this model has largely evolved from laboratory research with rats and pigeons, many prominent educators, such as Eisner (1984), have questioned its utility in the classroom. However, the question of utility is largely an empirical issue. Research that contrasts the operant model with other conceptual frameworks for classroom management (e.g., Gordon's teacher effectiveness training, Dreikurs social discipline model, Glasser's reality therapy model, and Canter's assertive discipline model) would be immensely helpful in determining what overall approach is most useful in classroom management.

Despite apparent gaps in classroom management research, some variables have received quite adequate attention. Feedback, modeling, peer cooperation, group contingencies, tangible reinforcers, activity reinforcers, response cost, and generalization training are some of the valuable procedures strongly represented in classroom management research. Although not receiving extensive coverage, other treatment variables, such as testing, time limits, response delay training, interspersal training, home-based reinforcers, reinforcement sharing, functional contingencies, antecedent exercise, in-school suspension, positive practice overcorrection, negative preference management, DRL schedules, and DRO schedules appear to have considerable promise for improving student performance, sometimes in very unexpected ways. For example, shortening time limits seems to improve not only the pace of student work but the quality also.

Future Trends. With the exception of a decrease in 1983, publication of classroom management research has steadily increased in quantity since 1980. That trend is very likely to continue through the decade, especially if classroom management researchers join the bandwagon of educational reform. How these researchers approach their involvement in the reform process will determine whether the anticipated proliferation of classroom management research has a decisive impact on the practice of education.

Two types of studies are necessary for classroom management research to have an optimal impact on the reform process: (a) carefully controlled studies in which treatment effects are clearly isolated; (b) less well controlled studies that test the efficacy of treatment packages with large samples of students. The first kind of study would preserve the heritage that has characterized classroom management research (at least the operant perspective) since its formative years. These early studies were characterized by unitary applications of treatments, simplicity of research designs, and internal validity. Continuing this type of research would expand the base of precise cause–effect relationships in classroom management. The external validity of this base could then be tested by applying more complex treatment packages (comprised of manipulations of proven effectiveness) to broader samples of students.

There is some evidence from the 1980–83 studies that classroom management research may be moving beyond its emphasis on extrinsic motivation. Although token economy variables remained very popular during this period, some attenuation was noted toward the end of the period. For example, the token economy packages peaked in 1981 (11 applications) and diminished to six applications in 1982 and six in 1983. Activity and tangible reinforcers, widely used in token economics, peaked in 1981 and 1982 and declined substantially in 1983. Reponse cost, a technique for weakening behavior often used with token economics, dropped from a frequency of four applications each of the previous years to only one application in 1983. Although extrinsic incentives have been especially effective in reducing disruptive and off-task behavior, the time may be right to direct research attention more toward intrinsic motivation.

A desirable emphasis for the mid-to-late-1980s would be application of behavior management techniques to the instructional process. As previously noted, many instructional variables (e.g., task analysis, task difficulty, task presentation, concept formation training) received very little attention in the 1980–83 period. Although academic targets were heavily emphasized in the 1980–83 research, creative responding and problem-solving skills were seldom included among these targets.

Thus, various treatment applications and target behaviors warrant more attention in the instructional area. A lack of emphasis on the instructional domain will likely perpetuate dependency on extrinsic payoffs as a means of motivating students. On the other hand, a stream-lined technology of instruction could largely negate the need for extrinsic controls.

Educational reformers are emphasizing the role computers will play in the instructional process. Classroom management researchers need to apply their technology to refinement and evaluation of computerized instruction. What kinds of computerized instruction are likely to promote academic learning, an affinity for learning, and appropriate classroom conduct? Although no computer evaluation studies were located in the 1980–83 issues of the journals reviewed, a meta-analysis of 51 independent evaluations of computer instruction greatly extends our empirical assessment of this approach (Kulik, Bangert, & Williams, 1983). Kulik *et al.* selected studies at the high school level that had contrasted computer instruction with more conventional teaching approaches and that were free of major methodological flaws. In comparison to traditional approaches, computer-based instruction raised students' final exam scores from about the 50th to the 63rd percentile, but had smaller (yet positive) effects on exams given several months after instruction. The computer approach also produced a more positive evaluation of computers and course content taught by computers. Another major benefit of computer based instruction was a much faster rate of learning. Obviously, computerized instruction is a very promising area that should not be neglected in future classroom management research.

In summary, the impact of classroom management research on the actual practice of education and the discipline of educational psychology is more limited than it deserves to be. An extensive application of what researchers presently know about classroom management would likely produce pervasive improvement in educational practices. To accomplish this far-reaching application, classroom management researchers must get their work into the mainstream of educational psychology and must ambitiously address the issue of how best to train teachers to apply the many useful behavior management strategies.

ACKNOWLEDGMENTS. The author expresses deep gratitude to Ms. Mary Ann Hand, a graduate student in Special Education at The University of

Tennessee, for her extensive assistance in analyzing the research patterns described in this chapter.

References

Albion, F. M., & Salzberg, C. L. (1982). The effect of self-instructions on the rate of correct addition problems with mentally retarded children. *Education and Treatment of Children, 5*(2), 121–131.

Allen, L. D., Gottselig, M., & Boylan, S. (1982). A practical mechanism for using free time as a reinforcer in classrooms. *Education and Treatment of Children, 5*(4), 347–353.

Allison, M. G., & Ayllon, T. (1980). Behavioral coaching in the development of skills in football, gymnastics, and tennis. *Journal of Applied Behavior Analysis, 13*(2), 297–314.

Anderson, B. L., & Redd, W. H. (1980). Programming generalization through stimulus fading with children participating in a remedial reading program. *Education and Treatment of Children, 3*(4), 297–314.

Arlin, M., & Webster, J. (1983). Time costs of mastery learning. *Journal of Educational Psychology, 75*(2), 187–195.

Armstrong, B., Johnson, D. W., & Balow, B. (1981). Effects of cooperative vs. individualistic learning experiences on interpersonal attraction between learning-disabled and normal-progress elementary school students. *Contemporary Educational Psychology, 6*(2), 102–109.

Bachman, J. E., & Fuqua, R. W. (1983). Management of inappropriate behaviors of trainable mentally impaired students using antecedent exercise. *Journal of Applied Behavior Analysis, 16*(4), 477–484.

Ballowe, T., Marlowe, M., & Algozzine, B. (1981). Effects of success and failure on emotionally handicapped boys. *Contemporary Educational Psychology, 6*(1), 95–101.

Barton, E. J., & Bevert, J. (1981). Generalization of sharing across groups: Assessment of group composition with preschool children. *Behavior Modification, 5*(4), 503–522.

Bear, G. C., & Richards, H. C. (1980). An interdependent group-oriented contingency system for improving academic performance. *School Psychology Review, 9*(2), 190–193.

Bear, G. C., & Richards, H. C. (1981). Moral reasoning and conduct problems in the classroom. *Journal of Educational Psychology, 73*(5), 644–670.

Becker, W. C., & Gersten, R. (1982). A follow-up of follow through: The later effects of the direct instruction model on children in fifth and sixth grades. *American Educational Research Journal, 19*(1), 75–92.

Berler, E. S., Gross, A. M., & Drabman, R. S. (1982). Social skills training with children: Proceed with caution. *Journal of Applied Behavior Analysis, 15*(1), 41–53.

Bizzis, J., & Bradley-Johnson, S. (1981). Increasing the school attendance of a truant adolescent. *Education and Treatment of Children, 4*(2), 149–155.

Blechman, E. A., Kotanchik, N. L., & Taylor, C. J. (1981). Families and schools together: Early behavioral intervention with high risk children. *Behavior Therapy, 12*(3), 308–319.

Borg, W. R., & Ascione, F. R. (1982). Classroom management in elementary mainstreaming classrooms. *Journal of Educational Psychology, 74*(1), 85–95.

Boyd, L. A., Keilbaugh, W. S., & Axelrol, S. (1981). The direct and indirect effects of positive reinforcement on on-task behavior. *Behavior Therapy, 12*(1), 80–92.

Brophy, J., Rohrkemper, M., Rashid, H., & Goldberger, M.

(1983). Relationships between teachers' presentations of classroom tasks and students' engagement in those tasks. *Journal of Educational Psychology, 75*(4), 561–571.

Bryant, L. E., & Budd, K. S. (1982). Self-instructional training to increase independent work performance in preschoolers. *Journal of Applied Behavior Analysis, 15*(2), 259–271.

Budd, K. S., Leibowitz, J. M., Riner, L. S., Mindell, C., & Goldfarb, A. L. (1981). Home-based treatment of severe disruptive behaviors: A reinforcement package for preschool and kindergarten children. *Behavior Modification, 5*(2), 273–298.

Burgio, L. D., Whitman, T. L., & Johnson, M. R. (1980). A self-instructional package for increasing attending behavior in educable mentally retarded children. *Journal of Applied Behavior Analysis, 13*(3), 443–459.

Buzas, H. P., & Ayllon, T. (1981). Differential reinforcement in coaching tennis skills. *Behavior Modification, 5*(3), 372–385.

Campbell, C. R., & Stremel-Campbell, K. (1982). Programming "loose training" as a strategy to facilitate language generalization. *Journal of Applied Behavior Analysis, 15*(2), 295–301.

Carnine, D. (1981). High and low implementation of direct instruction teaching techniques. *Education and Treatment of Children 4*(1), 43–51.

Center, D. B., Dietz, S. M., & Kaufman, M. E. (1982). Student ability, task difficulty, and inappropriate classroom behavior: A study of children with behavior disorders. *Behavior Modification, 6*(3), 355–374.

Cohen, R., Polsgrove, L., Rieth, H., & Heinen, J. R. (1981). The effects of self-monitoring, public graphing, and token reinforcement on the social behaviors of underachieving children. *Education and Treatment of Children, 4*(2), 125–138.

Collins, F. L., Epstein, L. H., & Hannay, H. J. (1981). A component analysis of an operant training program for improving visual acuity in myopic students. *Behavior Therapy, 12*(5), 692–701.

Copeland, A. P., & Weissbrod, C. S. (1980). Effects of modeling on behavior related to hyperactivity. *Journal of Educational Psychology, 72*(6), 875–883.

Cuvo, A. J., & Riva, M. T. (1980). Generalization and transfer between comprehension and production: A comparison of retarded and non-retarded persons. *Journal of Applied Behavior Analysis, 132,* 315–331.

Dickerson, E. A., & Creedon, C. F. (1981). Self-selection of standards by children: The relative effectiveness of pupil-selected and teacher-selected standards of performance. *Journal of Applied Behavior Analysis, 14*(4), 425–433.

Dickie, R. F., & Finegan, S. (1980). The use of a common overcorrection procedure in eliminating topographically and functionally dissimilar "autistic" behaviors in several children. *Education and Treatment of Children, 3*(1), 21–31.

Drew, B. M., Evans, J. H., Bostow, D. W., Geiger, G., & Drash, P. W. (1982). Increasing assignment completion and accuracy using a daily report card procedure. *Psychology in the Schools, 19*(4), 540–547.

Dunlap, G., & Koegel, R. L. (1980). Motivating autistic children through stimulus variation. *Journal of Applied Behavior Analysis, 13*(4), 619–627.

Dyer, K., Christian, W. P., & Luce, S. C. (1982). The role of response delay in improving the discrimination performance of autistic children. *Journal of Applied Behavior Analysis, 15*(2), 231–240.

Egel, A. L. (1981). Reinforcer variation: Implications for motivating developmentally disabled children. *Journal of Applied Behavior Analysis, 14*(3), 345–350.

Egel, A. L., Richman, G. S., & Koegel, R. L. (1981). Normal peer models and autistic children's learning. *Journal of Applied Behavior Analysis, 14*(1), 3–12.

Eisner, E. W. (1984). Can educational research inform educational practice? *Phi Delta Kappan, 65*(7), 447–452.

Evertson, C. M., & Veldman, D. J. (1981). Changes over time in process measures of classroom behavior. *Journal of Educational Psychology, 73*(2), 156–163.

Fantuzzo, J. W., & Clement, P. W. (1981). Generalization of the effects of teacher- and self-administered token reinforcers to nontreated students. *Journal of Applied Behavior Analysis, 14*(4), 435–447.

Filipczak, J., Archer, M., & Friedman, R. M. (1980). Inschool social skills training: Use with disruptive adolescents. *Behavior Modification, 4*(2), 243–263.

Fishbein, J. E., & Wasik, B. A. (1981). Effect of the good behavior game on disruptive library behavior. *Journal of Applied Behavior Analysis, 14*(1), 89–93.

Fitterling, J. M., & Ayllon, T. (1983). Behavioral coaching in classical ballet: Enhancing skill development. *Behavior Modification, 7*(3), 345–368.

Forman, S. G. (1980). A comparison of cognitive training and response cost procedures in modifying aggressive behavior of elementary school children. *Behavior Therapy, 11*(4), 594–600.

Fowler, S. A., & Baer, D. M. (1981). "Do I have to be good all day?" The timing of delayed reinforcements as a factor in generalization. *Journal of Applied Behavior Analysis, 14*(1), 13–24.

Gallant, J., Sargeant, M., & Van Houten, R. (1980). Teacher-determined and self-determined access to science activities as a reinforcer for task completion in other curriculum areas. *Education and Treatment of Children, 3*(2), 101–111.

Gang, D., & Poche, C. E. (1982). An effective program to train parents as reading tutors for their children. *Education and Treatment of Children, 5*(3), 211–232.

Gettinger, M. (1982). Improving classroom behaviors and achievements of learning disabled children using direct instruction. *School Psychology Review, 11*(3), 329–336.

Gettinger, M. (1983). Student behaviors, teacher reinforcement, student ability, and learning. *Contemporary Educational Psychology, 8*(4), 391–402.

Glover, J. A., Zimmer, J. W., Filbeck, R. W., & Plake, B. S. (1980). Effects of training students to identify the semantic base of prose materials. *Journal of Applied Behavior Analysis, 13*(4), 655–667.

Goetz, E. M., Ayala, J. M., Hatfield, V. L., Marshall, A. M., & Etzel, B. C. (1983). Training independence in preschoolers with an auditory stimulus management technique. *Education and Treatment of Children, 6*(3), 251–261.

Grabe, M. (1982). Effort strategies in a mastery instructional system: The quantification of effort and the impact of effort on achievement. *Contemporary Educational Psychology, 7*(4), 327–333.

Gresham, F. M. (1983). Use of a home-based dependent group contingency system in controlling destructive behavior: A case study. *School Psychology Review, 12*(2), 195–199.

Gross, A. M., & Ekstrand, M. (1983). Increasing and maintaining rates of teacher praise: A study using public posting and feedback fading. *Behavior Modification, 7*(1), 126–135.

Hallahan, D. P., Lloyd, J. W., Kneedler, R. D., & Marshall,

K. J. (1982). A comparison of the effects of self- versus teacher-assessment of on-task behavior. *Behavior Therapy, 13*(5), 715–723.

Halpin, G., & Halpin, G. (1982). Experimental investigation of the effects of study and testing on student learning, retention and ratings of instruction. *Journal of Educational Psychology, 74*(1), 32–38.

Haskins, R., Walden, T., & Ramey, C. T. (1983). Teacher and student behavior in high- and low-ability groups. *Journal of Educational Psychology, 75*(6), 865–876.

Haynes, N. M., & Johnson, S. T. (1983). Self- and teacher expectancy effects on academic performance of college students enrolled in an academic reinforcement program. *American Education Research Journal, 20*(4), 511–516.

Heaton, R. C., & Safer, D. J. (1982). Secondary school outcome following a junior high school behavioral program. *Behavior Therapy, 13*(2), 226–231.

Hendrickson, J. M., Strain, P. S., Tremblay, A., & Shores, R. E. (1982). Interactions of behaviorally handicapped children: Functional effects of peer social initiations. *Behavior Modification, 6*(3), 323–353.

Hertz-Lazarowitz, R., Sharan, S., & Steinberg, R. (1980). Classroom learning style and cooperative behavior of elementary school children. *Journal of Educational Psychology, 72*(1), 99–106.

Hundert, J. (1982). Training teachers in generalized writing of behavior modification programs for multihandicapped deaf children. *Journal of Applied Behavior Analysis, 15*(1), 111–122.

Hundert, J., McMahon, S., & Kitcher, P. (1982). Increasing students' use of hearing aids: An analysis of teacher feedback and public posting. *Behavior Modification, 6*(2), 240–249.

Johnson, D. W., & Johnson, R. T. (1981a). Effects of cooperative and individualistic learning experiences on interethnic interaction. *Journal of Educational Psychology, 73*(3), 444–449.

Johnson, D. W., & Johnson, R. T. (1981b). The integration of the handicapped into the regular classroom: Effects of cooperative and individualistic instruction. *Contemporary Educational Psychology, 6* (4), 344–353.

Johnson, D. W., Johnson, R., Tiffany, M., & Zaidman, B. (1983). Are low achievers disliked in a cooperative situation? A test of rival theories in a mixed ethnic situation. *Contemporary Educational Psychology, 8*(2), 189–200.

Kazdin, A. E., & Geesey, S. (1980). Enhancing classroom attentiveness by preselection of back-up reinforcers in a token economy. *Behavior Modification, 4*(1), 98–114.

Kazdin, A. E., & Mascitelli, S. (1980). The opportunity to earn oneself off a token system as a reinforcer for attentive behavior. *Behavior Therapy, 11*(1), 68–78.

Kelley, M. L., & Stokes, T. F. (1982). Contingency contracting with disadvantaged youths: Improving classroom performance. *Journal of Applied Behavior Analysis, 15*(3), 447–454.

Kendall, P. C. (1982). Individual versus group cognitive-behavioral self-control training: 1-year follow-up. *Behavior Therapy, 13*(2), 241–247.

Kendall, P. C., & Zupan, B. A. (1981). Individual versus group application of cognitive-behavioral self-control procedures with children. *Behavior Therapy, 12*(3), 344–359.

Keer, M. M., Strain, P. S, & Ragland, E. U. (1982). Teacher-mediated peer feedback treatment of behaviorally handicapped children: An analysis of effects on positive and negative interactions. *Behavior Modification, 6*(2), 277–290,

Kim, N. S. (1980). Cognitive-behavioral treatment for students' adaptation to academic major departments and improvement of academic performances. *Behavior Therapy, 11*(2), 256–262.

Kindall, L. M., Workman, E. A., & Williams, R. L. (1980). The consultative merits of praise-ignore versus praise-reprimand instruction. *Journal of School Psychology, 18*(4), 373–380.

Kirby, K. C., Holborn, S. W., & Bushby, H. T. (1981). Word game bingo: A behavioral treatment package for improving textual responding to sight words. *Journal of Applied Behavioral Analysis, 14*(3), 317–326.

Kirschenbaum, D. S., Dielman, J. S., & Karoly, P. (1982). Efficacy of behavioral contracting: Target behaviors, performance criteria, and settings. *Behavior Modification, 6*(4), 499–518.

Kirschenbaum, D. S., Malett, S. D., Humphrey, L. L., & Tomarken, A. J. (1982). Specificity of planning and the maintenance of self-control: 1 year follow-up of a study improvement program. *Behavior Therapy, 13*(2), 232–240.

Konarski, E. A., Jr., Johnson, M. R., Crowell, C. R., & Whitman, T. L. (1980). Response deprivation and reinforcement in applied settings: A preliminary analysis. *Journal of Applied Behavior Analysis, 13*(4), 595–609.

Konarski, E. A., Jr., Crowell, C. R., Johnson, M. R., & Whitman, T. L. (1982). Response deprivation, reinforcement, and instrumental academic performance in an EMR classroom. *Behavior Therapy, 13*(1), 94–102.

Koop, S., & Martin, G. L. (1983). Evaluation of a coaching strategy to reduce swimming stroke errors with beginning age-group swimmers. *Journal of Applied Behavior Analysis, 16*(4), 447–460.

Koorland, M. A., & Oseroff, A. (1980). Effects of an instructor's written comments on teacher-trainee behavioral statements. *Educational Technology, 20*(7), 32–36.

Kulik, J. A., Bangert, R. L., & Williams, G. W. (1983). Effects of computer-based teaching on secondary school students. *Journal of Educational Psychology, 75*(1), 19–26.

Lancioni, G. (1982). Normal children as tutors to teach social responses to withdrawn mentally retarded schoolmates: Training maintenance, and generalization. *Journal of Applied Behavior Analysis, 15*(1), 17–40.

LaRowe, L. N., Tucker, R. D., & McGuire, J. M. (1980). Lunchroom noise control using feedback and group contingent reinforcement. *Journal of School Psychology, 18*(1), 51–57.

Litrownik, A. J., & Fretas, J. L. (1980). Self-monitoring in moderately retarded adolescents: Reactivity and accuracy as a function of valence. *Behavior Therapy, 11*(2), 245–255.

Lordeman, A. M., & Winett, R. A. (1980). The effects of written feedback to parents and a call-in service on student homework submission. *Education and Treatment of Children, 3*(1), 33–44.

Luce, S. C., & Hall, R. V. (1981). Contingent exercise: A procedure with differential reinforcement to reduce bizarre verbal behavior. *Education and Treatment of Children, 4*(4), 309–327.

Luce, S. C., Delquadri, J., & Hall, R. V. (1980). Contingent exercise: A mild but powerful procedure for suppressing inappropriate verbal and aggressive behavior. *Journal of Applied Behavior Analysis, 13*(4), 583–594.

Luiselli, J. K., & Rice, D. M. (1983). Brief positive practice with a handicapped child: An assessment of suppressive and re-educative effects. *Education and Treatment of Children 6*(3), 241–250.

Lutzker, J. R., Crozier, J. L., & Lutzker, S. Z. (1981). The paradoxical effects of "moral" stories on children's behavior. *Education and Treatment of Children, 4*(2), 115–124.

Mace, F. C., Cancelli, A. A., & Manos, M. J. (1983). Increasing teacher delivery of contingent praise and contingent materials using consultant feedback and praise. *School Psychology Review, 12*(3), 340–346.

Maher, C. A. (1982). Behavioral effects of using conduct problem adolescents as cross-age tutors. *Psychology in the Schools, 19*(3), 360–364.

Mayer, G. R., Butterworth, T., Nafpaktitis, M., & Sulzer-Azaroff, B. (1983). Preventing school vandalism and improving discipline: A three-year study. *Journal of Applied Behavior Analysis, 16*(4), 355–369.

Mayhew, G. L., & Anderson, J. (1980). Delayed and immediate reinforcement: Retarded adolescents in an educational setting. *Behavioral Modification, 4*(4), 527–545.

McKenzie, M. L., & Budd, K. S. (1981). A peer tutoring package to increase mathematics performance: Examination of generalized changes in classroom behavior. *Education and Treatment of Children, 4*(1), 1–15.

McLaughlin, T. F. (1981). The effects of individual and group contingencies on reading performance of special education students. *Contemporary Educational Psychology, 6*(1), 76–79.

Moreno, R., & Hovell, M. F. (1982). Teaching survival English skills and assessment of collateral behavior. *Behavior Modification, 6*(3), 375–388.

Murphy, H. A., Hutchison, J. M., & Bailey, J. S. (1983). Behavioral school psychology goes outdoors: The effect of organized games on playground aggression. *Journal of Applied Behavior Analysis, 16*(1), 29–35.

Murray, J., & Epstein, L. H. (1981). Improving oral hygiene with videotape modeling. *Behavior Modification, 5*(3), 360–371.

Nau, P. A., Van Houten, R., & O'Neil, A. (1981). The effects of feedback and a principal-mediated timeout procedure on the disruptive behavior of junior high school students. *Education and Treatment of Children, 4*(2), 101–113.

Neef, N. A., Iwata, B. A., & Page, T. J. (1980). The effects of interspersal training versus high-density reinforcement on spelling acquisition and retention. *Journal of Applied Behavior Analysis, 13*(1), 153–158.

Neef, N. A., Shafer, M. S., Egel, A. L., Cataldo, M. F., & Parrish, J. M. (1983). The class specific effects of compliance training with "do" and "don't" requests: Analogue analysis and classroom application. *Journal of Applied Behavior Analysis, 16*(1), 81–99.

Nungester, R. J., & Duchastel, P. C. (1982). Testing versus review: Effects on retention. *Journal of Educational Psychology, 74*(1), 18–22.

Ollendick, T. H., Matson, J. L., Esveldt-Dawson, K., & Shapiro, E. S. (1980). Increasing spelling achievement: An analysis of treatment procedures utilizing an alternating treatments design. *Journal of Applied Behavior Analysis, 13*(4), 645–654.

Ollendick, T. H., Dailey, D., & Shapiro, E. S. (1983). Vicarious reinforcement: Expected and unexpected effects. *Journal of Applied Behavior Analysis, 16*(4), 485–491.

Pace, D. M., & Forman, S. G. (1982). Variables related to effectiveness of response cost. *Psychology in the Schools, 19*(3), 365–370.

Paine, S. C., Hops, H., Walker, H. M., Greenwood, C. R., Fleischman, D. H., & Guild, J. J. (1982). Repeated treatment effects: A study of maintaining behavior change in socially withdrawn children. *Behavior Modification, 6*(2), 171–199.

Pelham, W. E., Schnedler, R. W., Bologna, N. C., & Contreras, J. A. (1980). Behavioral and stimulant treatment of hyperactive children: A therapy study with methylphenidate probes in a within-subject design. *Journal of Applied Behavior Analysis, 13*(2), 221–236.

Pratt-Struthers, J., & Struthers, T. B. (1983). The effects of the add-a-word spelling program on spelling accuracy during creative writing. *Education and Treatment of Children, 6*(3), 277–283.

Ragland, E. U., Kerr, M. M., & Strain, P. S. (1981). Social play of withdrawn children: A study of the effects of teacher-mediated peer feedback. *Behavior Modification, 5*(3), 347–359.

Rapport, M. D., Murphy, H. A., & Bailey, J. S. (1980). The effects of response cost treatment tactic on hyperactive children. *Journal of School Psychology 18*(2), 98–111.

Rapport, M. D., Murphy, H. A., & Bailey, J. S. (1982). Ritalin vs. response cost in the control of hyperactive children: A within-subject comparison. *Journal of Applied Behavior Analysis, 15*(2), 205–216.

Ratholz, D. A., & Luce, S. C. (1983). Alternative reinforcement strategies for the reduction of self-stimulatory behavior in autistic youth. *Education and Treatment of Children, 6*(4), 363–377.

Reese, S. C., & Filipczak, J. (1980). Assessment of skill generalization: Measurement across setting, behavior, and time in an educational setting. *Behavior Modification, 4*(2), 209–224.

Reese, S. C., Murphy, R. J., & Filipczak, J. (1981). Assessment of multiple behavioral procedures on academic and social classroom behavior. *Psychology in the Schools, 18*(3), 349–355.

Repp, A. C., Barton, L. E., & Brulle, A. R. (1983). A comparison of two procedures for programming the differential reinforcement of other behaviors. *Journal of Applied Behavior Analysis, 16*(4), 435–445.

Robinson, P. W., Newby, T. J., & Ganzell, S. L. (1981). A token system for a class of underachieving hyperactive children. *Journal of Applied Behavior Analysis, 14*(3), 307–315.

Rosen, H. S., & Rosen, L. A. (1983). Eliminating stealing: Use of stimulus control with an elementary student. *Behavior Modification, 7*(1), 56–63.

Rosenbaum, M. S., Creedon, D. L., & Drabman, R. S. (1981). Training preschool children to identify emergency situations and make emergency phone calls. *Behavior Therapy, 12*(3), 425–435.

Russo, D. C., Cataldo, M. F., & Cushing, P. J. (1981). Compliance training and behavioral covariation in the treatment of multiple behavior problems. *Journal of Applied Behavior Analysis, 14*(3), 209–222.

Saigh, P. A., & Umar, A. M. (1983). The effects of a good behavior game on the disruptive behavior of Sudanese elementary school students. *Journal of Applied Behavior Analysis, 16*(3), 339–344.

Salend, S. J., & Henry, K. (1981). Response cost in mainstreamed setting. *Journal of School Psychology, 19*(3), 242–249.

Schofield, J. W., & Francis, W. D. (1982). An observational study of peer interaction in racially mixed "accelerated" classrooms. *Journal of Educational Psychology, 74*(5), 722–732.

Schunk, D. H. (1981). Modeling and attributional effects on children's achievements: A self-efficacy analysis. *Journal of Educational Psychology, 73*(1), 93–105.

Schunk, D. H. (1983). Ability versus effort attributional feedback: Differential effects on self-efficacy and achievement. *Journal of Educational Psychology, 75*(6), 848–856.

Seidner, M. L., & Kirschenbaum, D. S. (1981). Behavioral contracts: Effects of pretreatment information and intention statements. *Behavior Therapy, 11*(5), 689–698.

Shapiro, E. S., & Klein, R. D. (1980). Self-management of classroom behavior with retarded/disturbed children. *Behavior Modification, 4*(1), 83–97.

Sharpley, A. M., Irvine, J. W., & Sharpley, C. F. (1983). An examination of the effectiveness of a cross-age tutoring program in mathematics for elementary school children. *American Education Research Journal, 20*(1), 103–111.

Sharpley, C. F. (1982). Elimination of vicarious reinforcement effects within an implicit reward situation. *Journal of Educational Psychology, 74*(4), 611–617.

Sherman, C. F., & Anderson, R. P. (1980). Modification of attending behavior in hyperactive children. *Psychology in the Schools, 17*(3), 272–279.

Singh, N. N., Dawson, M. J., & Manning, P. (1981). Effects of spaced responding DRL on the stereotyped behavior of profoundly retarded persons. *Journal of Applied Behavior Analysis, 14*(4), 521–526.

Skon, L., Johnson, D. W., & Johnson, R. T. (1981). Cooperative peer interaction versus individual competition and individualistic efforts: Effects on the acquisition of cognitive reasoning strategies. *Journal of Educational Psychology, 73*(1), 83–92.

Smith, B. M., Schumaker, J. B., Schaeffer, J., & Sherman, J. A. (1982). Increasing participation and improving the quality of discussions in seventh-grade social studies classes. *Journal of Applied Behavior Analysis, 15*(1), 97–110.

Smith, K., Johnson, D. W., & Johnson, R. T. (1981). Can conflict be constructive? Controversy versus concurrence seeking in learning groups. *Journal of Educational Psychology, 73*(5), 651–663.

Speltz, M., Shimamuira, J. W., & McReynolds, W. T. (1982). Procedural variations in group contingencies: Effects on children's academic and social behaviors. *Journal of Applied Behavior Analysis, 15*(4), 533–544.

Strain, P. S., Lambert, D. L., Kerr, M. M., Stagg, V., & Lenkner, D. A. (1983). Naturalistic assessment of children's compliance to teachers' requests and consequences for compliance. *Journal of Applied Behavior Analysis, 16*(2), 243–249.

Swain, J. J., Allard, G. B., & Holborn, S. W. (1982). The good toothbrushing game: A school-based dental hygiene program for increasing the toothbrushing effectiveness of children. *Journal of Applied Behavior Analysis, 15*(1), 171–176.

Tobin, K. G., & Capie, W. (1982). Relationship between classroom process variables and middle-school science achievement. *Journal of Educational Psychology, 74*(3), 441–454.

Trice, A. D., Parker, F. C., Furrow, F., & Iwata. (1983). An analysis of home contingencies to improve school behavior with disruptive adolescents. *Education and Treatment of Children, 6*(4), 389–399.

Trovanto, J., & Bucher, B. (1980). Peer tutoring with or without home-based reinforcement for reading remediation. *Journal of Applied Behavior Analysis, 13*(1), 129–141.

Van Houten, R., & Little, G. (1982). Increased response rate in special education children following an abrupt reduction in time limit in the absence of a token economy. *Education and Treatment of Children, 5*(1), 23–32.

Van Houten, R., & Nau, P. A. (1980). A comparison of the effects of fixed and variable ratio schedules of reinforcement on the behavior of deaf children. *Journal of Applied Behavior Analysis, 13*(1), 13–21.

Van Houten, R., Nau, P. A., MacKenzie-Keating, S. E., Sameoto, D., & Colavecchia, B. (1982). An analysis of some variables influencing the effectiveness of reprimands. *Journal of Applied Behavior Analysis, 15*(1), 65–83.

Wacker, D. P., & Berg, W. K. (1983). Effects of picture prompts on the acquisition of complex vocational tasks by mentally retarded adolescents. *Journal of Applied Behavior Analysis, 16*(4), 417–433.

Wall, S. M. (1983). Children's self-determination of standard in reinforcement contingencies: A re-examination. *Journal of School Psychology, 21*(2), 123–131.

Webb, N. M. (1982a). Group composition, group interaction, and achievement in cooperative small groups. *Journal of Educational Psychology, 74*(4), 475–484.

Webb, N. M. (1982b). Peer interaction and learning in cooperative small groups. *Journal of Educational Psychology, 74*(5), 642–655.

Webb, N. M., & Cullian, L. K. (1983). Group interaction and achievement in small groups: Stability over time. *American Educational Research Journal, 20*(3), 411–423.

Whitman, T., & Johnston, M. B. (1983). Teaching addition and subtraction with regrouping to educable mentally retarded children: A group self-instructional training program. *Behavior Therapy, 14*(1), 127–143.

Whitman, T. L., Scibak, J. W., Butler, K. M., Richter, R., & Johnson, M. R. (1982). Improving classroom behavior in mentally retarded children through correspondence training. *Journal of Applied Behavior Analysis, 15*(4), 545–564.

Williams, J. A., Koegel, R. L., & Egel, A. L. (1981). Response-reinforcer relationships and improved learning in autistic children. *Journal of Applied Behavior Analysis, 14*(1), 53–60.

Williamson, D. A., Calpin, J. P., Dilorenzo, T. M., Garris, R. P., & Petti, T. E. (1981). Treating hyperactivity with dexedrine and activity feedback *Behavior Modification, 5*(3), 399–416.

Witt, J. C., & Adams, R. M. (1980). Direct and observed reinforcement in the classroom: The interaction between information and reinforcement for socially approved and disapproved behaviors. *Behavior Modification, 4*(3), 321–336.

Witt, J. C., & Elliott, S. N. (1982). The response cost lottery: A time efficient and effective classroom intervention. *Journal of School Psychology, 20*(2), 155–161.

Workman, E. A., Helton, G. B., & Watson, P. J. (1982). Self-monitoring effects in a four-year-old child: An ecological behavior analysis. *Journal of School Psychology, 20*(1), 57–64.

Zwald, L., & Gresham, F. M. (1982). Behavioral consultation in a secondary class: Using DRL to decrease negative verbal interactions. *School Psychology Review, 11*(4), 428–432.

CHAPTER 15

The Elusive Search for Teachable Aspects of Problem Solving

Richard E. Mayer

The purpose which runs through and strengthens all educational purposes—the common thread of all education—is the development of the ability to think.

We should be teaching students how to think; instead we are primarily teaching them what to think.

It is strange that we expect students to learn yet seldom teach them anything about learning.

Introduction

The ideas just presented serve to motivate the present chapter and its central question, "Can problem solving be taught?" These quotes are, respectively, from the National Education Association's (1961) *The Central Purpose of American Education,* the introduction to Lochhead and Clement's (1979) *Cognitive Process Instruction,* and Norman's (1980) chapter in Tuma and Reif's (1980) *Problem Solving and Education.* These quotes point to both the promise and the pitfalls of research on problem solving. The promise refers to the possibility of a scientifically based understanding of how to teach people to think. The pitfalls

refer to the possibility of raising expectations about the teachability of problem solving that can only be met by a yet another wave of educational fads and cults.

Emphasis on "good habits of mind" is, of course, not a new goal in education. Rippa (1980) points out that as early as 1712 the curriculum of the Boston Latin School required that students read, write, and speak Latin as well as have some knowledge of Greek and mathematics. The Latin School approach, which was still strong a century ago, was based on the idea that learning Latin and Greek and geometry would foster the traits of mental discipline and logical thinking. The demise of the Latin School approach was brought about by the practical demands of an emerging technological and democratic society and by the growing body of educational research indicating that skills learned from Latin did not transfer easily to practical situations. Although they give lip service to the development of the mind, today's schools

Richard E. Mayer • Department of Psychology, University of California, Santa Barbara, Santa Barbara, CA 93106.
This chapter was written while the author was on sabbatical leave at the Center for the Study of Reading. This material is based on work supported by the National Science Foundation under Grant No. MDR-8470248.

stress the teaching of objectively measurable behaviors. However, current research in the psychology of problem solving has again raised the possibility of succeeding where the Latin Schools failed. While retaining the Latin School's goal of teaching "good habits of mind," current attempts to teach problem-solving skills are bolstered by one hundred years of scientific research on problem solving.

The study of problem solving traditionally has had a modest but consistent place in educational psychology. For example, much of the early work concerning transfer of training actually involved studies of the teachability of problem-solving skills (e.g., Thorndike, 1923). More recently, a review of the contents of the *Journal of Educational Psychology, Contemporary Educational Psychology,* and the *Educational Psychologist* reveals a consistent interest in problem solving. Problem solving is not heavily represented in undergraduate texts in our field (see Ash & Love-Clark, 1985), but there continues to be a broad interest in problem solving and the development of problem-solving skills.

The purpose of this chapter is to determine whether there are aspects of problem solving that might be learnable (Gagne, 1979). In order to address this question, this chapter first provides some basic definitions and a brief historical overview of the problem-solving literature. Then, this chapter explores classic issues concerning the teaching of problem-solving ability, such as whether to use discovery or direct instruction, whether to focus on the product or the process of problem solving, whether to teach general skills applicable in many domains or specific skills applicable in more restricted domains, and whether to teach a wholistic approach to solving problems or an analytic approach that focuses on the component processes. Finally, the chapter closes with a discussion of implications for future research.

Definitions

In order to study human problem solving, it is useful to agree on the definitions of key terms, such as problem, problem solving, types of problems, and reasoning. The information processing approach to problem solving (Mayer, 1983) yields the following definitions.

A problem consists of: (a) *a given state,* that is, certain conditions or objects are present at the be-

ginning, (b) *a goal state,* that is, certain conditions or objects are desired at the end, and (c) *obstacles,* that is, certain difficulties prevent the problem solver from directly transforming the given state into the goal state. Thus, a problem occurs when some situation exists, the problem solver desires the situation to be changed into a different one, but there is no direct or obvious way to accomplish the change. A task that is a problem for one person may not be a problem for another person; for example, finding an answer for "What is 3 + 5?" is a problem for a preschooler who has not yet memorized all the number facts but not for a normal adult.

Problem solving is (a) *cognitive,* but is inferred from behavior, (b) *a process* that involves a series of manipulations on knowledge in a person's mind, and (c) *directed* towards to solution of a problem. Thus, problem solving involves what Polya (1968) calls, "finding a way out of a difficulty, a way around an obstacle, attaining an aim that was not immediately obtainable." Hayes (1981) analyzes problem solving into two major parts: *representing* the problem and *searching* for a way to solve the problem. For example, if a person is presented with an algebra story problem, the person might represent the problem as an equation and then search for a solution by applying the rules of algebra and arithmetic.

It should be noted that behaviorists and cognitivists differ with respect to the definition of problem solving. The behaviorists content that empirically observable behavior must be the primary data of psychology; because internal cognitive processes cannot be directly observed, they have no place in psychology. The cognitivist position is that behavior is just the result of thinking but internal cognitive processes can be inferred from behavior; thus, the goal of psychology should be an understanding of the mechanisms that underlie behavior.

There are many different types of problems. For example, Greeno (1978a) has distinguished among (a) *problems of inducing structure,* such as series completion or analogy problems, (b) *problems of transformation,* such as chess and checkers, and (c) *problems of arrangement,* such as anagram or cryptarithmetic problems. Reitman (1965) has listed four types of problems, based on the specificity of the given and goal states: (a) *well-defined given state and well-defined goal state,* such as, "How can you turn a sow's ear into a silk purse?" (b) *well-defined given state and poorly defined goal state,* such as, "How can you redesign a Cadillac to get better gas mileage?" (c) *poorly defined given state and well-defined goal state,* such as, "Explain the mechanisms responsible for sun spots." (d) *Poorly defined given state and poorly defined goal state,* such as, "Understand problem solving." Guilford (1959) distinguished between *convergent thinking,* that is, thinking that proceeds towards a single answer, such as arithmetic computation problems, and *divergent thinking,* or thinking that moves outward from the problem in many possible directions, such as "list all the uses for a brick." School learning tasks generally favor well-defined problems requiring convergent thinking—although most practical living problems are poorly defined problems requiring divergent thinking.

The roots of modern issues in problem solving can be found in the philosophers' study of inductive and deductive reasoning tasks. In inductive reasoning tasks, the problem solver is given a number of instances or examples and must induce a rule. Examples include concept learning, series completion, and analogy problems. In deductive reasoning tasks, the problem solver is given premises and must logically deduce a conclusion using the rules of logic. Examples include categorical, linear, and conditional syllogisms. Early problem-solving research focused on these types of reasoning tasks (Revlin & Mayer, 1978).

Cognitive Analysis of Problem Solving

Earlier in this volume, DiVesta showed how cognitive psychology has become the dominant source of new ideas in educational psychology. As has been pointed out elsewhere (Mayer, 1981a), the contributions of cognitive psychology rest mainly in providing a set of tools for analyzing and describing knowledge and processes. In the area of problem solving, the most fundamental analysis involves breaking problem solving into two phases: (a) *problem representation,* in which the problem statement is represented mentally by the problem solver, and (b) *problem solution,* in which mental operations are performed on the representation in order to achieve solution.

The historical roots of analyzing problem solving into stages can be traced to Wallas' (1926) classic book, *The Art of Thought.* Using case studies of famous problem solvers, Wallas suggested a series of four stages in problem solving: preparation, incubation, illumination, and verification. Polya's (1945) classic book, *How to Solve It,* also described four stages in problem solving: understanding the problem, devising a plan, carrying out the plan, looking back. The first two of Polya's stages and first three of Wallas's stages correspond to problem representation, whereas the remaining stages correspond to problem solution. Similarly, classic Gestalt research (e.g., Duncker, 1945) revealed that different problem representations lead to different solution procedures. More recently, computer simulations of problem solving have required distinctions between understanding and solving (Hayes, 1978).

Two tools that are relevant to problem representation are schema and problem space; two tools that are relevant to problem solution are strategies and algorithms. These four tools are described in this section.

Schema. A *schema* for a problem refers to a problem solver's general mental representation of the structure of the problem. The historical roots of the concept of schema in psychology can be traced to Bartlett's (1932) classic book on prose memory, *Remembering,* as well as Piaget's (1954) classic discussion of intellectual development. However, the term has been used in a far more restricted sense when applied to problem solving. For example, Hinsley, Hayes, & Simon (1977) studied people's schemata for various types of algebra story problems. In one study, high school and college students were given a collection of story problems and asked to sort the problems into categories. The results indicated that subjects were able to perform this task with high levels of agreement, yielding 18 categories such as work, interest, time-rate-distance, mixture, and so on. These results provide some evidence that people have developed schemata for various types of algebra story problems.

Greeno (1980) and Riley, Greeno, and Heller (1983) have described children's schemata for simple word problems. One kind of problem involves a "cause/change" schema, such as: "Joe had 3 marbles. Then Tom gave him 5 more marbles. How many marbles does he have now?" Another kind involves a "combine" schema, such as: "Joe has 3 marbles. Tom has 5 marbles. How many marbles do they have altogether?" A third kind is "compare," such as: "Joe has 3 marbles. Tom has 5 more marbles than Joe. How many marbles does Tom have?" Kindergartners and first graders performed well on the first two problems but

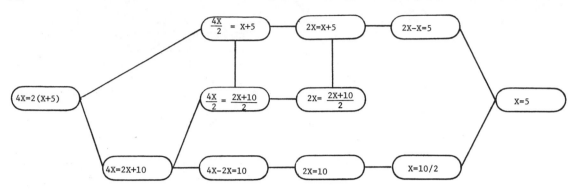

Figure 1. Partial problem space for an equation problem.

poorly on the last one, whereas second and third graders performed well on all three. These results encourage the idea that children begin with one or two basic schemata, such as cause/change, and develop more differentiated schemata, such as compare, as they acquire more experience.

In order to gain a broader perspective, Mayer (1981b) surveyed the exercise problems given in a set of standard algebra textbooks. Of the approximately 1,100 problems found, there were about 20 general categories of problems similar to those found by Hinsley, Hayes, and Simon. In addition, for each general type, there were often many subtypes. For example, for time-rate-distance problems the subtypes included a round trip, two vehicles converging, two vehicles traveling in opposite directions, one vehicle overtaking another, and so on. A tally of the frequency of each subtype revealed that some versions of a problem were far more common than others.

In a follow-up study, Mayer (1982) presented eight story problems to subjects and then asked the subjects to recall the problems. When subjects made errors, they tended to change an uncommon version of a problem into a more common version. This type of error suggests that subjects have schemata for common subtypes of problems and try to use these schemata for interpreting problems.

Problem Space. Problem space refers to the problem solver's mental representation of the initial state, goal state, all intermediate states, and the operations that can be made to move from one state to another. The historical roots of this approach may be traced to Duncker's (1945) classic attempts to diagram the solution path that subjects used to solve his tumor problem. In Duncker's analysis, the problem solver continuously reformulated the statement of the givens or goal.

The modern concept of problem space was heavily influenced by developments in computer science, and was popularized by Newell & Simon's (1972) classic book, *Human Problem Solving*. For example, Figure 1 shows the problem space for the problem of solving the following equation for X: $4X = 2(X + 5)$. Each node represents a problem state and each arrow represents a transformation from one state to another. As can be seen, the initial state is $4X = 2(X + 5)$ and the goal state is $X = 5$. The legal operators are the rules of algebra and arithmetic, such as dividing both sides of the equation by 2 or subtracting X from both sides.

Strategy. Once a problem has been represented as a problem space, solving the problem involves figuring out a way to search through the space. A strategy is a general procedure or rule of thumb that helps the problem solver determine how to go about solving the problem. Means–ends analysis is one strategy for searching a problem space, and has been used widely in computer simulations of problem solving (Newell & Simon, 1972). In means–ends analysis, the problem solver always works on one goal at a time by asking, "What means do I have to achieve the ends I desire?" If a goal cannot be directly achieved, the problem solver establishes a subgoal of removing an obstacle that is in the way, and so on.

Figure 2 summarizes three major kinds of goals as described by Newell and Simon (1972): (a) Transform State A into State B. For example, the first goal in the equation problem given previously is to transform the given state, $4X = 2(X + 5)$, into the goal state, $X = \_\_$. However, there is an obstacle in the way, namely there is an X on the right side of the equation. Thus the outcome of the attempt to transform is recognition of a difficulty—

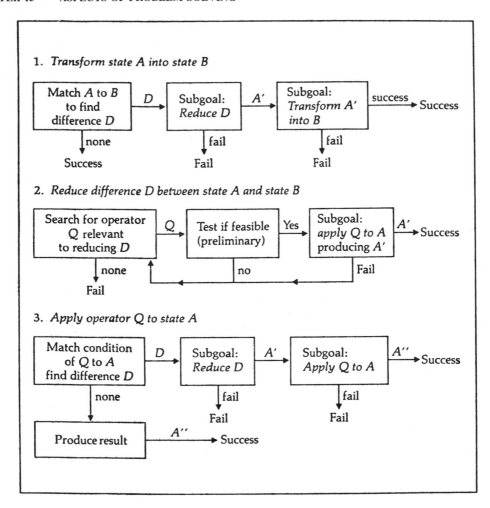

Figure 2. Subgoals in means–ends analysis.

namely X is on the right side. (b) Reduce the difference between State A and State B. Once the problem solver recognizes that there is an obstacle or difficulty, the goal is set to reduce this obstacle. The result of the reduce goal is to identify an operator to use in trying to eliminate the obstacle. For example, in the math problem, the operator that is chosen is to subtract X from both sides of the equation. (c) Apply Operator Q to State A. Once an operator is selected, the next goal is to apply it. If successfully applied, this will create a new state. However, in the example given there is an obstacle that will not allow the problem solver to carry out directly the operation—namely, the X on the right is in parentheses.

Goals are placed in a goal stack until they are carried out. As you can see in the math example,

the transform goal could not be carried out so it is placed in the stack. Then, the reduce goal and the apply goal were not carried out, so they are placed in the stack. Next, the problem solver will try to reduce the obstacle of having parentheses on the right. This can be achieved by clearing the parentheses. The goal of applying this operator is successful, resulting in a new state, $4X = 2X + 10$. Now the old goal in the stack—subtracting $2X$ from both sides—can be carried out resulting in a new state $2X = 10$. Eventually, the last goal of transforming the given state into the goal state is the only one left in the stack; when it is achieved it can be eliminated and the problem is solved.

The means–ends analysis strategy can also be expressed as a production system (Anderson, 1984; Newell & Simon, 1972). A production system is a list of condition–action pairs. For example, a condition–action pair for the equation problem could be, "If there is an *X* on the right side, subtract *X* from both sides." A detailed description of means–ends analysis is presented in Mayer (1981a).

Algorithm. An algorithm is a well-defined procedure that leads automatically to an answer. Examples include the procedure for long division or for three column subtraction. The historical roots of procedural analyses can be traced to the work of Donders (1868/1969) and the history of chronometric techniques has been described by Posner (1978). Early advances in task analysis, such as Gagne's (1968) learning hierarachy were also attempts to break an intellectual task into smaller parts. More recently, Sternberg's (1977) "componential analysis" has focused on the analysis of cognitive processes into parts. Following the conventions used in computer programming, psychologists have used flowcharts to specify algorithms. For example, Figure 3 shows a flow chart for three column subtraction. The boxes represent states, the diamonds represent decisions, and the arrows represent the flow from one step to the next.

Brown and Burton (1978) have shown how children's performance on tests of subtraction can be described in terms of their underlying algorithms. Children were asked to solve a series of subtraction problems; for each child, Brown and Burton tried to find an algorithm that would generate the same answers, including any errors. Some children made no errors, and thus presumably used a procedure like the one in Figure 3. Some seemed to make random errors that could not be modeled. However, others made errors that could be described by saying that the children used the procedure in the figure but with one or more "bugs" (i.e., erroneous steps in the procedure) added. For example, suppose a child gave the following answers:

$$876 - 453 = 423$$
$$547 - 356 = 211$$
$$713 - 342 = 431$$
$$455 - 322 = 133$$
$$674 - 555 = 121$$

This child seems to possess a bug that Brown and Burton call "smaller from larger," that is, the smaller number in a column is always subtracted from the larger number. Thus, the child is con-

sistently using an algorithm, but the algorithm contains a bug. Other common bugs observed by Brown and Burton included "borrowing from zero" such as $205 - 126 = 179$, and "move over zero" such as $205 - 126 = 29$.

Groen and Parkman (1972) and Woods, Resnick, and Groen (1975) have developed algorithmic models to describe how young children add and subtract small numbers. Fuson (1982) has argued that there is a developmental trend in which the procedures become more sophisticated and eventually automatic. Recent research by Siegler (1978) and by Case (1978) suggests that as procedures become automatized, this allows the problem solver to incorporate them within more complex procedures.

Historical Example

The history of research on problem solving has produced two quite distinct views of the problem-solving process—the associationist view and the Gestalt view. According to the associationist view, problem solving involves exercising existing associations between the stimulus (i.e., the problem situation) and various responses. For example, in Thorndike's (1898) classic study of cats solving the problem of how to get out of a puzzle box, the stimulus was being in the puzzle box and the associated responses included meowing, pouncing, scratching, and pulling a string (the response that opened a door to let the cat out). Thorndike observed that the cat solved the problem by "trial and error and accidental success." On the first few trials the cat engaged in many irrelevant activities before accidentally pulling the string, but after many trials the cat pulled the string almost immediately upon being placed in the puzzle box. Thorndike's explanation of the cat's problem-solving behavior was straightforward: based on past experience the cat tried responses that were associated with the stimulus with the most strongly associated response being the most likely to be tried. In addition, Thorndike proposed his famous law of effect: if a response is followed by a pleasing state of affairs (such as getting out of the puzzle box) it will become more strongly associated with the stimulus; if a response is followed by an unpleasing state of affairs (such as not getting out of the puzzle box) its association to the stimulus will be weakened. The instructional implication for teaching of problem solving is that the learner should

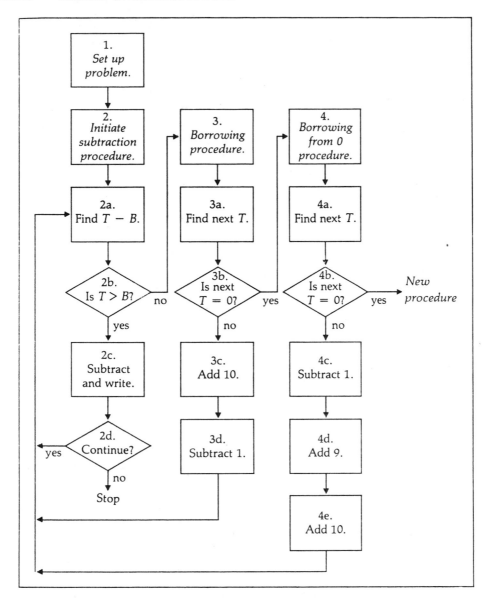

Figure 3. A procedure for three column subtraction problems.

engage in drill and practice, with each solution response being immediately reinforced.

In contrast, according to the Gestalt view, problem solving involves understanding how the givens in the problem fit together in order to satisfy the requirements of the goal. For example, in one of Kohler's (1925) classic studies of problem solving in apes, a caged ape was given some sticks and some fruit out of reach outside the cage. The ape did not engage in random trail and error; rather, the

ape reflected on the situation and invented the solution of using the sticks as a tool for raking in the fruit. According to Kohler, the ape achieved "structural insight" by seeing how all the parts of the problems fit together into a coherent structure. The instructional implication for teaching is that the learner needs to learn in a meaningful way, with emphasis on how to represent problems.

The associationist and Gestalt views of problem solving offer quite different directions for how to teach problem solving. The associationists focus on the product of problem solving—that is accurate application of a solution procedure—whereas the Gestaltists focus on the process of problem solving—that is, techniques for representing and planning. The associationists focus on reproductive problem solving—using already learned responses to solve a problem—whereas the Gestaltists focus on productive problem solving—creating a novel solution. The associationist view focuses on teaching of specific skills whereas Gestalt theory focuses on general skills. These three issues—product versus process, reproductive versus productive, and general versus specific—have their roots in the classic confrontation between the associationist and Gestalt views. Yet, they are also contemporary issues that are still central to the development of an effective instructional program in problem solving.

Teaching for Transfer: Rote versus Meaningful Learning

Issue.   The issue of transfer has been a major battleground for the confrontation between the associationist and Gestalt views of problem solving. *Transfer* refers to the degree to which a learner can apply existing knowledge to accomplish new tasks. Thus, the issue of transfer concerns how to teach in a way that will foster creative problem solving. Three traditional categories of instructional method are rule, discovery, and guided instruction. In rule instruction, the to-be-learned rule is explicitly given to the learners, along with drill and practice in using the rule. In discovery instruction, learners are given a challenging environment and allowed to search for the to-be-learned rule on their own. Guided instruction represents a compromise between rule and discovery methods, in which learners actively participate in the learning process and also receive guidance to keep them on track. Similarly, several theorists have distinguished between rote and meaningful learning (Ausubel, 1968; Katona, 1942; Wertheimer, 1959). Rote learning involves being able to retain exactly what was taught, whereas meaningful learning involves being able to use information creatively in new ways. Figure 4 shows the three methods of instruction and two kinds of learning. As you can see, any of the three instructional methods can lead to either rote or meaningful learning.

TYPES OF LEARNING OUTCOMES

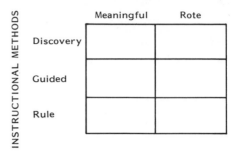

Figure 4. Distinction between instructional method and learning outcome.

An Example.   Can we teach in a way that fosters productive problem solving? Let us begin with an example from the work of the well-known Gestalt psychologist, Max Wertheimer (1959), in his book *Productive Thinking*. One problem Wertheimer presents concerns how to find the area of a parallelogram. Wertheimer states that there are two ways of teaching students how to solve parallelogram problems: (a) learning by rote, and (b) learning by understanding.

In learning by rote, the student is taught to draw a perpendicular line inside the parallelogram, to measure the height of the perpendicular and the length of the base, and then to multiply height times base in order to determine the area. In short, the student learns how to apply the formula, Area = Height × Base, as shown in the bottom of Figure 5. Wertheimer refers to this method of learning as ''senseless'' or as building ''arbitrary associations.''

In learning by understanding, the student is encouraged to discover that he or she could cut off a right triangle from one end of the parallelogram, place it on the other end, and thus form a rectangle. In this method, the student sees that a parallelogram takes the same amount of area as a corresponding rectangle; since the student already knows how to find the area of a rectangle, the problem is solved. This method is summarized in the top of Figure 5. Wertheimer refers to this method of learning as ''structural insight'' or ''meaningful apprehension of relations'' because the student understands the structural relationship between a parallelogram and a rectangle.

According to Wertheimer, students taught under either method will be equivalent in their ability to solve standard parallelogram problems like those

LEARNING BY UNDERSTANDING

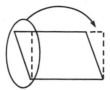

A PARALLELOGRAM CAN BE CHANGED INTO A RECTANGLE.

LEARNING BY ROTE

AREA = H x B

Figure 5. Two methods for teaching students how to find the area of a parallelogram.

given during instruction. However, if students are given a transfer problem that is quite different from those given during instruction, the rote learners will say, "We haven't had this yet," whereas the meaningful learners will be better able to solve it. Wertheimer's claim, then, is that the payoff for teaching problem solving in a meaningful way is not in improved retention but in improved transfer.

Although Wertheimer's work is now several decades old, examples such as the parallelogram problem raise important issues that are still relevant to the current study of problem solving. First, Wertheimer suggests that there are qualitatively different kinds of learning. Instead of focusing on how much is learned, Wertheimer's work raises the intriguing idea that we should focus on what is learned. Recently, in examining the problem of "what is learned," cognitive psychologists have begun to develop techniques for representing people's knowledge, including their knowledge of how to solve problems. Second, Wertheimer's work suggests that we should focus on the process that students use for solving problems rather than focus solely on the product (or outcome) of problem solving. Recently, from examining students' problem-solving protocols, cognitive psychologists have developed programs of "cognitive process instruction" in which problem-solving instruction focuses on process. Finally, Wertheimer asserted that the key to evaluating the success of

instruction in problem solving concerns evaluating how well the student can transfer what was taught to new situations. Recently, there have been renewed efforts to provide serious evaluations of currently available problem-solving courses, with special focus on whether training transfers to new situations.

The distinction between learning by rote and learning by understanding is a major contribution of the Gestalt psychologists (Katona, 1942; Kohler, 1925; Wertheimer, 1959). Although their works provided many interesting examples of the distinction, the cognitive theory underlying the distinction was not well spelled out and the educational applications were not well tested. In particular, their work suggested that meaningful methods of instruction would help students to use creatively newly learned information in problem solving whereas rote methods would help students only in retention. In this section, we investigate three well-known attempts to provide "meaningful" methods of instruction: structure-oriented methods, discovery methods, and inductive methods.

Structure-Oriented Methods. One aspect of "learning by understanding" in Wertheimer's parallelogram problem is that the underlying structure of the problem was made concrete, that is, by physically cutting a triangle off one end and placing it on the other. Structure-oriented methods refer to the use of concrete objects to represent structures underlying problem solving ideas. In mathematics instruction, for example, "concrete manipulatives" include Dienes blocks, Montessori beads, attribute blocks, cuisenaire rods, bundles of sticks and geoboards.

What is the theoretical basis for mapping procedures onto concrete objects and actions? Bruner's (1964) theory of intellectual development provides the basis for a cognitive theory of structure-oriented methods. According to Bruner's theory, children's thinking develops through three modes of representation of information: the *enactive mode,* using actions such as counting on one's fingers during computation; the *iconic mode,* using visualization, such as visualizing bundles of sticks that can be grouped by tens; and the *symbolic mode,* using language or some other symbol system, such as numerals. The development of understanding must progress through the same stages as intellectual development: first understanding by doing, then by seeing, and eventually by symbolic representation. Bruner & Kenney (1966, p. 436) state this idea as follows:

We would suggest that learning mathematics may be viewed as a microcosm of intellectual development. It begins with instrumental activity, a kind of definition of things by doing. Such operations become represented . . . in the form of . . . images. Finally, with the help of symbolic notation, the learner comes to grasp the formal or abstract properties of the things he is dealing with.

Bruner's theory suggests that concrete manipulatives may be useful in making the transitions from enactive to iconic to symbolic modes of representation.

One of the earliest empirical studies of a structure-oriented instructional method was conducted by Brownell and Moser (1949). Third graders were taught how to solve two-column subtraction problems such as,

$$\begin{array}{r} 65 \\ -28 \\ \hline \end{array}$$

One group of children was taught using a standard method that focused only on the symbols; a second group was taught using a meaningful method that showed how the symbols related to sticks that could be bundled into groups of tens. On posttests, both groups were able to solve two-column subtraction problems similar to those given during instruction, but the children who learned with a concrete model performed better than the standard group in learning to solve different kinds of problems. As predicted by Brownell (1935), the advantage of meaningful learning can be seen when students are asked to transfer what they have learned to new situations.

The more recent body of empirical research (Mayer, 1985; Resnick & Ford, 1981; Silver, 1985) has been consistent with Brownell's findings in that meaningful mathematics instruction is favored over rote instruction; however, it still is not clear which particular meaningful approach is most useful, or why. For example, Resnick and Ford (1981, p. 126) noted that "the structure-oriented methods and materials have not been adequately validated by research and we know little from school practice about [their] effects."

Discovery Methods. Another aspect of Wertheimer's approach to the parallelogram problem is that meaningful learning involves active discovery on the part of the learner—that is, the problem solver was encouraged to find the solution independently. Discovery methods refer to requiring the learner to find the to-be-learned rule or principle. For example, in Suchman's (1960, 1966) "inquiry training" the student is shown some interesting scientific phenomenon and asked to make predictions and explanations, which are then tested empirically, and so on.

The theoretical justification for discovery methods is generally traced to Bruner's (1961) famous essay, "The Act of Discovery." Bruner distinguished between expository instruction—in which the teacher tells the student how to solve the problem—and hypothetical instruction—in which the student actively discovers the new rule or principle. According to Bruner, the expository mode encourages the student to memorize material whereas the hypothetical mode encourages students to learn how to become creative problem solvers.

During the 1960s, Bruner's assertions led to a flurry of research studies that made comparisons among two or more of the following methods of instruction: *pure discovery,* in which the student receives representative problems and must solve them with little or no teacher supervision; *guided discovery,* in which the student receives representative problems to solve but the teacher provides hints and questions that systematically keep the student on track; *expository instruction,* in which the final answer or rule is presented to the student for each problem (Shulman & Keisler, 1968). For example, Kittel (1957) trained students to solve oddity problems (e.g., given four items choose the one that does not belong) using each of these three methods. The guided discovery group performed much better than the expository group on a transfer test, even though both groups performed at the same level on a retention test. The pure discovery group performed much worse than the other groups on both transfer and retention, presumably because subjects often failed to discover the to-be-learned principles. Similarly, Gagne and Brown (1961) found that students who learned to solve series sums problems under a guided discovery method required more time to learn than students who learned under an expository method, but guided discovery students performed much better on transfer tasks than expository students.

Apparently, pure discovery methods have the drawback that some students fail to discover the underlying principle and expository methods have the drawback that students fail to learn in a meaningful way; however, a carefully planned guided discovery sequence can overcome these difficulties and still produce strong transfer effects. More recently, Papert (1980) has argued strongly for a sort of "pure discovery" approach to computing. According to Papert, children will acquire "powerful intellectual skills" if they are left on their own to have "hands-on" experience with a computer system. However, there is almost no research support to encourage Papert's suggestion. For example, Bayman and Mayer (1983) found that students who learned to write BASIC programs through "hands-on" experience developed a large assortment of incorrect conceptions of computer programming.

Inductive Methods. Another aspect of Wertheimer's learning by understanding is that learning proceeds inductively from the givens to a underlying rule, whereas learning by rote proceeds deductively from a statement of rule to its application.

The theoretical justification for inductive methods of instruction comes from the idea that productive learning involves connecting new material to existing knowledge. Ausubel (1968) and Mayer (1975) refer to this idea as assimilation theory. Under inductive methods, students are exposed to long periods of mental searching before they can verbalize the rules; during this searching, students have more opportunities to activate existing knowledge. Thus, inductively taught students are more likely to encode new material within a broad

context of existing knowledge as compared to deductively taught students.

Early research by Winch (1913) supported the idea that deductive methods were better for retention and inductive methods were better for fostering certain kinds of transfer. A half century later, Hermann (1969) confirmed that there was still qualified support for these observations. For example, Roughead and Scandura (1968) used inductive and deductive methods to teach children how to solve series sum problems. In the deductive method, the rule was stated and applied to several problems, and then the student applied the rule to several problems of the same type. In the inductive method, the student solved several problems all of the same type, then the rule was presented and applied to the problems. The deductive group learned faster during original instruction but the inductive group learned faster during transfer.

In another study, Mayer and Greeno (1972) used inductive and deductive methods to teach students how to solve binomial probability problems. The inductive method began by presenting familiar ideas such as "trial" and "success" and "probability of success" and gradually worked them together into a formula. The deductive method began with the formula and showed how it applied to other ideas. Although both methods provided the same basic information and sample problems, performance on a posttest was strongly affected by method of instruction. The deductively sequenced instruction produced superior performance on solving problems similar to those given during instruction but the inductively sequenced instruction produced superior performance on solving problems that required far transfer.

Research on the sequencing of problem-solving instruction indicates that deductive methods are better when the goal is to teach students how to solve a small set of problems but inductive methods are better when the goal is to help students be able to transfer to new situations. More recently, Collins and Stevens (1982) showed how a computerized tutor can use an inductive or Socratic method to teach topics such as geography.

Summary. What have we learned about the issue of teaching for transfer? The history of research and practice in this area has been marked by cycles of very strong claims, curriculum changes, and disappointment. Yet the research results suggest that meaningful methods of instruction—using structured materials, guided discovery, or guided induction—can be effective in increasing students' transfer performance. Mayer (1975, 1984) has identified three conditions of meaningful learning: (a) reception of the to-be-learned material in working memory, (b) availability of appropriate prerequisite knowledge in long-term memory, and (c) actively searching and connecting existing knowledge with new learning. When the material is extremely familiar to the learner, then meaningful methods may not be needed because the learner can naturally engage in these three processes. When undirected discovery or inductive methods are used, the learner may fail to receive the to-be-learned rule; when too much direction is used, the learner may fail to activate prior knowledge. Thus, for meaningful methods to be effective they must provide enough guidance for the learner to discover the to-be-learned rule, but must provide enough challenge for the learner to search actively and connect existing knowledge with new learning.

The remainder of this chapter focuses on the characteristics of effective problem solving instruction in four exemplary areas: reading comprehension, writing of essays, mathematical problem solving, and intelligence.

Teaching Problem Solving in Reading

Teaching of reading comprehension is one area in the curriculum that involves problem-solving instruction. Although a review of research on teaching of reading strategies is beyond the scope of this chapter, this section explores representatives of two different approaches: SQ3R, which involves teaching of general or context-free strategies, versus schema training, which involves teaching of specific tools for representing information.

SQ3R (Robinson, 1961) consists of five steps that a reader should carry out when confronted with a new reading assignment: survey, in which the reader skims the title and headings and summaries in order to get an idea of what the passage is about; question, in which the reader generates a question for each subsection of the passage; read, in which the reader reads each subsection with a goal of answering the question for that subsection; recite, in which the reader answers each question in his or her own words based on information from the passage; review, in which the reader goes over

the entire passage and tries to recall as much as possible from each subsection.

As can be seen, SQ3R focuses mainly on general techniques for encoding text. The SQ3R method has been adopted, in various modified forms, in many of the popular basal reading series used by millions of school children and in many of the remedial study skills programs found in nearly every college campus and school district. However, as several reviews have pointed out (Cook & Mayer, 1983; Forrest-Pressley & Gillies, 1983; Johns & McNamara, 1980), there is very little evidence to support the claim that SQ3R actually helps students modify processing in effective ways. Shepherd (1978) pointed out that students tend to find the technique to be too cumbersome. Like many popular programs for teaching problem-solving skills, the support for SQ3R is rooted more in opinion than in fact. For example, Forrest-Pressley and Gillies (1983, p. 149) observe:

We sadly conclude this section by noting that virtually every college campus in North America has a remedial study skills program that is often based largely on the unproven SQ3R technique. . . . It would appear that we have made very little progress over the past 75 years, at least as far as substantiating our teaching methods is concerned! Given the prevalence of the need for study skills interventions, research on them should have high priority.

In summary, the SQ3R method, although widely used, lacks a firm theoretical or research base. Cook & Mayer (1983) pointed out that similar conclusions can be drawn for other widely used reading comprehension methods.

In contrast, recent research on prose processing has pointed to the importance of the reader's schema in comprehension. DiVesta's chapter in this volume described the concept of schema as a major contribution of cognitive psychology. The appropriate use of schemata may also be relevant for being able to understand expository text. For example, Cook (1982) devised a schema training program for readers of scientific text. The purpose of the training is to help readers learn to organize scientific information in a way that will enhance their ability to use creatively the information on subsequent problem-solving tests.

Cook's training program involved teaching junior college students to recognize several different types of passage structures found in their chemistry textbooks. For example, students learned to recognize the following three kinds of structures:

generalization, in which a main idea is followed by supporting evidence; *enumeration,* in which a list of facts is presented; and *sequence,* in which a chronologically ordered process is given. Then, students were trained to outline each type of passage structure and were given practice in outlining sample passages for each type of structure. A control group received no strategy training.

In order to assess the effectiveness of the training program, Cook gave students pretests before training and posttests after training. The tests involved scientific passages using the same prose structures but from content areas other than chemistry, that is, content areas different from that used during training. The results showed that the strategy-trained group showed an increase in recall of important information but not in unimportant information as compared to the control group. More interestingly, the strategy-trained group showed a strong increase in problem-solving performance on questions from the prose but did not show an increase in retention of facts as compared to the control group. Apparently, training in schemata that are commonly found in the domain of science texts helped students learn how to organize meaningfully scientific information, and thus allowed them to more creatively use the information to solve problems.

Other researchers have also reported success in the use of other types of schema training programs (Holley & Dansereau, 1984). For example, in the networking technique (Holley & Dansereau, 1984), readers of expository prose are trained in how to identify the main "nodes" in a passage and how to recognize six kinds of "links" among nodes: part of, type of, leads to, analogous to, characteristic of, and evidence for. Students receive practice in converting passages into diagram networks that contain the nodes in circles and the links as arrows. The networking technique is inspired by recent cognitive theories of memory organization, and is supported by positive results in a series of experimental tests.

In summary, many of the widely used methods for teaching reading comprehension are not based solidly on research or theory. These methods tend to teach very general skills that can be applied in many content domains. In contrast, more recent schema training techniques are inspired by cognitive theory and have an encouraging research track record. These methods tend to teach specific skills related to specific content areas.

Teaching Problem Solving in Writing

Can we improve students' performance in creatively answering essay questions? This has been a goal of several "creativity training" programs, as described in more detail by Mayer (1983). One approach to creativity training is to teach general skills, independent of specific content domains—for example, a special course in problem solving. A second approach is to teach specific skills for essay writing within specific subject matter domains—for example, an integrated course that teaches problem solving within the context of each subject matter domain.

The Productive Thinking Program (Covington, Crutchfield, & Davies, 1966; Covington, Crutchfield, Davies, & Olton, 1974; Olton & Crutchfield, 1969) is an example of a "context–free" program that has enjoyed wide use in schools. The program was designed to teach general problem-solving skills to fifth and sixth graders. Specifically, students read and answered questions about mystery and detective stories that were presented in a series of 15 cartoon-like booklets. For example, in one booklet, two children—Jim and Lila—learn about and try to solve "the riverboat robbery."

The Productive Thinking Program focused on the process of problem solving (such as, "restating the problem in your own words" or "generating ideas to explain the mystery") and used imitation of models as the key instructional method (such as characters in the booklets). However, the problem-solving training was intended to be "context–free" so that students would use the techniques in a wide variety of situations calling for creative essays.

In a review of a dozen studies that have evaluated the effectiveness of the Productive Thinking Program, Mansfield, Busse, and Krepelka (1978) found that there have been many cases in which a trained group performs better on a problem-solving posttest than a control group. However, the effects of the Productive Thinking Program are generally smaller in well-controlled studies and seem limited to problems that are like those given in the lessons. Because the mystery story domain is not a typical subject matter area, failure to transfer beyond that domain is disconcerting. Concerning the lack of evidence for transfer of problem solving skills,

Mansfield *et al.* (1978, p. 522) concluded: "it is unclear whether the effects of training are sufficiently generalizable to be useful in real-life problem solving situations." Apparently, it is possible to teach students to perform well on one type of problem (such as mystery/detective problems), but there is not strong evidence that such training transfers to other academic or real-world domains. Similarly, there is a glaring lack of research support for many popular creative training programs, such as attribute listing (Crawford, 1954), braistorming (Osborn, 1963), synectics (Gordon, 1961), and CoRT (deBono, 1983). Although creativity training programs often have an impressive list of testimonials, the relationship to theory is weak and the research base is thin (Bransford, Arbitman-Smith, Stein-Vye, 1985; Davis, 1973; Edwards, 1978; Polson & Jeffries, 1985).

In contrast to teaching general skills in a content-free course, Bloom and Broder (1950) attempted to teach question-answering skills to university students within the context of specific subject matter domains. Although the training did not involve actual writing, it did focus on increasing students' oral fluency. The subjects for Bloom and Broder's study were University of Chicago students who were unable to pass comprehensive exams in various subject matter areas, in spite of the fact that these students were just as motivated, studied as hard, and scored as high on scholastic achievement tests as students who did pass the exams.

What should be the content of the instructional program? Bloom and Broder distinguished between the *products of problem solving,* such as whether or not the student produced the correct answer, and the *process of problem solving,* such as the thought process that a student engages in. Furthermore, Bloom and Broder decided that the instructional program should focus on teaching of useful problem-solving strategies and processes, rather than on reinforcing students for emitting correct responses.

What should be the instructional method for the program? The program could have been based on having students master a set of problem-solving principles as presented by the teacher. Instead, Bloom and Broder decided to let the remedial subjects compare their solution strategies with those of successful problem solvers. For example, a remedial student and a successful problem solver were each asked to "think aloud" as they solved the same problem. Then, the remedial subject could point out the similarities and differences between his solution strategy and that of the successful problem solver. Thus, the method of instruction involved modeling of successfully worked out problems, rather than memorizing a list of principles and procedures from the teacher.

In a typical experiment, subjects who received 10 to 12 training sessions tended to score much higher on an exam and expressed more self-confidence than equivalent students who had not received the training. In spite of their apparent success in teaching problem solving skills, Bloom and Broder (1950, p. 76–77) warned that it is not possible to teach general problem skills that are unrelated to specific knowledge:

> It became clear that some specific information was necessary for solution of the examination problems and that a certain amount of background in the subject was indispensable. It became apparent that methods of problem solving, by themselves, could not substitute for basic knowledge of the subject area.

In summary, Bloom and Broder's work foreshadowed three themes of the modern information approach to teaching of problem solving: (a) focus on process rather than product, (b) teach by giving students practice in modeling successful problem solvers, and (c) recognize that general strategies and specific knowledge are both needed (e.g., Tuma & Reif, 1980).

Teaching Problem Solving in Math

Teaching of mathematical problem solving is another area in the curriculum that involves problem-solving instruction. Although a review of research on mathematical problem solving is beyond the scope of this paper (see Mayer, 1985), this section explores representatives of two different approaches: Polya's (1945, 1968) four-step approach to mathematical problem solving, which involves teaching of general or context-free strategies, and heuristic training, which involves teaching of specific tools for planning soultions.

Figure 6 shows a mathematics problem. The goal is to find the volume (V) of the frustrum of a right pyramid. The givens are the lengths of the upper base (U) and lower base (L), as well as the height of the frustrum (H). This could be called the pyramid problem and is presented by Polya (1968) in his book, *Mathematical Discovery.*

THE PROBLEM:

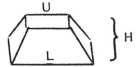

Find the volume V of the frustrum of a right pyramid with square base given the length L of the lower base, the length U of the upper base, and the height H of the frustrum.

THE SOLUTION PLAN:

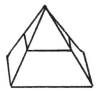

Subtract the volume of the smaller pyramid from the volume of the larger pyramid.

Figure 6. Polya's frustrum problem.

According to Polya, there are four stages in solving problems like the pyramid problem. The first step is to *understand the problem*. The problem solver must understand what is given—such as the values of U, L, and H—what is unknown—such as V—and which operations are allowed—such as the rules of algebra and geometry. The second step is to *devise a plan*. The problem solver must determine a general plan for attacking the problem. One plan might be to restate the frustrum problem so that it is more like a familiar problem. For example, to determine the volume of the frustrum, the problem solver could subtract the volume of small pyramid on the top from the full pyramid that includes the top and the frustrum. The third step is to *carry out the plan*. The problem solver must make the appropriate computations, such as computing the volume of the small and large pyramids. The fourth step is to *look back*. Here, the problem solver looks over the solution to see what can be learned.

Polya has suggested many techniques to help with each phase of problem solving, with particular focus on *devising a plan*. Some of the general strategies that Polya suggests are to find a related problem, to work backwards, to break the problem into smaller parts, and so on. Although Polya's

system has been influential among mathematics educators, there has not been overwhelming eagerness to test empirically its effectiveness. Thus, there is an annoying lack of research on the question of whether or not it is possible to teach successfully general problem-solving strategies such as Polya's four steps.

Instead of teaching general problem-solving strategies that are expected to apply to wide-range domains, more recent problem-solving training programs have focused on teaching strategies within well-defined domains. For example, Schoenfeld (1979) taught the following five problem-solving heuristics to mathematics students: (a) Draw a diagram. (b) If there is an integer parameter, look for an inductive argument. (c) Consider arguing by contradiction or contra-positive. (d) Consider a similar problem with fewer variables. (e) Try to establish subgoals.

In Schoenfeld's study, strategy training consisted of five sessions. On each session one of the heuristics was described and then students were asked to use that heuristic in solving four problems. Each of the four problems could be solved by using the target heuristic. In contrast, the control group solved the same 20 practice problems but was not told about the five heuristics. Also, for the control group, the problems in each session were not all solvable by the same heuristic.

In order to evaluate the effectiveness of strategy training, Schoenfeld gave students a pretest before training and a posttest after training involving mathematical problems similar to those used during instruction. The trained group showed a large pretest to posttest gain but the control subjects did not. Although the sample size in this study was small, the results suggest that it might be possible to teach heuristics within the context of a specific mathematical domain.

In summary, many of popularly used methods for teaching mathematical problem solving are not based solidly on research or theory. These methods focus on general skills that can be applied to a wide array of problems. In contrast, more recent heuristic training techniques have begun to accumulate some research support. These methods tend to teach specific skills related to specific kinds of mathematics problems.

Teaching Problem Solving for Intelligence Gains

Can we increase a student's intelligence through training in problem-solving techniques? Although a review of the research is beyond the scope of this chapter (see Detterman & Sternberg, 1982), this section explores representatives of two different approaches: the Head Start program, aimed at increasing general intellectual functioning in children, and componential training, aimed at teaching the specific component processes required for various reasoning tasks.

Head Start was begun in 1965 in order to increase the intellectual ability of disadvantaged children in the United States. Although the program was enthusiastically proclaimed and eventually consumed over $6.5 billion, there is not convincing evidence that Head Start has lasting effects on the intellectual functioning of children (Caruso, Taylor, & Detterman, 1982). According to Caruso et al. (1982), most studies show that compensatory programs result in either no gain in IQ or gains that are largely lost as the child gets older. Nurss and Hodges (1982) provide a similar summary of evaluation studies. According to Caruso et al. (1982, p. 52), the Head Start program failed because it lacked a clear research base:

the program had lost all contact with research, and, instead, drew its scientific justification from what we call the "Joyce Brothers data base"—ideas endorsed by the public at large but not necessarily supported by research.

More recently, Carter (1984) collected data on the achievement of 100,000 elementary students as they progressed through three successive years of compensatory education under Title 1. Although some high-level students showed temporary gains across a year, the low-level students did not; in addition, there is not strong evidence that the gains lasted in subsequent years. Again, large-scale school programs aimed at improving intellectual ability have not been overwhelmingly successful. Apparently, good intentions, massive funding, and common sense are not sufficient ingredients for a successful training program.

In contrast to the atheoretical and general approach of compensatory programs, the componential analysis of cognitive processes (Sternberg, 1977) suggests a much more specific approach to training people's problem-solving skills. Componential analysis involves selecting some reasoning task, such as solving verbal analogies or series completion problems, and analyzing the cognitive processes that a person would have to engage in to solve the problem. Componential process training involves providing training and practice in each of the major processes required for solving the problem. For example, let us consider a series completion problem taken from Thurstone's (1938) test of intelligence: abcmbcdlcdek _ _ _ _. In this problem, the subject's task is to fill in the missing letters in the series.

Simon and Kotovsky (1963) and Kotovsky and Simon (1973) have analyzed this task into four major processess: (a) "Detection of interletter relations" refers to relations between letters such as "next," "backwards next," and "identity." For example, in progressing from the first position to the fifth position to the ninth position, the relationship is "next." (b) "Discovery of periodicity" refers to the interval at which the relation or break in the relation occurs. For example, in the sample problem the periodicity seems to be four. (c) "Pattern description" refers to formulation of a rule; for example, "beginning with Position 1 every fourth position uses the next letter in the alphabet". (d) "Extrapolation" refers to applying the rule to fill in the missing spaces; for example, thirteenth space in the above problem is "d" because d comes next after c (in the ninth position).

Holzman, Glaser, and Pellegrino (1976) developed a componential process training program for series completion problems, based on Simon and Kotovsky's componential analysis. The training involved four 30-minute sessions in which elementary school children practice detection of relations backwards next, and identify—through a series of oddity problems such as, "cd xy lm mx" or "aa cc mn vv." For periodicity training, students were asked to place slash marks in problems such as, "aaaxxxmmm" or "mkfmtzmbd". Students given componential process training showed strong pretest-to-posttest gains in solving series completion problems, as compared to a control group that received no training.

In another line of research, Sternberg (1977) provided a componential analysis of analogy problems of the form, "A is to B as C is to __." The five major processing steps in these problems are as follows: (a) "Encoding" refers to identifying the terms, A, B, and C. (b) "Inference" refers to determining the relation between A and B. (c) "Mapping" refers to applying the above relation to the C term. (d) "Application" refers to generating a D term based on the above mapping. (e) "Response" refers to the problem solver selecting the correct response. Sternberg & Ketron (1982) were able to teach specific strategies, based on the componential analysis, for solving analogy problems.

In summary, componential process training has been used successfully to teach students how to solve specific kinds of reasoning problems, such as items that are often found on intelligence tests. Some authors, such as Whimbey & Lochhead (1979), have even attempted to build problem-solving courses around the componential approach. However, one shortcoming of componential process training is that the effects of training on any one task may be extremely limited, and there is no evidence that training transfers to other kinds of tasks.

In summary, the literature on teaching of intelligence is somewhat paradoxical. Well-controlled, theoretically based laboratory studies can succeed in training performance on intellectual tasks (such as IQ test items), but large-scale school programs are not overwhelmingly successful. However, the resolution of this paradox may be the way in which laboratory research and instructional practice are merged. For example, Caruso *et al.* (1982) suggest that intervention programs should build upon a sol-id research base and begin on a small scale. The recent theoretical developments in the analysis of cognitive processes suggests that cognitive process instruction can be effective when specific processes for specific content domains are taught.

The Future of Problem-Solving Research

Validating Current Findings. The theme that emerges from the foregoing review is that there are distinct differences between effective and ineffective (or unproven) programs of problem-solving instruction. The effective programs are based on cognitive theory and careful research, whereas the ineffective (or unproven) programs are motivated by practical demands and common sense. The effective programs teach specific problem-solving skills within the context of existing subject matter domains rather than general problem solving in domain-free courses. The effective programs focus on teaching the processes of problem solving (e.g., how to represent problems and plan solutions) rather than on the product of problem solving (e.g., making the correct response). The effective programs depend on an artful combination of meaningful learning (e.g., active participation by the learners) and guided instruction (e.g., guiding the learner) rather than rote learning (e.g., passive memorization of solution procedures) or pure discovery (e.g., no teacher guidance).

The dream of teaching students how to improve their minds has had a disappointing history, marked by the failure of the Latin School movement, and more recently by the failure of compensatory programs, curriculum reforms of the 1960s, and by untested or unproved industrial and school programs in problem solving.

The cognitive revolution in psychology has rekindled the dream of teaching students how to control their cognitive processes, that is, of teaching students how to think and how to learn. The cognitive approach offers tools for clearly describing the to-be-learned problem-solving skills. As suggested by the brief review given in this chapter, there is a growing collection of isolated examples of success in teaching specific problem-solving skills. The cognitive approach offers the opportunity of building programs based on our current understanding of human problem solving. In order to have a chance of succeeding where so many previous attempts have failed, it is useful to learn from and try to confirm the results of previous efforts to teach problem solving.

First, research on teaching for transfer, such as the discovery learning literature and on teaching problem-solving skills, such as Bloom and Broder's work, indicates that good problem solvers need also to have a lot of specific knowledge of the subject matter. Apparently, discovery learning cannot be effective when the student has little or no knowledge of content, and general habits of mind cannot replace a rich knowledge of the subject matter domain. Future research is needed in order to help explain why general problem skills and specific subject matter domain are so closely connected. At the present time, it makes more sense to integrate problem-solving training within subject matter domains (such as algebraic problem solving or engineering) rather that to teach problem solving as an independent subject area (Glaser, 1984). Future research is needed to confirm and explain this finding.

Second, research on teaching problem-solving skills has indicated that the effects of training are usually quite restricted; in cases where successful evaluations have been conducted, problem-solving training seems to enhance performance mainly on problems similar to those given. Thus, there is no reason to believe that training in solving logic problems, for example, would help a person solve other kinds of problems, such as problems in chemistry or social studies. The current state of the literature suggests that successful training of problem solving skills involves teaching very specific rather than very general skills. Future research is needed to help confirm and explain this finding.

Third, the more grandiose the claims are for a problem solving course, the less likely that there is adequate research evidence for the effectiveness of the course. There are many commercially available courses but almost none of them has been evaluated in a scientifically valid way. Davis and Scott (1978) have correctly pointed out that researchers have tended to ignore the commercially available problem-solving courses. Future research is needed to determine which aspects of existing courses are useful, and why.

Extending Current Findings. Let us continue our list of future research directions by examining topics that extend current work in cognitive psychology. The cognitive revolution seemed first to focus on the field of perception, as summarized in Neisser's (1967) *Cognitive Psychology,* and later examined the field of memory, as summarized in Klatzky's (1980) *Human Memory.* Finally, within the last decade, the cognitive revolution has begun to take hold in the field of problem solving, as summarized in Mayer's (1983) *Thinking, Problem Solving, Cognition.* Some additional suggestions for future research based on the cognitive approach are summarized in the following.

This chapter has briefly described techniques for the cognitive analysis of problem-solving strategies, processes, and representations. Future research is needed to continue to apply these techniques to classroom problem-solving tasks in subject matter areas ranging from mathematics to science to social studies. One exciting direction involves analyzing the strategies of experts in subject matter areas such as physics (Larkin, McDermott, Simon, & Simon, 1980), with the hopes of developing instructional programs that help novices. A related direction involves the computer simulation of problem solving in classroom tasks such as geometry (Greeno, 1978b). By clearly specifying the strategies that students have, we might be better able to develop instructional programs to help students acquire more useful strategies. Future research is needed to determine the possibility of moving from various examples, such as those cited previously, to a more extensive evaluation of students' problem solving across all relevant school domains.

The cognitive analysis of intelligence (Hunt, 1978; Pellegrino & Glaser, 1979) suggests new ways of conceiving of problem-solving ability. Future research is needed in order to determine whether these new measures of intelligence are more useful for educational practice than the traditional psychometric measures. In addition, future research is needed to determine the extent to which intellectual abilities can be modified through instruction.

The cognitive analysis of intellectual development (Case, 1978; Siegler, 1978) suggests that the components of cognitive growth can be specified in detail. For example, when a simple procedure becomes automatized, the learner can incorporate that procedure within a more sophisoticated procedure. Future research is needed to determine the teachability of these components.

Research on comprehension, learning, and problem solving has suggested the important role played by metacognitive factors—for example, the problem solver's awareness of his own problem-solving processes (Brown & Smiley, 1977, 1978). Most of the currently successful training efforts have focused on lower level strategies. Future research is needed to determine the role of metacognition in problem solving, and whether metacognitive skills can be taught.

Research on problem solving has tended to ignore noncognitive factors in problem solving, including personality, emotion, affect, and motivation. Future research is needed that integrates the rational and affective sides of human mental life.

Educational issues have been traditionally a substantial part of the history of research on problem solving. For example, the Gestalt psychologists made the educationally relevant distinction between productive learning—that is, learning in a way that results in creative problem solving—and rote learning—that is, learning in way that does not promote transfer (Mayer, 1983). Similarly, educational psychologists have long been interested in studying the teachability of thinking skills, as was reflected in Thorndike's (1931) early work on transfer of training and Gagne's (1979) more recent survey of the learnable aspects of problem solving. In both cases, results seem to indicate that there is no shortcut to becoming a productive problem solver; the implication of both papers—spanning a half century—is that successful problem solving requires plenty of knowledge, that is, ''a variety of experiences in problem solving'' (Gagne, 1979, p. 25).

Finally, let us close with a new version of the Latin School movement—what could be called the Computing School movement. Proponents of this school argue that when children are allowed to freely interact with specially designed computer programs—such as LOGO—the children's minds will grow and develop. Papert (1980), for example, claims that children will acquire ''powerful ideas'' when they are allowed to program a computer—that is, when children teach the computer how to solve problems. However, to date there has been almost no reliable data to support this claim. A recently published study (Clements & Gullo, 1984) found that LOGO learners showed gains in measues of creative thinking and metacognition; however, this promising result is based on only a single study involving nine LOGO learners and nine controls. In the future, research is desperately needed to determine whether interacting with computers has positive effects on children's intellectual development.

In summary, past research in problem solving has searched for an understanding of how people learn to solve problems. The future of this search is an exciting one. Yet, after a century of scientific study on problem solving, a clear understanding of how people learn to think rests more in the future than in the past.

References

Anderson, J. R. (1984). *The architecture of cognition.* New York: Oxford University Press.

Ash, M. J., & Love-Clark, P. (1985). An historical analysis of the content of educational psychology textbooks, 1954–1983. *Educational Psychologist, 20,* 47–55.

Ausubel, D. P. (1968). *Educational psychology: A cognitive view.* New York: Holt, Rinehart & Winston.

Bartlett, F. C. (1932). *Remembering.* London: Cambridge University Press.

Bayman, P., & Mayer, R. E. (1983). Diagnosis of beginning programmers' misconceptions of BASIC programming statements. *Communications of the ACM, 26,* 519–521.

Bloom, B. S., & Broder, L. J. (1950). *Problem-solving processes of college students.* Chicago, IL: University of Chicago Press.

Bransford, J. D., Arbitman-Smith, R., Stein, B. & Vye, N. J. (1985). Improving thinking and learning skills: An analysis of three approaches. In J. W. Segal, S. F. Chipman & R. Glaser (Eds.), *Thinking and learning skills: Volume 1, Relating instruction to research* (pp. 113–206). Hillsdale, NJ: Erlbaum.

Brown, A. L., & Smiley, S. S. (1977). Rating the importance of structural units of prose passages: A problem of metacognitive development. *Child Development, 48,* 1–8.

Brown, A. L., & Smiley, S. S. (1978). The development of strategies for studying texts. *Child Development, 49,* 1076–1088.

Brown, J. S., & Burton, R. (1978). Diagnostic models for procedural bugs in basic mathematical skills. *Cognitive Science, 2,* 155–192.

Brownell, W. A. (1935). Psychological considerations in the learning and teaching of arithmetic. In *The teaching of arithmetic: Tenth yearbook of the National Council of Teachers of Mathematics.* New York: Columbia University Press.

Brownell, W. A., & Moser, H. E. (1949). Meaningful vs. mechanical learning: A study on grade 3 subtraction. In *Duke University Research Studies in Education, No. 8.* Durham, NC: Duke University Press.

Bruner, J. S. (1961). The act of discovery. *Harvard Educational Review. 31,* 21–32.

Bruner, J. S. (1964). The course of cognitive growth. *American Psychologist, 19,* 1–15.

Bruner, J. S., & Kenney, H. (1966). Multiple ordering. In J. S. Bruner, R. R. Oliver, & P. M. Greenfield (Eds.), *Studies in cognitive growth.* New York: Wiley.

Carter, L. F. (1984). The sustaining effects study of compensatory and elementary education. *Educational Researcher, 13,* 4–13.

Caruso, D. R., Taylor, J. J., & Detterman, D. K. (1982). Intelligence research and intelligent policy. In D. K. Detterman & R. J. Sternberg (Eds.), *How and how much can intelligence be increased* (pp. 45–65) Norwood, NJ: ABLEX.

Case, R. (1978). Intellectual development from birth to adulthood: A neo-Piagetian interpretation. In R. S. Siegler (Ed.), *Children's thinking: What develops?* (pp. 37–72) Hillsdale, N.J.: Erlbaum.

Clements, D. H., & Gullo, D. F. (1984). Effects of computer programming on young children's cognition. *Journal of Educational Psychology, 76,* 1051–1058.

Collins, A., & Stevens, A. L. (1982). Goals and strategies of inquiry teachers. In R. Glaser (Ed.), *Advances in instructional psychology* (Vol. 2, pp. 65–119). Hillsdale, NJ: Erlbaum.

Cook, L. K. (1982). *The effects of text structure on the comprehension of scientific prose.* Unpublished doctoral dissertation. University of California, Santa Barbara, CA.

Cook, L. K., & Mayer, R. E. (1983). Reading strategies training for meaningful learning from prose. In M. Pressley & J. R. Levin (Eds.), *Cognitive strategy research* (pp. 87–131). New York: Springer-Verlag.

Covington, M. V., Crutchfield, R. S., & Davies, L. B. (1966). *The productive thinking program.* Berkeley, CA: Brazelton.

Covington, M. V., Crutchfield, R. S., Davies, L. B., & Olton, R. M. (1974). *The productive thinking program.* Columbus, OH: Merrill.

Crawford, R. P. (1954). *Techniques for creative thinking.* New York: Hawthorn.

Davis, G. A. (1973). *Psychology of problem solving: Theory and practice.* New York: Basic Books.

Davis, G. A., & Scott, J. A. (1978). *Training creative thinking.* Huntington, NY: Krieger.

DeBono, E. (1983). *CoRT Thinking.* Oxford: Pergamon Press.

Detterman, D. K. & Sternberg, R. J. (1982). *How and how much can intelligence be increased.* Norwood, NJ: Ablex.

Donders, F. C. (1969). On the speed of mental processes. *Acta Psychologica, 30,* 412–431. (Translated by W. G. Koster from paper originally published in 1868.)

Duncker, K. (1945). On problem solving. *Psychological Monographs, 58* (5, Whole No. 270).

Edwards, M. W. (1968). A survey of problem solving courses. *Journal of Creative Behavior, 2,* 33–51.

Forrest-Pressley, D. L., & Gillies, L. A. (1983). Children's flexible use of strategies during reading. In M. Pressley & J. R. Levin (Eds.), *Cognitive strategy research: Educational applications* (pp. 133–151). New York: Springer-Verlag.

Fuson, K. C. (1982). An analysis of the counting-on solution procedure in addition. In T. P. Carpenter, J. M. Mosner, & T. A. Romberg (Eds.), *Addition and subtraction: A cognitive perspective* (pp. 67–81). Hillsdale, NJ: Erlbaum.

Gagné, R. M. (1968). Learning hierarchies. *Educational Psychologist, 6,* 1–9.

Gagné, R. M. (1979). Learnable aspects of human thinking. In A. E. Lawson (Ed.), *The psychology of teaching for thinking and creativity* (pp. 1–28). Columbus, OH: Association for the Education of Teachers of Science, ERIC.

Gagné, R. M., & Brown, L. T. (1961). Some factors in the programming of conceptual learning. *Journal of Experimental Psychology, 62,* 313–321.

Glaser, R. (1984). Education and thinking: The role of knowledge. *American Psychologist, 39,* 93–104.

Gordon, W. J. (1961). *Synectics.* New York: Harper & Row.

Greeno, J. G. (1978a). Natures of problem solving abilities. In W. K. Estes (Ed.), *Handbook of learning and cognitive processes* (Vol. 5, pp. 239–270). Hillsdale, NJ: Erlbaum.

Greeno, J. G. (1978b). A study of problem solving. In R. Glaser (Ed.), *Advances in instructional psychology.* (Vol. 1, pp. 13–75). Hillsdale, NJ: Erlbaum.

Greeno, J. G. (1980). Some examples of cognitive task analysis with instructional implications. In R. E. Snow, P. Federico & W. E. Montague (Eds.), *Aptitude, learning, and instruction.* Vol. 2. Hillsdale, NJ: Erlbaum.

Groen, G., & Parkman, J. M. (1972). A chronometric analysis of simple addition. *Psychological Review, 79,* 329–343.

Guilford, J. P. (1959). The three faces of intellect. *American Psychologist, 14,* 469–479.

Hayes, J. R. (1978). *Cognitive psychology.* Homewood, IL: Dorsey.

Hayes, J. R. (1981). *The complete problem solver.* Philadelphia, PA: Franklin Institute Press.

Hermann, G. (1969). Learning by discovery: A critical review of studies. *Journal of Experimental Education, 38,* 58–72.

Hinsley, D., Hayes, J. R., & Simon, H. A. (1977). From words to equations. In P. Carpenter & M. Just (Eds.), *Cognitive processes in comprehension.* Hillsdale, NJ: Erlbaum.

Holley, C. D., & Dansereau, D. F. (Eds.). (1984). *Spatial learning strategies.* New York: Academic Press.

Holzman, T. G., Glaser, R., & Pellegrino, J. W. Process training derived from computer simulation theory. *Memory & Cognition, 4,* 349–356.

Hunt, E. (1978). The mechanisms of verbal ability. *Psychological Review, 85,* 109–130.

Johns, J. L., & McNamara, L. (1980). The SQ3R study technique: A forgotten research target. *Journal of Reading, 23,* 705–708.

Katona, G. (1942). *Organizing and memorizing.* New York: Columbia University Press.

Kittel, J. E. (1957). An experimental study of the effect of external direction during learning on transfer and retention of principles. *Journal of Educational Psychology, 48,* 391–405.

Klatzky, R. (1980). *Human memory.* New York: Freeman.

Kohler, W. (1925). *The mentality of apes.* New York: Harcourt Brace Jovanovich.

Kotovsky, K., & Simon, H. A. (1973). Empirical tests of a theory of human acquisition of concepts for sequential patterns. *Cognitive Psychology, 4,* 399–424.

Larkin, J. H., McDermott, J., Simon, D. P., & Simon, H. A. (1980). Expert and novice performance in solving physics problems. *Science, 208,* 1335–1342.

Lochhead, J., & Clement, J. (1979). *Cognitive process instruction.* Philadelphia, PA: Franklin Institute Press.

Mansfield, R. S., Busse, T. V., & Kreplka, E. J. (1978). The effectiveness of creativity training. *Review of Educational Research, 48,* 517–536.

Mayer, R. E. (1975). Information processing variables in learning to solve problems. *Review of Educational Research, 45,* 525–541.

Mayer, R. E. (1981a). *The promise of cognitive psychology.* New York: Freeman.

Mayer, R. E. (1981b). Frequency norms and structural analysis of algebra story problems into families, categories, and templates. *Instructional Science, 10,* 135–175.

Mayer, R. E. (1982). Memory for algebra story problems. *Journal of Educational Psychology, 74,* 199–216.

Mayer, R. E. (1983). *Thinking, problem solving, cognition.* New York: Freeman.

Mayer, R. E. (1984). Aids to prose comprehension. *Educational Psychologist, 19,* 30–42.

Mayer, R. E. (1985). Mathematical ability. In R. J. Sternberg (Ed.), *Human abilities.* New York: Freeman.

Mayer, R. E., & Greeno, J. G. (1972). Structural differences between learning outcomes produced by different instructional methods. *Journal of Educational Psychology, 63,* 165–173.

National Educational Association. (1961). *The Central Purpose American Education.* Washington, DC: Author.

Neisser, U. (1967). *Cognitive psychology.* New York: Appleton-Century-Crofts.

Newell, A., & Simon, H. A. (1972). *Human problem solving.* Englewood Cliffs, NJ: Prentice-Hall.

Norman, D. A. (1980). Cognitive engineering and education. In D. T. Tuma & F. Reif (Eds.), *Problem solving and education* (pp. 97–107). Hillsdale, NJ: Erlbaum.

Nurss, J. R. & Hodges, W. L. (1982). Early childhood development. In H. E. Mitzel (Ed.), *Encyclopedia of educational research* (pp. 489–508). New York: Macmillan.

Olton, R. M., & Crutchfield, R. S. (1969). Developing the skills of productive thinking. In P. Mussen, J. Langer, & M. V. Covington (Eds.), *New directions in developomental psychology.* New York: Holt, Rinehart & Winston.

Osborn, A. F. (1963). *Applied imagination.* New York: Scribners.

Papert, S. (1980). *Mindstorms.* New York: Basic Books.

Pellegrino, J. W., & Glaser, R. (1979). Cognitive correlates and components in the analysis of individual differences. In R. J. Sternberg & D. K. Determan (Eds.), *Human intelligence* (pp. 61–88). Norwood, NJ: Ablex.

Piaget, J. (1954). *The constructional of reality in the child.* New York: Basic Books.

Polson, P. G. & Jeffries, R. (1985). Instruction in general problem-solving skills: An analysis of four approaches. In J. W. Segal, S. F. Chipman & R. Glaser (Eds.), *Thinking and learning skills: Volume 1, Relating instruction to research* (pp. 417–455). Hillsdale, NJ: Erlbaum.

Polya, G. (1945). *How to solve it.* Princeton, NJ: Princeton University Press.

Polya, G. (1968). *Mathematical discovery.* New York: Wiley.

Posner, M. (1978). *Chronometric explorations of mind.* Hillsdale, NJ: Erlbaum.

Reitman, W. R. (1965). *Cognition and thought: An information processing approach.* New York: Wiley.

Resnick, L. B. & Ford, W. W. (1981). *The psychology of mathematics for instruction.* Hillsdale, NJ: Erlbaum.

Revlin, R. & Mayer, R. E. (1978). *Human reasoning.* New York: Winston/Wiley.

Riley, M. S., Greeno, J. G., & Heller, J. I. (1983). Development of children's problem-solving ability in arithmetic. In H. P. Ginsburg (Ed.), *The development of mathematical thinking* (pp. 153–196). New York: Academic Press.

Rippa, S. A. (1980). *Education in a free society: An American history.* New York: Longman.

Robinson, F. P. (1961). *Effective study.* New York: Harper & Row.

Roughead, W. G. & Scandura, J. N. (1968). What is learned in mathematical discovery. *Journal of Educational Psychology, 59,* 283–289.

Schoenfeld, A. (1979). Explicit heuristic training as a variable in problem solving performance. *Journal for Research in Mathematics Education, 10,* 173–187.

Shepherd, D. L. (1978). *Comprehensive high school reading methods.* Columbus, OH: Merrill.

Shulman, L. S., & Keisler, E. R. (1966). *Learning by discovery.* Chicago, IL: Rand McNally.

Siegler, R. S. (1978). The origins of scientific reasoning. In R. S. Siegler (Ed.), *Children's thinking: What develops?* (pp. 109–149). Hillsdale, NJ: Erlbaum.

Silver, E. (1985). *Teaching and learning mathematical problem solving: Multiple research perspectives.* Hillsdale, NJ: Erlbaum.

Simon, H. A., & Kotovsky, K. (1963). Human acquisition of concepts for sequential patterns. *Psychological Review, 70,* 534–546.

Sternberg, R. J. (1977). *Intelligence, information processing, and analogical reasoning.* Hillsdale, NJ: Erlbaum.

Sternberg, R. J., & Ketron J. L. (1982). Selection and implementation of strategies in reasoning and analogy. *Journal of Educational Psychology, 74,* 399–413.

Suchman, J. R. (1960). Inquiry training in the elementary school. *Science Teacher, 27,* 42–47.

Suchman, J. R. (1966). *Inquiry development program in physical science.* Chicago, IL: Science Research Associates.

Thorndike, E. L. (1898). Animal intelligence: An experimental study of associative processes in animals. *Psychological Monographs, 2,* No. 8.

Thorndike, E. L. (1923). The influence of first-year Latin upon the ability to read English. *School and Society, 17,* 165–168.

Thorndike, E. L. (1931). *Human learning.* New York: Century.

Thurstone, L. L. (1938). *Primary mental abilities.* Chicago, IL: University of Chicago Press.

Tuma, D. T., & Reif, F. (Eds.). (1980). *Problem solving and education.* Hillsdale, NJ: Erlbaum.

Wallas, G. (1926). *The art of thought.* New York: Harcourt.

Wertheimer, M. (1959). *Productive thinking.* New York: Harper & Row.

Whimbey, A., & Lochhead, J. (1979). *Problem solving and comprehension: A short course in analytic reasoning.* Philadelphia, PA: Franklin Institute Press. -

Winch, W. A. (1913). *Inductive versus deductive methods of teaching.* Baltimore, MD: Warwick & York.

Woods, S. S., Resnick, L. B., & Groen, G. J. (1975). An experimental test of five process models for subtraction. *Journal of Educational Psychology, 67,* 17–21.

CHAPTER 16

Research on Teaching and Classroom Processes

VIEWS FROM TWO PERSPECTIVES

Carolyn M. Evertson and Mark A. Smylie

The search for knowledge to understand and improve the quality and effectiveness of teaching is an endeavor in which educational researchers have been engaged for decades. The focus of this search, however, has changed over time. It has shifted from efforts to identify teacher characteristics that were thought to result in improved student learning, to the development of strategies for training teachers to implement specific curricula. The search has also shifted to the identification of classroom procedures and instructional processes that correlate empirically with greater rates of student academic achievement. The means by which researchers have collected data to guide the search have been diverse, as have the theoretical constructs they have employed to focus their inquiry.

One question that runs throughout this line of research is "What is effective teaching?" Studies conducted in and before the early 1960s yielded for the most part disappointing answers to this ques-

tion. Early reviews of this research regularly reported insignificant and contradictory findings (Dunkin & Biddle, 1974). In the last 15 years, new approaches emerged from different disciplines, including psychology, sociology, linguistics, and anthropology, to address the issue of teacher effectiveness. Researchers have adapted constructs and methodologies from these disciplines and have developed new ways to study a wider variety of educational events. These advances have significantly expanded our aggregate knowledge of teaching and classroom processes.

Despite this expansion of knowledge, the question "What is effective teaching?" remains only partially answered. It remains so for several reasons. First, there are many questions about the nature and processes of teaching and learning that have yet to be asked or to be investigated. Second, the different perspectives and methods employed to view and analyze classroom events often yield only fragments of classroom reality. Third, recent advances in knowledge coming from the various disciplines and research traditions that have engaged the issue of teaching effectiveness have been made in relatively uncoordinated fashion and have remained virtually unintegrated. As a consequence, we have been discovering more and more

Carolyn M. Evertson • Department of Teaching and Learning, Peabody College, Vanderbilt University, Nashville, TN 37203. Mark A. Smylie • Department of Curriculum Instruction and Evaluation, University of Illinois, Chicago, IL 60680.

pieces of a complicated puzzle but we are not certain how those pieces might fit together or if they belong to the same puzzle at all. Therefore, to develop a more comprehensive understanding of teaching and classroom processes, it seems crucial to identify and to integrate knowledge derived from different traditions of research (Bolster, 1983; Gage, 1985; Sergiovanni, 1984; Soltis, 1984).

In this chapter, we review selected findings from two traditions of educational research that have made significant contributions to our knowledge of teaching and classroom processes—process–product research and sociolinguistic research. We examine each of these traditions as lenses through which we view the events of the classroom. We shall describe each lens and contrast each focus. Then, highlighting findings of several major studies we consider how each presents a different but complementary view of teaching in three areas: (a) teacher planning and decision making, (b) classroom management, (c) academic instruction. Our purpose extends beyond a comparative synthesis of research on teaching. In this discussion we attempt to make a broader argument for an integrative perspective to draw together heretofore disparate bodies of knowledge.

Ryle (1949) suggests a useful point of departure for developing an integrative perspective. While we will not engage the debate of the logic behind the definitions or the reduction of his terms (see Hartland-Swann, 1956, Roland, 1961), Ryle's distinction between knowledge related to facts and propositions—"knowing that"—and knowledge related to process and practice—"knowing how"—lead us to argue that we should be concerned with discovering, not only the relationships that exist between behavior and outcomes, but how particular relationships come about. In other words, we should be concerned with knowing not only *that* a particular relationship exists between behavior *x* and outcome *y,* but with knowing *how* behavior *x* functions in its relationship to *y.*

Until now much of classroom research from the psychological perspective has been concerned with identifying normative models of teacher behaviors that relate to student outcomes across time and context. This approach has been in the mainstream of research on teaching for the last 15 years. It has served and continues to serve an important function of mapping unknown territory and identifying important general relationships that exist between teaching practices and student outcomes (Evertson

& Green, 1986). However, in order to understand more completely classroom realities, we must, as Wittrock (1985) suggests, begin to enlarge the perspective of teaching–learning processes presented by educational psychology (see also Gage, 1985; Shulman, 1986). We must try to determine how the processes identified from the psychological perspective function in specific contexts on an evolving basis. Sociolinguistic research provides one important way to gain this understanding. Together, sociolinguistic and process–product research provide equally important perspectives to construct and understanding of the *that's* and the *how's* of teaching and classroom processes.

This review is a first attempt and a first step toward looking across research traditions to knowledge and understanding of teaching. The findings we present are illustrative rather than inclusive. We chose to review and compare aspects of process–product and sociolinguistic research traditions not to imply that these bodies of knowledge present a complete picture of classroom events. To the contrary, there exist other important bodies of research from sociological, psychological, and anthropological traditions that significantly add to our understanding of teaching and learning. Further, we do not propose to cover completely each of the traditions included in our discussion. We have, instead, been selective to show how two traditions examine in different ways different aspects of several of the same broad areas of classroom activity.

Two Lenses—Different Perspectives

The first tradition we examine has developed from what has been called the process–product research paradigm. Process–product research generally focuses on the teacher and looks *across* a large number of classrooms to identify teacher behaviors (processes) that correlate with student outcome measures (products). This can be considered a macro view of classrooms. Investigations using this approach are concerned with examining variation *between groups* and with developing a summary model of classroom teaching processes. They are less concerned with the specifics of context and variation within groups.

The second tradition is sociolinguistic research. This tradition is part of a broader area of research on communication (see e.g., Gumperz, 1982;

Gumperz & Hymes, 1972; Hymes, 1974). It considers teaching and learning as linguistic processes. The focus of sociolinguistic research in classrooms is on face-to-face communicative interactions between the teacher and students and among students themselves. This approach looks *within* the structure of formal processes in single or small numbers of classrooms to examine contextual and functional features of everyday interactions, the meanings that participants attribute to those interactions, and how those interactions promote or constrain access to learning. As compared with process–product research, the findings from sociolinguistic studies we present provide a relatively micro view of events in the classroom.

In short, both of these research traditions may be considered a lens through which researchers view classroom events. Before we examine what is seen through these lenses, we consider further their construction and foci. Each lens—each research tradition—is based on different assumptions and constructs, poses different questions, and examines different phenomena. These differences yield complementary perspectives on what transpires in the classroom.

The Process–Product Lens

The process–product research tradition defines legitimate inquiry in terms of relations between overt, categorical teacher behaviors and student outcomes (Doyle, 1977; Gage, 1963, 1978, 1985). The studies we include here are based on a predictive model with roots in behavioral psychological research. In general, criteria of teacher effectiveness (student outcomes) are defined *a priori,* either by empirical criteria or by theory (Dunkin & Biddle, 1974). Then, the task of the researcher becomes the identification of the best "predictors" of the criteria. Those predictors—teacher behaviors—are most often defined *a priori* as well.

Rosenshine (1971) describes the basic stages of most process–product research:

1. The development of an instrument that can be used systematically to record frequency of certain specified behaviors
2. Use of the instrument in natural settings to record classroom behaviors of teachers and their pupils
3. A ranking of classrooms according to a measure of pupil achievement adjusted for initial difference among the classes

4. A determination of the behaviors whose frequency of occurrence is related to adjusted class achievement scores.

Once those relationships are identified, they may again be tested through experimental investigation (Rosenshine & Furst, 1973). In such studies, experimental groups of teachers are trained to implement practices identified through correlational analyses. Then, changes in student outcome measures in classes of the experimental groups are compared to changes in outcome measures of control classes to further establish the influence of the behavior. Process–product research may also look in detail at teacher behavior in previously identified high-achieving classrooms and compare that behavior with teacher behavior in lower-achieving classrooms.

Process–product research has examined a number of outcome measures, including student scores on standardized tests of academic achievement, students behavior (e.g., misbehavior, student engagement, time on task), and student attitudes. In this research tradition, student outcome measures are aggregated both at the classroom level and across classrooms. They are further examined across the variety of events and activities that occur across time and across the specific contexts of individual classroom settings.

Several assumptions underlie process–product research that bear directly on the view it portrays of classrooms (Doyle, 1977; Gage, 1963). First, this research tradition assumes teacher primacy, that teacher behaviors have a direct causal impact on student outcomes. The effects of teacher behavior on student outcomes is assumed to be linear and unidirectional. Second, this research isolates frequency as the most salient dimension of teacher behavior. The implication is that the presence or absence of a behavior or the number of times that behavior occurs determines the magnitude of its effects. Third, the tradition generally assumes stability of teacher behavior across contexts and across time. Indeed, most process–product research seeks to control contextual variables rather than consider variations in teacher behavior and student outcomes within various contexts.

The Sociolinguistic Lens

Sociolinguistic research consists primarily of comparative descriptions of verbal and nonverbal communication used by people in interaction with one another (Peterson & Cherry-Wilkinson, 1984). Instead of focusing primarily on the teacher, as is characteristic of process–product research, the sociolinguistic approach considers the teacher and students as participants in the communicative environment of the classroom. This approach is based more on theories of social group processes than on theories that view classroom activity as teacher-to-individual-student interaction. Sociolinguistic research seeks to understand the teaching-learning process by determining how language is used to establish and maintain goals and expectations for student behavior and academic performance, influence student participation in classroom tasks, and promote or constrain access to learning (Bloome & Green, 1984; Green, 1983b).

Of central importance to this research tradition is assessment of the context, function, history, and meaning of communicative interaction in the classroom (Cazden, 1986; Green, 1983b). As Green and Wallat (1981) indicate, this tradition considers conversations as more than random strings of words whose purpose is the simple verbal exchange of ideas, opinions, and sentiments. Sociolinguistic research views conversations as complex interpersonal social phenomena that include nonverbal and social properties in addition to, or concurrent with, the verbal characteristics of the exchange. These properties have function and communicate meaning and goals to participants for social behavior and academic performance.

Several constructs guide this line of inquiry as it relates to teacher–student interactions (Green, 1983a, b). First, classrooms are viewed as communicative environments in which teachers and students are constantly assessing what is occurring and how it is occurring. There is an assumption of a recursive model of interaction among classroom participants. Second, interactions in the classroom are considered to be rule governed and goal oriented. This does not mean that teachers and students follow fixed scripts or that conversations and activities do not vary (Green, 1983b). Rather, "rule governed" means that expectations for performance exist that are determined by the culture of the classroom. These expectations guide participation in conversation and activities toward goals and act to constrain the options of what can and will occur in classrooms. Further, expectations for conversation and participation in activities vary from one activity to another and differ by groups of students within the classroom. It is the task of the teacher and students to monitor different demands, shift ways of participation, and change behaviors to meet each different situation. The third construct that guides sociolinguistic research is that meaning from communication is derived from context and that contexts are continuously constructed and reconstructed during interactions. In all, then, the sociolinguistic perspective considers events in classrooms as parts of a dynamic interactive process that requires both structural and functional communicative knowledge and skills on the part of teachers and students (Peterson & Cherry-Wilkinson, 1984).

Sociolinguistic research has examined a number of student outcomes similar to those measured in process–product studies. These outcomes include student attention and participation in classroom tasks and activities, student responses in communicative interactions, and student perceptions and attitudes. What distinguishes the sociolingistic tradition from the process–product tradition is in its view of outcomes. Sociolinguistic research examines outcomes in relation to the specific contexts in which they are identified. In addition, sociolinguistic research views student outcomes in relation to a myriad of factors including the teacher, the social and communicative dynamics of the classroom, and the history, function, and meaning of discourse and interaction. As noted above, process–product research views student outcomes as a direct result of teacher behavior and most studies in this tradition seek to control for contextual variation.

Sociolinguistic researchers use a variety of approaches to study events in classrooms, including ethnography of communication and sociolinguistic analysis (Green, 1983b; Green & Wallat, 1981). These approaches are quite different from those traditionally applied in process–product research. The object is to look within classrooms in systematic, principled ways for recurrent patterns of language use, to observe how messages are received and responded to, to identify typical cases of interaction within and across various classroom activities.

The primary investigative technique in sociolinguistic research is long-term participant observation. Each study begins with a mental grid composed of a series of assumptions derived from theory and previous research (see Green, 1983b). These assumptions guide initial, general participant observation in the classroom. Once observations are under way, initial questions become re-

Table 1. Primary Focus of Research Traditions by Area of Classroom Activity

Area of classroom activity	Foci of research traditions	
	Process–product	Sociolinguistic
Planning and decision making	Preactive measures to plan the learning environment and academic work	Moment-to-moment responsiveness during classroom activity
Classroom management	Formal rules and procedures implemented to structure the physical aspects of the classroom, manage resources, and control student behavior	Functional rules and expectations that create communicative contexts, govern communication and behavior, and determine access to classroom discourse
Academic instruction	Frequencies and sequences of teacher behavior	Patterns and functions of language use in instruction and influence on instruction, participation, and access to learning.

fined as the observer explores them in specific activities and contexts. The phenomena under study become more focused as does the researcher's understanding of when, where, and how they occur within and across a variety of activities and contexts. The investigation can be narrowed in a variety of ways. For example, participant observation can be topic-centered (e.g., a focus on literacy, reading groups, or classroom processes). It can also involve observation of natural experiments used to explore what has been identified in topic-centered observation. Such explorations, therefore, can move from topic-centered observation *in situ* to natural experiments back to topic-centered observation in a cyclical manner (Green & Bloome, 1983). This allows identification of naturally occurring phenomena and close exploration of those phenomena (Cook-Gumperz, Gumperz, & Simons, 1981). Data collected through observation are analyzed in a variety of ways such as mapping (see Green & Wallat, 1981; Green & Rasinski, 1985; Weade, 1985) and may also be used for secondary analyses.

Looking across Traditions

Taken as lenses, these two research traditions provide a dramatically different view of events in classrooms. It is not that through these lenses we see the same events differently. Rather, each looks at the nature of classrooms in different ways, cx-

poses different kinds of events, and views student outcomes differently.

In the following sections of this chapter, we present examples of the views of classrooms from each research tradition in three areas of teacher activity: (a) planning and decision making, (b) classroom management, and (c) academic instruction. In these sections, we present representative findings from each tradition that illustrate the differences in views. Our reviews of the literature are not comprehensive. They are not intended to be. Rather, we seek to present sufficient findings to illustrate the views and to make the case that an integrative approach is required for a more complete understanding of teaching.

As an introduction to our discussion of the research, Table 1 presents the primary foci from each tradition in each of the three areas of teacher activity. In the areas of planning and decision making, process–product research focuses on preactive measures that teachers take to plan the learning environment and academic work. Sociolinguistic research examines moment-to-moment responsiveness of teachers and students during classroom activity. In the area of classroom management, process–product research focuses on the formal rules and procedures that teachers implement to structure the physical aspects of the classroom, manage resources, and control student behavior. Sociolinguistic research, on the other hand, examines functional rules and expectations that create communicative context, govern conversation and behavior in classrooms, and determine who has access to classroom discourse. Finally, in the area of academic instruction, process–product research identifies a sequence of teacher instructional behaviors. Sociolinguistic research looks within several of these behaviors to examine patterns and functions of language used in instruction, and ways language use and understanding influence participation in tasks, access to learning, and teacher evaluation of student performance.

Both traditions examine the importance of student attention and differentiation in instruction among groups in classrooms. These are two of several points where the traditions seem to converge. Although the overall purpose of this chapter is to compare different perspectives of these traditions, we include findings in these areas of overlap because they relate directly to findings in several other areas we address. We now begin our review of findings from each tradition in the area of planning and decision making.

Planning and Decision Making

Most research on teacher planning and decision making has grown out of studies of human decision making and problem solving. This work examines primarily the cognitive processes that underlie teachers' judgments and decisions. It considers the functions of those judgments and decisions and how they relate to teacher behavior in the classroom. Although this area of research is critically important to understanding teaching, it falls outside the purview of the present review (see National Institute of Education, 1975; Shavelson 1976, 1983; Shavelson & Stern, 1981; Shulman & Elstein, 1975; for comprehensive reviews of this literature). Here, we examine a more limited group of studies that explore relationships among different aspects of planning and decision making and student outcomes measures, and the role of decision making in the communicative environment of the classroom.

Process–product and sociolinguistic studies view different aspects of teacher planning and decision making. In general, process–product research focuses on the formal steps teachers take to prepare for classroom activity. Few attempts have been made in process–product research to examine teacher decision making during classroom activity

and its relationship to student achievement. On the other hand, sociolinguistic research looks primarily at the more informal, moment-to-moment judgments and decisions teachers make during that activity.

The two foci are quite complementary. As we shall see, the preactive plans teachers make provide frameworks for what is possible or even likely to occur in classrooms. In practice, these frameworks do not function as rigid scripts for teacher and student activity. Instead, they seem to set directions and establish boundaries in which moment-to-moment decision making occurs (Clark, 1983).

The Process–Product Perspective

Few process–product studies examine specific elements of teacher planning and decision making. Rather, most infer the importance of certain types of plans and decisions that seem necessary for teachers to behave and for classrooms to function in academically productive ways. These types of plans and decisions include (a) preparing the learning environment, and (b) planning academic work. Where applicable, we highlight the little work that has been done directly relating specific aspects of planning and decision making to student outcome measures.

Preparing the Learning Environment. Process–product research suggests that establishment of a classroom environment that facilitates student learning begins with advance preparation. Studies of academically successful elementary school classrooms point to the importance of planning for the management of physical space and preparing the classroom for use by students to help maximize the degree to which they benefit from learning activities (Brophy & Putnam, 1979; Evertson & Emmer, 1982; Good & Brophy, 1978). In these classrooms, plans are made before the school year begins to arrange furnishings to accommodate anticipated instructional activities, to facilitate smooth and quick transitions between those activities, and to promote the teachers' abilities to monitor student work and behavior. Also, plans are made to place and store equipment, instructional materials, and students' personal belongings to facilitate easy access. Before the school year begins, routines and traffic patterns are developed for the physical movement of students around and in and out of the classroom. In addition, procedures are developed for the efficient completion of paperwork and other routine non-academic class business, including record keeping, so that instructional time can be maximized (Evertson & Emmer, 1982; Kounin, 1970).

In structuring the social environment of the classroom, academically successful elementary teachers develop rules for establishing and maintaining appropriate student behavior throughout the year (Brophy, 1983). As we shall see in our discussion of the process–product view of managing student behavior, these teachers teach rules and standards for appropriate behavior to students at the beginning of the school year. The importance of such planning and instruction is seen in the relatively few incidents of disorder in these classrooms. In less well-managed classrooms, teachers appear to struggle throughout the year to maintain order (Emmer, Evertson, & Anderson, 1980).

Process–product research identifies the importance of planning the learning environment in secondary classrooms as well (Evertson & Emmer, 1982; Evertson, Weade, Green, & Crawford, 1985; Moskowitz & Hayman, 1976; Sanford & Evertson, 1981). These studies also suggest that preparing for the effective use of space and for the physical movement of students are key elements of successful management. Although teachers in secondary classrooms generally need not place as much emphasis on teaching students appropriate social behavior as teachers in elementary classrooms, it is no less important at the secondary level that before the school year begins teachers plan rules for student behavior to establish classroom norms and expectations as well as plan strategies for maintaining appropriate student behavior throughout the school year (Evertson *et al.*, 1985; Moskowitz & Hayman, 1976).

Another area of planning the learning environment is decisions teachers make about grouping students for instruction. The ways teachers group students in classrooms have important consequences for student learning and social development (see Good & Marshall, 1984). These findings indicate that academically and socially productive grouping requires careful preparation. Such preparation includes accurate assessment of students' academic abilities and learning needs (a topic we examine later), choice of academic work appropriate to the group, and consideration of how students within groups will work and interact with one another. As students complete activities and learning progresses, group assignments need to be reassessed and, where appropriate, new assignments to

groups made. Research on grouping suggests that without this type of planning and reassessment, groupings become static, often to the detriment of academic progress (Eder, 1982; Rist, 1970).

Planning Academic Work. Process–product studies have generally found little relationship between the time that teachers spend planning academic work and student academic performance. Indeed, one experimental study reveals a negative relationship between additional time spent planning and student achievement (Peterson, Marx, & Clark, 1978). This study also found no consistent relationships between student achievement and attitude and the relative attention teachers gave to planning lesson objectives and content, instructional processes, and materials.

Although the relative amounts of time teachers spend planning may not relate directly to student outcome measures, other process–product studies indicate that in one way or another specific elements in the conducting of academic work be considered. The first consideration in planning for academic work is assessment of student ability and learning needs. Studies that address methods of assessment reveal that teachers assess students in many ways, ranging from checking for understanding during review of class work and question and answer activities, to checking daily seatwork and homework assignments, to more formal measures of evaluation, such as periodic written tests and examinations. Studies that investigate methods of assessing students find them related to student achievement (see, e.g., Evertson, Anderson, Anderson, & Brophy, 1980; Good & Grouws, 1979; Stallings, 1980). Indeed, the need for systematic student assessment is illustrated by other findings showing that the sequencing and pacing of instructional activities have important relationships to student learning (Barr, 1975, 1980; Good, 1983; Rosenshine & Stevens, 1986). Appropriate sequencing and pacing of instructional activities require that teachers accurately determine students' levels of understanding and skill before students are allowed to progress to the next, more difficult level. Student assessment provides important information that teachers need to make this determination.

A second crucial element of planning for academic activities is selection of subject matter to be taught (Berliner, 1982). There is a clear relationship in process–product research between coverage or emphasis on subject matter and student achievement. The opportunity to learn a given content area is one of the most potent factors in accounting for differences in student achievement in that area (Berliner & Rosenshine, 1977; Cooley & Leinhardt, 1980; see also Fisher *et al.*, 1978). Basically, students do not learn what they are not exposed to. The choice of subject matter, therefore, becomes an important component of planning for instruction.

The research in this area indicates that despite state and local curriculum and textbook requirements, teachers are final arbiters of what is taught in classrooms. Schwille *et al.* (1981) found, for example, that perceived effort required to teach particular subject matter, the perceived difficulty of the subject matter for students, and personal feelings of enjoyment while teaching a particular subject matter influence the teacher's choice of content. As Berliner (1982) notes, decisions to emphasize, deemphasize, or exclude particular content from classroom instruction are only casually made and often based on personal disposition (see also Buchmann & Schmidt, 1981).

A third important element of planning involves allocating appropriate amounts of time for instructional activities and the correct pacing of those activities. Teachers in academically successful classrooms seem to plan both how to maximize instructional time and how to divide it appropriately among different instructional activities and subject matter areas. These teachers also seem to plan the implementation of activities that minimize time when students have nothing to do. In addition, effective planning of instructional activities includes determining the pacing of those activities consistent with students' learning needs and with subject matter skills to be learned. A more elaborate discussion of time and the pacing of instructional activities is found in the later section on classroom management.

The importance of decision making in adjusting and adapting lessons is strongly inferred but remains virtually unexamined in process–product research. One of the primary correlates of student outcomes identified in research on classroom processes is the smooth flow of instructional activity (Brophy, 1983; Kounin, 1970). The failure of previously planned activities introduces classroom disruption, management problems, and, potentially, reduced learning (Kounin, 1970). When students' attention to the task is interrupted, or when the instructional activity itself fails, teachers must be able to make decisions to change or adjust plans to maintain the flow of instructional activity and to maintain student cooperation.

The one process–product study that did examine the relationship between teacher decision making during instruction and student achievement presented interesting findings (Peterson & Clark, 1978). In this instance, teachers were asked to evaluate decisions they made to continue or change their behavior during a lesson. In general, when teachers perceived the lesson going well and made decisions not to change their behavior, positive correlations were found with student achievement. When teachers perceived that the lesson was not going well and then chose to continue the lesson in the same manner anyway, negative correlations with achievement were found. Interestingly, when teachers perceived that the lesson was not going well and decided to change behaviors, positive correlations were found with abstract achievement but negative correlations were found with factual and concrete achievement. Although this study seems to raise more questions than it answers, we have discussed it here to show the limited inquiry of process–product research into in-class teacher decision making. We now turn to the sociolinguistic research that provides a more detailed picture of this teacher activity.

The Sociolinguistic Perspective

Sociolinguistic analyses of teacher planning and decision making focus on the moment-to-moment responsiveness of teachers to students during classroom activity. As Green (1983b) noted, the sociolinguistic perspective views teacher decision making as extending beyond the preactive stage focused on in process–product research. Instead, teacher decision making is considered an ongoing process in which teachers continuously make judgments while they are teaching (Cole, Griffin, & Newman, 1978–1981). According to this perspective, the decision-making process for teachers occurs within lessons and is based primarily on teacher assessments of student responses during interactions.

The findings of this research related to teacher decision making rest on two assumptions. First, teachers continuously make judgments during lessons and those judgments are triggered by teachers' ongoing assessments of student responses. Second, the judgments teachers make are revealed in their verbal and nonverbal behavior and in their differentiated behavior toward different students in the classroom. In general, the findings point to factors teachers consider when they make decisions and how they differentiate their communicative exchanges, presumably on the basis of those judgments. However, this research has not directly examined the process by which teacher perceptions and assessments are translated into behavior.

The following discussion is divided into two sections. The first identifies types of information teachers consider during moment-to-moment decision making. The second section outlines various areas of behavioral differentiation. We consider this topic again in our discussion of academic instruction later in this chapter.

Inputs to Decision Making. The primary source of information for teacher decision making is student responses during classroom discourse (Green, 1983b). These responses may take many forms, including answers to questions, the questions students ask, and comments during lessons (see DeStefano & Pepinsky, 1981). Another type of student response is level of attention. Levels of student attention are gauged on the basis of observed cues from students, including eye gaze, body movement and orientation, inability to respond to questions, talking, and interference with others' activities (May, 1981). Such responses provide a basis for teachers and make judgments about student interest and academic performance during teaching (Cole *et al.*, 1978–1981).

These bits of information are generated and gathered throughout the course of a lesson and seem to be considered in conjunction with other information that teachers have before the lesson begins, such as knowledge of student academic abilities and learning needs (Cole, Griffin, & Newman, 1979, 1978–1981), the teacher's theories of pedagogy (Petitto, 1982), and the purposes and structures of the activities implemented as part of the lesson (Merritt & Humphrey, 1981). In evaluating students' language ability, teachers also appear to compare student responses to an adult model or an ideal model of discourse (e.g., narrative structure) (Cook-Gumperz & Worsley, 1981; Michaels & Cook-Gumperz, 1979).

Differentiation in Teacher Communication. Sociolinguistic research has uncovered different ways that teachers change or differentiate their communication in response to the information they receive and the decisions they make during class activities. In general, differentiation in teacher communication has been observed and reported in relation to the different levels of academic ability of students in the classroom.

Teachers differentiate the amount of content covered according to the academic ability of student groups in the classroom. They require different levels of thinking on the part of students and hold students accountable in different degrees for errors made in academic work. Where differentiation occurs, teachers are likely to cover more content and require higher levels of thinking from higher-achieving students (Cole *et al.*, 1978–1981; Collins, 1981; Cook-Gumperz, Gumperz, & Simons 1981; McDermott, 1976, 1978). In contrast, they are more likely to hold lower-achieving students accountable for errors in factual and concrete knowledge (Collins, 1981; Eder, 1982). Finally, teachers have been found to differentiate their use of praise, positive and negative behavioral sanctions, and reprimands (Cahir & Kovacs, 1981; Erickson, Cazden, Carrasco, & Guzman, 1979–1981; Guzman, 1981).

Classroom Management

Process–product and sociolinguistic research traditions emphasize the importance of management functions in the classroom. Both traditions deliver a clear message: teachers play a crucial role in creating classroom conditions that influence student learning. However, these views of classrooms differ. In general, process–product research focuses on formal stated rules and procedures constructed *a priori* and implemented to structure the learning environment, manage resources, and control student attention and behavior. Sociolinguistic research, on the other hand, examines the functional rules and expectations that govern communicative interaction in the classroom. These rules are constructed and evolve during interaction, shifting and changing according to task. Whereas the focus of process–product research is often on the form of rules and procedures, sociolinguistic research examines the development and function of rules, norms, and expectations within the context of specific classroom activities.

The Process–Product Perspective

Process–product research has found at least moderate positive relationships between student achievement and teachers' abilities to manage their classrooms and keep students productively engaged in academic activities. Through the process–product lens, academically successful classrooms appear to be orderly, students seem cooperative and well-focused on academic tasks and activities, and there appears to be a smooth and continuous flow of instructional activity (Brophy, 1983; Brophy & Evertson, 1976; Good, 1983; Kounin, 1970).

According to process–product research, the relationship between managing the instructional setting and student learning pivots on the effective use of class time. The amount of time allocated for instruction as well as how that instructional time is used are significantly correlated with student achievement (Berliner, 1979; Denham & Lieberman, 1980; Good, 1983; Karweit, 1983; Stallings, 1980; Walberg, Schiller, & Haertel, 1979). The opportunities for teachers to devote significant portions of class time to instruction and to use that instructional time in productive ways is determined in large part by the rules and procedures teachers implement to structure and maintain their classroom environment.

In this section, we discuss the findings of process–product research related to five general areas of organization and management: (a) structuring physical space in the classroom, (b) managing physical movement, (c) developing procedures and routines for handling nonacademic class business, (d) managing student behavior, and (e) managing instructional time.

Structuring Physical Space in the Classroom. Process–product studies of well-managed elementary and secondary classrooms find that teachers arrange furnishings to accommodate different types of planned activities, minimize disruptive movement around the classroom, and facilitate teacher monitoring of student work and behavior (Emmer *et al.,* 1980; Evertson & Emmer, 1982; Moskowitz & Hayman, 1976). Further, teachers locate instructional equipment, materials, and students' personal belongings so that they are readily accessible to both teacher and students.

By arranging classroom furnishings and student seating, disruption of ongoing instructional activities can be minimized and teachers can devote more time to students' academic needs. Easy access to equipment and materials facilitates smooth transitions between activities and preserves instructional time. Further, routines established wherein students take primary responsibility for obtaining and returning equipment and materials for instruction increase the opportunity for teacher instructional time with students (see Good, 1983). Other studies show that changes in the physical environment of the classroom can bring about changes in students' choices of activities (Morrow & Weinstein, 1982; Nash, 1981; Phyfe-Perkins, 1979; Weinstein, 1977).

Managing Physical Movement. As with managing physical space, studies of classrooms at the elementary and secondary levels indicate that routines for physical movement promote smooth and quick transitions between learning activities and thus relate to increased amounts of time available for academic work (Brophy, 1983; Emmer *et al.,* 1980; Evertson & Emmer, 1982; Moskowitz & Hayman, 1976; see also Arlin, 1979; Kounin, 1970). These routines are related to lower rates of disruption that may lead to student behavior problems. They further relate to continuity of instructional activity and to maintenance of student task engagement (Arlin, 1979).

Procedures and Routines for Nonacademic Class Business. Process–product research identifies a clear negative relationship between the time teachers spend completing nonacademic business during class and the time available for instruction (Evertson & Emmer, 1982; Stallings, 1980). Procedures and routines to minimize class time spent completing paperwork, taking roll, making announcements, records keeping, and other classroom business relate to increased amounts of time available for instruction.

Managing Student Behavior. There are negative relationships between the number of behavioral sanctions required of teachers during class instructional time and student achievement (Berliner, 1979; Brophy, 1979; Cooley & Leinhardt, 1980; Rosenshine, 1979; Stallings, 1980). When teachers must deal with disruptive behavior it is at the expense of instructional time. More and less effective classroom managers, however, react to instances of student misbehavior in much the same way (Kounin, 1970). What distinguishes the more effective managers is their use of preventive techniques (Brophy, 1983).

In successful elementary classrooms, appropriate behavior is taught early in the school year. Further, it is modeled by teachers for their students and practiced with them until that behavior is learned. Studies of well-managed secondary classrooms reveal less emphasis on formally teaching appropriate behavior to students. However, teachers do introduce rules and procedures to students at the beginning of the year in a clear and systematic way (Evertson & Emmer, 1982; Sanford & Evertson, 1981).

Successful behavior management also depends on following through on expectations for appropriate behavior. Teachers in well-managed classrooms continuously monitor student behavior; they remind students of rules and reintroduce or reteach them if necessary (Brophy, 1983; Emmer *et al.*, 1980; Evertson & Emmer, 1982). Teachers who manage their classroom well detect inappropriate behavior and act before it becomes a problem (Kounin, 1970).

Managing Instructional Time. Process–product research has consistently found significant relationships between time spent on learning and student achievement (e.g., Anderson, 1976; Bloom, 1974; Fisher *et al.*, 1980; Stallings, 1980; Walberg, 1982). However, this body of research indicates that how instructional time is used is more important than the amount of time spent on academic activities (Karweit, 1983; Stallings, 1980). The amount of time students spend engaged in academic tasks with high success rates has been found to be more significantly related to academic achievement than the amount of time spent *per se* on those tasks (Bloom, 1976; Borg, 1980; Fisher *et al.*, 1978; Sirotnik, 1982; Walberg *et al.*, 1979).

Among the most important factors in the effective use of class time is good classroom management (e.g., Arlin, 1982; Good, 1983). Teachers who take steps to increase the amount of time spent on learning activities and ensure that the time spent on those activities is continuous and relatively free of disruption are likely to be more successful academically with their students. These teachers also ensure that students' attention is well focused on academic tasks during instruction and that downtime is minimized (Brophy, 1983; Kounin, 1970). Other management functions related to effective use of classroom time are as follows:

1. *Explaining learning goals and activities to students.* Several studies have found that clearly communicating learning goals to students and explaining directions for learning activities relates positively to student achievement (Berliner, 1982; Fisher *et al.*, 1980). Both student attention rates and achievement improve when teachers spend more time communicating goals and giving directions (Berliner, 1982).

2. *Pacing instruction and student work.* Another important aspect of managing instructional time is appropriate pacing of classroom instruction and student work (Barr, 1975; Berliner, 1982). Pacing can account for as much as 80% of the difference in achievement among high and low performers (Barr, 1980). Effective pacing requires a match between students' achievement levels and the difficulty of the instructional activity (see Brophy, 1979). For example, high-achieving students require a faster pace of work with a higher degree of challenge whereas low-achieving students require

a slower pace with an opportunity to overlearn (Rosenshine & Stevens, 1986). With appropriate pacing, teachers know when to move the class along while still maintaining a critical balance with successful completion of academic activities (Barr, 1975; Brophy, 1979).

3. *Maintaining student focus of attention.* Effective teachers take steps to engage student attention and then to maintain that attention throughout the course of instruction (see Anderson, Evertson, & Brophy, 1979; Brophy & Evertson, 1976; Bruner, 1981; Emmer *et al.*, 1980; Fisher *et al.*, 1980; Rosenshine, 1979). Students are more likely to attend to academic work if full attention is required when important information is presented. This seems to be particularly important when teachers explain learning goals to students and give directions for the completion of learning activities. Once students' attention is focused and they are engaged in learning activities, continuous, active monitoring by the teacher is necessary to detect signs of confusion or inattention. If students become inattentive or disengaged from their work, teachers should act quickly to refocus student attention by using cues (e.g., variations in voice, movement, pacing, and/or gesturing) and questions, or by implementing contingency plans in substitution for unsuccessful activities.

These strategies to engage and maintain students' attention on learning activities are reinforced by the creation of physical conditions in the classroom that reduce the likelihood that students' attention will wander. We mentioned several of these conditions earlier. Another factor related to increased student attention is the selection of activities and materials that hold students' interest. Activities and materials should be challenging but allow for student success. Academic work should also be varied within any given instructional period (Anderson & Scott, 1978; see also Bossert, 1979).

The Sociolinguistic Perspective

According to the sociolinguistic tradition, the rules and expectations that govern classroom communication comprise participation structures. These structures provide a framework for communicative interaction and serve to constrain the options for what can and will occur during classroom discourse. As Green (1983b) pointed out, rules and expectations for interaction are communicated throughout class time. Management of communication occurs simultaneously with academic instruction. Within a lesson, a teacher not only presents academic subject matter but also orchestrates participation in conversation to maintain the flow of classroom activity.

Norms and expectations for conversation create communicative contexts that provide meaning for classroom participants. These contexts are not static. They are continuously constructed and reconstructed by teachers and students as they engage in face-to-face interactions. The teacher, as instructional leader, is ultimately responsible, however, for what occurs during classroom discourse (Green 1983b). Throughout the course of conversation, the teacher's expectations dominate. As the teacher and students interact, the teacher guides the flow of activity, and signals rules and expectations for when students can talk, how they are to talk, and how they are to interpret the meaning of the interaction. Still, even though rules and expectations exist and are communicated, this research finds that interactions cannot be predicted with certainty. There is great potential for variation in the flow of conversation, which makes classroom communication a dynamic process.

In this section, we examine participation structures and how rules for speaking are communicated during classroom activity. Then, we present findings from two other areas of sociolinguistic research related to classroom management—teachers' use of sanctions and the nature of student attention.

Participation Structures. Participation structures are defined in sociolinguistic research as the demands and expectations for participation in communicative activity and the varying rights and obligations that can occur within and across activities (Green, 1983b). Research on participation structures had demonstrated that they vary within classrooms across different activities. Indeed, they range from being ritualistic (e.g., calling roll and collecting assignments) to being almost spontaneous (Erickson, 1982). An individual lesson may be divided into parts with each part setting different expectations and rules for participation (Cook-Gumperz et al., 1981; Florio & Shultz, 1979). As the lesson progresses from one activity to another, requirements and obligations for participation shift for students in the classroom (Cherry-Wilkinson, 1981; Erickson, 1982; Green & Harker, 1982; Gumperz, 1977, 1981).

Demands for participation are set by rules for speaking. Before we discuss those rules and how they are communicated, it is important to note that appropriate performance within participation structures depends on how a student reacts to the demands of that structure. Failure to read the demands correctly can lead to inappropriate performance (Green & Harker, 1982). And, performances within participation structure relate directly to teacher evaluation of student ability and to student achievement (Michaels & Cook-Gumperz, 1979). These findings underscore the importance of how norms and expectations for speaking are communicated and how student competence to perform within structures is developed.

Rules for Speaking. Rules for speaking are culturally determined expectations for how and when to speak, to whom, and for what purpose (Hymes, 1974). These rules form frames of reference and create contexts for participants in face-to-face interactions on both a general level and for specific activities (Green, 1983b).

In general, rules for speaking function to regulate access to classroom discourse. They signal appropriate ways to enter conversations, such as taking turns, waiting to be called on, raising hands, and waiting until another person is finished speaking (Merritt & Humphrey, 1981; Michaels & Cook-Gumperz, 1979). They also determine the appropriate content of present interactions (Merritt & Humphrey, 1981). Classroom participants usually bring to a given conversational situation frames of reference developed from participation in past similar situations. However, in the dynamic linguistic environment of the classroom, the specific rules and expectations for performance in each conversation are signaled by participants as they interact and build on each other's messages (DeStefano & Pepinsky, 1981; Erickson & Shultz, 1981; Green, 1983b; Merritt & Humphrey, 1981). In this way, frames of reference that regulate classroom discourse and create communicative context are in a state of constant flux.

Rules for speaking are signaled both verbally and nonverbally through contextualization cues (Erickson, 1982; Green, 1983b). These cues may be explicit statements of literal meaning or they may be implicit and require participants to infer meaning. Implicit cues may be signaled through choice of vocabulary, order of words, verbal pitch, rhythm, and intonation. They may also be signaled through eye and body position and movement (Cook-Gumperz & Gumperz, 1976; Erickson, 1982; Erickson & Shultz, 1981).

Contextualization cues are signaled continuously throughout the course of conversation. They may reinforce existing rules applied to a specific situation or they may serve to amend or create new rules. Apart from those that carry literal meaning, students must actively interpret cues and infer their meaning (DeStefano & Pepinsky, 1981).

The development of meaning of rules and expectations for interaction seems to be influenced by several factors. The first is the frame of reference an individual brings to the conversational situation. The second is how participants view the "local history" of the situation (Green, 1983b). In other words, the development of meaning for any given situation will be influenced in part by events immediately preceding that situation. Finally, making inferences can be complicated by different messages sent concurrently in an individual interaction and by multiple functions of single messages (Green, 1983b).

As we mentioned earlier, frames of reference classroom participants bring to and construct in interactions are modified as interactions occur. Such modification comes from both overt and covert feedback during conversation and serves to maintain the flow of activity (Frederiksen, 1981; Tannen, 1979). However, when one participant's frame of reference changes and another participant's does not, or when two participants bring or hold different frames for the same situation, a frame clash can occur (Elkind, 1979; Green & Harker, 1982; Heap, 1980; Mehan, 1979). These clashes, when translated into conversation, signal to the teacher inappropriate behavior on the part of the student. As such, frame clashes often lead to negative evaluations of student performance and may result in teachers' use of sanctions (Griffin, Newman, & Cole, 1981; Michaels & Cook-Gumperz, 1979).

Use of Sanctions. Sociolinguistic research identifies six categories of sanctions used by teachers during whole class instruction (Merritt & Humphrey, 1981). The first category includes placement sanctions. These sanctions are used in response to student talk that occurs in wrong places during the lesson, such as when another student or the teacher is talking or when a student responds out of turn. The second category includes delivery sanctions where the placement of student talk is correct but the manner of utterance, such as volume or tempo, is inappropriate. Responsive sanctions comprise the third category. In these responses, the teacher corrects inappropriate placement of student talk but acknowledges the content of the student's utterance. The fourth category is composed of what are termed double-takes.

Here, the teacher first sanctions student talk because its placement is incorrect. Then, the teacher revises the sanction in response to an emergency signaled in the interaction. The fifth category includes curt responses in which the teacher responds to the content of a student's talk, but the curtness of the response indicates the teacher's dissatisfaction with the placement. The final category is behavior sanctions. This category includes teacher sanctions of inappropriate student behavior. Other types of sanctions associated with individual student work time have also been identified. These include sanctions to rechannel interactions to other participants, defer attention to a later time, and squelch inappropriate talk (Merritt & Humphrey, 1981).

Whereas process–product research focuses primarily on teacher behavior to control and sanction overt student misbehavior, sociolinguistic research suggests that behavioral sanctions comprise a very small proportion of the total sanctions issued by teachers during class time. Indeed, the vast majority of teachers' sanctions appear directed toward the management of the flow of conversational discourse. For example, one study found that almost 95% of the sanctions used by teachers related to the management of communication (Merritt & Humphrey, 1981). And, of these sanctions, 90% were directed toward the inappropriate placement of student talk.

Managing Student Attention. Process–product research stresses the importance of having students focus on and engage in academic work. Sociolinguistic research provides a different perspective on the nature and management of student attention.

According to the sociolinguistic perspective, the teacher and students do not begin an activity with a shared understanding of the rules and requirements for attention. The teacher's role is to direct student attention to the activity and the relevant rules. As our earlier discussion suggests, when the teacher fails to communicate the relevant rules, students may draw on rules that relate to different activities and inappropriate performance, including inappropriate levels of attention, may result (see DeStefano & Pepinsky, 1981; Merritt, 1982).

Sociolinguistic research indicates that the role of attention is not always clear. Not all learning requires constant attention, and attention requirements differ across various types of classroom activity (May, 1981). For example, attention requirements may differ during the presentation of new learning material, making assignments and giving directions, independent seatwork, tests, and free time. An additional consideration is that attention and inattention may be masked by different types of overt behavior. For example, a student may appear inattentive (e.g., with head on the desk) but may actually be attending to what is being said in the classroom. Further, students can give attention without understanding what is happening during an activity (May, 1981) and cover up that inattention through the use of procedural displays that allow students to appear as if they are behaving appropriately (Bloome & Argumedo, 1983).

Teachers' decisions to tolerate different levels of inattention relate to the individual student in question, the group of which that student is a part, the activity at hand, and the teacher's goal for that activity. Furthermore, teacher tolerance of inattention relates to the type of inattentive behavior exhibited by the student. Generally, teachers tend to ignore inattentive behavior that can be ignored (May, 1981). However, when inattentive behavior involves loud talk or student movement from one place in the room to another without permission, lasts a long time, or disrupts the attention of other students, teachers usually act to sanction behavior and refocus attention (May, 1981).

Academic Instruction

We have seen in our reviews of both process-product and sociolinguistic research the importance of planning, decision making, and classroom management for establishing the conditions of learning. In this section, we consider a third area of teacher activity—academic instruction. The two research traditions focus on different facets of instructional processes in classrooms. Process–product research examines various types of instructional behavior, whereas sociolinguistic research investigates the patterns and functions of language use in instruction.

The Process–Product Perspective

Over the past 15 years, process–product research has examined relationships between instructional processes and student learning (see Brophy & Good, 1986, and Rosenshine & Stevens, 1986, for reviews). This research has not identified one

instructional method that consistently relates to improved student achievement. However, it does reveal a pattern of instructional behaviors related to higher levels of student learning.

Central to this pattern of instructional behavior identified in process–product research is the concept of interactive teaching. Interactive teaching takes many forms, including presentation and explanation of new material, questioning sessions and discussions, and monitoring seatwork where the teacher actively moves from student to student, provides feedback, and reteaches material if necessary. The time teachers spend interacting with students is positively related to student learning. Also the amount of student–teacher interaction is positively associated with student task engagement (Evertson & Emmer, 1982; Fisher et al., 1978; Stallings, 1980). And, as we have described earlier, the amount of time students are off-task is negatively associated with learning.

Findings from a number of process-product studies of classroom teaching show a general picture of instructional behavior (Rosenshine & Stevens, 1986). That pattern contains the following elements:

1. Review of the previous day's work
2. Presentation of new academic material
3. Initial student practice, feedback, and correctives
4. Independent student work
5. Daily, weekly, and other periodic reviews

Although many of these elements of instruction were first identified in studies of basic skills instruction in elementary grades, subsequent research has found them (with minor variations) in secondary classrooms as well. We describe each of these elements in the following.

Reviewing the Previous Day's Work. Significant relationships have been found between beginning instructional activities with a review of relevant work from the previous day and student learning gains (Rosenshine & Stevens, 1986; Good & Grouws, 1979). This type of review allows teachers to check for student understanding of prerequisite content and skills for the day's activities. Process–product research identifies several ways in which these reviews could be conducted. Teachers can ask questions orally, check homework with students, or review the previous day's presentation or seatwork. In areas where students are having difficulty, the material may be retaught or additional practice can be provided to ensure student understanding. Although teachers may conduct these reviews in different ways, the importance of this activity is that these types of reviews be carried out, particularly if learning new material is predicated on the mastery of formerly presented content and skills. Experimental studies show that reviews of previously presented material relate to student achievement gains at both elementary and secondary levels (Emmer, Sanford, Clements, & Martin, 1983; Good & Grouws, 1979).

Presenting New Learning Material. Process–product research identifies three characteristics of effective presentation of new learning material to students. First, research at both elementary and secondary classrooms finds that teachers who are successful in promoting learning gains spend proportionately more time presenting instructional material to their students than their less successful counterparts (Evertson, Emmer, & Brophy, 1980; Good & Grouws, 1979). Successful teachers used additional presentation time to provide explanations, used a variety of examples, checked for student understanding, retaught material when necessary, and generally gave sufficient instruction so that students could complete independent seatwork activities with minimal difficulty. Second, the clarity of teachers' presentations is related to student learning gains (Bloom 1976; Fisher *et al.,* 1978; Kennedy, Bush, Cruickshank, & Haefele, 1978; Stallings, 1980). Third, effective presentation involves appropriately sequencing hierarchical learning materials to ensure that students first master material they will need to apply to subsequent learning tasks (Good, 1983; Rosenshine & Stevens, 1986).

Rosenshine and Stevens (1986) have identified several components of effective classroom presentations from process-product research (see also Gage, 1978; Kennedy *et al., 1978*). These components include:

1. Clarifying goals and main points in lessons by
   (a) stating the goals or objectivesof the presentations
   (b) focusing on one point (direction) at a time
   (c) avoiding digressions
   (d) avoiding ambiguous phrases and wording
2. Presenting material step-by-step by:
   (a) organizing and presenting the material so that one point is mastered before the next point is given
   (b) giving explicit, sequential directions
   (c) presenting an outline when material is complex
3. Providing specific and concrete procedures by:
   (a) modeling the skills when appropriate
   (b) giving detailed and redundant explanations for difficult points;
   (c) provide students with concrete and varied examples
4. Checking for students' understanding by:
   (a) being sure that students understand one pont before proceeding to the next
   (b) asking the students questions to monitor their comprehension of what has been presented
   (c) having students summarize the main points in their own words
   (d) reteaching the parts of the presentation that students have difficulty comprehending, either by further teacher explanation or through students tutoring each other

The importance of pacing and evaluation is explicit in these components of classroom presentation. Teaching lower-ability students often requires that new material be presented in smaller steps, whereas higher-ability students might progress in larger steps at a faster rate (Brophy & Evertson, 1976; Evertson, 1982; Rosenshine & Stevens, 1986).

Providing Initial Student Practice, Feedback and Correctives. Findings from process–product studies show that in more academically successful classrooms, presentation of new material is followed by initial teacher-led student practice. During initial student practice, teachers conduct question/answer sessions or assign practice problems or exercises to check for student understanding. It is important that all students have opportunities to respond to questions or exercises in this period (Anderson *et al.,* 1979; Brophy & Evertson, 1976; Fisher *et al.,* 1978; Good & Grouws, 1979; Kennedy *et al.,* 1978; Stallings & Kaskowitz, 1974; Stallings, 1980). Teachers in more academically successful classrooms monitored student work closely and provided immediate and frequent content-specific feedback to students about their performance, in contrast to undirected praise or criticism (Brophy, 1979; Rosenshine,

1979). They moved quickly to correct individual student errors by rephrasing questions, providing clues and prompts, and reteaching material if error rates were high (Anderson *et al.*, 1979; Good & Grouws, 1979; Stallings & Kaskowitz, 1974).

An important part of interactive teaching is the detection and correction of errors before students practice mistakes for a long period of time (Good, 1983; Rosenshine & Stevens, 1986). Findings suggest that initial student practice should probably continue until students demonstrate understanding and make few errors (Fisher *et al.*, 1978).

Assigning Independent Student Work. Process–product studies conducted in academically successful classrooms found that after students demonstrated reasonably high success during initial student practice, teachers assigned independent seatwork so that newly acquired skills could be practiced. The most common forms of independent work were individual seatwork and homework. However, unless these independent work activities are well-monitored, problems can occur. Studies conducted in elementary and secondary classrooms indicate that students spent more time working alone at seatwork than any other activity; estimates range as high as 70% of class time (Evertson, Anderson, *et al.* 1980; Evertson, Emmer, *et al.*, 1980; Fisher *et al.*, 1978; Stallings, Cory, Fairweather, & Needels, 1977). This research further indicates that students were less engaged during seatwork than they were during other types of instruction. For example, the Beginning Teacher Evaluation Study found that average student engagement was 84% during teacher-led discussion but only 70% during unsupervised seatwork (Fisher *et al.*, 1980).

Seatwork is more effective if it is well distributed across class time. Students seem less likely to get off-task if they are not exposed to one activity for too long a period. In addition, these findings suggest that for seatwork or any other form of independent work to be beneficial, students must be adequately prepared. This preparation includes clear, explicit, and even redundant instructions for the completion of independent work. In addition, teachers must monitor student work and provide substantive instruction, feedback, and explanation when students experience difficulty. Effective teachers actively circulate around the classroom, monitor student work, ask questions, and give explanations during independent seatwork. All these teachers activities are related to increased levels of student task engagement that is in turn related to student achievement (Evertson, Emmer, Sanford, & Clements 1983; Evertson *et al.*, 1985; Fisher *et al.*, 1980; Good & Grouws, 1979).

Conducting Periodic Reviews. Effective instruction includes periodically reviewing instructional routines and reteaching material in areas in which students experience lapses (e.g., Emmer *et al.*, 1982; Good & Grouws, 1979). These reviews provide additional opportunities for teachers to check for student understanding and to ensure that students have adequately learned material necessary as a foundation for future knowledge and skills. Reviews also provide teachers with the opportunity to assess the effectiveness of learning activities and materials selected (Rosenshine & Stevens, 1986).

Process–product research identifies two other areas that relate to each of these elements of instruction and have an impact on student academic outcomes. These areas are teacher expectations for student learning and accountability for academic work.

Communicating Expectations for Student Learning. Process–product studies have consistently found relationships between teachers' expectations for student academic performance and student achievement in basic skills. When teachers set high but attainable goals for student performance, achievement usually increases; when teachers set goals for performance that are low, achievement usually declines (Berliner, 1982; Brookover, Beady, Flood, Schweitzer, & Wisenbaker, 1979; Brophy & Good, 1974; Cooper, 1979). The likelihood that teachers' expectations will become self-fulfilling prophecies for student learning is greatest when those expectations are inaccurate and inflexible.

Process–product research has identified several ways that teachers communicate expectations for student learning through differentiation in their instructional behavior. For example, some teachers have been found to tolerate more behavioral interruptions when working with low-achieving than with high-achieving students (Evertson, 1982). And, as indicated by other process–product research, the number of behavioral interruptions that occur in the classroom is negatively related to student achievement (e.g., Cooley & Leinhardt, 1980; Stallings, 1980). Teachers sometimes provide low achievers fewer opportunities to perform academically than high achievers and thus give fewer opportunities for low achievers to receive the necessary corrective feedback for learning. In addition, some teachers require more seatwork of low than of high achievers, whereas they devote more interactive teaching time to high rather than to low achievers. When called upon to answer questions, some teachers give low achievers less time to answer than high achievers, and when given incorrect answers, some teachers prompt high-achieving students more than low-achieving students in the proper direction (Brophy & Good, 1974; Cooper, 1979). Although these differential teacher behaviors may serve to keep *any* activity ongoing in the classroom, they seem to communicate low expectations for academic performance to low achievers, that, in turn, contribute to further low achievement and to widening the achievement gap among students.

Establishing Accountability for Academic Work. Several process–product studies found that teachers in high-achieving classrooms consistently held students accountable for academic work. Accountability appeared to be conveyed through teachers' expectations for student learning, through their efforts to make effective use of instructional time, and through maintaining student focus on learning activities. Another way teachers demonstrated that students were accountable for learning was by requiring that work be completed on time (Brophy, 1983; Good, 1983). Teacher expectations and classroom work procedures appear to be significant influences on establishing an accountability system that increases student cooperation in academic activities that, in turn, relate to achievement gains (see Emmer *et al.*, 1980; Evertson & Emmer, 1982; Moskowitz & Hayman, 1976).

The Sociolinguistic Perspective

From the sociolinguistic perspective, teaching is more than academic instruction. We have seen that during the course of lessons, teachers also present information to students about rules and expectations for participation and norms for behavior (Erickson, 1982; Green & Harker, 1982; Wallat & Green, 1982). In the linguistic environment of the classroom, instructional and managerial communication occur simultaneously.

Sociolinguistic research asserts that the language used by teachers and students provides information about the teacher's implicit instructional goals and implicit theories of pedagogy (Cook-Gumperz & Gumperz, 1982; Green & Harker,

1982; Hymes, 1981). The ways that teachers interact with students within and across various activities, the types of feedback and sanctions given to students, both literally and tacitly communicate to students what is expected of them academically and socially and how instructional activity is to progress.

We examined how rules and expectations for participation and norms for behavior are established and communicated in our discussion of classroom management. In this section, we present findings from sociolinguistic research that relate more specifically to various aspects of academic instruction. Findings that relate to academic instruction fall generally into two broad categories: (a) patterns and functions of language use in instruction and (b) differentiation in language use and function among groups of students during instruction. Like process–product research that has focused primarily on teacher instructional behaviors, the findings from sociolinguistic research reveal behaviors as they relate to instructional interaction. However, sociolinguistic research goes further to identify the functions and meanings of various types of instructional communication in classrooms.

Patterns of Language Use in Instruction. According to the sociolinguistic perspective, instructional communication is framed within academic task structures (Erickson, 1982). These structures serve to organize academic work for students by presenting a logic for the subject matter taught, designating steps for the presentation of subject matter, and providing cues and strategies for completing instructional activities (Green, 1983b). In general, sociolinguistic research finds that certain types of teacher-directed lessons begin with a relatively high density of one-way communication in which the teacher designates and enforces the order and structure of the lesson and explains the activities that will follow (DeStefano & Pepinsky, 1981; Guzman, 1980; Morine-Dershimer & Tenenberg 1981). Then, throughout the course of the lesson, instructional communication is dominated by teacher-initiated exchanges. The greatest proportion of teacher talk centers on concrete information rather than discussion of process (DeStefano & Pepinsky, 1981).

Sociolinguistic research examines in detail a variety of types of communicative exchanges. Two types of teacher–student communication that have been related to student achievement will be discussed here. The first type is teacher questioning.

According to this perspective, questioning serves a variety of functions including instruction and evaluation. The exploration of the relationship between questioning and student learning is limited. However, Morine-Dershimer and Tenenberg (1981) found a positive relationship between individual student participation in classroom discourse and academic achievement. Further, they found that student responses and participation are influenced by the ways questions are asked and student perceptions of the functions of those questions.

Morine-Dershimer and Tenenberg (1981) also focused on student perceptions of classroom language. Students reported that they generally answered questions because "someone asked." However, their rates of responses to questions were usually greater when the same question was asked of a number of students or when the teacher asked a series of questions to one student for clarification or evaluation. Students also reported that their responses were more salient to both themselves and the teacher when teachers initiated exchanges.

Students' perceptions of the function of questions also related to the frequency of their participation in discussions. The more students perceived questions as instructional and informative, the more likely they were to participate (Morine-Dershimer & Tenenberg, 1981). In general, students perceive the use of questions to teach or tell (Green, 1983b). However, students of higher-academic achievement, who had higher academic status with their teacher and peers, more frequently viewed questions as instructional. Students of lower status tend to attribute no particular function to questions teachers ask.

This difference in perceptions may be attributable to the ways teachers differentiate language use and behavior among higher- and lower-achieving students. As we have seen, teachers sometimes require less of lower-achieving students. Such differentiation may relate to differential student perceptions of teachers' communications, to their participation in academic discourse, and, in turn, to their academic performance.

Sociolinguistic research indicates that the instructional function of questioning is not only served during students' direct interaction with the teacher. Students learn from other students' answers to questions. During question-and-answer sessions, students listen to their peer's responses to find out the correct answers and to check their own answers (Morine-Dershimer, 1981). Their atten-

tion rates to responses are higher when peers answer lower-level convergent and higher-level divergent questions (Morine-Dershimer & Tenenberg, 1981).

The second type of exchange examined by sociolinguistic research is teacher praise. Like other areas of communication, praise is a differentiated linguistic phenomenon (Green, 1983b). Praise functions to focus attention and confirm and reward appropriate behavior (Green, 1983b). Morine-Dershimer and Tenenberg (1981) found that strong praise (a) was highly salient, (b) was recalled more frequently by students, even though its actual occurrence was less than other forms of communication, and (c) was more likely to be distributed among higher-achieving, high-status students than lower-achieving, low-status students (Morine-Dershimer & Tenenberg, 1981).

One important outcome of differentiated praise for student learning is again related to student participation in classroom discourse. Students who believe that praise is deserved—for example, for good ideas or good answers—are more likely to participate in question–answer sessions and discussions (Morine-Dershimer & Tenenberg, 1981). And, as we have indicated, such participation is related to student achievement. These findings are one more indication that differentiation in the instructional language of teachers has important implications for student learning. We now examine other ways that teachers differentiate their instructional communication.

Differentiation in Instruction. Teachers differentiate instruction within lessons for high- and low-achieving groups of students (Guzman, 1980). They also vary feedback about rules for participation in discourse and expectations for student performance (Cherry-Wilkinson, 1981; Collins, 1981; McDermott, 1976; Stoffan-Roth, 1981). Other studies have found that the amount of content teachers cover is usually greater for higher-achieving groups (Cole *et al.*, 1978–1981; Petitto, 1982). In lower-achieving reading groups, teachers place greater emphasis on pronunciation, grammatical errors, and single word decoding. Less emphasis is placed on reading for content and meaning (Collins, 1981). However, in high-achieving groups, teachers encourage students to develop meaning. While emphasizing higher-level thinking, teachers often ignore errors in pronunciation, grammar, and decoding of higher-achieving students (see also Allington, 1983, and Eder, 1981).

The differentiation of language use within lessons reflects differences in teacher instructional style (Erickson, 1982; Green & Harker, 1982). Indeed, differences in instructional approaches to different groups of students may be due to differing theories about the instructional needs of students. Rather than applying a single theory of pedagogy, teachers shift instruction according to their perceptions of different student needs (Petitto, 1982).

Conclusion

We have presented findings from two research traditions that illustrate different but complementary ways to look at classroom teaching. Each tradition views classrooms in different ways. Process–product research focuses on the teacher and looks across a large number of classrooms to identify teacher behaviors that correlate with student outcome measures. This tradition assumes teacher primacy and that teacher behaviors have a direct causal relationship to student outcomes. The relationship between teacher and student is considered linear and unidirectional and contextual variables are generally controlled. Sociolinguistic research, on the other hand, looks within classrooms to determine how language and face-to-face communicative interactions function in the teaching-learning process. This research focuses on communication between the teacher and students and among students themselves and is based on a recursive model of interaction among classroom participants. Classroom social group context, goals, and expectations are central to the sociolinguistic tradition.

Each research tradition exposes different classroom events. In the area of planning and decision making, process–product research focuses on preactive measures that teachers take to plan the learning environment and academic work. Sociolinguistic research examines the moment-to-moment responses of teachers and students during the course of classroom activity. In the area of classroom management, process–product research identifies the formal rules and procedures teachers implement to structure the physical aspects of the classroom, manage resources, and control student behavior. Sociolinguistic research explores the functional nature of rules and expectations that create a communicative social context, govern conversation and behavior, and determine access

to classroom discourse and, thus, access to learning. Finally, in the area of academic instruction, process–product research focuses on sequences of teachers' instructional behaviors. Sociolinguistic research focuses on patterns and functions of language use in instruction.

These research perspectives illustrate two important dimensions of knowledge that are crucial to develop a more complete understanding of teaching and learning processes. The first is of the general processes and behaviors that relate to student learning across a variety of situations. Of equal importance is knowledge that explains *how* those processes operate and function within specific contexts across time. It is important to develop these two bases of knowledge about phenomena and to distinguish between knowing *that* relationships among them exist and knowing *how* those relationships function. Studying phenomena from the process–product perspective has provided useful information that addresses the *that's;* research from the sociolinguistic perspective is useful for understanding the *how's*. Without both perspectives we are left with a partial understanding of classroom phenomena that limits efforts at program and policy development, and programs to improve teaching.

Without a view that looks across classrooms, we cannot identify the broad frameworks of behavior and activity that seem to promote learning. Without a view that looks within classrooms, we cannot anticipate how interventions and innovations will function. As research on change and innovation makes clear (e.g., Fullan, 1982), it is at the classroom level that efforts to understand teaching and ultimately to improve teaching will either succeed or fail.

References

Allington, R. L. (1983). The reading instruction provided readers of differing reading abilities. *Elementary School Journal, 83,* 548–559.

Anderson, L. M., Evertson, C. M., & Brophy, J. E. (1979). An experimental study of effective teaching in first grade reading groups. *Elementary School Journal, 79,* 193–223.

Anderson, L. W., & Scott, C. C. (1978). The relationship among teaching methods, student characteristics, and student involvement in learning. *Journal of Teacher Education, 29*(3), 52–57.

Anderson, L. W. (1976). An empirical investigation of individual differences in time to learn. *Journal of Educational Psychology, 68,* 226–233.

Arlin, M. (1979). Teacher transitions can disrupt time flow in classrooms. *American Educational Research Journal, 16,* 42–56.

Arlin, M. (1982). Teacher responses to student time differences in mastery learning. *American Journal of Education, 90,* 334–352.

Barr, R. C. (1975). How children are taught to read: Grouping and pacing. *School Review, 83,* 479–498.

Barr, R. C. (1980, April). *School, class, group, and pace effects on learning.* Paper presented at the annual meeting of the American Educational Research Association, Boston.

Berliner, D. C. (1979). The Beginning Teacher Evaluation Study: Research to inform policy. *The Generator, 9,*(1), 7–8, 15.

Berliner, D. C. (1982, March). *The executive functions of teaching.* Paper presented to the annual meeting of the American Educational Research Association, New York.

Berliner, D. C., & Rosenshine, B. (1977). The acquisition of knowledge in the classroom. In R. C. Anderson, R. J. Spiro, & W. E. Montague (Eds.), *Schooling and the acquisition of knowledge* (pp. 375–396). Hillsdale, NJ: Erlbaum.

Bloom, B. S. (1974). Time and learning. *American Psychologist, 29,* 682–688.

Bloom, B. S. (1976). *Human characteristics and school learning.* New York: McGraw-Hill.

Bloome, D., & Argumedo, B. (1983, March). *Procedural display and classroom instruction at the middle school level: Another look at academic engaged time.* Paper presented at the annual meeting of the American Educational Research Association, Montreal.

Bloome, D., & Green, J. (1984). Directions in the sociolinguistic study of reading. In D. Pearson, R. Barr, M Kamil, & P. Mosenthal (Eds.), *Handbook of reading research* (pp. 395–421). New York: Longman.

Bolster, A. S. (1983). Toward a more effective model of research on teaching. *Harvard Educational Review, 53,* 294–308.

Borg, W. R. (1980). Time and school learning. In C. Denham & A. Lieberman (Eds.), *Time to learn* (pp. 33–72). Washington, DC: National Institute of Education.

Bossert, S. T. (1979). *Tasks and social relationships in classrooms.* New York: Cambridge University Press.

Brookover, W., Beady, C., Flood, P., Schweitzer, J., & Wisenbaker, J. (1979). *School social systems and student achievement: Schools can make a difference.* New York: Praeger.

Brophy, J. E. (1979). Teacher behavior and its effects. *Journal of Educational Psychology, 71,* 733–750.

Brophy, J. E. (1983). Classroom organization and management. *Elementary School Journal, 83,* 265–285.

Brophy, J. E., & Evertson, C. M. (1976). *Learning from teaching: A developmental perspective.* Boston, MA: Allyn & Bacon.

Brophy, J. E., & Good, T. L. (1974). *Teacher-student relationships: Causes and consequences.* New York: Holt, Rinehart & Winston.

Brophy, J. E., & Good T. L. (1986). Teacher behavior and student learning. In M. Wittrock (Ed), *Handbook of research on teaching* (3rd edition), New York: Macmillan.

Brophy, J. E., & Putnam, J. (1979). Classroom management in the elementary grades. In D. Duke (Ed.), *Classroom management* (pp. 182–216). The 78th Yearbook of the National Society for the Study of Education, (Part II). Chicago, IL: University of Chicago Press.

Bruner, J. (1981, August). *On instructability.* Paper presented at the annual meeting of the American Psychological Association, Los Angeles.

Buchmann, M., & Schmidt, W. H. (1981). *The school day and teachers' content commitments,* (Research series No. 83). East Lansing: Michigan State University, Institute for Research on Teaching.

Cahir, S. R., & Kovacs, C. (1981). *Exploring functional language.* Washington, DC: Center for Applied Linguistics.

Cazden C. (1986). Classroom discourse. In M. Wittrock (Ed.). *Handbook of research on teaching* (3rd ed.). New York: Macmillan.

Cherry-Wilkinson, L. (1981). Analysis of teacher-student interaction-expectations communicated by conversational structure. In J. L. Green & C. Wallat (Eds.), *Ethnography and language in educational settings.* (pp. 253–268). Norwood, NJ: Ablex.

Clark, C. M. (1983, February). *Research on teacher planning: An inventory of the knowledge base.* Paper presented at the annual meeting of the American Association of Colleges for Teacher Education, Detroit, MI.

Cole, M., Griffin, P., & Newman, D. (1979). *They're all the same in their own way,* (Mid-quarter report, NIE G-78-0159). Washington, DC: National Institute of Education.

Cole, M., Griffin, P., & Newman, D. (1978–1981). *Mid quarter reports.* (NIE G-78-0159). Washington, DC: National Institute of Education.

Collins, J. (1981). Differential treatment in reading instruction. In J. Cook-Gumperz, J. Gumperz, & H. Simons, *School-home ethnography project* (Final report, NIE G-78-0082). Washington, DC: National Institute of Education.

Cook-Gumperz, J. & Gumperz, J. (1976). Context in children's speech. In J. Cook-Gumperz & J. Gumperz (Eds.) *Papers on language and context, Working paper # 46.* Berkeley, CA: Language Behavior Research Laboratory, University of California.

Cook-Gumperz, J., & Gumperz, J. (1982). Communicative competence in educational perspective. In L. Cherry-Wilkinson (Ed.), *Communicating in the classroom (pp. 13–24). New York: Academic Press.*

Cook-Gumperz, J., Gumperz, J., & Simons, H. D. (1981). School-home ethnography project, (Final report, NIE G-78-0082). Washington, DC: National Institute of Education.

Cook-Gumperz, J., & Worsley, L. (1981). Report on the narrative discourse study. In J. Cook-Gumperz, J. Gumperz, & H. D. Simons (Eds.), *School-home ethnography project.* (Final report, NIE G-78-0082). Washington, DC: National Institute of Education.

Cooley, W. W., & Leinhardt, G. (1980). The instructional dimensions study. *Educational Evaluation and Policy Analysis, 2,* 7–25.

Cooper, H. (1979). Pygmalion grows up: A model for teacher expectation communication and performance influence. *Review of Educational Research, 49,* 389–410.

Denham, C., & Leiberman, A. (Eds.). (1980). *Time to learn.* Washington, DC: National Institute of Education.

DeStefano, J., & Pepinsky, H. (1981). *The learning of discourse rules of culturally different children in first grade literacy instruction* (Final report, NIE G-79-0032). Washington, CD: National Institute of Education.

Doyle, W. (1977). Paradigms for research on teacher effectiveness. In L. S. Shulman (Ed.), *Review of research in education,* Vol. 5, Itasca, IL: Peacock.

Dunkin, M., & Biddle, B. (1974). *The study of teaching.* New York: Holt, Rinehart & Winston.

Eder, D. (1981). Ability grouping as a self-fulfilling prophecy: A microanalysis of teacher–student interaction. *Sociology of Education, 54,* 151–162.

Eder, D. (1982). Differences in communicative styles across ability groups. In L. Cherry Wilkinson (Ed.), *Communicating in the classroom* (pp. 245–264). New York: Academic Press.

Elkind, D. (1979). *Child and society,* New York: Oxford University Press.

Emmer, E., Evertson, C., & Anderson, L. (1980). Effective management at the beginning of the school year. *Elementary School Journal, 80,* 219–231.

Emmer, E., Sanford, J., Clements, B., & Martin, J. (1982). *Improving classroom management: An experimental study in junior high classrooms,* Austin, TX: Research and Development Center for Teacher Education, The University of Texas.

Erickson, F. (1982). Classroom discourse as improvisation: Relationships between academic task structure and social participation structure in lessons. In L. Cherry-Wilkinson (Ed.), *Communicating in the classroom* (pp. 153–181). New York: Academic Press.

Erickson, F., Cazden, C., Carrasco, R., & Guzman, A. (1979–81). *Social and cultural organization of interaction in classrooms of bilingual children.* (Mid-quarter Report, NIE G-78-0099). Washington, DC: National Institute of Education.

Erickson, F., & Shultz, J. (1981). When is a context? Some issues and methods in the analysis of social competence. In J. L. Green & C. Wallat (Eds.), *Ethnography and language in educational settings* (pp. 147–160). Norwood, NJ: Ablex.

Evertson, C. (1982). Differences in instructional activities in higher- and lower-achieving junior high English and math classes. *Elementary School Journal, 82,* 309–327.

Evertson, C., Anderson, C., Anderson, L., & Brophy, J. (1980). Relationships between classroom behaviors and student outcomes in junior high mathematics and English classes. *American Educational Research Journal, 17,* 43–60.

Evertson, C., & Emmer, E. (1982). Effective management at the beginning of the school year in junior high classes. *Journal of Educational Psychology, 74,* 485–498.

Evertson, C., Emmer, E., & Brophy, J. (1980). Predictors of effective teaching in junior high mathematics classrooms. *Journal of Research in Mathematics Education, 11,* 167–178.

Evertson, C., Emmer, E., Sanford, J., & Clements, B. (1983). Improving classroom management: An experiment in elementary school classrooms. *Elementary School Journal, 84,* 173–188.

Evertson, C., & Green, J. (1986). Observation as inquiry and method. In M. Wittrock (Ed.), *Handbook of research on teaching,* (3rd ed.), New York: Macmillan.

Evertson, C., Weade, G., Green, J., & Crawford, J. (1985). *Effective classroom management and instruction: An exploration of models.* Final rept. (NIE G-83-0063), Washington, DC: National Institute of Education.

Fisher, C., Filby, N., Marliave, R., Cahen, L., Dishaw, M., Moore, J., & Berliner, D. (1978). *Teaching behaviors, academic learning time, and student achievement,* (Final report of Phase III-B, Beginning Teacher Evaluation Study, Technical Report V-I). San Francisco: Far West Laboratory for Educational Research and Development.

Fisher, C., Berliner, D. C., Filby, N. N., Marliave, R., Cahen, L. S., & Dishaw, M. M. (1980). Teaching behaviors, academic learning time, and student achievement: An overview. In C. Denham & A. Lieberman (Eds.), *Time to learn* (pp. 7–32). Washington, DC: National Institute of Education.

Florio, S., & Shultz, J. (1979). Social competence at home and at school. *Theory into Practice, 18,* 234–243.

Frederiksen, C. (1981). Inference in preschool childrens' conversations—a cognitive perspective. In J. L. Green & C. Wallat (Eds.), *Ethnography and language in educational settings,* (pp. 303–334), Norwood, NJ: Ablex.

Fullan, M. (1982). *The meaning of educational change.* New York: Columbia University, Teachers College Press.

Gage, N. (1963). Paradigms for research on teaching. In N. L. Gage (Ed.), *Handbook of research on teaching* (1st ed., pp. 94–141). Chicago: Rand McNally.

Gage, N. (1978). *The scientific basis of the art of teaching.* New York: Teachers College Press.

Gage, N. (1985). *Hard gains in the soft sciences: The case of pedagogy.* Bloomington, IN: Phi Delta Kappa, Center on Evaluation, Development, and Research.

Good, T. (1983). *Classroom research: A decade of progress.* Paper presented at the annual meeting of the American Educational Research Association, Montreal.

Good, T., & Brophy, J. (1978). *Looking in classrooms.* (2nd ed.). New York: Harper & Row.

Good, T., & Grouws, D. (1979). The Missouri Mathematics Effectiveness Project. *Journal of Educational Psychology, 71,* 355–362.

Good, T., & Marshall, S. (1984). Do students learn more in heterogeneous or homogeneous groups? In P. L. Peterson & L. Cherry Wilkinson (Eds.), *The social context of instruction* (pp. 15–38). Orlando, FL: Academic Press.

Green, J. (1983a). Research on teaching as a linguistic process: A state of the art. In E. Gordon (Ed.), *Review of research in education.* (Vol. 10). Washington, DC: American Educational Research Association.

Green, J., & Bloome, D. (1983). Ethnography and reading: Issues, approaches criteria, and findings. *The thirty second yearbook of the National Reading Conference.* Rochester, NY: National Reading Conference.

Green, J., & Harker, J. (1982) Gaining access to learning: Conversational, social, and cognitive demands of group participation. In L. Cherry-Wilkinson (Ed.), *Communicating in the classroom* (pp. 183–221). New York: Academic Press.

Green J., & Rasinski, T. (1985). *Teacher style and classroom management: Stability and variation across instructional events.* Paper presented at the American Educational Research Association, Chicago, IL.

Green, J., & Wallat, C. (1981). Mapping instructional conversations. In J. Green & C. Wallat (Eds.), *Ethnography and language in educational settings* (pp. 161–205). Norwood, NJ: Ablex.

Griffin, P., Newman, D., & Cole, M. (1986, August). *Activities, actions, and formal operations: A Vygotskian analysis of a Piagetian task.* Paper presented at a meeting of the International Society for the Study of Behavioral Development, Toronto.

Gumperz, J. (1977). Sociocultural knowing in conversational inference. In M. Saville-Troike (Ed.), *28th annual round table monograph series on language and linguistics.* Georgetown, VA: Georgetwon University.

Gumperz, J. (1981). Conversational inference and classroom learning. In J. Green & C. Wallat (Eds.), *Ethnography and language in educational settings,* Norwood, NJ: Ablex.

Gumperz, J. (1982). *Discourse strategies,* New York: Cambridge University Press.

Gumperz, J., & Hymes, D. (1972). *Directions in sociolinguistics.* New York: Holt, Rinehart & Winston.

Guzman, A. (1980, December). *Theoretical and methodological issues for the ethnographic study of teachers' differential treatment of children in bilingual bicultural classrooms.* Paper presented at the annual meeting of the American Anthropological Association, Washington, DC.

Guzman, A. (1981). *A multidimensional ethnographic framework for studying classroom organization and interaction.* Qualifying paper, Harvard University.

Harker, J. (in press). Contrasting the content of two story reading lessons: A propositional analysis. In J. Green, J. Harker, & C. Wallat (Eds.), *Multiple perspectives analysis of classroom discourse.* Norwood, NJ: Ablex.

Hartland-Swann, J. (1956). The logical status of "knowing that". *Analysis, 16,* 111–115.

Heap, J. (1980). What counts as reading? Limits to certainty in assessment. *Curriculum Inquiry, 10,* 265–292.

Hymes, D. (1974). *Foundations of sociolinguistics: An ethnographic approach.* Philadelphia, PA: University of Pennsylvania Press.

Hymes, D. (1981). *Language in education: Ethnographic essays.* Washington, DC: Center for Applied Linguistics.

Karweit, N. (1983). *Time-on task: A research review.* (Report #322). Baltimore, MD: The Johns Hopkins University, Center for the Social Organization of Schools.

Kennedy, J., Bush, A., Cruickshank, D., & Haefele, D. (1978, March). *Additional investigations into the nature of teacher clarity.* Paper presented at the annual meeting of the American Educational Research Association, Toronto.

Kounin, J. (1970). *Discipline and group management in classrooms.* New York: Holt, Rinehart & Winston.

May, L. (1981). Spaulding school: Attention and styles of interaction. In D. Hymes (Ed.), *Ethnographic monitoring,* (Final Report NIE G-78-0038). Washington, DC: National Institute of Education.

McDermott, R. (1976). *Kids make sense: An ethnographic account of the interactional management of success and failure in one-first grade classroom.* Unpublished doctoral dissertation, Stanford University.

McDermott, R. (1978). Relating and learning: An analysis of two classroom reading groups. In R. Shuy (Ed.), *Linguistics and reading.* Rawley, MA: Newbury House.

Mehan, H. (1979). *Learning lessons,* Cambridge, MA: Harvard University Press.

Merritt, M. (1982). Distributing and directing attention in primary classrooms. In L. Cherry-Wilkinson (Ed.), *Communicating in the classroom.* New York: Academic Press.

Merritt, M., & Humphrey, F. (1981). *Service-like events during individual work time and their contributions to the nature of communication in primary classrooms* (NIE G-78-0159). Washington, DC: National Institute of Education.

Michaels, S., & Cook-Gumperz, J. (1979). A study of sharing time with first grade students: Discourse narratives in the classroom. In *Proceedings of the Berkeley Linguistic Society, 5,* 87–103.

Morine-Dershimer, G. (1981). *Who hears whom: Classroom status variables and pupil attention to the comments of other pupils.* Paper presented at the annual meeting of the American Educational Research Association, Los Angeles.

Morine-Dershimer, G., & Tenenberg, M. (1981). *Participant perspectives of classroom discourse.* (Final Report, Executive Summary, NIE G-78-0161). Washington, DC: National Institute of Education.

Morrow, L. M., & Weinstein, C. S. (1982). Increasing children's use of literature through program and physical design changes. *Elementary School Journal, 83,* 131–137.

Moskowitz, G., & Hayman, M. (1976). Success strategies of inner-city teachers: A year long study. *Journal of Educational Research, 69,* 282–289.

Nash, B. (1981). The effects of classroom spatial organization on four- and five-year-old children's learning. *British Journal of Educational Psychology, 51,* 144–155.

National Institute of Education. (1975). *Teaching as clinical information processing.* Report of Panel 6, National Conference on Studies in Teaching. Washington, DC: National Institute of Education.

Peterson, P., & Cherry-Wilkinson, L. (1984). Instructional groups in the classroom: Organization and processes. In P. Peterson & L. Cherry Wilkinson (Eds.), *The social context of instruction.* Orlando, FL: Academic Press.

Peterson, P., & Clark, C. (1978). Teacher's reports of their cognitive processes during teaching. *American Educational Research Journal, 15,* 555–565.

Peterson, P., Marx, R., & Clark, C. (1978). Teacher planning, teacher behavior, and student achievement. *American Educational Research Journal, 15,* 417–432.

Petitto, A. (1982, March). *Culturally motivated goals and calculating devices: Learning arithmetic in elementary schools.* Paper presented at the annual meeting of the American Educational Research Association, New York.

Phyfe-Perkins, E. (1979, April). *Children's behavior in preschool settings: A review of research concerning the influence of the physical environment.* Paper presented at the annual meeting of the American Educational Research Association, San Francisco.

Rist, R. (1970). Student social class and teacher expectations: The self-fulfilling prophecy in ghetto education. *Harvard Educational Review, 40,* 411–451.

Roland, J. (1961). On the reduction of "knowing that" to "knowing how," In B. O. Smith & R. H. Ennis (Eds.), *Language and concepts in education,* Chicago, IL: Rand McNally.

Rosenshine, B. (1971). *Teaching behaviors and student achievement.* Windsor, Berkshire, England: National Foundation for Educational Research in England and Wales.

Rosenshine, B. (1979). Content, time, and direct instruction. In P. Peterson & H. Walberg (Eds.), *Research on teaching: Concepts, findings, and implications.* Berkeley, CA: McCutchan.

Rosenshine, B. & Furst, N. (1973). The use of direct observation to study teaching. In R. M. W. Travers (Ed.), *Handbook of research on teaching.* (2nd edition) Chicago, IL: Rand McNally.

Rosenshine, B., & Stevens, R. (1986). Teaching functions. In M. Wittrock (Ed.), *Handbook of research on teaching* (3rd ed.), New York: Macmillan.

Ryle, G. (1949). *The concept of mind.* Chicago, IL: The University of Chicago Press.

Sanford, J., & Evertson, C. (1981). Classroom management in a low SES junior high: Three case studies. *Journal of Teacher Education, 32,* 34–38.

Schwille, J., Porter, A., Belli, G., Floden, R., Freeman, D., Knappen, L., Kuhs, T., & Schmidt, W. (1981). *Teachers as policy brokers in the content of elementary school mathematics.* East Lansing, MI: Michigan State University, Institute for Research on Teaching.

Sergiovanni, T. J. (1984). Expanding conceptions of inquiry and practice in supervision and evaluation. *Eductional Evaluation and Policy Analysis, 6,* 355–365.

Shavelson, R. (1976). Teacher's decision making. In N. Gage (Ed.) *The psychology of teaching methods,* 75th Yearbook of the National Society for the Study of Education. Chicago: University of Chicago Press.

Shavelson, R. (1983). Review of research on teachers' pedagogical judgments, plans, and decisions. *Elementary School Journal, 83,* 392–413.

Shavelson, R., & Stern, P. (1981). Research on teachers' pedagogical thoughts, judgments, decisions, and behavior. *Review of Educational Research, 51,* 455–498.

Shulman, L. (1986). Research programs for the study of teaching: A contemporary perspective. In M. Wittrock (Ed.), *Handbook of research on teaching.*(pp. 3–36). New York: Macmillan.

Shulman, L., & Elstein, A. (1975). Studies of problem solving, judgment, and decision making. In F. Kerlinger (Ed.), *Review of research in education* (Vol. 3). Itasca, IL: Peacock.

Sirotnik, K. (1982). The contextual correlates of the relative expenditures of classroom time on instruction and behavior: An exploratory study of secondary schools and classes. *American Educational Research Journal, 19,* 275–292.

Soltis, J. (1984). On the nature of educational research. *Educational Researcher, 13,* 5–10.

Stallings, J. (1980). Allocated academic learning time revisited, or beyond time on task. *Educational Researcher, 9,* 11–16.

Stallings, J., Cory, R., Fairweather, J., & Needels, M. (1977). *Early childhood classroom evaluation.* Menlo Park, CA: SRI International.

Stallings, J., & Kaskowitz, D. (1974). *Follow-through classroom evaluation, 1972–73.* Report prepared for the Division of Elementary and Secondary Programs, Office of Planning, U.S. Office of Education. Menlo Park, CA: Stanford Research Institute.

Stoffan-Roth, M. (1981). *Conversational access gaining strategies in instructional contexts.* Unpublished doctoral dissertation, Kent State University.

Tannen, D. (1979). What's in a frame? Surface evidence for underlying expectations. In R. Freedle (Ed.), *Advances in discourse processing.* (Vol. 2). Norwood, NJ: Ablex.

Walberg, H. (1982). What makes schooling effective? An analysis and critique of three national studies. *Contemporary Education Review, 1,* 102–120.

Walberg, H., Schiller, D., & Haertel, G. (1979). The quiet revolution in educationalresearch. *Phi Delta Kappan, 61,* 179–183.

Wallat, C., & Green, J. (1982). Construction of social norms. In K. Borman (Ed.), *Social life of children in a changed society*(pp. 97–121). Hillsdale, NJ: Erlbaum.

Weade, R. (1985). *Lesson construction and instructional management: An explorationof social and academic content demands within lessons.* Paper presented at the annual meeting of the American Educational Research Association, Chicago, IL.

Weinstein, C. S. (1977). Modifying student behavior in an open classroom through changes in the physical design. *American Educational Research Journal, 14,* 249–262.

Wittrock, M. (1985, June). Enlarging the conception of educational psychology, *Newsletter for Educational Psychologists, 8,* 1–2. (Publication of Division 15, American Psychological Association).

CHAPTER 17

Future of Educational Measurement

Barbara S. Plake and Gerald J. Melican

Introduction

As a field, educational measurement has strong and essential ties to educational psychology. Practitioners in educational measurement, almost by definition, are closely linked to educational psychology for the basis of their theoretical and pedagogical principles. Researchers in educational measurement are often dependent on educational psychologists for the theoretical underpinning of the psychometric principles and applications they pursue in their scholarly endeavors. Reciprocally, educational psychologists rely on educational measurement for providing the essential psychometric tools for analyzing and applying their educational psychology theories and practices. The details of this close and necessary linkage between educational psychology and educational measurements will be addressed further in this chapter, which will focus on how this interrelationship may evolve and expand in the future.

The history of educational measurement has been marked by pragmatism, practicality, controversy, and critical analysis. Beginning with Binet's test to identify French students in need of re-

mediation and special schooling, through the Army Alpha era of categorizing military inductees on "general intelligence" measures, to the "minimum competency" movement of identifying students who have mastered certain minimal competencies necessary for high school graduation, the practitioners in the field of educational measurement have, to a large extent, reacted to perceived needs of society. The development of the field of educational measurement has, then, been directed at specific goals or definable objectives and will, in all likelihood, continue to be so directed. The future of educational measurement will likely follow in the directions (and misdirections) of its recent past.

One way to predict the future of educational measurement, then, is to analyze the criticisms and objectives that are currently being addressed, thereby identifying new directions that may become the vogue and identifying sources of criticism that will require expenditures of time and effort by educational measurement specialists. For example, one of the criticisms that has been leveled at educational measurement specialists is that they are too concerned with the "hows" instead of the "whys" of testing. Measurement experts are often viewed as interested in developing esoteric measurement tools or in concentrating on "data crunching" aspects instead of providing clear, lucid answers to practical measurement problems. In

Barbara S. Plake • Department of Educational Psychology, University of Nebraska, Lincoln, NE 68588. Gerald J. Melican • Educational Testing Service, Princeton, NJ 08541.

the future, as in the past, members of the measurement community will need to spend increased effort on explaining their "esoteric" theories in a manner less riddled with jargon and with an eye toward applications. Teachers, students, and test takers are the consumers of the measurement specialists' products and educating these consumers about the usefulness of measurement tools should be as high a priority as is refining and developing new tools.

There are a few sources that can be used to identify what may be reasonably important to the future of educational measurement. One such source is the National Council on Educational Measurement (NCME), a major organization for professionals in educational measurement. Recently, NCME's board of directors sponsored the development, administration, and analysis of an instrument designed to identify topics of interest to the members of its organization. The survey was mailed in the summer of 1983 to all active members of NCME, who were asked to rate a list of 26 measurement topics using a 1 to 5 scale (1 = little or no interest, 5 = extremely pertinent topic). Specific details of the results are summarized elsewhere (Plake & Berk, 1984), but generally, the top three rated topics were (a) computer applications to testing, (b) issues in test construction, and (c) alternative methods of testing. Least popular topics were (a) bilingual testing, and (b) measurement in the health area. The results of the survey of NCME membership did clearly identify topics of keen interest to the membership and those of markedly less interest. If this measure of interest can be used as an index of the directions of the field, which seems reasonable, then future emphasis in educational measurement might be on computerized testing, new developments in the arena of testing and item construction, and toward alternative methods of testing. In general, somewhat less emphasis would be given to specific subgroup needs in testing.

One important external impact on the future directions of educational measurement is from litigation and legislation. Legal decisions over the past couple of decades have produced profound effects on educational programming and opportunity (e.g., *Brown vs. Board of Education,* 1954; *Hobson vs. Hansen,* 1967). Several recent court cases have focused more directly on the role of measurement and testing in the educational process and decision making. Decisions from *Larry P. vs. Riles* (1979) and *PASE vs. Hannon* (1980), for

example, both concern the validity of intelligence tests for decision making with minority groups. More recently, legal cases have focused on the curriculum validity of minimum competency tests (*Debra P. vs. Turlington,* 1981). An important feature of the legal decision process is that the final outcome of these cases rests in the hands and minds of non-psychometrically trained personnel (juries and judges). Even though psychologists, educators, and psychometricians may appear in the legal process as expert witnesses, the ultimate decisions are being formulated by persons who are to a large extent psychometrically naive.

In addition to legal decisions as an external source of direction for the field of educational measurement, legislation involving education and testing is being considered at most state levels. Many states have passed (or are considering) bills that require minimum levels of academic competency for high school graduation, teacher certification, and/or recertification. As was true with the legal system, the decision making body for these legislative actions are, for the most part, not expert in the areas of measurement and testing.

Another useful source for predicting the future directions of educational measurement is a volume currently in preparation in a series entitled the *Buros/Nebraska Symposium Series on Measurement and Testing.* This volume (Plake & Witt, 1986) contains a collection of invited papers on several important areas of educational measurement: aptitude and achievement testing, minimum competency and criterion referenced testing, and computerized applications to testing.

This chapter will focus on three major areas of educational testing: use of aptitude and achievement tests, use of computers in assessment, and use of tests for decision making. These areas were selected because they are directly related to the major themes revealed by the NCME survey and the Buros volume. A fourth section will be dedicated to the impact of the American Educational Research Association (AERA)/American Psychological Association (APA)/National Council on Measurement in Education (NCME) *Joint Technical Standard for Educational and Psychological Tests* (1985). This revised manual of technical criteria for educational and psychological tests promises to have a dramatic impact on the development, application, and evaluation of educational and psychological tests. The final section of the chapter will then attempt to integrate these sections into a meaningful unit and to provide a logical framework for a set of conclusions pertaining to the future of educational measurement.

Aptitude and Achievement Testing

The major thrust of educational measurement has always been achievement and aptitude testing. Since its early history in America, one of the primary purposes of educational measurement has been the measurement of educational abilities (or aptitudes) and outcomes (or achievements). Although the emphases have purportedly changed since the introduction of the initial educational instruments, the most remarkable element over these decades is the limited change in the test instruments themselves. Paper and pencil, multiple choice tests continue to be the most frequently used method of testing.

Recently, however, there have been some important influences on traditional approaches to the measurement of aptitudes and achievements. In particular, cognitive psychology has provided radically different conceptions of human intelligence and subject area capabilities. Further, the refinement of latent trait theories has affected some important elements of aptitude and achievement test construction and use. In addition, typical methods of reporting the results of achievement tests have come under fire. These influences will be examined in greater depth in the subsections that follow.

Influences of Cognitive Psychology. The field of cognitive psychology has been providing an array of theoretical developments targeted toward understanding intellectual processing (see Glaser, 1981; Messick, 1984; Sternberg, 1984). The specifics of the theories vary, but the general trend is toward conceptualizations of information processing and cognitive capacity in multidimensional terms (Whitely, 1981). These recent developments, therefore, are far different from the earlier unidimensional conception of aptitude and achievement (see Anastasi, 1984; Ebel, 1969). These multidimensional models have been translated into some recent aptitude batteries. For example, the K-ABC (Kaufman & Kaufman, 1983) was based on the theoretical framework of sequential and simultaneous information processing models (e.g., Beller, 1970; Neisser, 1967; Das, Kirky, & Jarman, 1975). The Kit of Factor-Referenced Cognitive Test (Ekstrom, French, Harman, & Derman, 1967) was based on the theoretical model suggested by Merrifield (1975) for a Tetrahedral Model of Intelligence. Evidence for the merit of these recent reconceptualizations of intelligence is being gathered slowly because of the time required to demonstrate the predictive validity or utility of these instruments.

Item Response Theory. Aptitude and achievement testing have also benefited from the recent attention to latent trait theories, particularly Item Response Theory (IRT) (Bejar, 1983). Latent trait theories involve specifying mathematical functions relating observed behavior (e.g., job performance by a teacher) to underlying, unobservable traits (e.g., knowledge of pertinent field, ability to communicate knowledge, ability to interact with students). IRT is a family of mathematical functions used to relate performance on test items to an underlying ability. If the particular IRT function is appropriate, the probability that an examinee of a particular level of ability will answer any item correctly can be ascertained, even if similar items have never been administered to similar examinees. The ability to make probabilistic statements in this manner has great implications for educational measurement, especially in the areas of equating, preequating, assessment programs such as the National Assessment of Educational Progress (NAEP), and adaptive testing.

In testing programs it is often necessary to develop multiple forms of an examination in order to provide test security or to keep the test material current. No matter how well the test development effort is performed, there will be differences in the difficulties between these examinations. Reporting scores as the number correct or as the percentage of items answered correctly would be misleading to examinees who took different test forms because of the differences in difficulty between test forms. For example, a raw score of, say, 25 on one form of the examination may not denote the same level of ability as a raw score of 25 on a second form because of these differences in difficulty. Statistical procedures have been developed to transform the scores on one or both forms of these separate examinations to a common scale so that "scaled scores" of equal magnitude will denote equal ability. After equating, it should be a matter of indifference to an examinee which form of the examination is administered. Classical methods of equating have been most commonly used but methods based on IRT are becoming commonplace. One reason for this switch to IRT methods of equating is that equatings based on IRT may be more accurate and stable than classical equating methods over a reasonably long chain of equatings (Peterson, Cook, & Stocking, 1983). As an example of such a chain of equatings, consider a sequence of four test forms, A, B, C, and D, where B is equated to A and the scores from both placed on a common scale. Form C is now equated for form B and the scores from C are placed on the common scale and, finally, form D is equated to form C and the scores of form D are placed on the same scale as A and B (and C), even though form D was not directly equated to forms A or B. As testing programs grow and develop over time, the need for equating over such chains of equating is becoming more common.

One typical equating using classical methods involves having an overlap of items between the "old" form of the examination and the "new" form (Angoff, 1984). These overlap items are a minitest (often called the "anchor test") designed to mimic the content and difficulty of the total test so as to provide a link between the old and new forms. Therefore, with classical methods it is necessary to administer the examination intact so that the total score and the score for this minitest can be computed for each examinee before equating can be performed. This requirement leads to a rather long time interval between the administration of an examination and the reporting of results.

IRT affords the first real possibility of performing "preequatings" (placing scores from a form onto the common scale before the form is administered) because with IRT it is the items themselves that are analyzed (or "calibrated") and the item parameters that are equated to a common scale. New items are introduced into the calibrated item pool through a process of pretesting. This involves placing the items into a current form but not using these items when computing an examinees' score. Because the operational items in the test have all been calibrated previously using pretesting, the conversion table for establishing scaled scores for each examinee is already known. The pretest items can be calibrated after scores have been reported and then parameters for these items can be placed onto the scale common to the established pool of items. These items can now be placed into a new form of the examination and used as operational items to establish scores for examinees while a new set of pretest items is being administered for calibration as the cycle continues (see Cowell, 1982). Therefore, the equating analy-sis that previously required substantial time after the administration to complete because the equating algorithms were dependent (in part) on current examinee test performance can be completed before the administration by using the preequating of items via IRT methodology. Preequating, then, will eliminate the long time interval that was previously required to complete test equations after administration of the test form before scores could be reported.

Another important application of IRT technology is the development of pools of calibrated items to be used for on-line computerized adaptive testing. In adaptive testing, the examinee's answer to some of the items can be used to identify the next set of items to be administered. A series of correct answers will lead to the administration of an item set requiring higher or equal ability whereas incorrect answers will prompt the administration of an item set requiring lower or equal ability. In this way the ability or achievement level of the examinee can be estimated with fewer items. Therefore, it is no longer be necessary for an individual student to be administered an achievement battery containing large numbers of items that are at an inappropriate developmental level (Green, 1983). The probability that one examinee will receive the exact same items as any other examinee, however, should be very low (approaching zero as the size of the item pool increases). Consequently, establishing a common scale for comparing these test scores would not be possible using classical test theory. Although theoretically feasible via IRT methodology, some recent studies suggest that establishing a common scale for scores from adaptive testing may not be always possible even with IRT methodologies (Dorans & Kingston, 1984; Stocking, 1984).

Although promising, the utility of these IRT methodologies for aptitude and achievement tests will be determined by the ability of these techniques to improve educational decision making and/or educational programs. Without such preliminary research, early adoption of IRT technology into testing programs may be somewhat risky leaps into an unknown realm of practice before thorough testing.[1] One wonders what a measurement organization equivalent to the Food and

---

[1]Several major programs have made the transition from theory into practice after reasonable amounts of research, e.g. Test of English as a Foreign Language (TOEFL), California Test of Basic Skills (CTBS).

Drug Administration would say about the early adoptions of new techniques prior to the safety research required in the parallel drug field. Without such a governance regulation board, however, consumers of educational measurement are often at the mercy of unethical or overzealous test developers, or misled groups in decision-making roles (such as judges or legislators).

A great deal of research in the near future will be devoted to evaluating the practicability of IRT methodology for common applications (i.e., uncomplicated equatings), comparing types of IRT models to each other and to the classical models, finding new applications, and integrating the methodology with instructional design. A major area that needs to be addressed is the integration of IRT capabilities with the Bayesian concepts of prior information and utility. A marriage of Bayesian techniques with Item Response Theory will facilitate the decision-making process in educational practice (Lord, 1980; Weiss & Kingsberry, 1984).

Grade-Equivalent and Age-Equivalent Scores. Another important controversy in educational achievement and aptitude testing involves the use of grade-equivalent or age-equivalent scores. Relying heavily on sciences in which scales as height/weight are easily conceptualized, analogous scales have been developed for education. The information in grade- (or age-) equivalent scores summarize the grade level (or age) of the group of students for which a particular score was typical (i.e., the median score in the distribution of scores for that grade, or age, level). This is analogous to reporting a particular weight as being the typical weight of a specific age (or height) group of children. Although most people are not tempted to generalize height- or age-equivalent scores (as in the weight example) to the extremes of proposing that 10-year-old children whose weights are equal to a typical 18-year-olds be treated or dressed like their age equivalent, grade-equivalent scores in achievement testing are often subject to precisely these kinds of interpretations. Arguments regarding grade-equivalent scores vary from the practical ("nobody can understand them or make reasonable decisions based on the information contained in them"), to the applied ("unequally interpretable grade/age equivalent scores are found at the extremes of grade/age distributions"), to the theoretical ("what does it mean conceptually to have a grade equivalent beyond the upper limits of the testing instruments?"). Much of the controversy, however, stems from inade-

quate education of users, unsound test development/scaling practices, or incomplete conceptualization of the theoretical framework for the score scales rather than an inherent problem with the scaling system itself (see Hoover, 1984). Developing better ways to educate test users and the public regarding these concepts has not received the attention it should. The future should include more attempts to explain these concepts clearly and accurately. John Hills has presented several short articles in *Educational Measurement: Issues and Practice* (e.g., 1983, 1984) that clarify several areas that have been confusing to test users. Wider dissemination of these types of articles would be highly beneficial to the consumers of testing.

Summary

Major predictions for the future of aptitude and achievement testing lie in the direction of developing new instruments to match recent conceptual developments in the areas of intellectual processing. Furthermore, the adoption of Item-Response-Theory-based technology will provide the mechanism through which several advances in test administration and analysis will be feasible.

Probably one of the most pervasive influences in the area of aptitude and achievement testing is that of computer applications to testing. The next section of this chapter is devoted to this topic, with specific reference to achievement and aptitude testing.

Future of Computers in Educational Measurement

A major technological development that will continue to have a dramatic effect on the field of educational measurement is that of computers, both mainframe and micro. In some cases the degree of activity is predictable, expected, and not unique to the measurement field. Other uses and involvements, on the other hand, are more surprising and specific to measurement. This section will outline the ways in which computers may influence the field of educational measurement. It will draw heavily on recent and current ventures into the uses of computers in education, building on the strengths and weaknesses of these forays. Further, continuing the theme begun earlier in this chapter, this section will focus on specific outcomes or uses for which computers may become a vehicle for educational measurement. The first three sections identify the areas in the testing process where computers are predicted to have substantial impact: test development, test administration, and test scoring and reporting. Next, a discussion is presented on the probable impact of the computer on the role of measurements in educational research. A separate subsection then addresses the development of computerized searchable data bases of educational and psychological instruments. A final subsection providing a glimpse into a classroom of the future follows and forecasts ways in which computers may become integrated into the ongoing future classroom environment. This section concludes with a summary that focuses on the philosophical and technological issues of the computer in educational measurement.

Test Development

The test development sequence begins with the formulation of tables of specification typically based on extensive reviews of the content area or curriculum. Only after establishing the tables of specification, which should include descriptions of appropriate item types, should item writing begin. There already have been several attempts at incorporating the computer into the item-writing process of test development. Some of these attempts are quite mundane, basically using the computer as a storage and retrieval device, perhaps taking advantage of data base options. Others have used the computer in somewhat more imaginative ways, for example, in having the computer supply randomly chosen phrases or grammatical structures to item stems or alternatives (Roid, 1986). This is particularly attractive for mathematical items in equation solving where, by having the computer generate numbers at random, a unique set of "parallel" items may be developed. Even though these uses of the computer in item writing have been described as more imaginative than the clerical procedures mentioned earlier, it is still in the drill and practice mode, with little more than a computer generated "fill in the blank." This use of computers is limited and does not fully utilize the capacity of the equipment.

Jason Millman has been doing some of the more adventurous work in the area of item development via computers. His work involves the establishment of a network of foundations and concepts from a subject field (e.g., mathematics, agriculture) and building into the computer the rules and connecting linkages between concepts and foundations for the subject field (Millman, 1984). Through this structure, it is theoretically possible to have the computer generate the test items that will become part of the test. Although this work is only fledgling, it does represent a first step in the direction of truly computer-generated item development. Researchers in the fields of psychometrics and artificial intelligence will be developing comprehensive theories and techniques that will apply to this area of item development and generation.

Item Statistics. A further way that the computer has affected test development is in the area of calculating and summarizing descriptive item statistics. Once test items have been written and pretested they should be subjected to a thorough review concerning their psychometric properties because, in most cases, faulty items (i.e., items that have been miskeyed or items that are ambiguous) can be detected using simple item statistics, such as the percent answering correctly and the correlation of the item with the total test score. Further, when new forms of an examination are constructed using previously used items (e.g., from an item bank of precalibrated items), items with borderline or poor statistics can be eliminated or revised. The computer provides the capability of analyzing item performance for large numbers of examinees, numbers that would need to be drastically reduced without computer access. It is interesting to note, however, that even with extremely large samples, faulty items may not be detected (Wainer, 1983), because large numbers can not replace human judgment. In any case, items should generally not be excluded (or included) in a test simply for statistical reasons. If the items are not flawed, items with poor statistics that cover the content area are superior to items with better statistics that are only tangential to the content area.

The computer also facilitates developing item statistics through establishing their IRT parameters. These calculations are quite laborious, and in many cases, impractical (and possibly impossible) without the computer. The computer will allow for easier computation of item bias statistics. Collection of demographic information for large numbers of examinees and calculations of item basis statistics, including IRT parameters, will be facilitated.

Test Administration

Once a test has been fully developed, pretested, and equating systems prepared, the next involvement of computers is in the actual administration of the instrument. The administration of tests themselves via computers opens the door to a variety of new and interesting dimensions of test presentation and recording. In addition to the possibility of varying the specific items delivered to individual examinees via computers (as was discussed under adaptive testing), it is also possible to measure a variety of other test-taking behaviors aside from choice of answer. For example, response time or lag, use of touch screen, and physiological receptors sensitive to, for example, changes in skin response and heart rate (Roid, 1986) are all feasible with interactive computerized testing. In addition, computer technology allows for unique kinds of item presentation. The computer can be programmed to deliver items that simulate "real life" situations through the use of pictorial or figural displays. For example, an item that previously required a long introduction in order to describe the conditions for a problem in conservation of liquid using Piagetian theory could be shown through a series of changing visual displays. Items for a physics or chemistry examination that may require motion or change also could be enhanced by utilizing computerized delivery of item stems or alternatives. Coupled with other technology, the computer can present interactive videodisk simulations of real problem-solving cases that also allow for potentially more valid and realistic measurement of skills and achievements. This is already being planned in the field of emergency room medicine, where rather than having the physician read a description of a crowded, pulsing emergency room with accident victims arriving momentarily (providing the foundation for a planning problem, for example) the examinee in the interactive videodisk presentation of this item would hear the screeching sirens approaching, see the conditions of the emergency room, and then be asked the relevant questions regarding planning. Simulation items, including items using videodisk simulations, add an extra feature of realism to items that in previous years required long and sometimes complex text introductions. In addition to making the items more realistic and therefore potentially more valid, the use of visual and/or auditory presentation along with written test items may remove some of the potential confounding of these previous items due to their earlier heavy reliance on reading comprehension, vocabulary, and other predominantly verbal skills.

The field of medicine has been a front runner in the use of interactive test administration for a number of years. One frequently used technique in the medical field, in tests for licensure and/or certification, is called a "Patient Management Problem" (PMP). In PMPs the examinee's responses to a question determine the next step that an examinee will take. Some PMPs are linear in nature, with each examinee following the same path of questions as each other examinee. In linear PMPs, the examinees vary in the number of responses they make to a question before moving on to the next question; one examinee may choose Option "C" to Question 1 and be directed to Option "D" before moving on to Question 2 whereas a second examinee may choose Option "D" first and be immediately directed to Question 2. Some PMPs are truly branching with the possibility of examinees following different paths than other examinees. For example, an examinee who answers "D" to Question 1 may be told to go on to Question 3 whereas the examinee who answers "C" may be told to go on to Question 2. This mode of testing requires a specialized test booklet or computer program. Such a procedure leads to a number of technical problems in the analysis of PMP test results (for example, some of the branches are more difficult than others, and depending on the scoring procedure, may yield higher scores than another branch that might lead to more immediate resolution of the patient's problem). However, the realism of PMPs has been identified as a strength of the technique (Kane, 1986) and recent advances in videodisk technology will allow even more realistic simulations. With computer coordination, the number of branches (alternative routes) will be limited only by the test writer's ability to anticipate real world responses. Further, psychometric developments in the areas of scoring and reliability may solve some of the more pervasive technical problems surrounding this test administration strategy.

Although computerized test administrations appear to be a fertile area in educational measurement, there are still a number of issues, technical and practical, that need to be resolved. Many educators and psychometricians question the validity and interpretability of normative comparisons possible with adaptive testing. Further, the IRT theory required is extremely complex and sophisticated, removing the direct interpretability of the test results away from the teacher, who no doubt will be curious about how students who take different items on a test can be compared on a common score continuum.

Furthermore, the high expense of the support machinery and technical staff to provide computerized adaptive testing and alternative modes of testing may, at least at the present, price these techniques out of the range of many school systems and testing programs. Finally, there are some important technical problems that impede the general acceptance of adaptive testing that are still being addressed by researchers in the field. Obviously, several problems and concerns will need to be answered by the field of educational measurement before the standard use of adaptive and computerized testing will become a reality.

Test Scoring and Reporting

Computerized scoring, in addition to facilitating the traditional total score determination, allows for complex variations of scoring, such as the assignment of differential weights to options (Roid, 1983), and analyses of patterns of errors in diagnostic achievement test scoring (Birenbaum & Tatsuoka, 1982, 1983). The incorporation of computerized scoring algorithms by test publishers has already allowed for better and more reliable test interpretation and recording. Some recent advances in IRT theory allow for the calculation and identification of aberrant test performances, thereby allowing for consideration of such undesirable test taking behaviors as random marking or cheating.

By using the data base features of the computer, it is now easily possible to provide such interpretative information as local norms, large city norms, and conditional score distributions by groups such as age and aptitude. This kind of information has already made its way into many school systems' annual reports and evaluation guides. As noted previously, separate forms of the same examination are not generally of equal difficulty and reporting results as raw scores or percent of items correct is usually considered inappropriate. Although classical linear equating methods can be performed without the computer, the time and effort can be considerable and nonlinear methods would almost never be performed without the computer. IRT methods are virtually impossible without the aid of the computer.

Educational Research

Measurement often plays a vital role in educational research by providing instrumentation for the quantification of the dependent variables. In addition to changing and enhancing many of the aspects of test-item development, delivery, and analysis of instruments used in educational research, the computer also has the potential for improving the types and kinds of research questions that may be addressed in educational research (Johnson, 1983). Basically, the computer has the potential for impact on educational research in three ways: (a) in providing additional control of the delivery of educational treatments or conditions, (b) in facilitating the measurement of specific dependent variables, and (c) in allowing for consideration of variables that previously were only tangentially measurable in educational research.

By using the computer as a controlling device for the delivery of educational research materials, treatment delivery can be standardized in ways that were previously nearly impossible. For example, in prose comprehension research, time on task is often a confounding variable in a study designed to investigate the impact of specific adjunct aids developed to improve the retention of material. Using the computer as the deliverer of the test content, it is more feasible to control subjects for time on task than by the utilization of assistants with stop watches. More importantly, it is possible to control exactly what the subject is attending to (and not allowed to inspect visually) via computer delivery of text content. Therefore, the computer allows for systematic control of many previously confounding variables in many types of educational research.

Further, the computer facilitates the ability to deliver unique material to treatment groups, including the option of individualizing the treatment materials to the subjects within a treatment condition. In the case of prose comprehension research, a confounding variable related to time on task is individual reading rates. By presenting subjects with a preliminary set of reading materials and directions to stroke specific keys to signal test completion, the computer can serve as a mechanism to first calculate the reading rate of an individual subject and then to deliver the prose materials at a specific rate for that particular subject. Another example of this aspect of enhanced research design can be seen in studies investigating adaptive testing and programmed learning techniques.

As mentioned earlier, the computer can be used to keep track of and measure some subject variables that have been traditionally difficult to assess. For example, the computer can be programmed not only to record the subject's responses to questions displayed via a computer terminal, but also to record the time required to respond to that question and the intensity of the key stroke. Therefore, in a study to measure the degree of cognitive dissonance created by pairing of two objects for a preference choice, for example, the computer could not only note the final choice, but also record the time required by the subject to determine his or her preference. Other possibilities mentioned earlier include sensory monitors attached to the keyboard and/or subjects to record simultaneously skin temperature or heart rate. Through the coupling of sensory and computer technology, it is possible to complement the set of dependent variables in, for example, a motivation study.

There are some additional dimensions of the integration of computer technology and educational research that have only recently begun to be recognized and utilized in educational research. By incorporating the computer totally into the research design it is possible to address some important educational research questions that were only tangentially accessible before. One example of such an application of computer methodology to educational research is in a study designed to investigate the cognitive processing demands of certain types of measurement items. Many researchers in educational measurement have attempted to quantify the conceptual demands of educational materials (see Seddon, 1978). Recently Plake, Glover, Kraft, & Dinnel (1984) have utilized a methodology developed by Britton (e.g., Britton & Tessor, 1981; Britton, Glynn, Meyer, & Penland, 1982) to examine this research question. This methodology employs the computer in several ways. First, items that are hypothesized to differ in cognitive processing demands are presented randomly, one at a time, to subjects using a computer monitor. Occasionally, while the item is displayed, and at randomly determined intervals, a tone is emitted by the computer. Time to respond to the tone (subjects are instructed to strike the space bar as rapidly as possible upon hearing the tone) is tracked by the computer. Current research using this methodology shows a marked difference in mean reaction time by subjects to items that were designed to require more cognitive processing as opposed to those designed to require less cognitive processing. Therefore, by using a cognitive psychology technique and the computer, it is possible to address a cognitive processing question regarding test items that was elusive to educational researchers prior to computer technology.

Although the computer has served to advance the control and quality of educational research, it has also introduced a set of problems unique to this research methodology that require consideration. First, in order to gather data via computer, each subject must have access to a computer facility. Many times this entails serial delivery of the research study to the subjects, requiring hours and weeks of individualized scheduling and monitoring of the subjects. Second, many of the research delivery programs will be written under a specific operating system that restricts the transportability of the procedure to other computers without minor (or, in some cases, major) modifications. This has clear implications for replicability of these studies. Because the field of microcomputer hardware and software is still in a transition state where several noncompatible machines are competing for large shares of the consumer market, and because software designed to convert one language system to another is still in early developmental stages, current educational researchers are most likely bound by the hardware and software specifically designed for the computer equipment at hand at the researcher's locale. Third, there are also unique problems with confidentiality and consent of subjects when utilizing computer technology for educational research studies. Some subjects might find the addition of assessing and monitoring body functions in the research study confusing and/or threatening and institutional research review boards will probably need further explanation of this kind of educational research. Fourth, there is some preliminary research that suggests that the use of the computer as a medium for delivering research instruments may distort the applicability of the existing norms and validity data gathered previously via a paper and pencil method (Roid, 1986). Thus, problems of accessibility, replicability, confidentiality, and comparability of existing norms need to be addressed and solved before educational research incorporating computer technology can achieve its highest and most promising possibilities.

Searchable Data Bases

Another important application of computer technology to educational measurement is the incorporation of information about test instruments onto a computerized data base. For example, the Buros Institute of Mental Measurements, in cooperation with the Bibliographic Retrieval Service, is in the process of establishing, updating, and refining a searchable data base containing psychometric information and reviews of many educational and psychological instruments (Mitchell, 1984a). By taking advantage of the data base features of computer technology, it is possible to search for specific instrument types, conditioning on many relevant psychometric dimensions (e.g., reliability values and/or target population). Although this application of computer technology is not unique to the field of educational measurement, the advantages to researchers and practitioners are remarkable.

Computer Integration in the Classroom

An interesting frontier for computers in educational measurement is their integration into an ongoing process within the educational system. In this integration the feedback loop between achievement, assessment, and instructional planning would be connected and facilitated by the computerized system. Cole (1983) has described a "fantasy into the classroom of the future." Admitting that this was her own fantasy, conditioned by her personal values and expectations, Cole presented a picture of the future of education that relied heavily on computers in the classroom. The hypothetical teacher presented classroom group exercises through that medium, and based on diagnostic information derived from the class performance, additional drill and practice was made available to students needing specific instruction. Diagnostic testing was done via the computer, as was the delivery of specialized remediation activities. The teacher was able to monitor students' performance, keeping current records of progress and problems. The teacher's computer was also tied into the computer network serving the administrative unit of the school and district as well as each child's home computer. Therefore, continual communication was possible with the parents and school administration. All achievement testing was done on line and was adaptive with immediate scoring and interpretation reports provided to the communication network, under a security lock system. Education was individualized, diagnostic, and communication was open.

Cole's fantasy, however, is not without its problems and controversies. First, the financial underpinnings of her educational future are staggering under current fiscal constraints. Every child would be provided with a computer terminal at school, home computers would be necessary for every family, and a computer network system for the administration communication link would need to be developed. Problems of compatibility and feasibility obviously exist for this fantasy. A more pervasive problem though is the educational philosophy on which it is based. Humanism might become secondary to efficiency and achievement highlighted over self-esteem and social competency. However, these problems are not a function of computerized integration *per se,* but are due to current limitations in software and teacher awareness. Most current computer programs are mechanical and, at the present time, most teachers view the computer as a tool to provide drills and practice. When more complex educational software becomes available, increase in other types of usage will result. Appropriate educational software will be such that, after instruction (by the teacher or, periodically, by the computer) the student will sit at the computer terminal for practice sessions during which the student will be provided with problems and/or scenarios that encourage and challenge the student. These exercises will allow the computer and teacher to identify areas in need of further explanation and work so that diagnosis of weak areas is nearly immediate. Thus, the computer will not decrease the teacher's work load but instead allow for more appropriate use of the teacher's time. The student will not have a computer as the main source of instruction but, instead, will have the computer as a tutor, textbook, workbook, and examination booklet rolled into one. The human interaction not only will still be available but, if computer assisted instruction is applied appropriately, will be of higher quality.

The challenge for the education community is to develop the appropriate and effective software and to increase teachers' knowledge and acceptance of the machines. The measurement challenge is to coordinate the testing area with tutorial aspects to provide students with diagnostic feedback and teachers with information sufficient for their teaching and grading needs.

Summary

The potential for computer technology to have a major impact on educational measurement is great. It is hard to imagine a future test development sequence that does not rely heavily on computer technology for item development, storage, retrieval, and analysis. Additional aspects of computer integration in the testing process include item delivery, adaptive testing, and score reporting. Illustrating the heavy reliance of testing on computer technology in the future, a recent volume titled *New Horizons in Testing* (Weiss, 1983) focuses exclusively on Latent Trait Test Theory and Computerized Adaptive Testing, both of which place heavy emphasis on computer coordination in testing.

The impact of computer technology on educational measurement, however, is more pervasive than just in test design, development, delivery, and documentation. Computers have the potential for enhancing measurement tools and techniques for the educational researcher. Perhaps even more dramatic, however, is the potential for computer technology to influence the entire educational environment. The glimpse into the future provided by Cole suggests an educational system that involves the computer at nearly every level and stage. The interrelationship between education and measurement, in a direct feedback loop of information and decision making, is connected more strongly with the integration of computers in the classroom and school environment. Many of the potential problems and concerns, then, that may appear at the surface to be related only to the educational system, and not directly to the field of educational measurement, become increasingly more relevant to educational measurement. For example, an educational system totally integrated with computer technology, as conceived by Cole, depends to a large degree on the validity of the measurement information for making adequate and correct decisions about what additional or unique educational materials should be made available to the student. The current state of the art in such educational decision making lacks sufficient sophistication to allow for such implementation. In addition, a research base is not sufficiently developed to demonstrate that specially designed materials to augment or complement learning style strengths is necessarily advantageous or desirable. Thus, although the ability to provide volumes of data about a child's educational needs and achievements will be enhanced by integration of the computer in the classroom, the application of that data in making improved or valid educational decisions regarding the educational needs of students has yet to be realized.

Further, how computers fit into the field of educational measurement in the future is in large part a function of many unresolved educational and philosophical issues. Although the technology exists, and in isolated cases has already been put into practice, the incorporation of the computer into an integrated educational process has not been fully accepted by educators. Many educators question the desirability of computer integration in meeting the educational goals of the students. Some believe that the amount of information that can be presented via the computer is too limited to be effective. Others are concerned with the possibility that the ultimate effect will be a limiting of the person to person interaction and of the dynamics of the teacher-student-classroom climate. The field of education has faced similar philosophical debates before, but the resolution of this issue will no doubt have major implications for the integration of computer technology into the educational system. As the field of education is reevaluating itself, and as society is reevaluating the importance of the educational system, issues of computerized educational systems will become more salient. Whether the day will come when the teacher is a technician monitoring an educational process controlled by a computerized educational program depends on the degree of acceptance of the computer by educators and the amount of involvement they have in the software development.

Testing for Decision Making

The end of the baby-boom era has decreased the number of students who will take college admission examinations but, on the other hand, there has been an increase in the number of people taking licensing and certification examinations. There has also been an increase in the number of professions desiring to establish licensing or certification requirements. Combined with the minimum competency movement, the result is an intense interest in criterion-referenced testing. Although the criterion-referenced concept is not new, the uses of criterion-referenced tests (CRTs) has now surpassed many of the methodologies available for appropriate test development, analysis of item behavior, and for establishing passing levels.

Results from criterion-referenced examinations are meant to provide information regarding where the examinee stands with regard to some external performance standard (e.g., an examinee's score on the bar examination should be related to performance as an attorney). The interpretation is intentionally different from the interpretations one applies to the results of a norm-referenced test

(NRT), where the scores provide information regarding where an examinee falls with reference to a peer group (e.g., 30% of the examinees have scores below the examinee's score). In the bar examination example, an examinee passes or fails the examination on the basis of his or her standing relative to the criterion (or standard), not on the basis of his or her relative standing to a norm group. If the examinee's score is above the standard, he or she passes regardless of the number of fellow examinees above or below the examinee's score.

Item Statistics.   Typically, items from CRTs are indistinguishable from NRT items. However, the statistics used to review the quality of items in these two types of examinations are (or should be) distinctively different. NRTs are based on the theory that each and every score point indicates a different level of performance from any other score point, implying that the whole continuum of ability or achievement is of interest. A typical application of CRTs involves the use of cutoff scores, for example, assignment to pass/fail or license/nonlicense groups. This use of CRTs is based on the premise that a threshold level exists: a point below which the examinee is not competent and above which the examinee is competent (ignoring error of classification). In other words, the score continuum for this application of CRTs is viewed as a dichotomy with the passing point identifying the point above which all scores have the same meaning (pass) and below which all scores have the same meaning (fail).

Classical statistical indexes employed for evaluating the quality of NRT items and examinations reflect their reference to the total ability continuum. For example, the indexes for determining the discriminability of items generally involve correlating item responses (e.g., right/wrong) with overall performance on the examination (e.g., number of items answered correctly). The statistical indexes traditionally used to review the discrimination of an item in an NRT, point biserials and biserial correlations, are based on the premise that better performing examinees throughout the score continuum will be more likely to answer more items correctly. The biserial (or point biserial) correlation is between a variable that is dichotomous (item performance: pass or fail) and one that is continuous (test performance: total score).

For CRTs this inference regarding the entire score continuum is somewhat strained because the relationship between item performance and overall performance on a CRT should not be linear beyond the passing point or "cut-score." Because, in CRT, both the item performance and test performance are dichotomously scored (item performance: right or wrong; test performance: pass or fail), correlational indexes for NRTs are inappropriate. Phi or phi/phi max coefficients may be more applicable than biserial correlations as evidence of the discriminating power of an item in this circumstance because these coefficients are relationship indexes between two variables that are dichotomously scored. There is no universal agreement as to which discrimination indexes are appropriate (for either CRTs or NRTs) and further research is needed before any definitive statements are possible.

Reliability.   Another area in need of research concerns the concept of CRT reliability. Again, reliability analogs found in NRT are generally based on the reference to the whole ability–achievement continuum. Classical indexes of reliability are generally interpreted as correlations, answering in one manner or another the question, "Will examinees with high scores on one form of an examination (or on one administration of a single form) have high scores on another form (or on another administration of the same form)?" This question is irrelevant for CRTs, where the important question is, "Will examinees who pass one form of an examination (or one administration of a single form) pass another form (or another administration of the same form)?" This question has been the subject of much research and many reliability indexes have been proposed as possible solutions. Coefficients such as those by Huynh (1976), Livingston (1972), and Subkoviak (1976) are just a few of the indexes that have been proposed. The Livingston coefficient is a direct application of the classical concept of reliability being equal to true score variance divided by total score variance. Livingston added a second term to both the numerator and the denominator, the square of the difference between the population mean on the examination and the cut-score—thus complementing NRT with CRT information. The Huynh and Subkoviak coefficients are estimates of consistency of categorization. That is, they are estimates of the degree to which the pass/fail status of examinees will be consistent from one testing situation to the next. The future of educational measurement will be replete with studies comparing these and other indexes for the reliability of CRTs.

Determination of Cut Scores. Problems regarding item statistics and CRT reliability indexes, however, are trivial compared to the problem of setting standards or "cut" scores for CRTs. If the steps of determining the appropriate content, developing test specifications, generating items, and constructing an examination form have all been completed adequately, the results would still be for naught if an inappropriate standard (passing score) is used.

Livingston and Zieky (1983) have described the major existing methods for establishing a passing score (except for the recent method proposed by Jaeger, 1978). Each of these standard-setting methods is based on different assumptions. The large body of research concerning comparisons of results obtained via these methods suggests that the standards derived by one method are likely not to be the same as those that would result if another method had been employed.

All standard-setting methods, however, require judgments—either judgments involving the items themselves and/or judgments concerning members of the target population. Any new methods for deriving standards will necessarily also include a judgmental component. If judgments of the minimum acceptable score are made by qualified individuals with adequate information and preparation, the judgmental aspect of standard setting is not necessarily a problem. The training of judges to make these decisions, then, becomes paramount. The methods for defining the "minimally competent candidate" need to be fully described in order to guide researchers and practitioners who are establishing standards for the first time. Further, research concerning methods of collecting useful information (e.g., performance on experimental subjects on all or a selection of the items) and methods for using these data (e.g., training the judges to replicate the collateral information or adjusting the judges' final results by a constant difference) needs to be carried out. Finally, research concerning methods for increasing individual judges' coherence (assigning the same rating to items of similar difficulty and content) should be pursued.

Any application of a cut score or standard will lead to errors of classification. Regardless of where the standard is set, competent examinees will fail and less than competent examinees will pass. Adjusting the standard to decrease the probability of one type of classification error (e.g., failing a competent examinee) will have the resultant effect of increasing the probability of the other type of error (e.g., passing an incompetent examinee). Adjustments to the standards established by the judgments of an expert committee are common in practice (e.g., setting the operational standard at one standard error of measurement below the standard actually established by the committee). Beuk (1984) has suggested a technique for devising a standard that adjusts the committee's standard by a factor dependent on their separate judgment about the percentage of examinees expected to pass the examination. Notice that this adds an element of norm referencing in the establishment of the standard. Methods that allow adjustments based on external information (e.g., other judges' opinions or previous performance of experimental subjects on selected items), and on utilizing information about the relative effects of error of classification are only a few of the areas in need of research and explication.

Summary

The field of educational measurement has grown beyond the exclusive use of traditional NRTs to examinations that provide specific information for decision making. Beyond addressing the psychometric issues of reliability, item analysis, and cut-score setting, for CRTs, there are philosophical questions to challenge the measurement community. One of the philosophical issues is whether testing for minimal competency will lead to mediocrity (Madaus, 1981; Popham, 1981). If students, for example, need to pass an examination to receive a high school diploma, will they concentrate on the courses that are most likely to increase their probability of passing to the exclusion of courses that are more challenging but less test specific? Will teachers continue to drill on the content of courses required for graduation to the detriment of the enrichment material? Answers to questions such as these will have an important impact on the direction, focus, and emphasis of tests for decision making in the future of educational measurement.

Implications of the Revised Joint Technical Standards on the Future of Educational Measurement

One of the major sources of influence on practitioners of educational measurement has been the set of standards developed by the AERA, APA, and NCME. These groups combined to prepare a replacement of the *Standards for Educational and Psychological Tests* (1974). Draft forms of these revised standards were accepted, in principle, by the executive committees of these three organizations by August, 1984.

Although in many ways these revised standards represent a confirmation of the previous set of standards prepared by these cooperating organizations (AERA, APA, & NCME, 1974), the *Revised Standards* differ in some very important aspects. Most notably, the revised set of standards provides clarification of the kinds and types of validity evidence that test publishers must provide, and adds new and critical standards for computerized testing and testing for decision making.

The purpose of this section of the chapter is to identify the potential impact of the *1985 Standards* on the future of educational measurement. Consistent with the other sections of this chapter, the specific areas of aptitude and achievement testing, computers in testing, and testing for decision making will be addressed. Obviously, the impact of the *Revised Standards* will have a broader impact on the field of measurement than just these subareas. Therefore, this section will take a limited view of the impact of the revised standards on educational measurement.

Aptitude and Achievement Testing

The major impact *Standards* will probably have is in clarifying the definition of validity. These changes are really clarifications of what most psychometricians believe to be true of validity. That is, they emphasize that the different components of validity separately identified in previous editions of the standards are really separate elements of a unified concept. Previously, validity was subdivided into the triumverate of content, criterion (predictive and concurrent), and construct validities. Many users of the previous standards elected to take this separation of validity as evidence for the existence of three distinct concepts of validity. The *Revised Standards* attempts to clarify this problem by stating that

validity . . . is a unitary concept. Although evidence may be accumulated in many ways, validity always refers to the degree to which that evidence supports the inferences that are made from the scores. It is the inferences regarding specific uses of a test that are validated, not the test itself. Traditionally, the various means of accumulating validity evidence have been grouped into categories called *content-related, criterion-relat-*

ed, and construct-related evidence of validity. These categories are convenient, . . . but the use of the category labels should not be taken to imply that there are distinct types of validity or that a specific validation strategy is best for each specific inference or test use. Rigorous distinctions between the categories are not possible. Evidence normally identified with the criterion-related or content-related categories, for example, also is relevant in the construct-related category. (p. 1)

The clarification of the concept of validity will not eliminate debates over the relative merits of the three types of evidence. Ebel (1983), for example, provided several cogent arguments for the preeminence of content (intrinsic rational) validity. Ebel's major point was that the other types of evidence (criterion and construct) place the burden on a criterion other than the instrument itself and that, if one has to make judgments anyway, it is better to make them about the instrument in question. Others argue for different relative ratings of the importance of validity evidence (see Cronbach, 1983). The *Revised Standards* call for the test developer to justify the manner of establishing validity and to explain further why other forms of evidence were not collected. Therefore, regardless of which source of validity is favored as the most relevant or important in a particular testing situation, the *Revised Standards* call for a consideration of all forms of validity evidence.

Tests for Decision Making

The previous *Standards* (1974) contained no identifiably separate standards for criterion-referenced tests. Although in some cases it was possible to infer reasonable standards, many of the standards developed for NRTs were inappropriate for CRTs. The *Revised Standards* will contain a separate section devoted to CRT's.

Examples of specific standards referring to the educational uses of tests designed for decision making are the following:

1. Test and instructional domain information should be described in enough detail to allow the match between domain and content domain to be evaluated. (Standard 9.5)
2. Specially designed technical reports and manuals should be developed and disseminated. (Standard 9.6)
3. Information about the results of the tests should be reported promptly, including a description of the test, what was measured, the conclusions and decisions that are based

on the test results, and the obtained score. Information on how to interpret the reported score and about the methods used to establish the classifications are requested. (Standard 9.7)

4. Multiple opportunities should be allowed for students to demonstrate mastery of skills or knowledge. (Standard 9.9)

Chapter 11 of the *Revised Standards* addresses standards for licensure and certification examinations. Consistent with the standards reported for CRTs in educational settings, these standards emphasize establishment of validity evidence that matches the content domain of the test with the importance of competent performance in the occupation or outcome being certified or licensed. These standards specify that tests such as these must meet a dual set of criteria: be psychometrically sound and legally defensible. Many technical problems still exist that present obstacles to reaching these ''minimal standards'' (e.g., choice of appropriate psychometric indices, cut-score methods). However, it is a step in the right direction to have the special, critical, and idiosyncratic area of decision making be recognized and delineated in the *Revised Standards*.

Computers in Testing

The impact of the *Revised Standards* on the role and use of computers in testing is expected to be substantial. First, many of the specifications regarding the need for psychometric evidence and supporting materials will result in even more involvement of computers in the test development and reporting phases. Second, due to the unique nature of computerized testing, the *Revised Standards* includes specific statements regarding the uses of computers in educational and psychological testing.

The evidence to be required by the *Revised Standards* for quantitative indexes of reliability and validity reinforces the integral role of computers in test development and publication. For example, the extensive research for documenting the validity of tests for a variety of educational and psychological purposes will need to be based on large data sets from representative samples of the population. Additionally, evidence to document the reliability of a test should include not only information about relevant sources of error, but also the types of decisions anticipated to be based on the test scores and

the expected level of aggregation of the test scores, (individuals versus groups).

The *Revised Standards* will have a more direct impact on computers in educational measurement because of the inclusion of special standards for computerized testing. In particular, the *Revised Standards* specify:

1. That the rationale and supporting evidence for procedures used in selecting items for administration, in stopping the test, and in scoring the test for adaptive testing be described in the test manual (Standard 3.9)

2. That sensitivity of test performance to improvements with practice, coaching, or brief instruction should be part of the research program of test publishers, especially on performance tests or computer-administered tests (Standard 3.14)

3. That score report forms and instructional materials for a test should be designed to facilitate interpretations, especially in the case of computer programs or computerized reports provided to test takers (Standard 3.16)

4. That computer services offering test interpretations make available information on the rationale of the test and a summary of the evidence supporting interpretations given (Standard 5.11)

5. That test users should not use computer-interpreted test results unless they have a manual for that test including information on the validity of the computer interpretations for the intended applications and on the samples on which they are based (Standard 8.14)

6. That testing environment should be one of reasonable comfort and minimal distractions; testing materials should be readable and understandable. In computerized testing, items displayed on a screen should be properly legible and free from glare, and the terminal should be properly positioned (Standard 15.3)

Summary

The *Revised Joint Technical Standard for Educational and Psychological Tests* provides the basis for substantial impact on the development, publication, and administration of educational tests. The degree of compliance with such standards by test developers, however, does not suggest ready acceptance (Mitchell, 1984b). Thus, whether these *Revised Standards* will actually make a marked impact on the field of educational measurement will depend to a large extent on the somewhat voluntary nature of the applications of these standards by professional test developers and users. The manner of dissemination and the degree of education regarding the standards will also influence their impact.

Conclusions

The future of educational measurement has been considered as an extension of the past developments and philosophical foundations of the field. Given its pragmatic and practical past, the field is predicted to remain reactive. However, in its efforts to develop and refine instruments and methods to aid in answering societal needs, the field of educational measurement will need to address some fundamental theoretical issues. These issues and concerns will likely bring the field closer to a unifying theoretical base. As an example, the new conceptualizations of intellectual processing will require a large amount of theory building by researchers and practitioners in educational measurement. Further, as research into the dynamics, dimensions, and applications of latent trait theories continues, new and exciting roles of testing in assessment and evaluation of educational goals will become possible.

There appears to be a number of areas in educational measurement for which exciting and important changes will occur in the future.

1. Continuing as the major thrust in educational assessment, aptitude and achievement testing will be affected by the development of instruments to assess new conceptualizations of intellectual functioning. In addition, aptitude and achievement tests will be refined through application of advances in equating and adaptive testing made possible by latent trait theories such as IRT.

2. Computers will become even more important in educational measurement. Beyond aiding the test development process by organizing and sorting item banks, it will also become a vehicle for developing conceptually sound test items.

3. Test and item analyses will become more sophisticated due to adherence to the recommendations from the *Revised Joint Technical Standards for Educational and Psychological Tests*. Increased sophistication will also be more likely due to computer support systems for test and item analyses.

4. Test administration will often involve the computer in the test delivery mode, either as a means of presenting realistic simulations or as a method for individualizing test administration (as in adaptive testing).

5. Test scoring procedures will become more varied, including in some cases analyses of error response patterns. Additional item performance information will also be assessed possibly through complex integration of sensory receptors connected to subjects.

6. Score reports will continue to become more complete and complex. Conditional distributions of test results already common in most large scale testing, will accompany more tests. Computerized score interpretations will also be utilized more in the future.

7. A concentration of intellectual and financial resources will be dedicated to development of instrumentation and psychometric procedures to accompany criterion-referenced tests. Initially, these effects will be in the direction of rapid technological and psychometrics advancements. Long-term predictions, however, are for more emphasis on the theoretical aspects regarding appropriate uses and functions of criterion-referenced systems of assessment.

8. Increased involvement in testing issues by external forces is expected. Legal and legislative systems will continue and expand their influences by requiring more and clearer justification for outcome decisions from licensure, admission, certification examination, and in the establishment of standards and guidelines for school graduation.

9. Expansion of the use of tests for granting educational credit is predicted. As more nontraditional students enter higher education, the possibility for backgrounds and experiences equalling undergraduate course material becomes greater. Further, programs at the secondary school level designed to match and complement the advanced educational needs of gifted and/or specialized students will increase. This will further the need for examination availability for awarding course credit.

10. Increased concerns and problems surrounding issues of minority representation, access, and test bias is anticipated due to several important and

possibly contradictory movements in education and measurement. On the one hand, cries for increased excellence have been echoed by educators, parents, students, and legislators (Payton, 1984). As a result, procedures have been proposed, and in several instances adopted, to increase the level of educational attainment of secondary students by (a) increasing the academic requirements for high school graduation, (b) changing the definitions of high school certification to include academic and nonacademic diplomas, and (c) requiring a standard of academic performance for high school graduation, typically measured by means of an examination. In addition, colleges and universities with teacher preparation programs have responded to the call for excellence in education with plans for increased academic credentials required for admission to their teacher preparation programs. However, the impact of immediate implementation of these collective sets of standards for graduation and/or teacher education programs will be to disallow access of a larger proportion of minority than majority group members (Navarro, 1984). Therefore, several minority group members, through their recent exposure to inadequate educational opportunities, will be denied access to teacher preparation programs at many institutions that have set reactive admission standards quickly and without consideration of alternative programs for applicants with potential but who are inadequately prepared to meet the revised standards.

Summary

In the three areas of concentration considered in this chapter (achievement and aptitude testing, computers, and decision making) a common theme was the need for education. Better descriptions of the uses and abuses of achievement and aptitude test results, better understanding of the techniques and the meaning of such terms as equating and grade-equivalent scales are needed. Many of the criticisms leveled at the educational measurement field are the result of a concerned but confused public. As the "truth in testing" movement grows and evolves, and as the sophistication of methods and theories increases, the need for appropriate educational training programs will also increase. A responsive and responsible profession, such as educational measurement, is expected to meet this need with a program of education for the consumers of its professional labors. John Hills' attempts in *Educational Measurement: Issues and Practice* (e.g., 1984) provide a limited model. More attempts of this sort coupled with wider dissemination are called for.

Predicting the future is a risky business. Even though the influencing factors and issues may be incorporated into an "intellectual algorithm" to determine the prediction, it is always possible, albeit at a later date, to validate and evaluate the quality and accuracy of these predictions. Robert L. Thorndike (1971) provided the field of educational measurement with his predictions of the field for the 1970s. In his projections for this recent era, he focused on aspects of (a) the impact of technological development, particularly item banks and computer-generated tests, sequential (adaptive) testing, and test scoring; (b) conceptual developments, focuses on the meaning and relative importance of the contributing aspects of test validity, issues involving the theoretical underpinnings of testing for decision making, and the initial stages of realistic item presentation (e.g., Patient Management Problems), and (c) social and political issues, concerning the impact of testing on educational practice, issues of fair use of tests with minority groups, and the importance of the maintenance of test quality via test criticisms and standards. It is interesting to note that whereas many of the specific developments and outcomes predicted by Thorndike have, in fact, transpired in the decade of the seventies, many of the same issues and concerns from that era are important ones for the eighties and beyond. This is not an indication of lack of progress for the field of educational measurement, but rather, a reality of the continual and unfolding development of any progressing field. The future is seen not only in the crystal ball of the futurist but, perhaps even more clearly, in the rearview mirror of the practitioners and researchers in the field.

References

AERA/APA/NCME Joint Committee. (1985). *Joint technical standards for educational and psychological testing*. Washington, DC: American Psychological Association.

Anastasi, A. (1984). Aptitude and achievement testing: The curious case of the indestructible strawperson. In B. S. Plake (Ed.), *Social and technical issues in testing: Implications for test construction and usage* (pp. 129–140). (Buros-Nebraska Symposium on Measurement and Testing) Hillsdale, NJ: Erlbaum.

Angoff, W. H. (1984). *Scales, norms, and equivalent scores* (pp. 85–127). Princeton, NJ: Educational Testing Service.

APA/AERA/NCME Joint Committee. (1974). *Standard for*

educational and psychological tests (rev. ed.). Washington, DC: American Psychological Association.

Bejar, I. I. (1983). *Achievement testing: Recent advances.* Beverly Hills, CA: Sage.

Beller, H. K. (1970). Parallel and serial stages in matching. *Journal of Experimental Psychology, 84,* 213–219.

Beuk, C. H. (1984). A method for reaching a compromise between absolute and relative standards in examinations. *Journal of Educational Measurement, 21(2),* 147–152.

Birenbaum, M., & Tatsuoka, K. (1982). On the dimensionality of achievement test data. *Journal of Educational Measurement, 19,* 156–266.

Birenbaum, M., & Tatsuoka, K. (1983). The effect of a scoring system based on the algorithm underlying the students' response pattern on the dimensionality of achievement test data of the problem solving type. *Journal of Educational Measurement, 22,* 17–26.

Britton, B. K., Glynn, S. M., Meyer, B. J. F., & Penland, M. S. (1982). Effects of text structure on use of cognitive capacity during reading. *Journal of Educational Psychology, 74,* 51–61.

Brown v. Board of Education, 347 U.S. 483 (1954).

Cole, N. S. (1983, October) *Future directions for educational achievement and ability testing.* Paper presented at the Buros-Nebraska Symposium on Measurement and Testing, Lincoln, NE.

Cowell, W. R. (1982). Item response theory pre-equating in the TOEFL testing program. In P. W. Holland & D. B. Rubin (Eds.), *Test equating* (pp. 149–161) New York: Academic Press.

Cronbach, L. (1983). What price simplicity? *Educational Measurement: Issues and Practice, 2(2),* 11–12.

Das, J. P., Kirby, J. R., & Jarman, R. F. (1975). Simultaneous and successive synthesis: An alternative model for cognitive abilities. *Psychological Bulletin, 82,* 87–103.

Debra P. v. Turlington, 474 F. Supp. (M.D. Fla. 1979).

Dorans, N., & Kingston, N. (1984). Item location effects and their implication for IRT equating and adaptive testing. *Applied Psychological Measurement, 8(2),* 146–154.

Ebel, R. L. (1983). The practical validation of tests of ability. *Educational Measurement: Issues and Practice, 2(2),* 7–10.

Ebel, R. L. (1984). Achievement test items: Current issues. In B. S. Plake (Ed.), *Social and technical issues in testing: Implications for test construction and usage* (pp. 129–140). (Buros-Nebraska Symposium on Measurement and Testing. Hillsdale, NJ: Erlbaum.

Ekstrom, R. B., French, J. W., Harman, H. H. & Derman, D. (1976). *Manual for Kit for Factor-Referenced Cognitive Tests.* Princeton, NJ: Educational Testing Service.

Glaser, R. (1981). The future of testing: A research agenda for cognitive psychology and psychometrics. *American Psychologist, 36,* 923–936.

Green, B. F. (1983). Adaptive testing by computer. In R. B. Ekstrom (Ed.), *Measurement, Technology, and Individuality in Education* (New Directions for Testing and Measurement No. 17, pp. 5–12). San Francisco: Jossey-Bass.

Hills, J. R. (1983). Interpreting grade-equivalent scores. *Educational Measurement: Issues and Practice, 2(1),* 15.

Hills, J. R. (1984). Interpreting NCE scores (Hill's Handy Hints), *Educational Measurement: Issues and Practice, 3(3),* 25–26.

Hobson v. Hansen, 269 F. Supp. 401 (D.D.C. 1967), aff'd sub nom. Smuck v. Hobson, 408 F.2d 175 (D.C. Cir. 1969)

Hoover, H. D. (1984). The most appropriate scores for measuring educational development in the elementary schools: GE'S. *Educational Measurement: Issues and Practice, 3(4),* 8–14.

Huynh, H. (1976). On the reliability of decisions in domain-referenced testing. *Journal of Educational Measurement, 13,* 253–264.

Jaeger, R. M. (1978). *A proposal for setting a standard on the North Carolina High School Competency Test.* Paper presented at the spring meeting of North Carolina Association of Research in Education, Chapel Hill, NC.

Johnson, J. W. (1983). Things we can measure through technology that we could not measure before. In R. B. Ekstrom (Ed.), *Measurement, technology, and individuality in education.* (New Directions for Testing and Measurement, No. 17, pp. 13–18). San Francisco, CA: Jossey-Bass, Inc.

Kane, M. T. (1986). The future of testing for licensure and certification examinations. In B. S. Plake & J. C. Witt (Eds.), *Future Directions for Testing* (Buros-Nebraska Symposium on Measurement and Testing). Hillsdale, NJ: Erlbaum.

Kaufman, A. S., & Kaufman, N. L. (1983). *Kaufman - Assessment Battery for Children (K-ABC).* Circle Pines, MN: American Guidance Service.

Larry P. v. Riles, 495 F. Supp. 926 (N.D. Cal. 1979), *appeal docketed,* No. 80-4027 (9th Cir., Jan. 17, 1980)

Livingston, S. A. (1972). Criterion-references applications of classical test theory. *Journal of Educational Measurement, 9,* 13–26.

Livingston, S. A., & Zieky, M. J. (1982). *Passing scores: A manual for setting standards of performance on educational and occupational tests.* Princeton, NJ: Educational Testing Service.

Lord, F. M. (1980). *Applications of item response theory to practical testing problems.* Hillsdale, NJ: Erlbaum.

Madaus, G. F. (1981). NIE clarification hearing: The negative team's case. *Phi Delta Kappan, 63,* 92–94.

Merrifield, P. R. (1975). Review of Cattell's Abilities: Their structure, growth, and action. *American Educational Research Journal, 4(12),* 515–521.

Messick, S. (1984). Abilities and knowledge in educational achievement testing: The assessment of dynamic cognitive structures. In B. S. Plake (Ed.), *Social and technical issues in testing: Implications for test construction and usage* (pp. 155–172). (Buros-Nebraska Symposium on Measurement and Testing) Hillsdale, NJ: Erlbaum.

Millman, J. (1984, April). *Computer assisted test construction.* Invited address. National Council on Measurement in Education. New Orleans, LA.

Mitchell, J. V., Jr. (1984a). Serving the test user: New developments from the Buros Institute. *Educational Measurement: Issues and Practice, 3(2),* 51–52.

Mitchell, J. V., Jr. (1984b). Testing and the Oscar Buros lament: From knowledge to implementation to use. In B. S. Plake (Ed.), *Social and technical issues in testing: Implications for test construction and usage* (pp. 111–126). (Buros-Nebraska Symposium on Measurement and Testing) Hillsdale, NJ: Erlbaum.

Navarro, M. S. (1984, October). *Efficiency and equality: The impact of state standards on college access.* Paper presented at the 1984 Educational Testing Service Invitational Conference on Educational Standards, Testing, and Access, New York, NY.

Neisser, U. (1967). *Cognitive psychology.* New York: Appleton-Century-Crofts.

PASE v. Hannon, 506 F. Supp. 831 (N.D. Ill. 1980)

Payton, B. F. (1984, October). *Improving access and standards: What kind of education do we want?* Paper presented at the 1984 Educational Testing Service Invitational Conference on Educational Standards, Testing, and Access. New York, NY.

Peterson, N. S., Cook, L. L., & Stocking, M. L. (1983). IRT versus conventional equating methods: A comparative study of scale stability. *Journal of Educational Statistics, 8(2),* 137–156.

Plake, B. S. (1984, November). Computer technology in educational research: Possibilities and Problems. *Significant Perspectives Newsletter,* pp. 2–11.

Plake, B. S., & Berk, R. A. (1984). Listening and responding to voices from NCME members: Development and analysis of survey about NCME's annual meeting. *Educational Measurement: Issues and Practice, 3,(2),* 40–44.

Plake, B. S. & Witt, J. C. (Eds.). (1986). *Future directions for testing* (Buros-Nebraska Symposium on Measurement and Testing). Hillsdale, NJ: Erlbaum.

Plake, B. S., Glover, J. A., Kraft, R. G., & Dinnel, D. (1984). Cognitive capacity usage in responding to test items. *Journal of Psychoeducational Assessment, 2,* 333–343.

Popham, W. J. (1981). The case for minimum competence testing. *Phi Delta Kappan, 63,* 89–91.

Roid, G. H. (1983, August). *Generalizations of continuous norming: Cross-validation of test-score means estimates.* Paper presented at American Psychological Association, Anaheim, CA.

Roid, G. H. (1986). Computer technology in testing. In B. S. Plake & Witt, J. C. (Eds.), *Future directions for testing.*

(Buros-Nebraska Symposium on Measurement and Testing) Hillsdale, NJ: Erlbaum.

Seddon, G. M. (1978). The properties of Bloom's taxonomy of educational objectives for the cognitive domain. *Review of Educational Research, 48,* 303–323.

Stocking, M. L. (1984). *Two simulated feasibility studies in computerized adaptive testing* (ETS Research Report #84-15). Princeton, NJ: Educational Testing Service.

Sternberg, R. J. (1984). What cognitive psychology can (and cannot do for test development. In B. S. Plake (Ed.), *Social and technical issues in testing: Implications for test construction and usage* (pp. 39–60). (Buros-Nebraska Symposium on Measurement and Testing) Hillsdale, NJ: Erlbaum.

Subkoviak, M. J. (1976). Estimating reliability from a single administration of a mastery test. *Journal of Educational Measurement, 13,* 265–276.

Thorndike, R. L. (1971). Educational measurement for the seventies. In R. L. Thorndike (Ed.), *Educational measurement* (pp. 3–14). Washington, DC: American Council on Education.

Wainer, H. (1983). Pyramid power: Searching for an error in test scoring with 830,000 helpers. *The American Statistician, 37,* 87–91.

Weiss, D. J. (1983). (Ed.). *New horizons in testing: Latent trait test theory and computerized adaptive testing.* New York: Academic Press.

Weiss, D. J. & Kinsgbury (1984). Application of computerized testing to educational problems. *Journal of Educational Measurement, 21,* 361–376.

Whitely, S. E. (1981). Measuring aptitude processes with multicomponent latent trait models. *Journal of Educational Measurement, 18,* 76–93.

PART IV

Perspectives on Educational Psychology

The first four chapters in this section are diverse in style and content, much as the contributions of these authors to the field of educational psychology have taken very different forms. Our intent was to have scholars who have made important contributions to the field give their personal perspectives on what educational psychology has been and where it is going. The final chapter is our attempt to summarize the volume.

CHAPTER 18

Peaks and Valleys of Educational Psychology

A RETROSPECTIVE VIEW

Robert M. Gagné

My interest in psychology as a field of study dates back to youthful years, although nothing in my uneventful childhood can be recalled as giving rise to such an interest. Our middle-class family provided me with few cultural and intellectual influences, even though books and radio were readily available. It was the public schools that stimulated and nurtured my search for knowledge in many different areas—in the arts, literature, and in a variety of fields of science and technology. Although I am now keenly aware of how limited such knowledge was, I nevertheless realize that the school was the primary source of stimulation for my interest in books and in the knowledge they contained.

Most people, I suppose, have periods of their lives that are peaks of memorability. High school years are one of these peaks in my memory. Besides the usual turbulence of adolescence, these years are for me remembered as a period of concentrated learning, of many new experiences, and of valuable and gratifying friendships. I was a good student, and had little difficulty in completing school assignments. Much of the remaining time I spent in reading all kinds of books—new and old, serious and humorous, fictional and technical. Among the books I ran across that dealt with subjects of systematic study were those of psychology. I came to think of this subject as "the new science," although of course it was not new, even at that time. My interest in psychology continued until high school graduation, when it became the subject of a speech I was required to deliver as class valedictorian.

My plans for attending college were somewhat tentative; the time was, after all, the depth of the depression, and our family finances were not flourishing. But a scholarship offer from Yale made it possible for me to accept and to go. This surely was a place where I could study psychology, I thought.

Well, it was, but not right away. First I had to choose a distribution of subjects for the freshman year—English, two languages, biology and chemistry. So it was in my second year that I took a first course in psychology. The first-rate instructors, one of whom later became my undergraduate major advisor (E. S. Robinson) and the scholarly text (Woodworth's) failed to make psychology either a coherent or a greatly interesting subject of study. However, courses at advanced levels reversed this

Robert M. Gagné • Department of Educational Research, Florida State University, Tallahassee, FL 32306.

effect, and reinforced my positive attitude toward psychology. Two influences on my future development are particularly notable. One of my instructors introduced me to the "early papers" of Clark Hull, in which he was describing how S-R theory could account for a number of kinds of complex behavior in animals (see Amsel & Rashotte, 1984). I found these articles fascinating examples of incisive thinking. The second event, occurring during my senior year, was the taking of a semester course in educational psychology. This course happened to be taught by James J. Gibson, whose brilliant unconventional wisdom made an inevitable impression on me, an effect that continued during many later years of close association and friendship.

As an undergraduate major in psychology, it was evident to me that serious pursuit of the subject required graduate study. My advisor encouraged me to make application to several universities. I accepted the offer of an assistantship in the program at Brown University, where I joined an outstanding group of graduate students, a good number of whom have since become research psychologists of distinction. The department at Brown was headed by Walter S. Hunter. I usually describe Professor Hunter as an "old behaviorist" (to indicate his professional generation as that of Watson, but not of Skinner). Much of Hunter's work sought evidences of symbolic thought in animal behavior, through what he called a "representative process."

My major professor at Brown was Clarence H. Graham, known for his studies of vision and theories of retinal mechanisms in perception. A brilliant scholar, Graham was a friendly and kindly man, who set high standards of scholarly research and thought for his students. I was intrigued with his attempts to apply in the field of learning the precise mathematical approach to theory that was familiar to him in the field of visual processes. This point of view led to studies of learning in white rats in a very simple situation: leaving a starting box and running to a goal box on a straight elevated runway. Measures of latency of response yielded average learning curves that were conceived as exhibiting increasing response strength. This conception of the nature of learning continued to dominate psychologists' thought for many years. Today, I would not be sure how to account for the learning curves that were reported in my doctoral thesis.

During the 1930s, scientific studies of learning were sometimes done with animals, sometimes with human beings, and there was a strong prevailing belief that many of the results obtained with one organism were generalizable to the other. My own interest in human learning continued during my first academic appointment at Connecticut College, where I began the preparation of materials for investigation of the immediate memory span. This work was interrupted in 1941 by a call to Army training that later extended into the period of World War II.

The Aviation Psychology Program, headed in the Office of the Air Surgeon General by Colonel John C. Flanagan, made it possible for many psychologists to serve the war effort by making applications of their knowledge to the selection and training of crew members in military aircraft. This was a highly organized program with definite goals, which is acknowledged to have resulted in the saving of an enormous number of dollars and a good many lives. Many distinguished psychologists served in this program in uniform. My impression is that in most cases their experiences in making valuable practical applications of psychology had a profound effect on their attitudes in approaching all of their subsequent work. This surely was true of me.

My main assignments during this period were with units having responsibility for test development. There were tests for psychomotor abilities that had to be manufactured, inspected, and tested for their durability of operation, before giving consideration to the reliability and predictive validity of the scores they yielded (Melton, 1947). Another kind of development was motion picture tests of perceptual abilities. These had their own peculiar difficulties of construction, validation, and use, including the limitations that had to be placed on size of the viewing group (Gibson, 1947). For a short period before being discharged, I was assigned to a unit whose mission was research in a field that came to be called "human engineering" (Fitts, 1947).

I returned to academic pursuits after the war, first in a brief interim appointment at the Pennsylvania State University, and then again at Connecticut College. During this period I taught courses in general and systematic psychology, as well as in educational psychology. I recall thinking that available textbooks in the latter subject were terrible, particularly because they dealt so scantily with what teachers actually had to do in supporting student learning.

As I reflect back on my early life and schooling, I think I would mention the following influences that have supported my interest in educational psychology: (a) good experiences in school settings, both in learning and in relations with people; (b) early fascination with the idea of scientific study of human behavior; (c) developing knowledge of psychology as a science in undergraduate and graduate years in universities; and (d) wartime experience of a variety of important psychological problems in the assessment and training of human capabilities.

Early Postwar Research

Many of the tests given to aviation cadets in World War II represented the tasks they would later perform as aircrew members (pilots, navigators, bombardiers, gunners). Although they were not exactly "job-sample" tests, many of them did represent small portions of the activities involved in aircrew operations. This was true, for example, of such psychomotor tests as Complex Coordination and Rudder Control, as well as a number of others (see Melton, 1947). This broad class of human activities continued to interest me as learning tasks in the postwar period, and I devised several learning tasks requiring responses to patterns of lights and switches (Gagné & Baker, 1950; Gagné & Foster, 1949). I thought of them as "motor" tasks, but this classification continued to seem unsatisfactory to me, because the motor actions involved were already well learned, and the patterning of stimuli and responses defined the learning requirements. The inadequacy of traditional task categorization in psychology was revealed by these research studies, a shortcoming that persists even today. In terms of my own attempts at classification, most of these tasks would later be called "intellectual skills."

These studies aimed to illuminate a topic long known to educational psychology, namely, the conditions of transfer of training. During this period at Connecticut College, my colleagues and I attempted to devise sensible measures of the effects of transfer (Gagné, Foster, & Crowley, 1948) and to investigate the effects of such variables as amount of similarity in stimulus conditions and in response requirements. Probably we were able to shed some light in this general area. But the problem of how best to "teach for transfer" remains complex, and resists a satisfyingly clear solution down to the present day.

Research on Training of Military Personnel

Following a few years of undergraduate teaching at Connecticut College, I was attracted to the prospect of full-time research, and was persuaded to join an Air Force organization called the Human Resources Research Center, whose technical director was Arthur W. Melton. This organization established a number of research programs on the training of several kinds of Air Force specialities, which were added to an existing program of research on the assessment of human abilities for personnel selection. I became the technical director of a laboratory having an orientation to basic research on perceptual and motor skills. Later the parent organization was changed in title to the Air Force Personnel and Training Research Center, and I was assigned (in 1953) as technical director of a laboratory at Lowry Air Force Base, Colorado, whose mission was research on training of electronic maintenance personnel.

Three notable trends stand out as accomplishments of the Lowry laboratory (entitled the Maintenance Laboratory), each of which reflects the participation of a professional staff of outstanding research psychologists. The first was a conviction arising from analysis of existing training practices to the effect that the sources for training improvement could not be found in application of traditional principles of learning, such as contiguity, repetition, and the law of effect. If improvements were to take place, it was necessary to examine the structure of the content of training, its sequence and organization. This was the idea I tried to express a few years later in a presidential address to the Division of Military Psychology of the American Psychological Association (Gagné, 1962). In contemporary terms, one would say that training improvement has its basis in the organization of training content (a) for effective utilization of prior knowledge and (b) for encoding that assures ready accessibility in retrieval.

The second development of this period (1953–1957) was the application of new ideas in devices for training. Training devices were generally conceived as instruments for the practice and refinement of motor skills (such as aircraft maneuvers in the Link Trainer). In the realm of electronic maintenance, however, few motor skills were involved. Instead, activities such as adjustments, alignment, parts replacement, and system troubleshooting partook of intellectual skills. Guided in part by checklists and symbolic diagrams, the incumbent of a maintenance job needed to do a great deal of rule following, rule selection, and problem solving. The new inventions of the Maintenance Laboratory were training devices that provided practice in the intellectual skills and problem-solving activities of electronic maintenance. We realized that such devices, although most continued to require manipulation of switches and connectors, were actually a variety of *teaching machine*. Some of the ideas of the latter movement were infused into the plans and formulations of research of the Maintenance Laboratory, as reported by Briggs (1959a, b) and Lumsdaine (1959).

The third strand of our work in the Maintenance Laboratory may have been the most pioneering of all. We were asked to participate in the weapon systems planning of the Air Force by forecasting requirements for selection and training of personnel. To accomplish these aims, we had to devise novel methods of analyzing man–machine systems, of describing the projected jobs, and of deriving requirements for selection and training of personnel. Original contributions for methods of task description and task analysis were made by R. B. Miller (1956, 1962); a variety of other procedures and refinements were contributed by many members of the laboratory's professional staff. As methods of deriving "personnel requirements information," many of the procedures, or parts of them, are still in use in the Air Force today. As contributions to the field of educational psychology, the techniques of task description, task analysis, and the specification of instruction have been of considerable value. The linkage they make with the definition of *instructional objectives* I undertook to describe in a conference on programmed instruction (Gagné, 1965).

School Subjects as Learning Tasks

Returning once again to academic haunts (1958), I became engaged in the education of undergraduate and graduate students in psychology at Princeton University. It was a time of program design and staff building for the department. My research was concerned with the learning of intellectual skills and problem solving. Training in electronic maintenance had often included objectives of this sort. However, in orienting the work to nonmilitary goals, I began to use tasks in mathematics, some of which were portions of established

curricula, whereas others were of novel design, unfamiliar to school students. In attempting to study human problem solving, I found the most difficult problem of the investigator was to select or devise tasks whose characteristics lent themselves readily to experimental manipulation and assessment of outcomes. It seems to me this continues to be the case.

One of the intellectual tasks I employed during this period was "deriving a formula for the sum of N terms in a number series." An initial study examined some variables in the learning of this task via programmed instruction. Incidental observations of students made during this and other related studies led me to think that lack of success on the final task by particular students may have been caused by apparent gaps in their knowledge of mathematical procedures (such as finding multiples of numbers, or simplifying fractions). I decided to investigate this idea, using the same number-series task. In doing this, I had first to analyze the task into its simpler component activities. The identification of subtasks that represented "what the student really had to do" yielded the first set of surprises in this research. Further, I quickly realized that these subordinate tasks were themselves analyzable into even simpler subtasks; and that if I were going to look for gaps in student knowledge, I would have to identify these simpler skills as well. Thus was born the idea that these intellectual skills formed a hierarchy. The target task was analyzable into progressively simpler skills (usually those that had been earlier learned), until one reached skills that could be assumed to be highly familiar to particular samples of students.

To find the gaps of student knowledge in this hierarchy, I began to test each individual student beginning with the target task and proceeding downwards until those tasks were reached that the student clearly knew how to do. Then, beginning with these, I gave brief instructions for the next "higher" task and tested it again, proceeding upwards through the hierarchy in this manner until the target task was reached. For an investigator used to assessing learning in terms of average performances of groups, some of the most startling surprises were observed in the behavior of these individual students. When the learning hierarchy was used in a manner that sought the combining of subordinate skills, this method brought about learning that was both successful and satisfying to students. Their "aha!" experiences in such learning were almost visible.

Research on learning hierarchies was continued in collaboration with a mathematics project at the University of Maryland. A few years later, the basic idea of learning hierarchies could be applied in a somewhat liberalized fashion to the structuring of lessons in the development of a science curriculum called *Science—A Process Approach,* sponsored by the American Association for the Advancement of Science. I participated actively in this project, as a member of the commission that made its plan, and also of the teams that developed its instruction. *Process* meant that the instruction was aimed at the teaching of intellectual skills that appear to be involved in the understanding of science as a participant as opposed to a spectator—the basic skills that compose the activities of observing, classifying, measuring, communicating, experimenting. Although evaluation studies were made, it is interesting to note that no convincing evidence was obtained that this program, or any of the several other elementary science curriculum programs, "made a difference" in the later development of student interest and competence in the study of the sciences. The tracing of causal effects of this sort over a number of years of individual development and schooling has so far appeared too tough a job for educational evaluation to tackle.

The Period of Development of Laboratories and Centers

For several years (1962–1965) I held the position of Director of Research in a private nonprofit research organization, the American Institutes for Research. This was a very busy period, affording me a wide variety of experience with research projects partaking of systems analysis, performance measurement, and design of programs of education and training. During this period, I occasionally consulted with people working under the direction of Robert Glaser at the University of Pittsburgh, planning and initiating the research programs of the Learning Research and Development Center. This experience with a federally funded organization for educational research was to be of value in my next job. When I moved to the University of California, Berkeley, I found that their Department of Education, in collaboration with other educational agencies, had been making plans for a proposal to establish a regional laboratory. I was persuaded to become the director of the Far West Laboratory for Educational Research and Development during its initial formative period.

The task of establishing the regional laboratory began almost from scratch, albeit with the formal support of educational agencies and school systems in northern California. It was necessary for a small staff to find and rent space in a suitable location, hire office personnel, obtain necessary office equipment, and carry out various other logistic activities. We submitted to the Office of Education several progress reports containing plans for laboratory and research management, and proposals for R & D in such areas as overcoming cultural deficiencies of students, requirements for the education of school personnel, dissemination of R & D products, instructional methods, and curriculum development. Perhaps the most satisfying task I accomplished, after months of such activity, was assuring that the governing board for the laboratory had a chance to consider several fine candidates for the position of laboratory director, and so to make the excellent choice of John K. Hemphill.

What significance does the establishment of Centers and Regional Laboratories have for educational psychology? These organizations provide opportunities for educational psychologists, along with other educational specialists, to apply their knowledge by participation in research, development, and evaluation efforts that are of much larger scale than can be undertaken within the framework of single local school systems. Some projects of this large-scale variety have been conducted with moderate success. Many of them have enlarged and enriched the field of educational psychology, by providing good examples of application of the results of psychological research. It would be a good idea if more reporting of such studies were done in textbooks of educational psychology.

At Berkeley, I was a member of an educational psychology section in a department of education. I suppose it was at this time that I functioned in a full sense as an educational psychologist. The graduate students whose work I supervised came from a variety of educational disciplines besides psychology—art, music, language, mathematics, and science. Educational psychology is often the "research" component in the study of instruction and learning within these and other specialized fields of education. If educational psychologists can play such a role, graduate education in a college of education is inevitably enriched.

Development of Ideas about Instructional Psychology

It is surely not possible for me to identify any particular event that gave rise to the central idea embodied in the title of *The Conditions of Learning*. My various experiences in attempting to apply learning principles to military training, to professional education, and to education in the schools, led to an abiding conviction that the different human performances resulting from learning were causally affected by correspondingly different factors. Although there were common causes for changes in performance (such as reinforcement), in a practical sense there were *different conditions* under which different learning outcomes were attained. In the first edition of this book, I attempted to describe these conditions for the various learning prototypes that were traditional categories of investigation at that time, including classical conditioning, operant conditioning, paired-associate learning, and concept learning. Although somewhat less frequently covered by research, the categories of rule learning and problem solving were added to the list. Viewed as a whole, the attempt was to build a bridge between psychological research on learning and what appeared to be the kind of knowledge needed to account for learning in practical situations of education and training. Subsequent editions reflected increasing concern with the learning that takes place in classrooms and other educational settings, and a decreasing emphasis on the traditional concepts of laboratory learning studies.

In meeting the challenge of making an address as retiring President of The American Educational Research Association, I had decided to report the results of my reflection on the question, ''What kinds of things are learned in school?'' I called these types of learned capabilities ''domains of learning'' (Gagné, 1972), and identified them as intellectual skills, verbal information, cognitive strategies, motor skills, and attitudes (Gagné, 1984). In the third and fourth editions of *The Conditions of Learning,* these categories of learning outcomes replaced those of earlier editions as major organizing sections; the laboratory-based prototypes, such as the conditioned response, were treated as ''basic forms of learning.'' This change meant that the book's coverage extended to a great variety of educational and training objectives, and potentially to all varieties.

The second major change in later editions of *The Conditions of Learning* was the introduction of the information-processing model of learning and memory, following particularly the version described by Atkinson and Shiffrin (1968). Although a behaviorist orientation is usually detected in my writings, it should not be surprising that an information-processing model was described in my chapter called ''Human functions in systems'' published in 1963, including the levels of processing entitled ''sensing,'' ''identifying,'' and ''interpreting.''

The information-processing model permits a description of learning in terms of the kinds of processing involved in transforming stimulus inputs to memory structures and to human performances as outputs. Learning occurs whether or not there is any instruction. But each of the processes of learning may be influenced in some manner by events external to the learner. When such events are deliberately planned to support the internal processes of learning, they are called *instructional events,* or given the collective name *instruction.* Thus it may be seen that the processes of learning, as identified by information-processing theory and research, provide a rationale for instructional events. As recently formulated (Gagné & Briggs, 1979), nine of these supporting events make up instruction, beginning with ''gaining attention'' and running through ''enhancing retention and transfer.'' This second theme, instructional events, ties the ideas of *The Conditions of Learning* to cognitive learning theory, and forms the basis for what is called *instructional theory* (Gagné, 1985).

The primary application of a theory of instruction is to the design of instruction as embodied in materials, lessons, courses, and media. Designing and developing instruction in this detailed sense is an essential part of the larger enterprise usually referred to as *instructional systems design.* Over a period of years, I have had frequent opportunities to describe the principles of instructional theory to educational system designers of many sorts, and in many locations. Currently, I see these ideas as influential in the design of training programs in various industries, and also in the design of lessons for use in computer-based instruction.

It is my belief that a systematic view of instruction and how it affects the human learner, such as is reflected in instructional theory, is one of the capabilities most essential for a teacher to possess. In terms of cognitive learning theory, it is the *schema* that teachers need to guide their pedagogy and into which their various bits of new subject matter knowledge and new elements of teaching experience may be fitted. There are scores of studies of "teaching behaviors" that give evidence of the effects of isolated variables (such as allocation of time, questioning, use of feedback, and others) on favorable teaching outcomes. But manipulation of any of these individual features of teaching performance can only be done within the framework of a schema that models the effects of instruction on the human learner. As trained professionals, teachers need to have the kind of schema worthy of the "expert."

Some Reflections on Educational Psychology

The previous account should surely make clear that the abiding interest in my professional life has been in understanding how human beings learn, in describing what they learn, and in discovering how such knowledge can be put to use in educational programs to improve human competence and the satisfactions of life. I began to investigate learning as an experimental psychologist, and the scientific customs of that discipline, particularly the values it places on operationally defined theoretical concepts and their empirical validation, have remained influential in my work and thought. Viewed from such a vantage point, educational psychology has over the years experienced peaks and valleys—peaks during which worthwhile developments in the parent discipline have been incorporated and used to advantage, and valleys in which some near crack-brained notions have been given undeserved attention and publicity. I shall not try to list the latter, although I think they would collectively make an interesting history. Obviously, though, I think the current trend of interest in cognitive learning theory is a definite peak.

Textbooks in educational psychology must now be meeting reasonably good markets; there seem to be many of them. I have examined a number of these texts, and have taught classes using one or two that are currently available. From these books I gain a strong impression: the psychology in them is out of date. Perhaps the parent field has progressed so rapidly that authors of educational psychology texts find it difficult to keep up. Or perhaps the field of psychology itself is experiencing difficulty adapting to the paradigm shift of cognitive psychology. Whatever the reason, I have the definite impression that the psychology in these textbooks is characteristic of the field of about 30 years ago. Surely paired-associate learning merits some mention; but its findings occupy no more than a limited place in the interpretation of the phenomena of school learning. This is but one example of the tendency I see for texts in educational psychology to communicate obsolete knowledge. (See, for example, an article by Estes, 1982, contrasting old and new conceptions of learning phenomena.) Improvements in such texts will come when authors take the trouble to inform themselves about contemporary developments in psychology before they undertake to tell prospective teachers how to apply psychological knowledge.

It appears to me that there are four major pedagogical topics that should be well covered by texts in educational psychology. These topics may best be presented in ways that aim for the teaching of four different schemata that will guide the teacher's behavior and future learning. The first, already mentioned, is a schema about the nature of instruction as the external means of supporting processes of learning. A second and related schema pertains to the students' learning to learn—the learnable skills and strategies that learners can themselves employ to engage in effective study and self-initiated learning. A third schema essential for pedagogy consists of the array of techniques used by teachers to observe the outcomes of their teaching, including a range of actions from unscheduled observations of student behavior to the formal means of achievement testing. And a fourth schema, not at all least in importance, pertains to what is called classroom management—the allocation of tasks, on-task behavior, the maintenance of order, the encouragement of appropriate behavior in the classroom situation. Of course, there are other topics for an educational psychology course to cover—socialization, personality, moral development, and others. But so far as the main job of teaching is concerned, these four comprise the kind of knowledge needed by the teacher.

I believe that the kind of pedagogical knowledge just described seldom comes directly from empirical studies of the classroom or of other educational situations. The reason, as educational psychologists know well, is that worthwhile studies of this sort are carried out very infrequently, because they must extend over long time periods and are too expensive. These essential schemata, therefore, must be made up of knowledge obtained from psychological studies of learning, memory, performance measurement, and the theories that are derived from them. Current theory and research in cognitive psychology provide rich sources of ideas that cry out for application to the educational scene.

References

Amsel, A., & Rashotte, M. E. (1984). *Mechanisms of adaptive behavior: Clark L. Hull's theoretical papers, with commentary.* New York: Columbia University Press.

Atkinson, R. C., & Shiffrin, R. M. (1968). Human memory: A proposed system and its control processes. In K. W. Spence & J. T. Spence (Eds.), *The psychology of learning and motivation* (Vol. 2, pp. 89–195). New York: Academic Press.

Briggs, L. J. (1959a). Teaching machines for training of military personnel in maintenance of electronic equipment. In E. Galanter (Ed.), *Automatic teaching: The state of the art* (pp. 131–145). New York: Wiley.

Briggs, L. J. (1959b). Teaching machines: History and possible applications to Air Force education and training programs. In *Symposium on training media* (pp. 150–195). Washington, DC: National Academy of Sciences-National Research Council.

Estes, W. K. (1982). Learning, memory, and intelligence. In R. J. Sternberg (Ed.), *Handbook of human intelligence* (pp. 170–224). Cambridge: Cambridge University Press.

Fitts, P. M. (1947). *Psychological research on equipment design.* Report No. 19, AAF Aviation Psychology Program Research Reports. Washington, DC: U.S. Government Printing Office.

Gagné, R. M. (1962). Military training and principles of learning. *American Psychologist, 17,* 83–91.

Gagné, R. M. (Ed.). (1963). *Psychological principles in system development.* New York: Holt, Rinehart & Winston.

Gagné, R. M. (1965). The analysis of instructional objectives for the design of instruction. In R. Glaser (Ed.), *Teaching machines and programed learning, II. Data and directions* (pp. 21–65). Washington, DC: National Education Association.

Gagné, R. M. (1972). Domains of learning. *Interchange, 3,* 1–8.

Gagné, R. M. (1984). Learning outcomes and their effects. *American Psychologist, 39,* 377–385.

Gagné, R. M. (1985). *The conditions of learning* (4th ed.). New York: Holt, Rinehart & Winston.

Gagné, R. M., & Baker, K. E. (1950). Stimulus predifferentiation as a factor in transfer of training. *Journal of Experimental Psychology, 40,* 439–451.

Gagné, R. M., & Briggs, L. J. (1979). *Principles of instructional design* (2nd ed). New York: Holt, Rinehart & Winston.

Gagné, R. M., & Foster, H. (1949). Transfer of training from practice on components in a motor skill. *Journal of Experimental Psychology, 39,* 47–68.

Gagné, R. M., Foster, H., & Crowley, M. C. (1948). The measurement of transfer of training. *Psychological Bulletin, 45,* 97–130.

Gibson, J. J. (1947). *Motion picture testing and research.* Report No. 7, AAF Aviation Psychology Program Research Reports. Washington, DC: U.S. Government Printing Office.

Lumsdaine, A. A. (1959). Teaching machines and self-instructional materials. *Audio-visual Communications Review, 7,* 163–181.

Melton, A. W. (1947). *Apparatus tests.* Report No. 4, AAF Aviation Psychology Program Research Reports. Washington, DC: U.S. Government Printing Office.

Miller, R. B. (1956). *A suggested guide to position-task description.* (Technical Memo ASPRL-TM-56-6.) Lackland Air Force Base, TX: Air Force Personnel and Training Research Center.

Miller, R. B. (1963). Task description and analysis. In R. M. Gagné (Ed.), *Psychological principles in system development* (pp. 187–228). New York: Holt, Rinehart & Winston.

CHAPTER 19

Quantitative Methodology

THEN, NOW, AND THE FUTURE

Lloyd G. Humphreys

In this chapter I shall discuss quantitative methodology as it was at the outset of my career, as I see it now, and as it may be in the future. The topic in one sense is considerably broader than the specialty called educational psychology, but one can also consider that specialty to include the whole of general psychology. The particular area of application or the particular age group used in research does not set apart a subdiscipline of psychology from general psychology.

When I added "the future" to "then" and "now" in my title, I was asserting a hope that there would be appreciable improvement in the methodology of psychological research. This hope does not depend on the development of new methodology, although it is certain that new developments will appear. I make the point instead that psychologists are not using well the tools they currently have available. Many inadequacies and downright errors are well entrenched in text books and in graduate training. These inadequacies and errors are also entrenched in the evaluations of editors as well as in the design of studies and analyses of data by researchers. In many cases it will be impossible to cite recognized authorities in support of my recommendations, although other ac-

tive research people are thinking and writing along similar lines. Readers will frequently have to evaluate present practices against the logic of the alternatives recommended.

Methodology Then

I undertook my first research project under the guidance of Robert Holmes Seashore in 1932–1933 in my sophomore year at the University of Oregon. This was followed by two more projects prior to the B.S. degree in 1935. I left Oregon for a master's degree at Indiana in 1936 and from there went to Stanford for my Ph.D. in 1938. After a one year postdoctoral fellowship taken at Yale, I became an instructor at Northwestern University. This brief resume defines "then" for my purposes.

Differences between Means. Relatively few psychologists knew about population estimates or the t-distributions in my early days. The standard error of a mean equaled the sample standard deviation divided ordinarily by the square root of sample size. It was recognized that this procedure was inadequate for small samples so a rule-of-thumb was used. For $N < 10$ the sample standard deviation was divided by $N - 3$, for $N > 10 < 20$ $N - 2$ was used, and for $N > 20 < 30$ $N - 1$.

Lloyd G. Humphreys • Department of Psychology, University of Illinois, Champaign IL 61820.

The standard error of a difference was the square root of the sum of the two squared standard errors. There was no pooling of sample variances in computing the standard error of a difference. The difference in means divided by its standard error, a critical ratio, was referred to a table of the normal probability surface.

These computational procedures, in spite of their lack of elegance, resulted in fewer alpha errors than are currently committed for at least one reason. The generally accepted level of the critical ratio required for rejection of a zero population difference was 3.00. In large samples p is less than .0027 for a two-tailed test. There may also be a second reason for a small number of alpha errors in the early literature. With many more psychologists doing research today, more null results may be buried in file drawers and never submitted for publication.

Use of an unbiased estimate of the population variance and referral of ratios to the appropriate t distribution has not been an unhallowed blessing for reasons that go beyond the generally accepted alpha level of .05. Many research people seem to believe that lack of bias in statistics is an adequate basis for the use of small samples. They neglect the fact that random error increases monotonically with the increase in systematic error in sample variances as N decreases. When the need for unbiased estimates is greatest, the amount of random error is also greatest and is unaffected by correction for bias. Most psychological research is done with sample sizes that are too small to provide the kinds of answers needed to advance our science.

Reporting Correlations.   It used to be the standard operating procedure to report a sample correlation plus or minus its probable error. The latter can be thought of as an approximation to the 50% confidence interval for the population correlation. The probable error reported was not an accurate estimate. It was .6745 times an approximate standard error of the sample correlation and produced a confidence interval misleadingly symmetric about the sample correlation. A critical ratio was formed by dividing the sample correlation by either its probable error or its standard error. The two ratios required for rejection of the null hypothesis were commonly 4.00 and 3.00, respectively, even though these ratios do not lead to identical probabilities.

Reporting the probable error along with the sample correlation had one great advantage over most present day reporting procedures. It was a constant reminder that there was more to the interpretation of correlations than the dichotomy of significant and nonsignificant. It was also a constant reminder, no matter how large the sample, that one did not have a completely determined relationship, accurate to two or three decimal places, between X and Y.

The Fisher z transformation for linear correlations constituted a major step forward in the analysis of data, but it was just beginning to be used by 1940. Fisher's t test for the hypothesis that the population regression slope is zero had a similar early history, but its popularity grew more rapidly. The z transformation and the standard error of z should be used more frequently, the t test less frequently. For all too many psychologists there is only one population parameter of any importance: rho is zero and $H_o\rho$ is accordingly zero. It does not seem to matter whether rho might be .01 or .99 as long as .00 can be rejected.

Partial and Multiple Correlations.   Computational procedures for higher-order correlations were well understood, but we were handicapped by the capabilities, or lack thereof, of mechanical computers. Ingenious psychologists had moved computations beyond desk calculators to IBM punched card equipment, most of which had not been designed for statistical purposes, but the gain was a good deal less than an order of magnitude effect. The computational load for higher-order correlations increases exponentially with the number of variables. As late as the mid-fifties in Air Force personnel research we used an iterative procedure to compute multiple regression weights. Even here there was a side benefit. The weights cross-validated to new samples with less shrinkage if we set a gross convergence criterion.

The hazards involved in the interpretation of these statistics were well recognized in the literature. Beta weights "bounced" from sample to sample. Holding constant a particular measure in a partial correlation could "throw the baby out with the bath." Just because two observed measures had different names was not a sufficient basis for treating them as perfectly reliable and valid measures of different traits.

Although well recognized by sophisticated psychologists, the hazards were not widely recognized. Partial and multiple correlations, and multiple regression weights, were probably as inaccurately interpreted generally then as they are today. Path analysis had been proposed by Sewell Wright (1921), a geneticist, several years earlier.

Almost certainly the primary reason it was not misused by psychologists more frequently in my early days was the computational problem. In the absence of experimental control, inferences about cause and effect are difficult enough when one is able to estimate an errorless latent trait. The causal interpretation of measures of observed variables is so hazardous that one is tempted to recommend banning all such interpretations.

Test Theory. The publication of Thurstone's *Reliability and Validity of Tests* (1931) brought together contributions from many sources dating back to Spearman and Pearson and established in much its present form what is now called classical test theory. A final contribution was made by Kuder and Richardson (1937) in their article on the measurement of test homogeneity.

Carrying out the required computations was laborious and shortcuts had to be taken. Item intercorrelations were out of the question. Biserial correlations between items and total score, especially with the item removed from the total, were generally not feasible. Item analyses started typically by splitting the distribution of total scores into upper and lower criterion groups. Kelley (1939) had established that 27% tails in a normal distribution maximized power once the decision to dichotomize had been made. The split was made only once so that the correlations were part–whole and spuriously large. The correlation itself was a difference between means of the criterion groups, a phi coefficient, or an estimate of the biserial from widespread classes. Did the predictive validities of tests constructed in accordance with the theory and based on shortcut computational strategies suffer? The answer is an unequivocal "no."

Factor Analysis. Spearman (1927) had developed methods for the detection of a general factor, but multiple factor analysis did not become really feasible for large correlation matrices until Thurstone (1935) developed the centroid method. In the beginning, the use of orthogonal rotations by Thurstone (1938) obscured the general factor. Holzinger and Swineford (1937) provided the bi-factor method that preserved the general factor of Spearman, but bi-factoring required an initial clustering. This made it less flexible. In contrast, the more elegant least squares method of Hotelling (1933) and Kelley's (1935) principal axis procedure, could reasonably be applied only to small numbers of variables.

Flanagan (1935) did use Kelley's computational routine for his analysis of the four Bernreuter Personality Inventory scales. The application of those findings by the Stanford University Press constitutes a dramatic early example of the error of reification of dimensions revealed by statistical analysis. Similar errors are being made today. Flanagan found that two principal components described quite accurately the variance-covariance matrix of the four Bernreuter scores. The Stanford press obtained permission to use the new scoring keys and henceforth offered test users six different keys and six different trait names obtained from the test. Users were not warned that they must choose between two and four traits and that the choice of four was contraindicated by the Flanagan analysis.

I learned the centroid computations and made a start on learning multiple factor theory during my graduate year at Indiana under Merrill Roff. Merrill had come to Indiana that same year from a postdoctoral appointment in Thurstone's laboratory. I managed to include a centroid analysis with rotated factors in my unpublished master's thesis. I factored for a reason that has been repeated by myself and others many times over the years: I had a correlation matrix.

I took additional work in factor analysis at Stanford with George Kuznets who had replaced Quinn McNemar for a year's leave of absence. I also published a couple of papers in the area, although I worked with Jack Hilgard on an eyeblink conditioning problem for my dissertation. Thus, when Thurstone's *Primary Mental Abilities* (1938) was published during my postdoctoral year at Yale, I was the best qualified member of Don Marquis' seminar to review the monograph.

A centroid analysis was tedious and time consuming, but it was at least feasible for quite large matrices. It is also true that it can quite closely approximate the principal axis solution. The centroid is close to the factor determined by least squares. The more elegant method was unthinkable for the problems that Thurstone and his students were tackling. Use of the centroid method cannot be used as a basis for discarding research completed before the advent of high-speed electronic digital computers.

There were problems then and now with regard to determining the number of common factors and the position of axes following rotation. There were more problems then than now with respect to the digital accuracy of computations. Electronic computers are highly satisfactory on this dimension. There are probably more problems now than then, however, in deciding what to compute. The people who use modern computers can and do make egregious errors.

Factor analyses are performed in a less sophisticated fashion today. It is too easy to read a manual for a canned computer program and to assume that one can make intelligent choices among the options and interpret adequately the output after a one-year graduate course in statistics. Today's Ph.D. in psychology is probably less well qualified quantitatively to use the highly sophisticated programs available than predecessors who had to compute on desk calculators. Sophisticated hardware and software may indeed have reduced the sophistication of the user and the quality of the research being produced.

Canonical Analysis. Harold Hotelling (1935) had also developed canonical analysis before I was in graduate school, but it was little more than a gleam in the eye of the psychologist at the time. Again the problem was a computational one. The only substitute, and not necessarily an undesirable one, was to compute a correlation between two composites with each being based on elements given *a priori* weights. When weights are not determined from the observations, there is no cross-validation problem. When weights are based on observations, the problem of cross-validation becomes severe when components are moderately to highly intercorrelated. Such components are characteristic of much psychological data. Use of a priori weights was also possible for one composite and a single criterion measure, thereby avoiding the cross-validation problem in multiple regression.

Analysis of Variance. I did not become acquainted with the analysis of variance until my postdoctoral year. Don Marquis asked Jim Calvin and me to review Fisher's *Design of Experiments* (1935) in his seminar. I immediately became enthusiastic about the methodology, and the following year at Northwestern introduced the technique in the graduate statistics course. Allen Edwards and my wife, Dorothy, among others, were students in that course. Allen's dissertation represented a between and within mixed design, but we did not use an appropriate method of analysis. This lack was filled shortly thereafter in an experimental study of time perception by Raymond Gilliland and Dorothy Humphreys (1943). Linquist at Iowa probably included the analysis of variance in his course prior to 1939. There may have been others

as well, but the one at Northwestern was one of the first.

The analysis of variance was highly appropriate for many problems in psychology, but it became too popular. For many years the content of the typical required graduate course in statistics contained little else. As a result it has been applied in research for which it is at best a crude way of analyzing that data, at worst an inaccurate, misleading way. Categories based on individual differences are not the equivalent of levels of treatment of an independent variable. Ben Underwood (1957) described these differences well in his discussion of subject variables. Humphreys and Fleishman (1974) described the spurious relationships that can be produced by categorizing individual differences variables and pretending that they are therefore under experimental control.

The analysis of covariance was also available in Fisher, but I did not teach it at the outset. This was unfortunate. It is widely applicable in many psychological experiments, but its essential function has been widely misunderstood. It is primarily a method of reducing the size of the error term and only more or less incidentally adjusts group means for the random errors generated by random assignment to levels of treatment. Thus it is primarily a method for increasing the power of statistical tests.

The essential assumption in the use of covariance is random assignment to treatments. Additional control can be obtained by imposing random assignment within strata. It is essential to be able to assume that the population difference on the covariate is zero. On the other hand, covariance analysis is inadequate as a way of controlling for existing differences between treatment groups.

A different inadequate methodology for the problems associated with doing research on existing groups was commonly used before 1940, even though the fallacy in selecting individuals from different populations who "match" on one or more variables was well understood by methodologists. Some understandings disseminate slowly, however, and individual matching continues to this day. The matching fallacy is closely related to the misuse of the analysis of covariance in similar situations. It is also closely related to the error in the single group experiment in which subjects are selected from the tail of a distribution, allowing capitalization on regression effects.

What We Have Added

There has been nothing added in the way of new methodology that is one-tenth as important as the introduction of electronic computers. If research people today were restricted to the methodologies of 1940, their research horizons would be increased by more than an order of magnitude by our computational facilities. Among other advantages it has become possible without invoking a computational burden to do research on large enough samples to be able to estimate the size of differences between means and the size of correlations within reasonably narrow bounds. This advantage, however, is being largely neglected.

Although the pace of computer improvement in speed and capacity has been very rapid, in my perception the big gain was made early. I still remember the awe with which I viewed the inverse of a 20×20 matrix produced by ILLIAC I in the early fifties. The difference between an almost impossible computing task and minutes to compute was more dramatic than the difference between minutes and seconds that followed subsequently.

Although computers have made the largest difference, there are also some useful methodologies that have been added to the research person's repertoire. I shall discuss these in their appropriate categories.

Multiple Correlation and Multiple Regression. Several techniques for the partial control of the "bouncing betas" problem have been introduced. These include ridge regression and jackknifing and are effective in reducing shrinkage in cross-validation. Gains have also been made in substituting statistical estimates of cross-validation shrinkage for the empirical procedure. As with all small-sample techniques, availability is an insufficient reason for settling for a smaller N when a larger one can reasonably be obtained.

Factor Analysis. Several new factor analytic methods have entered our repertoire, and the centroid method has been abandoned. Only two methods are at all widely used, however, with such methods as alpha and image analysis being treated by most investigators as intellectual curiosities. The typical choice is between the principal axis and the maximum likelihood methods.

When the intent is to rotate and to make psychological interpretations of factors, the principal axes should be computed with estimates of communalities in the principal diagonal of the R matrix.

These are the principal factors of the R matrix. Principal components is the term applied when unities are placed in the principal diagonal. Components include both common and unique variance. At times the choice of the diagonal term makes little difference, but the point is that it can make a difference. Because the correct model can be used at little extra cost, why settle for something else that can create problems in interpretation? Psychological variables do not automatically have high reliability and minimal specific variance.

Among the possible choices for initial estimates of communalities, squared multiple correlations of each measure with all of the others has proven to be highly satisfactory. After the initial estimation one can iterate the communality estimates until some criterion of change has been met, but iteration is not always desirable. One can capitalize on small random variations among the correlations and produce untenable final estimates. Iterated communalities should always be inspected for reasonableness. Values greater than one are mathematically unreasonable, but other anomalies can only be detected by a criterion of psychological meaningfulness.

The most widely used criterion for deciding on the number of factors is Kaiser's (1961) number of roots greater than 1.0 in the R matrix in which unities have been placed in the diagonal as the initial step. This is not adequate. There are frequently occurring circumstances in which this criterion is known to overestimate the number of common factors, and there are other circumstances in which underestimation occurs. The scree test is a useful source of evidence, but there are typically several breaks in the curve defined by the latent roots. Less widely used, but deserving of greater use, is the parallel analysis criterion of Montanelli and Humphreys (1976). The latter requires estimates of the latent roots obtained from an R matrix in which distributions of random normal deviates based on the same sample size as used in the research are substituted for the same number of psychological variables.

The maximum likelihood method is more expensive in computer time, but it provides a chi square test of the hypothesis that m common factors can be rejected as an adequate explanation of the intercorrelations. This would appear to be an important asset. However, in Monte Carlo studies the method was less accurate in recovering the known number of factors than the parallel analysis criterion (Humphreys & Montanelli, 1975) and made consistent overestimates in other matrices (Tucker, personal communication, 1984).

Whether the principal factors or maximum likelihood factors are computed, one has the rotational problem. If there is no interest in higher order factors, the Varimax program is highly satisfactory. It well deserves its popularity. If one looks only at the factor patterns, the results from several different oblique rotational programs have a great deal of communality. There is no point in using an oblique program, however, unless one plans to at least interpret the factor intercorrelations. Second-order factors are dependent on one's confidence in the intercorrelations of the first-order factors. It is uncertain at this point in time which oblique rotational program should be recommended for this purpose, but Tucker (1984) has a program that has been highly promising in several Monte Carlo comparisons with other oblique solutions.

Analysis of Variance. The general linear model has been slowly replacing the traditional analysis of variance. It is simply unfortunate that the trend has not developed more rapidly. Dummy coding of categorical variables makes the use of regression statistics applicable, and regression analysis is more flexible. Unequal Ns are handled without distortion, and it has become more acceptable to report measures of strength of relationships in addition to the traditional F ratios.

A second important addition is multivariate ANOVA, but use of this useful, even required method of experimental design and analysis is growing more slowly. Psychology is essentially a multivariate discipline, but many experimenters elect to use a single dependent variable, sometimes chosen quite arbitrarily, when several are easily possible. The need for several arises because many dependent variables in use are factorially complex. The total variance of the dependent variable may not be affected by the experimental treatment. If only one component of variance is affected, this can only be determined by means of a careful selection of dependent variables.

I demonstrated quantitatively (Humphreys, 1943) the presence of two independent factors in various measures of strength of conditioned eyelid responses in the human. Razran (1935) had argued theoretically that there were physiological and psychological bases for two factors. Two factors, defined by latency and amplitude, respectively, were apparent in my intercorrelations and in the well-nigh redundant factor analysis. In typical experi-

ments, however, amplitude, latency, and frequency as well were all correlated similarly with the number of reinforced acquisition trials. Seemingly independent factors among standard dependent variables were of little significance. Two factors were revealed, however, in the comparison of 50% and 100% reinforcement (Humphreys, 1939). This treatment affected the latency factor but not the one defined by amplitude. If the analysis of individual differences reveals more than a single factor among possible dependent variables, one will be able to find an independent variable that will show differential effects.

Fitting Factor and Path Models. Following the development of the LISREL methodology by Joreskog and associates, the fitting of factor and path models has grown rapidly. It had been possible to rotate toward a model by means of so-called Procrustes rotations, but this provided no statistic of goodness of fit. Use of the maximum likelihood criterion in LISREL provides a chi square that can be used to reject the fit of a given model to the observations. When applied to common factor models, a distinction is made between exploratory analyses, in which principal factors are rotated to simple structure, and confirmatory analyses, in which the observations are fitted to a theoretical model.

The principal advantage of maximum likelihood fitting is the attendant chi square, but this index is being treated commonly as a descriptive rather than a statistical index of goodness of fit. There are grounds for doing this in that chi square, as t and F, is a function of sample size. Thus, if a model is tried out on very large samples, any model can be rejected. Interpreting statistically significant chi squares in this way, however, is presently highly subjective and occasionally even erroneous. I have seen a criterion proposed in terms of a value less than some constant times the number of degrees of freedom, but this neglects the important variable of sample size. If one is interested in a descriptive statistic, there is no need for maximum likelihood. Start with a LISREL model, use a least squares criterion of goodness of fit, and report mean squared error.

In every application of fitting observations to a theoretical model it is typically possible to find alternative models that provide equally good fits. This principle becomes especially important in the fitting of factor models. If a model involving m factors provides an acceptable fit to the observations, one can find by rotation an infinite number of models that will fit equally well. Also, if m

factors provide an acceptable fit, $m+1$, $m+2$, etc., factors will provide acceptable fits as long as one does not run short of degrees of freedom. Routine testing of alternative models provides a firmer foundation for conclusions about a particular model.

Fitting path and other models with LISREL is attractive because the coefficients are those for latent traits that are not subject to measurement error. This controls one of the major sources of bias in drawing causal inferences from observed variables. However, there are also errors of estimation. The requirement that each construct be defined by three measures is an essential minimum; more than three are desirable. The methodology represents a leap forward, not merely a step, but important problems remain in making causal inferences from data that are not controlled experimentally. The constructs estimated are all too often reified by those who interpret the results. More importantly, the very difficult problem of being able to develop measures of all necessary constructs remains. The identification of important variables requiring statistical control is much more difficult. The problem of the important variable that has not been measured or perhaps not even considered for measurement is ever present.

Item Response Theory. Item response theory (IRT) has taken psychometricians by storm. Use is growing rapidly, and the methodology is also changing rapidly. It is much too early to predict long-term impact, but initial enthusiasm needs to be tempered by a little skepticism. There are several applications that need careful evaluation, and the computational algorithm may not deliver everything the model promises.

A basic problem is that a literal interpretation of the assumption of unidimensionality may lead to undesirable consequences psychologically. I have argued elsewhere (Humphreys, 1979, 1985) that the most important human traits are broad ones, such as general intelligence or its two major components, Vernon's (1960) verbal-numerical-educational and spatial-mechanical-practical group factors. Broader factors are probably more important in the personality domain as well. It is possible to construct broad tests so that only one dominant dimension is measured, but such tests are not unidimensional in the strict sense.

The IRT model is also being widely used to investigate item "bias" in comparisons of various demographic groups. This use, remembering the connotations of bias, is unfortunate. The primary outcome is a difference. A subsequent judgment is required before an emotionally laden label is applied. This is especially important as the IRT methodology is presently used because the focus is on the displacement between two item characteristic curves. This obscures the important difference between slope and intercept, which for items are discrimination and difficulty. It also ignores the difference between the regression of the item on the latent trait and the regression of the trait on the item.

A difference in item discrimination can arise artifactually as a result of floor and ceiling effects or from a differential degree of range of talent in the two groups. A large difference in the absence of these artifacts, however, indicates a substantial cultural difference between the two groups. One group does not understand the item and is unable to respond to it in a meaningful way. Here use of bias is appropriate. In contrast, within wider limits than random sampling theory would allow, differences in difficulty can arise as a function of incomplete overlap, in the groups being compared, of the multiple determinants underlying the response to the item. There is no basis for the common belief that item responses are determined by an entity or unitary trait. From the point of view that some moderate dispersal of item difficulties is intrinsic to behavioral measurement, it is a mistake to call such differences bias. A difference in one direction can readily be corrected in the total score by a difference in the other.

The full implications of a difference between the two regressions are unclear to me at present. It is clear, however, that an item can discriminate equally well in two groups when one of the two regressions is compared, but can discriminate unequally when the other regression is the focus. IRT obtains the regression of the item on the estimate of the latent trait. Although classical item analysis rarely if ever compared regressions, if a regression were to be selected, it would logically be that of the total score on the dichotomous item. This regression is linear, for obvious reasons, and the point biserial is therefore an acceptable component of the regression statistic. Should the score one will use to predict an external criterion be estimated with equal accuracy in two groups by the items, should the items be estimated with equal accuracy in the two groups by the hypothetical trait, or should both regressions be approximately equal?

IRT analysis as a method for detecting item bias is also affected by a statistical principle that extends to all comparisons of observed data to a model. If sample size is sufficiently large, all psychological models can be rejected by any of the tests of statistical significance. Given a nonzero difference of any size in the population, t, F, and X^2 will at some point become sufficiently large that the null hypothesis can be rejected. It seems highly probable that there are no zero differences or zero correlations in nature, although there may be many trivial differences and correlations. It is important, therefore, to evaluate the size of the group difference when studying item differences. It is neither good science nor good social policy to label items as biased when the difference between two groups is small descriptively.

Problems in Psychological Research

I have strong convictions about the nature of psychological research and methods of analysis of data that I shall describe and justify in this section. In spite of high rejection rates in our journals I believe that there is a great deal of published research that does little to advance the science. Indeed some published research creates retrogression.

What Researchers Do.   Research is basically the search for relationships or correlations among variables. The popular contrast between correlational research and experimental research is misleading. It is more accurate to recognize that all of us are concerned with correlations, but the difference is between experimental control and its absence. Whatever one's philosophic preference may be with respect to the meaning of causation, correlations obtained under experimental control can be given causal interpretation with more confidence than those in which experimental control is absent.

In addition to the control of stimulus and situational variables that are capable of biasing the results, it is necessary to assign subjects at random, with or without a covariate, to experimental treatments. One cannot do an experiment on intact groups unless multiple groups can be randomly assigned to treatments. One cannot ever do an experiment on a subject or individual differences variable. One cannot assign subjects at random to male and female groups or to levels of general intelligence. A subject variable can be a covariate or a dependent variable but never an independent variable.

The statistics of sampling variability such as t, F, and X^2 tell only part of the story about the correlations discovered in research. They provide information about the sampling *stability* of the correlation, but provide no information about its size. Holding size constant these statistics vary directly with sample size. If one knows t and the number of degrees of freedom on which it is based, one can quickly compute the product-moment (point biserial) correlation between the independent and dependent variables. This statistic varies between zero and one, and its population estimate is independent of sample size. (The bias in the sample statistic is typically quite small.) If one knows F and the number of degrees of freedom for both the numerator and the denominator, one can quickly compute the nonlinear correlation (eta). Obtaining the population estimate of eta is more critical than doing the same for r because, with more than two levels of treatment, the bias in the sample is larger. Eta also has a range from zero to one, and its population estimate is independent of sample size. To know the size of a correlation discovered in research the obvious solution is to compute a correlation.

Probably because experimental has been contrasted with correlational, experimentalists have been slow to adopt the use of correlations. The fixation on tests of significance has been a handicap. All differences between means and even correlations tend to be categorized as significant or not significant. The problem becomes acute when individual differences variables become the target of research. By categorizing the continuous distribution of some measure, creating levels for an analysis of variance, and reporting an F ratio only, some research people act as if they had converted a correlational problem into an experiment.

When converting F ratios into correlations, it is highly desirable to follow the advice of Peters and Van Vorrhis (1940) rather than Hays (1963). The latter described the use of omega square, which is the population estimate of the sample correlation ratio in which the denominator includes all of the variance contributed by other independent variables and their interactions in addition to the variance of the component of variance of immediate interest. The earlier authors used a different name, epsilon square, for the partial correlation between the given component of variance and the dependent variables with all other experimentally controlled sources of variance held constant. The population estimate of the correlation between an independent and a dependent variables that is con-

411

founded with other sources of variance that the experimenter has inserted in the design is essentially meaningless.

Misuses of Hypothesis Testing. Hypothesis testing is widely used incorrectly. In a first experiment, the statistical hypothesis of no differences between population means is rejected at a given level of confidence. In a second experiment in which the independent and dependent variables appear to be identical, the statistical hypothesis of a zero population difference cannot be rejected. The author concludes that there has been failure to replicate, but the hypothesis that there has been failure to replicate has not been tested. It is essential that the difference in the size of the two differences be evaluated directly. There is an appropriate t test for the direct comparison of two differences, and the F ratio for the interaction of the independent variable with the two experiments is the square of the t for the difference between differences when a pooled estimate of the population variance has been obtained (Humphreys, 1980).

The folly of comparing two differences independently with a hypothetical population value of the difference of zero and concluding that the significant difference is larger than the nonsignificant one reaches its zenith when the sample size is smaller for the nonsignificant difference. Most psychologists when asked the direct question will respond that the null hypothesis cannot be proved, but they discuss their findings as if the null hypothesis were true. Inability to reject the null hypothesis is *not* the equivalent of acceptance. Depending on sample size, inability to reject a zero population difference could be accompanied in the same data by inability to reject a population difference of substantial size.

Differences between correlations present a completely parallel situation. One correlation is significant at some acceptable level of significance, a second is not. The researcher discusses the two correlations as if the first were greater than the second. In this case, also, the two correlations must be compared directly with each other if one expects to draw an inference concerning their respective sizes in the population. A given correlation can be greater than a population value of zero at an acceptable level of significance, but not be greater than a sample correlation of zero or even a small negative value. Standard errors of differences are larger than the standard errors of the separate statistics.

The necessity of comparing sample correlations,

or differences between means, directly with each other does not arise only in attempts to replicate. Suppose that one has a single criterion and n different predictors. Some of the n possible correlations with the criterion are statistically significant and some are not, but one cannot conclude that some predictors are correlated with the criterion and some are not. One must still compare the sample correlations directly with each other. Failure to make the direct comparison constitutes what is probably the most common statistical error committed by psychologists.

Compulsive Hypothesis Testing. Suppose that one is reporting correlations greater than .7 and sample size is several hundred. The author of the article places asterisks after each correlation, and the footnote reports that p is less than .05. For an N of 227 and a sample correlation of .707, t for the hypothesis that rho is zero is 15. The p value is obviously smaller than .05 raised to a rather sizeable power. No one competent to read the results of the research needs to be told that p is less than .05. Some other hypothesis may be relevant. Is the sample correlation of .707 greater than a population value of .6?

Several years ago we published some research involving dichotomous individual differences variables in a factorial design in which the maximum sample size was approximately 100,000 (Humphreys, Lin, & Fleishman, 1976). The statistical equivalents of the main effects and their interactions were reported in the form of correlations. We did not compute a single F ratio for the excellent reason that we had no interest in interpreting correlations of .01. An editorial consultant condemned the manuscript because there were no mean squares and F ratios. He advised us to do an analysis of variance. We did interpret some fairly small correlations, but we had the satisfaction of knowing that a correlation of .15 was greater than .14 and less than .16.

This discussion also points up a common misunderstanding concerning the definition of the null hypothesis. A test of a null hypothesis does not require that the statistical hypothesis be a zero difference between means, a zero difference between differences, a zero correlation, or a zero difference between correlations. The null hypothesis is defined as a zero difference between the observed statistic and the statistical hypothesis no matter what the size of the latter may be.

The Alternative to Hypothesis Testing. Although hypothesis testing as used in psychological research can be more sophisticated than it is currently, it is not the paradigm of choice in basic research. In applied research it may be necessary to make a decision pro or con at the conclusion of a study, but in basic research the scientist can always withhold judgment and gather more data. As a matter of fact, the application of hypothesis testing par excellence is to quality control. There must be a decision rule for stopping the machinery and adjusting it.

Consider the following examples of how little the hypothesis testing paradigm contributes to psychological knowledge. The correlation between a selection test and an important criterion is statistically significant. Although a population correlation of zero can be rejected, a rho of .01 cannot be rejected. Or suppose that a rho of zero cannot be rejected, but neither can a rho of .5 be rejected. Should the correlation in the first of these two examples be considered important and useful, but the second not?

These examples become even more ludicrous if one allows sample size to vary. In the first studies, following passage of civil rights legislation, of the predictability of performance of blacks in comparison to whites, the size of the black sample was typically much smaller than the size of the white. Thus it became possible for a correlation of .4 in the black sample to be nonsignificant whereas a correlation of .20 in the white sample could be statistically significant. The correlation of .40 was interpreted as if it were zero and therefore smaller than the one of .20.

The substitution of confidence intervals for tests of significance provides a means of interpreting psychological data more validly. A particular statistical hypothesis represents only one of an infinite number of possible population parameters. A confidence interval recognizes this and provides for an infinite number of tests of hypotheses. It does not matter whether one is concerned with means or with correlations, any difference or any correlation falling within the confidence interval represents a possible hypothesis that cannot be rejected with alpha equal to one minus the level of confidence used in forming the interval. By the same token, any difference or any correlation falling outside the confidence interval represents a possible hypothesis that can be rejected at the same level of alpha. When there is a great deal of overlap between the confidence intervals for two or more differences or two or more correlations, it becomes obvious that one cannot conclude that the larger statistic having the confidence interval that excludes a particular statistical hypothesis represents a larger population parameter than the statistic that has the confidence interval that includes the same statistical hypothesis.

If confidence intervals were reported routinely, it would become clear that the typical study in our journals furnishes relatively little information about the phenomenon being investigated. The typical hypothesis tested is the zero difference between means or the zero correlation. Rejection of the hypothesis tells one that the sign of the relationship is either positive or negative, nothing more, whereas correlations can vary between zero and one. Although the size of the correlation between an independent and dependent variable in an experiment can never be determined to point accuracy, experiments using large samples, effective covariates, or both can narrow the confidence interval and allow more precise predictions of outcomes than the sign of a correlation.

The proper use of confidence intervals allows one to define a testable hypothesis in the situation in which one would like to support the null hypothesis rather than reject it. One proceeds by defining in advance of doing the study a range of differences or correlations that one will consider to be trivial in size. Then, if the sample statistic falls within the trivial interval *and* if the entire confidence interval about the sample statistic also falls within the trivial interval, one has the support required. Support for a conclusion that a difference or a correlation is trivial in size requires a design with a great deal of power. A sample statistic falling within the trivial range but with a confidence interval falling well above the positive or negative limit, let alone beyond both limits, does not represent a trivial degree of relationship.

Reporting Research. Psychology is a quantitative science. Numbers are more meaningful than many pages of interpretive comments by the author. Authors should write for the sophisticated reader, and the latter should be given enough information that he or she can interpret the data without assistance from the author. Present editorial policies are typically at the other end of these continua.

A complete summary table should be published when the analysis of variance is used. There is information in small F ratios, but the fixation on hypothesis testing neglects these. Means and variances should also be routinely reported. I have seen articles in which the author concentrated on the significance of the difference, but the reader had to infer the direction of the difference.

Tables of correlations and factor loadings should be published in their entirety. Again there is information in small correlations and in small factor loadings that should not be disregarded. Readers should not be encouraged to infer that the small correlations commonly omitted from tables are zero correlations. There is, of course, a high probability that unsophisticated readers will misinterpret small correlations, but a scientific journal is not published for the benefit of unsophisticated persons. The latter should sign up for courses and read text books.

There is widespread neglect of the effects on correlations, especially those obtained under conditions of experimental control, of errors of measurement and restriction of the range of "talent." These matters are not a part of test theory *per se*, but are an integral part of measurement theory. A careless experimenter must be concerned with measurement error in both independent and dependent variables; a careful experimenter needs to worry about the reliability of the dependent variable only. It takes more than careful experimentation to assure high reliability of the dependent measure.

Reduction of the generally acceptable level of alpha from .05 to .01 alone, would have useful affects on the quality of research. Abandonment of the critical ratio of 3.00 by psychologists was not based on the error arising from failure to use unbiased estimates to population variances and the distributions of t associated with the varying number of degrees of freedom. Because there is no single distribution of t, Fisher published tables for selected values of p. He selected fairly large values of p because it is typically more difficult to obtain large samples in agricultural than in psychological research. Unless there are limitations on sample size imposed by the nature of the research, psychologists should be held to a higher standard of significance. Concern about beta errors can always be met by increasing sample size to the point that the beta error reaches a trivial size. As a side benefit of this change, there would be less publication pressure on our journals!

Psychological Measurement Scales. There is inadequate recognition of the problems associated with psychological scales of measurement. Variation of the size of the units of measurement at different levels of the distribution of scores can produce spurious interactions, spurious differences in variance, and nonlinearity of regressions. Counting the number of items correct on a psychological test does not produce an interval scale of measurement. Each rater who uses a rating scale imposes his or her own zero and size of units on the ratings.

If there is a difference in the amount of measurement error in the distributions of scores on a test for two different samples of examinees, correlations of those scores with another measure will be differentially attenuated. Perhaps a number of items are biased in their measurement properties for one of the groups. The less reliable test is expected to have smaller correlations with other measures, but the numerical slope of the regression of those other measures on the test is expected to be steeper. The explanation for this seeming paradox is that the units of measurement in the two groups are not equal.

Raw scores on tests and observed ratings furnish ordinal information only. Nonlinear transformations of scores based on theory may allow one to move from ordinal to interval information, but the transformed scores should be treated somewhat tentatively. It does not follow, however, that one should use only nonparametric statistics with tests and rating measures. Use of parametric statistics does require sophistication and, like the defense of freedom, eternal vigilance. Whenever possible, research should be designed so that the conclusions are independent of monotonic transformations of the dependent variable (Birnbaum, 1982).

Psychologists tend to avoid looking at variances of their dependent variables, but seemingly not because they are concerned about their units of measurement. Their focus is entirely on measures of central tendency. The potential inequality of units of measurement in different parts of the scale is not a problem when two samples from the same population have similar means but different variances. It rarely occurs to the researcher that an independent variable might have an effect on a measure of variability.

It is also true that inspection of variances when there are differences in measures of central tendency can reveal a problem with the measurement scale. It is generally stated that heterogeneity of variance does not make a critical difference in the interpretation of F ratios, but an important qualification is not added. When the distribution of variances is highly correlated with their accompanying means, a measurement scale problem is ensured.

Training of Students. There is reason for

concern about the training of graduate students in psychology. It is too easy to input data into a computer and obtain an output. The manual that describes computer programs cannot educate the user to the point that allows sophisticated choice of options and interpretation of the data. A one-year graduate course following a brief, inadequate undergraduate exposure to quantitative methodology is not a sufficient basis for a career in psychological research or teaching.

What is needed? A psychologist should have an undergraduate major or minor in mathmatics including, in addition to the traditional courses, matrix algebra. Add computer science. In graduate school there should be at least two full years in methodology courses or the equivalent in independent study. Course work is not essential, but knowledge is. Availability of a digital computer with large capacity is a necessary but not sufficient condition for the use of LISREL and other multivariate methodologies.

References

Birnbaum, M. H. (1982). Controversies in Psychological measurement. In B. Wegener (Ed.), *Social attitudes and psychophysical measurement* (pp. 401–486). Hillsdale, NJ: Erlbaum.

Fisher, R. A. (1935). *The design of experiments*. Edinburgh: Oliver & Boyd.

Flanagan, J. C. (1935). *Factor analysis in the study of personality*. Palo Alto, CA: Stanford University Press.

Gilliland, A. R., & Humphreys, D. W. (1943). Age, sex, method, and interval as variables in time estimation. *The Journal of Genetic Psychology, 63*, 123–130.

Hays, W. L. (1963). *Statistics for psychologists*. New York: Holt, Rinehart & Winston.

Holzinger, K. J., & Swineford, F. (1937). The bi-factor method. *Psychometrike, 2*, 42–54.

Hotelling, H. (1933). Analysis of a complex of statistical variables into principal components. *Journal of Educational Psychology, 24*, 417–441, 498–520.

Hotelling, H. (1935). The most predictable criterion. *Journal of Educational Psychology, 26*, 139–142.

Humphreys, L. G. (1939). The effect of random alternation of reinforcement on the acquisition and extinction of conditioned eyelid reactions. *Journal of Experimental Psychology, 25*, 141–158.

Humphreys, L. G. (1943). Measures of strength of conditioned eyelid responses. *Journal of General Psychology, 29*, 101–111.

Humphreys, L. G. (1979). The construct of general intelligence. *Intelligence, 3*, 105–120.

Humphreys, L. G. (1980). The statistics of failure to replicate: a comment on Buriel's conclusions. *Journal of Educational Psychology, 72*, 71–75.

Humphreys, L. G. (1985). General intelligence: An integration of factor, test, and simplex theory. In B. Wolman (Ed.), *Handbook of intelligence* (pp. 201–224). New York: Wiley.

Humphreys, L. G., & Fleishman, A. (1974). Pseudo-orthogonal and other analysis of variance designs involving individual differences variables. *Journal of Educational Psychology, 66*, 464–472.

Humphreys, L. G., & Montanelli, R. (1975). An investigation of the parallel analysis criterion for determining the number of common factors. *Mutivariate Behavioral Research, 10*, 183–206.

Humphreys, L. G., Lin, P., & Fleishman, A. (1976). The sex by race interaction in cognitive measures. *Journal of Research in Personality, 10*, 42–58.

Kaiser, H. F. (1961). A note on Guttman's lower bound for the number of common factors. *British Journal of Statistical Psychology, 14*, 1–2.

Kelly, T. L. (1935). *Essential traits of mental life*. Cambridge, MA: Harvard University Press.

Kelly, T. L. (1939). The selection of upper and lower groups for the validation of test items. *Journal of Educational Psychology, 30*, 17–24.

Kuder, G. F., & Richardson, M. W. (1937). The theory of estimation of test reliability. *Psychometrika, 2*, 151–160.

Montanelli, R., & Humphreys, L. G. (1976). Latent roots of random data correlation matrices with squared multiple correlations on the diagonal: A Monte Carlo study. *Psychometrika, 41*, 341–348.

Peters, C. C., & Van Voorhis, W. R. (1940). *Statistical procedures and their mathematical bases*. New York: McGraw-Hill.

Razran, G. H. S. (1935). Conditioned responses: An experimental study and a theoretical analysis. *Archives of Psychology, #191*.

Spearman, C. (1927). *The abilities of man*. New York: Macmillan.

Thurstone, L. L. (1931). *The reliability and validity of tests*. Ann Arbor, MI: Edwards Brothers.

Thurstone, L. L. (1935). *The vectors of mind*. Chicago, IL: University of Chicago Press.

Thurstone, L. L. (1938). *Primary mental abilities*. Psychometric Monographs, No. 1. Chicago, IL: University of Chicago Press.

Underwood, B. J. (1957). *Psychological research*. New York: Appleton-Century-Crofts.

Vernon, P. (1960). *The structure of human abilities* (rev. ed.). London: Methuen.

Wright, S. (1921). Correlation and causation. Journal of *Agricultural Research, 20*, 557–585.

CHAPTER 20

Perspectives on Educational Psychology

Ernest R. Hilgard

The comments that follow are based on a long career, primarily through my professorship in academic psychology in the School of Humanities and Sciences at Stanford University, but secondarily through a professorship held jointly in the School of Education, beginning a half-century ago. Professional affiliation with education began in the summer of 1927, when in the midst of my graduate study in psychology at Yale I spent the summer as a teaching assistant in courses in vocational guidance under Harry D. Kitson at Teachers College, had course work there with Ben D. Wood, and became well acquainted with Goodwin Watson. I had only a single graduate course in educational psychology at Yale under V. A. C. Henmon, who had interrupted his career at the University of Wisconsin to teach for a time at Yale. In addition to teaching educational psychology to graduate students in education at Stanford, I spent a sabbatical year at the University of Chicago in 1940–1941 to work with Daniel Prescott in a special program in the Department of Education on child development and teacher personnel. I was chairman of a Yearbook of the National Society for the Study of Education on theories of learning and instruction (Hilgard, 1964). Although I have not been very active in educational societies, I have

had contact with more recent developments through my membership in the National Academy of Education. At present I have completed a book on the history of twentieth-century psychology in America, and in the preparation of a chapter on educational psychology I have reviewed some of the matters touched upon here, and I have made use of some of the material from that chapter.

The Nineteenth-Century Background in America

The history of educational psychology cannot be divorced from the development of educational theory and practices during the years that educational psychology was implicit rather than explicit. From Europe came the influence of Pestalozzi, Herbart, Froebel, and their American representatives. William T. Harris (1835–1909) was a powerful figure, not only as superintendent of the schools in St. Louis, but as Commissioner of Education. He was an innovative administrator and an educational reactionary at the same time. Although he wrote an educational psychology (Harris, 1898) as a Hegelian in philosophy, he had no use for experimental psychology, and opposed Colonel Parker, John Dewey, and progressive education. Still he was the first to make the kindergarten part of the public school system, and made curricular innova-

Ernest R. Hilgard • Department of Psychology, Stanford University, Stanford, CA 94305.

tions. From the side of psychology G. Stanley Hall (1844–1924) with his role in the child study movement, his journal *Pedagogical Seminary,* and his students, both at Johns Hopkins and at Clark University, made a developmental psychology (then called genetic psychology) explicit for educators, most notably in his major work *Adolescence* (Hall, 1904), published after he had already been teaching, lecturing, and promoting for two decades. Another encouragement was given to a possible educational psychology by William James in his *Talks to teachers* (1899). James' book appeared after he had already become recognized as America's leading psychologist.

The Influence of Global Perspectives

A general theory in psychology is something like a political platform, in that its policies are stated as of large scope, and in a form to encourage enthusiastic adherents, and often equally committed opponents. At another level, there are details of procedure, methods, and practices that may have more in common than the general platforms suggest. There were two overriding positions in American education for many years. One was that of John Dewey (1859–1952), who preferred to call his position "experimentalism" or "instrumentalism," actually his variety of pragmatism. The second was that of Edward L. Thorndike (1874–1949), whose *stimulus-response* became the foundation for what was called the scientific movement in education. Like major party platforms, both were essentially positivistic, for certainly Dewey's pragmatism and Thorndike's positivism have much in common in their scientific logic and both men valued the word "experimental." The differences rested in part on their general political views, with Dewey the liberal and school reformer, and Thorndike the conservative, accepting the conventional values of society as reflected in the schools as they exist. At another level, they differed in the criteria to be met to determine the effectiveness of their recommendations when applied to practice. Dewey wanted to free the child's intelligence for self-initiated creative activity, problem solving, and social responsibility; Thorndike wanted the child to be equipped for effectiveness in performing necessary tasks by acquiring a mass of learned connections between stimuli and situations. The product that Dewey hoped for

could be judged and evaluated by the child's productive behavior, particularly in social situations; Thorndike wished to have the evidence come by measurement, with the famous dictum that everything that exists exists in some amount, hence can be measured. The difference became reflected in the practice of progressive education, as espoused by Dewey and his disciples, and in conventional education, judged by achievement tests, by those who followed Thorndike. Eventually both progressive education and the scientific movement in education were failures as major orientations, but this gets ahead of the story.

Of course pitting Dewey against Thorndike is only a small part of the turmoil that all along characterized educational psychology. Another strong figure was Charles H. Judd (1873–1946), better trained in experimental psychology than Dewey, but in the functionalist tradition of James, Dewey, and the University of Chicago, despite his Ph.D. under Wundt in Leipzig. In some ways he fell between Dewey and Thorndike, with a sensible position of the kind that influences students but does not make visibly committed disciples. In educational psychology, one of his emphases was on the teaching of the special school subjects, thus recognizing that content to be taught bears on how it should be taught. Unlike Thorndike, he preferred to emphasize the higher thought processes leading to generalizations from what is learned, but like Thorndike he also valued disciplined experimentation in the schools.

Eventually, alternative perspectives began to have influence upon educational psychology: Watsonian behaviorism, never fully endorsed by Thorndike, Gestalt psychology, and psychoanalysis.

Educational Research and Innovation between Two Wars

Largely as a consequence of Thorndike's insistence on measurement in all aspects of education, supported by the prominence that intelligence and achievement testing had received just before and after World War I, the decade of the 1920s was one in which educational psychology flourished. Educational psychologists, of all educational specialists, appeared to be best qualified to do the necessary research on student abilities and the most efficient methods of instruction. One leading educator and historian of education, Elwood P. Cubberley, was emboldened to call psychology "the master science" for education (Cubberley, 1920).

In a review of the period 1918–1927, W. S. Monroe and his associates (1928) noted the forward surge that was given to educational research by the establishment of the Commonwealth Fund in 1918, which began to subsidize educational research. The American Council on Education, with an aim to improve education, was founded in 1919. Monroe and others were able to assemble 3,700 references to studies that made worthwhile contributions during the period under review. Of them, they selected for favorable comment five major research projects: (a) the University of Chicago studies of reading associated primarily with Judd, Guy Buswell, and W. S. Gray; (b) the extensive study by Thorndike and his associates of intelligence in the years 1922–1925, culminating in *The Measurement of Intelligence* (Thorndike, Bergman, Cobb, Woodyard, & Staff 1926); (c) the initiation of Terman's study of gifted children and the appearance of its first two volumes; (d) the nature–nurture studies in the Yearbook of the National Society for the Study of Education that appeared in 1928; and (e) an investigation directed by George D. Strayer, an authority on educational administration, known as the Educational Finance Inquiry, published in 13 volumes appearing between 1923 and 1925. It may be noted that of the five selected studies from the current educational research, only the last fell outside of educational psychology. Of the others, three had to do primarily with testing. Only one in their listing, the investigations of reading, used laboratory methods and was directed to a topic basic to the school curriculum. This is hardly what would have been expected, with the prominence, in theory, given to the scientific movement.

The Failure of the Scientific Movement

Psychologists, who could understand Thorndike and Judd as educational psychologists of their own stripe, felt comfortable in using their familiar research methods in the study of learning and of individual differences in the schools. Thorndike, the experimentalist and quantifier, was the model. In the 1930s, along with the other trends in education, the more familiar attempts to experiment and measure went on, and became summarized in another Yearbook of the National Society of Education (1938) under the chairmanship of Frank N. Freeman (1880–1961), long a professor at the Uni-

versity of Chicago and later Dean of Education at the University of California (Berkeley). The book was a summarization of the contributions of research in 37 chapters, with two final chapters on the science and philosophy implied, one written by Dewey, the other by Freeman. To a general psychologist the book reads little like the expected summaries of research because of the essay character of many of the chapters, the limited amount of quantitative data, and the few citations of the most convincing research studies. The impression is left that there was something wrong about the directions taken. The type of concrete study with which Thorndike had been identified was only tangentially represented, although many of the chapters were by his students. Judd's contribution was limited to his chapter on school surveys. Freeman, in his concluding chapter, hints at his dissatisfaction with the approach:

This review of the achievements of the scientific movement in education during the past generation makes an impressive showing. The ultimate significance of this movement, however, is not determined beyond question by such a review. It is possible, after examining these achievements, to view them as essentially superficial in character, as concerned with the husk rather than the kernel of the educational process. Science can, in this view, evaluate the means but not the ends; it can estimate the efficiency of the process but cannot determine or even influence its direction. It has, therefore, gone about as far as it can in improving education. (Freeman, 1938, pp. 487–488)

This is about as negative a statement as could have been written by an editor whose volume was intended to celebrate the achievements of the scientific movement, dominated as it was by educational psychology, of which he was a representative.

The Rise and Decline of Progressive Education

Dewey's idealized hopes of reforming and democratizing the schools, with the ultimate aim of transforming society, in the end fared no better than the scientific movement. The Progressive Education Association, founded in 1920 on Dewey's principles, had always been more committed to innovation than to research, and looked askance at intelligence and achievement tests as divisive. In fairness to him, it must be noted that Dewey was critical of the Association, and never joined, although he was given honorary status.

Later leaders saw that a more positive approach was needed if progressive education was to make its case in terms of the outcomes of its practices. Hence, a new conception of measurement was introduced that would reflect the aims of education better than the standardized achievement tests. A leader in the new type of appraisal, that went by the name of *evaluation* was inaugurated by an educational psychologist, Ralph W. Tyler, who was for a number of years chairman of the Department of Education and Dean of the School of Education at the University of Chicago. The concept of evaluation caught on as a way of justifying modern educational practices (e.g., Leonard & Eurich, 1942), but it was subject to abuse as it departed from any precise relationship to measurement, with purely narrative description occasionally accepted as evaluation.

A final burst of activity to justify progressive education took place in the Eight-Year Study. Under the auspices of the Progressive Education Association through its Commission on the Relation of School to College established in October of 1930, a long-range investigation was undertaken. Thirty secondary schools, willing to make radical changes according to democratic objectives of education, began an 8-year program of change and recordkeeping in 1933, and 29 of them completed the 8 years. Of the 29 completing the study, 12 were public high schools, two were high schools connected with state universities, three with private universities, and the remaining 12 were private schools. Although the original language appeared to stress measurement, the "scores" were primarily those of new evaluation instruments (Smith, *et al.*, 1942).

How did it all come out? Five volumes were published on various aspects of the program, under the general title of *Adventure in American education*. The general overview was presented by Wilford M. Aiken, the Director, with the title *The Story of the Eight-Year Study* (1942). A follow-up study, *Did They Succeed in College?* (Chamberlin, Chamberlin, Drought, & Scott, 1942) compared 1,475 graduates of the schools with a matched group, based on aptitude or intelligence tests, the graduates all studying at the same time in the same colleges and universities. The results were quite favorable in showing that it was not necessary to prepare according to fixed courses and units in high school in order to meet college requirements. In general (except for inferiority in foreign languages), the students from the 29 schools did as well or better than their matched controls.

The hope of the Eight-Year Study had been to revitalize progressive education. Even its friendly critics realized that progressive education was in crisis (Bode, 1938). Why did such an extensive, forward-looking, and successful program have so little impact on secondary education? A major factor may have been that the reports appeared during World War II when the war effort took all the attention, professional societies did not meet on a regular basis, and it was not a time for innovation. There was no great debate, mostly lack of interest as shown by the infrequent citations later. Even the few critical voices received little hearing (e.g., Johnson, 1946). The momentum was lost and never regained. The Progressive Education Association died in 1955, and its journal *Progressive Education* ceased publication in 1957. Dewey's ideas were not actually dead, and the John Dewey Society for the Study of Education and Culture continued, but the "movement" no longer existed.

It is little wonder that educators generally, accompanied by educational psychologists, turned to new viewpoints in psychology.

The conflicting psychological viewpoints among behaviorism, Thorndike's connectionism, and Dewey's instrumentalism, did not serve to resolve psychological conflicts among educational theorists, as had been noted by Boyd H. Bode, an educational philosopher, in an earlier book entitled *Conflicting Psychologies of Learning* (1929). Bode expressed the hope that the newer Gestalt psychology might promise a way out, and indeed there was a flurry of educational psychology texts based on Gestalt theory. At the same time, psychoanalysis was bringing a searchlight upon the individual that strengthened those who were seeking to adapt education to the needs of the child. Some interest in psychoanalysis was developing in the broader culture, but its influence was slow to enter education.

The years after World War II brought other changes, but it may prove informative to retrace steps somewhat to see what was being taught in courses in educational psychology, which often did not go deeply into matters of educational policy.

Because nearly all students in their preparation to become teachers had a course in educational psychology, and because many (perhaps most) American college teachers through the years relied on textbooks in their courses, the textbooks give some idea of what psychology was taught to prospective teachers over the years. There were, in general, two major types of textbooks for use in educational psychology courses. The first type attempted to teach what psychology the teacher ought to know, with little reference to schoolroom practices except to hold the student interest. This is a fair characterization of Thorndike's massive three-volume *Educational Psychology* (1913–1914), with the titles of each volume: 1. *The Original Nature of Man;* 2. *The Psychology of Learning;* and 3. *Mental Work and Fatigue, and Individual Differences and their Causes.* To be sure, these topics were likely to have been treated lightly in the general psychology texts of his day, making a special educational psychology text desirable, but there is little direct reference in texts of this kind to the practices of the teacher. By contrast, Judd's *Psychology of High School Subjects* (1915) takes the other position, that educational psychology should apply psychology to the teacher's problems and hence should move in a different direction, thus representing a second type of text. His position was later represented by Reed (1927). To be sure, Thorndike also wrote specialized books, such as *The Psychology of Arithmetic* (1922) and *The Psychology of Algebra* (1923), but these were considered to be textbooks concerned with specific aspects of the accepted curriculum rather than of general policy for educational psychology.

Two books by Arthur I. Gates (1890–1972) illustrate the relationship that commonly existed between textbooks in educational psychology and those in general psychology. He is a good representative to select because he was in a sense Thorndike's educational psychology disciple at Teachers College, and, with collaborators, authored a leading educational psychology textbook in revised versions over many years. His *Psychology for Students of Education* (1923), as its name implies, was intended to teach psychology to educators. With very little change it could be modified to become also his *Elementary Psychology* (1925), a book successful as a text in general psychology, and adopted as such at Yale when I began as a teaching assistant there in 1928. (Both the educational and general editions were revised later, a year apart, in 1929 and 1930.) It is of some interest to follow the changes in educational psychology textbooks over the years.

In an early review of three current textbooks in educational psychology (one of them that by Gates) Goodwin Watson (1926), then a young and

popular teacher at Teachers College, showed about equal numbers of pages devoted to tests and measurements, school subjects (especially reading, writing, and arithmetic), laws of learning (including general aspects of teaching methods), and physiology of sense organs, brain, and nervous system. Today's reader will note the absence of emphasis on child development, socialization, personality, and mental hygiene.

In a later summarization of educational psychology textbooks by Gates, Jersild, McKillop, Rivlin, Shoben, and Watson (1956), covering 83 textbooks published between 1920 and 1956 (with extensive revisions counted as new books), some interesting trends were noted by decades. In the later books, by contrast with those that Watson reviewed, the chief decline was in the number of pages devoted to the physiology of the brain and nervous system, despite a more than doubling of the pages devoted to the various topics categorized. If corrected for the general increases in pages per topic, emphasis on laws of learning and tests declined (though not as much as physiology) whereas the emphases on personality dynamics (counseling and guidance, unconscious motivation, mental hygiene) received four times as many pages and social processes (group dynamics, attitudes, etc.) received six times as many pages in the 1950–1956 period relative to their share on the basis of total pages in the 1920s.

Gates and his collaborators give a summary statement that is illuminating with respect to the changes:

It would seem that the productive innovations in theory in educational psychology during the past 25 years did not spring from intensive development of Thorndike's early work on original natur, laws of learning, and individual differences, nor from the innumerable experiments on teaching school subjects. The new light came rather from the impact of research carried on outside the field of learning and teaching. We understand the psychology of education better today than we did a generation ago largely because of the case studies and theories which came from psychoanalytic and other "depth psychology" clinics; because of the altered picture of mental processes which came from laboratory studies of perception; because of the experiments of some social psychologists on group cohesion, leadership, morale, and productivity; and because other social psychologists observed the formation of social norms, attitudes, and prejudices. (Gates *et al.*, 1956, 214)

It was true that psychological processes were better understood, but it was not clear that educational psychology had finally found itself, that is, was now contributing to the improvement of education in ways it was not able to do before. Some important developments lay ahead.

Instructional Psychology in the Late Twentieth Century

The cognitive revolution in psychology that began in the 1950s did not leave education unmoved. Piaget, standing as a symbol for cognitive growth, became a hero for education as he did for developmental psychologists (e.g., Green, 1978). His was not an educational psychology, and he sometimes had to answer requests for applications of his theory by referring to Montessori schools (Piaget, 1970). His emphasis on sensorimotor learning no doubt had some influence on the growth of Montessori schools in America after a relatively quiescent period (Elkind, 1967).

There were, however, other influences that led to an emphasis on cognitive processes. There was the shock of the Russian launching of Sputnik, with the fear that America had lost its lead in technology. This led to government support of education in traditional fields of mathematics and language learning, to which schools accommodated. This, however, merely accelerated developments that were already taking place.

Educational Technology

Technical aids to education had a long history; any review would have to recognize the importance of printing that made available books other than the handwritten copies that had to be chained to the tables of the libraries where they were consulted, the introduction of slates and blackboards, workbooks, outline maps, and the various other instructional aids. For our purposes, however, the more recently developed audiovisual aids and devices for programmed instruction were far more significant in the postwar period.

Audiovisual Aids. Projection lanterns for slide projection were available early, but they were cumbersome and expensive and not widely used in the classroom until the 35 mm. slide projectors with film strips became available, along with the 16 mm. and 8 mm. motion picture projectors. The early phonograph found some use, but mostly for music, and was not convenient for recording, except in the cylinder form of the early dictaphones.

The audio side of technology came into use with the sound motion picture and then with the electromagnetic recorder, at first the wire recorder, then the tape recorder. These changes moved rapidly, and their uses for instruction were greatly accelerated by the training done in the military forces during World War II (Glaser, 1962).

Audiovisual aids were important enough to have a yearbook devoted to them in 1949 (Corey, 1949). Dale (1954) brought instructional use of the methods to the attention of teachers. A good deal of research was done later, for example, how to make films instructive through response instead of a merely passive experience (e.g., May & Lumsdaine, 1958). The language laboratory was another important development because the audio equipment permitted hearing the correct spoken form, and allowed comparison of the production by the student with that of the language model. Through the use of a monitoring control system, a teacher could provide assistance to a number of students who were moving at their own levels. Language laboratories in high schools expanded rapidly after 1945 (Haber, 1963).

The apparent advantages of these aids did not always hold up when there were careful evaluations. Hoban (1960), after reviewing 400 investigations of teaching films concluded that people learn from films, but no strong assertions could be made in relation to success as compared with other kinds of teaching. Carroll (1963) showed a very mixed record of success of language laboratories in foreign language teaching.

The Media. The radio and the television added technological opportunities for instruction, while at the same time causing problems through the many hours that children spent before the television screen without guidance regarding the value of what they were watching. Psychologists and educators had to take into account the effects of television viewing because it became such a large part of the child's experience. In addition, however, it proved effective as a teaching aid, particularly in developing countries (e.g., Chu & Schramm, 1967).

Programmed Learning: Teaching Machines and Computer-Assisted Instruction. Programmed learning gained impetus after B. F. Skinner published an article entitled "The science of learning and the art of teaching" in the *Harvard Educational Review* (Skinner, 1954), and a second article on "Teaching machines" in *Science* (Skinner, 1958). It is true that Pressey had used a simple teaching machine as early as 1927 (see Pressey, 1964), but Skinner's proposal was widely influential whereas Pressey's had not been. One reason was perhaps that Pressey's was described as related to simple drill learning, whereas Skinner conceived the machine as a tutor that would lead the learner along by "shaping" of the behavior through reinforcement according to the learning principles that he had long espoused. The arrangements according to which particular goals could be achieved required a *program* of small steps, so that the procedure came to be called programmed learning or programmed instruction. The details of theory and application were soon published in a number of books, of which that edited by Arthur A. Lumsdaine and Robert Glaser, *Teaching Machines and Programmed Learning* (1960) is a good example, sponsored as it was by the National Education Association to bring the original papers and subsequent developments to the attention of the educational audience.

There were many developments after Skinner's initiative, such as the replacement of teaching machines with programmed books, including those that substituted branching programs for simple linear ones (e.g., Crowder, 1959). The introduction of computer-assisted instruction (CAI) added so many new dimensions that it cannot be considered a simple derivative of the teaching machine or the kind of programmed learning that Skinner introduced (Atkinson & Wilson, 1969). Still Skinner's programs were its immediate ancestors.

The new technology of programmed and computer-assisted instruction had at least three consequences for educational psychology: first, the new technology opened many possibilities for individualizing instruction, for teaching diagnostically, and for obtaining accurate records of progress; second, the usefulness was so immediate that the research was conducted in real school settings with the materials to be learned such as those taught in the school, rather than artificial laboratory material; third, the technological problems were sufficiently difficult and intriguing that a whole new group of well-trained psychologists needed no persuasion to interest themselves in problems of instruction. It is quite possible that this last consequence is as important as any, and reversed the belief expressed by Freeman (1938) that science had gone about as far as it could go to improve education. With the infusion of trained scientists with their advantage of far more powerful tools, the scene had changed.

Theories of Teaching

An important new area of concern became that of the theories of teaching, as well as theories of learning, as proposed by Nathaniel L. Gage (1963), a professor of educational psychology at Stanford, and repeatedly stressed by him later, including a yearbook that he edited on teaching methods (Gage, 1976). Newer textbooks on educational psychology became focused more directly on helping the prospective teacher to understand his or her task in the school setting (e.g., Cronbach, 1954, 1977; Gage & Berliner, 1975, 1979).

The flavor of later books on the impact of research on education was more hopeful than the reviews of a few years earlier, which seemed to strain to find signs of progress in the various subfields of education. Careful reviews showed that research had in fact left permanent residues on educational practices and policies, and the newer methods and technologies were interpreted as holding genuine promise for the future (Cronbach & Suppes, 1969; Suppes, 1978; Travers, 1983).

The Influence of Cognitive Psychology

Despite the gains that were made through the application of educational technology, there was a lingering dissatisfaction that psychology was not yet getting at the heart of its responsibility toward education. The objectives that became so carefully defined in programmed learning did not seem to carry the full meaning of the ends that education was intended to serve. When a taxonomy of education was worked out, it became recognized that there were a variety of different knowledge structures that were appropriate to the meeting of the objectives, and even in the standard subject-matter fields, the course content required that learning be specially tailored to a variety of different cognitive demands (Bloom, 1956; Dreeben, 1968). The development of cognitive psychology produced a great change in the relationship between psychology and education. As already noted, the training psychology that developed during and after World War II had already brought more experimental psychologists into investigations on instruction via programmed learning and computer-assisted instruction. As cognitive psychology advanced, many of the same investigators, including some who had been trained in the behaviorist tradition, accepted the new theoretical stance, and their ranks were enlarged by the accretion of a new generation of cognitive psychologists. The changes in learning theory were pronounced during these years, the 1960s and the 1970s (Greeno, 1980).

The *Annual Review of Psychology,* which had had occasional chapters on educational psychology and related topics, began a regular series of reviews on instructional psychology, one about every 3 years, beginning in 1969 (Gagné & Rohwer, 1969). These reviews became increasingly oriented to cognitive psychology as it related to education. By 1977 the authors of the review chapter could say:

The current shift emphasizes the study of central cognitive and affective associationistic and holistic processes by which the learner selects, transforms, and encodes the nominal characteristics of experience into functional, meaningful representations. A cognitive perspective implies that a behavioral analysis of instruction is often inadequate to explain the effects of instruction on learning. (Wittrock & Lumsdaine, 1977)

By 1981, the change had continued in the same direction:

Instructional psychology is no longer basic psychology *applied* to education. It is fundamental research *on* the processes of instruction and learning . . . Instructional psychology, like most research on human learning and development, is now largely cognitive; it is concerned with internal mental processes and how their development can be enhanced through instruction. (Resnick, 1981)

The Future of Educational Psychology

The political, economic, and social forces that shape education, and the resistance to change, place many constraints on the modification of instruction as embodied in the curriculum and in schoolroom practices. The investigations of psychologists interested in affecting education cannot be limited to improving instruction in narrow areas of teaching, even though division of labor requires that precise work of this kind should continue.

Education is a process embedded in society, and it is likely that social psychology, as it develops in relation to neighboring social science disciplines, will find an increasing role in education. If a search is made, there have already been many starts in this direction. Getzels, writing in the *Handbook of Social Psychology* (1963), complained of the neglect of an interest in education by social psychologists, rather than the neglect of social aspects by the educators. There has long been a sociology of education (e.g., Brookover, 1955;

Halsey, Floud, & Anderson, 1961), but the serious incorporation of social aspects of educational administration and educational reform into educational psychology was slow, partly because of psychologists' early preoccupation with short-term laboratory studies of learning and memory, and with testing procedures, as the core of psychology's responsibility for educational practices.

The increasing pertinence of the psychology of instruction may continue the salutary effect of causing research psychologists to conduct their investigations directly in the school settings where learning and teaching go on, where classroom management and other contextual aspects of the school experience become part of the psychologist's background information. Too often in the past the problems of classroom management and the arrangements of learning opportunities were left to the administration or to curriculum supervisors who may have had a minimum competence in psychological knowledge or in research competencies. The psychologists, in turn, although they sometimes collected their data from test results in the schools, more commonly conducted their learning experiments in artificial settings with artificial materials and over short time spans. When research goes on in the classroom, the teacher has a participant role with the psychologist-investigator, and this is bound to have a wholesome effect on producing desirable consequences for the educational process.

The advances in educational psychology that have brought research directly into the classroom augurs well for the future, provided sufficient attention is paid to the total educative influences—positive and negative—in the home, community, and larger culture, all of which must be given their proper places as essential aspects of lifelong education.

References

Aiken, W. M. (1942). *The story of the eight-year study. Adventure in American education* (Vol. 1). New York: Harper.

Atkinson, R. C., & Wilson, H. A. (Eds.). (1969). *Computer-assisted instruction.* New York: Academic Press.

Bloom, B. S. (Ed.). (1956). *Taxonomy of educational objectives. Handbook I: Cognitive domain.* New York: Longmans.

Bode, B. H. (1929). *Conflicting psychologies of learning.* New York: Heath.

Bode, B. H. (1938). *Progressive education at the crossroads.* New York: Newsom.

Brookover, W. B. (1955). *A sociology of education.* New York: American Book Company.

Carroll, J. B. (1963). Research on teaching foreign languages. In N. L. Gage (Ed.), *Handbook of research on teaching.* Chicago, IL: Rand McNally.

Chamberlin, D., Chamberlin, E., Drought, N. E., & Scott, W. E. (1942). *Did they succeed in college? Adventure in American education,* Vol. 4. New York: Harper.

Chu, G. C., & Schramm, W. (1967). *Learning from television: What the research says.* Stanford, CA: Institute for Communication Research.

Corey, S. M. (Chairman). (1949). *Audio-visual materials of instruction. Forty-Eighth Yearbook of the National Society for the Study of Education, Part I.* Chicago, IL: University of Chicago Press.

Cronbach, L. J. (1954). *Educational psychology.* (3rd ed., 1977) New York: Harcourt Brace Jovanovich.

Cronbach, L. J., & Suppes, P. (Eds.). (1969). *Research for tomorrow's schools: Disciplined inquiry for education.* New York: Macmillan.

Crowder, N. A. (1959). Automatic tutoring by means of intrinsic programming. In E. H. Galanter (Ed.), *Automatic teaching: The state of the art* (pp. 109–116). New York: Wiley.

Cubberley, E. P. (1920). *History of education.* Boston, MA: Houghton Mifflin.

Dale, E. (1954). *Audio-visual methods in teaching.* New York: Dryden.

Dreeben, R. (1968). *On what is learned in school.* Reading, MA: Addison-Wesley.

Elkind, D. (1967). Piaget and Montessori. *Harvard Educational Review, 37,* 535–545.

Freeman, F. N. (Ed.). (1938). *The scientific movement in education. Thirty-seventh yearbook of the National Society for the Study of Education, Part 2.* Bloomington, IL: Public School Publishing.

Gage, N. L. (Ed.). (1963). *Handbook of research on teaching.* Chicago, IL: Rand McNally.

Gage, N. L. (Ed.). (1976). *Psychology of teaching methods. Seventy-fifth yearbook of the National Society for the Study of Education, Part I.* Chicago, IL: University of Chicago Press.

Gage, N. L., & Berliner, D. C. (1975). *Educational psychology* (2nd ed., 1979). Boston, MA: Houghton-Mifflin.

Gagné, R. M., & Rohrer, J. H. (1969). Instructional psychology. *Annual Review of Psychology, 20,* 381–418.

Gates, A. I. (1923). *Psychology for students of education* (2nd ed., 1930). New York: Macmillan.

Gates, A. I. (1925). *Elementary psychology.* New York: Macmillan (2nd ed., 1929).

Gates, A. I., Jersild, A. T., McKillop, A. S., Rivlin, H. N., Shoben, E. J., Jr., & Watson, G. (1956). Educational psychology. *Review of Educational Research, 26,* 241–267.

Getzels, J. W. (1969). A social psychology of education. In G. Lindzey & E. Aronson (Eds.), *Handbook of social psychology* (Vol. 5, pp. 459–537). Reading, MA: Addison-Wesley.

Glaser, R. (Ed.). (1962). *Training research and education.* Pittsburgh, PA: University of Pittsburgh Press.

Greeno, J. G. (1980). Psychology of learning, 1960–1980: One participant's observations. *American Psychologist, 35,* 713–728.

Groen, G. J. (1978). The theoretical ideas of Piaget and educational practice. In P. Suppes (Ed.), *Impact of research on education* (267–317). Washington, DC: National Academy of Education.

Haber, R. N. (1963). The spread of an innovation: High school language laboratories. *Journal of Experimental Education, 31,* 359–369.

Hall, G. S. (1904). *Adolescence,* 2 vols. New York: Appleton.

Halsey, A. H., Floud, J., & Anderson, C. A. (Eds.). (1961). *Readings in the sociology of education.* New York: Free Press of Glencoe.

Harris, W. T. (1898). *Psychologic foundations of education.* New York: Appleton.

Hilgard, E. R. (Ed.). (1964). *Theories of learning and instruction. Sixty-third yearbook N.S.S.E., Part 2.* Bloomington, IL: Public School Publishing Co.

Hilgard, E. R. (1987). *Psychology in America: A historical survey.* San Diego: Harcourt Brace Jovanovich.

Hoban, C. F. (1960). The usable residue of educational film research. In W. Schramm (Ed.), *New teaching aids for the American classroom.* Stanford, CA: Institute for Communication Research.

James, W. (1899). *Talks to teachers on psychology.* New York: Holt.

Johnson, H. G. (1946). Weakness in the eight-year study. *School and Society, 63,* 417–419.

Judd, C. H. (1915). *Psychology of high school subjects.* Boston, MA: Ginn.

Leonard, J. P., & Eurich, A. C. (Eds.). (1942). *An evaluation of modern education.* New York: Appleton-Century.

Lumsdaine, A. A., & Glaser, R. (Eds.). (1960). *Teaching machines and programmed learning.* Washington, DC: National Education Association.

May, M. A., & Lumsdaine, A. A. (1958). *Learning from films.* New Haven, CT: Yale University Press.

Monroe, W. S., Odell, C. W., Herriott, M. E., Englehart, M. D., & Hull, M. R. (1928). Ten years of educational research, 1918–1927. *University of Illinois Bulletin, 25,* No. 42.

Piaget, J. (1970). *Science of education and the psychology of the child.* New York: Viking.

Pressey, S. L. (1964). Autoinstruction: Perspectives, problems, potentials. In E. R. Hilgard (Ed.), *Theories of learning and instruction. Sixty-third N.S.S.E. yearbook, part I* (pp. 354–370). Chicago, IL: University of Chicago Press. University of Chicago Press.

Reed, H. B. (1927). *Psychology of elementary school subjects* (rev. ed., 1938). New York: Ginn.

Resnick, L. B. (1981). Instructional psychology. *Annual Review of Psychology, 32,* 659–704.

Skinner, B. F. (1954). The science of learning and the art of teaching. *Harvard Educational Review, 24,* 86–97.

Skinner, B. F. (1958). Teaching machines. *Science, 128,* 969–977.

Smith, E. R., Tyler, R. W., and Evaluation Staff. (1942). *Appraising and recording student progress. Adventure in American Education,* Vol. 3. New York: Harper.

Suppes, P. (Ed.). (1978). *Impact of research on education.* Washington, DC: National Academy of Education.

Thorndike, E. L. (1913–1914). *Educational psychology,* 3 vols. New York: Teachers College.

Thorndike, E. L. (1922). *The psychology of arithmetic.* New York: Macmillan.

Thorndike, E. L., Cobb, M. V., Orleans, J. S., Symonds, P. M., Ward, E., & Woodyard, E. (1923). *The psychology of algebra.* New York: Macmillan.

Thorndike, E. L., Bergmann, E. O., Cobb, M. V., Woodyard, E., & Staff. (1926). *The measurement of intelligence.* New York: Columbia University Press.

Travers, R. M. W. (1983). *How research has changed American schools.* Kalamazoo, MI: Mythos Press.

Watson, G. (1926). What shall be taught in educational psychology. *Journal of Educational Psychology, 17,* 577–599.

Wittrock, M. C., & Lumsdaine, A. A. (1977). Instructional psychology. *Annual Review of Psychology, 28,* 417–459.

CHAPTER 21

Retrospect and Prospect in Educational Psychology

John E. Horrocks

Change is supposedly the essence of progress. If it is indeed true that change represents progress then one can say of educational psychology that the past 50 years, the span of my time in the field, has brought much progress. Yet, one wonders. Change there has been, but has it represented progress? Of course, it is a matter of point of view and against point of view it is vain to argue. We all tend to have some feeling, however vigorously we may deny it, that our own times were the best of times and that new ways and interests, although perhaps of some value, still leave much to be desired.

In all fairness one must admit that times and conditions do change. Adaptations to these changes, like those that would be made in an applied discipline such as educational psychology, may have, given new ways and objectives, an internal justification all of their own. What was once good may be less so given materially changed conditions. It is neither my interest nor my purpose here to evaluate the culture of today against that of yesteryear but only to indicate what I see as changes in the field and in the approaches to the field of educational psychology over the past few decades. Others can make the relative evaluations of good and bad.

I liked my times in educational psychology but I

hope I can appreciate the value and even the necessity of change. Certainly I have no desire to denigrate the present or to overpraise the past. Perhaps it would be best to back off from a view limited solely to personal experience, add some 40 years to my own time, and look at educational psychology in retrospect following the closing years of the first decade of the 20th century. To do so is to start with those times when what is now called educational psychology was still known by some as experimental pedagogy and educational psychology as a separate field was really only an applied branch of psychology.

Nearly any psychologist of those years was apt to give some consideration to the problems of the child learner. As a matter of fact, G. Stanley Hall called his 1911 two-volume work on what really was psychology in education *Educational Problems* and included chapters such as "The Pedagogy of Sex" and "The Pedagogy of the Kindergarten." Indeed there was even a chapter, hardly to be found in the textbooks of today, on "Children's Lies: Their Psychology and Pedagogy." But by then what was to become the mainstream of educational psychology was already underway in the laboratory of Edward L. Thorndike, whose early work in measurement and learning was written up and copyrighted in 1914 under the title of *Educational Psychology*. His 1924 edition of *Educational Psychology: Briefer Course* became the

John E. Horrocks • Department of Psychology, Ohio State University, Columbus, OH 43210.

textbook of choice in what may well have been the majority of educational psychology courses around the nation.

A look at the table of contents of Thorndike's 1924 edition yields an interesting picture of what was considered fundamental in educational psychology some 60 years ago. The chapters were grouped under three headings: *The Original Nature of Man, The Psychology of Learning,* and *Individual Differences and Their Causes.* The heart of the book, exceeding the combined lengths of the other parts, was devoted to the psychology of learning. In Thorndike's book measurement as such was not an issue but thanks to the measurement and classification work of psychologists in World War I measurement, particularly of intellectual functions, was much in the thinking of educational psychologists and courses in measurement were becoming, as the 1920s proceeded, standard features in the educational psychology programs of the era.

Thus, in the 1920s we see educational psychology as clearly emerging from general applied psychology as a recognized specialty in its own right. A whole new generation of psychologists, calling themselves educational psychologists but with a background of specific training in aspects of psychology bearing little relation to education, was appearing on the scene and beginning to assume leadership roles in the development of educational psychology.

Among such men were Arthur Gates of Columbia, Sydney Pressey of Ohio State, and Charles Judd of the University of Chicago. These three, among others, were the men whose textbooks were to become the defining influence in the development of the field of educational psychology. What leaders such as Pressey or Gates or Judd said educational psychology should be was what it became in the thinking of the rapidly increasing corps of educational psychologists. The various successive editions of the Pressey and of the Gates textbooks present a story of continuing change and adaptation in the field of educational psychology. Here we have a contrast to the present. There are a great number of textbooks in educational psychology today and even more are appearing on the horizon as publishers vie with each other to bring out best selling ephemera. Inevitably a few, but only a few, of these textbooks are excellent indeed, but none can be said to dictate the content and direction of educational psychology as those earlier books did.

Perhaps the field today has become so complex and so fragmented that it is unlikely that any small group, let alone any single figure, will emerge as predominant or as a defining leader. And then, of course, in those earlier days textbook publishers were far less likely to succeed, or even attempt, to dictate the content, the format, or the point of view to be expressed by the author than one suspects may be the case today. Certainly there was less tendency to "write down" to the readers or to entertain them. Where among today's textbooks would one find such a statement as that in Thorndike's 1914 preface:

Certain topics are included which are a little beyond the interests and capacities of the lowest third of college students. . . . I make no apology for including them. If education is to be a serious profession, preparation for it should not avoid matters which require study and are beyond the interests of dull minds.

Incidentally, there were no pictures, wide margins, color, or print of varying contrasts in these earlier textbooks. Just straight exposition relieved by data presenting graphs and tables. Dull, nonmotivating, and nonattentive to student "felt needs"? Perhaps, but the reader might find it of interest to leaf through a dozen or so of the modern versions of textbooks in educational psychology with a view to evaluating them as college level expositions in a worthy and integrated discipline.

But, to return to the founding figures and their successors in educational psychology. A developing field needs new recruits if it is to prosper and in educational psychology many such were gained through the setting up of graduate programs in the field designed not only for instruction for teachers in service and in training but for the production of Ph.D.s specifically trained in educational psychology. Today, in the penultimate decade of the 20th century, we have at hand the fifth generation of such persons. The present writer is of the second generation. It has been his privilege to have known some of the early figures personally and in the case of S. L. Pressey to have worked with one as a colleague at Ohio State. But an intervening generation was to make its appearance on the scene before his time in educational psychology and it was this first generation group who accomplished so much to broaden the field of educational psychology as they modified existing Ph.D. training programs or instituted new ones and as in their own teaching and research they carried on and extended the work begun by their own mentors.

The writer assumed his place in the second generation as he took his Ph.D. in educational psychology under the direction of M. E. Troyer at Syracuse who in his turn had done his graduate degree under the direction of S. L. Pressey at Ohio State. In a former day psychologists tended to be interested in tracing back their own academic blood lines and I am still amazed at how quickly as late as 1940 one could trace back to the earliest days of educational psychology. Today, I suppose, personal origins are both harder to find and of far less interest, yet the retrospective point being made is that the educational psychologists of some 45 years ago tended to have a real sense of the continuity of their own field and of their place in that continuity.

As we entered the decades of the 1950s and the 1960s I seem to have sensed less cohesiveness among educational psychologists and certainly less appreciation of the continuity of their field of endeavor. A retrospective view, then, sees educational psychology in its earliest days and well into the 1930s as being primarily concerned with learning as such, both in terms of its general principles and in terms of its application to specific school subjects.

Following World War I measurement became increasingly a preoccupation of educational psychologists and with it came a growing recognition of the need for a thorough grounding in statistics. The 1920s and the 1930s were exciting years for educational psychologists as they expanded their work and expertise in measurement and statistics and as they applied their work in learning to the various school subjects. Factor analysis made its appearance and increasing sophistication in statistical analysis gave new meaning to research.

Every educational psychology program of any worth included such courses as *Psychology of the Elementary Subjects* and *Psychology of the Secondary Subjects* with Homer B. Reed's two volumes acting as a kind of common handbook. Many schools included specialized courses, not necessarily seminars, on such topics as psychology of algebra and psychology of reading. In the writer's day as a graduate student Thurstone's *Vectors of the Mind* (a little later his *Multiple Factor Analysis*), Guilford's *Psychometric Methods,* Peters and Van Voorhis *Statistical Procedures and their Mathematical Bases* and Murchison's *The Foundations of Experimental Psychology* were at least on the shelves or within the life space of alert graduate students of educational psychology although, unfortunately perhaps, not very firmly within their minds.

At least the expectation of our mentors as to what we should know was clear enough. There was a great deal of interest in the application of learning theory to education and such persons as Hull, Tolman, and Guthrie were believed to have much to contribute as witness some of the year books of the National Society for the Study of Education. But the work of Piaget was unknown to most of us and indeed continued to be so until well into the 1950s. As a graduate student the writer never did encounter a course in Personality or Social Psychology. Most of us had heard about something called Guidance and sometimes wondered what the course was about and finally decided it must be about career information and *ipso facto* outside the field.

As a graduate student I knew about Jones' textbook but never got to read it. It was perhaps an innocent world in the early 1940s and we could all admire the measurement compendia of O. K. Buros, read Clark Hull's Principles and in a seminar even encounter Thorndike's *The Measurement of Intelligence* and his *Psychology of Learning.* We were familiar with Baldwin and with G. Stanley Hall but did not read them directly and hence pretty much misinterpreted what they actually had to say. The work of Gesell was much admired.

But an apple tree was growing in our Eden and upon that tree was an apple soon to be known as the individual child. The work of John Dewey and of his followers such as Boyd Bode was having a great impact on colleges of education everywhere and indeed in school practice across the nation. In the early 1920s a department of the NEA had issued a fiat that the American secondary school was a school for all the children of all the people. In 1927 Thayer's *Passing of the Recitation* made its appearance. In 1940 we were laughing at *The Saber Tooth Curriculum* by J. Abner Peddwell (with co-authors listed as "several Tequila Daisies"). We were perturbed to read in the late 1930s the New York State Regents' Report, which pronounced that social adjustment was the primary business of the New York State schools, although not as perturbed as when we heard that one professor of elementary education was talking about the first grade teacher and her pupils as "co-changers of society." But then we were consoled when we remembered (I hope we did) that even in the Roman Forum geese were to be found.

The work of the Progressive Education Association was seen by educational psychologists as a ground-breaking contribution to education as were the publications of the Social Science Research Council. Paul Horst's *The Prediction of Personal Adjustment* opened new horizons as did Allport's classical monograph on the analysis of personnel documents and the growing list of reports on community research. Looking back, it seems curious today that ethical issues regarding the collection of data simply were not raised. Personal rights, so important in our research thinking today, were not an issue in the culture of the time.

Most of the educational thinking of the time was gradually being incorporated into our thinking and into our work as educational psychologists. We even embraced the jargon.

The field expanded rapidly in the 1940s and the 1950s and as it did it fragmented and numerous subspecialties arose. In the 1920s and 1930s the educational psychologist tended to be a generalist. Measurement tended to be the main specialty or sometimes it was an aspect of learning such as transfer of training or memory. There was much interest in finding principles and then applying them. We liked to talk about applications of theory and spent much time doing so.

Perhaps the greatest change other than the inclusion of the individual and his personal needs to the content of educational psychology was the specific inclusion of the developmental point of view and the continuing addition of a whole array of developmental courses to the point that the orientation of some departments of educational psychology was primarily that of development. Unfortunately this tended to exacerbate the split that had grown to exist on most university campuses between the department of educational psychology and the "regular" department of psychology. Oftentimes duplicate courses in development occurred, particularly in large universities.

In general, the psychology of learning aspect of the educational psychology programs found increasing de-emphasis in the 1960s and 1970s although as we get into the 1980s there seems to be developing a return to a greater interest in learning as such, particularly as development has become increasingly an interest of instructional departments outside the colleges of education. Certainly the trend toward more interest in social behavior has been more and more on the scene in educational psychology than in the years before World War II.

As I was writing this chapter I wondered if it would be possible or even worthwhile to set down a whole list of points of demarcation in educational psychology—points that could be categorized as representing times after which (and, obviously, because of which) major changes occurred. Such times do occur in science, as for example the time before which and after which the Pearsonian *r* was introduced (1904). But I think that such a listing is not practical. Most of the major changes in educational psychology did not arise from single incidents but from the gradual interaction of whole groups of incidents and of changes in thinking and in attitudes. Possibly the best approach is to look at widely accepted textbooks in educational psychology to see what their preoccupation has been at different periods in the developmental history of educational psychology.

This can best be done by considering differences from edition to edition of those textbooks that have had a long run. The 1923 edition of Arthur Gates' *Psychology for Students of Education* is a far cry from the 1930, the 1942, and the 1948 editions (the last bore the title *Educational Psychology* under the authorship of Gates, Jersild, McConnell, and Challman). The same progression may be observed in S. L. Pressey's 1933, 1944, and 1957 editions, the last edition appearing as *Psychology in Education* by Pressey, Robinson, and Horrocks. It is significant that the 1944 title was *Psychology and the New Education*. Obviously by 1957 the new education had become the old education. What should one call the education of 1985? Apparently it is safe to assume that whatever it may be called in 1985 the name will be less appropriate in 2000.

What of the future of educational psychology? No one can predict the future with any certainty but predictions can have heuristic value. In actuality they are really part of the retrospective view because they tell more about the predictor and his summary view than they ever can of what is yet to be. The most certain prediction is that change and adaptation to new ways will continue. It seems most probable that educational psychologists in general will continue to react rather than to lead in future relationships either with the parent field of psychology or with the application context of education. This is nothing new and although less than optimally desirable it is not all bad. Traditionally, educational psychology has been a service area whose main function is to interpret psychology to education and to exemplify scientific methodology in the collection and interpretation of data. Most educational psychologists of any stature have been and will continue to be research oriented and to produce research of their own although the research will be most productive and representative of their field if it is directed to the uncovering and solution of problems of direct interest to the educator.

The most effective research laboratory for educational psychologists is in the schools and in the community where education in all its complexity is in process. This is where the educational psychologist justifies his existence as a research specialist.

Yet it is in this very area that educational psychology has been falling behind. As of today there seem to be few indications that the trend will reverse at least in the immediate future. University promotion and tenure systems have been downplaying the teaching role in favor of research productivity and such productivity can be made to appear more plentiful if the researcher confines himself to the collection of in-house data on topics of minor importance, often having little if any relationship to anything happening in education or to children in the real world context of home, community, and school. The day of a ministudy of, say, Piagetian conservation with a fortuitously selected sample of 17 available college freshmen is very much with us. Even worse is the "party line" argument without substantive research backing that one so often finds, particularly in the textbook writing of educational psychologists. If the field is to prosper it will simply have to make a more substantive contribution.

There are and probably will continue to be too many educational psychologists who feel that distancing themselves from education as such is the road to prestige. That is not to say that educational psychologists should not, if they are to fulfill their interpretation role, keep in close touch with the parent discipline. But, in doing so they need to remember that they are educational psychologists with a specific and important helping role in education as such.

We will continue to have separate departments of educational psychology as long as colleges of education and the college departmental organization system continue to exist. Merging of educational and regular departments as was done at Ohio State, Penn State, and a few other institutions produced less than optimal results and most such combinations have been abandoned. I see no future return to attempts to merge. Yet, at the same time it is important for the educational psychologist to maintain his identity as a psychologist working in education.

There have been in the past and probably will continue to be in the future many attempts to disperse educational psychologists among the various specialties of education to the point that the educational psychologist gradually becomes less and less identifiable as a psychologist. An erstwhile educational psychologist dealing solely with an instructional unit in a Foundations of Education course is virtually out of his field. Of course the continuing fragmentation into subspecialties makes the educational psychologist more vulnerable to a watering down of his role. This writer feels that a return to the generalist in the training of an educational psychologist is the most effective and useful way to go. He can not, however, predict that the generalist will represent the direction of the future. Quite the contrary, and that is why he has a certain pessimism about the long-term future of educational psychology as a separate and viable discipline either in or out of education.

There is one particularly happy possible development for the future, however, a development that has been too long deferred. That development will represent an increasing realization that the educational psychologist's main interest is in the process of education and that such processes are not confined to children and teachers in a public or private elementary or secondary school or even in a college. A learner is a learner, whatever his age, and there are many contexts for learning. There are schools both in industry and in the military dealing with people of all ages. Learning as such is not confined to a school any more than it is a concern only of children and their teachers.

This point of view may well become increasingly accepted by educational psychologists with the result that the future will find substantial numbers of educational psychologists expanding their fields of interest and their employment opportunities beyond the education of children in rather narrowly conceived contexts. That is why I have espoused the training of educational psychologists as generalists and why as I conclude these retrospective-prospective notes I reverse my previous prediction and forecast that the wave of the future in educational psychology bears upon its crest the generalist—providing, of course, that there is indeed the development of a recognition of the existence of expanded fields of endeavor for educational psychologists.

CHAPTER 22

Conclusion

Royce R. Ronning and John A. Glover

Overview

This book touched on the history of educational psychology from its antecedents in the 16th to 18th century. However, primary attention was devoted to the period from the late 19th century to the present. The historical treatment reveals the diverse roots of educational psychology in philosophy and psychology. At the same time, it demonstrates how the never clearly integrated field of educational psychology has splintered into subject areas that now hold the status of disciplines in their own right.

Despite the diversity, it is clear a nucleus of topical areas remain central to what is now educational psychology. From our perspective this nucleus includes (a) tests and measurements; (b) individual differences (closely allied, of course, to tests and measurements); (c) behavioral psychology; (d) instructional psychology; (e) cognition; and, to a lesser extent, (f) humanistic psychology. Even this nucleus seems to have two quite different areas of focus: the first, measurement and individual differences, emphasizes assessment, whereas the second aims more generally at the task of understanding and changing human behavior.

In sum, educational psychology appears to have a substantial and broad body of psychological and educational content. Practitioners, however, apparently desire a clearer identification with a specific area, hence the continued distancing of closely related disciplines, such as school and counseling psychology. The remainder of this chapter represents a highly individualistic response to the historical sections of the book. It is, of course, based on the chapters presented to us, yet it is influenced by the attitudes and perspectives we have as practicing educational psychologists reflecting on our field.

The "Splinter" Groups

The areas that have put greater distance between themselves and educational psychology appear to have kept their roots in the two foci just mentioned. Thus, school psychology has retained its identification with tests and measurements, individual differences, and more recently, behavioral and instructional psychology. Counseling psychology and guidance emphasized the role of understanding the learner from, initially, a humanist view; more recently counseling and guidance are beginning to incorporate aspects of social psychology as well as instructional psychology and cognition. At the same time, a somewhat different division is evidenced by the move of many doctoral level counseling psychologists away from work in school settings toward therapeutic efforts in private practice more akin to clinical than to educational

Royce R. Ronning and John A. Glover • Department of Educational Psychology, University of Nebraska, Lincoln, NE 68588-0440.

psychology. Worth noting is the fact that many programs in counseling psychology and school psychology join clinical psychology as areas of psychological practice accredited by the American Psychological Association.

Because, as we noted in chapter one, less than half of doctorates in educational psychology are awarded by psychology departments, it may appear that counseling and school psychology represent groups more closely identified with psychology than with education. Thus one might hypothesize that approved training programs in counseling and school psychology would more often appear in Departments of Psychology than in Educational Psychology or other units.

Data from a recent list of fully accredited doctoral programs in professional psychology (American Psychological Association, 1984, pp. 1470–1472) do not support the hypothesis. Of the 34 counseling psychology programs, 10 are in Departments of Psychology, five in Departments of Educational Psychology, seven in Departments that include Educational Psychology (but not Psychology) as part of the department title, and 12 in administrative units with other names. Of the 26 school psychology programs, five are in Departments of Psychology, six in Departments of Educational Psychology, one in a Department that includes Educational Psychology in the title, and 13 in units with other names. There is one accredited program in a Department of School Psychology. In contrast, clinical psychology training occurs in 105 Departments of Psychology and in 20 other units with varying names, none of them Educational Psychology. Thus, more than four fifths of the clinical programs are located in Departments of Psychology, whereas less than one third of School or Counseling programs are so located.

The training site data provided demonstrate the efforts of school and counseling psychology to find identities separate not only from educational psychology but from traditional psychology departments as well. Indeed, for both groups, the most frequent program identification is neither psychology nor educational psychology.

Even as groups such as those listed moved away from an earlier identification with educational psychology, specialization appeared within the fields that are still, at least nominally, a part of the domain of educational psychology. Such specializations include evaluation and classroom management, as well as topical emphases, such as teacher effectiveness, comprehension processes, and even

as relatively narrow a topic as problem solving. In each specialization and topical emphasis, a voluminous literature has developed such that it is difficult, if not impossible, to retain high levels of knowledge and expertise across all of them. Furthermore, interest in many of the topic areas cuts across simple discipline lines. Although none of the areas listed above appears to be overtly separate from educational psychology, many of them *do* have national professional organizations of fairly narrow scope. One such example is the National Council on Measurement in Education (NCME), which was formed to serve the interests of education professionals interested in measurement. NCME publishes its own journal and holds national and regional meetings.

Given past history, further increase in specialization appears to be inevitable. However, as a counter example one may offer school psychology, which at present is struggling with the perceived constraints posed by the narrow title *School Psychology*, so that the group has seriously considered changing to a title (such as Educational Psychology!) that more nearly represents the present scope of school psychology practice.

Problems of Definition

Given the fragmentation described earlier, what do we make of educational psychology? How is the field to be defined? Careful reading of Parts I and II of the volume leads us to the conclusion (drawn on pp. 9–10 of the introductory chapter) that a simple definition does not exist. The disparate activities described in this book defy definition beyond the obvious: educational psychology is what educational psychologists do. On the other hand, considerable consensus exists for a description of educational psychology as, simply, the application of psychological principles to education. Examination of Parts I and II does, however, reveal recurring themes—themes worth spelling out.

In Chapter 2, Professor Charles suggests that not until the 1920s did educational psychologists appear as a group separate from psychologists. As he noted, the functionalist movement, with its emphasis on making psychology useful, led psychologists to carry out research in school settings. Furthermore, practical problems of education—how to teach children to read, or to solve arithmetic problems—became legitimate objects for study. Nonetheless, in main, these activities were carried out by persons who considered themselves psychologists, not educational psychologists. Thus, formal identification of educational psychology as a discipline separate from psychology has existed since only about 1920. The relationship of educational psychology to psychology seems similar to that of some aspects of engineering to physics, however, the role of theory appears to be more pronounced in educational psychology than in engineering, especially because education as a discipline continues to suffer from a lack of adequate theory to drive practice.

Educational psychology's formal relation to education has been an uneasy one. Educational psychologists often have been accused of being too "theoretical," "impractical," or "insensitive to the needs of children (or teachers)." Although colleges of education have long required one or two undergraduate courses in educational psychology as part of the professional education sequence, all too often these courses are not well integrated into the formal preparation program.

Early Educational Psychology Content

The chapters in Part II of the volume list and briefly describe the early history and current status of topics significant in the establishment of educational psychology: individual differences (particularly in intelligence), measurement, child study, guidance, and school psychology.

In order to provide a manageable chapter, Professor Jensen chose to model the recent history of individual differences by tracing the development of attempts to understand one individual differences variable—intelligence. His treatment shows the impact of theories of intelligence on education and psychology. The problems posed by efforts to gain "pure" measures of intellect stimulated intense activity in the area of measurement, but also led educational psychology to reexamine a continuing and deeper problem: the logical and psychological analysis of intelligent behavior into its genetic and environmental roots. Methodological efforts (such as factor analysis) to deal with issues of intellectual assessment began to shape curriculum in educational psychology. Such methodological efforts led applied measurement and statistics to flourish as a "core" area of educational psychology.

Professor Carroll's chapter on measurement nicely illustrates the impact of practical problems on the shape of educational measurement. The use of psychological testing for the Army in World War I provided a model quickly adapted to achievement testing. As "new type" (objective) tests were developed, thoughtful researchers recognized the need to provide a sounder basis for understanding tests as well as the necessity for a testing technology that dealt with issues ranging from the simpler aspects of test-item writing to much more profound problems of scaling items (and tests). These efforts led to the development of test theory and to such well known topics as reliability and validity, which have had substantial impact not only on educational psychology, but on other areas of psychology and education as well.

At the same time that techniques and statistical procedures were being developed to deal with the measurement and individual differences issues just mentioned, pressures from outside the field of educational psychology led to consideration of increasingly sophisticated research designs for exploring educational problems. The work of Fisher (1925) in (primarily) agriculture directed educational researchers toward increasingly complex multivariate research designs. These designs came into use with the recognition that many educational questions of interest cannot be dealt with in simple two- or three-group comparisons.

School psychology early adopted a differential psychology model that led to the focus on developing powerful tests for assessing individual differences. This search also led to measurement as a core of that discipline. However, as Professor Kramer's chapter points out, time demands on school psychology practitioners for testing increasing numbers of children became uneconomic. Diagnostic testing has proved not only expensive but also, in the final analysis, only a stopgap measure. Given the realities of numbers of students, improvement in education—increasing the capabilities of schools and teachers to develop environments for productive student learning—could occur only by spending more time with teachers rather than with children. Thus, the testing component is slowly, but quite surely, from the perspective of school psychologists, becoming a tool that provides a basis for consultation with teachers. Consultation models, although initially clinical, more recently have borrowed heavily from behavioral psychology. Whereas assessment (hence measurement) issues are still clearly in the domain of school psychology as well as educational psychology, school psychology has distanced itself from educational psychology through the consultation model.

The guidance movement has roots in many ways similar to those of the child study movement and humanistic psychology. The child study movement (see Chap. 4) began as an educational movement dedicated to nurturing children. It rose out of much of the same forces of protest, social reform, and idealism as those Professor Dixon ascribes to the formation of the guidance movement. However, the child study movement, consistent with the educational psychology of Rousseau and the writings of Herbart and Pestalozzi, moved to a search for an empirical pedagogy—the development of educational methods that would most effectively nurture children. The methods of study tended to be informal, diary like, rather than taking on the trappings of formal educational measurement. As the relatively unscientific methods of child study were contrasted to the demands for rigor in measurement and research design, the movement refocused on the scientific study of human development. This was especially clear, as Professors Davidson and Benjamin recount, with the formation of the various child research centers, such as Iowa Child Welfare Station.

Whereas the child study movement focused particularly on early childhood, turn of the century social forces, such as industrialization and the division of labor, led guidance to focus on the postschool vocational adjustment of young men and women. This orientation apparently borrowed little from the methodology and theory of psychology. Professor Dixon details the vocational adjustment emphasis of the early guidance movement with its focus on discovering means for determination of characteristics of the self—particularly emphasis on the development of measures of aptitudes and interests. Thus, measurement became an integral part of the guidance movement.

Almost coincidental in time with the guidance movement was the mental hygiene movement. The emphasis on mental illness led to the development of a psychotherapy movement among such mental health practitioners as Carl Rogers, which ultimately led, following World War II, to the formal development of counseling psychology as a subdiscipline clearly different in goals from the guidance movement.

Whereas the vocational guidance movement focused on self appraisal for the purpose of identifying a satisfying career, the humanist movement approaches self from an existential/phenomonological perspective growing out of the work of persons such as Snygg and Combs (1949). The humanist orientation to the study of the "whole" person was advanced in the period from 1950–1980 as an alternative view of psychology in contrast, particularly, to behavioral emphases, such as those described by Professors Kratochwill and Bijou. In our view, the humanistic movement has had relatively little force in educational psychology, at least in part because of its lack of a clear theoretical and conceptual base. Yet humanist influences are clear in studies of classroom climate, teacher–student interaction, and definitions of effective teaching, as well as some aspects of both guidance and counseling. Professor Hamachek nicely characterizes the movement as a "theoretical umbrella [providing] a framework and language for understanding the inner person."

Demands for mental health professionals substantially increased in the period following World War II. As efforts to meet these demands grew, clinical psychology programs expanded in numbers and in size. At the same time, "counseling" psychologists appeared, initially trained, apparently, to deal with vocational decisions and with relatively "minor" mental health problems. Differential emphasis on therapeutic, as opposed to education, interventions soon resulted in a division within the guidance movement that led to the development of counseling psychology as a separate discipline, though one without a clearly delineated "home."

By 1960, the independence of school psychology and counseling psychology from educational psychology was quite evident. The humanistic movement had been largely (although not exclusively) absorbed into aspects of school psychology, guidance, and counseling psychology. Thus, educational psychology was perhaps at its most empirical stage. Measurement, individual differences, learning, and child development appeared to be the core of the discipline.

Change, however, was in the air. Learning, long a central part of educational psychology and closely, perhaps even slavishly, allied with Hullian learning theory of the 1940s and 1950s was under attack for its lack of relevance to schooling. The hypothetico-deductive method of Hull seemed singularly inapplicable to the problems teachers faced in helping students to learn. The surge of interest in the work of B. F. Skinner, coupled with Skinner's eagerness to attack educational problems, led to substantial reformulation of the study of learning in educational psychology. Kratochwill and Bijou detail the evolution of this movement. The old "mentalism" of motivation, intervening variables, hypothetical constructs, and so forth, was directly attacked from the perspective of a set of (presumably) simple and directly observable events: stimuli, responses, and consequences of the responses. An extensive literature on classroom management quickly appeared based on this paradigm. This perspective (also widely adopted by school psychology as part of the consultive repertoire) became in a short time the dominant approach to a classroom oriented educational psychology of learning.

Educational Psychology 1960–1987

By 1940, educational psychology was well established as a field. Many departments with that title had been formed. Courses in educational psychology were a part of virtually every teacher preparation program, and graduate programs leading to master and doctoral degrees were well in place. World War II set in motion events that had direct impact on the discipline. Perhaps first among these events was the demand placed on educational psychology for techniques that permitted efficient training of great numbers of individuals for the armed services. As instructional design met modest, but nonetheless impressive, success in meeting military needs, recognition came for the need to consider training demands more intensively. These demands led to the development of three clearly identifiable movements within educational psychology: behaviorism (behavior modification), humanistic psychology, and cognitive psychology.

Instructional psychology's roots in educational technology are briefly described in Professor Dick's chapter. From an early emphasis on the comparative value of various media, instructional psychology quickly moved to the study of man–machine interactions, with emphasis on the study of learners in the environment in which they were expected to perform. This led to the development of task analysis, to systems analysis, and ultimately instructional design. As the development of sophisticated weapons systems occurred in World War II, concern for personnel selection mounted. Thus, testing and evaluation techniques received increasing attention. Because most of these events took place in military (as opposed to university) contexts and under pressure to "help win the

war," concerns for carefully controlled, methodical laboratory research were put aside. Evaluation techniques were developed to provide, in many cases, after the fact evidence for the usefulness of a particular program. Recognition by the military of the value of instructional psychology resulted in the continuance following World War II of efforts aimed at increasing the effectiveness of armed service training programs.

The publication of B. F. Skinner's research in programmed instruction had obvious implications for military training as well as for education more broadly conceived. Coupled in the 1950s with enormous renewed interest in education as a means for competing with the USSR, programmed instruction led not only to concern for how curriculum could be most effectively presented to learners, but also to the question of the nature of curriculum itself. Thus instructional design, with its focus on behavioral objectives, task analysis, and the like, began to develop so that by 1980 instructional designers were preparing for educational *systems* that encompassed a broad spectrum of activities ranging from formulating goals for instruction, to development of instruction, to assessment of the effectiveness and costs of instruction.

As programmed instruction developed interactively with the instructional design, a slightly different focus, operant analysis of human behavior, appeared. Behavior modification encompassed much of the work that led to programmed instruction, but with clearer recognition of the individual–environment interaction. Operant conditioning became a major tool not only for the design of instruction, but more frequently for the analysis and amelioration of individual problems in learning. Thus, "behavior modifiers" used the technology of operant conditioning to arrange environmental contingencies so as to maximize attainment of an educational goal. Professors Kratochwill and Bijou provide a brief history of the development of that movement, whereas Professor Williams provides an estimate of the current status of classroom management technology. What, perhaps, is most significant in both chapters are descriptions of well-specified techniques that could be tested in many educational arenas. With clearly specified objectives and behavioral response criteria, the success of an educational program (an intervention) can be readily accessed. However, the behavioral focus of this technology, and even perhaps its success, led to concerns from two areas: humanistic psychology and cognitive psychology. Humanists argued that there is more to human behavior and to education than arrangements of contingencies, whereas cognitive psychologists argued that operant analysis of complex behavior, such as human problem solving, revealed little of the significant internal events giving force and shape to such complex behaviors.

Humanistic psychology, dismissed earlier as having little force as a movement, nonetheless had considerable influence on educational psychology. Much of that influence comes from an emphasis on the need to study motivation, affect, and the nature of teacher–student affective interactions if learning in classroom settings were to be adequately conceptualized, much less understood. Professor Hamachek makes an eloquent plea for the potential of education to free students to learn—a perspective many educational psychologists find unattractive given a quite different goal—to make psychology a "science." It is still difficult to assess the impact of humanistic psychology as a "third force" in the field of educational psychology. A part of this difficulty comes from view of the self and its development, which suggests that neither education nor psychology has much to offer to the educational process. This extreme view, as Hamachek notes in Chapter 8, appeared to suggest that the development of the self required little by way of structure or organization, negating the influence of curriculum or teacher on learning by the individual. However, the apparent return to the examination of constructs such as self-esteem, values, and the like has kept educational psychologists mindful of the broad array of human behavior for which they have taken responsibility.

The second countervailing force to behavioral psychology, cognitive psychology, emerges from a concern for the nature of understanding—a persistent question that presumes a categorical (cognitive?) structure that cannot be examined by simple observation of behavior in environments, but rather requires analysis of learner context as well as instructional environment. As Professor Di Vesta describes the contextualist—constructivist position with its roots in the rationalism of Kant, it becomes clear that to some degree the position subsumes the humanist perspective (see Don Norman's (1980) "Twelve issues for cognitive science,"—affect, belief systems, consciousness, thought and the like are all considered a part of the domain of cognitive science). Questions about the structure and organization of human memory, the nature of human expertise, and decision-making processes, once remote from psychological study are now significant research areas. Clearly, cognitive psychology offers a plethora of area educational psychology can choose to study in naturalistic (i.e., school) settings. Such study is just now getting under way.

The Future of Educational Psychology

Futurists we are not! Yet our reflections on selection of chapter topics for this work early forced us to consider what is to come. Despite the fact that they are often housed in departments of educational psychology, it seems clear to us that school psychology and counseling psychology are already conceptually set off from educational psychology. Other areas, measurement for example, may also separate from educational psychology. However, what may well happen instead, we believe, is a continuing trend toward specialization within educational psychology. In effect, our chapter topics for Part III of the book suggest our sense of what already exists in the field. The six chapters in Part III (comprehension processes, teacher effectiveness, classroom management, measurement, evaluation, and problem solving), *do* suggest our picture of the future of educational psychology. Although our chapter selections were not random, they were chosen so as to represent the wide variety of specialization already in existence. Clearly, our sense is one of increased specialization. Each of the six chapters attempts to provide a concise overview of a significant present day topic in educational psychology.

Professor Andre takes a "narrow" topic—reading comprehension—and shows how a variety of models of text comprehension bring structure to that topic. Recent research and theory in reading comprehension has stressed a cognitive view growing out of the contextualist-constructivist perspective Di Vesta describes in Chapter 11. Chapter 17, problem solving, also takes a heavily cognitive perspective. Yet from the topics covered, and from the volume of research generated, it is clear that research on comprehension processes may (and will) be conducted by persons only tangentially knowledgeable of the problem-solving research Professor Mayer describes. Yet one may consider, and wish for, a merger of views so that reading comprehension is more consistently treated as a problem solving process. Although many educational psychologists admit that comprehension is a problem-solving process, our reading of the research literature suggests that members of our discipline increasingly see themselves as studying "reading comprehension," *or* "development of problem-solving skills," *or* "development of expertise." This narrowness of specialization inevitably seems to be self-defeating, and indeed some signs of research that considers comprehension and problem solving in domain specific areas such as mathematics (see the work of Greeno and Kintsch) suggests recognition of the shortsightedness of very narrow perspectives.

Yet it is revealing that the references cited by Professors Evertson and Smylie in their chapter on teacher effectiveness have virtually no overlap with the references cited by Professor Williams in his classroom management chapter or with the references provided by Professor Mayer in his chapter on problem solving. Certainly, effective teaching depends on effective management skills as well as on problem-solving skills—indeed, teaching might be viewed as a complex problem-solving process. The observation that these chapters review practically no literature in common is not meant as criticism so much as it is noted to illustrate an issue of training and research. All three chapters are, in the editors' judgment, thoughtful and comprehensive. All three areas seem widely acceptable as appropriate to the domain of educational psychology. Yet can our discipline continue to study them in such isolation?

Equally revealing is the chapter on measurement. Professor Plake's chapter suggests the complexity of the problems measurement must deal with. Even a cursory reading of her chapter suggests that measurement has become a highly refined specialty. At the same time, Professor Brown's careful critique of evaluation suggests that this, too, has become an area requiring intensive study—an area of expertise. Inevitably, such intensive study comes at cost of breadth of training.

Our reading of the future of the field suggests that such isolation is likely to continue. After all, we could have chosen a variety of additional current topics had we so desired and space permitted. What we did instead was to choose six areas we felt were representative of topics of continuing interest to educational psychologists. Is such specialization appropriate? The question is extremely difficult to answer in any simple way. One may

argue that an in-depth approach (intensive study of one area) is the only approach likely to yield fruitful insights into an area. Thus, if one is interested in effective teaching, one examines, in some fashion, the characteristics and behavior of teachers (and teachers in classrooms) who are by some criterion "effective" or "ineffective." On the other hand, one may argue that analysis of teaching behavior into "problem solving behaviors," "management behaviors," etc., followed by observation of teaching *in situ* from that broader perspective may, though more complex, prove to provide a more complete and satisfying view of effective teaching.

The final section of this volume offers a variety of, in this case, "elder statesperson's" opportunities to reflect on topics in educational psychology. Our request for comments was very general. Essentially, the writer of each of these sections provided his own perspective. Professor Hilgard comments on educational psychology from the perspective of an academic psychologist. He suggests a need to study instruction in school settings taking into consideration the social setting in which much school learning occurs, as well as consideration of the entire cultural milieu in which instruction takes place. Professors Gagné and Horrocks both speak to the issue of understanding schooling, but from different views. Gagné appears to feel that educational psychology will make a contribution to instruction through empirical, controlled experiments that are then generalized to classroom settings. With considerable justification, he argues that empirical studies conducted in the classroom are too difficult to carry out for the long time periods necessary. Horrocks, on the other hand, speaks to the need to prepare educational psychologists who can, and do, study learning in a wide variety of settings—far beyond those that take place only in schools. Professor Humphreys chose a quite different tack. His comments bear upon change in quantitative methodology in educational psychology. His comments on the need to require substantial quantitative training for researchers are presented with force and conviction.

Concluding Remarks. The future of educational psychology seems assured for at least another two to three generations. However, the shape of educational psychology of the future is uncertain. One might argue that the increased depth of specialization seen in present day educational psychology has resulted in a substantial increase in the knowledge base of the discipline. Furthermore, by exploring topics such as problem solving, behavior management, and teacher effectiveness in natural settings, the ecological validity of findings from such study is more clearly assured. One may well argue that developing sufficient expertise in a single area, such as any of those suggested in Part III, is all that an individual may be reasonably expected to complete in the course of a scholarly career. On the other hand, one may also argue that the role of an educational psychologist is to examine human behavior from a broader, more inclusive perspective, searching for means for classifying and understanding human behavior that cut across narrow topical lines. However, this is not an "either/or" choice.

Instead, it seems to us that educational psychology has made visible progress of which it can be proud. Although discipline boundaries are not clear, well-defined topical areas have been developed in educational psychology and are being explored in the psychological tradition of depth first, then breadth. From our experience in reading the field, educational psychology today is closer than ever before to the goal of accumulating a substantial fund of usable knowledge. This accumulation is not simply a result of more research, but, instead, of the intensive study of rather narrowly defined topics in naturalistic settings. To achieve this wealth of information, specialization appears to be necessary. Of course, a potential threat,

raised earlier, is that educational psychology will continue to pursue topics in depth, but that the assimilation across topics—breadth—will not occur. A challenge to educational psychologists now and in the next 20 years is to provide the balance of knowledge and judgment necessary to use both strategies. Clearly, programs for the preparation of future educational psychologists must insure understanding and appreciation of both. Finally a move toward collaborative research (now becoming evident), which cuts across narrow topical areas, is likely to alleviate problems of excessive specialization. If these hopes are realized, the educational psychologist at the turn of the next century should be deeply immersed in a specialty area, yet fully capable of seeing the impact of the specialty area as it is joined with other specialties to provide an integrated understanding of our cognitive, affective, social, and behavioral roles.

References

American Psychological Association. (1984). APA-Accredited doctoral programs in professional psychology: 1984. *American Psychologist, 39,* 1470–1472.

Fisher, R. A. (1925). *Statistical Methods for Research Workers.* Edinburgh and London: Oliver & Boyd.

Norman, D. A. (1980). Twelve issues for cognitive science. *Cognitive Science, 4,* 1–32.

Snygg, D., & Combs, A. W. (1949). *Individual behavior: A new frame of reference for psychology.* New York: Harper.

Index

Ability grouping, 299
Academic performance, 298
Achievement testing
    educational measurement, 375–377
    Revised Joint Technical Standards, 386
Adolescence
    behaviorism and, 152
    child study movement and, 55
    historical perspective on, 22
Advance organizers, 215–216
Affect, 227
Age–equivalent scores, 377
Algorithm, 332
Allport, Gordon, 167
American Association for Humanistic Psychology, 160, 165
American Association of Counseling and Development (AACD), 109
American Psychological Association (APA), 4
    behaviorism and, 147
    counseling psychology, 108–109
    educational psychology, 27
    founding of, 22
    guidance and counseling, 113–114
    humanistic psychology, 163
    professional standards, 10
    school psychology, 123
Analogy, 221
Analysis of variance, 406, 408
Angell, James R., 24
ANOVA technique, 96
    computer, 408
    measurement, 99–100
Antecedent exercise, 311
Applied behavior analysis, 141–147
Aptitude testing
    educational measurement, 375–377
    Revised Joint Technical Standards, 386

Aquinas, Thomas 64
Aristotle, 64
Assessment, 240
Association for the Advancement of Behavior Therapy (AABT), 147–148
Associationism
    behaviorism and, 132–133
    problem solving, 332
Association of Counselor Education and Supervision (ACES), 109
Attendance. *See* Compulsory attendance
Attention management (classroom), 361–362
Attribution, 227–228
Audiovisual aids, 420
Ausubel, David, 171

Bain, Alexander, 132
Baldwin, James Mark, 53, 57, 63
Barnes, Earl, 51–52
Bechterev, Vadimir, 133
Behavior
    environment and, 131
    experimental analysis of, 139–140
    humanistic psychology and, 165
Behavioral coaching, 313
Behavioral psychology
    educational psychology and, 9
    instructional design and, 186–187
Behaviorism, 131–157
    applications of, 150–153
    applied behavior analysis, 141–147
    associationist school, 132–133
    conditioning and, 133
    educational psychology and, 7–8
    empiricist roots of, 132
    historical perspective on, 138
    humanistic psychology and, 161
    impact of, 149–150

Behaviorism (*Cont.*)
  learning research and, 133–137
  neobehaviorism, 137–138
  professional developments in, 147–149
  reading comprehension and, 263
  Skinner, 138–141
Behavior management, 297–325
  classroom management research evaluation, 317–321
  instructional manipulations, 299–302
  parents interventions, 304–305
  participant types, 297–298
  peer control, 302–304
  reinforcement procedures, 307–311
  self–administered strategies, 305–307
  target behaviors, 298–299
  treatment packages, 313–317
  treatment strategies, 299–317
  weakening techniques, 311–313
  See also Classroom management; Teaching
Behavior modification
  behaviorism and, 131
  behavior management and, 314
Behavior therapy, 313
Berkeley, George, 132
Bessel, F. W., 66
Bijou, Sidney, W., 142–145
Binet, Alfred, 68, 70–72
Boy Scouts, 55
Briggs, Leslie, 184
Bruner, Jerome, 171
Buhler, Charlotte, 160

California (Berkeley), University of, 28
Canonical analysis, 406
Carr, Harvey, 24
Cattell, James McKeen, 23, 46, 69
Cattell, Raymond Bernard, 79, 80–81
Chicago, University of, 28
Child study movement, 41–60
  criticism of, 53–54
  demise of, 55–57
  educational psychology and, 5
  eighteenth and nineteenth centuries, 41–44
  founding of, 46–48
  goals of, 41, 48–49
  human nature and, 41–42
  influence of, 54–55
  kindergartens and, 42–43
  legacy of, 57–58
  literature of, 51
  methods of, 51–53
  nation–wide, 50–51
  psychology and, 48–54
  school psychology and, 122
  urbanization and, 44–46
Clark University, 29, 49–50, 51
Classroom
  humanistic psychology, 175
  See also Teaching

Classroom behavior management. *See* Behavior management
Classroom management, 357–362
  See also Behavior management
Classroom processes. *See* Teaching
Clinical psychology, 126
Clubs, 45
Cognition
  intelligence and, 81
  problem solving, 328, 329–332
  reading comprehension, 280–281
Cognitive movement, 203–233
  current, 208–210
  educational psychology and, 206–208
  empiricism and, 204–205
  expertise, 225–226
  external facilitators, 213–218
  illustrative strategies, 220–222
  information processing, 210–213
  motivation, 226–228
  rationalism, 205–206
  school subjects, 223–225
  skills and control processes, 218–220
  skills training, 222–223
  understanding and, 204
Cognitive psychology
  educational measurement, 375
  educational psychology, 8
  humanistic psychology, 170–171
  influence of, 421–422
  instructional design and, 193
  reading comprehension and, 262–263
Columbian Exposition, 50
Columbia University, 28–29
Communication
  behavior management, 304–305
  teaching, 357, 364–365
Communication theory, 252–253
Compliance training, 313–314
Comprehension. *See* Reading comprehension
Compulsory attendance, 44
Computer
  instructional design, 186, 193–194
  measurement, 100–101, 377–383
  quantitative methods, 407–410
  Revised Joint Technical Standards, 387
  See also Quantitative methods; Statistics
Computer assisted instruction, 420–421
Conditioning. *See* Operant conditioning
Context, 217–218
Contextualist–constructivist position (cognitive movement), 208–210
Contracting, 314
Cornell University, 29
Correlations (statistical), 404–405, 407
Correspondence training, 314
Council for Accreditation of Counseling and Related Education Programs (CACREP), 109
Counseling. *See* Guidance and counseling

Counseling psychology, 108–109
Counselor education, 109–110
Criterion–referenced test, 96
    educational measurement, 383–385
    instructional design, 187, 191
Crowder, Norman, 185–186
Curiosity, 227
Curriculum, 238

Darwin, Charles, 19, 44–45, 54, 65, 67
Decision making
    educational measurement, 383–385
    evaluation, 239–240, 242–243, 246
    Revised Joint Technical Standards, 386–387
    teaching strategies, 354–357
Demography, 11–13
Descartes, René, 132
Developmental psychology
    child study movement and, 52
    educational psychology and, 6–7
    intelligence testing and, 71
Dewey, John, 23–24, 56, 57
Differential reinforcement of low rate of responding (DRL), 312
Differential reinforcement of other responses (DRO), 312–313
Discovery problem solving, 336–337
Discussion skills training, 314–315
Doctoral programs
    counselor education, 109
    educational psychologists, 11–12, 432
    guidance and counseling, 115
Durkin, D., 283

Ebbinghaus, Hermann, 70–71
    counseling psychology, 108–109
    counselor, 109–110
    educational psychology, 3–4
    evaluation professionals, 248
    guidance and counseling, 110–111, 115
    humanistic psychology, 171–172
    instructional design, 194–196
    school psychology, 123–124
Educational measurement, 373–391
    aptitude and achievement testing, 375–377
    computers in, 377–383
    criticisms of, 373–374
    decision making, 383–385
    educational psychology, 373
    law and, 374
    Revised Joint Technical Standards, 385–388
    See also Measurement
Educational psychology
    behaviorism and, 149, 152–153
    bahavior management and, 318
    cognitive movement and, 206–208
    current, 420–421, 435–436
    definitions of, 5–10, 183, 432–433
    educational measurement and, 373

Educational psychology (*Cont.*)
    emergence of, 17–38
    evaluation and, 238–239
    future of, 422, 425–429, 436–438
    global perspective on, 416–420
    humanistic psychology and, 176–179
    institutions and, 28–35, 399
    instructional design and, 196–200
    learning tasks, 398–399
    nineteenth century, 415–416
    personnel in, 10–14
    psychology and, 3–4
    reading comprehension and, 261–263
    retrospective view of, 395–402
    school psychology and, 121, 125–128
    "splinter" groups, 431–432
Education for All Handicapped Children Act of 1975, 124–125
Education programs, 11
Elaboration
    cognitive movement, 221–222
    reading comprehension, 277–280
Empiricism
    behaviorism, 132
    child study movement, 45–46
    cognitive movement, 204–205
    intelligence and, 65
Employment opportunity
    educational psychologists, 13
    guidance and counseling, 115
Environment
    behavior and, 131
    humanistic psychology and, 162
Erikson, E., 165
Evaluation, 237–257
    classroom management research, 317–321
    clients/audience in, 244–245, 251
    conducting of, 241–244
    defined, 239–241
    educational psychology and, 9
    historical perspective on, 237–239
    instructional design, 184, 188
    methods and process of, 250–251
    professionalization and, 247–249, 255
    purpose of, 249–250
    tests and testing, 102
    use enhancement of, 251–255
    use of information from, 245–247
Existentialism, 163–165
Expectancy training, 299
Expertise, 225–226
Eysenck, Hans, J., 141

Factor Analysis
    computer and, 407–408
    individual differences and, 72–81
    measurement and, 97–98
    quantitative methods, 405–406
Fading, 299–300

Federal government. *See* Government
Feedback
    behavior management, 300
    peer control, 303
    teaching, 363–364
Freud, S., 161–162
Froebel, Friedrich, 42–43
Functionalism, 23–24

Gagńe, Robert, 184, 187–188
Galton, Francis, 19–20, 65, 66–70, 94
Games. *See* Play behavior
Generalization training, 315–316
Genetics
    historical development and, 19–20
    individual differences and, 67
    intelligence and, 83–85
George Peabody College for Teachers, 32–33
Gesell, Arnold, 57
Gestalt psychology
    cognitive movement, 207–208
    problem solving, 332–334
    reading comprehension, 263–264
Goddard, Henry H., 72
Goodman, K. S., 265–267
Government
    evaluation and, 238
    guidance and counseling, 114–115
    instructional design and, 185, 186
    intelligence and, 84
    school psychology and, 122, 124–125
Grade–equivalent scores, 377
Graham, Clarence H., 396
Guidance and counseling, 107–119
    counseling psychology, 108–109
    counselor education, 109–110
    current status of, 116–117
    educational psychology and, 9, 432
    education in, 110–111
    mental hygiene movement, 113
    National Defense Education Act of 1958 and, 114, 115
    1960s, 114–115
    1970s, 115–116
    psychology and, 113–114
    psychotherapy and, 113
    testing and, 112–113
    variety in, 107–108
    vocational guidance movement and, 112
Guilford, Joy Paul, 79–80
Gulick, Luther, 5
Guthrie, Edwin, R., 137

Hall, G. Stanley, 22–23, 41, 46–48, 49, 50, 53–54, 55, 56, 58, 425
Harvard University, 29–30
Health services, 238
Herbart, Johann, 18, 43
Heredity. *See* Genetics

Huey, Edmund B., 26–27, 206–207, 262
Hull, Clark L., 137–138
Humanistic psychology, 159–182
    behavior and, 165
    behaviorism and, 161
    cognitive psychology and, 170–171
    contributions to, 167–168
    criticisms of, 168–169
    defined, 160
    early origins of, 160–161
    educational psychology and, 176–179
    education and, 170–171
    evolution of, 162–163
    implications of, 171–172
    phenomenology and existentialism in, 163–165
    psychoanalysis and, 161–162
    self and, 166–167
    strengths of, 169–170
    teaching and, 172–175
Human nature
    child study movement, 41–42
    definitional problems and, 6–9
Hume, David 132
Hunter, Walter S., 396

Ignoring strategy, 311
Imagery, 220–221
Immigration, 44
Indiana University, 30
Individual differences (intelligence), 61–88
    Binet and, 70–72
    educational psychology and, 6–7
    education and, 85–86
    factor analysis and, 72–81
    Galton and, 66–70
    genetics and, 83–85
    information processing theories and, 81–83
    prescientific era and, 63–66
    psychology and, 63–66
    relevance of, 61–62
    scientific era and, 66–67
Individually Prescribed Instruction (IPI), 189
Inductive problem solving, 337
Industrial Revolution, 44–46
Information processing
    cognitive movement and, 210–213
    intelligence and, 81–83
Institutions
    child study movement and, 45
    measurement and, 101
Instructional design, 183–202
    conceptual revolution in, 186–189
    current status of, 192–194
    defined, 183
    educational psychology and, 9, 196–200
    instructional systems and, 189–192
    origins of, 183–184

Instructional design (*Cont.*)
  personnel in, 194–196
  programmed instruction and, 184–186
Instructional games, 300
Instructional Systems Development (ISD) model, 190–191
Intelligence
  problem solving, 342–343
  See also Individual differences (intelligence)
Interspersal training, 300–301
Item response theory (IRT), 96
  computer and, 409–410
  educational measurement and, 375–377

James, William, 5, 21–22, 48, 53, 63
Journal of Educational Psychology, 5–6
Journals
  behaviorism, 147
  child study movement, 51
  counseling psychology, 108–109
  instructional design, 196–198
  measurement, 101–102
Judd, Charles, 26
Juvenile delinquency
  behaviorism, 152
  child study movement, 45

Kelley, Truman, 95
Kindergartens, 42–43
Kinstch, W., 268–269

Labor laws, 45
Law
  educational measurement, 374
  labor laws, 45
  See also Government
Learning theory, 7
Legislation. *See* Law; *entries under name of specific law*
LISREL methodology, 408–409
Locke, John, 65
Luckey, G. W. A., 48, 51–52

Mager, R. F., 187
Maslow, H., 165, 167, 171–172
Master's degree
  counseling and guidance, 110
  educational psychology, 12–13
Mathematics, 340–342
McClelland, J. L., 267–268
McKee, P., 263
Means (statistical), 403–404
Measurement, 89–106
  behaviorism, 139
  educational psychology and, 7
  evaluation and, 238
  factor analysis, 97–98
  institutional/organization arrangements, 101
  necessity for, 89–90
  professional organizations/journals, 101–102

Measurement (*Cont.*)
  research design in, 99–100
  technology and, 100–101
  testing methods, 90–91
  test publishing, 102
  test review/evaluation procedures, 102
  test theory, 94–97
  test validity, 98–99
  theory of, 91–94
  See also Educational measurement; Tests and testing
Media, 193
Medical model, 379
Medication. *See* Pharmacology
Memory
  cognitive movement, 210–213, 221
  reading comprehension models, 271
Mendel, Gregor, 67
Mental ability. *See* Individual differences (intelligence);
    Intelligence
Mental age, 71
Mental hygiene movement, 113
Metacognition
  cognitive movement, 219–220
  reading comprehension, 280–281
  See also Cognition; Cognitive movement; Cognitive
    psychology
Metaphor, 274–277
Michigan, University of, 30–31
Mill, James, 132
Mill, John Stuart, 132
Millman, Jason, 378
Minnesota, University of, 31
Missouri, University of, 31
Mnemonic aids, 221
Modeling
  behavior management, 301
  peer control, 303
Morality, 45
Mother
  child study movement, 42
  See also Parents
Motivation
  cognitive movement, 226–228
  educational psychology, 7,9
Mowrer, O. Hobart, 138
Multiple correlations, 404–405, 407
Multiple regressions, 407
Münsterberg, Hugo, 53, 54–55
Music, 43

National Association of School Psychology, 124, 127
National Council on Education Measurement, 374
National Defense Education Act of 1958 (NDEA), 114, 115
Native equipment. *See* Human nature
NEA, 49–50
Nebraska, University of, 31
Negative preference management, 312
Neobehaviorism, 137–138

New York University, 31–32
Norm-referenced tests, 187
Norms, 92

Objective measurement, 91
Objectivism, 132
Ohio State University, 32
Operant conditioning
    behaviorism, 138–141
    children and, 142–145
Organization, 216–217

Parents
    behaviorism and, 150–151
    behavior management, 304–305
    child study movement and, 49, 51
    teacher communication with, 304–305
Partial correlations (statistics), 404–405
Patient Management Problem (PMP), 379
Pavlov, Ivan P., 133
Pearson, Karl, 70
Peer interactions, 298, 302–304
Pennsylvania, University of, 33
Pestalozzi, Johann Heinrich, 18, 42, 43
Pharmacology, 311
Phenomenology, 163–165
Piaget, J., 80–81
Plato, 63–64, 205
Play behavior
    behavior management, 300
    child study movement and, 43
Play movement, 55
Positive practice overcorrection, 312
Pressey, Sidney, J., 141, 186, 420–421
Problem solving, 327–347
    centrality of, 327–328
    cognitive analysis of, 329–332
    definitions, 328–329
    intelligence and, 82, 342–343
    math, 340–342
    reading comprehension, 338–339
    research directions, 343–345
    research history, 332–334
    transfer issue in, 334–338
    writing and, 339–340
Process–product perspective
    academic instruction, 362–365
    classroom management, 357–359
    described, 350–351
    planning and decision making, 354–356
Productive Thinking Program, 339
Professional organizations
    behaviorism, 147–149
    counselor education, 109
    educational psychology, 410
    measurement, 101–102
    school psychology, 122, 124
    *See also entries under names of specific professional
        organizations*

Professional standards. *See* Standards
Program evaluation. *See* Evaluation
Programmed instruction, 141–142, 184–186, 420–421
Progressive movement
    child study movement and, 45
    educational psychology and, 417–420
    humanistic psychology and, 170
Prompting, 301
Psychoanalysis
    history of, 22
    humanistic psychology and, 161–162
Psycholinguistic guessing games, 265–267
Psychology
    child study movement and, 48–54
    educational psychology and, 3–4, 6
    guidance and counseling, 112, 113–114
    historical precursors of, 17–19
    individual differences and, 63–66
    military personnel, 397–398
    nineteenth century, 19–20
    scientific method and, 43
    teacher training and, 20
    twentieth century, 21–27
    World War II, 396–397
    See also entries under names of various specialties
Psychometrics. *See* Educational measurement;
        Measurement; Tests and testing
Psychopathology, 49
Psychotherapy, 113
Public school
    child study movement, 44
    school psychology, 122

Quantitative methods, 403–414
    computer and, 407–410
    past, 403–406
    research problems, 410–414
    See also Computer; Statistics
Questionnaires
    child study movement, 46–47, 52–53
    scientific pedagogy, 49–50
Quintillian, 64

Rationalism, 205–206
Reading comprehension, 259–296
    bottom–up, data driven models of, 264–265
    centrality of, 259
    dimensions of models in, 271–272
    educational psychology and, 261–263
    elaboration and, 277–280
    interactive models of, 266–269
    metacognitive components in, 280–281
    metaphor in, 274–277
    models of, 263–272
    problem solving and, 338–339
    research issues in, 272–281
    schemata concept in, 261
    schema–theoretic view, 269–271
    syntactical factors in, 272–274

Reading comprehension (*Cont.*)
  teaching skills of, 282–288
  top–down, conceptually driven models of, 265–267
Reciprocal teaching, 287–288
Reliability
  educational measurement, 384
  test theory, 94–95
Religion, 44
Repetition, 213–215
Research design, 99–100
Response cost strategy, 311–312
Response delay training, 302
Revised Joint Technical Standards, 385–388
Rogers, Carl, 113, 165, 167, 170, 178–179
Rousseau, Jean-Jacques, 41–42
Rumelhart, D. E., 267–268
Rural prejudice, 47

Sanctions, 361
Scales, 92–93
Schema, 329–330
Schema–theoretic views, 269–271
Scholastic Aptitude Test (SAT), 96
School psychology, 121–130
  clinical psychology and, 126
  developmental analysis of, 121–126
  diversity in, 128–129
  educational psychology and, 9, 125–128, 432
  recent development and, 124–125
  specialization and, 123–124
Scientific method
  child study movement, 51
  humanistic psychology, 168
  psychology and, 18–19, 43
Scientific pedagogy, 49–50
Sechenov, Ivan M., 133
Self
  behavior management, 305–307
  humanistic psychology, 166–167
Sentimentality, 168–169
Shinn, Millicent, 52
Signaling, 217
Skinner, B. F., 138–141, 161, 183, 185
Social Darwinism, 45
Social skills training, 315
Socioeconomic class
  behaviorism and, 151–152
  child study movement and, 43–44
  morality and, 45
  Pestalozzi and, 42
  social Darwinism, 45
  urbanization and, 44
Sociolinguistic perspective
  academic instruction, 365–367
  classroom management, 359–362
  described, 351–353
  planning and decision making, 356–357
Speaking rules, 360–361
Spearman, Charles Edward, 71, 72–77, 94–95, 97

Specialization, 123–124
Spencer, Herbert, 65, 132
Sputnik, 184–186
SQ3R, 338
Standards
  educational psychology, 10–11
  teachers, 44
Stanford University, 33–34
Statistics
  ANOVA design, 99–100
  educational measurement, 378, 384
  individual differences, 72–81
  measurement, 93, 99–98
  technology, 100–101
  test theory, 94–97
  See also Computer; Quantitative methods
Structure–oriented problem solving, 335–336
Suspensions, 311
Syntax, 272–274

Tasks, 301
Teachers
  behavior management, 298
  evaluation and, 245
  feedback and, 300
  humanistic psychology and, 172–175
  parent communication with, 304–305
  qualifications of, 44
Teachers College (Columbia University), 25
Teacher training
  child study movement and, 48–50, 51, 54, 55
  instructional design and, 198–199
  psychology and, 20, 27–28
  standards in, 44
Teacher training packages, 316–317
Teaching, 349–371
  academic instruction, 362–367
  behavior management, 299–302
  classroom management, 357–362
  effectiveness and, 349–350
  instructional design, 188
  planning/decision making, 354–357
  problem solving, 334–338
  process–product research paradigm, 350–351
  reading comprehension skills, 282–288
  sociolinguistic research, 351–353
  theories of, 421
Teaching machines, 141–142, 186, 420–421
Terman, Lewis Madison, 72
Tests and testing
  aptitude and achievement, 375–377
  behavior management, 301–302
  child study movement and, 49
  computer in, 378–380
  evaluation and, 237–238
  guidance and counseling, 112–113
  instructional design, 184, 187
  IQ, 62
  measurement, 90–91

Tests and testing (*Cont.*)
  publication of, 102
  reading comprehension and, 263
  review/evaluation procedures, 102
  school psychology and, 122
  scoring and reporting, 380
  technology and, 100–101
  theory, 94–97
  validity, 98–99
  See also Educational measurement; Measurement
Test theory, 405
Theory
  definitional problems and, 6, 10
  educational measurement, 375–377
  empiricism, 45–46
  evaluation, 241, 242, 243, 252–253
  intelligence, 81–83
  measurement, 91–94
  programmed instruction, 185
  reading comprehension, 263–272
  teaching, 421
  tests and testing, 94–97
Thorndike, E. L., 5, 6, 7, 24–26, 65, 77–79, 89, 91–92, 133–134, 332
Thurstone, Louis L., 79, 97–98
Time limits, 302
Token economy, 315
Tolman, Edward C., 137
Tufts University, 34
Tutoring
  parent intervention, 304
  peer control, 303–304
Twin studies
  historical development and, 19–20
  intelligence and, 83
Tyler, Ralph, 238

Understanding, 204
Urbanization, 44–46
U–shaped curve, 219

Validity
  quantitative methods, 405
  tests and testing, 98–99
Values
  evaluation, 243
  humanistic psychology, 169–170
Van Dijk, T. A., 268–269
Verbal reprimands, 312
Vienna Circle, 136–137
Vietnam War, 115
Vives, Juan, 17–18
Vocational guidance movement, 112

Watson, John Broadus, 83–84, 132, 134–136
Weakening behavior techniques, 311–313
Wechsler, David, 72
Winship, A. E., 49
Wisconsin, University of, 34–35
Wissler, Clark, 70
Wolfe, H. K., 48, 51
Woodworth, Robert S., 24
World War II
  instructional design and, 184
  psychology and, 396–397
Wrenn, C. Gilbert, 116
Writing skills, 339–340
Wundt, Wilhelm, 19, 46, 66, 67–68, 206

Yale University, 35
YMCA, 45, 55